Travel Geography

Travel Geography

SECOND EDITION

Rosemary Burton

PITMAN
PUBLISHING

PITMAN PUBLISHING
128 Long Acre, London WC2E 9AN

A Division of Longman Group Limited

First edition published in Great Britain in 1991
Second edition published in 1995

© Rosemary Burton 1995

ISBN 0 273 60203 9

British Library Cataloguing in Publication Data
A CIP catalogue record for this book can be obtained from the British Library

10 9 8 7 6 5 4 3 2 1

Typeset and illustrated by PanTek Arts, Maidstone, Kent.
Printed and bound by Clays Ltd, St Ives plc

The Publishers' policy is to use paper from sustainable forests.

CONTENTS

PREFACE

Tourism is a growing phenomenon in the world today, both in terms of its penetration into new parts of the world and in terms of the numbers of people participating in travel and holiday-making. The social and ecological problems it may bring in its wake are also increasing. A more environmentally aware society is beginning to express concern about the effects of tourism on the environment. Its economic impact is also growing but the policies that lead developing countries to promote tourism (despite its environmental impacts) are also being questioned. Tourism is therefore a controversial activity but one that gives pleasure to millions.

This book is concerned with two main aspects of travel geography: first, the world's geographical resource base for tourism, and second, the spatial patterns of world tourist activity. The book illustrates the world distribution of natural and manmade tourist resources and provides the student with some understanding of the interactions between the tourist and the resource. Chapters 7 to 14 introduce some of the theories that describe and explain the cyclical nature of tourist development and the seeming inevitability of the process of intensification of tourism at the most popular destinations. Tourism appears to change the nature of the resource it consumes. Chapter 14 discusses the various policy options that aim to contain tourism's growth and impact, but readers may draw their own conclusions as to the ease with which these may be implemented.

The second part of the book is concerned specifically with the spatial variation in tourist activity throughout the world; it will give the reader some understanding of the distribution of tourism in the different regions of the world, and it offers geographical explanations of these patterns. The text also outlines the range of factors that lead to changes in travel flows and patterns of tourist development. In order to understand these processes the student must be aware of tourists' motivations and the other social, political and economic circumstances that both generate tourism

and control its spatial expression. This is discussed in Chapter 15.

Students, particularly those wishing to work in the travel trade, must also know the world distribution of geographical resources that function as tourist attractions (described in Chapters 2 to 6), the way in which transport networks evolve to link tourist generating regions with potential destinations (see Chapter 16), and their regional expression (see Chapter 17).

The bulk of the text analyses, in greater detail, the world's regional patterns of tourism that result from the interaction of these factors. Four main regions are identified:

1 **Europe** – the world's focus of international tourism generation and the world's primary destination region (see Chapters 18–28, plus parts of Chapter 29).
2 **North America** – an equally significant world tourist region in terms of the volume of tourist movement, whose general patterns of tourist development show striking similarities with those of Europe (see Chapters 31 and 32).
3 **The Pacific and Australasia.** The world's most rapidly growing tourist region (see Chapters 34 to 37).
4 **The peripheral regions of the world** (South Asia, Subsaharan Africa, the Middle East and Central and South America). These regions are peripheral in terms of their economic relationships with the developed world and in terms of their tourist linkages with the major Western tourist generating regions (see Chapters 29, 30, 33 and 38).

It should be noted that for ease of reference for vocational students, Chapters 18–38 are organised on a continental basis rather than explicitly on the basis of these functional regions, but it is hoped that this does not obscure the functional regions of the world.

The text provides the student with a knowledge of the major tourist attractions and resources of each destination. It outlines the level of tourist development there and the reasons for the development (or lack of it). It analyses the spatial distribution of tourist activity in individual countries, indentifying their congested, developing and untouched regions and their potential for different types of tourism, indicating potential points of conflict between domestic and international tourists. The book will, therefore, give geography students an understanding of the geographical processes shaping spatial pattern of tourism, while those preparing to work in the tourist industry will also acquire the basic geographical knowledge that will allow them to provide an informed service to potential travellers.

It does not pretend to be a substitute for an atlas, in fact the student will gain more if the book is read alongside an atlas. The maps provided here add to the geographical information available and complement the atlas. Nor does the text aim to be a complete catalogue of tourist attractions, that is the role of travel guides and encyclopedias. Rather, the book is designed to give the reader an understanding of the changing patterns of tourism and the vocational student in particular with the knowledge to work effectively within an ever-changing environment. The assignments are specifically designed to help develop the skills that will enable the vocational students to use and apply their geographical knowledge to practical effect in their work environment.

ACKNOWLEDGEMENTS

Thanks are due to all those who have played a part in the production of the book: Paul Dyke and the other cartographers, colleagues, friends and family, who have both provided help and shown great tolerance while the book was being prepared, and particular thanks to Helen Davis for the typing.

Specific thanks go to Dr V Costello for Fig 4.2, Miss C Peace for Figs 4.3, 12.2 and 12.3 and Mrs G Horsman for Figs 6.1, 6.2 and 29.5.

CHAPTER 1

Introduction

This book is about the geographical distribution of tourism throughout the world: it seeks to describe and explain the spatial patterns of tourist activity and development on regional, national, international and world scales. It is about the location of tourist resources and the factors (e.g. economic, political etc) that influence when, how and where they are used for tourism. It is about the people who are tourists, where and why they travel, and the effect they have on the places they visit. There are many different types of tourist:

1 **Foreign tourist.** Any person visiting a country (other than that in which he usually resides) for a period of at least 24 hours (OECD definition).
2 **Excursionist.** Persons travelling for pleasure for a period of less than 24 hours (OECD definition).
3 **Visitor.** Any person visiting a country (other than that in which he has his usual place of residence) for any reason other than following an occupation remunerated from within the country visited (OECD definition) (i.e. this includes people travelling for pleasure, business, educational or religious purposes etc, as well as excursionists).
4 **Domestic tourist.** A person who travels away from home for a distance of at least 50 miles (one way) for business, pleasure, personal affairs or any other purpose except to commute to work, whether he stays overnight or returns the same day (USA definition).

The common factor running through these definitions is that the tourist travels away from home for a variety of reasons (other than work). The definitions differ in that they make distinctions between:

1 **The length of time a person travels.**
2 **The combination of non-work purposes motivating the travel.**
3 **The place visited.**

The essence of tourism is, therefore, that it involves:

- travel
- to a location that is not the tourist's home.

Thus the simplest spatial model of the tourist system is shown in Fig 1.1. The system consists of three spatial elements:

- the tourist's home area (the tourist generating region)
- the places people travel to (the destination regions)
- the routes people follow between the generating and destination regions.

Travel geography is concerned with the study of all three elements of the system, at all spatial scales (from the study of domestic tourism within a city region, through to world patterns of intercontinental travel). It is concerned with (*a*) the economic and physical character of the tourist generating regions and the motivations of tourists (that add up to the 'push' factors that make people wish to travel); (*b*) the nature of the destination areas (the 'pull' factors that attract travellers to particular places); (*c*) the routes and organisation of the transport systems and services that enable the tourist to get from home to the tourist destination.

Travel geography must therefore take account of both the factors motivating tourists and the way in which the travel industry is organised in as much as they influence the spatial development of tourism. These are major areas of study in their own right and are discussed fully elsewhere (e.g. Holloway). It is not the purpose of this book to examine these topics in depth, although they are discussed at appropriate points. The main focus of this book is the spatial elements of the tourist system.

Part 2 of this book describes the location and character of the world's main tourist generating regions and briefly discusses the various forms of

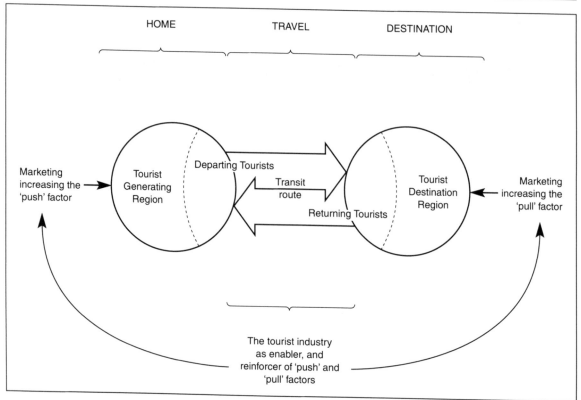

HOME   TRAVEL   DESTINATION

Marketing increasing the 'push' factor

Tourist Generating Region

Departing Tourists

Transit route

Returning Tourists

Tourist Destination Region

Marketing increasing the 'pull' factor

The tourist industry as enabler, and reinforcer of 'push' and 'pull' factors

Fig. 1.1 The tourist system
(*Source*: After Leiper, 1981)

transport and routes that link people's homes to their tourist destinations. Although the journey is often an important part of the tourist experience itself, most of this book is devoted to the tourist destinations and to a description of world patterns of tourism, so Part 1, Section 1 begins with a description of the nature of the world's resources that make destinations appealing to different types of tourist and the world distribution of these resources. Section 2 analyses the way in which these resources are used for tourism, concentrating on the interaction between the tourist and the destination, the cycle of changes that tourism brings about and the process of the spatial spread of tourism. This section discusses the various models that seek to describe and explain these processes and the political responses of decision makers to these changes. The first half of the book thus provides a general overview of the world

tourist systems with an emphasis on the spatial location and patterns of use of tourist resources. The second half of the book (Part 3) describes the tourist regions of the world in more detail. Information is provided not only on the specific resources and attractions (on a country by country basis), but also on the nature, scale, growth and spatial distribution of tourism within each region and country. The principles described in the first half of the book can be followed through and illustrated in these succeeding sections. The book concludes with a brief comment on the very significant role of world politics as an overall influence on world tourism development.

FURTHER READING

Holloway, J C (1994) *The Business of Tourism*, 4th edn, Pitman

PART 1

Tourism and the Environment

World geographical resources for tourism

INTRODUCTION

The book begins with a study of tourist destinations and the geographical resources that make them attractive for tourists, and seeks to answer the following questions.

1 What geographical features of the world attract travellers to them; i.e. which types of climate are most suitable for different types of tourist activity; what sorts of coast and landscapes do tourists find attractive? Which historical, cultural and wildlife resources have the potential for tourism?
2 Where are these features located in the world, i.e. what is the world distribution of climatic, landscape, coastal, wildlife, historical and cultural resources for tourism?

Each chapter in this section examines the attraction and world distribution of each type of resource. Where appropriate, the chapters include case studies illustrating the relationship between the nature of the resource and the type of tourism that it supports. The cumulative evidence of the chapters together indicate that there are two regions of the world where there are strong concentrations of attractive tourist resources (ideal climates and beaches, with outstanding historic and cultural resources set in attractive landscapes all grouped around the sheltered waters of enclosed seas). These two regions are:

1 **the Mediterranean basin**, which lies directly to the south of the main European tourist generation region; and
2 **the Gulf of Mexico/Caribbean Sea**, which is similarly situated to the south of the population concentrations that generate most North American tourists.

The tourist resources of the huge Pacific region (the third major tourist generation region of the world) are more dispersed, but on the whole its most attractive resources are also located between the generating populations and the Equator. Resources with a high tourist potential are more widely scattered throughout the economic periphery, while the world's best wildlife resources are almost entirely now confined to the remoter parts of the world.

CHAPTER 2

Climatic resources for tourism

LEARNING OBJECTIVES

After reading this chapter you should be able to
- explain how the climate affects human bodily comfort
- identify the climatic factors that limit tourist activities
- locate the climatic regions of the world most suited to tourist development
- locate the parts of the world where there are severe climatic limitations to the development of tourism
- understand the effects of relief on temperature and precipitation, and the special character of mountain climates
- be aware of the importance of reliability and length of season for both tourists, tour operators and the providers of tourist infrastructures.

INTRODUCTION

In order to enjoy their holiday, tourists must be physically comfortable in the climatic conditions at the holiday destination. They must be comfortable irrespective of their activity, be it passive (sunbathing) or at the other extreme, very active (e.g. surfboarding, horse riding, snow skiing, and so on). Second, the climate of the holiday destination must be attractive. People tend to be more relaxed and cheerful when it is sunny and clear than when skies are overcast and gloomy.

CHARACTERISTICS OF CLIMATE ASSOCIATED WITH HUMAN COMFORT

Temperature and relative humidity

The normal body temperature of a human being is 36.5° C. This will rise with physical exertion or exposure to heat (such as bright sunshine). Body temperature is controlled by evaporation from the skin by sweating. Our body temperature would rise by 2° C per hour if we did not sweat. The ability of the air to take up moisture depends on its relative humidity (RH). If the relative humidity is too high –

generally over 70 per cent – the air will not take up enough moisture from the skin to cool it, and the body will begin to overheat and the person will feel uncomfortable. In conditions of high relative humidity, there may be a risk of heat stroke at temperatures of only about 26° C, whereas in dry conditions bodily stress may not occur until the temperature nears 36° C. Figure 2.1 shows the range of temperature and relative humidity conditions within which a human feels comfortable.

The coincidence of high temperatures and high relative humidity thus renders climates unsuitable for tourist development, as holiday activities cannot be limited to air-conditioned buildings and vehicles alone. The equatorial regions of the world are, therefore, not generally developed for tourism to any great extent.

Dry heat is more tolerable, as long as the body is shielded from direct sunshine, and it takes in sufficient water to replenish the moisture lost by sweating. The discomfort and danger of hot desert climates comes as much from dehydration as from the body overheating. Both adventure holidays and package tours are now extending into the more accessible fringes of the hot deserts and outings to a Saharan oasis is now an option on package tours to the North Africa coasts.

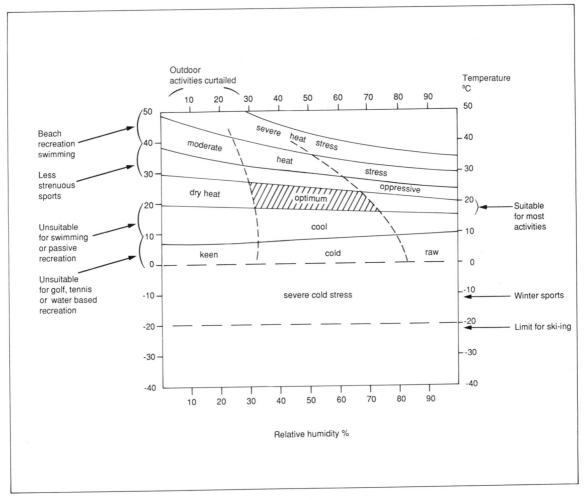

Fig. 2.1 Temperature and relative humidity conditions for human comfort
(*Source*: After Terjung, 1966)

It has been noted that any physical exertion raises the body temperature; land-based activity holidays will thus have a slightly different spatial distribution needing slightly lower temperatures than water sports and 'sun, sea and sand' holidays. Figure 2.1 shows the range of comfortable climatic conditions for a range of tourist activities.

Wind

The comfort chart (shown in Fig 2.1) indicates that conditions begin to feel uncomfortable for a lightly clothed, sedentary person at temperatures below about 16° C to 18° C. The body begins to feel cold when the temperature drops to 10° C and at this point extra clothing is necessary. Heat loss is accelerated by the wind because this not only increases the speed of moisture evaporating from the skin, but it also increases the rate of heat lost directly from the skin to the adjacent moving air. A breeze may thus reduce overheating and restore comfort at high temperatures, but the wind causes the body to chill quickly and brings intense discomfort at lower temperatures. This action of the wind in effectively reducing the air temperature is known as the **windchill factor**. In the Polar regions and the high mountains of the world, the air temperature may be at or below freezing point for much of the year. In such conditions, windchill considerably increases the level of discomfort, and the risk of frostbite, as wind strength increases, which in turn reduces the potential of such areas for winter sports activities.

CHARACTERISTICS OF CLIMATE RELATED TO TOURIST NEEDS

Whatever a tourist's choice of activity, a holiday is much enhanced if the weather is fine. Tourists want as near as possible to a guarantee of good weather for their visit: they are not concerned if it is cloudy and wet at other times of the year. On the other hand, the tour operator and property developer may be very interested in the seasonal distribution of sunshine and rainfall, particularly if they wish to develop an infrastructure providing for both summer tours and winter sun holidays in the same location. Thus, it is the reliability and seasonal distribution of sunshine, cloud cover and rainfall rather than the total amounts of each that are crucial for tourist development.

Rainfall

Most of the main tourist generating areas are in the Northern Hemisphere. A resort catering for these markets will thus be more attractive if it is sunny and dry during the Northern Hemisphere's summer months (June–September), whereas for the Southern Hemisphere tourist, December–February are the crucial months. Figure 2.2 shows the seasonal distribution of rainfall throughout the world. The subtropical and Mediterranean climates are characterised by long, reliable summer drought seasons when virtually no rain falls at all. The quantity and spatial distribution of rainfall are locally variable, even within a given climatic regime because of the influence of topography on precipitation. This may be particularly pronounced in mountain areas. Rainfall induced by high land is known as **orographic rainfall**.

The nature of rainfall may also be significant for tourism. Short, sharp downpours mixed with long, sunny and dry periods (e.g. tropical climates, Mediterranean winter weather) are preferable to

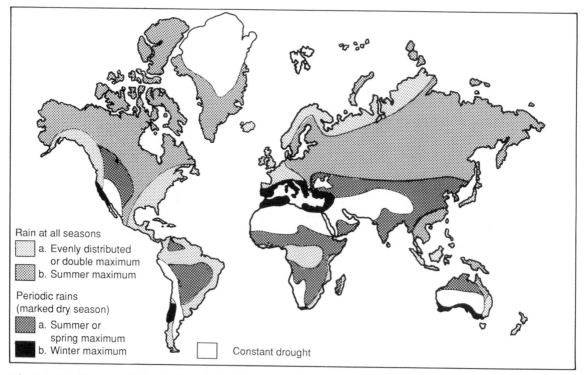

Fig. 2.2 World seasonal distribution of rainfall

the overcast sky and hours of drizzle and light rain that frequently occurs in Western European temperate climates.

Cloud cover

Cloud cover is obviously related to patterns of rainfall, though not invariably. In some locations there may be high amounts of cloud or fog which produce little in the way of precipitation, for example along the Californian coast where cold sea water cools the air passing over it and produces foggy conditions, but little rain when the air reaches the coast. On the other hand, some equatorial climates have good sunny periods each day in spite of very high rainfall totals.

Sunshine

This is perhaps the most difficult climatic characteristic to measure accurately, and some resorts may be guilty of over-optimistic interpretations of their sunshine records. By definition, the total daily hours of sunshine can never exceed the hours of daylight which vary according to latitude and season. Amounts of sunshine must be inversely proportional to rainfall and cloud cover; that is when rainfall and cloud cover increases, the total amount of sunshine must decrease. Air pollution will, however, reduce the clarity of the sunshine, and in extreme cases (e.g. Los Angeles) will even produce smog which dramatically cuts down the penetration of sunlight.

WORLD CLIMATES AND THEIR SUITABILITY FOR TOURISM

We have noted that clothing can modify the effect of the climate on bodily comfort by insulation, thus creating a more comfortable internal microclimate. This operates in both hot and cold climates. The loose, flowing robes characteristic of the traditional dress of the Bedouins and Nigerians, for example, shield the body from excessive radiation from the sun while still allowing evaporation to cool the skin. On the other hand, clothing can protect the body by reducing heat loss in the cold

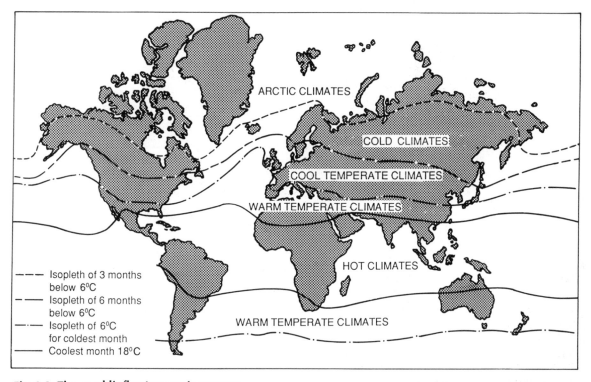

Fig. 2.3 The world's five temperature zones

climates. The climates of the world have been classified according to conditions of human comfort and the amount of clothing needed to maintain comfort. The world's climates fall into six clothing zones which can be further subdivided according to their seasonal pattern of temperature and rainfall. These seasonal variations will finally determine the overall attractiveness of the climate for tourism at different times of the year.

There are five temperature zones in the world, (*see* Fig 2.3), with each zone corresponding to one of the clothing zones (*see* Fig 2.4).

Hot climates: minimum clothing zone

A nude man begins to feel cold below 30° C so some clothing is required, yet any clothing at all may impede evaporation from the skin and increase discomfort. Such climates may not be suited to tourism depending on the season.

Hot climates can be subdivided according to their pattern of rainfall.

Equatorial climates

These climates are limited to a zone within about 10° N and 10° S of the Equator forming the central part of the hot climatic zone. They are typically very hot (over 26° C) and humid (over 75 per cent

relative humidity) and have heavy rainfall all year round, mainly in violent regular afternoon downpours. Such climates are not attractive to tourists as the heat and humidity make any outdoor activity exhausting. However, particular circumstances may lead to specialised forms of tourism being developed in the equatorial zone.

Case study: Singapore

Singapore, a tiny city state, lies just 1° north of the Equator. Figure 2.5 shows that it has a typical equatorial climate.

The combination of temperature and humidity makes the air feel oppressive, the moist heat feeling like a smothering wall when leaving the shelter of air-conditioning. Nevertheless, Britain recognised Singapore's strategic location and developed the island as a trading base from 1819 to 1942, when it became a major communications and commercial centre for South East Asia, through the development of its port facilities. Later a major international airport was added, which now functions not only as a hub and gateway to SE Asia, but also as a major interchange and stopover location for round the world flights. Apart from business tourism, its main tourist function is for stopovers rather than as a site for long stays. With the help of air-conditioning, short stay visitors can tolerate the climate for a day or so. In spite of the high annual rainfall total, the days can be quite sunny, as the rainfall comes in regular late afternoon deluges.

Latitude	Temperature zone and climatic type	Corresponding clothing zone
Equator	1 Hot (Equatorial, tropical and desert)	Minimum clothing and light protective clothing
	2 Warm temperate (Mediterranean and eastern margin climates)	One layer clothing
	3 Cool temperate (marginal and continental types)	Two layer clothing
	4 Cold climates	Three layer clothing
	5 Arctic and polar climates	Maximum clothing
Poles		

Fig. 2.4 Temperature and clothing zones

	Average temp (°C)	Average rainfall (mm)	Average relative humidity (RH) %
Jan	27	253	80
Feb	27	172	74
Mar	28	195	73
Apr	29	189	76
May	29	174	76
Jun	29	174	76
Jul	29	171	76
Aug	29	171	75
Sep	29	179	76
Oct	29	210	75
Nov	28	256	77
Dec	27	259	80

Fig. 2.5 Singapore's climate

Outdoor activity is, therefore, possible, but must be taken at a leisurely pace to avoid heat exhaustion. Light loose cotton clothing is most comfortable.

Tropical climates

These are hot climates (generally over 23° C) with moderate to heavy summer rainfall and a clearly defined slightly cooler dry (or drier) winter season. These climates occur in the zones of latitude roughly at 10–25° N comprising East and South Asia, the West African coast (around the Gambia), the Caribbean and the coast of Mexico, and Hawaii.

A similar zone 10–24° S of the equator covers northern Australia, Mauritius and Madagascar, parts of the South American coast and many of the South Pacific Islands.

The oceanic islands and the eastern coast locations (i.e. on the eastern margins of the continent) tend to have rain throughout the year but with a clear summer maximum, and are subject to seasonal tropical storms of great intensity (known as hurricanes, cyclones or typhoons). These occur most frequently in summer.

The western margin locations (i.e. on the west coast of the continents) have a much more pronounced completely dry winter period and much heavier summer rainfall. The monsoon climates of South and East Asia are even more extreme with a prolonged winter drought and a torrential summer wet season (the 'monsoon'). Monsoon climates also suffer the risk of severe cyclonic storms.

At the outermost limits of the tropical zone (around 24–26° N and S), the temperatures are a little lower, and the dry season less distinct.

Case study: Jamaica (18° N)

This Caribbean island has an east margin tropical climate. Its capital, Kingston, has 870 mm rainfall a year – on the low side for a subtropical climate. This is mainly due to the fact that Kingston itself lies in the rain shadow of the Blue Mountains which rise to over 2200 metres. In contrast the west-facing coasts of many of the other mountainous Caribbean Islands (such as Montserrat) have 1280 mm to 1660 mm of rain a year. In short, the total amount of rainfall is very dependent on aspect and topography; windward coasts and mountainous islands receive the heaviest rainfall, and the flat islands (e.g. Aruba and the Bahamas) may get very little.

The wettest months in Jamaica are May to October. In spite of this, many visitors come in July and August (the Northern Hemisphere summer) though the rest of the wet season (May/June and Sept/Oct) is the low point of Jamaica's tourist year. Most visitors come in the dry season (January–April) for Northern Hemisphere winter holidays (*see* Fig 2.6).

	Average temp °C	Rainfall mm	RH%	Number of staying visitors to Jamaica 1987 (thousands)
Jan	25	26	61	79.6
Feb	25	16	62	69.9
Mar	25	26	62	87.4
Apr	26	31	66	68.2
May	27	110	68	59.5
Jun	27	105	68	49.5
July	28	43	65	59.5
Aug	28	95	70	79.3
Sept	28	105	70	47.5
Oct	27	192	73	43.5
Nov	26	79	68	50.6
Dec	26	26	62	44.0

Fig. 2.6 Jamaica's climate (Kingston)

Tourism levels will have inevitably dropped since 1987 as Jamaica was hit by Hurricane Gilbert in September 1988. The 110 mph winds did much damage – the hurricane caused 500 deaths and billions of dollars worth of damage as it gathered momentum on its passage through the Caribbean and across the Yucatan peninsula. The track of Hurricane Hugo in 1989 followed a more northerly track, well clear of Jamaica, but it devastated Guadeloupe, Montserrat, the Virgin Islands and San Juan in Puerto Rico. Jamaica's tourist resorts have been rebuilt but tour operators and investors in tourist facilities must take account of the risk of hurricane damage. The hurricane season runs from July to October with the greatest incidence in August and September.

Case study: Darwin (12° S)

Darwin is on the north coast of Australia and it has a monsoon type of tropical climate. Tourism in Darwin is more clearly seasonal and is focused on the National Parks inland rather than on coastal resources. The summer rains (November to April) are very intense and make travelling on unsealed roads difficult; many of the adventure safaris and other trips from Darwin operate only between May and October. The climate in these months is dry and hot, and is just on the upper limits of the optimum comfort zone (*see* Fig 2.1) but the low relative humidity makes it just suitable for all kinds of activity and adventure holidays. Tropical cyclones in this part of the world are a little less frequent than in the Caribbean, but Darwin also suffered devastation in 1974 from Cyclone Tracey, but has since been completely rebuilt.

	Av temp °C	Rainfall mm	RH%
Jan	29	381	75
Feb	28	305	76
Mar	29	254	73
Apr	29	102	62
May	28	25	55
Jun	26	0	54
Jul	25	0	52
Aug	26	0	54
Sep	28	25	57
Oct	30	51	59
Nov	30	127	63
Dec	29	229	69

Fig. 2.7 Darwin's climate

Darwin's climate is nearer the monsoonal variation of tropical climate, though it is not quite as extreme as the Northern Hemisphere monsoons of the Indian Subcontinent. Bombay, for example, has a maximum of 610 mm in its peak summer wet month (July) and a total of 1827 mm, but a five-month complete winter drought.

Other variants of tropical climates

Western margin tropical climates
Banjul in the Gambia on the West African coast, and Acapulco on the Pacific coast of Mexico, have many climatic similarities. The summer period of rainfall is pronounced (but not quite as intense as in a monsoonal climate). Neither region is subject to cyclones, and the winter dry season is ideal for winter sun, sea and sand holidays, though the relative humidity at Acapulco is a little on the high side for more active holidays (between 73 and 79 per cent).

	Av temp °C	Rainfall mm	RH%
Jan	23	0	27
Feb	24	0	26
Mar	25	0	29
Apr	25	0	41
May	26	5	49
Jun	27	74	61
Jul	26	280	72
Aug	26	504	78
Sep	27	257	73
Oct	26	95	65
Nov	24	5	47
Dec	25	3	36

Fig. 2.8 Banjul's climate (16.8° N)

Oceanic tropical climates
The Pacific islands, e.g. Hawaii and Cook Islands, have variable amounts of rain, depending on their precise location and topography. In spite of less clearly defined dry seasons with virtually all year round rainfall and high humidity values, the islands may be developed for 'sun, sea and sand' tourism, which are relatively less strenuous holidays. Sea breezes also make the climate feel more comfortable. The extent to which the islands are developed for tourism depends on their accessibility, most of the islands being very isolated.

The hot deserts

In these regions, mean temperatures rise above 33° C with daily maxima well over 37° C and there is persistent sunshine. Some clothing is necessary to protect the body from the sun but it must be loose and light to allow cooling by evaporation to continue, e.g. Insalah (Algerian Sahara), *see* Table 2.1.

The hot deserts have virtually no rain at all. Winters are not quite so hot as the summer months, but at all seasons there is a very wide diurnal range of temperature. The nights may be cold enough for slight frosts in winter, but all year round the daytime temperatures climb rapidly. Maxima of over 45° C in the shade have been recorded in the peak of summer. The relative humidity is very low (about 30 per cent or less), and the discomfort of the dry heat is increased by frequent strong and gusty winds.

| | | | | | Av temp °C | | | | | | |
Jan	Feb	Mar	Apr	May	Jun	Jul	Aug	Sep	Oct	Nov	Dec
12.6	14.8	19.8	24.2	29.7	34.1	37.0	35.8	33.0	26.4	19.8	14.3

Table 2.1 Insalah, Algeria

	Av temp °C	Rainfall mm	RH%
Honolulu (Hawaii) Latitude 20.8° N.			
Jan	22	105	71
Feb	22	67	71
Mar	22	79	69
Apr	23	29	67
May	24	26	67
Jun	24	18	66
Jul	25	23	67
Aug	25	26	68
Sep	25	36	68
Oct	25	29	70
Nov	24	64	71
Dec	23	105	72
Rarotonga (Cook Is) Latitude 21° S.			
Jan	26	256	78
Feb	26	225	81
Mar	26	276	80
Apr	25	179	79
May	24	174	72
Jun	23	107	77
Jul	22	95	75
Aug	21	125	74
Sep	22	125	73
Oct	23	131	74
Nov	24	143	75
Dec	25	233	76

Fig. 2.9 Oceanic tropical climates

Tourism in the hot deserts is limited in two ways; in summer the daytime temperatures are too high and in winter the night-time temperatures may drop too far for comfort. At all times dehydration is a danger, causing discomfort in the eyes and nose, but creating a real danger of illness if enough liquid is not taken at frequent intervals. Tourism is possible in the desert environment, for example, cruises and tours to the ancient Egyptian sites in the Nile valley, if the hottest season is avoided (at Aswan, the June–August average temperatures reach 33° C).

Arid zones

These are hot regions of the world on the margins of the hot deserts, but which have up to 250 mm of rainfall a year.

Case study: Alice Springs (23° S)

Alice Springs is in the 'red centre' of Australia. The proximity of Ayers Rock and the Olgas National Parks has led to the development of tourism in Alice Springs.

The average monthly temperature does not rise above 28° C but the daily range is, nevertheless, very great.

	Av temp °C	Minimum temp	Maximum temp	Rainfall mm	RH%
Jan	29	13	41	46	27
Feb	28	13	40	43	29
Mar	25	10	38	31	31
Apr	20	4	34	20	34
May	15	1	31	18	40
Jun	12	−2	27	16	45
Jul	11	−3	27	10	40
Aug	15	−1	31	10	32
Sep	19	2	35	10	27
Oct	23	6	38	18	24
Nov	26	10	40	26	24
Dec	28	12	41	41	26

Fig. 2.10 Alice Springs' climate

This leads to problems in managing the safety of tourists. The energetic climb to the top of Ayers Rock must be undertaken in the relative cool of the early morning to lessen the risk of heat exhaustion. Twenty-seven people have died climbing Ayers Rock, from heat exhaustion, heart attacks induced by heat stress, and from falls. Except for the more energetic bush walks and safaris (which are offered from April to around September) all the tours and trips from Alice are offered all year round, although, of course, transport is air-conditioned. The rainfall very rarely disrupts tourism, but rainfall in arid zones is notoriously variable. There may be several years with no rain at all followed by a brief period of torrential downpours which may cause extensive flooding and make travel on the unsealed roads hazardous. In 1988 Alice experienced such floods at Easter when many sections of roads were washed away, so that many communities were effectively isolated until the floods receded and repairs were carried out.

Warm temperate climates – one layer clothing zone

These climates can provide the optimal conditions of temperature and humidity for human comfort and some are ideal for tourism which may be possible all year round. Mean monthly temperatures are generally within the range of 10° C in winter up to 25° C in the summer, but daily maxima sometimes reach the 30s. The torso may need the protection of light clothing but not the body's extremities. Relative humidities are generally low enough to make activity holidays possible, though maximum temperatures may be high enough to enforce a midday siesta. The winters are cooler than the summer but are never cold (average winter temperatures do not fall below 6° C). Such climates occur roughly in the zone of latitude 25° N–40° N and 25°–40° S of the Equator (*see* Fig 2.3 on page 9).

The characteristics of the warm temperate climates vary according to their location. The western margins of the continents enjoy the classic Mediterranean climate, with hot, dry summers and rainfall only in the winter. The eastern margins of the continents are exposed to rainbearing onshore winds all year round and are much more humid and their rainfall is much more evenly distributed throughout the year. (This pattern of variation between east and west coasts is similar to that shown by the tropical climates.)

Mediterranean climates

The world location of these climates coincides with the regions of winter rainfall as shown in Fig 2.2 on page 8. The Mediterranean basin itself

is the most extensive area, and the continental influence of the surrounding land masses accentuates the extremes of the climate: in summer the temperatures rise much higher than in this type of climate elsewhere in the world, and in winter (in the northernmost parts of the Mediterranean) night temperatures can occasionally fall low enough for a frost. Similarly, in the heart of the Mediterranean basin, the summer drought may be several months longer than in other parts of the world. These differences make the climate even more suitable for tourism, particularly summer sun holidays.

Case study: Athens (37° N)

Athens is located more or less in the centre of the Mediterranean basin. In July and August the average temperature reaches 27° C but the maximum can go as high as 38° C. Such summers can be graphically described as baking as the summer is very dry, with the period April to September receiving negligible amounts of rainfall. Sunshine totals are high, with 2737 hours of sunshine a year. The sunniest summer month has 362 hours of sunshine (compared with 203 in London). The relative humidity is low, making the heat much more bearable than in comparable temperatures in the more humid tropical climates (*see* Fig 2.11). Not surprisingly, Greece has developed sun, sea and sand packages for the European market, extending

	Av temp °C	Rainfall mm	RH%	Av sunshine hours per day
Jan	9	62	70	5
Feb	10	37	66	6
Mar	11	37	63	6
Apr	15	23	57	7
May	19	23	54	7
Jun	24	14	54	10
Jul	27	6	41	12
Aug	27	7	41	11
Sep	23	15	50	9
Oct	19	51	61	7
Nov	14	56	70	4
Dec	11	71	71	3

Fig. 2.11 Athens' climate (37.58° N)

tourism to the less developed areas as some of the Athens beaches have become more polluted. The northern Europeans, from Britain, Scandinavia, Switzerland and Austria, single out the climate as the main reason for choosing Greece as a holiday location. The reliable heat and sunshine provide a welcome contrast to the greyer climates of the north of Europe.

Although the climate is suitable for this type of holidaymaking all the summer (from May through to October), the demand is heavily concentrated in July and August. Greece has tried to extend the holiday season, both for sun holidays but also for cultural tourism. City breaks and tours of the historic resources of Athens and its hinterland have been promoted, particularly in the spring, when the maximum temperatures stay below 26° C, making sightseeing much less exhausting than in the August heat. In this way, the season has been spread a little into the spring (*see* Fig 2.12).

It has been noted that Athens is one of the hotter examples of a Mediterranean climate. The other parts of the world that enjoy Mediterranean climates are narrow coastal strips on the western sides of the continents. The proximity to the open ocean moderates the summer temperatures, though in other respects (such as sunshine, rainfall and humidity) they conform to the pattern set by Athens.

Fig 2.13 shows the average temperature of the warmest summer month in the Mediterranean climates in the other continents of the world. The winter conditions of Mediterranean climates make winter sun holidays possible, though the winter provides less reliable and more variable weather than in the summer. Some locations (e.g. some of the Spanish costas) have promoted winter holidays for the retired who can benefit most from the milder winter conditions without needing the high levels of sunshine offered by many competing winter sun destinations.

Eastern margin warm temperate climates

These climates have temperature regimes very similar to the Mediterranean climates (though a few degrees cooler than the central Mediterranean basin), but are more humid and have rainfall all year round, e.g. Sydney, Australia.

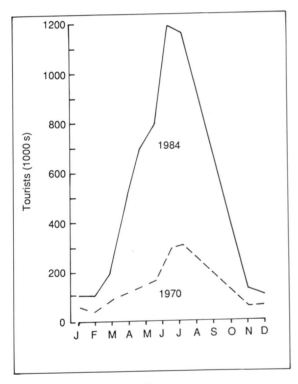

Fig. 2.12 Athens' tourist flow

Location	Latitude	Continent	Highest average summer month temperature
Los Angeles	34° N	North America	August 22°C
Valparaiso	33° S	South America	January 19.5°C
Cape Town	34° S	South Africa	January/Feb 21°C
Perth	32° S	Australia	January/Feb 23.5°C

Fig. 2.13 World Mediterranean climates

	Temp °C	Rainfall mm	RH%
Jan	22	95	66
Feb	21	110	68
Mar	20	123	69
Apr	18	143	70
May	15	131	70
Jun	13	123	70
Jul	12	123	68
Aug	13	77	64
Sep	15	74	61
Oct	18	82	61
Nov	19	72	63
Dec	21	74	64

Fig. 2.14 Sydney's climate (34° S)

Case study: Florida, USA (25° N)

The best known tourist area with a eastern margin temperate climate is the State of Florida, USA: indeed, some claim that it is the leading tourist destination in the world. Florida lies on the extreme southernmost boundary of the warm temperate climatic zone (extending from about 26° N to roughly 31° N) so the southern tip of the Florida peninsula may occasionally suffer from hurricanes straying north from the tropical Caribbean region. Thus, it shows some transitional features between tropical and warm temperate, but is generally classified with the warm temperate climates.

Miami is located well to the south of Florida, and thus shows maximum temperatures comparable to nearby tropical locations.

	Minimum temp °C	Maximum temp °C	Rainfall mm	RH%
Jan	6	28	50	72
Feb	7	29	48	70
Mar	8	30	58	69
Apr	12	31	99	68
May	17	33	163	69
Jun	20	34	188	73
Jul	22	34	170	73
Aug	22	34	178	73
Sep	22	33	241	76
Oct	17	23	208	75
Nov	10	30	71	72
Dec	7	28	43	73

Fig. 2.15 Miami's climate

Florida has a range of attractions, from the beach for sun, sea and sand holidays, the Everglades National Park for outdoor activities, and a wealth of indoor and entertainment facilities, such as the Epcot centre and Disneyworld, and Miami has diversified into conference and business tourism. Not surprisingly, Florida has all year round tourism. With an average winter temperature of 20.5° C and under 50 mm of rainfall per month from December to February, the winter is the peak season. The majority of winter visitors fly in from the freezing weather of the north east of the USA. In spite of the high summer rainfall totals, there are almost as many visitors in the second and third quarters of the year as in the peak winter season (see Fig 2.15).

1985 Air and auto arrivals in Florida (millions)			
	Air	Auto	Total arrivals
Jan–March	4.87	3.70	8.57
April–June	3.28	4.32	7.60
July–Sept	2.85	4.21	7.06
Oct–Dec	3.30	3.55	6.85

Fig. 2.16 Seasonal distribution of visitors to Florida

The number of overseas visitors gradually increases from April to August, peaking in the wettest season. The final quarter of the year (Oct–Dec) has only slightly fewer visitors than the other periods of the year. So in spite of the high rainfall and humidity of the summer months, Miami (and Florida as a whole) is virtually a non-seasonal destination.

Cool temperate climates – two layer clothing zone

Cool temperate climates are typified by the Western European climates. Mean monthly temperatures range from about 0° C in mid-winter to 16° C in mid-summer, making only the main summer months really suitable for the more passive tourist pursuits. A large proportion of tourist generating areas lie within this climatic zone and tourists will be seeking a more comfortable and attractive climate than their own, e.g. Falmouth in the South of England, where the average temperatures are shown in Table 2.2.

	Jan	Feb	Mar	Apr	May	Jun	Jul	Aug	Sep	Oct	Nov	Dec
Temp °C	7.0	6.6	7.7	9.3	11.5	14.8	15.9	16.5	14.8	12.1	8.8	7.0
RH%	85	83	83	79	79	80	80	83	85	87	85	85

Table 2.2 Falmouth, UK

These climates have a definitely cold winter season (usually below 6° C) and rain occurs all year round.

In this zone the western coastal margins of the continents have their peak rainfall in the winter, and annual ranges of temperature are quite low. These climates are characterised by very variable weather with many sudden temperature and cloud cover changes. Rainfall levels and cloud cover are greatest on the most westerly margins, and decrease inland. Spells of settled hot weather may occur in the summer, but their timing cannot be predicted in advance with any certainty. Tourists, when planning and booking their holidays, will want some guarantee of the weather they might expect, and are thus likely to opt for the locations with more predictable and reliably hot, sunny climates such as those of the Mediterranean countries. The interiors of the continents in the cool temperate zone have much greater ranges of temperature throughout the year (even up to a range of 30° C). Neither variant of this type of climate is ideally suited for tourism except in the peak summer months of July and August. This zone covers the main tourist generating areas rather than any significant tourist receiving areas. Many of the older coastal tourist resorts in the cool temperate zone are experiencing a significant decline in visitors due to increasing competition from resorts in more attractive climates in other parts of the world.

The cold climates – the three layer clothing zone

The average temperature in this zone for at least six months of the year is below 6° C. In these latitudes the winter days are very short and the summer days are long. Summers are short and cool (June–August) and the season changes rapidly from winter to summer. Such areas may be suitable for scenery and activity holidays but the tourist season is inevitably short too. The continental interiors in this zone have much more extreme climates, with intense winter cold, below minus 30° C (way below freezing) but with summer averages climbing to 19° C.

The Arctic and polar climates – maximum clothing zone

These climates are always cold, with less than three months' average temperature above 6° C. The tundra climates have a short period when the ground is free from snow but in the more northerly areas there is permanent snow cover. It may be possible in the future to develop the Arctic regions for special interest tourism, for example, wildlife cruises to Antarctica, but the potential of such areas is thought to be very limited.

Mountain climates

Mountain regions will generally follow the climatic regime of the region where they are situated: mountains in desert regions will be dry, while those in tropical zones will have rainfall according to the local seasonal pattern. However, their height modifies their climate in three ways.

1 The effect of altitude on temperature. The temperature drops at a regular rate as the land rises above sea level, e.g. in the Alps the temperature decreases by 0.75° C per 100 metres on north-facing slopes. So upland areas are cooler than surrounding lowlands. The actual temperature at the summit will depend on two variables: the height of the mountain and the air temperature at the bottom of the mountain (which is determined by latitude). Thus, on the Equator, mountains are cold enough for there to be snow all year round at heights above 5500 metres. Moving away from the Equator into cooler temperature zones (*see* Fig 2.3 on page 9) the 'snowline' (i.e. the height at which snow lies all year round) drops (*see* Fig 2.17).

Temperature zone	Latitude	Mountain	Mountain height	Snowline height
Arctic	70° N	–	–	sea level
Cold	62° N	Glitter Fjeld	2598 m	1200 m
Cool temperate	46° N	Mont Blanc	4807 m	2750 m
Warm temperate	28° N	Everest	8834 m	4800 m
Hot	Equator	Chimborazo	6243 m	5500 m

Fig. 2.17 **Height of snowline in temperature zones**

2 Effect of altitude on air pressure. The air gets thinner with increased altitude, so that at 5500 metres the air pressure is only half that at sea level, and there is less oxygen available in such a rarefied atmosphere. Thus, at about 2500–3000 m humans begin to feel breathless and lethargic (a condition known as 'mountain sickness') which will make any energetic activity difficult.

3 The effect of altitude on rainfall. Mountains generally experience greater rainfall than lowlands similarly placed. This is caused by the air being cooled as it is forced up the slope of the mountain side, and as it cools, the moisture in the air condenses to form rain. The effect is most pronounced where high land forms a barrier to rain-bearing winds.

In summary, mountains are often cooler, wetter and at high altitudes, less comfortable places than the surrounding lowlands. Nevertheless, many mountainous regions are important tourist destinations. First, in hot, humid, equatorial and tropical climates, the very coolness of the mountains may make them attractive hot season resorts (such as Simla in the Himalayas). Second, the scenery of the mountains may attract tourists, even in spite of unfavourable weather conditions. Indeed, in many resorts in the European Alps, summer visitors outnumber winter tourists, although the mountains are at their wettest in the summer. Finally, the mountains may be developed for winter sports. Skiing needs a very particular combination of climatic conditions: good snow quality (dry and powdery), abundant sunshine, little wind, and a long enough winter season (at least 120 days) with snow lying to make the very substantial investment in ski facilities (lifts, tows, hotels etc) economically worthwhile. In addition, the resort must necessarily be well below the height at which people start to feel the effects of mountain sickness.

This specification is most closely met in the European Alps, where snow falls in autumn and early winter but high pressure then builds over the mountain chain bringing very cold, sunny and settled weather for long periods. The clear air, although very cold, allows the sun's rays to penetrate with little loss of intensity. The sunshine warms the skin and will quickly produce a deep tan, so although the air temperatures are very low (e.g. average January temperature is −7° C in Davos, Switzerland) skiers will not feel uncomfortably chilled.

	Av temp °C	Precipitation mm
Jan	−7	46
Feb	−5	56
Mar	−3	56
Apr	2	56
May	5	59
Jun	10	102
Jul	12	125
Aug	11	128
Sep	8	95
Oct	3	69
Nov	−1	56
Dec	−6	64

Fig. 2.18 **Davos' climate (47° N) – altitude 1564 metres**

There may be great local variations in ski conditions within a mountain region: the amount and quality of snow and length of time it persists depend very much on aspect and will vary considerably from slope to slope. Similarly, one part of a valley may be much windier than another, depending on local air circulation. The precise location of ski resorts and ski slopes within a mountain region will be constrained by these local factors.

FURTHER READING

Hobbs, J E (1980) *Applied Climatology*, Butterworth, (particularly pp. 62–74, 'Climate and comfort').

Pearce, E A and Smith, C G (1984) *The World Weather Guide*, Hutchinson.

QUESTIONS AND DISCUSSION POINTS

1 Locate Los Angeles on a world map and study

Los Angeles (Latitude 34° North)

	Av temp °C	*Rainfall mm*	*RH%*
Jan	13	79	57
Feb	14	76	64
Mar	15	71	64
Apr	16	25	69
May	17	10	73
Jun	19	3	73
Jul	21	1	71
Aug	22	1	71
Sep	21	5	67
Oct	17	15	62
Nov	16	30	50
Dec	14	66	52

Total rainfall (mm): 382
Total annual hours of sunshine: 3500
Average number of rainy days: 50.

Table 2.3

the climatic data for the city shown in Table 2.3. What type of climate does Los Angeles have? Suggest reasons why the relative humidity is so high in July and August, even though there is negligible rainfall. Is this likely to constrain the development of the tourist potential of this location?

2 Identify the world locations of the most ideal climates for tourism. Where are these climatic zones

in relation to the main tourist generating regions of the world (see also Chapters 17 and 15).

3 Which climatic zones of the world are climatically unsuitable for all but certain very specialised forms of tourism? Why are they unsuitable for mass tourism?

ASSIGNMENTS

1 Assessment of Palma's climate for tourist activities. Trace the human comfort chart (from Fig 2.1) onto squared paper. Plot the monthly temperature and relative humidity figures for Palma on the chart using the figures from Table 2.4. Which months' values fall within the 'optimum' zone? What range

Palma de Mallorca, Balearic Islands, Latitude 39° N

	Av temp °C	*Rainfall mm*	*RH%*
Jan	10.7	43	78
Feb	11.8	39	76
Mar	13.1	39	75
Apr	15.3	36	72
May	18.5	31	72
Jun	22.2	20	68
Jul	25.5	9	68
Aug	25.8	17	70
Sep	23.8	44	74
Oct	19.2	77	77
Nov	14.4	50	78
Dec	11.3	55	77

Table 2.4

of tourist activities (other than beach activities) could take place in a climate such as Palma's?

2 You work for a tour company wishing to expand its winter sun holidays for the British market. You have been asked to identify three possible locations with ideal climates for winter sun holidays.

Select and map three locations, and using the

CHAPTER 3

Coastal resources and the sea

LEARNING OBJECTIVES

After reading this chapter you should be able to
- list the characteristics of the sea coast that are of significance for tourism
- locate the areas of the world where the best natural conditions exist for sun, sea and sand tourism
- understand the relationships between climate, and the processes of erosion and deposition that fashion the coastline
- be aware of some of the physical factors that constrain or facilitate coastal tourist development.

INTRODUCTION

For many people, going on holiday means going to the seaside. In Britain about 70 per cent of domestic holidays have traditionally been to the coast and 'sun, sea and sand' holiday packages are overwhelmingly the most popular overseas trips. After the climate, the coast and the sea are perhaps the most important geographical resources for tourism, the nature and quality of the coast and beaches play a very important part in making a successful and enjoyable holiday.

WHAT THE TOURIST IS LOOKING FOR

The sea

The tourist is first and foremost looking for a clean, sandy beach that is comfortable to sunbathe on and safe for swimming, with gentle waves that allow children to play at the water's edge. There must be no dangerous tidal or offshore currents that might sweep the unwary swimmer, small boats or inflatables out to sea. A shelving beach may also get the non-swimmer into trouble though the sea must still be deep enough inshore (perhaps chest deep) to give the more serious swimmers scope to enjoy themselves.

The beach

A wide and fairly flat beach provides plenty of room for all the holidaymakers and their beach equipment (which may include tables, chairs and parasols). On the other hand, the sea must not be too far away for the swimmer to walk to, so a low tidal range is ideal. Finally, the beach should be only a few yards away from the tourists' accommodation; a long walk or a climb up and down a steep cliff can be tiring and inconvenient.

From the tourist developer or tour operator's point of view, access to the beach is also crucial. Level land suitable for hotel development as close as possible to the beach makes for a more attractive product. For them, the winter climate is another important factor as development close to the high watermark may be vulnerable to wind and wave damage if there are winter storms. The long-term stability of the coast is an additional consideration as investment in such development is pointless if erosion by the sea will eventually undermine the buildings or wash away the sandy beach.

Specialised sea-based sports such as surfing, angling, diving, sailboarding, sailing and other forms of boating may require additional or even perhaps totally contrasting features. For example, the best surfing beaches need very much bigger, regular, slowly breaking waves rolling in to a sandy beach. The sailboarders, however, need a relatively quiet rather sheltered sea where the inexperienced or less fit sailboard enthusiast will be safe.

The experienced yachtsman may relish more of a challenge and in common with other boating people will need launching facilities or deeper water inshore for anchorage. The anglers and divers will be looking for clean, unpolluted waters where marine wildlife abounds. Although the real specialist will be pleased to find these qualities anywhere, the ideal situation would have such coasts alongside the best swimming and sunbathing beaches for the perfect holiday. Thus it is clear that the following physical characteristics of the beach and coast are of crucial importance for tourism:

(a) composition of the beach (its lithology) – for comfort.

(b) the nature and size of the waves – for safety.

(c) the tides and currents in the sea – for convenience and safety.

(d) cleanliness and pollution – for health and comfort.

(e) the shape of the beach in plan and in profile – for safety and convenience.

(f) The shape and character of the land above high watermark – for ease of access and development.

(g) The stability of the beach and coast – for long-term investment.

THE COMPOSITION OF THE BEACH

This is perhaps the most important characteristic. A sandy beach is an attractive beach, a shingly or muddy beach is of relatively little use for tourism. Of course, the type of rock that makes up the coast is important as this may form the immediate source of the sand or mud that accumulates on the shore. A soft sandstone will easily crumble under the action of the wind and rain to yield sand for the beach, but chalk on the other hand will dissolve away leaving a residue of rounded flint nodules which form the shingly beaches which are typically found under the White Cliffs of Dover on the south coast of England. The purer limestone rock of the Dalmatian coast of Croatia produces neither sand nor pebbles, so the coastline consists mainly of bare rock. However, where the characteristics of beaches are examined on a world scale

there seems to be a distinct regional pattern of occurrence of sandy, muddy and shingly beaches, and surprisingly enough this pattern seems to be more closely associated with the climate (past and present) than with the present characteristics of the rock that makes up the coast.

Figure 3.1 shows that pebbly beaches are much more common in the high latitudes; these coincide with those parts of the world dominated by icecaps either now or in the glaciations of over ten thousand years ago. The icecaps and glaciers leave a coating of mixed crushed and broken rocks and gravel which are reworked by the sea to form shingly beaches. Figure 3.2 shows the distribution of the types of material of which beaches are made, according to their latitude. This shows that while shingle is dominant in high latitudes, mud is much more common nearer to the Equator (0–20° latitude).

The present equatorial climate, with its hot, wet conditions, allows rapid chemical decomposition of rocks to take place, so that they eventually disintegrate into mud. This zone of intense chemical weathering is shown on Fig 3.1. The great equatorial rivers (e.g. the Amazon and Congo) also add vast quantities of mud to the coast in these parts of the world. Although Chapter 2 suggests the climate of this zone to be far from perfect for tourism, there are some attractive tourist beaches in the hot climate zone, namely, coral beaches. Where the warm waters of the tropics are clear and shallow, coral grows in abundance, and corals may be ground up by the sea to form attractive beaches of coral and shell sand – the white beaches typical of the tropical coral island. The Great Barrier Reef off the Queensland coast of Australia is perhaps the world's most spectacular area of live coral, with a wealth of opportunities for tourists to snorkel and scuba dive to look at the coral, fish and other marine wildlife.

Figure 3.2 shows that sand is most frequently found in latitude 20–40° N and S, coinciding roughly with the world distribution of the types of climate most suitable for tourism (i.e. tropical and warm temperate climates).

It appears that the characteristics of the waves and currents in this zone of the world also tend to encourage the accumulation of sand. However, shingle does occur on some of the coasts of the semi-arid and desert areas where the humidity is too low to allow chemical weathering of rock to take place.

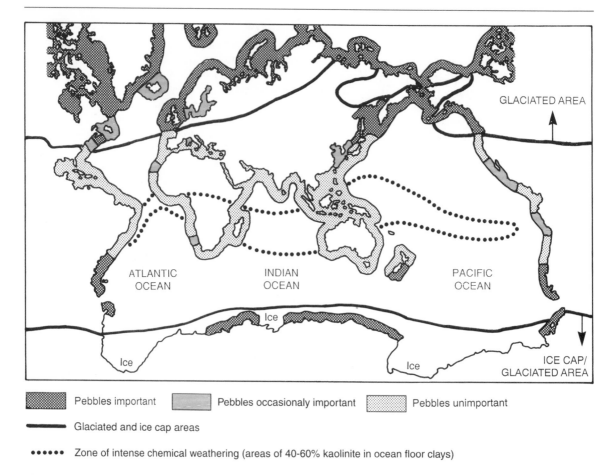

Fig. 3.1 World distribution of pebbly beaches showing the importance of pebbles as a beach material
(*Source*: After Davies, 1972)

THE WAVES

It has been noted that size and nature of the waves are significant for the safety and enjoyment of the tourist in the summer. The waves, along with tides and currents, are also major factors in determining the processes which erode or build up the beach and coast. However, the climate is once again the underlying factor that controls these processes, because the waves themselves are created by the action of wind on the surface of the sea.

Storm waves

Certain types of climate are windier than others, some of the windier being the cool temperate climates that are found in latitudes 40°–60° (*see* Fig 2.3).

It is in these latitudes that most storms occur. These frequent storms and winds generate big energetic waves which crash onto the coasts of these zones causing wear and tear and erosion. Figure 3.3 shows the world distribution of these 'storm wave environments'.

These waves carve out dramatic coastal landforms such as cliffs, stacks and caves, in the hard rocks that are abundant in this zone. The erosion also tends to shift and erode away sand to create and reform the beaches. The storm waves tend to be short, steep and rapid, with the next wave breaking before the first has completed its backwash. This may make paddling or swimming in the surf zone uncomfortable and even dangerous in rough weather particularly on a steeply sloping beach. In the winter, waves over 7 metres high

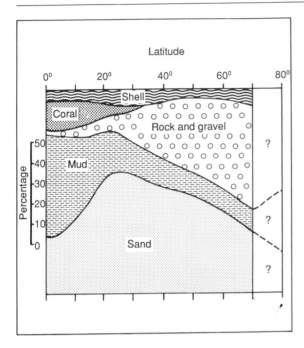

Fig. 3.2 Distribution of types of materials that form beaches

have been recorded which are capable of doing great damage to any buildings or constructions near the high watermark. However, the cool temperate climates are characterised by their variability and the storm waves that wash the beaches are as ephemeral and variable as the weather that created them. In summer, of course, the weather is generally calmer, when weather and waves may combine to produce ideal paddling and bathing conditions.

Severe storms (called **cyclones**) do also occur in tropical latitudes (*see* Fig 3.3), for example the hurricanes in the Caribbean. Although these storms cause more damage to buildings than the storms experienced in higher latitudes, they are too infrequent and localised to affect landforms and beaches to any great extent.

In summary, it can be concluded that the storm wave environments of latitudes 40°–60° are areas of high wave energy, though of course there are periods of calm seas in the summer season. The action of such waves creates gently sloping shores often leading up to cliffed coasts. Beaches are limited in development and frequency and are often pebbly. However, where sand does accumulate

locally to form beaches they are often backed by sand dunes creating an attractive beach for the tourist. It must be remembered that this is a broad generalisation, and local variations in geology and climate will lead to some variations in coastal characteristics within this general pattern.

Swell waves

The waves created by high winds in mid latitude zones radiate outwards through the oceans like ripples on a pond, penetrating into the parts of the world with much less windy climates. These ripples form the sea swell which makes waves break on shores many thousands of miles away from the winds that created them. This swell causes waves to break on the coasts in the low latitudes (0°–40°) even when there are no winds blowing in the vicinity.

In the South Pacific, persistently strong westerly winds blow, which build up huge waves that radiate out from the centre of the south of the Pacific Ocean. It is these big regular swell waves that create the best surfing conditions. The most popular surfing beaches are found where such waves meet the shore head on, such as Bondi Beach on the eastern Australian coast at Sydney and the famous Californian surfing beaches on the other side of the Pacific. On some Pacific beaches, however, the combination of big waves and local currents can create dangerous swimming conditions.

Swell waves in the other oceans are generally smaller and less steep than the Pacific swell. They are also less frequent, so that the backwash is able to return to the sea before the next wave arrives. This creates an environment wherein the tourist is both safer and more comfortable. In addition, this type of wave is far less destructive than storm waves and tends to encourage the accumulation of the sand and mud on the shore.

The coasts of the world in latitudes 20°–40° thus show the coincidence of all the factors favourable for seaside tourism. The best climates, abundant sand, good surfing or gentle reliable and regular waves that tend to accumulate the sand into offshore sandbars, lagoons, spits and some of the best and biggest sandy beaches of the world. Hard rocks and cliffs are rarely found in these latitudes, though pebbly beaches may be found on the coasts of semi-arid desert areas.

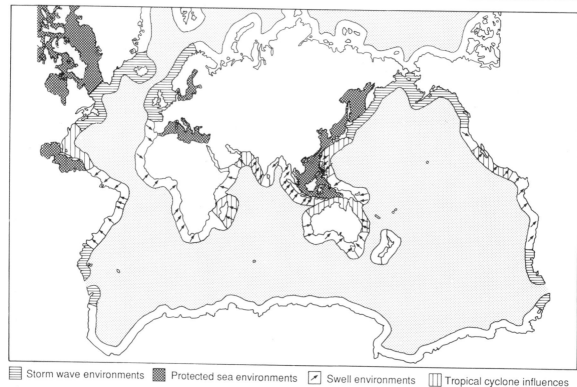

Storm wave environments   Protected sea environments   Swell environments   Tropical cyclone influences

Fig. 3.3 Wave conditions round the coasts of the world
(*Source*: After Davies, 1972)

THE TIDES

The tides are caused by the gravitational pull of
the moon on the body of water of the seas. The
range of the tide (i.e. the difference in height of the
water at low and at high tide) varies over the
world. The world distribution of tidal range at
spring tides (those very high tides occurring when
the sun reinforces the gravitational pull of the
moon) is shown in Fig 3.4. In the open oceans the
range is generally about two metres but this may
be considerably greater where the configuration of
a coast line may form a funnel. This is particularly
the case around Great Britain. The Severn Estuary
is a classic example of this; at Avonmouth the tidal
range at spring is 16.3 metres. The significance of
tidal range for tourism is the fact that the greater
the tidal range the wider the beach tends to be.
The erosive power of the sea is spread over a wide
area between the tidal limits and the sea tends to
cut a wide, very gently sloping beach platform.

Although this may at first glance seem an advantage for tourism in that it provides plenty of space
on the beach, another consequence of this is that
the sea may recede a very long way from the shore
at the lowest tides, giving the tourist a very long
walk to find the sea! Also, having reached it, the
sea is often too shallow for swimming (e.g. as at
Weston Super Mare in Avon).

An additional problem in such areas is that the
tide may come in unexpectedly rapidly on wide,
very gently sloping beaches, which may catch the
unsuspecting tourist unawares. A fast incoming or
outgoing tide is also often associated with dangerous tidal currents. In the British Isles, some of the
fiercest tidal currents are experienced in the shallow,
funnel-shaped estuaries, rendering them unsafe for
swimming and some even too dangerous for boating and sailing (e.g. on the Severn Estuary).

Dangerous tidal currents may also occur
around and between islands, (e.g. the Menai
Straits in Wales) and off promontories. There is

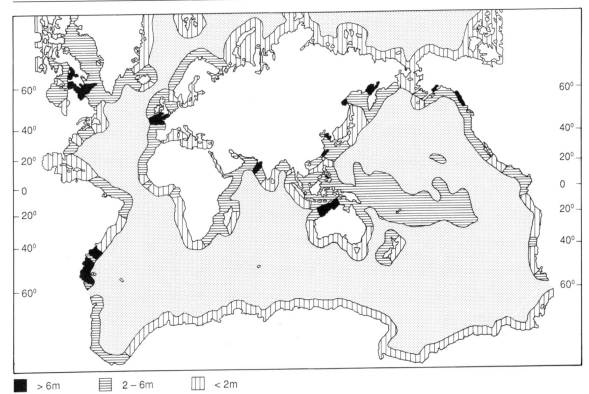

■ > 6m   ▤ 2 – 6m   ▥ < 2m

Fig. 3.4 World distribution of tidal range at spring tides
(*Source*: After Davies, 1972)

one advantage of a reasonably high tidal range for tourism: the tide acts as a very effective cleaning and scouring agent, carrying away rubbish and resorting the sand (though rubbish may be deposited and accumulate at the winter high watermark). Beaches in areas such as the Mediterranean which has a very low tidal range may have to be cleaned manually.

THE ENCLOSED SEAS

Figure 3.3 classifies certain of the seas of the world as 'protected seas'. These are bodies of water linked to the main oceans but which are almost cut off by the configuration of the land masses, e.g. the Mediterranean, or by strings of islands (for example, the Gulf of Mexico). Because they are relatively small bodies of water, the effect of the moon on the tides is less. In fact, many of these seas have very small tidal ranges or are virtually tideless.

Because they are effectively enclosed, these seas are not affected by the waves and swell created in the high latitudes of the open oceans, so these seas experience only very small waves, even in winter. This pattern is only disturbed by local weather conditions when bigger waves may be temporarily generated. The waves have little power to cause erosion, so safe, sandy beaches are frequently found: all in all, a perfect tourist environment.

Finally, the enclosed seas although benefiting on the whole from their protected character suffer one disadvantage: because the water in the enclosed sea does not circulate and mix with the water of the open ocean, any pollution entering the sea is not dispersed or diluted, and indeed pollution tends to build up virtually irreversibly in such locations. This is a particular problem in the Mediterranean. Due to the restricted flow of water through the narrow Straits of Gibraltar, it takes 75 years for the whole of the water of the Mediterranean to be replaced by fresh Atlantic water. In the late 1980s the northern Adriatic coastal resorts were badly hit due to the consequences of the build up of pollution.

SEA POLLUTION

There are five main types of pollutants that affect the sea:

1 Solid debris washed up at high tidemark. The debris such as bottles, plastic containers and boxes originates both from coastal towns, rivers washing into the sea and from ships at sea.
2 Oil, in the form of liquid slicks floating on the surface and as coagulated lumps of tar. Oil may come from urban onshore industrial centres, from ships cleaning out their holds or from accidental spillages both at sea and at coastal oil terminals.
3 Other chemical pollution dissolved or suspended in water entering the sea. This originates mainly from fertilisers in the run off from farmland, or from industrial effluent containing industrial waste products.
4 Sewage, either treated or raw. This comes from urban areas onshore.
5 Hot water that has been used for cooling purposes, either in industrial process or in power stations. This is perhaps the only form of pollution that has no undesirable effects on tourism.

The first four types of pollution make the beaches less desirable for tourism but some forms of chemical pollution and raw sewage effluent may make them totally unusable on health grounds. Oil pollution is perhaps the most obvious and visible form of pollution and has received most attention in the press; consequently, tourist resorts have given more priority to overcome this pollution problem than any of the others.

WORLD POLLUTION

Oil

In 1983 48 per cent of the volume of world marine oil pollution came from land-based sources and 52 per cent from ships. Only about one third of the ship-generated oil pollution was due to accidental spillages, and only a tiny proportion from the oil

and gas fields. Thus, industry and routine shipping are the major sources. Surveys completed in 1978 not surprisingly showed the greatest concentration of oil pollution along shipping lanes and in coastal waters, where tourism is concentrated. Virtually the whole of the Mediterranean falls into the highest category of pollution; the fact that it is an enclosed sea prevents the dispersal or dilution of the oil.

Natural biological processes may remove the oil in time, but the solid tar balls may be swept on shore before these processes are complete. Where the tar arrives depends on winds, waves, and currents, but in general terms it will tend to accumulate in the same places and by the same processes as sand and other sediments. The solid tar will tend to be concentrated where sand is accumulated, i.e. on the most extensive sandy beaches.

Detergents are successfully used to clean the beaches, but it must be recognised that these detergents are themselves as much a pollutant as the oil and can damage marine wildlife, although it is a more acceptable form of pollution (at least in visual terms) to tourists.

Other forms of pollution

Sewage and chemical pollution are the other most serious hazards to tourists on health grounds. Chemical pollution can sometimes be very dangerous but perhaps the resident population (i.e. the population that is continually exposed to the chemical) is at greater risk than visitors of a week or so's duration.

On the other hand, untreated sewage is just as dangerous to residents and tourists alike. The technology exists to treat all sewage products to a high standard but tourist resorts may not be willing or able to afford to install the equipment capable of meeting the extra volume produced in the few months of the peak holiday period. The excess sewage produced in July and August may be pumped straight into the sea with partial or no treatment at all. Beaches polluted in this way are not only visually repellent but are also, of course, a great health hazard. Research in the USA has shown that of all the bathers swimming in their areas of sewage polluted waters, 18 out of every 1000 succumb to some form of pollution-related illness (such as gastroenteritis, skin allergies, ear, nose or throat infections).

In Europe, the EC has set standards of cleanliness and water quality that bathing beaches should meet. In Britain, the Government monitors 392 beaches, and by 1988, 75 per cent of these beaches had been brought up to the EC standard. However, 22 beaches in the North West, including Blackpool, and some of the beaches in South East England failed to meet the standard. Most of the beaches of South West England were adequate.

TOURIST DEVELOPMENT ON THE COAST

However attractive a beach may be, it cannot be developed for tourism unless it is both accessible and has space for development to landward. This depends on the location of the beach in relation to the landforms above high watermark. Very attractive pocket, bayhead and bayside beaches may be found along irregular cliffed upland coasts, the beaches being found in the bays of various sizes interspersed between the headlands which are composed of harder, more resistant rock. The attractive beaches of the Lleyn and Gower peninsulas of Wales are generally of these types.

Bayhead beaches may sometimes be found where valleys are cut into the higher land, with the river valley providing an accessible route to the coast. Or they may occur where the cliffs are lower and less rugged. In either case, some low level land may be available for tourist development and small resorts may develop. However, where such beaches are backed by high or steep cliffs, land that can be developed is scarce, and is both difficult and very expensive to build on. This may lead to very exclusive development of cliff top hotels, having access to their own small private beaches. No long-term development at all is possible where the coastline is unstable. Some geological features such as cliffs made of soft clays, glacial deposits or rock consisting of alternate horizontal layers of soft and harder rocks, are particularly susceptible to erosion. The sea can accelerate the erosion, particularly during winter storms by undercutting the cliff foot and rapidly removing material that falls onto the beach from the cliff face. These circumstances combine to create a highly mobile, unstable cliff, often charac-

terised by slumping, landslides and sometimes even mudflows. The undercliffs at Lyme Regis in Dorset are a classic example of an unstable area generated by repeated landslips on the cliff face which prohibits any development. Access to beaches at the foot of such mobile unstable cliffs is also often difficult, as any steps or stairways built down the cliff face will need repeated replacement every year or so, e.g. as at St Marys Bay, Brixham.

Where erosion is a continuous problem, attempts may be made to reinforce the shore by building sea walls, bulkheads or revetments. These are generally of concrete or stone, and are designed to dissipate the energy of the breaking wave so that less damage is done. These sea defences are typical of many of the coastal resort areas in the high latitude storm wave zone, where the waves generated by winter storms can do great damage to tourist installations. However, it is unusual for the defences to be anything other than temporary expedients, needing eventual repair and replacement.

In mid latitudes, where marine erosion is more common than the accumulation of sand, the beaches themselves may also be very changeable. As the waves and the tides repeatedly flow over them, the sand is shifting, sorted, rearranged and replaced. Where the supply of sand brought by the waves and currents to the beach is less than that renewed by the sea, then the beach is eroded. In general, sand is moved along the beach if the waves break on the beach at an angle. Where beach material is on the move, a tourist resort has great interest in artificially retaining or increasing the amount of sand on its beach.

Groynes may be constructed to trap the sand and help build out the beach. The beach sand accumulates on the updrift side and is removed on the downdrift side leading to differences in height or size of beach on either side of the groyne. This may, however, create a potential danger for paddlers or swimmers stepping over the groyne into deep water.

A more drastic and expensive solution is to replenish the sand at the same rate, or faster than it is being removed. This is possible if there is a suitable source of sand, and the resort can afford the cost of the engineering work. Bournemouth beach has been reinforced by sand dredged up from Poole Harbour. In the storm wave environments at this latitude there is always the risk that winter storms will render such actions ineffective.

The violent storms of February 1990 rearranged the sand at Bournemouth, eroding some and depositing the rest on coastal roads.

Elsewhere in the world, other tourist resorts have also tried to improve their beaches. In Magalluf, in Mallorca, for example, the resort was so popular that the beach was just not large enough for all the tourists. The local authority responded by importing sand and widening the beach. In the enclosed sea environment of the Mediterranean this is likely to be a more successful long-term investment. Thus, it is possible for engineers to modify and possibly improve the natural qualities of the beach and coast for tourism. The amount of public money spent to control pollution, stabilise or improve the beach depends on the investment decisions of the local authority (or other agency that is responsible for the infrastructure) and the extent to which they perceive the promotion of tourism to be in the public interest.

REFERENCES AND FURTHER READING

Those texts marked with an asterisk are particularly recommended for further reading.

*Caines, R (Ed) (1991) *The Good Beach Guide,* Marine Conservation Society, Ebury Press.

Davies, J L (1972) *Geographical Variation in Coastal Development*, Oliver and Boyd.

QUESTIONS AND DISCUSSION POINTS

1 What are the advantages and disadvantages of an enclosed sea location for coastal tourism?

2 In what ways is the build up of marine pollution a threat to coastal tourism? In what types of location is the danger greatest?

3 In which climate zones of the world are the best natural conditions for coastal tourism to be found? Where are these zones in relation to the main tourist generating regions of the world? (*See also* Chapters 1 and 2.)

ASSIGNMENTS

1 You work for a tour operator who specialises in sun, sea and sand tours to the Mediterranean region for the UK market. Your Chief Executive wishes to diversify into summer sun, sea and sand packages in *other* parts of the world and has asked you to select the regions of the world likely to provide the ideal combination of climatic and coastal conditions for this type of holiday.

Prepare a short report (illustrated with world maps) indicating those stretches of coast where these conditions are likely to coincide, and where your company might start to search for suitable sites to develop and promote.

2 You work in a travel agency. A customer arrives who is a surfing enthusiast, and he asks you to advise him where in the world the best surfing conditions are likely to occur, and when would be the best times of year to visit these places. Write notes for this customer, listing:

(a) the general world locations, where the best surfing conditions are likely to be found; and

(b) the months of the year when the climate is most suitable for beach activities in these places. List the range of temperatures he might expect during this period. The customer wants this information for each of the regions of the world you have identified under (a).

CHAPTER 4

Landscape and wildlife resources for tourism

LEARNING OBJECTIVES

After studying this chapter you should be able to
- list the qualities that make a landscape attractive for tourism
- assess the attractiveness of a landscape for tourists
- locate the areas of the world that have the greatest potential for scenic tourism
- appreciate the role of world conservation bodies and national governments in the protection of scenic and wildlife resources for tourism
- understand the differences between the British and the world National Parks
- locate Britain's main landscape resources for tourism.

INTRODUCTION

Tourists visit the countryside for many reasons; their motivations may be much more complex and varied than those that generate coastal tourism.

1 Visitors may travel to rural areas to appreciate the natural wonders of the world – features such as great waterfalls (e.g. the Niagara Falls) volcanic phenomena (hot springs, sulphur pools, geysers such as Old Faithful in Wyoming, USA etc), geological phenomena such as caves or rock formations (e.g. Ayers Rock), or spectacular views (e.g. across the Grand Canyon).

2 People may use the countryside in order to pursue activities that require a rural setting or that depend on rurally located resources, rather than for the scenic quality of the rural backdrop. Activities such as sailing, canoeing, potholing, shooting, climbing, hang-gliding and skiing are examples of the latter where the quality of the resource is more significant than the landscape in which it is set, whereas activities such as cycling, horse riding and walking perhaps depend more closely on high quality landscapes.

3 Touring holidays, where the travel is the focus of the experience rather than the destination, will also be best enjoyed in a region with a variety of attractive landscapes and picturesque villages.

4 On the other hand, people may wish to visit the countryside as a destination in its own right in order to experience a non-urban way of life for a period, as a relief from the congestion and pressures of the urban environment. This may be motivated by the wish to participate in a real or imagined rural lifestyle as exemplified by holidays on working farms or dude ranches in the USA.

5 Nature tourism is a specialised, though developing, market. With the increasing interest in environmental issues, and the experience of seeing television films of animals in the wild, people now wish to see wildlife in its natural habitat rather than in the zoo or safari park setting.

6 Finally, people may indeed visit the countryside purely for the pleasure of looking at, and being in attractive rural landscapes.

LANDSCAPE ELEMENTS

There are three basic geographical elements that make up any landscape.

1 The landform and geology, which determine the shape of the land and its relief. The landform also

determines the presence or absence of many of the features on which activity-based rural tourism depends (e.g. caves for potholing, rocky peaks for climbing, cliffs or scarps for hang-gliding, very steep slopes for skiing etc). The other important physical element of the landscape is the water which shapes and drains the landscape, in the form of rivers, lakes and inland seas.

2 The natural vegetation of the land, and the animals that depend on it. On a world scale, this ranges from the tropical rainforest of equatorial regions, to the grassy plains and savannas of Africa, through to the forests of the north which give way to the scrub and mossy plains of the open tundra and finally to the arctic ecosystems of the polar regions. The nature of vegetation and wildlife is obviously closely related to the pattern of world climates. The landform and vegetation when untouched by man create the natural landscape and wilderness areas of the world.

3 The third element of the landscape is the presence of man. Much of the natural vegetation has been greatly modified by man through agricultural and forestry practices. The landscapes that are created by human modification and exploitation of the natural vegetation can be called the 'land use' landscape. Buildings, roads, power lines and other man-made constructions add artificial elements to the land use landscape. Human interaction with the natural features of the land has created a variety of cultural landscapes across the world, from the detailed, intimate landscapes of enclosed fields and hedges in the English lowlands, or the terraced hillsides of Southeast Asia, to the vast open landscapes of the North American prairies.

In certain circumstances each of these three elements may individually dominate the landscape, e.g. in the dry deserts, the landform is the dominant element, while the city centre is dominated by the man-made landscape. In a tropical rainforest the natural vegetation masks all the other elements. In general, however, most landscapes consist of combinations of the three elements, in fact the landscape itself is the product of the interaction between the three elements. The way in which the elements combine to create particularly attractive

landscapes is hard to define. Attempts have been made to assess the appeal of landscapes for recreation and tourism but it is a difficult task since 'beauty is in the eye of the beholder'. It is evident that different people have different tastes and preferences depending on their background, culture, education and personal experiences. Nevertheless, studies of the perception of and preference for landscapes do seem to show that there are certain types of landscape that appeal widely to people of westernised cultural backgrounds.

Preferences for landform landscapes

Research on landscape preferences, and indeed tourist behaviour, indicate that landscapes with high relative relief are the most dramatic and most attractive to visitors. Relative relief is the difference in height between the highest point (e.g. the top of a mountain, hill or plateau) and the lowest point of a landscape (be it a river valley, lake surface or low-

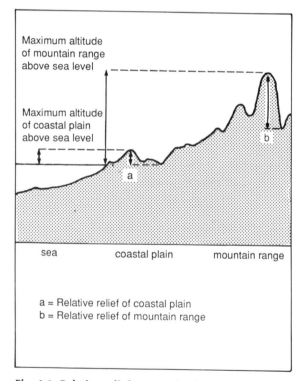

Fig. 4.1 Relative relief versus absolute relief

land plain). Relative relief thus differs from absolute relief (that is, the height of land above sea level) as it is a measure of vertical scale and degree of dissection of a landscape, rather than its altitude (*see* Fig 4.1).

A landscape of high relative relief will be characterised, for example, by deep valleys, or by cliffs and scarps (*see* Fig 4.2). High relative relief provides the opportunity for long or dramatic views. The presence of water in such a landscape always adds even more to its dramatic quality, perhaps because the water surface (by definition truly horizontal) provides a sharp contrast to the surrounding hill slopes, and reflections in still water (such as lake surfaces) appear to add depth to the view in another dimension.

The fjords along the coast of Norway are a classic example of this type of landscape where the mountains plunge thousands of metres into the sea; another world-famous landscape with a very high relative relief is the Grand Canyon where the River Colorado has cut a gorge over a mile deep into the flat plains of the Colorado desert. Landscapes of low relative relief, be they undulating lowland plains or plateau surfaces, tend to afford shorter views; truly flat landscapes (therefore, with zero relative relief) provide featureless vistas or long views interrupted only by trees or buildings. Such landscapes tend to be perceived as boring, though of course in some parts of the world they can provide very dramatic land and skyscapes (*see* Fig 4.3).

Landforms may be described and classified according to their relative relief. Linton's system (*see* Fig 4.4) provides a comprehensive classification, combining relative and absolute relief.

Fig. 4.2 A landscape of high relative relief: Yosemite National Park, California

Fig. 4.3 A landscape of very low relative relief: the salt plains of Australia

Lowlands	Areas below 500' (150 m) in height
Rolling countryside	500–1500' (150–450 m) with relative relief <400' (120 m)
Upland plateau	1500' + (450 m+) high with relative relief over 400' (120 m)
Hill country	(a) 500–1500' (150–450 m) high with relative relief over 400' (120 m)
	(b) 500'–2000' (150–600 m) with relative relief 400–600' (120–180 m)
Bold hills	(a) 2000' + (600 m) in height with relative relief 400–800' (120–250 m).
	(b) 1500–2000' (450–600 m) with 600' + (180 m+) relative relief.
High hills	Over 2000' (600 m) high with over 800' (250 m) relative relief.
Mountains	Over 2500' with 2000' + (600 m) relative relief.

Fig. 4.4 Definitions of landform

This classification was adopted in a research project (by A Gilg of Exeter University) designed to discover people's preferences for different types of landform. A group of 50 geography students were shown a series of 38 photographs of landscapes representing the range of possible landforms. The students were invited to rate the pictures according to the strength of their preferences: the higher the score the greater the appeal of the landscape.

	Average score of different landforms out of 95
Lowlands	37
Low uplands	46
Plateau uplands	47
Hill country	53
Bold hills	61
Mountains	75 – most attractive landform

Fig. 4.5 Preferences for landforms

Figure 4.5 shows the average score given to each type of landform, and clearly indicates a preference for landscapes of high relative relief.

NATURAL LANDSCAPES AND THEIR WORLD DISTRIBUTION

Natural vegetation of the world

Throughout the world, trees will grow and dominate the vegetation wherever it is mild and wet enough to support them. The type of dominant tree species will vary with soils and climate. In more extreme climatic conditions, trees are replaced as dominant vegetation usually by smaller, tougher plants that can withstand long periods of very hot or very cold temperatures and can survive where water is rarely available (especially in hot deserts, or in freezing conditions). From the Equator to the Poles, there is a series of vegetation zones (corresponding roughly with the temperature zones shown in Fig 2.3 on page 9). A similar type of zonation of vegetation is seen on mountain slopes, as the climate changes with increasing altitude.

Generalised vegetation and climatic zones of the world

Hot climates

1 Equatorial tropical forest. Dense forest, very rich in species of both plants and animals. The climate is hot and wet, allowing for vigorous plant growth all year round.

2 Tropical savannah grasslands. Dominated by tall grasses but with some scrub and forest patches. The growth of trees is limited by the pronounced dry season. The grasslands support vast numbers of grazing animals and large carnivores that prey on them.

3 Hot deserts. Too hot and dry for even grasses to survive. No vegetation at all, or only scattered cactus or thorn scrub.

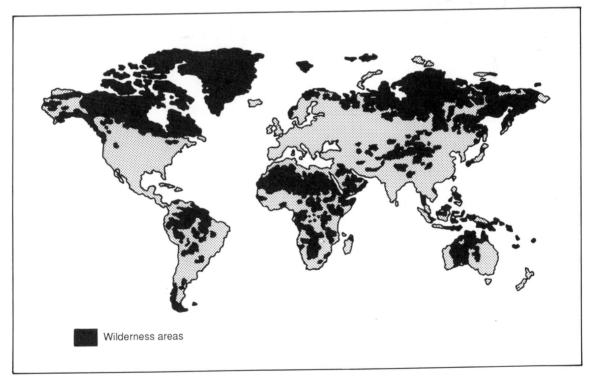

Fig. 4.6 World distribution of wilderness areas

Warm temperate climates

1 Mediterranean scrub (known in different parts of the world as garigue, maquis, or chapparal). A mixture of drought-resistant, often evergreen trees and shrubs mixed with open areas of grass and herbs. Again, the prolonged summer drought limits tree growth.

2 Cool temperate climates

Temperate forests: forest lands of the wet but cooler regions. Often deciduous tree species.

3 Cold climates

Coniferous forests: needle-bearing trees adapted to withstand the cold and dry conditions of harsh winter seasons.

4 Arctic and polar climates

(*a*) Arctic and alpine tundra. Temperatures and growing season, too low for tree growth. This type of vegetation is dominated by grasses, herbs, moss and lichens.

(*b*) Cold deserts of polar regions. No vegetation.

In many parts of the world particularly where the climate is suitable for agricultural production, the natural vegetation has been replaced by agricultural plant species and thus the natural landscape replaced by a man-made landscape.

Figure 4.6 shows the areas of the world where the vegetation and natural ecosystems have been largely untouched by man, and, therefore, shows the parts of the world where wild landscapes still exist. The majority of these (over 60 per cent) are open, treeless tundra and hot desert areas (*see* Fig 4.7).

Vegetation type	% of total world wilderness
Tundra	41.7
Warm deserts/semi deserts	19.4
Temperate needle leaf forests	18.3
Tropical forests	9.3
Mixed mountain systems	4.1
Cold winter deserts	3.1
Tropical grassland/savannahs	1.5
Temperate forests (rainforest and deciduous)	1.5
Temperate grasslands	0.6
Evergreen forests (Mediterranean type)	0.4
Island systems	0.2
	100% = 48 069 951 km²

Fig. 4.7 Percentage of wilderness left (1988)

The vast majority (nearly 80 per cent) of this wilderness lies in only ten countries (*see* Fig 4.8).

		Million km²
1	Antarctica	13.2
2	Soviet Union	7.5
3	Canada	6.4
4	Australia	2.2
5	Greenland	2.1
6	China	2.1
7	Brazil	2.0
8	Algeria	1.4
9	Sudan	0.7
10	Mauritania	0.7

Fig. 4.8 Distribution of wilderness areas

Preference for natural landscapes

Although vegetation has often been shown to be a significant factor in shaping landscape preferences few landscape research projects have explicitly investigated the strength of preferences for different types of natural vegetation cover. The preference study already referred to on page 32 grouped all non-forested wild landscapes together, and these averaged a preference score of only 50 out of 95 though when wild landscapes were combined with mountain terrain they became far more attractive. Forest landscapes on the other hand were found to be highly attractive, irrespective of the topography. This finding is supported by research done on a wider cross-section of the British population (not only students but adults, recreationists etc) who when offered the chance, not only picked out forested landscapes but overwhelmingly preferred oak woodland, the natural vegetation of most of the British Isles.

Preference for the land use landscape

Through agriculture and other forms of resource exploitation and development, much of the world's natural landscapes have been greatly modified by man. Preference for the resulting land use landscapes may well depend on people's cultural backgrounds and the type of managed landscapes that they are used to seeing in their everyday life.

Gilg's study was limited to British students responding to European (including Britain) landscapes but for what it is worth it shows clearly that varied landscapes (be they varied forest and moorland or varied farmland) were liked better than urban landscapes or treeless farmland (*see* Fig 4.9).

Landscape type	Average score for different land uses out of 95 (NB the higher the score, the greater the preference)
Urban/industrial	39
Treeless farmland	42
Wild landscapes	50
Moorland	51
(a semi natural but man-created landscape)	
Varied forest/moor	54
Varied farmland	59
Forest	69

Fig. 4.9 Preference for natural or land use landscapes

To summarise, according to Gilg's study, mountains or any landscape with high relative relief, particularly when combined with wild landscapes or forests appear to be the most attractive, and any water feature adds to a landscape's appeal.

THE CONSERVATION AND PROMOTION OF TOURISM IN WILD LANDSCAPES

The next section will discuss the ways in which attractive landscapes are defined, managed and conserved, and how they are made available for tourism. The United Nations and the International Union for the Conservation of Nature and Natural Resources (IUCN) have played leading roles in promoting the management and conservation of landscapes throughout the countries of the world.

World Heritage Sites

In 1972 UNESCO set up the World Heritage Convention, designed to protect the most outstanding examples of the world's cultural and natural heritage. The Convention came into force in 1978 and by 1983 76 member states accepted the Convention and agreed to identify, conserve and protect world heritage sites. Member states also contribute to a fund whereby the poorer nations of the world can be financially aided to protect their world heritage sites.

Natural landscapes that have been accepted nationally and internationally as world heritage sites include the Galapagos Islands (with their unique fauna), the Ngorongoro conservation area in Tanzania (a dramatic extinct volcanic crater where African savannah wildlife now abounds), the Tai National Park in the Ivory Coast (one of the last vestiges of West African tropical rainforest), the Kakadu National Park in the wetlands of north Australia, the Grand Canyon of Colorado, USA, and the Nahanni National Park in northern Canada which is characterised by turbulent rivers and hot sulphur springs.

Biosphere reserves

The International Union for the Conservation of Nature and Natural Resources also aims to encourage nations to conserve their wildlife and landscapes. The IUCN advises that countries should establish a range of types of protected areas; these may vary in 'naturalness' from untouched areas of undisturbed wildlife that should be protected from any disruption by humans ('strict nature reserves') or 'National Parks' where natural habitats should be protected from all forms of exploitation other than tourism, through to 'protected landscapes' which may include land use landscapes considerably modified by man. The two categories of protected area that have most significance as tourist resources are the IUCN's National Parks and protected landscapes. The IUCN collects world data on the National Parks of the world, on behalf of the United Nations. Figure 4.10 shows the world distribution of conserved landscapes.

International National Parks

In order to be included in the UN list of National Parks and equivalent reserves, a National Park should enjoy legal protection against all human exploitation of its natural resources. Agriculture, hunting, fishing, forestry, mining or water gathering would all be prohibited; and no residential,

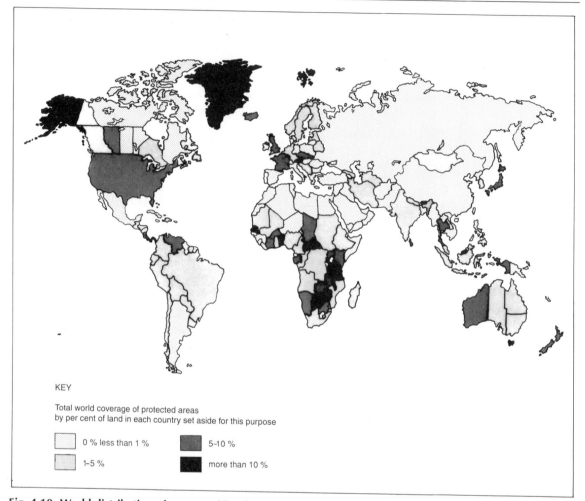

Fig. 4.10 World distribution of conserved landscapes

commercial or industrial development, road or railway construction would be allowed. The only exception would be tourism, since tourism is one of the major reasons for the existence of the Park, so road construction, hotel building, provision of camp sites, interpretation centres and other services and infrastructure for tourism are allowed in internationally recognised National Parks. However, most Parks are zoned for different levels of tourist use: some areas are accessible for mass tourism; and some areas are accessible only to visitors on horseback or on foot. The National Park should be free of all resident population other than those needed to administer the Park and manage its tourism.

Although many countries of the world have designated National Parks, two regions (the USA and the Central African countries of Kenya, Uganda and Tanzania) are particularly noted for their Parks and the tourist activity associated with them.

Case study: National Parks in USA

The USA began the world National Park movement by being the first to designate a National Park, the Yellowstone National Park in 1872. A hundred years later, the USA had 38 National Parks, covering about 5.8 million hectares. The Parks cover a wide variety of types of landscape and natural features, ranging from the forested mountain landscapes of Yellowstone in Wyoming, the snowy peaks of Mount McKinley in Alaska, the active volcanoes of the Hawaiian National Park, to the low-lying tropical swamps of the Everglades in Florida. American National Parks may also be focused on particular landscape elements such as the Sequoia and Redwood National Parks in California that include stands of the giant trees (the biggest trees in the world), or the Carlsbad caverns in New Mexico, again the largest known cave system in the world.

The US National Parks system is extensively used for tourism with 287 million visits in 1987. Most parks contain accommodation and camp sites, though the location of tourist development is controlled and parts of the National Parks are set aside as 'Wilderness Areas' where no tourist vehicles are allowed and where the intensity of tourist use is deliberately kept very low.

In a developed and affluent economy such as the USA, the legal powers and financial resources are available to maintain the natural habitats of the National Parks in a relatively undisturbed form. In such a large country the pressures for the economic use of the land can be diverted to other parts of the territory but the pressures are such that land may be very intensively developed right up to the national park boundary which may threaten the wildlife environment within the Park (Jenner and Smith, 1992, Hendrix and Morehead, 1983). The main problem is the product of their success and popularity – the control and management of tourist pressures on the environment (Lindsay, 1986).

Case study: the East African National Parks

The African National Parks are far greater in size even than those in the United States. The National Parks south of the Sahara in Africa together cover an area of 53.6 million hectares (an area only slightly smaller than the whole of France). The abundant and (for tourists) easily visible wildlife of the open savannah grasslands is the main reason for the Parks' designation and their main tourist attraction. Vast herds of wildebeeste, zebra and antelope mix with elephants, giraffe and buffalo. Groups of lions appear to be quite tolerant of the approach of tourists in vehicle convoys, although the weight of tourist numbers may be beginning to affect the wildlife. The threat to the African National Parks is not so much one of controlling tourism, but of managing the whole ecosystem so that the numbers of animals are maintained, and of controlling the illegal poaching of the animals (for meat, ivory, horn or skins) by the native population in response to national and international demands for these products. The main pressures on the parks are therefore agriculture and poaching. Agricultural land around the parks may be fenced; this disrupts the migration routes of the wild animals as they search for grazing outside the National Parks in dry seasons and in drought years. This leads to both the death of many animals and the overgrazing of the ranges in the National Parks (Curry and Morvaridi, 1992, Pullen, 1983). Illegal poaching is the second major problem. Poaching is concentrated on particular species that yield products that are very valuable on the black market (e.g. ivory, rhino horn, animal skins). Figure 4.11 shows that the elephant (*see* Poole and Thomsen, 1989) and the black rhino have suffered particularly badly. Zimbabwe is attempting to protect its remaining 500 black rhino through a dehorning programme, so that the animals are no longer a target for the poacher.

	1969	1973	1979	1980	mid-1980s	1989
Kabelega Falls NP (Uganda)						
Elephant	–	14 000	–	200	–	–
Ruwenzori NP (Uganda)						
Elephant	3 000	153	–	–	–	–
Buffalo	18 000	4 200	–	–	–	–
Kenya as a whole						
Black rhinos	1 800	–	1 500	–	500	–
Elephant	167 000	–	60 000	–	–	16 000

Fig. 4.11 Loss of wildlife in East Africa 1969–89

Poaching in some areas has caused drastic reductions in animal populations – *see* Fig 4.11. Illegal hunting tends to increase during periods of national and international disturbances which have characterised this part of Africa since 1964. The presence of sophisticated firearms and plentiful ammunition, plus the disruption to both local food supplies and to wildlife protection systems (generated by civil or international instability) all encourage the destruction of the animals. Another threat to the integrity of the National Parks in Africa comes from the pressure for economic developments. The economic benefits from wildlife-based tourism may in the end not be sufficient to contain the pressure for economic development (e.g. for farming or water gathering).

Attempts have been made to reimburse residents for the agricultural losses due to wildlife conservation with both government compensation and by channelling tourist revenues more directly to local people (Western, 1982, Curry and Morvaridi, 1992). In spite of all the management problems, the numbers of visitors to many of the African National Parks continue to climb: visitors to Kenya's parks grew from 986 000 in 1985 to 1.5 million in 1991.

Thus the effectiveness of National Park designation varies from country to country although the framework for protection exists.

To summarise, international National Parks are defined by the following criteria:

1 They are authorised by the central government of the country concerned; in many countries the land of the Park is nationally owned.
2 They have legal protection from economic exploitation, backed up by having a minimum level of staff to implement the protection and conservation of the landscape and wildlife, and a defined annual budget allocated for the same purpose.
3 The national government allows or itself organises and promotes tourism within the National Park.

Protected landscapes

According to IUCN, the purpose of designating areas as protected landscapes is 'to maintain nationally significant, natural landscapes which are characteristic of the harmonious interaction of man and land, while providing opportunities for public enjoyment through recreation and tourism within the normal lifestyle and economic activity of these areas'.

Thus, in contrast to international National Parks, protected landscapes include land use landscapes: the cultural landscapes that have evolved over time as a result of human activity over a period of thousands of years.

Many countries of the world have developed different hierarchies of protected landscapes (excluding the areas internationally recognised as National Parks). For example, Australia has a system that ranges from State Recreation Areas, through Nature Parks, Environmental Parks, Parks, to State Parks. The USA's protected landscapes include designations such as National Reserves, National Wildlife Refuges, Parks, National Historic Parks, to National Recreation Areas and other areas.

As virtually all of Britain's landscape has been much artificially modified, all the designated landscape areas are classified internationally as protected landscape, even the National Parks of England and Wales. These National Parks are not

Designation	Number	Area(km²)	
National Parks	10	13 745	(9% of England and Wales)
Equivalent Areas	2	662	
National Scenic Areas (Scotland)	40	10 018	(12.9% of Scotland)
AONBs (England & Wales)	37	17 084	(11.3% of England and Wales)
AONBs (N Ireland)	9	2 803	
Heritage Coasts	40	1 370	(31.05% of coastline of England and Wales)

Fig. 4.12 UK areas of protected landscapes (May 1987)

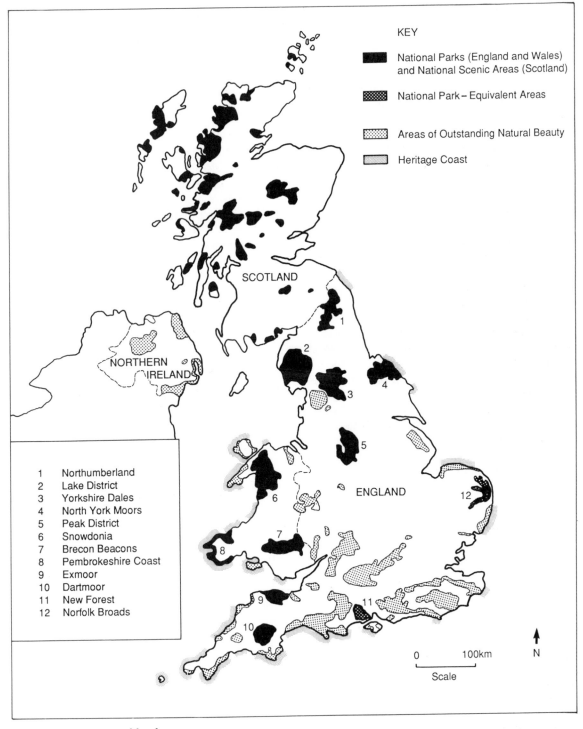

KEY

National Parks (England and Wales)
and National Scenic Areas (Scotland)

National Park – Equivalent Areas

Areas of Outstanding Natural Beauty

Heritage Coast

SCOTLAND

NORTHERN
IRELAND

1   Northumberland
2   Lake District
3   Yorkshire Dales
4   North York Moors
5   Peak District
6   Snowdonia
7   Brecon Beacons
8   Pembrokeshire Coast
9   Exmoor
10   Dartmoor
11   New Forest
12   Norfolk Broads

ENGLAND

0   100km

Scale

N

Fig. 4.13 UK protected landscapes

recognised as full international National Parks as they do not meet any of the international criteria set out.

The British National Parks are not nationally owned; the landscapes are extensively exploited for economic purposes and agriculture is explicitly encouraged; visitors do not have legal rights of access over the whole of the Parks – indeed, there may be policies for the constraint of recreation and tourism rather than for its promotion. England and Wales have ten National Parks and two Equivalent Areas (the New Forest and the Norfolk Broads). The corresponding landscape designation in Scotland are the National Scenic Areas: areas of national scenic significance which are considered to be of unsurpassed attractiveness and which must be conserved as part of the national heritage. The second level designation is the Area of Outstanding Natural Beauty (AONB). These are parts of the countryside of England and Wales which, while they lack extensive areas of open country (suitable for recreation) are nonetheless of such fine scenery that there is a national as well as local interest in keeping them so. In spite of the relative lack of opportunity for outdoor recreation, the AONBs are still the focus of much tourist activity. AONBs are also designated in Northern Ireland but there is no equivalent category in Scotland.

Stretches of attractive and undeveloped coastline may be designated as Heritage Coasts in England and Wales. In these areas there are often conflicts of interest between the conservation of the coastal landscape and its development for tourism.

Finally, certain areas whose characteristic landscape depends entirely on the maintenance of a particular traditional form of agricultural practice, are designated as Environmentally Sensitive Areas. These cover over one million hectares in the UK.

Figure 4.13 shows the distribution of protected landscapes and therefore the main landscape resources for tourism within Britain. The ten National Parks and the Scottish National Scenic areas are concentrated in the Upland and mountain areas of the North and West of Britain, reflecting people's preferences for landscapes of high relative relief. The two other areas of England and Wales equivalent to National Parks are landscapes where elements other than landform are dominant. The New Forest is a lowland area of mixed moorland and varied coniferous and deciduous forest,

whereas the Norfolk Broads is a series of shallow lakes and extensive navigable waterways. It is a major centre for water recreation and tourism based on boating.

The Heritage Coasts are clustered on the south and west coast. The majority of the Heritage Coasts are dramatic cliffed coastlines, again reflecting preferences for landscapes of high relative relief and the presence of water as a major feature in the landscape. The Areas of Outstanding Natural Beauty are also mostly located in the south and west of England (i.e. south and west of a line drawn from the Dee to the Thames). This leaves the heavily populated and industrialised centre and eastern quadrant of England relatively undersupplied with high quality landscape resources.

REFERENCES AND FURTHER READING

Those texts marked with an asterisk are particularly recommended for further reading.

*Cartwright, J (1991) 'Is there hope for conservation in Africa', *Journal of Modern African Studies*, Vol.29, No.3, pp.355–71.

Curry, S and Morvaridi, B (1992) 'Sustainable tourism: illustrations from Kenya, Nepal and Jamaica' in Cooper, C P and Lockwood, A (Eds) *Progress in Tourism Recreation and Hospitality Management*, Vol.4, Belhaven, pp.131–9.

*EIU (1991) 'Managing tourism and the environment: a Kenyan case study', *Travel and Tourism Analyst*, No.2, pp.78–87.

Gilg, A W (1975) 'The objectivity of Linton type methods of assessing scenery as a natural resource', *Regional Studies*, Vol.9.

Hendrix, G and Morehead, J (1983) 'Everglades National Park: an imperiled wetland', *Ambio*, Vol.12, No.3/4, pp.153–7.

Jenner, P and Smith, C (1992) 'The tourism industry and the environment', Economist Intelligence Unit, *Special Report*, No.2453.

Lindsay, J J (1986) 'Carrying capacity for tourism development in the National Parks of the United States', *Industry and Environment*, Vol.9, No.1, UNEP.

*Linton, D L (1968) 'The assessment of scenery as a natural resource', *Scottish Geographical Magazine*, Vol.84, December.

Lucas, P H C (1992) *Protected Landscapes – A Guide for Policy Makers and Planners*, IUCN, Chapman and Hall.

Poole, J H and Thomsen, J B (1989) 'Elephants are not beetles: implications of the ivory trade for the survival of the African elephant', *Oryx*, Vol.23, No.4, pp.188–98.

*Poore, D and J Poore, (1987) *Protected Landscapes – The United Kingdom Experience*, Countryside Commission, DoE, IUCN.

Pullen, R A (1983) 'Do National Parks have a future in Africa?', *Leisure Studies*, Vol.2, No.1, pp.1–18.

Western, D (1982) 'Amboseli National Park: enlisting landowners to conserve migratory wildlife,' *Ambio*, Vol.6, No.5, pp.302–8.

QUESTIONS AND DISCUSSION POINTS

1 To what extent is tourism a threat or a benefit to the international National Parks?

2 Why are British National Parks ineligible for recognition as international National Parks?

3 What features make the landscape shown in the photograph below attractive for scenic and wildlife tourism?

ASSIGNMENTS

1 Select a tour company brochure selling scenic holiday tours (e.g. a 'lakes and mountains' brochure). Analyse the content of the photographs of landscapes in the brochure. What landform, landuse, and natural vegetation features do the photographs depict? How effective are these pictures likely to be in selling the holidays?

You have been asked to redesign and update the brochure for next season. Would you suggest any changes to the illustrations? If so, what changes would you recommend?

2 A group of American tour operators (specialising in tours for Americans to American National Parks) have arrived in Britain for a study tour of the British National Parks. You are a tourism officer employed by one of the British National Park authorities. You have been invited to give a welcoming speech to the party and show them something of your National Park. The brief you have been given for your speech is:

(*a*) to explain the British system of landscape and wildlife protection to the party; and

(*b*) to outline the tourism potential, tourism-policies and tourist development in British National Parks. (You may use your own park as an example where appropriate.)

Draw the party's attention to the similarities and differences between the British and American National Park systems.

Write notes for your speech. (You may decide yourself which National Park Authority you work in. Reference should be made to the appropriate National Park plan, where available.)

CHAPTER 5

Historic resources for tourism

LEARNING OBJECTIVES

After reading this chapter you should be able to
- **define a historic resource**
- **explain why tourists are attracted to historic resources**
- **understand the processes by which historic resources have survived, and some of the problems facing the organisations who are responsible for maintaining them for future tourist use**
- **locate the major world concentrations of historic resources.**

INTRODUCTION

Historic resources are the surviving physical remnants from past civilisations and past eras. They include architectural, landscape and archaeological features as well as the artefacts and day-to-day objects that have survived from the past. Places associated with significant historical, religious or mythical events may also be regarded as historical resources even though the place may have physically changed out of all recognition or have no architectural evidence of past events.

HISTORIC RESOURCES

Tourists find these resources attractive for several reasons.

1 Tourists may simply be attracted by the age of ancient relics of past civilisations and at the technological achievements of those ancient cultures. This is a particularly important factor for North American visitors to Western Europe. The first sustained European colonisation of America dates only from about the beginning of the 16th century, so these ex-European colonies are obviously without physical traces of West European culture from before this date. Americans must, therefore, come to Europe in order to experience the cities and buildings of their own cultural background dating from before 1500 AD.

Many people apart from the North Americans go to marvel at the extreme age of buildings and artefacts, and the technical ability and physical skills of the people that constructed them without the aid of any modern machinery, whether it be Stonehenge, the Egyptian pyramids (built about 4500 years ago) or the 15th and 16th century cities of the Incas in which the stones were cut with such accuracy that the walls needed no cement.

2 Tourists of varying cultural backgrounds may enjoy visiting historic sites purely for the appreciation of the beauty of the art and architecture. For example, it is the beauty of the Greek temple at Sounion, set on a dramatic promontory that attracts visitors to it in preference to the many other temples accessible from Athens. Similarly, the Taj Mahal in India, named by many as the most beautiful building in the world, attracts increasing numbers of both Indian and international visitors, *see* Fig. 5.1.

3 Visitors may be attracted to buildings and places for their historic meaning rather than their visual appeal. The Viking excavations in York reveal fascinating details of the social life of the ninth century inhabitants which can stimulate the imagination of the visitors to the sites. Similarly, places associated with great historical or mythical exploits and events can be of great interest; visiting Mycenae in Greece with its association with Agamemnon and the Trojan wars adds an extra dimension to the reading of the stories of Odysseus in Homer's Iliad.

Fig. 5.1 The Taj Mahal, Agra, India

In Britain, Stratford-upon-Avon is visited for its association with Shakespeare rather than for its aesthetic qualities. Places such as Runnymede or the battlefields of Flanders in Belgium may hold the tourists' interest simply because they are the locations of events of great political significance.

Similarly, places may hold great religious meaning.

HOW DO HISTORIC FEATURES SURVIVE?

There are certain geographical factors which enable ancient buildings to survive.

Protection from atmospheric weathering

The stonework of ancient buildings is subject to the same process of weathering as the rocks which break down to form the sand and pebbles of the beach (*see* Chapter 3). Buildings from the past will only survive if this process of weathering is slow. The dry, unpolluted air of the desert has had little effect in weathering the granite monuments in Egypt, although even here, more weathering can be observed on the monuments near Cairo where there is some slight rainfall than the statues in the drier parts of Egypt. Even limestone and marble rock which is very susceptible to weathering in a mild, damp climate such as the British Isles may survive undamaged for thousands of years in a dry Mediterranean climate such as Athens. Many of the stone carvings on British cathedrals dating from the 15th century have needed considerable restoration in recent years, whereas the sculptures on the frieze of the Acropolis were still in excellent condition after thousands of years when removed by Lord Elgin to Britain in the 19th century.

More recently, however, air pollution caused by an increase in sulphur dioxide in the atmosphere has accelerated these processes of weathering in both Britain and Greece. In 1975 UNESCO concluded that air pollution had already had a significant detrimental influence on the buildings and monuments of the Acropolis and in 1977/8 some controls on the use of high sulphur domestic fuels were introduced in Athens in an attempt to reduce the level of sulphur dioxide in the air. In spite of these efforts, considerable restoration work has been necessary. The industrialisation and spread of atmospheric pollution to the hitherto undeveloped countries of the Middle East and Central Asia are a substantial threat to the survival of existing and potential historic tourist attractions in these areas.

Archaeological and historic remains may be protected from atmospheric weathering by being covered with the accumulated dust and vegetation of the years. Their preservation depends on the presence or absence of oxygen.

In temperate latitudes, archaeological remains are protected and preserved by being buried under the fragments of rock and soil created by erosion and weathering and deposited by soil creep and rainwash. In Britain, Roman villas dating from before 450 AD have been excavated from beneath nearly two metres of rock waste (representing an accumulation of about 0.3 m per 200 years). As oxygen is present in the soil all but the stonework has decayed.

In totally oxygen-free environments, such as in acid bogs, or on the sea bed, wood, leather and metal may not decay. This may allow the recovery of well-preserved objects such as the Mary Rose, the flagship of Henry VIII, which, when subsequently preserved and restored using modern technology, became a major tourist attraction.

Changes in settlement patterns

Settlements are located at particular sites for many reasons. For example, towns may be located at sites that were easy to defend, or they may be market centres for rich agricultural regions; they may be sited close to highly localised physical resources (e.g. water for power, sandy beaches for tourism, minerals for industrial use etc.) or they may develop at crucial points along routeways such as ports or river crossings. Settlements that retain this function continue to grow and thrive and the old buildings at their original core are renewed and replaced as technological demands change. If, however, there is a change in these geographical factors (e.g. if a river on which a port is situated silts up) the settlement may be bypassed by more modern development rather than being rebuilt.

Thus, the original street layout and many of the original buildings may not be destroyed by more modern development, though if the site is abandoned completely then the fabric of the buildings will decay and their condition will depend on their age and on the weathering factors mentioned above. The seven cities of Delhi were built by successive Mughal rulers between 1193 and 1648 and each abandoned as a new seat of government was built (*see* Fig. 5.2). The ramparts of the oldest city are incomplete whereas the last two cities, dating from about 1540 and 1640 have most of their buildings intact. Most of the seven cities have now been surrounded by modern development as the suburbs of Delhi spread out, but the sites themselves remain untouched.

Barely a hundred years after the last city of Delhi was being built in India, the industrial

Fig. 5.2 Tughluqabad, third city of Delhi, dating from 1320–1350 AD

revolution was underway in Britain. The early industrial developments in the Ironbridge Gorge in Shropshire were sited there because industry depended on water for both power and transport at the time. However, the discoveries of Abraham Derby at his iron works in Coalbrookdale in the 1760s changed the whole basis of industry and the subsequent industrial developments took place on the major coalfields. This left the Ironbridge sites abandoned until the recent interest of historians in industrial archaeology led to their excavation and the interest of tourists led to its restoration and development as a tourist attraction. Many of the major historic towns of Britain were also bypassed by the industrial revolution. Towns such as York, Winchester, Norwich and Wells had important commercial, ecclesiastical or administrative functions in medieval times but have retained much of their medieval character, since, while they retained a local significance as a market centre, they were located well away from the centres of growth during the industrial revolution. Chester, sited at a critical crossing point of the Dee, was originally an important port in Roman and medieval times but was replaced by Liverpool as the major port for the northwest of England as the River Dee progressively silted up. Modern industrial development thus bypassed Chester and its centre survived much 20th century redevelopment. A similar pattern of events occurred at Bruges (a major commercial centre of the medieval world) which was overtaken as a port by cities such as Antwerp. In this way Bruges has retained much of its medieval character. These historic towns were not industrialised but over the centuries they still retained some economic functions as a local administrative or market centre so that the buildings retained some economic use and were, therefore, occupied and maintained in good repair rather than being abandoned to decay. However, in the 20th century a major problem facing these historic tourist centres is finding new economic uses for the buildings in order to pay for the escalating cost of the upkeep of the ageing buildings. The small scale of the buildings and the tortuous medieval street patterns with difficult access make them unattractive for many modern office, commercial or even residential uses. Their medieval character and inaccessibility, which form their major tourist attraction, make them totally uneconomic locations for any other activity other than residential use or tourism.

Venice is facing this problem today; although the major palaces on the Grand Canal are reasonably well maintained, many of the other buildings (which individually may not be of outstanding architectural significance but together make up the distinctive character of the city) are empty and decaying. The problems of subsidence and flooding make the whole situation worse as it raises the cost of maintenance.

Retaining and continuing traditional uses

In contrast to the problems discussed above, some buildings have survived relatively intact because they have retained their original use, and have been maintained but little modified through the centuries. The ancient universities of Oxford and Cambridge, the great cathedrals and churches and some of the historic country houses which are family homes in the English countryside are examples of this in Britain.

Conservation of historic resources

During the last century there has been a growing realisation of the value of historic features, both for their intrinsic worth and their contribution to the attractiveness of our living environment. Many countries have gradually evolved systems of protective legislation and new approaches to the planning and redevelopment of historic areas which puts the emphasis on the protection and conservation of buildings and features of historic importance.

MAJOR WORLD DISTRIBUTION OF HISTORIC FEATURES

Early civilisation

Modern tourists are fascinated by relics associated with early man. Some of the earliest human fossils (1½ million years old) were found in the Olduvai Gorge (south of Lake Victoria in Tanzania, East Africa) but early man quickly spread to many parts of the world.

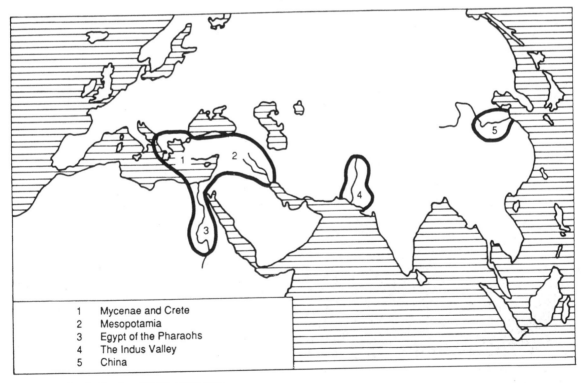

1	Mycenae and Crete
2	Mesopotamia
3	Egypt of the Pharaohs
4	The Indus Valley
5	China

Fig. 5.3 Early civilisation (3500–1500 BC)

The first urban civilisations, that have left remnants of buildings for posterity, date from the period 3500–1500 BC. It is believed that urban civilisation started in the arid but fertile alluvial valleys of the Tigris and Euphrates, a region known as Mesopotamia that is now part of modern Iraq.

The Iran-Iraq war of the 1980s and the crisis in the Gulf in 1990 have inhibited any tourist development of these sites. However, there was a series of scattered civilisations (*see* Fig 5.3) that flourished in similar environments at about the same time, some of which have been exploited as tourist attractions. To the west of Mesopotamia the main centres were along the Nile valley (the Egyptian pharaohs in 3000–1000 BC) and circled round the Aegean Sea (Mycenae, Crete and Troy).

The archaeological sites of this period which lie to the east of Mesopotamia have not been fully developed for tourism due to modern political instability or restrictions. Notable ancient civilisations are located in the Indus valley (in modern Pakistan) and in northern China.

The classical world

The civilisations of this era spread, developed, evolved and were replaced, until in the period 1000 BC to AD 500 there was a more or less unbroken chain of empires which made up the 'classical world' (*see* Figs 5.4 and 5.5). This formed a zone of civilised life in Europe and Asia from the Mediterranean to the Pacific coast of China, some of which is roughly bounded by the Tropic of Cancer (23.5° N) and 40° N. Particular regions within this zone came to prominence at different times during the 1500 year period.

Each had its own particular style of architecture and many of the great historic monuments of the Mediterranean and Middle East date from these centuries. In general, the surviving buildings are built on a lavish scale and consist of public buildings, temples, palaces and tombs of kings and leaders, all expressions of the civilisation's wealth and power, and illustrating the peaks of artistic skills and technical achievements.

The smaller scale, less substantial buildings of the ordinary citizens rarely survive intact in other

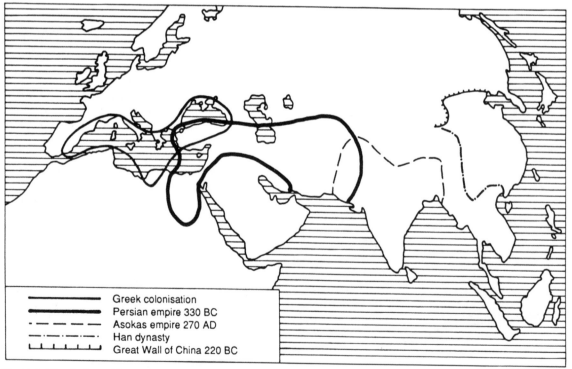

Fig. 5.4 Classical world (1000 BC – 500 AD)

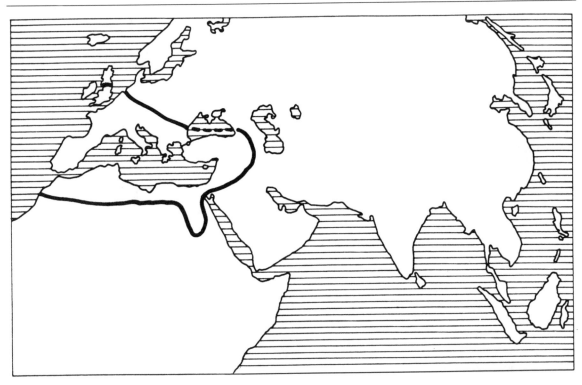

Fig. 5.5 Roman world (1000 BC – 500 AD)

than exceptional circumstances as occurred at Pompeii where the entire Roman town was engulfed in and preserved by the lava and ash from the volcano, Vesuvius. The greatest concentrations of historic remains are inevitably centred on the core of each empire. Thus, the Aegean region is rich in Greek buildings, Iran in Persian buildings, and Italy in Roman constructions, though examples are found throughout the territory of each empire. For example, notable Roman ruins are seen in even the farthest flung corners of the Roman world such as Hadrian's Wall in Northumberland, and the coliseum in Tunisia, North Africa. Similarly, the Great Wall of China was built during the period 300–100 BC, at the northernmost limits of the Han empire.

The age of migrations

The classical world, with civilisations based on stable, urban communities came to an end around the fifth century AD, when the nomadic peoples from the north of Asia (e.g. tribes such as the Angles, Saxons, Huns, Goths and Mongols) became dominant over wide areas of Europe and Asia. The rural and nomadic way of life of these peoples left few major built monuments for posterity. The only areas of urban civilisations to withstand or adapt to these invasions were the Byzantine empire (which covered the territory of present-day Greece and Turkey) and the Chinese kingdoms which were eventually reunified in the sixth and seventh centuries with the emergence of the Tang Dynasty, which survived from 618 to 907 AD. However, the period of the age of migrations also saw the spread of two major religions that now dominate the culture of much of the present-day world: Christianity (from first century AD) and Islam from 632 AD. As these religions spread from their origin in Israel and Saudi Arabia, substantial buildings such as churches, monasteries, and mosques were constructed (see Fig 5.6). Again, the best of each culture's artistic and technical skills were invested in the buildings, many of which attract tourists to them purely for their beauty, in addition to those who visit them for religious purposes and on pilgrimages.

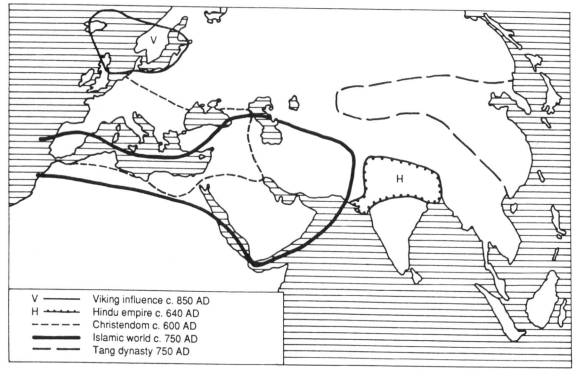

V ———— Viking influence c. 850 AD
H ∙∙∙∙∙∙ Hindu empire c. 640 AD
– – – – Christendom c. 600 AD
▬▬▬▬ Islamic world c. 750 AD
— — — Tang dynasty 750 AD

Fig. 5.6 Civilisations (500–900 AD)

The recovery of Europe

Medieval times

From about 950 AD there was a re-establishment of urban-based civilisations in Europe, which developed in parallel with economic change, population growth and the creation of wealth by trade. The period was typified by the rise of the small rival city states, for example in Italy, dominated by cities such as Florence, Naples and Milan and by the rich merchant cities such as Venice, Genoa, Pisa and Dubrovnic.

Further north in Europe too, a similar form of political and economic organisation developed which created the wealth of historic city centres that tourists now can enjoy. On the western and northernmost fringes of Europe, however, society was characterised by the establishment of feudal monarchies and the major heritage of this period is the scattering of defensive strongholds and castles built by the conquering feudal rulers in the nation states of England, France, Portugal, Scandinavia and Spain.

14th-16th centuries

The Renaissance, a period spanning the 14th to the 16th centuries, was a time when the great wealth generated by trade allowed the aristocracy and the rich merchants to become patrons of the arts. Their wealth was expressed in the architecture and art of the cities, much of which have survived intact, particularly in those cities bypassed by the subsequent development of the industrial revolution in Europe from the 17th century onwards. The most outstanding examples are, of course, the buildings and the art in the churches and galleries of Florence and Venice.

17th century to the present

Once again, the outstanding architectural features of more recent years tend to be the religious buildings or homes of the rich and powerful, who built themselves new homes and palaces on a grand scale using the best architects and designers of the period. On the other hand, few settlements retain the essence of the character of the times, because (apart from Victorian cities developed in new locations during the industrial revolution) the overall settlement pattern stabilised, and sites have been continuously occupied. Thus, towns grew organically with a mixture of buildings of different dates and styles, with new development replacing or modernising the older buildings. However, there are major exceptions, for example, the towns based on the early development of the tourist trade, which sprang up in hitherto undeveloped locations, such as the spa town of Bath, and many Georgian and Victorian seaside resorts which characterise the style and taste of their period. Similarly the ghost towns of the new world which sprang up very rapidly with the development of particular economic resources (e.g. in the California gold rush) and were completely abandoned once they become obsolete, for example, as resource was worked out or lost its value or economic relevance. In California, most of the 19th century gold rush towns remain deserted ruins but some have been preserved as tourist attractions (such as Old Sacramento and Columbia State Historic Park).

There has been a growing interest in the history and architecture of the industrial revolution, and many of the northern industrial towns of Britain have begun to preserve, renovate and market their industrial heritage for tourism, e.g. Gladstone Pottery Museum in Stoke-on-Trent, the Black Country Museum in Dudley, and the promotion of the whole city of Bradford; industrial conservation and tourism has also been built into many of the dockland redevelopment schemes in Britain, for example the Arnolfini, the SS Great Britain and the Watershed (all in Bristol) the maritime museums and other attractions in Cardiff and in Swansea.

Historic resources of the New World

Many peoples of the New World (i.e. outside Europe and Asia) have very ancient origins. It is maintained that the Aborigines of Australia represent the oldest unbroken culture of the world of about 40 000 years. But many of these peoples of the new world were nomadic hunter/gatherers,

living in small groups in ecological equilibrium with their environment. Thus, these cultures, in spite of their immense age, leave few buildings or monuments as historical resources.

However, the more urban-based civilisations of Central America were one exception. The ancient Mayan culture was at its peak around AD 300 but extended on to between 800 and 900 AD. Their major centres are located mainly in present-day Mexico, but their influence also extended into Guatemala and Honduras.

In later years the urban civilisations of the Toltecs around the 11th and 12th centuries and the Aztecs from the 13th century dominated Mexico, while in the central Andes during the 15th century the Inca empire extended over a region 320 km wide and 3200 km long, covering parts of present-day Ecuador, Peru, Bolivia and the northern parts of both Chile and Argentina.

The world distribution of historic resources is thus very patchy. The greatest wealth of historic resources exists in the western Mediterranean from Italy, through the Aegean to the Middle East. These regions retain well preserved remnants of the most ancient civilisations, which are complemented by rich examples of the art and architecture of later periods of history too. China can also boast a similar wealth of historic resources.

Some of these regions have the wealth and political stability to both protect and develop their historic resources for the benefit of the tourist. In the other areas, however, political instability not only inhibits the development of tourism but also more critically it may threaten the very survival of the historic features themselves.

Many historic sites and cultural properties are included on the list of World Heritage Sites and enjoy the same support and protection as the natural landscapes referred to in Chapter 4. Examples are drawn from every historic period from the archaeological ruins at Moenjodaro in the Indus valley in Pakistan, the Egyptian pyramids, the rock-hewn churches in Lalibela in Ethiopia, the Maya site of Copan in Honduras, Chartres Cathedral, the historic centre of Florence through to the Auschwitz concentration camp which was run by Nazi Germany in Poland during World War II.

FURTHER READING

Barraclough, G (Ed) (1978) *The Times Atlas of World History*, Times Books.

QUESTIONS AND DISCUSSION POINTS

1 Which country in Europe has the widest range of historic resources of different ages?

2 Explain the processes that are leading to the loss of historic resources. How can historic features be protected from destruction?

3 Locate the historical resources that are effectively out of bounds for tourism due to modern political problems.

ASSIGNMENTS

1 Your tour company wishes to develop new European tours with a special interest in history. You have been asked to construct a 14-day itinerary to include sites characteristic of each main period of European history. Write a brief report to your chief executive, outlining your suggested itinerary and explaining the reasons for your choice of stops, showing how your selection represents each main period of European history.

2 The local council of your home town is considering promoting the town's tourist potential. You have been commissioned by them to (a) make an assessment of the historic resources of the town and (b) make recommendations to the council as to whether or not the historic resources have the potential for this form of tourist promotion, and whether the council should go ahead with their planned promotion campaign.

Write a brief report for the Chairman of the Leisure and Tourism Committee of the local council, assessing the historic resources of the town, and advising the committee on the course of action they should take.

CHAPTER 6

Cultural entertainment and manmade resources for tourism

LEARNING OBJECTIVES

After reading this chapter you should be able to
- define cultural and ethnic resources
- explain why tourists are attracted to cultural and ethnic resources
- locate the areas in the world where ethnic tourist resources are most likely to be found
- understand some of the factors that influence the location of manmade and entertainment facilities
- appreciate the importance of modern cultures as tourist resources.

INTRODUCTION

The term 'cultural tourism' has been applied to a bewildering array of different tourist activities. A nation's or ethnic group's 'culture' can be described as their way of life, norms and values – that is their whole style of life including their religion, language, customs and behaviour, their expression in the performing arts (music, dance and drama), as well as their political and social organisation.

Cultural tourism must therefore include all tourist activity that involves exposure to and appreciation of another group's culture, and also the enjoyment of aspects of one's own culture. Cultural resources are thus not only the performing arts (from 'serious' culture such as opera, ballet and drama, through to 'popular' culture or entertainment in the form of shows, cabaret and pop concerts) but also the whole living expression of existing cultures. This includes the dress, cuisine, religious rites, traditions and customs of the different peoples of the world.

The attraction of cultural and entertainment resources to tourists

Cultural resources engage the tourist's mind: they can educate, inform and entertain. However, it has been suggested that tourists can be divided into two types, 'wanderlusters' and 'sunlusters', each of whom have significantly different motivations and therefore different interests in cultural and entertainment resources (Gray, 1970).

Wanderlusters

These are tourists who visit more than one destination and are actively seeking cultural experiences. These cultural experiences may range from personal experiences of exotic cultures such as tours to the hilltribes of Thailand (this is termed 'ethnic tourism' by Harron and Weiler, 1992) to visits to other countries where the tourist enjoys the different culture as part of the tourist experience but it is more a backdrop to sightseeing activity rather than the specific focus of travel. This second form of tourism is more generally known as 'cultural tourism'.

The wanderluster's motivation ranges from curiosity about other cultures and a wish to learn about them, to a wish to participate in and enjoy a different cultural environment from their own. The tourist has some interest in and sensitivity towards the culture they visit, though not always an understanding of it.

Sunlusters

These tourists tend to visit one destination which is chosen for its physical character (be it the sun and beach, water resources for water sports or snow fields for skiing, etc). The culture of the people in whose region or country these resources occur is of no particular interest to the 'sunluster', whose motivation is recreation, relaxation and entertainment. This type of tourist is a more passive recipient of cultural experiences and tends to expect culturally familiar forms of entertainment. The western tourist therefore expects to find facilities for western style entertainment at the destination (e.g. forms of popular culture and entertainment such as shows, cabaret, discos, gambling, etc).

The sunluster does not seek learning experiences or intellectual stimulation and development, but is looking for opportunities to relieve the stresses caused by his/her own day-to-day life. For western tourists these stresses may range from tension (relieved by passive entertainment) to boredom (relieved by forms of entertainment that involve thrill and risk – such as gambling, going on white-knuckle rides in theme parks or watching exciting sports, etc).

This general theory of dividing touristic behaviour into the 'wanderlust' or 'sunlust' modes does not suggest that individuals are always of one type or the other; rather, the two types described represent two extremes and many tourists will fall somewhere between, showing different combinations of motivations at different times, though one type of motivation is usually dominant.

CULTURAL RESOURCES

World pattern of cultures

Different cultures have evolved in different parts of the world as a result of people's varied social organisation and unique adaptation to their physical environment, their different histories (*see* Chapter 5) and styles of economic and political development.

Each region of the world thus shows a different pattern of cultural development, providing rich resources for the cultural tourist. It is clear that much of western Europe has a similar historic background, shares a religion, has a common basis for language (dating from the Latin of the ancient Roman empire) and a similar political way of life. But within this relative unity there is, however, a myriad of regional differences – regional both in terms of the differentiation between the countries of western Europe and in terms of more local differences within countries. These variations in language and dialect, in cuisine, dress and customs and traditional events, have led in recent years to a much greater consciousness of regional, ethnic and provincial identity (leading sometimes to political expressions of regional independence – for example, the Basque separatist movement in Spain and, to some extent, the Welsh and Scottish Nationalists in Britain). These regional variations are of great significance for tourism. Travellers within Europe find such variations attractive in that they are novel and interestingly different from their own regional culture, but reassuringly similar in that the basic way of life, manners, customs and style of life is the same as their own. Tourists can thus be assured that the local cuisine or customs will not be offensive or repellent, neither will the tourists' normal behaviour be liable to misinterpretation by the local residents.

Outside Europe there are much wider variations in culture. In the areas of European colonisation of the New World many of the indigenous nomadic races and their cultures have been more or less wiped out so that very little of their authentic culture remains. This is very much the case in North America and Australia. Similarly, other parts of South America, Africa and the South Pacific have had western values superimposed so that indigenous cultures have been stifled, suppressed or so undervalued that much has been lost, and what remains is in danger of being trivialised for the benefit of the tourist.

On the other hand, the eastern cultures of the Islamic, Hindu and Buddhist worlds are less influenced by westernisation. Indeed, some countries such as Myanmar are still virtually closed to the outside world, and some have only recently been opened to western influence. Travel in and out of Japan has only really developed since the 1960s and China's disrupted 'open door' policy dates only from the 1980s. These cultures, founded on the three main types of religion, are based on very different beliefs, traditions and codes of behaviour, which may inhibit tourism development. Strict adherents to Islam, for example, will not consume alcohol and will expect women to dress and behave modestly in public. Thus, the Islamic fundamentalist states (e.g. Libya, Iran and Saudi Arabia) do not welcome westernised tourists, whose behaviour is often not compatible with Islamic beliefs. Buddhism and Hinduism are inherently more tolerant religions and some regions have deliberately managed and marketed their religion and culture for tourism, the Hindu island of Bali being a classic example.

However, there is still a great potential for mutual misunderstanding between tourists and hosts. This is particularly the case in Japan, a country which superficially appears very westernised but whose society is based on fundamentally different customs and values. Individualism, unconventionality and self-expression do not fit comfortably into the Japanese way of life. The convention of politeness, the unwillingness of the Japanese to say 'no' to a request that cannot be met and the formalities of bowing etc, can lead to misunderstanding and frustration.

There are also some completely non-westernised parts of the world where people still live in a traditional way, with their own unique patterns of social organisation, customs and religion which the tourist is unlikely to understand unaided. These areas tend to be small, isolated and unaccessible, qualities that have protected the cultures from change. It is these cultures that form the resource for the specialised form of cultural tourism known as *ethnic tourism*. Examples occur in contrasting parts of the world but mainly from areas that are still relatively untouched wilderness (*see* Fig. 4.6, page 33, Chapter 4), e.g. Eskimo tourism in the polar/tundra regions of Alaska, and Aboriginal tourism in the remote parts of the Northern Territory of Australia, and the mountain peoples of the remote Himalayas (in Bhutan and Ladakh) and the hill tribes of the mountainous interior of Thailand (*see* Figs 6.1 and 6.2). The remoteness and inaccessibility of these regions often precludes access by vehicle, and so many of these ethnic tours include 'adventure' elements of travel on foot (trekking) or by local forms of transport such as horse or bullock carts, canoe or raft, or even by elephant.

Fig. 6.1 Hilltribe in Northern Thailand

Fig. 6.2 Ladies of the Padaung ('long-necked') tribe of Northern Thailand

Another characteristic of ethnic tourism is the involvement of tour guides to bridge the cultural gap between tourist and ethnic groups, explaining and interpreting the groups' customs and arranging for tourists to have access to rituals, meals, customs, dancing and other activities. The guides enable the tourist to communicate with the group and obtain the 'authentic' experience that this type of cultural tourist wants.

There is thus a great range of cultural resources in different parts of the world but it appears that relative isolation (be it political, economic or physical isolation) maintains the extremes of cultural diversity of different peoples and ethnic groups.

MANMADE AND ENTERTAINMENT RESOURCES

On the face of it, manmade attractions and entertainment resources may seem to be very different in nature from the cultural resources described above. Cultural resources are very much tied to specific locations where particular groups of people live. Manmade facilities on the other hand can be created wherever man chooses to build them. Nevertheless, there are some clear spatial patterns in the location and distribution of manmade attractions: firstly, they will be located throughout the western world to meet the leisure and entertainment needs of resident westernised populations, and secondly, they will occur where the 'sunluster' type of western tourist is found. Indeed, these attractions can be seen as the trappings of contemporary westernised culture, generated by certain social and psychological needs created by modern western society. These needs include:

1 **The need for thrills, risk taking and cathartic experiences.** The manmade leisure and tourism activities that meet these needs include:

- white-knuckle rides in theme parks
- gambling and sex tourism
- spectator sports events.

2 **The need for entertainment, relaxation and social contact.** Activities meeting these needs include:

- concerts, shows, cabaret, films, theatre, festivals, carnivals
- drinking and eating out
- dancing
- entertainment spectacles at, for example, theme parks.

3 **Consumerism – the need to purchase non-essential and luxury goods.** Activities meeting these needs include:

- leisure shopping
- visiting exhibitions.

The facilities that meet these needs have several characteristics in common:

- They appeal to tourists, day trippers and non-tourists.
- They rely on a mass market for their economic viability.
- They generally require high levels of investment and are fairly high risk business ventures.

These three characteristics exert a strong control over the location of manmade facilities – particularly the bigger ones. Because they rely on the mass market they are generally located in either a major urban region (where they can draw their clientele from both tourists and residents and enjoy all year round trade), or in a major all year round 'sunluster' type tourist destination such as Florida (*see* Chapter 2). Also, they must be highly accessible to the mass market, so will be located either in city centres, or out of town but close to good mass transport links (e.g. motorway intersections or airports). Many of the manmade attractions are indoor facilities, so they are independent of the climatic controls that influence the use and location of many other tourist resources.

These attractions include theme parks, leisure shopping complexes, indoor resorts, exhibition and conference venues, gambling and sex tourism, and hallmark events. The character and spatial distribution of these attractions is discussed below, in order to illustrate some of these points.

Fig. 6.3 Disneyland – themed area

Theme parks

Theme parks are most definitely a modern western cultural leisure and tourism concept: the first (Disneyland) was opened in 1955 in California, USA. By 1987 another 29 large scale theme parks had been established in the USA, each of which attracted over 1 million visitors a year. By 1990, 40 parks had achieved the 1 million attendance figure. In Europe by the late 1980s there were 21 parks that attracted at least 300 000 visitors per annum. Theme parks are large amusement or leisure parks, with white-knuckle rides and entertainments and attractions grouped by themes (e.g. the sea, nature, the jungle, cartoon characters or fairy tales, etc) which are replaced and updated from time to time, needing continuous investment (*see* Figs 6.3 and 6.4). They are generally set in a parkland environment away from towns but in very accessible locations. Though some of the entertainments are indoors (e.g. Lotte World in Seoul), most are large scale outdoor attractions, so these parks have conflicting locational requirements: they need to be located in good climates on the one hand, but close to the tourist generating region on the other. The European distribution of theme parks shows that the latter is dominant; most European theme parks are located in the western maritime climatic zone of northern Europe – which are the most affluent and densely populated parts (*see* Fig. 6.5). In the USA, theme parks are concentrated in the main tourist destinations with the best climates: in 1989, 38 per cent of the top USA theme parks were located in Florida and California, while only 21 per cent were located in the north-eastern states (the densely populated economic core of New York, Pennsylvania and Ohio) (Millman, 1993).

Although theme parks are perceived to be mainly tourist facilities, surveys show that the majority of users are day visitors: a sample of eight European parks showed 70–95 per cent of the visitors to be day trippers, with more than 60 per cent of the visitors travelling less than two hours.

In the USA, 75 per cent of the parks' visitors were day trippers, drawn from a 150-mile catchment area (Lyon, 1987). Only the USA Disney parks (which are located in tourist destinations in good climatic zones) attract a significant number of overnight tourists.

Fig. 6.4 Disneyland, California – showing four different types of ride (and taken from a fifth)

Country	Number of parks opened	Planned
W Germany	6	
Belgium	4	
UK	2	
Netherlands	3	
France	2	7
Denmark	2	
Spain	1	
Sweden	1	

Fig. 6.5 European Theme Parks (1987)
(*Source*: Brown and Church, 1987)

Leisure shopping, entertainment and conference centres

These three rather different types of tourist facility also rely on regular all year round use by non-tourists to stay in business. Their attraction to the tourist is enhanced if they are clustered together. They are normally found in easily accessible locations in big cities, often in or near the city centre. Indeed, they may be concentrated in specialised districts of the inner city, e.g. the West End of London, Broadway in New York, Castlefield in Manchester and Albert Dock, Liverpool (*see* Chapter 13).

Leisure shopping

Surveys of tourist behaviour generally show that visitors spend a lot of time shopping – browsing and window shopping – and having meals, as well as actually purchasing goods. Urban planners often seek to encourage this behaviour by increasing the attractiveness of shopping environments, for example, by pedestrianising streets, allowing street entertainment, providing good parking and car access, and enhancing the street scene with trees, flowers, attractive seats, signs, lighting and so on. In many city centres this type of environment has evolved from existing shopping streets, but successful new shopping complexes can be created from the adaptation of redundant buildings such as Covent Garden in London or Albert Dock in Liverpool. Established city centre shopping areas are now facing competition from new, out of town, shopping and leisure developments. These are often indoor centres (shopping malls) in locations with very good access and an abundance of parking space, often on the urban fringe or even outside the

city itself. Leisure attractions (such as multiplex cinemas, sports facilities and even hotels) are built into the development. The larger centres, for example, West Edmonton Mall in Canada (opened in 1985) attract tourists as well as residents, but normally these shopping facilities cater more for local urban residents (Jansen-Verbeker, 1991).

Entertainment and conference facilities

These facilities span the range of cultural interests from art galleries, museums, concert halls, theatres, clubs to bars, cafés and restaurants.

The same locational factors influence the distribution of entertainment attractions, resulting in their concentration on the urban scale in the centres but also on a national scale in national or regional capital cities.

Conference and exhibition centres are also concentrated in capital cities. International congresses are concentrated in the most accessible capitals and 'international' cities of the countries of the world's economic core: in 1990 Paris was the leading European conference destination, hosting 361 events, followed by London, Brussels, Vienna, Geneva and Berlin. Singapore (with 136 congresses) and Washington DC (101) were the leading non-European international conference centres that year. On a national and city scale, these facilities are more closely tied to good transport (airport, rail and motorway links) and a good supply of hotel accommodation, than the other attractions that are concentrated in the city centre.

Indeed, many of the struggling coldwater coastal resorts of northern Europe have attempted to diversify into business tourism by building new conference centres in the hope that the combination of abundant hotel accommodation and purpose-built modern conference facilities will lure the business tourist away from the regional and national capital cities (*see* Chapter 8).

Hallmark events

These are major fairs, festivals, expositions and cultural events. They may be held regularly – annually, or on a regular cycle of every two or four years, for example – or on a one-off basis. Many of the regularly held major events (e.g. World Travel Fair in London, Rio Carnival,

Edinburgh Festival) are located in major world cities, for the locational advantages as discussed above. Some may be deliberately staged in the shoulders of the peak tourist season in order to spread demand. However, the main objective for a city staging a hallmark event is to provide the city with the opportunity to make a big impact on the tourist industry and thereby to attract additional tourists, over and above those who visit specifically for the event itself. Thus existing tourist markets are boosted and new markets may be created and developed. So, hallmark events tend to be distributed among a wide variety of settlements – some already well established tourist centres (e.g. Cannes Film Festival), some wishing to create a tourist industry (e.g. the Olympics in Seoul, South Korea), and even some small villages wishing to promote tourism in rural regions (e.g. the Eurovision Song Contest in the village of Millstreet, Ireland).

There are also major international sporting events that can be classed as major events (such as the Olympic Games or the World Cup football finals) which are held regularly but not necessarily in the same country each time. These provide the host city (and country) with a unique opportunity to sell itself, its culture and its attractions directly to a wide international audience (for example, as at the opening ceremony of the Olympic Games in Barcelona in 1992). New transport and accommodation facilities may be built specifically for the event in the hope that it will trigger off new tourist demand. There is evidence that the awareness of such venues does increase, at least in the short term, for example, the Winter Olympics at Calgary, Canada (Ritchie and Smith, 1991) and that tourism can be boosted – for example, the Americas Cup in Perth, Australia's bicentennial and the Brisbane World Expo all appeared to accelerate the growth of international tourism to Australia in the late 1980s.

Hallmark events can be on a much smaller scale (even down to local community and arts festivals), but their function – to bring the economic benefits of tourism to the locality by promoting its tourist image – remains the same, as does their locational pattern, spread widely throughout a range of different settlements in regions with or without an established tourist industry (Hall, 1989).

Gambling and sex tourism

Commercialised gambling and sex tourism, along with the consumption of alcohol, represent aspects of modern culture that are not universally acceptable; in some cultures they are banned. For example, the stricter Islamic countries (e.g. Libya, Saudi Arabia) prohibit the consumption of alcohol, and prostitution is not officially allowed in Thailand, although the authorities may 'turn a blind eye'.

These activities are often geographically widespread throughout the countries where they are legal, both in the urban (tourist generating) regions and the tourist destinations – particularly the resorts that cater for the 'sunluster' type of tourist where these additional forms of entertainment are welcomed.

On a world scale, centres that cater specifically for sex tourism or gambling may be clustered on political boundaries – just across the borders of countries where the activities are outlawed. Tourists cross the border to locations where they can then indulge in these pursuits legally. For example, Monte Carlo owes its origin to the fact that gambling used to be illegal in France and visitors to the French Riviera resorts of Nice and Cannes crossed into the 'country' of Monte Carlo to gamble in the Casino. Tweed Heads (on the New South Wales side of the Queensland state border in Australia) fulfilled the same function for Queenslanders up to 1985 (when slot machines etc were legalised in Queensland). Currently, Lesotho and Swaziland provide these facilities for South Africans (Leiper, 1989). Similarly, prostitution (packaged as sex tourism) may be highly organised in some patriarchal countries (e.g. the Philippines) where it is tolerated or even encouraged because it brings in desperately needed foreign currency (Hall, 1992).

CONCLUSIONS

Cultural and entertainment resources are geographically widespread throughout the resort regions and the city regions of any country, because they cater for both tourist and resident together. Nevertheless, this chapter has suggested that there are some fairly consistent locational patterns associated with each type of attraction. Figure 6.6 presents a generalised summary of the most important spatial relationships.

These resources and activities are not tied to the geographical pattern of the world's physical resources: their locations are more related to man's social behaviour and to financial and economic forces that govern tourism development decisions.

REFERENCES AND FURTHER READING

Those texts marked with an asterisk are particularly recommended for further reading.

Brent Ritchie, J R, and Smith, B H, (1991) 'The impact of a mega-event on host region awareness: a longitudinal study', *Journal of Travel Research*, Vol. 30, No. 1 pp. 3–10.

*English Tourist Board and Jones Lang Wootton (1989) *'Retail, Leisure and Tourism'*.

Brown, J and Church, A (1987) 'Theme parks in Europe', *Travel and Tourism Analyst*, pp. 35–46, Feb.

*Getz, D (1991) *'Festivals, Special Events and Tourism'*, New York: Van Nostrand Reinhold.

Gray, H P (1970) *'International Travel – International Trade'*, Lexington, MA: D C Heath.

Hall, C M (1989) 'The definition and analysis of hallmark tourist events', *Geojournal*, Vol. 19, No. 3, pp. 263–68.

*Hall, C M (1992) *'Hallmark Tourist Events – Impacts, Management and Planning'*, Belhaven.

Hall, C M (1992) 'Sex tourism in South East Asia' in Harrison, D (Ed) *'Tourism and the Less Developed Countries'*, Belhaven.

Harron, S, and Weiler, B, (1992) 'Ethnic Tourism' in Weiler, B and Hall, C M (Eds) *'Special Interest Tourism'*, Belhaven.

Tourist attraction or activity	Location						
	Capital city/major city, centre or tourist quarter	Outside city but in city region	Peripheral town or region	Coastal resort or major destination area	Cross-border resort	Adjacent country	Remote region
Heritage 'cultural' resource	Yes	Yes	Yes				
Arts attraction	Yes	Yes					
Arts festival/event	Yes	Yes	Yes				
Conference/exhibition centre	Yes			Yes			
Leisure shopping	Yes						
Theme park and other attractions		Yes		Yes			
Hallmark events			Yes				
Sex tourism	Yes			Yes	Yes	Yes	
Gambling	Yes			Yes	Yes		
Cultural tourism						Yes	
Ethnic tourism							Yes

Fig. 6.6 Typical locations of cultural, entertainment and manmade tourist resources

*Jansen-Verbeker, M (1988) 'Leisure, recreation and tourism in inner cities', *Netherlands Geographical Studies*, No. 58, Amsterdam.

Jansen-Verbeker, M (1991) 'Leisure shopping – a magic concept for the tourism industry?' in *Tourism Management*, Vol. 12 March.

*Law, C M (1993) *Urban Tourism – Attracting Visitors to Large Cities*, Mansell.

Leiper, N (1989) 'Tourism and gambling', *Geojournal*, Vol. 19, No. 3, pp. 269–75.

Lyon, R (1987) 'Theme parks in the United States', in *Travel and Tourism Analyst*, Jan., pp. 31–43.

McEniff, J (1993) 'Theme parks in Europe', *Travel and Tourism Analyst*, No.5, pp. 52–73.

Millman, A (1993) 'Theme parks and attractions' in Khan, M, Olsen, M and Var, T (Eds) in *VNR's Encyclopedia of Hospitality and Tourism'*, New York: Van Nostrand Reinhold.

QUESTIONS AND DISCUSSION POINTS

1 Why should tourists be aware of the customs and values of the host communities that they visit?

2 What factors motivate tourists to seek ethnic, cultural and entertainment experiences when on holiday?

3 Why is Paris a successful international conference centre?

ASSIGNMENTS

1 You are the manager of a company wishing to develop a new theme park in the UK. You are preparing to write a brief for your assistant who has the task of seeking out a selection of possible sites that you might consider buying for the new development. In which region of the UK would you start looking for a suitable site and why? In what sort of location (within the chosen region) would you expect to find the 'best' site? In order to guide your assistant in the search for suitable sites, write out a list of the locational factors which would make an ideal location for your new theme park.

2 You work in the tourism marketing section of your local authority, which is considering promoting a themed festival or special event sometime in the future in order to develop the region's tourist image and increase the number of inbound tourists. The head of your section has organised a 'brainstorming' session to generate some new and original ideas for the new event. Write out your suggestions for either a completely new event, or an existing event that could be expanded and promoted as a 'hallmark' tourist event for your area.

The use of geographical resources for tourism

INTRODUCTION

This section of the book is concerned with the way in which tourist resources develop into tourist destinations, how they are used by tourists and the spatial patterns of tourist resource development. Section 2 seeks to answer the following questions:

1 How do the world's physical, historical and cultural resources become developed for tourism? What part do the tourists themselves, the tourist industry and the host community play in this process of development?

2 How are the world's tourist resources used, who uses them, and what impact does tourism have on the resources?

3 How does tourist development spread to new destinations throughout the world? Is this spatial spread of tourism inevitable?

4 How do host communities react to the development and spread of tourism? Do they encourage it or seek to control it through their economic and planning policies?

Many researchers into tourism have proposed theories of the way they think tourist development occurs. These include theories about the motivation of the tourist, the travel industry and the host community and how the behaviour of these groups fuels the process of development. Other researchers have put these ideas together to construct theoretical models of how the process of destination development occurs. These models have been applied most often to the development of seaside resorts, but they also apply to the development of landscape, wildlife, historic, cultural and urban tourist resources to a certain extent. Tourism does change the nature of each resource as it grows, but other socioeconomic forces and other land uses may well have bigger impacts than tourism. Host governments appear to have contrasting attitudes to tourism; some countries encourage it because tourist development can help them achieve other social and economic policy objectives, while other countries seek to curb the seemingly inevitable spread of tourism in order to protect the character of the tourist resource and to limit its undesirable effects. 'Sustainable' tourism has been put forward as a solution to the world problem of the increasing spread and impact of tourism, but a closer analysis of the concept reveals its limitations.

CHAPTER 7

Theories of tourist development

LEARNING OBJECTIVES

After reading this chapter you should be able to
- **understand the motivations of different types of tourist, the travel industry, and the different elements of the host community**
- **describe the product life cycle**
- **list the stages of the destination life cycle model**
- **understand the process of the spatial spread of tourism to new destinations.**

INTRODUCTION

The first chapter of this book describes tourism in terms of a simple origin – destination model; Chapters 2–6 describe the character and global distribution of the world's natural and cultural resources for tourism. This chapter seeks to introduce a further theme – the process by which these tourist resources are developed and used for tourism. An understanding of the process will help explain the current spatial pattern of tourist activity in tourist destination regions. The process of tourist development also operates both in space (leading to the spatial spread of tourist development and tourist activity) and through time (leading to changes in the amount and type of tourism in one specific destination over a period of years).

It is suggested here that the process can be explained mainly in terms of human motivation and behaviour, namely:

1 the motivation and behaviour of the tourist (i.e. what the tourist wants from the travel experience, and how the tourist behaves in choosing and taking the holiday);
2 the motivation and behaviour of the travel industry in seeking to develop and promote services in and to particular destinations;
3 the motivation and behaviour of the host community as it responds to the impact of tourist development.

This chapter will start by summarising what is known about the motivation of these groups, and will go on to discuss the possible spatial outcomes of the actions of the groups and the interactions between them (as proposed in different theories put forward by different authors).

TOURIST MOTIVATION

At the beginning of Chapters 2–6 it is suggested that tourists seek and obtain enjoyable experiences from the world's natural and cultural resources, for example, physical comfort from being in a suitable climate, aesthetic pleasure from viewing a beautiful landscape or building, excitement from theme park rides or gambling, etc. Each individual tourist may be seeking a range of these different pleasures in the course of their travel, depending on their psychological needs.

It is assumed that potential tourists are motivated to travel in order to meet these needs (Uysal and Hagan, 1993). Many authors (e.g. Crompton, 1979, Leiper, 1984) have suggested what these needs might be; the following list indicates some:

1 **Physical needs,** which range from
   - the need for rest from physical fatigue, to
   - the need for activity and exercise.
2 **Social needs,** ranging from
   - the need to strengthen social relationships, to
   - the need to escape from social duties and pressures.

Need		Examples of tourist activity that might meet each need
Physical	– Relaxation – Activity	Lying on the beach Mountain trekking
Social	– Social relationships – Escaping from social duties	Family holidays, 18–30 group holidays, honeymoons, in urban places Solitary holidays in remote places
Status	– Conformity – Status	Going to the most popular seaside resort Going to an exclusive resort frequented by popstars, royalty or film stars
Intellectual	– Rest – Intellectual stimulation	Passive entertainment (shows, watching traditional dancing) Heritage – educational or ethnic tourism
Mental	– Relaxation from tension – Escape from boredom	Going on an organised totally inclusive tour White-knuckle rides at theme parks, bungee jumping, gambling

Fig. 7.1 Tourist activities that might meet psychological needs

3 **Status needs,** varying from
  ● the need to conform, to
  ● the need for social status by being different in a way that people admire.
4 **Intellectual needs**
  ● the need for rest from mental fatigue, to
  ● the need for intellectual stimulation.
5 **Mental needs**
  ● the need for relaxation from mental tension and situations of conflict and risk, to
  ● the need to escape from boredom through exciting, risky and cathartic experiences.

These needs are created by the potential tourist's life style – the sum of the personality, family status, work, economic and social environment. Fulfilling these needs may involve the tourist in avoiding certain things (for example, the social pressures, tension and conflict situations, etc, that are part of daily routine) or actively seeking to do something that is absent from normal, everyday life (for example, risk taking, new intellectual experiences, etc).

Most leisure and recreation activities can meet these needs to some extent. The distinguishing fea-ture of tourism is that the individual seeks to meet these needs away from his/her everyday home environment. Tourism may therefore be more effective than home-based leisure and recreation because travelling to a completely different social and physical environment may remove the pressures and inhibitions that make the individual behave in a routine way at home; travel may thus allow the individual to behave differently, to do different things and to 'break the mould'. Also, money and time for the holiday are 'saved up' during the rest of the year – to be spent in one concentrated block. This may allow the tourist to take part in activities that are normally too time-consuming, not available, or too expensive, in everyday life. Some authors (e.g. Graburn, 1983) suggest that tourists go so far as to do the exact opposite of what they do at home. This may be overstating the case for the majority, but it is clear that people do choose to travel for the differences and contrasts between their home and holiday destination. Iso-Ahola (1982) has summarised this by classifying tourists' motives into 'desires to escape from circumstances' and 'desires to achieve particular things' as follows:

1 Desires to escape

- (a) from the personal environment (personal troubles, problems, failures)
- (b) from the interpersonal (i.e. social) environment – social roles and social duties towards other members of the family, to colleagues at work, friends.

2 Desires to achieve

- (a) psychological rewards and intrinsic personal rewards (rest, relaxation, education, ego enhancement)
- (b) interpersonal (social) rewards (more social interaction, making friends).

The 'desires to escape' may be equated with the 'push' factors that make people want to travel to a different environment away from home, while the 'desires to achieve' (the 'pull' factors) may lead to people choosing particular destinations that have the specific characteristics that they require. This interpretation of motivation is broadly consistent with the simple origin–destination model presented in Chapter 1.

These types of models are complicated by the fact that one individual may have many different combinations of motivations, and even conflicting motivations (e.g. for rest at some times and for activity at others). So, the same tourist may want to do a whole range of different things at the same destination. However, there is enough consistency in tourists' behaviour for researchers to attempt to identify common 'tourist types' – that is, groups of people who show similar holiday and travel choices and tourist behaviour patterns. It is assumed that they are likely to share similar motivations, values and attitudes. The division of tourism markets into these groups is called psychographic segmentation (Brayley, 1993).

Reference has already been made (see Chapter 6) to Gray's division of tourist behaviour into the wanderlust and sunlust types. Wanderlust is 'that basic trait in human nature which causes some individuals to want to leave things with which they are familiar and to go and see at first hand different exciting cultures and places. The desire to travel may not be a permanent one, merely a desire to exchange temporarily the known workday things of home for something exotic.' Wanderlusters would therefore be people who would prefer cultural tourism and tours that visit several destinations, and may be predominantly long-haul trav-

ellers. They may be people in which the 'push' factors (i.e. the desire to escape) are dominant over the 'pull' factors (i.e. the qualities of a particular destination). In contrast sunlust 'depends on the existence elsewhere of different or better amenities for a specific purpose than are available locally'. These amenities may be a hotter climate (for sun, sea and sand tourism), but may equally be a colder one (for skiing) or a beautiful landscape, abundant wildlife, heritage attractions, or any one of the resources described in Chapters 2 to 6. The sunluster (or snowluster, landscape luster, wildlife luster, etc) therefore tends to choose one specific destination that has the desired qualities, but is quite happy to travel in a familiar social group with his/her own secure cultural 'bubble' of familiar food, language and customs. Domestic tourism and short-haul travel may be able to meet the sunluster's needs.

There is a second widely quoted model of tourist types. Dr S C Plog worked in the United States and his research led him to suggest that there are two extremes of tourist motivation and behaviour: 'psychocentric' and 'allocentric'. McIntosh and Goeldner (1990) explain these terms as follows:

> The term 'psychocentric' is derived from *psyche* or *self*-centred, meaning the centring of one's thoughts or concerns on the small problem areas of one's life. 'Allocentric', on the other hand, derives from the root word *allo*, meaning 'varied in form'. An allocentric person, thus, is one whose interest patterns are focused on varied activities. Such a person is outgoing and self-confident and is characterised by a considerable degree of adventure and a willingness to reach out and experiment with life. Travel becomes a way for the allocentric to express inquisitiveness and satisfy curiosity.

The allocentric will therefore actively seek out new destinations and the unfamiliar in the form of educational, ethnic or adventure tourism. The psychocentric, on the other hand, is anxious, self-inhibited and unadventurous, seeking the 'safe bet' in well known and culturally familiar destinations such as popular resorts and theme parks. Plog's research showed that allocentrics are more likely to be found at the lower end of the income spectrum. But, of course, the majority of people can be classified as somewhere in between these two extremes – in the 'midcentric' category (see Fig 7.2). Midcentrics display a balance of all the normal/usual motivations – such as relaxation, the aesthetic

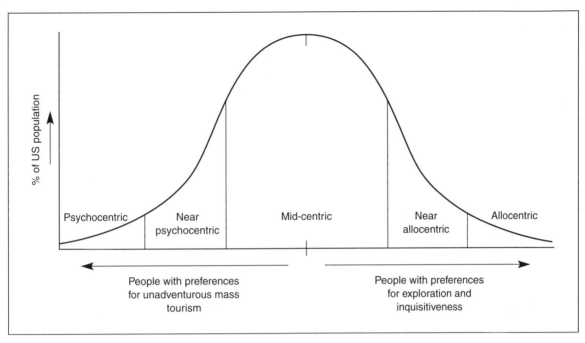

Fig. 7.2 Plog's division of the US population into different tourist types. (The curve represents a 'normal' distribution. The vast majority clusters around the middle, with smaller percentages of the population at either extreme.) (*Source*: After Plog, 1972)

pleasures of natural and historic features, need for a change, for sensual pleasure (food, climatic comfort, romance and sex, etc), for pleasant social interaction with friends and relatives and so on.

In geographical terms, the allocentrics are most likely to be the 'pioneers' who 'discover' new or remote long-haul destinations and who are prepared to try new, special forms of tourism. The psychocentrics will be the type most likely to be repeat customers of well developed domestic resorts. Midcentrics will enjoy the vast range of holiday experiences that lie between these two extremes.

There are other models of tourist types – Cohen's (1972) relates to the tourist's level of dependence on the tourist industry and on their relationship with the host community. His categories show some similarities to Plog's; they are

1 The drifter who avoids contact with the tourist industry and identifies with the host community – living with them and adopting their customs, and even working temporarily in the community.
2 The explorer who arranges their own trip alone, and seeks to 'get off the beaten track' but will use

comfortable tourist accommodation and retain the basics of their normal life style, though they are motivated by the need for cultural experiences.
3 The individual mass tourist who uses many of the services provided by tour operators but decides their own itinerary, though they will visit the popular 'sights'.
4 The organised mass tourist who is the least adventurous, and who relies on the tour operator to decide and arrange the complete holiday experience. They travel in their own 'environmental bubble' and may stay completely separate from the members of the host community.

Smith (1977) (*see* Fig 7.3) amplifies these groups, and relates the type of tourist to their total number and their attitude to the cultures they visit.

Again, these tourist types are likely to be segregated spatially, with the 'explorers' being found in the remote regions and the charter tourist at the other extreme, in the most popular resorts.

The translation of these potential tourists (with all their varied motivations) into real tourists who purchase holidays and actually travel depends

Type of tourist	Number of tourists	Adaptations to local culture
Explorer	very limited	accepts fully
Elite	rarely seen	adapts fully
Offbeat	uncommon but seen	adapts well
Unusual	occasional	adapts somewhat
Incipient mass	steady flow	seeks western amenities
Mass	continuous flow	expects western amenities
Charter	massive arrivals	demands western amenities

Fig. 7.3 Types, numbers and attitudes of tourists
(*Source*: Smith, 1977)

primarily on their social and economic circumstances (their disposable income, time available, family commitments, etc). Demand studies and market segmentation are based on the assumption that people of similar cultural attitudes and background, occupation, family situation and income and so on, are likely to behave more similarly to each other than to people with different socioeconomic characteristics. The general relationship between affluence and the growth of tourism is touched on in Chapter 15. Suffice it to say here that the frequency of holiday taking, and the distance travelled appears to increase with greater wealth.

MOTIVATIONS OF THE TOURIST INDUSTRY

The tourist industry aims to make a profit by supplying the services that enable the tourist to get to, stay in and enjoy the destination. The industry provides transport and accommodation and makes the attractions at the destination (which motivate travel) available to the tourist. The tourist's experience, which is the result of the enjoyment of all these services combined, can be called the tourist 'product'.

The industry is fragmented, made up of many different businesses, each supplying part of the service. The businesses are dependent on one another and must co-operate in order to provide a satisfactory total experience (or product) to the traveller and ought to co-operate to conserve the features that attract the tourist in the first place.

But in a free market, the individual businesses in each particular part of the industry are also in competition with each other: their survival depends on providing a 'better', different or new product, or the same product more cheaply.

The interaction between the industry's competitive behaviour and the purchaser (the tourist's) motivation and behaviour will, over a period of time, lead to a cyclic change in the type and nature of the product (that is, the set of services that makes up the tourist experience).

This product life cycle (first proposed by Vernon, 1966) has four stages (*see* Fig 7.4):

1 Introduction. The initial market (of 'pioneer') tourists is small. Because of the high cost and high risk of providing tourist services at a new, untested destination for this small market the cost to the tourist is high, but profits to the few businesses concerned are also high. Competition is low, and visitor numbers grow only slowly.

2 Growth. To increase numbers, promotion is stepped up, visitor numbers increase and profits reach peak level. But competition increases as more businesses enter the market to provide similar (and highly profitable) services. In consequence, prices begin to fall, enabling different types of customers to purchase the product.

3 Maturity (or saturation). Demand stabilises at a high level, with many people (i.e. the mass tourist) purchasing the product. Competition between businesses is at its maximum and prices are at their lowest, while profits begin to go down.

4 Decline. Sales go down as the product goes out of fashion. Profits are low, competition decreases and the price starts to rise (thus accelerating the decline).

Spatially, this means that there is constant pressure to either replicate facilities or services at a

	Introduction	Growth	Maturity	Decline
Characteristics				
Sales	Low	Fast growth	Slow growth	Decline
Profits	Negligible	Peak levels	Declining	Low or zero
Cashflow	Negative	Moderate	High	Low
Customers	Innovative	Mass market	Mass market	Laggards
Competitors	Few	Growing	Many rivals	Declining number
Responses				
Strategic focus	Expand market	Market penetration	Defend share	Productivity
Marketing expenditures	High	High (declining %)	Falling	Low
Marketing emphasis	Product awareness	Brand preference	Brand loyalty	Selective
Distribution	Patchy	Intensive	Intensive	Selective
Price	High	Lower	Lowest	Rising
Product	Basic/ unstandardised	Improved/ standardised	Differentiated	Rationalised

Fig. 7.4 Implications of the product life cycle
(*Source*: Doyle, 1976)

successful destination (during the growth and maturity phases), or to repeat the facility in a new or different place (as a response to the maturity phase), or to develop new and different services in new locations (starting a new cycle at the introduction stage). Butler has applied the concept of the product life cycle to the process of tourist development as it occurs in one particular resort over time (*see* Fig 7.5). This model labels the different stages of development.

1 **Exploration** } equivalent to the 'introduction'
2 **Involvement** } stage of product life cycle
3 **Development:** equivalent to the 'growth' stage of the product life cycle
4 **Consolidation:** equivalent to the 'maturity' stage of the product life cycle
5 **Stagnation:** equivalent to the 'decline' stage of the product life cycle.

The model defines each stage in terms of visitor numbers and changes in the tourist industry and its relationship with the local community (rather than with the spatial or land use changes). It is a widely accepted model and has frequently been applied to the study of seaside resorts (*see* Chapter 8). Its significance here is that it suggests a range of possible future changes that might occur in the existing resorts that have now reached 'stagnation' (that is, at the end of the product life cycle). It suggests that resorts might be rejuvenated or continue to grow at

a reduced rate; or that they might continue in their present form indefinitely (i.e. stabilise); or that they will continue on a path of decline (the path that the logic of the model suggests, in the absence of action by the industry, tourism planners and politicians and host community).

The cycle of development is also fuelled by another motivation of the tourist industry: to increase the number of tourists who use the services provided by the industry. This is done by advertising which increases potential tourists' knowledge of possible destinations but also plays on the potential tourists' motivations. Advertising may aim to increase the strength of the 'push' factors in the tourist generating region, but more frequently it seeks to increase the 'pull' factors of the development destination by emphasising (or even over-emphasising) the qualities of the destination that can meet the tourists' needs.

The industry also seeks to minimise risk at the introduction stage of the product life cycle when making new investments and developing new destinations. It is very unusual for tourist infrastructure (in the form of transport and accommodation) to be provided in a totally unknown destination and then marketed: it is much more likely that the industry will follow into destinations that have first already been shown to have tourist appeal by the drifters/explorers/allocentrics. It is suggested that the first organised tours into such new desti-

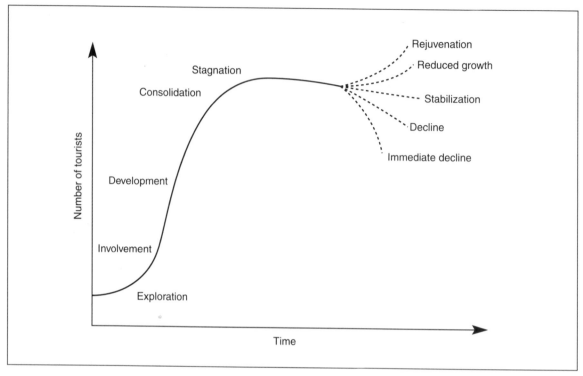

Characteristics of a resort at each stage of the model.

Exploration: difficult access, no facilities, destination unchanged.

Involvement: facilities provided by local people. Visitor numbers increasing.

Development: rapid expansion of facilities. Increasing investment by non-local companies to develop accommodation, natural, cultural and manmade attractions.

Consolidation: growth of visitor numbers slows down.

Stagnation: destination no longer fashionable, needs sustained marketing, problems emerge.

Decline: Local involvement increases, tourists switch to competing newer resorts, tourist accommodation etc changed to non-tourist uses.

Rejuvenation: attractions changed to appeal to new markets.

Fig. 7.5 Butler's model of resort development

nations are more likely to be adventure/camping or safari trips that do not require a completely western standard of infrastructure and that take their own accommodation (camping equipment) with them. This equipment can be utilised elsewhere (and so the investment is protected) if the destination does not prove popular: the risk of providing a completely built infrastructure and facilities until demand has been established is too high. The only exception to this rule would be the duplication of a tried and tested form of development that is already popular in a new untouched location (integrated or catalytic development).

MOTIVATIONS OF THE HOST COMMUNITY

Just as the 'tourist' and the 'tourist industry' are made up of many different units or elements, each with different motivations, so is the host community.

The host community is defined as the people living and working in the destination resort or region. The host community will normally be made up of the following groups:

1 The holders of local economic power – for example, the land and property owners, and the local non-tourist businesses which seek to use local resources such as the sea, for non-tourist activities such as fishing.

2 Holders of local political power – for example, local politicians, decision makers.

3 Local residents with little direct/institutionalised power – the ordinary people who live and work in the locality. The level and type of influence that this group can have on local decision making depends on the host community's political organisation (e.g. tribal, democratic, dictatorship).

4 The government of the country in which the destination region is located – people who wield political and economic decision-making power at regional or national level. The nature and power of this group will vary and also obviously depends on the political and economic organisation of the country concerned. For example, they may be banks (making economic decisions about lending money for investment) or governments (making laws about what the local and visitor population may or may not do).

One individual may be a member of one or more of these groups – for example, a local resident may be a landowner and a local politician. Tourism development itself may change the composition of the host community. New jobs created by tourism may trigger off migration of workers into the destination area so that the 'host community' may no longer consist of a majority of 'local' people. This may be accentuated by certain sections of the host community leaving as a result of tourist development – for example, local landowners selling up and moving away, to be replaced sometimes by absentee or even foreign property owners.

Each of these groups may well have very different attitudes to tourism and different motivations, depending on whether or not they benefit financially from tourism or they experience the undesirable impacts of it. The way in which tourism is encouraged or resisted and the resulting pattern of the type, scale and location of tourist development may reflect the motivations of the key people within the host community rather than those of the majority of local people.

MODELS OF TOURIST DEVELOPMENT

Butler's model of tourist development describes the progress of the product life cycle as it occurs in a single destination. Other models seek to describe and explain how and why tourist development occurs in the places and at the times that it does. Many authors and researchers have put forward their ideas in an attempt to explain the distribution of tourism that they have observed. As Pearce (1987) suggests in *Tourism Today* each author deals with a part of the whole complex system, each looking at it from a different point of view.

It is clear by now that the spatial pattern of tourist development depends not just on where the potential resources for tourism are; it depends on the coincidence between the sorts of places that the tourist wants to go to (defined by tourist motivations), the sorts of places that the tourist industry can choose to develop and promote (depending on the industry's motivations) and the locations where the host community does not prevent it (dependent on the host community's motivation). Where tourism development occurs depends therefore on the interactions between these three groups: the tourist, the tourist industry and the host community.

The following discussion takes the motivation of each group as its starting point. It seeks to synthesise this with the models referred to earlier in this book (the simple spatial model of generating and destination areas, *see* Chapter 1), and the model of the evolution and spatial distribution of tourist demand with increasing economic affluence – *see* Chapter 15 – and Butler's cycle of resort development (*see* Fig 7.5). The discussion also seeks to fit together elements of other authors' models, to provide a generalised framework that represents the process of tourist development both spatially and also over time.

SPATIAL PROCESS OF TOURIST DEVELOPMENT

Stage 1

The starting point of tourist development is the existence of a populated area (a town/city/country) which has the potential to generate tourists, and the existence of distant potential destination areas, but as yet no developed tourist industry to

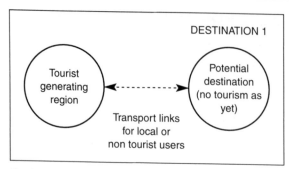

Fig. 7.6 Stage 1 of the spatial process of tourist development

the destination and have relatively little impact on the host community because of their numbers and style of travel. They return home, to talk and write about their experiences and show off things they have obtained, be it a tan, crafts or other purchases. The destination becomes prestigious, and is visited by the small number of tourists who can afford to travel. The host community responds by providing small scale services for them. In the absence of economic growth in the origin area, this situation is unlikely to change much.

link the two – only transport services and routes that have developed for other purposes, for example, trade (*see* Fig 7.6).

The process is started by the psychological need for travel expressed by a few unusual people resident in the tourist generating area, the allocentrics, explorers, or drifters, or they might be the affluent elite (*see* Chapter 15). These first travellers are motivated by curiosity, the need for education, interest in other cultures and so on (*see* pages 64–6), and they make their own travel arrangements using existing local forms of transport. They use local services at

Stage 2

If the standard of living of the generating region improves, and affluence begins to spread through the population (*see* Chapter 15), the next stage of tourist development takes place. The process of economic change itself may accelerate the growth in strength of the 'push' factors motivating people to travel, for example, increased tension or even boredom (*see* Chapter 6). So, more people wish to travel and as they get richer they are more able to travel but they are not the adventurous types who are prepared to explore for themselves and take risks.

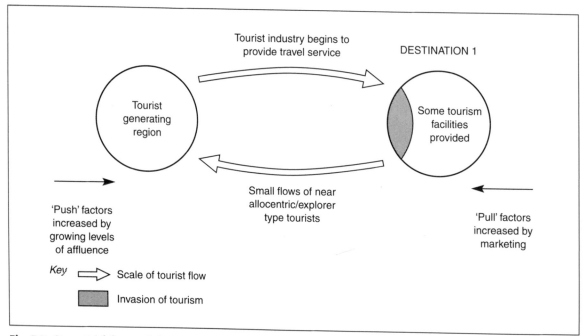

Fig. 7.7 Stage 2 of the spatial process of tourist development

At this stage in the process the 'tourist industry' enters the scene to provide the services that are sought by this new type of potential tourist, i.e. the near-allocentric, and the affluent. A new product is thus introduced and the product life cycle begins at the new tourist destination.

Those businesses that are prepared to take bigger risks by providing new and untried products enter the market first. They begin by providing direct travel service to the destination, and additional facilities at the destination and then proceed to sell them to the potential tourists, reinforcing the 'pull' factors that focus the attention of the potential travellers on this particular destination. The flow of tourists from the generating area to this destination begins to increase gradually, but they are slightly different types of tourist from those who originally visited the area in the first stage (*see* Fig 7.7).

The response of the host community is limited. Those who can benefit immediately and directly from tourism enthusiastically encourage it. Others may welcome the visitors, while those as yet unaffected may have no strong feelings.

Stage 3

As soon as the tourist industry begins to bring about changes in the destination through the development of the first commercialised (non-locally provided, non-traditional) tourist accommodation (hotels, campsites), the explorers, allocentrics and drifters will abandon this destination and find another, perhaps more distant and little known, destination. Stage 1 of the process will then begin anew in this second destination. Meanwhile, at the first destination, the tourist businesses that were not so prepared to take risks, enter the process, by replicating services and facilities which have already been provided and which have by now been demonstrated to be popular but more cheaply (this is the growth stage of the product life cycle). The speed and intensity of development very rapidly increase as the tourist businesses compete to provide more of the same with continuing economic growth in the region. The flow of tourists to the destination rapidly increases – as now the majority of the population (the midcentric, incipient mass or individual mass tourist) find

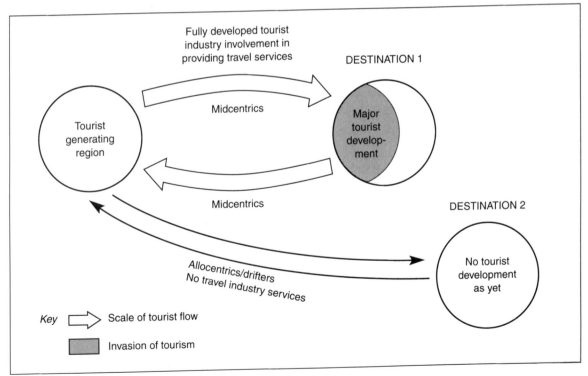

Fig. 7.8 Stage 3 of the spatial process of tourist development

the more fully developed resort/destination more attractive and can now also afford to travel to such destinations (as now they are relatively richer and the product is relatively cheaper due to the increasing number of tourist businesses offering these services) (*see* Fig 7.8).

The rapidity of the development in the destination and the increasing impact of much higher numbers of tourists and of different sorts of tourists, may lead to very mixed reactions in the host community. The rapidity of growth leads to immigration into the region as the local labour force is not big enough to provide all the services

needed. Land and property owners and local businesses will welcome tourist development, while the original local people who experience the changes to their way of life but get little financial benefit, may resent it. There may be strong local opposition to continued development. Regional and national politicians in the destination country may propose policies to either control or promote tourism development, depending on their perception of the balance between the benefits and disadvantages of tourism to their country as a whole, rather than the balance of advantage to the resort/destination region itself.

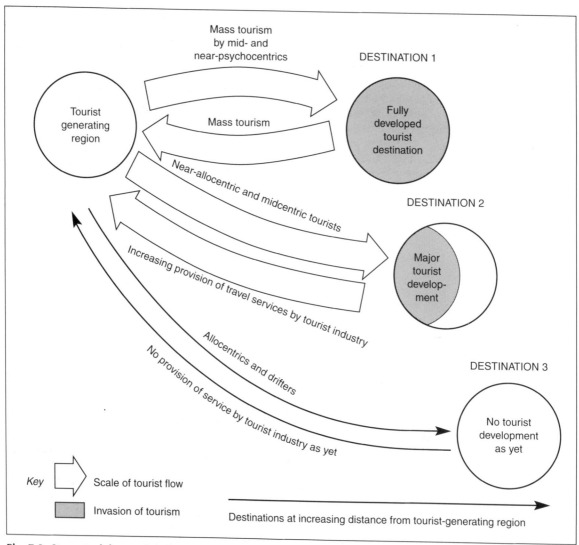

Fig. 7.9 Stage 4 of the spatial process of tourist development

Stage 4

Affluence continues to increase and spread through the population of the generating region. The destination is well known amongst the population as many of the midcentrics have been there. The resort/destination region is fully developed and has changed drastically from its original state. It now has different attractions and it has the potential to meet the needs of near-psychocentrics, the mass tourist, the organised mass tourist and charter tourist (whose travel motivations are discussed on page 65–6). Substantial flows of mid- and near-psychocentric tourists now visit the destination but a growing proportion of the midcentrics are now attracted to the second more distant destination that has by now reached Stage 2 of the process.

Destination 1 is thus losing tourists to Destination 2. The host community reacts by putting more effort to promote and support tourism in Destination 1, as by now the local economy is very dependent on tourism (even though this may generate more local opposition). The tourist businesses in Destination 1 react by trying to provide even cheaper services there, while other businesses expand their services in and to Destination 2.

Meanwhile Destination 2 now enters Stage 2 of the process, and the allocentrics abandon Destination 2 and 'discover' Destination 3 (*see* Fig 7.9).

Given continued economic growth in the generating area, the outcome of this process is thus the step by step spatial spread of tourism to ever more distant or different locations. The second outcome is the step by step progressive change in the type of tourism in each destination where tourism starts. This model describes in general terms what we think happens: it is a theory that brings together observations and conclusions that others have made when studying different parts of the process – the conclusions of researchers studying the impact of tourism on host communities and researchers studying the geographical development of particular destinations. Gordon and Goodall (1992) have married up the various models in a particularly useful way (*see* Fig 7.10). What happens in reality in a specific place may be much more complex and different in detail, depending on the influence of all the other factors, for example, political control, economic cycles, technological developments that may affect the speed and location of tourist development.

The following chapters describe the way the world's different tourist resources have been developed in reality; they discuss whether or not these models of tourist development really do make it easier to understand the existing patterns of development. They also examine the different impacts of tourist development (social/cultural, economic and physical) and the way in which different host communities have sought to influence, manage or control the development and its impacts.

Tourist typologies		Resort life cycle		Product life cycle
Plog (*see* Fig 7.2)	Smith (*see* Fig 7.3)	Butler model (*see* Fig 7.5)	Modified	(*see* Fig 7.4)
Allocentric	Explorer, elite off-beat	Exploration	Discovery	Introduction
		Involvement		
Midcentric	Incipient mass	Development	Growth	Growth
Psychocentric	Mass charter	Consolidation	Maturity	Maturity (saturation)
		Stagnation		
		Decline	Decline	Decline
		(Rejuvenation)	(Rejuvenation)	

Fig. 7.10 Integration of resort life cycles, product life cycles and tourist typologies
(*Source*: Gordon and Goodall, 1992)

REFERENCES AND FURTHER READING

Those texts marked with an asterisk are particularly recommended for further reading.

Brayley, R E (1993) 'Psychographic segmentation' in Khan, M, Olsen, M and Var, T (Eds), '*VNR's Encyclopedia of Hospitality and Tourism*', New York: Van Nostrand Reinhold.

Butler, R W (1980) 'The concept of a tourist area life cycle of evolution – implications for management of resources', *Canadian Geographer*, Vol. 24, pp. 5–12.

Cohen, E (1972) 'Toward a sociology of international tourism', *Social Research*, No. 39, pp. 164–82.

Crompton, J L (1979) 'Motivations for pleasure vacation', *Annals of Tourism Research*, Vol. 6, No. 4, pp. 408–24.

Doyle, P (1976) 'The realities of the product life cycle', *Quarterly Review of Marketing*, Vol. 1, pp. 1–6.

Gordon, I and Goodall, B (1992) 'Resort cycles and development processes', *Built Environment*, Vol. 18, No. 1, pp. 41–56.

Graburn, N H H (1983) 'The anthropology of tourism', *Annals of Tourism Research*, Vol. 10, No. 1, pp. 9–33.

Gray, H P (1970) *International Travel – International Trade*, Lexington, Mass: D C Heath.

Iso-Ahola, S E (1982) 'Toward a social psychological theory of tourist motivation – a rejoinder', *Annals of Tourism Research*, Vol. 9, No. 2, pp. 256–61.

*Johnson, P and Thomas, B (Eds) 1992 *Choice and Demand in Tourism*, Mansell.

Leiper, N (1984) 'Tourism and leisure – the significance of tourism in the leisure spectrum', pp. 249–53 in *Proceedings of 12th New Zealand Geographical Conference*, New Zealand Geographical Society, Christchurch.

*McIntosh, R W and Goeldner, C R (1990) *Tourism – Principles, Practices, Philosophies*, Wiley.

Pearce, D (1987) *Tourism Today – a Geographical Analysis*, Longman.

*Pearce, D (1989) *Tourist Development*, Longman.

Plog, S C (1974) 'Why destination areas rise and fall in popularity', *The Cornell Hotel and Restaurant Administration Quarterly*, Vol. 14, No. 4, pp. 55–58.

Plog, S C (1991) *Leisure Travel – Making it a Growth Market Again*, New York: Wiley.

Smith, V L (Ed) (1977) *Hosts and Guests - the Anthropology of Tourism*, Philadelphia: Pennsylvanian Press.

Uysal, M and Hagan, L-A R (1993) 'Motivation of pleasure, travel and tourism', in Khan, M, Olsen, M and Var, T (Eds) *VNR's Encyclopedia of Hospitality and Tourism*, New York: Van Nostrand Reinhold.

Vernon, R (1966) 'International investment and international trade in the product cycle', *Quarterly Journal of Economics*, Vol. 80, pp. 192–207.

QUESTIONS AND DISCUSSION POINTS

1 What are the differences and similarities between Plog's, Cohen's and Smith's classifications of types of tourists?

2 Why is it sometimes difficult to decide whether or not a tourist development is in the interests of the 'host community'?

3 Is the spatial spread of tourism to new destinations an inevitable process?

ASSIGNMENT

You are starting a research project in a tourist destination area, with the aim of identifying its stage of tourist development according to Butler's model. Make a list of :

(a) the information you would need to collect from existing documents, and

(b) the new surveys you would need to do in order to assess the destinations stage of tourist development.

CHAPTER 8

The use of coastal resources for tourism

LEARNING OBJECTIVES

After reading this chapter you should be able to
- **describe the land use structure of the normal seaside resort**
- **understand the sequence of land use changes that occur as a resort develops**
- **be aware of the impacts of coastal resort development on the destination area**
- **assess the policy options open to coastal resorts at different stages of the resort cycle.**

INTRODUCTION

The coast is used for a wide range of tourist activities, for example, snorkelling, diving, yachting, cruising, beach sports, fishing, scenic tourism, but sunbathing, swimming, beach and water activities, are by far the most popular. Numerous beach resorts have developed to provide accommodation, entertainment and other services for the mass tourist, while ports, fishing villages and yacht harbours provide the same range of services for those who enjoy the sea and coast by boat. This chapter is concerned with the geography of these two types of settlement, that is ports and beach resorts, their patterns of growth and development over time, and their impacts on the host region. In short, this chapter examines the land use, economic and social geography of such resorts as the cycle of tourist development (*see* Chapter 7) progresses. The impacts of the changes in the nature of the coastal resorts and their associated tourists may cause the host community some concern. The destination may therefore be subject to economic and physical planning policies that seek to influence and redirect, to control or even to speed up the cyclic process of development.

This chapter starts by describing the land use and urban structure (i.e. the morphology) of the beach resort and how this changes over time. This leads into a review of the resort cycle as applied specifically to beach resorts. The next part of the chapter highlights the problems, impacts and opportunities experienced by resorts in different geographical locations and at different stages of the resort cycle. This discussion raises the issues that host communities may view with concern, and goes on to outline the range of policies which address those issues, that have been (or might be) applied to resorts at various stages in the resort cycle, for example, from newly established resorts through to those facing stagnation and decline.

Coastal towns with major tourist port or harbour functions are briefly discussed. It should be noted that the use of the coast for scenic tourism is included in Chapter 9, as this form of tourism and its related impacts and policies has more in common with rural, landscape based tourism. Similarly, diving, snorkelling and other specialised forms of tourism based on marine wildlife are dealt with in Chapter 10 in the context of wildlife tourism.

BEACH RESORTS: LAND USE AND MORPHOLOGY

A beach resort is an urban settlement whose focus is a linear feature: the beach and coast. The first generalised descriptions of the land use patterns (i.e. models) of seaside resorts were put forward by Barrett (1958), Stansfield and Rickert (1970) and Lavery (1974). According to these models beach resorts are made up of three land use zones (*see* Figs. 8.1 and 8.2):

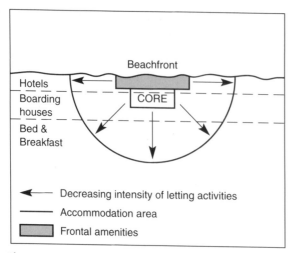

Fig. 8.1 Barrett's model of a seaside resort
(*Source*: After Barrett, 1958)

1 A specialised beach front zone of tourist amenities including shops and big hotels. The shops tend to only open in the tourist season and cater solely for leisure shopping. This seafront trading zone is known as the Recreational Business District (RBD).
2 A commercial core, situated just behind the RBD, consisting of the usual city centre land uses such as non-recreational shops, offices and services such as banks. This is the Central Business District (CBD).
3 Zones of tourist and residential accommodation, running parallel to the coast, decreasing in price and density with increasing distance away from the beach.

(*a*) The first zone extends out from either end of the RBD. It consists of the most expensive, fully serviced tourist accommodation, that is, hotels, in the prime locations overlooking the beach. They

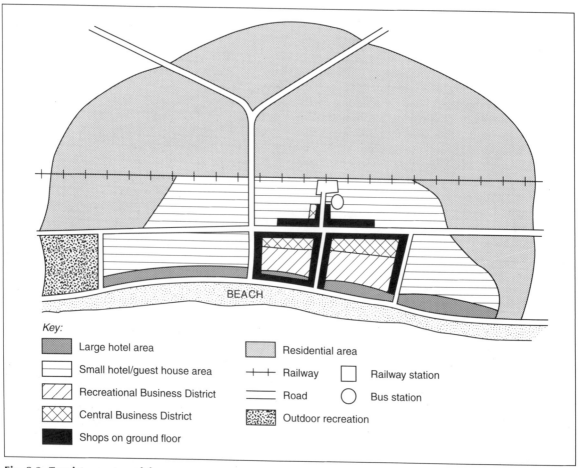

Fig. 8.2 Tourist resort model
(*Source*: After Lavery, 1974)

are built on the most valuable land, which is intensively developed, for example, with relatively high rise buildings providing as many tourist beds as possible on each site, in order to yield a high enough return to the developer and operator.

(*b*) On the next zone inland, land prices are a little lower so the density of development is a little lower and, at the time the models were produced, this was a zone dominated by boarding and guest house accommodation.

(*c*) The next zone contains the cheapest forms of accommodation (bed and breakfast) at a still lower density merging into

(*d*) a zone of residential accommodation.

It should be noted that these models reflect the pattern of tourist accommodation as it was in the 1950s to late 1960s when self-catering and caravan/camping were less popular than they are now.

Pearce (1987) suggests that most resorts still conform to this basic model, though it may be modified in detail by three sets of factors:

1 Site characteristics such as

(*a*) the size and shape of the beach (*see* Chapter 3). A resort on a small beach enclosed by rocky headlands may extend further inland, while a resort on a long straight sandy coast may be developed at a lower density and spread as a thin strip of development much further along the coast in each direction;

(*b*) the availability of flat, stable, well drained land (*see* Chapter 3).

Cliffs and very steep hillsides overlooking the sea are often left undeveloped but may be built on (for example, the Costa Brava or the French Riviera). They may need special construction techniques and almost certainly have tortuous and expensive access roads. Such developments therefore tend to be low rise and low density but very exclusive and expensive.

2 The other non-tourist urban functions of the settlement (which depend on the resort's size and its dependence on tourism). The resort may thus include other land use zones such as industrial use, port and fishing zones, residential zones for commuters or, perhaps, retirement homes.

3 The specific character of the tourist elements of the resort (e.g. types of attractions, access routes and railway or airport locations).

Pigram (1977) illustrates the significance of some of these factors in his analysis of the morphology of the Coolangatta – Surfers' Paradise resorts on the Queensland Coast.

THE EVOLUTION OF RESORT LAND USE PATTERNS

It has been noted that changes in demand for different types of accommodation since the 1960s has made the details of the Barratt and Lavery resort models slightly at odds with modern developments: land use patterns evolve to meet new needs and now most resorts include zones of apartments and a camping and caravan zone in their periphery. More recent research by Young (1983) and Smith (1991) has suggested that resorts go through various recognisable stages of land use change, from when the first tourists arrive at an undeveloped destination to the final stage at which a fully developed urban beach resort exists (*see* Figs 8.3 and 8.4). Both models start with a small coastal fishing or farming settlement with no tourism at all. At stage 2 second homes appear, followed by the first commercial tourist accommodation. By stage four of each model, tourism is established, and begins to trigger off changes in the host community (with new jobs, immigration and residential development). In stage 5 tourism expands until, in Smith's model, the Recreational Business District is established. The later stages of the two models differ slightly: Smith's envisages continued tourism intensification and culminates in the settlement becoming a complete city resort with distinct RBD and CBDs. Both models relate the process of land use change to other changes in the tourist system – i.e. changes in the number and types of tourist, the changing relationships between host and guests and the economic and environmental impacts of tourist development and the introduction of resort planning. These are all indications of progression through the destination (or product) life cycle (as outlined in Chapter 7). Various researchers have studied many resorts in different parts of the world to test these models to see if they do match up with reality – for example, the Isle of Man (Cooper and Jackson, 1989), Torremolinos (France and Barke, 1992) and Thailand (Smith, 1992). Their general conclusions are that resorts do vary a little in detail

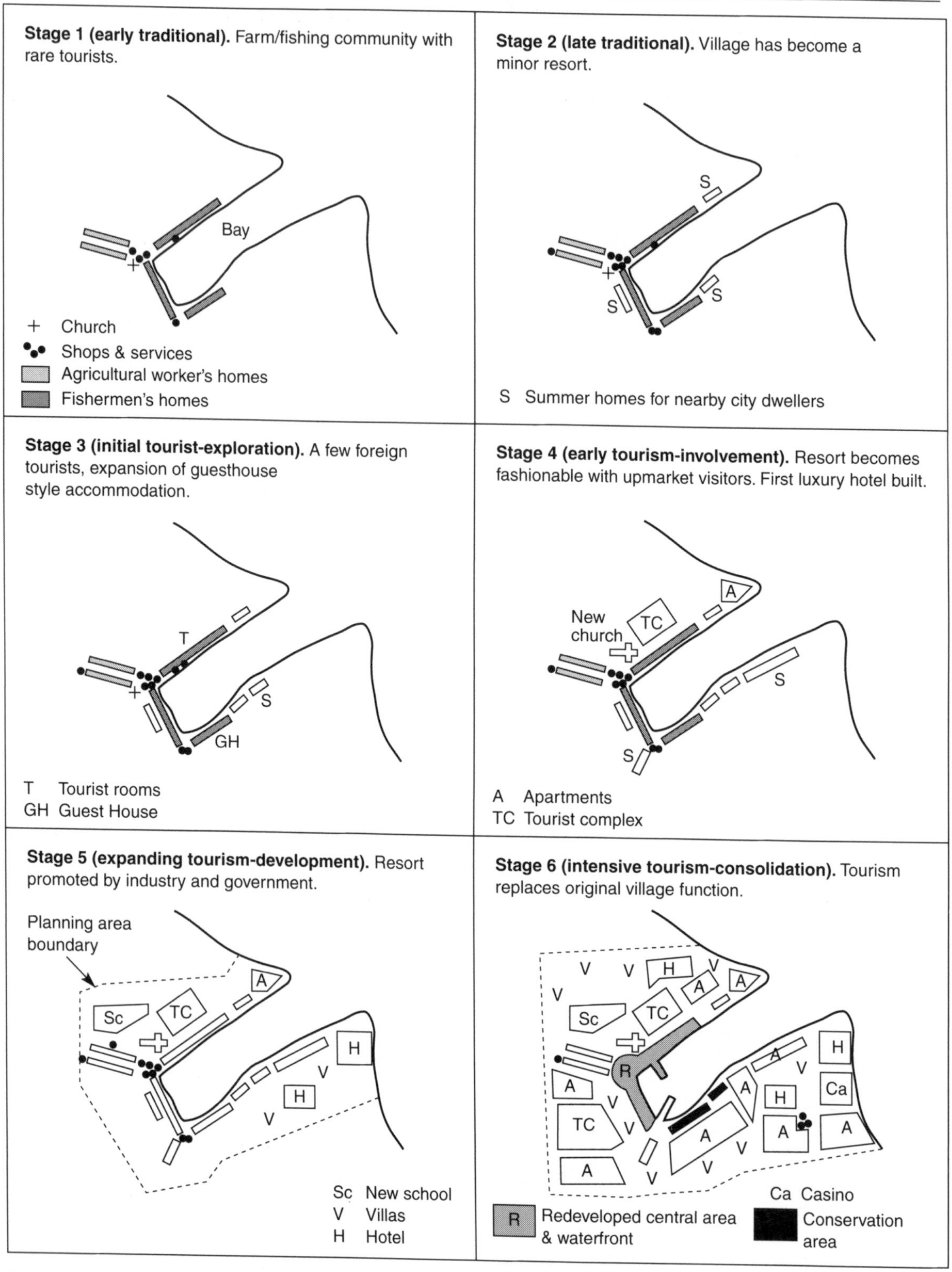

Stage 1 (early traditional). Farm/fishing community with rare tourists.

Bay

+ Church
•‚• Shops & services
▢ Agricultural worker's homes
▨ Fishermen's homes

Stage 2 (late traditional). Village has become a minor resort.

S   Summer homes for nearby city dwellers

Stage 3 (initial tourist-exploration). A few foreign tourists, expansion of guesthouse style accommodation.

T
S
GH

T   Tourist rooms
GH Guest House

Stage 4 (early tourism-involvement). Resort becomes fashionable with upmarket visitors. First luxury hotel built.

New church
TC
A
S
S

A   Apartments
TC Tourist complex

Stage 5 (expanding tourism-development). Resort promoted by industry and government.

Planning area boundary

Sc   TC   A
H
V
H
V

Sc New school
V   Villas
H   Hotel

Stage 6 (intensive tourism-consolidation). Tourism replaces original village function.

V V H V
V
Sc TC A A
R
A A H
TC V H Ca
A A A
A V V

Ca Casino
▨ R Redeveloped central area & waterfront
■   Conservation area

Fig. 8.3 A summary of Young's beach resort model
(*Source*: After Young, 1983)

and that clear stages in the process are difficult to identify. In reality, change happens gradually and continually rather than in sudden steps. Nevertheless, the land use models do provide a useful framework for explaining the structure and evolution of beach resorts. The only resorts that do not really fit the evolutionary pattern are certain modern resorts that have not grown slowly over time from existing villages, but have been planned and built as fully developed, integrated resorts (for example, the new resorts on the French Aquitaine coast and Cancun in Mexico). They appear at roughly stage 4 or 5 of Smith's model. They can be isolated from existing settlements because new transport, sewerage and other facilities are built with and for the resort. These separate tourist resorts are sometimes known as tourist 'enclaves'.

IMPACTS OF BEACH RESORT DEVELOPMENT ON THE HOST REGION

The various models of the destination life cycle have been discussed in Chapter 7, and beach resort models in the first part of this chapter. These models suggest that tourist development on the scale of major urban seaside resorts causes very great changes in the host community and the destination itself. These changes may be of four types.

1 **Cultural change.** Changes in the way of life, values and beliefs of a host community. This is likely to be most pronounced when westerners visit exotic cultures – this will therefore be discussed in detail in Chapter 12 on cultural tourism. In contrast, domestic seaside tourism may have very little cultural impact.
2 **Social change.** Change in the social structure and social behaviour of the local community. International and domestic beach tourism may both have considerable impacts on the social behaviour of the local people.
3 **Economic changes.** The spending power of tourists will change the nature of the local economy and employment structure.
4 **Physical impacts.** The land use models indicate that massive physical changes will occur as a result of the development of big urban beach resorts. Other environmental changes (such as increased pollution and loss of wildlife) may not be so easily visible but are just as significant.

The number and type of changes experienced by any one seaside resort will depend firstly on the scale and nature of tourism (the number of tourists, whether they are domestic or international etc), and on the speed of development (i.e. the speed at which the resort passes through the various stages of the development cycle as described by Young or Smith's models). The faster the development, the greater the physical and economic and social impacts will be. Hussey (1989) traces many such changes in Kuta, Bali, between 1970 and 1984 when the settlement changed from a small village to a resort with 60 000 tourists a year. Putting various models together, the general pattern of physical, economic and social change at each stage of the resort cycle can be summarised as follows:

Stage 1 – The first tourists arrive

This stage roughly covers Butler's 'Exploration' Stage, Young's 'Early traditional' and Smith's Stages 1 and 2.

Physical impact. Few tourists, no special facilities provided, very little physical impact.
Economic impact. Existing local services supply food, accommodation etc, to tourists, few new jobs created, but the slight increase in business means that profits from tourism are small but go directly into the locals' pockets.
Social impact. The locals may feel euphoria that their home area is appreciated by outsiders and their pride in their area motivates them to show it to the visitors. The local people retain control over their land and businesses.

Stage 2 – The first tourist flow

Butler's 'exploration and involvement', Young's 'initial tourism', Smith's Stage 2.

Physical impact. Small scale, low cost developments of summer homes and camping provided. Some damage to natural vegetation of the seashore.
Economic impact. Land is cheap, some is sold to domestic tourists (for second homes). Local suppliers increase their businesses and a few more jobs are created for local people. Some small scale facilities for tourists provided by local businesses.
Social impact. Local people perceive the possibility of big economic benefits from tourism but underestimate future costs to themselves.

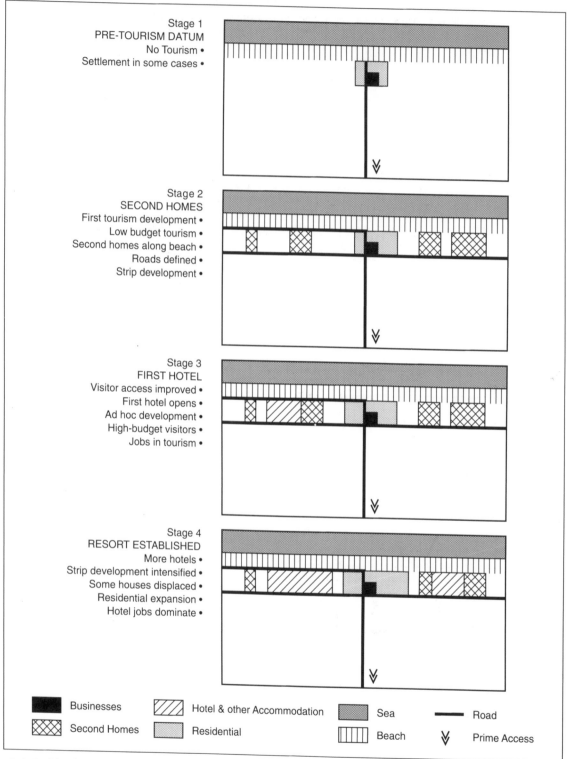

Fig. 8.4 Smith's beach resort land use model
(*Source*: Smith, 1991)

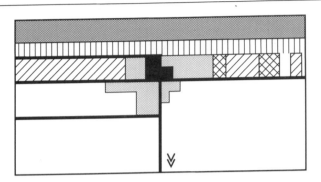

Stage 5
BUSINESS AREA ESTABLISHED
• More accommodation
• Visitor type broadens
• Non-hotel business growth
• Tourism dominates
• Large immigrant workforce
• Cultural disruption
• Beach congestion and pollution
• Ambience deteriorates

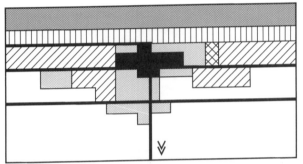

Stage 6
INLAND HOTELS
• Hotels away from beach
• Rapid residential growth
• Business district consolidates
• Flood and erosion damage potential
• Tourism culture dominates
• Traditional patterns obliterated
• Entrepreneurs drive development
• Government master plan

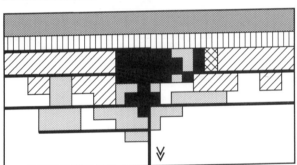

Stage 7
TRANSFORMATION
• Urbanized resort
• Rehabilitation of natural ambience
• Accommodation structural change
• Visitors and expenditures change
• Resort government fails

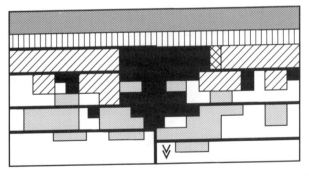

Stage 8
CITY RESORT
• Fully urbanized
• Alternative circulation
• District recreational and
  commercial business districts
• Lateral resort spread
• Serious pollution
• Political power to higher government

 Businesses   Hotel & other Accommodation   Sea   Road

 Second Homes   Residential   Beach   Prime Access

Stage 3 – Commercial tourism begins

Butler's 'involvement', Smith's Stage 3, Young's Stage 4.

Physical impact. First luxury hotels, destruction of local habitats and loss of local agricultural land. Some small scale pollution and depletion of local resources since local infrastructure such as water supply and sewage disposal, has not yet been improved to meet the new demands.

Economic impact. Hotels very profitable – catering for the fashionable upper class market. New jobs created in the new hotels and some more in local businesses.

Social impact. Development initiated and controlled by private entrepreneurs, some non-local, as locals do not have the capital for luxury hotel development. Two distinct separate social spheres exist – tourists and locals. Locals may become less enthusiastic about tourism.

Stage 4 – Rapid increase in tourist development

Butler's 'development' Stage, Smith's Stage 4, Young's Stage 5.

Physical impact. Rapid land use change, with the growth of large areas of varied tourist accommodation, with tourist facilities and entertainments. Residential expansion takes place on the inland side of the resort to house immigrants. Pollution problems may ease initially as local infrastructure is improved a little. The houses of the original inhabitants (now at the centre of the settlement, in prime sites) are bought up, converted to tourist use or demolished to make way for more intensive building.

Economic impact. Land speculation occurs on a big scale – speculators get rich as land prices rise fast. Tourist spending increases as the numbers of tourists grow, and the economic 'multiplier effect' begins to work by creating more turnover and employment in businesses that supply the tourist trade as well as in businesses directly serving the tourists. There is a rapid increase in the number of jobs created by these expanding (tourist and non-tourist) businesses. The local population is too small to provide enough labour so there is rapid immigration (of people seeking jobs) from outside the region into the resort. Central government may encourage these trends.

Social impact. There is a rapid decline of local involvement as external tourist companies move in. The local people are marginalised and outnumbered by tourists and immigrants. Locals may move away as they sell up their homes to developers. The developers are large non-local companies controlled by business people who may live outside the resort itself. Local social structures are broken down – there are no 'real' local people left – so local culture is adapted or imported for the tourists' entertainment.

Stage 5 – Fully developed resort

Butler's 'consolidation', Young's Stage 6, Smith's Stage 6.

Physical impact. Tourist numbers are high and the resort and beach become very congested, noisy and polluted. A great variety of different types of accommodation is built and spreads inland. Major new attractions are developed.

Economic impact. Major franchises and chains in the tourist industry are represented, and international chains move in. Local businesses control only the small-scale budget accommodation. There is growing 'leakage' of profits to businesses based outside the resort and its region. Labour is more expensive and becomes unionised. Top management jobs go to outsiders and non-nationals. Power and control over the process of development are still in the hands of the private sector (the tourism industry) but local government, recognising the undesirable environmental impact of tourism, begins to intervene with planning policies to improve environmental quality.

Social impact. The immigrants perceive themselves as locals and have an ambivalent attitude to the tourists. Imported (western) culture is promoted. Prostitution, crime and gambling grow. Power shifts towards local and national government as more control over the tourist industry is sought.

Stage 6 – Decline in numbers of tourists

Butler's 'stagnation and decline', Smith's Stages 7 and 8.

Physical impact. Serious pollution occurs as pressures outstrip the capacity of infrastructure and no reinvestment is made. Structural changes occur in tourist accommodation as hotels are converted into apartments (for lower cost holidays) or for other more profitable, non-tourist uses. General lack of investment in the updating and maintenance of the property as declining profits hit the businesses.

Economic impact. Tourist businesses fail; some are replaced by non-tourist businesses. Unemployment appears among resort residents.

Social impact. Social problems increase. Local government loses authority to national government as the problems of the resort are perceived to outweigh the current economic benefits.

POLICIES FOR BEACH RESORTS

It is clear that the balance between the economic benefits and the disadvantages of tourist development changes as the cycle of resort development progresses, and the distribution of the costs and benefits, between different socio-economic groups and spatially between the national and local community, also varies. The host community's reaction to the growth and decay of beach resorts may therefore be expected to change as the resort itself changes.

1 At the early stages of growth of the resort local and national perception of the economic benefits of development coincide. Policy responses may vary from a *laissez-faire* attitude (of allowing market forces to progress unimpeded) to a more positive approach aimed at speeding up the development process. This might include action to stimulate local responses, for example, the offering of low interest loans or grants to hoteliers to provide the initial capital for new businesses to become established, or action to accelerate the growth of tourist numbers through national promotion of the new destination, or public investment to speed up the development of the general infrastructure, for example, roads.

The national government's perception of the benefits of resort development may be so great that the government plans and initiates new integrated resorts in locations where there may be no local settlement or local population to act as a focus for development, in destinations as yet unvisited and undeveloped. Only a highly centralised government has the power and financial resources to do this, as high public investment in new infrastructure is usually necessary before any tourism income is received.

2 During the phases of rapid urbanisation, as the physical impacts of development become evident, sections of the community may exert pressure for stricter policies for land use and townscape control, for example, land use zoning, control of high rise development in prime sites, traffic management schemes. With the benefit of hindsight and observing the undesirable consequences of uncontrolled rapid resort development, some newly developed regions (e.g. Turkey) may introduce similar controls much earlier in the cycle of development in order to avoid environmental and land use problems. Local groups may also urge policies to constrain the social and cultural impact of tourism.

3 As tourist development is a fairly recent phenomenon, relatively few beach resorts have reached the stages of stagnation or decline. It is mainly the old domestic coastal resorts of the economic core countries that have experienced the biggest problems of decline. These have been established for around 100 years and their ageing building stock and their location in areas with less than ideal climates for beach tourism make them very vulnerable to competition from more recently established resorts in better climates. Nevertheless, some of the Mediterranean resorts that went through the 'development' stage in the 1960s (e.g. the Spanish Costas) began to experience some of the 'symptoms' of decline by 1990. The resort cycle models suggest that public policy makers became more involved in the process at this stage. Central government policy makers became involved in trying to influence the progress of the resort cycle because:

(a) They are concerned about the economic implications (on the national balance of payments) of the loss of domestic and/or international revenue to competing overseas resorts.

(b) They are concerned about rising unemployment in the resulting decline.

Local government may perceive additional problems:

(a) The loss of their share of a declining tourist market to competing domestic resorts.

(b) Decline in local environmental quality.

(c) Pressures for land use changes away from tourism accommodation into other forms of business and the knock-on effect of this decline in numbers of tourists on other tourist enterprises.

(d) Pressures for land use changes from one type of tourism to another.

The practical responses of central and local governments in different parts of the world depend on their powers and the strength of their economic and physical planning system. In Britain, policies have tended to respond to each of these issues one by one (incrementally) rather than form an integrated strategy for resort rejuvenation. Responses fall into three categories:

1 Marketing

(a) A marketing and management response – trying to improve and advertise the existing attractions of the resorts more effectively to its existing market. This may involve public and private investment in the restoration and renewal of existing attractions (e.g. Blackpool).

(b) Diversify into different tourist markets, that is, identify market segments whose specific needs are likely to match what the resort can offer (e.g. school parties, nuclear families, business tourism, etc). This may involve public investment in additional facilities e.g. indoor wet weather facilities, conference facilities, historic attractions (e.g. Portsmouth) and active marketing (e.g. Grimsby).

2 Environmental improvement

(a) Upgrading of sea water quality through public investment in sewage treatment.

(b) Improving litter clearance and visual quality of RBD.

(c) Upgrading the standard of tourist accommodation (through grant aid to encourage private sector investment).

(d) Introducing traffic management schemes in resort RBD and CBD.

3 Economic/employment responses

(a) Concentration on tourism – protection of existing tourism and resisting the contraction of the tourist industry by controlling land use changes that might reduce levels of employment in tourism or that might change the image of the resort, for example, by resisting changes of use of hotels into OAP homes or holiday apartments, bed and breakfast accommodation or residential accommodation (even though those might actually bring greater economic benefit to the settlement) or by resisting the expansion of the resort into different market-led forms of tourism (e.g. caravan sites).

(b) Promoting the expansion of non-tourist economic activity in order to provide a more diversified local economy and to provide other employment opportunities (i.e. economic diversification). The resort city/town seeks to reduce its reliance on tourism and even change its main economic function.

The 'success' of these policies for resort rejuvenation may be judged in two ways (depending on the overall objectives of the policy):

(a) By an increase in numbers of tourists (and, by implication, a revival of economic activity in the resort), or the maintenance of existing numbers, or the slowing of the rate of decline of tourist numbers.

(b) A decrease in unemployment and an increase in residents' prosperity which may be brought about by a strengthening of the tourist industry or by introducing new employment, or both.

In Britain it appears that the larger resorts have been the more 'successful', by adopting a strategy combining major public and private investment in tourism facilities and environmental quality and innovative marketing with economic diversification into other forms of employment. Protective policies appear the least effective. Goodall (1992) suggests that there is some level of 'critical mass' above which rejuvenation is more likely to be successful. This may be the existing size of the tourist market, or the size of the local population or the size of the potential employment market. Factors such as these might influence the investment decisions of tourist businesses considering upgrading or renewing attractions and the decisions of non-tourist businesses, which might consider locating in the resort settlement. The smaller resorts appear to lack the scale of public resources necessary and have tourism markets that have shrunk too far to interest the private sector (see Middleton, 1989, Lane, 1992, Cooper, 1990).

The Mediterranean resorts that have suffered decline in the last decade or so have selected a different combination of options; for example, Nice, on the Côte d'Azur, has diversified into 'clean' industry, using its accommodation, climate and coast to attract new industry that does not detract from local environment (the Californian coast has diversified its economic base in the same way).

The Spanish Costas and Balearics have tried to go 'up-market' through marketing and environmental improvement. They have sought to limit new accommodation to 4- or 5-star grades and to upgrade existing hotels. Environmental improvements have been made, while water quality is high on the agenda.

PORTS AND HARBOURS

Boat-based coastal tourism depends on port, harbour or mooring facilities with associated accommodation and other tourist facilities on shore. Settlements providing these tourist services are of four kinds:

1 Active functioning commercial ports that accommodate modern cruise liners as part of an existing town or city.
2 Recently redundant large scale commercial ports and docks (again part of an existing city) which have diversified into water sports, leisure boating and tourism to bring new economic activity into the region.
3 Fishing villages or old, small, estuary market towns/ports that have been taken over by tourism.
4 Purpose-built marinas or estuary barrages.

Thus cruising and boating are specialised forms of tourism (serving one market) and are grafted onto a settlement whose original and sometimes existing main function is not tourism.

Commercial ports

The primary function of the settlement is as a port which handles goods (imports and exports) and possibly ferry passengers, as well as cruise tourists. On many islands, the main port is one of the biggest urban areas and many function as the administrative 'capital' as well, i.e. the settlement is multi-functional. As the economics of cruising demands bigger and bigger cruise liners, the choice of available destinations (that have large enough berths) may be reduced. The receiving port does not need a supply of tourist accommodation as this is provided on board the cruise liner itself, but the port does need adequate facilities for handling large numbers of disembarking passengers. Land use conflicts may occur in the port area of the town

as tourist shops and restaurants will want to locate near the point of disembarkation – their environmental needs may be in conflict with the normal activities of the port. These areas become specialised tourist zones (Weaver, 1993).

Redundant ports and docks

Ports and docks (like beach resorts) may pass through an evolutionary cycle of economic activity, development and decline. By definition ports must have deepwater access and generally port facilities are successively expanded to accommodate bigger and bigger carriers and bulk container ships (as long as trade continues), until either:

1 the physical capacity of the site (or the river access to it) is reached and trade still exists: the port is then relocated on a greenfield site, leaving original docks redundant (e.g. Tilbury for Port of London, Avonmouth for Bristol);
or
2 the trade on which it was based declines and the port goes out of business (e.g. Swansea, Cardiff).

Ironically, water-based tourism uses are introduced by positive planning action and policies as a means of diversifying and rejuvenating the local economy (the reverse of the situation in the declining beach resort). The port and dock facilities are adapted into marinas (for privately owned small motor cruises and yachts) while the dockside environment is restored and gentrified. Warehouses and port buildings may be found new uses (e.g. restaurants, shops, maritime museums), while empty spare dockside land is developed for flats and apartments that are either holiday lets or sold as second homes for the boat owners for their use at weekends (thus financing some of the development costs). Tourist uses are thus integrated into an existing commercial settlement that would normally already possess all the other services needed by tourists (though not necessarily located near the waterfront).

Existing fishing villages and market towns

These are generally smaller settlements (villages or small towns) often on coasts of remote and rural regions, bypassed by modern industrial/commercial urban development, whose original *raison d'être* was the existence of sheltered water and harbours that were used for fishing or ferry terminals. These uses may have declined or been replaced by tourism but the settlement still retains boat-related businesses (e.g. boat building and chandlers). It may not have all the normal beach, urban entertainment and service facilities needed by a normal coastal resort, however, they are often picturesque settlements with unmodernised street patterns providing difficult access for large modern vehicles. Many of the original houses may be holiday lets or second homes and there may be pressure for expansion of the settlement on its outskirts (for new holiday homes/retirement homes/camp/caravan sites). On sandy coasts many such settlements have in the past formed the kernel of new seaside resorts (e.g. Lloret on the Costa Brava), but in other places the process of growth may have been inhibited by:

(a) strong planning controls (e.g. coastal villages in southwest England) preventing or severely limiting expansion; and

(b) the lack of any other tourist attractions, for example, estuarine fishing ports on muddy flat coast such as Burnham-on-Crouch and the Solent sailing centres, so the resort only has a real attraction for the limited boating market and has become just a boating/sailing centre. The relatively small scale of the boating market inhibits the development of other attractions.

Purpose-built marinas/barrages

Boat mooring facilities can be created where none existed by:

1 Building an artificial harbour, i.e. a marina to provide sheltered/safe mooring on an open coast. Capital costs are very high and these facilities are generally added to existing settlements/resorts where the rest of the infrastructure (roads, accommodation, services) already exists – sometimes as a means of diversifying tourism in a declining resort, for example, Brighton. Location is generally tied to an existing coastal settlement/resort.
2 Estuarine barrages. Another means of creating sheltered moorings is to dam an existing estuary and create a controlled/non-tidal lake suitable for water sports behind the barrage but with access to the open sea. In the development boom of the late 1980s in the UK, there was a spate of planning pro-

posals for such developments (again associated with the development of residential and tourist accommodation for sale, which recouped some of the development costs). There were 39 marina and barrage proposals in Wales alone. Such developments are generally tied to property development cycles; such big investment can only be made in an economic boom.

REFERENCES AND FURTHER READING

Those texts marked with an asterisk are particularly recommended for further reading.

Barrett, J A (1958) 'The seaside resort towns of England and Wales', unpublished PhD thesis, London.

Butler, R (1980) 'The concept of a tourist area cycle of evolution: implications for management of resources', *Canadian Geographer*, Vol. 24, No. 1, pp. 5–12.

Cooper, C (1990) 'Resorts in decline – the management response', *Tourism Management*, March, Vol. 11, pp. 63–7.

Cooper, C and Jackson, S (1989) 'Destination lifecycle: the Isle of Man study', *Annals of Tourism Research*, Vol. 16, No. 3, pp. 377–98.

France, L and Barke, M (1992) 'Torremolinos: the evolution of a resort' in *Tourism in Europe – The 1992 Conference*, Centre for Travel and Tourism (University of Northumbria and New College Durham).

Goodall, B (1992) 'Coastal resorts: development and redevelopment', *Built Environment*, Vol. 18, No. 1 pp. 5–11.

Hussey, A (1989) 'Tourism in a Balinese village', *Geographical Review*, Vol.79, pp. 311–25.

Lane, P (1992) 'The regeneration of small-to-medium-sized seaside resorts' in *Tourism in Europe – The 1992 Conference*, Centre for Travel and Tourism (University of Northumbria and New College Durham).

Lavery, P (1974) 'Resorts and recreation' in Lavery, P (Ed.) *Recreational Geography*, Newton Abbot: David and Charles.

Middleton, V (1989) 'Seaside resorts', *Insights*, English Tourist Board.

Pearce, D (1987) *'Tourism Today – a Geographical Analysis'*, Longman.

*Pearce, D (1989) *Tourism development* 2nd edn, Longman.

Pigram, J J (1977) 'Beach resort morphology', *Habitat International*, Vol. 2, No. 5/6, pp. 525–41.

Smith, R A (1991) 'Beach resorts – a model of development evolution', *Landscape and Urban Planning*, Vol. 21, pp. 189–210.

Smith, R A (1992) 'Beach resort evolution. Implications for planning', *Annals of Tourism Research*, Vol. 19, pp. 304–22.

Stansfield, C A and Rickert, J E (1970) 'The recreational business district', *Journal of Leisure Research,* Vol. 2, Part 4, pp. 213–25.

Young, B (1983) 'Touristization of traditional Maltese fishing/farming villages', *Tourism Management,* Vol. 4, No. 1, pp. 35–41.

Weaver, D B (1993) 'Model of urban tourism for small Caribbean islands', *The Geographical Review,* Vol. 83, No. 2, pp. 134–40.

QUESTIONS AND DISCUSSION POINTS

1 What economic factors lead to the concentration of certain tourist land uses in different parts of a beach resort?

2 Why do governments (both national and local) become involved with beach resort planning?

3 Is it inevitable that all seaside resorts will eventually face a decline in their tourist industry?

ASSIGNMENTS

1 You run a tourism consultancy. You have been asked by the Chief Executive of the local council of a small declining British seaside resort to produce a report to help them decide on their future strategy. Write a short report outlining:

(a) the general policy options facing the resort

(b) the problems and advantages of adopting each policy option.

2 You are the Tourism Minister for one of the world's less developed countries. Your country has few coastal resorts as yet and a foreign (western) company wishes to develop a luxury resort on your coastline on an undeveloped stretch of coast where there are currently just a handful of small fishing villages. How would you advise your Chief Minister to respond to the company's development proposal and why?

CHAPTER 9

The use of landscape resources for tourism

LEARNING OBJECTIVES

After reading this chapter you should be able to
- classify different forms of rural tourism
- assess the scale and impact of different forms of rural tourism
- be aware of the social and economic changes that occur in rural areas independently of tourism development
- list the sequence of changes brought about by tourism development in rural areas
- understand the relationships between agricultural and rural tourism policies in Europe.

INTRODUCTION

The attraction of rural landscapes depends on the qualities of their landform and land use (*see* Chapter 4). Most rural areas (other than untouched wilderness areas) are used for some form of economic production (forestry or agriculture) and their landscapes are, therefore, highly influenced and modified by man's activity, although by definition they contain no large urban developments. Rural areas do, however, contain scattered settlements (farms, hamlets, villages and small towns) but are characterised by low overall population densities. Tourism is attracted into these regions by their climate, natural features, landscape quality and rural way of life: because traditional agriculture creates the landscape and sustains the way of life, there is a very delicate relationship between tourism and agriculture. This chapter is concerned with the nature, location and growth of rural tourism in these agricultural regions, its impact and the policies that have been developed for its promotion or control. It should be noted that tourism in unsettled, untouched wilderness areas, where wildlife is the main attraction, is excluded from the definition of rural tourism (Dernoi, 1991).

This form of nature based tourism raises rather different management and policy issues and is discussed in Chapter 10.

THE NATURE OF RURAL TOURISM

Rural tourism can include a great variety of activities and can be classified in many different ways.

Firstly, it can be classified according to the **type of activity**. Figure 9.1 groups rural tourism activities into health related activities, sport and adventure pursuits, tourism that involves travelling through a landscape in a variety of different ways (for example, on foot, by horse, in boats), and tourism based on participating in a rural way of life.

Secondly, Fig 9.1 also groups activities according to the **type of rural resource** they require: some depend on a single natural feature (e.g. a cliff or cave), some need a combination of characteristics (e.g. climate and slopes), and some rely on the quality of the whole landscape.

Thirdly, rural tourism can be classified according to the **type of tourist** and their motivations and characteristic behaviour, for example, risk taking is an important part of the adventure tourist's experience (Johnston, 1992). Chapter 7 suggests that health, sport and adventure tourists are likely to behave more like 'sunlusters' as their enjoyment depends on the quality of a specific resource, rather than the overall landscape setting. Although some will wish to practise their sport in a peaceful and isolated rural setting, many may wish to have access to urban style resort facilities and entertainment in the evening. In contrast, the undeveloped quality of the landscape is essential to the tourer and rural life participant. For example, visitors to south-west England and northern Portugal ranked scenery, lack of congestion, lack of commercialisation and peace and quiet at the top of their list of criteria for choosing a country-side destination (Edwards, 1989). These are more likely to be the 'explorer' or 'allocentric' type of tourist (*see* Chapter 7).

Fourthly, rural tourism activities can be differentiated by the **type and location of accommodation** required. The existing pattern of small settlements that function as agricultural service centres provide the basic infrastructure, acting as nodes for tourist services and accommodation (Fagence, 1991). However, each type of rural tourism has its own particular ideal location. Sport and activity tourism ideally requires accommodation to be clustered as close as possible to the natural feature that is the basis of their pursuit (e.g. snow fields and slopes for skiing, water bodies for water sports, springs for health tourism etc). In contrast, touring activities require a wide choice of dispersed accommodation in towns, villages and hamlets scattered along routes throughout the landscape, while some adventure holidays and the more independent tourers may take their own mobile accommodation with them (in the form of tents or caravans) and so their distribution through the countryside is not constrained by the current settlement pattern. On the other hand, those wishing to participate in a rural way of life will be limited to accommodation in the existing working farms and villages. Finally, Fig 9.1 indicates that rural tourism can also be classified according to the **size of the market** and its **reliance on the tour operator**. Most rural tourism is small scale and occurs in small groups of family or friends. It is low intensity and spatially dispersed, because most visitors are seeking to get

away from the crowds. Most of these visitors travel independently and do not rely on a tour operator. The industry tends to cater either for specialised markets with special interest and adventure packages or for mass tourism (limited to winter sports, health tourism and coach touring in the rural context).

All these different ways of classifying rural tourism relate to differences in the scale and spatial distribution of rural tourism.

THE DEMAND FOR RURAL TOURISM

Rural tourism is an important element of European tourism: 25 per cent of all Europeans express an interest in holidays located in rural areas. It is an attractive destination for both international and domestic tourism: 25 per cent of French domestic holidays are to the countryside and an additional 17 per cent are to mountain resorts. In 1986, a total of 96 million tourist nights were spent in countryside destinations in the UK (ETB, 1988). Rural tourism is also an important element of the European short break market. In 1991 19 per cent of all the short break trips in Europe were touring holidays, 10 per cent were to mountain resorts outside the winter sports season and another 9 per cent were for countryside recreation, while 4 per cent were for winter sports and 3 per cent for other sports activities (European Travel Monitor). It is clear that general countryside, touring and mountain landscape tourism is a mass tourism activity.

Activity holidays that take place in a rural environment cater for smaller markets. BTA/ETB surveys of British domestic tourists (1986–88) show that over a quarter of all holiday makers went walking, hiking or rambling, but only 6 per cent (1.5 million) were 'serious' walkers (i.e. went hiking, rambling or hill walking). About half a million took part in each of the main countryside activities (e.g. cycling, fishing, horse riding, rock climbing), while the adventure activities (e.g. caving and parachuting) attracted far fewer people (Smith and Jenner, 1990).

Rural tourists and activity holiday makers are more likely to be drawn from the more affluent and better educated sections of the population.

Rural tourism activities	Natural resource	Intensity of tourism		
		Mass	Group	Individual
Health/spa	e.g. Climate, mineral or hot springs	✓		
Sport/activity associated with particular features				
e.g. Winter sports (skiing)	Climate, mountain	✓		
Climbing, abseiling	Cliffs, crags		✓	✓
Potholing	Caves (limestone regions)		✓	✓
Watersports (sailing, canoeing)	Lakes, rivers, canals		✓	✓
Adventure/high risk activities				
e.g. Whitewater rafting	Whitewater		✓	✓
Bungy-jumping, rap jumping	Cliffs, bridges etc		✓	✓
Hang gliding	High relative relief		✓	✓
Hot air ballooning	Access to safe, open landing places		✓	✓
Forms of touring/travelling through landscapes				
e.g. Coach, car, caravan and motorcycle touring	General landscape and spectacular features	✓	✓	
River cruising	Rivers, canals	✓	✓	
Cycling	Roads, paths and landscape		✓	
Walking (all forms)	Roads, paths and landscape		✓	✓
Pony trekking/riding	Bridlepaths		✓	✓
Activities based on economic activities/rural way of life				
Farm based activities, working/living/helping on farms	Farms		✓	✓
Second homes	Dispersed settlements			✓

Fig. 9.1 A classification of rural tourism

LOCATION OF RURAL TOURISM

Chapter 4 suggests that tourists find forested mountain landscapes the most attractive. Figure 9.1 indicates that many of the natural features that attract activity and adventure tourism are also located in mountainous regions. On a world scale, the mountain chains that combine accessibility with dramatic landscapes and climates suitable for commercial winter sports development are few and far between, but these are the most likely locations for all year round rural tourism on a mass scale. For example, it is estimated that the Alps attracted 250 million tourist nights and 60 million day visits a year at the beginning of the 1990s and an additional 10 million winter sports tourists. It is only in these regions that circumstances combine to create genuine, single purpose rural tourist resort settlements. Attractive upland landscapes that lack winter sports potential may be the focus for landscape and summer outdoor activity tourism but at a less intensive scale – here tourism will be dispersed throughout the existing small towns and villages. Tourism will be grafted on as an additional function for the settlements rather than forming their prime function. Lowland regions and the general farmed countryside of lower landscape quality may attract lower key, farm based, general touring and activity holidays, with accommodation even more thinly and widely dispersed amongst the farms, hamlets and villages.

TOURIST CYCLES IN RURAL REGIONS

Landscape based rural tourism

Because rural tourism is generally a low intensity and widely dispersed activity, it might be assumed that the destination cycle (*see* Chapter 7) has not progressed beyond the early stages of development. Many rural tourist businesses are still controlled by local people and the dominant behaviour of the rural tourist has most in common with the 'explorer', 'allocentric', 'drifter' or 'offbeat' tourist (*see* Chapter 7). These are also characteristics of destinations in the early, that is, discovery, exploration or involvement, stages of the destination life cycle. However, it is clear that landscape resources do go through a process of change and development as they become more popular for recreation and tourism. The process is similar to that experienced by coastal destinations, but demand for rural tourism is normally spread over a very large number of different attractions and a much larger physical area (in contrast to the concentration of demand for sun, sea and sand tourism on finite lengths of suitable coastline). Because of this, the physical expression of the progression of the destination life cycle is quite different. The industry responds to increasing demand by gradually intensifying the density of dispersed facilities instead of reproducing more facilities and accommodation concentrated in one resort location. The only exceptions to this pattern are the few examples of the world's most spectacular, world famous or unique landscape features such as Niagara Falls or Ayers Rock. Intensive demand is concentrated at these particular sites on a scale that generates an urban style tourist resort settlement.

The stages in the rural tourist resource development cycle might therefore be:

Stage 1

Destination. Untouched by tourism; an agricultural region with scattered farms and small villages. Roads single track, most traffic farm vehicles.

First tourists. Arrive in 4-wheel drive vehicles or travel on foot or by local transport, with camping equipment or stay in local inns. They are of the 'explorer' or 'adventurer' type of motivation.

Tourist facilities. None.

Stage 2

Tourists. Increase in number, but are still 'allocentrics'. Travel by car, some caravans.

Facilities. Bed and breakfast and farm-based accommodation provided by locals. No other facilities.

Destination. Some properties bought by outsiders and second homes. Landscape not much changed.

Stage 3

Tourists. Increase in number and length of season. 'Near allocentrics', travel by car.

Facilities. Still provided by locals – bed and breakfast, farm-based self-catering and small hotels or inns in villages. Car parking provided at beauty spots. Tea rooms open in villages or near beauty spots.

Destination. Traffic congestion at times leads to road improvements. Tourism beginning to have some visual impact.

Stage 4

Tourists. Increase in number and change in type. 'Allocentrics'/explorers visit elsewhere or visit this destination out of season or at non-peak times to avoid congestion.

Facilities. More commercial developments (gift shops, tea rooms, craft shops) in villages. Additional attractions open, based on local crafts and traditional activities. Toilets, litter collection, car parking, signposting, interpretation and traffic management offered at main beauty spots. Wide choice of accommodation offered.

Destination. Local property bought up by outsiders as holiday lets. Bigger hotels established. Roads improved. Large surfaced car parks.

Stage 5

Tourists. Midcentric and first psychocentrics visit main beauty spots and main tourist villages. Allocentrics and explorers cease to visit. Beauty spots congested at peak times.

Facilities. Roads improved, coach parks provided, viewing platforms and access trails built at beauty spots. Restaurants and visitor centres built at or near beauty spots. Additional entertainments and attractions opened. Pressure for caravan sites.

Destination. Main beauty spot and sights visited on coach tours by main tour operators. Beauty spots well developed but less accessible attractive areas of countryside unaffected. Dense network of accommodation, opportunities, some provided by non-local tourist businesses.

So the outcome of this cycle is an increase in the density of the dispersed accommodation attractions and facilities, a hierarchical development of beauty spots (the most dramatic being the most intensively developed and heavily used, but other attractive sites, often quite close to main beauty spots, being less developed, and some lesser places being quite unaffected by tourism) and the development of a small number of nodes of larger scale accommodation at the few landscape resorts, or at attractive and accessible small towns or villages that service the coach tours. Gunn (1993) suggests that attractions tend to cluster around these nodes within the destination zones (*see* Fig 9.2). However, spatial sorting of different types of tourist will occur. Those sensitive to crowds (allocentric type) may continue to visit the area until well on into the cycle, but modify their behaviour by concentration on the lower hierarchy beauty spots and by visiting the well-known beauty spots only at non-peak times. They will only abandon

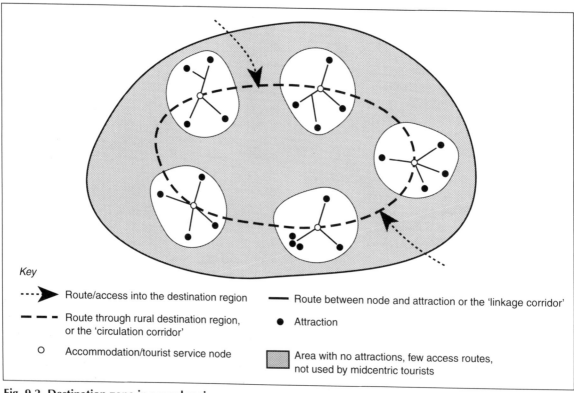

Key

- - - - ► Route/access into the destination region

— — — Route through rural destination region, or the 'circulation corridor'

○ Accommodation/tourist service node

—— Route between node and attraction or the 'linkage corridor'

● Attraction

▨ Area with no attractions, few access routes, not used by midcentric tourists

Fig. 9.2 Destination zone in a rural region
(*Source*: After Gunn, 1993)

the area when the permanent visual landscape impact of tourism development (road improvements, viewing platforms, buildings) became too intrusive and they perceive the area as too commercialised. The 'crowding tolerant' (midcentric to near psychocentric types) will be quite happy to view the landscape in the company of others and will continue to visit the well known sights.

Activity based rural tourism

The cycle of development of activity or special interest rural tourist resources is a little different from that of landscape resources. This is because:

1 The resource is generally spatially concentrated in particular locations.
2 There is a higher proportion of the 'sunluster' (or, in these cases, snowluster, rock climb-luster, caveluster) type of tourist amongst the visitors than wanderlusters/allocentrics.
3 The supply of top quality resources is limited.

It is therefore clear that these circumstances have more in common with coastal tourism than with landscape based tourism, and it might be expected that these resources would experience a process of development very similar to Butler's model (*see* Chapter 7, page 68). For ski fields, for example, the process may be as follows:

Stage 1

Tourists. First few pioneers of the sport bring their own equipment.
Facilities. None. Tourists stay in farm-based accommodation in the settlement nearest to the most accessible resource (ski field). They provide their own transport to the resource.
Destination. Physically little affected by tourism.

Stage 2

Tourists. As sport becomes more fashionable, they increase in number, but are mainly independent travellers and sporting skiers.
Facilities. Local community begins to invest in services for skiers (ski lifts, etc) and hotels in existing settlements.
Destination. Begins to change incrementally in nature, from depending on agriculture to depend-

ing on tourism. Some physical impact of ski runs and visual impact on landscape.

Stage 3

Tourists. Tour operators begin to provide packages as tourists dramatically increase in number, including 'social skiers' as well as 'sporting skiers'. The sporting skiers require less crowded and more specialised ski runs, beginners need easier slopes, i.e. segregation of different type of skier.
Facilities. Equipment for hire on location. Local settlements and transport facilities to ski fields at capacity. Investment by outside capital. Pressure for relocation of facilities closer to existing ski fields, or in new locations near better or different ski fields.
Destination. Integrated resorts developed at high altitude in best locations with a greater choice of ski slopes. (N.B. It should be noted that integrated resort development is often associated with other rural development policies (*see* Pearce 1989).) Urban and entertainment facilities grafted onto existing villages and included in the new resorts. Some erosion of over-used ski slopes, and damage to alpine pastures may disrupt traditional agricultural practices.

Stage 4

Tourists. Mass level tour operators involved to cater for the variety of demand.
Facilities. Settlements specialise in catering for different segments of the market. Some ski fields at capacity.
Destination. Proliferation of urbanised but still small resorts clustered round best, medium and lower quality resources. Older resorts in poorer locations decline in popularity.

The outcome of this process is a clustering of specialised (though physically quite small) resorts in and around the special natural resource. The resorts include a variety of non-resource based tourist attractions (cinemas, nightclubs, restaurants, shops, swimming pools, etc). The incidence of 'integrated', purpose-built resorts on green field sites may be higher than on the coast, as the original settlements of the ski regions fulfilled an agricultural function and their location was based on factors other than proximity to ski fields, i.e. the original settlement pattern of the mountains has little relationship to the location of the best ski fields, whereas in many coastal areas, tourist resorts have been grafted on to existing fishing settlements (i.e. settlements already located at the coast in close proximity to the required resource). The demand for other rural activities has not reached the mass scale of skiing, so the development of other resources, for example, climbing, water sports, horse riding, has not reached the same level of intensity, sometimes perhaps only Stage 2 or 3 of the cycle (for example, pony trekking in the Black Mountains of the Brecon Beacons, villages in the Norfolk Broads for water sports).

CYCLES OF ECONOMIC AND SOCIAL CHANGE IN RURAL AREAS

In many rural regions there are profound changes taking place in the rural economy and in the structure and distribution of the rural population. These changes are occurring quite independently of any changes initiated by tourism development. The changes appear to be cyclical and tend to be self-perpetuating. The introduction of tourism into these rural economies may be seen by politicians and planners to be the means of altering (or at least of influencing) the direction of rural change. Thus, in rural areas, tourism is as much a remedy for rural problems as it is a cause of social and environmental difficulties. This next section outlines the changes taking place in two different kinds of rural areas: the 'remote' and the 'pressured' rural regions.

The remote rural regions

These are, by definition, beyond the sphere of influence and a long way from a major urban area and have a small, very dispersed population. They show many of the socio-economic symptoms and characteristics of economic decline such as low incomes, high outmigration, declining and ageing populations, high unemployment etc (see Cloke, 1977). Such regions are mostly remote, inaccessible upland areas with poor, unproductive agricultural land that yields only a very modest income (sometimes only at subsistence level) to the farmer. As

young people move away in search of jobs and a better standard of living, the population falls. Local public services such as public transport, schools and medical services become more expensive to provide and are reduced; local businesses such as shops, become less viable and begin to close down. Each change makes the region less attractive to the young, so outmigration accelerates, leading to the eventual abandonment of farmland and settlements as the older generation retires or dies. Some parts of rural France, such as the Massif Central, are currently facing these problems. The introduction of tourism into such regions may provide the resident population with an alternative source of income and employment to that provided by agriculture. The economic multiplier effect of tourism has the potential to slow down or even reverse the cycle of economic decline. However, in the UK, policies for tourism promotion in such regions have often been controversial, as the local people may feel that the very earliest stages of the tourism cycle increase the problems they face. Smith and Young (see Chapter 7) suggest that the first tourist accommodation in new tourist regions takes the form of second homes for non-residents. The lack of housing demand from local people may have made suitable cheap property available in the first place. The increase in demand by tourists may drive prices back up beyond the reach of those locals who do wish to stay. The replacement of permanent residents by temporary summer visitors may also appear to reduce the demand for local services such as schools even further. So local people may perceive the incoming tourists to be the cause of their difficulties, as in Wales, for example, (Coppock, 1977) and the Lake District (Coté, 1987). This perception may be all the greater in attractive villages where second homes are concentrated. It is only a little later in the tourist cycle, when tourist numbers are high enough to start generating local jobs and boost local incomes, that the local people may change their attitude to tourism promotion.

Pressured areas

These are rural regions within the sphere of influence of major urban areas, where the countryside is used for daytrip recreation and is in demand for commuter housing. The intense housing demand drives rural property prices up and the overall population is growing. The regions are often more prosperous lowland agricultural areas, but they may also be losing agricultural employment through the mechanisation and modernisation of farms. Certain local services may be declining, such as shops and public transport, as the majority of the population (the commuters) are mobile and rely on their urban workplace for some services. However, the dominant process of change leads towards increasing pressures for the urbanisation of this type of rural area. The tourist use of these regions is dominated by day tourism to country-side beauty spots. They are the location of many manmade attractions which benefit from a rural setting, such as theme parks, Centre Parcs and safari parks. The process of increasing urbanisation of the population and landscape makes this type of countryside progressively less attractive to holiday tourism. Second home owners who may have originally bought rural properties fairly near their urban homes may sell up and relocate further away from the city's influence (*see* Pearce, 1989).

IMPACTS OF TOURISM IN RURAL REGIONS

Social impacts

The nature of the social impacts of rural tourism are consistent with those suggested in the early stages of the resort cycle models (*see* Chapter 7, pages 79 and 82–3). The smaller scale and more dispersed nature of rural tourism means that more tourist enterprises stay under the control of local people, though local attitudes to tourism in the more popular areas may turn to indifference or antagonism. The smaller scale of employment generated by rural tourism, and its extreme seasonal nature make it unlikely that tourism triggers off large scale immigration of tourism workers into rural regions, although it may provide enough local jobs to slow down population decline. These factors are of great importance, for the 'touring' visitors and those seeking to participate in a rural way of life as they expect to meet friendly, local people and value the contact with genuine local residents as part of their holiday experience (*see* Edwards, 1989).

Economic impacts

Tourist spending in rural regions triggers off the same economic processes as in other destinations, but local benefit varies with the type of tourist development. Second homes tend to generate less economic benefit as visitors may bring provisions with them, and use local services and tourist attractions less, while bed and breakfasts tend to generate bigger income multipliers as more of the expenditure is retained locally than with other types of service accommodation, i.e. hotels (*see* Pearce, 1989).

The leakage of profit outside the rural region may be higher in the case of the integrated activity resorts (e.g. ski resorts), as this depends on major injections of capital on a scale that most local rural economies do not possess, and these are generally financed by government or other outside agencies. Some of the smaller rural tourism enterprises may be supplementary to the operator's main businesses (for example, supplementary to agriculture or forestry) and function as an additional, rather than as the main source of income. Tourism may simply support the original enterprise, for example, farm tourism (Frater, 1982). Indeed many rural development policies encourage tourism for this very reason. Such businesses often start on a small scale and grow incrementally. These small businesses face many difficulties which include the lack of capital to invest in high quality facilities, the unwillingness to take risks and the lack of tourism business skills as the operator is trained and experienced in a different form of business operation (Evans and Ilbery, 1992). The successful businesses may grow, as the volume of tourism increases and as the operator gains experience and confidence, until tourism replaces the original enterprise. On the other hand many stay in tourism a relatively short time, dropping out perhaps as labour availability changes, or as profitability does not match the effort needed to sustain the venture.

Physical impacts

In addition to the changes in the settlement pattern and in the density of accommodation and attractions, rural tourism has an impact on the land and landscape itself. These impacts may be temporary or permanent.

Temporary impacts. These include the visual impacts of the tourists themselves, their cars, caravans and tents, all of which vanish when the tourists leave. There may also be the temporary ecological effects of visitors on vegetation and wildlife. At low intensities of use, trampled vegetation will recover and disturbed birds and animals will return to their territories after the tourists have gone.

Permanent impacts. Tourist developments such as car parks and road and footpath improvements, advertisements and new or converted buildings will all have a cumulative and permanent visual impact on the landscape. The rural landscape gradually becomes more urbanised. At high intensities of use, ecological impacts may become irreversible, for example, by disturbing wildlife breeding grounds or causing soil erosion. These effects are spatially concentrated at the most heavily used rural tourist sites and may be most critical at the special natural resources for tourism (e.g. cliffs, caves) that also form relatively rare landscape and wildlife habitats. On the other hand, a large proportion of the rural environment is unaffected. Such issues may be of concern to policy makers and tourists alike (or at least to the more 'allocentric' type of tourist), but it must be acknowledged that landscape and ecological change on a much larger and more widespread scale may be caused by other rural economic activities such as forestry or agriculture.

POLICIES FOR RURAL TOURISM

The European experience

In rural areas tourism is only one of the economic activities generating economic landscape and social change. The other issues of concern to rural communities and policy makers include:

1 Agriculture, forestry and other primary industry, as these underpin the rural economy and their practice determines the nature of the land use landscape (*see* Chapter 4).
2 The social welfare of the rural community, including the provision of services and the expansion or contraction of rural settlements.
3 The quality of the rural landscape. The present landscape is a result of thousands of years of man's activity and has historic as well as aesthetic meanings. The conservation of landscape character is an issue in many European countries, particularly in Britain.
4 Wildlife conservation – the countryside forms the habitat for much wildlife. Many conservationists view wildlife management in the general countryside as being of equal or at least comparable importance as conservation in the nature reserves and national parks.
5 Recreation and tourism together form an additional demand on rural resources.

Policies for rural areas are concerned with integrating the management of all these resources and demands. A genuine 'rural policy' will consider the interactions between different interests and activities. Some European countries such as the Netherlands and France, take a comprehensive approach to the planning and design of rural landscapes and have achieved integrated policies for rural change and rural tourism and recreation. However, in Britain, this has been very difficult in the past, as until recently agricultural policy has taken priority over other interests. This has led to many policy conflicts (e.g. between agriculture and landscape/wildlife conservation), while tourism and recreation have been promoted or controlled in the interests of achieving other policy objectives.

European agricultural policy and tourism

In Europe, the members of the EU have been subject to an agricultural policy that has encouraged agricultural intensification and restructuring of agricultural holdings. It has led to the massive overproduction of many agricultural commodities (for example, wine, beef, cereals and butter) beyond the needs of the population of the EU. The policy has involved the heavy subsidisation of agriculture which has maintained farmers' incomes but has proved very expensive for the governments concerned (*see* Blunden and Curry, 1988). Since the mid-1980s, the EU has attempted to curb overproduction and reduce spending on agriculture in several ways including:

1 gradually reducing price support for produce, effectively reducing farmers' incomes; and
2 encouraging and, more recently, requiring farmers to take land out of arable production (i.e. to set aside land).

Tourism has been seen by policy makers both as an appropriate form of alternative land use for surplus agricultural land and as a means of supplementing declining farm incomes. So UK farmers, particularly those in the lowland arable regions in the 'pressured' countryside, have been encouraged by grant aid, incentives and advice to diversify into recreation and tourism enterprises. Thus, certain types of tourism have been encouraged for reasons concerned with agricultural policy rather than because there was an unmet demand for rural tourism. Although this has doubtless increased the number and range of tourist opportunities in some parts of the countryside (particularly the remote regions and in the urban fringe), there is a danger that such policies can lead to the oversupply of tourist accommodation and facilities.

Tourism and UK landscape policies

In other parts of the UK countryside, policies for the promotion of tourism may be in direct conflict with landscape (and sometimes wildlife) conservation policies, on account of their physical and visual impacts. In the UK, conservation policies generally take precedence over tourism development (for example, as in the UK National Parks). The conflict is greatest in the designated landscapes (National Parks, AONBs, Heritage coasts – see Fig 4.13, page 39) which are deemed to be the most attractive and therefore under greatest pressure for tourist development. Most of these designated areas are hill or mountain regions where agriculture is marginal and where additional income from profitable diversification schemes would be most welcome. Planning policies for such areas seek to control the amount, location and landscape impact of new tourism developments in an attempt to maintain the quality of the main resource that attracts tourism in the first place: the landscape. In the UK therefore, the balance between the conflicting policies tends to change in different parts of the countryside:

1 In the designated landscape areas: (i.e. the 'protected' landscapes – see Chapter 4), a muted encouragement of 'appropriate' forms of tourism that support the local economy but strict controls over tourism developments that impinge on landscape quality.

2 The rest of the remote uplands: a general policy of support and encouragement of tourism in order to supplement farm incomes, support the local economy and maintain local communities.
3 The agricultural lowlands: general encouragement of farm diversification and use of set aside land for recreation and tourism enterprises.
4 The urban fringe: here, tourism policies are subject to policies for the curbing of urban development (in the green belts), so any proposed tourism enterprise involving major building development is likely to be restricted by planning policies.

Policies for integrated rural development in the rest of Europe

Attitudes to landscape change are perhaps a little less restrictive in other European countries, and different planning mechanisms allow a more integrated approach to be taken. In some of Europe's problem rural areas, for example Mezzogiorno in Italy and the Auvergne and the Languedoc-Roussillon regions of France, there have been major projects for the integrated development of forestry, agriculture, road infrastructure, industry and tourism (see page 162). Tourism development has been seen as a part of a coherent plan, rather than a separate area of policy.

REFERENCES AND FURTHER READING

Those texts marked with an asterisk are particularly recommended for further reading.

Blunden, J and Curry, N (1988) *A future for our countryside*, Blackwell.
*Bouquet, M and Winter, M (Eds) (1987) *Who From Their Labours Rest? Conflict and Practice in Rural Tourism*, Avebury.
Cloke, P J (1977) 'An index of rurality for England and Wales', *Regional Studies*, Vol. 11, No. 1, pp. 31–46.
Coppock, J T (1977) 'Social implications of second homes in mid and north Wales' in Coppock, J (Ed) *Second Homes: Curse or Blessing?*, Pergamon.
Coté, D (1987) 'Valle d'Aosta and the Lake District: a comparison of issues and approaches to recreational and residential growth' in Bouquet, M and Winter, M (Eds) *Who From Their Labours Rest? Conflict and Practice in Rural Tourism*, Avebury.
Dernoi, L (1991) 'About rural and farm tourism', theme issue, 'Rural and farm tourism', *Tourism and Recreation Research*, Vol. 16, No. 1, pp. 3–8.

Edwards, J (1989) 'Developments in rural tourism: a comparison of approaches in South-West England and Northern Portugal', in Botterill, D and Tomlinson, A (Eds) *Leisure Labour and Lifestyles, Vol. 9 – Tourism and Leisure*, Leisure Studies Association Conference Papers No. 40.

English Tourist Board (1988) *Visitors in the Countryside: a Development Strategy*.

Evans, N J and Ilbery, B W (1992) 'Farm based accommodation and the restructuring of agriculture: evidence from three English counties', *Journal of Rural Studies*, Vol. 8, No. 1, pp. 85–96.

Fagence, M (1991) 'Rural tourism and the small country town', *Tourism Recreation Research*, Vol. 16, No. 1, pp. 34–43.

Fox, M and Cox, L J (1993) 'Linkages between agriculture and tourism' in Khan, M, Olsen, M and Var, T (Eds) *VNR's Encyclopedia of Hospitality and Tourism*, New York: Van Nostrand Reinhold.

Frater, J (1982) 'Farm tourism in England and overseas', *Research Memorandum*, No.93, Centre for Urban and Regional Studies, Birmingham University.

Gunn, C A (1993) 'Tourism infrastructure and development' in Khan, M, Olsen, M and Var, T (Eds) *VNR's Encyclopedia of Hospitality and Tourism*, New York: Van Nostrand Reinhold, pp. 754–72.

Johnston, M (1992) 'Facing the challenges: adventure in the mountains of New Zealand' in Weiler, B and Hall, C M (Eds) *Special Interest Tourism*, Belhaven.

Pearce, D (1989) *Tourist Development*, 2nd edn, Longman.

Smith, C and Jenner, P (1990) 'Activity holidays in Europe', *Travel and Tourism Analyst*, No. 5, pp. 58–78.

Tourism and Recreation Research (1991) Vol. 16, No.1 (theme issue on rural and farm tourism).

QUESTIONS AND DISCUSSION POINTS

1 Does the promotion of rural tourism cause or prevent undesirable changes in rural areas?

2 Why are UK policies for tourism significantly different in the protected landscapes and the agricultural lowlands?

3 In what ways is the process of development of ski resorts different from that of landscape based rural tourism?

ASSIGNMENT

1 Choose one of the UK National Parks and obtain an O.S. map and tourist information (attractions, accommodation, tour operators) for the park. Map the tourist and landscape attractions, the access routes, accommodation, the 'circulation' and 'linkage' corridors (*see* Fig 9.2, page 92).

(a) Does the spatial pattern of tourist development resemble the theoretical model advocated by Gunn? Is it possible to identify any accommodation 'nodes'? What factors might explain the pattern you have demonstrated in your National Park?

(b) What stage of the theoretical cycle of tourist development do you think your Park has reached?

CHAPTER 10

The use of wildlife and wilderness resources for tourism

LEARNING OBJECTIVES

After reading this chapter you should be able to
- distinguish between rural tourism, nature based and wilderness tourism
- list the different types of nature based tourists
- assess the relative size of the nature based and wilderness tourism market
- assess the scale of the environmental impacts of wildlife and wilderness tourism
- apply the destination life cycle to the growth of wilderness and nature based tourism (i.e. list the sequence of changes brought about by wildlife and wilderness tourism)
- understand the relationship between nature based tourism policies and conservation policies in National Parks.

INTRODUCTION

Since the 1960s there has been a growing interest in and awareness of the world's wildlife and natural environments and man's impact on them. In the UK the media coverage of wildlife and conservation issues has grown enormously, with regular series of wildlife and conservation programmes on TV showing animals, birds and plants in their natural habitats. When travel to animals' natural habitats was impossible or very expensive, people were content to see wild animals in zoos. The animals were transported to the consumer, so wildlife viewing was a very popular part of the domestic tourist industry: attendances at London Zoo reached 3 million in the 1950s. But, as people's environmental awareness developed, they found viewing animals in cages less appealing. The domestic tourist industry responded by setting up Safari Parks. These provide an environment where the animals can be viewed in circumstances that allow for slightly more natural behaviour, even though the paddocks or parkland in which the animals roam are not their natural habitat. The

UK's first Safari Park was at Longleat, set up in 1966. The attendances at zoos began to decline (at London Zoo visitors had dropped to 1.3 million by 1988). In more recent years the Safari Parks have experienced reduced attendances and low profitability. In the early 1990s, London Zoo was threatened with closure and Windsor Safari Park (which had attendances of 950 000 in 1988) went out of business. At the same time there has been very rapid growth in nature based tours that make it possible for the tourist to travel to remote locations in the world and to observe wild plants, animals and birds in their natural settings.

DEFINITIONS

Nature based tourism

Nature based tourism involves travel to places for activities and experiences that are entirely dependent on nature. Valentine (1992) defines nature based tourism as being 'primarily concerned with the direct enjoyment of some relatively undisturbed phenomenon of nature'. Nature based tourism can therefore be distinguished from activity or adventure tourism such as climbing, skiing or sailing; the enjoyment of these pursuits may be enhanced by an undisturbed natural setting but is not entirely dependent on it (*see* Chapter 9).

Wilderness tourism

The appreciation of wild nature is also an integral part of the wilderness experience; wilderness tourists will seek the same undisturbed wild places as nature tourists. However, the wilderness tourist also requires solitude as an essential part of the wilderness experience (Hall, 1991), *see* Fig 10.1.

Ecotourism

Many writers think of nature tourism as being the same as 'ecotourism'. Caballos-Lascurain (1987) provides a widely quoted definition of ecotourism: 'travelling to relatively undisturbed or uncontaminated natural areas with the specific objective of studying, admiring and enjoying the scenery and its wild plants and animals, as well as any existing cultural manifestations (both past and present) found in these areas' (quoted in Jenner and Smith, 1992). If this definition of ecotourism is accepted, then it is clear that it involves:

1 Travel to 'unspoilt' natural environments where man's impact is minimal. These are areas of the world that have not been used for primary industry (forestry, agriculture, mineral extraction, etc). Such untouched areas are likely to be unpopulated, or only very sparsely populated. Chapter 4 describes the location and ecological character of the remaining areas of wilderness in the world.

2 Travel for the specific purpose of experiencing the natural environment. Ecotourism may include adventure type activities (for example, travel by canoe, horse, four-wheel drive, camping, etc), but these activities may be the only means of getting access to the wildlife areas – they are not the main purpose of the holiday.

If these definitions are accepted, it should be noted that no assumptions are made about visitor values or behaviour, or about the impact of tourism on the wildlife, or the management of that impact. However, some writers do use the term 'ecotourism' to refer only to nature based tourism that is:

- non-damaging, non-degrading, ecologically sustainable;
- a direct contributor to the continued protection and management of the natural areas used;
- subject to an adequate and appropriate management regime (Valentine, 1993); or
- an environmentally and culturally sensitive approach to travelling (quoted in Jenner and Smith, 1992).

Component	Nature of experience
Aesthetic/perception	Appreciation of wild nature and scenery
Religious/spiritual	The experience of God or self in the wilderness
Escapist	Finding freedom away from the constraints of urban living and alienation
Challenge	The satisfaction that occurs in overcoming dangerous situations
Historic/romantic	The opportunity to re-live or imagine the experiences of pioneers of the 'frontier' that helped form national culture and society
Solitude	The awe of being alone in a vast and indifferent setting
Companionship	Paradoxically, in relation to the previous category, the desire to share the setting with companions and reinforce social bonds and ties
Discovery/learning	The thrill of discovering or learning about nature in a natural setting
Vicarious appreciation	The pleasure of knowing that wilderness exists without ever having seen it

Fig 10.1 Components of the wilderness experience
(*Source*: Hall, 1991)

There is great potential for confusion until a generally accepted definition is established. (This chapter will generally follow Caballos-Lascurain's definition.) The management objectives and management methods used to regulate nature based tourism will be discussed later in this chapter, while the whole issue of the sustainability of tourism (as it applies to all forms of tourism) is dealt with in Chapter 14. This chapter will outline the motivations of nature based tourists and the growth of the market, the impacts of wilderness tourism on the natural environment, and finally the management of it.

MOTIVATIONS OF NATURE BASED TOURISTS

It has been suggested (Lindberg, 1991) that there are four basic types of nature based tourists:

1 **Hard core nature tourists.** These are scientific researchers or members of tours specially designed for educational or conservational purposes. This would include the 'science tourism' referred to by Laarman and Perdue (1989), but most definitions of tourism would exclude scientists working in the field as part of their jobs, although field trips for students would be included in educational tourism. Not surprisingly, these types of travellers tend to be very highly educated and predominantly Caucasian males.
2 **Dedicated nature tourists.** These are people who take trips specifically to see protected areas and who want to understand local natural and cultural history. A Canadian study showed that visiting tropical forests, wilderness, undisturbed nature and learning about nature were the most important motivations of this type of tourist (Eagles, 1992). Boo (1990) suggests that such tourists are less demanding in their requirements for luxury accommodation, food and entertainment and 'the nature traveller seems more willing to accept and appreciate local customs and foods'. Although there is little empirical evidence to confirm these assumptions, Eagles' study certainly showed that Canadian ecotourists were least interested in nightlife, shopping and resorts, while simpler lifestyles and experiencing new lifestyles were more important to them than to general tourists. Users of natural environments are typically university graduates, in professional jobs, earning above average incomes.
3 **Mainstream nature tourists.** These are people who visit wildlife destinations primarily to take an unusual trip. They may have no particular commitment to wildlife and would, perhaps, expect standards of accommodation and comfort equal to that of other non-environmentally based unusual holidays.
4 **Casual nature tourists.** These are people who partake of nature incidentally as part of a broader trip. Lindberg implies that both mainstream and casual nature tourists would expect better amenities than the 'serious' nature tourists and they may be tolerant of some crowding at the destination.

The total size of the ecotourist/nature based tourist market is difficult to estimate. Jenner and Smith report an estimated world spending on ecotourism of between $10 and $12 billion. Many ecotourism destinations, such as the Galapagos Islands, Parc National des Volcans in Rwanda, Monteverde Cloud Forest reserve in Costa Rica, have shown very rapid growth in tourist numbers particularly in the 1980s and general estimates of overall growth rate suggest 10–15 per cent growth per annum (Lindberg, 1991).

LOCATION AND DEMAND FOR NATURE BASED TOURISM

By definition, nature based tourism to undisturbed natural environments is limited to the world's wilderness areas, National Parks and to fragments of undisturbed habitats embedded in developed regions. The world's wilderness areas (*see* Chapter 4) are not exploited for intensive agriculture because of their inhospitable climates, the polar, mountain and tundra regions being too cold, the deserts and semi-arid zones being too hot and dry, and the tropical rain forests being too hot and wet. Such regions are only accessible, populated and developed if, for example, valuable mineral or timber resources are located in them. But generally such areas are climatically less than ideal for tourism, they are sparsely populated, with difficult access, and (except in some National Parks), lacking tourist infrastructure. In world terms, the National Parks of the USA attract most visitors. In 1991, 8 per cent of all US planned domestic summer vacations were to National Parks. Several individual parks attract well over 1 million visitors a year, for example, Great Smokey Mountains (11 million), Yellowstone (7 million visitors per annum in 1980s) and Yosemite (3.4 million visitors). But it must be remembered that the Parks cater for a wide range of landscape and activity holiday makers as well as those wishing to experience the wilderness and wildlife. Similarly, the Great Barrier Reef Marine Park off the Queensland Coast of Australia attracts activity holiday makers as well as ecotourists. Total tourist use of this Park is around 1 million passenger days per annum on all its tours and trips, but as 70 per cent of the Park's permitted tourist operations were for ecotourism, it is reasonable to assume that the majority of visitors go for nature based activities. Kenya (and East Africa) is perceived to be the major world centre for 'mass' wildlife tourism on account of this area's very visible and abundant animal herds. In 1990, just over 800 000 international tourists went to Kenya and all Kenya's National Parks together attracted 1.2 million visits (the most popular, Amboseli, with 208 000 visits in 1990). Wildlife tourism is developing in other East African countries but it is still on a relatively small scale. Only 155 323 non-resident visitor days were recorded in Tanzania's National Parks in 1989, a total of 137 800 leisure tourists to Botswana, and 17 136

visitors to Malawi's National Parks and game reserves. On the other hand, over 500 000 tourists (domestic and international) visited South Africa's Kruger National Park in 1988. Wetland habitats are also attractive destinations, even though the wildlife is more difficult to see (*see* Fig 10.2) and in less spectacular numbers. Kakadu (in Northern Australia) attracted nearly 250 000 tourists in 1988–9, while the Florida Everglades have always been heavily visited. Costa Rica's National Parks, which include rainforest habitats, received 161 828 international tourists in 1989, while the most recently developed ecotourism destination, the Antarctic, attracted 6500 in 1991–92. It is clear that nature based tourism has penetrated all types of environments and ecosystems, from tropical rainforests to polar ice caps. Total numbers are as yet quite small in terms of the scale of world tourism as a whole, although it has been noted that interest in ecotourism is growing rapidly.

THE IMPACTS OF NATURE BASED TOURISM

Much has been written on the negative environmental impacts of tourism in general and ecotourism in particular. However, this discussion must be put into context: it is quite clear that other primary industries (agriculture, forestry, fishing, mineral extraction and so on) have far more devastating and damaging ecological effects than tourism. Indeed, the World Wildlife Fund (WWF) in 1990 concluded that no major negative impacts (on the specific National Parks they had studied) had been revealed that were the result of tourist activity. The major threats to the wildlife of these valued ecosystems come from activities such as poaching, industrial pollution, present agricultural encroachment and past agricultural practices (for example, the control of non-native weed species and feral animals) and from pressures for new economic development, such as logging and mining. However, ecotourism/nature based tourism by definition is concentrated in those environments that are least modified by man; in many ecotourism destinations tourism is the only visible form of economic activity. Because ecotourists' and wilderness tourists' satisfaction depends on a pristine environment (unmodified even by their

Fig. 10.2 Wild saltwater crocodile in Kakadu National Park, Australia

own presence) attention has been focused on the ecological effects of tourism. Tourism can have three types of environmental impact:

1 Impacts of building development associated with tourism (e.g. accommodation, roads, information centres). This construction destroys the soil, plants and animals on the developed site and may initiate soil erosion, pollution and the consumption of local water supplies when the facilities are used. But these impacts are the same for any tourist development in any environment (urban or rural).

2 Widespread impacts caused by the presence of tourists themselves.

(a) Impacts on soil and water from chemical pollution (e.g. from oil, soap) and added nutrients (from faeces, urine, fire ashes, food waste). These impacts may be spread (in water) beyond the immediate site of tourist activity, but are generally greatest at tourist sites (e.g. campsites, trails etc.).

(b) The most widespread and ecologically potentially the most serious impact is the possible introduction of non-native weed species and pests into an untouched ecosystem (e.g. on tyres, boots, in horse/pack animal dung and feed, etc). These can spread throughout the ecosystem far beyond the sites to which tourists have access and have major ecological effects.

(c) Fire – wildfires can be started by tourists and can have widespread devastating effects, though fire is a natural part of many ecosystems.

(d) Impacts on the behaviour of animals and birds – the presence of people can disturb animals' feeding and breeding behaviour. Persistent disturbance could possibly threaten the viability of an animal or bird population.

3 Localised impacts on routes through the ecosystem caused by the passage of people or their means of transport and their activities.

(a) The trampling of human feet can kill vegetation, cause soil compaction and/or soil erosion (and kill coral in the marine environment). The passage of vehicles and pack animals may have an even greater effect.

(b) Consumption and removal of, for example, firewood, flowers, shell, coral, fossil specimens etc, and the introduction of litter. The precise nature of these impacts will depend on the type of activity of the tourist. Buckley and Pannell (1990) have listed some of the impacts that have been noted in Australian National Parks by a large number of researchers. The scale of impacts will depend on the numbers of tourists, their behaviour, their frequency of use and the sensitivity of the ecosystem. Most of the ecosystems valued for ecotourism are very sensitive to human use: for example in hot and dry and very cold environments, chemical reactions and plant growth tend to be slow, so the environment takes a long time to regenerate. Therefore tourist impacts (e.g. vegetation damage and litter) may be visible long after the tourists have gone. If the rate of tourist damage is faster than the rate at which the environment can recover naturally, then the tourist impacts are cumulative; it may eventually reach the stage at which the damage is irreversible, or where a sudden dramatic large scale environmental change is triggered off – Jenner and Smith refer to this as the 'shear point'.

Ecological carrying capacity

In theory it is possible to relate tourist numbers to a quantified assessment of their impact. Ecological carrying capacity represents 'an amount of tourist use above which unacceptable ecological results will occur and which can only be corrected by reduced use'. The fragile environments (e.g. sand dunes and hot/cold deserts) clearly have much lower carrying capacities than grasslands or forests. But, in practice, it is virtually impossible to quantify the relationship between tourist numbers and their impact because their effects depend as much on their behaviour as on their numbers.

The acceptability of the ecological changes induced by tourism is another grey area. Different types of tourist may vary in their evaluation of change: the hard core nature tourist may find the slightest environmental change unacceptable, while the dedicated nature tourist may tolerate only a little. The casual nature tourist at the other extreme may be unconcerned and may even be unaware that change has occurred. Similarly the various interest groups involved with the management of the tourist resource (e.g. the host community, National Park manager, tour operator) may also have differing opinions as to the acceptable level of change brought about by tourism.

Perceptual capacity

Just as tolerance of environmental change will vary between different types of tourist, so will their tolerance of the presence of others. For some, the quality of the wilderness experience depends on solitude. Burton (1974) showed that different types of visitors had different tolerance levels and different behavioural responses to crowding: the more highly educated visitors and those from non-urban home environments were the least tolerant of crowding and actively avoided crowded conditions, while the less well educated visitors were more gregarious. The crowding-sensitive visitors avoided congested places and peak times, so there was a spatial sorting of visitors. Although the research was carried out in a UK country park (a long way from wilderness conditions), comparable results were obtained (Hamitt and Patterson, 1991) in a genuine wilderness setting.

Clearly there is no easily identifiable carrying capacity (i.e., upper limit of tourist use that an environment can take). The ecological and perceptual capacity of an ecosystem depends on its own character, the behaviour of tourists and the attitudes of the tourists themselves. It is perhaps more useful to think of visitor populations as having a range of preferences and expectations, ranging through a continuum or spectrum, from the hard core nature tourists, who want to enjoy an untouched environment in solitude, at one extreme, to the gregarious, casual nature tourist, who is happy to share a substantially modified natural environment, at the other. Each type of tourist requires a different set of environmental conditions.

WILDERNESS AND NATURE BASED TOURISM AND THE DESTINATION LIFE CYCLE

It could be argued that the destination life cycle model (*see* Chapter 7) that is concerned with the process of resort development would have limited relevance for nature based wilderness tourism which relies entirely on the absence of urbanised development. On the other hand, the hard core nature tourist and the wilderness tourist may be the very initiators of the whole cycle of tourist development. By definition they seek untouched

sites where no human activity at all (let alone tourism) has yet occurred. Their penetration into remote areas may encourage tour operators to follow suit and provide opportunities for the dedicated nature tourist; this paves the way for different types of tourist and so the cycle progresses. Even if the cycle does not progress to the fully urbanised end point, it is clear that the principles apply to the evolution of wildlife and wilderness tourism, too. Indeed, Butler himself has applied his model to adventure tourism (Butler and Waldbrook, 1991). Keller (1987) notes that the model has yet to be applied to a case study of remote region tourism but suggests that Canada's North West Territories are at an early stage of development. In the context of wilderness and nature based tourism the process might operate as follows:

Stage 1. Discovery of the area by very small numbers of science tourists, hard core nature tourists and hard adventurers. Access to the destination is very difficult – by rivers, tracks, on foot, horse or canoe, or possibly, off-road, four-wheel drive vehicles. Accommodation is in temporary bivouacs or camps with no facilities. Environmental impact is low and the trips are long (in terms of weeks) due to the slow rate of travel and difficulty of access.

Stage 2. Organised groups of dedicated nature tourists arrive, through their own organisation or in small groups on four-wheel drive tours provided by tour operators with wilderness experience and local knowledge. The best camp sites are used fairly frequently, gravel tracks are established and there is some visible impact of tourism at the regularly used sites, for example, trampling, pollution, shortage of firewood etc. Tourist use spreads through the area as tour operators spread out, each seeking access to an 'untouched' area.

Stage 3. Levels of use increase; roads may be paved to the most heavily used sites and water supply, toilets, firewood supply and litter collection services are provided at the main camp sites. The crowding-sensitive visitors begin to modify their behaviour to avoid congested sites and peak times. The hard core visitors abandon the area.

Stage 4. Mainstream tourists begin to use the area as tourist facilities are increased (shower blocks, guided trails, information centres). Wildlife sites are protected by, for example, duckboard walks

Fig. 10.3 Tourist viewing platform with interpretation and information viewing boards

and railings (*see* Fig 10.3) and restrictions on visitor numbers or activities. Access is possible for two-wheel drive vehicles and coaches. Four-wheel drive tour operators seek new destinations.

Stage 5. A network of paved roads and a choice of built accommodation (hotels, hostels, safari lodges etc) is provided, allowing access to non-adventure and casual nature tourists. There may be air access. Viewing platforms and car parks are provided at many sites and policing/wardening of vulnerable sites may be necessary to protect wildlife. Visits are now short (possibly only a day) due to the greatly improved accessibility. Therefore income from tourism may decline even though total numbers are high. The area ceases to be a genuine wilderness area and nature based tourists may be outnumbered by mainstream or casual visitors. In a few cases, the cycle has progressed to the stage of resort development where a small settlement has been established specifically to meet tourists' needs, for example, Yulara for Ayers Rock in Australia. However, the cycle does not normally appear to progress to that final stage: those wilderness areas that are designated as National Parks are usually state-owned and have managing authorities that may have powers to intervene in market forces and control new development. The National Park policies towards tourism and its impact are therefore critical to the development of nature based and wilderness tourism, and to the progression of the destination life cycle.

NATIONAL PARK POLICIES FOR TOURISM

International National Parks are primarily conservation bodies (*see* Chapter 4) – their main role is to conserve and manage the natural environment and tourism is generally a secondary issue. However, the Park authorities face several policy dilemmas involving choices between the control or promotion of tourism. Each country and each Park service may resolve these dilemmas in different ways:

1 The Park is a public service and it could be argued that access to the Park should be available to the population that pays for it (through their taxes). So, control of access is politically difficult to justify.

2 On the other hand, as the environment is a 'common good', each member of the public or tourist industry has an incentive to over-use it for their own individual benefit as they do not directly bear the 'cost' of over-use (the costs are shared between all users). So, theoretically, some control of the individual Park user may be politically justified.

3 The Parks need to protect the ecosystem as a whole and individual species from tourist impacts as part of their conservational work. Management and control of tourism can be justified on these grounds.

4 The Parks need to strengthen the political will of most countries to support conservation, so the tourist use and demand for conservation (not to mention the potential tourism income) may be used as political justification for conservation expenditure. The Parks therefore have an incentive to promote themselves for tourism.

5 Park authorities must also balance local and national interests: local attitudes to tourism may range from positive exploitation of the environment for tourism through to resistance to tourist intrusions. In some circumstances local distribution of tourist income may also be used as a means of gaining local support for conservation measures. So here again, Park authorities may be led towards tourist promotion.

6 Finally, Parks in countries or states whose economies depend heavily on tourism may be under political pressure to develop tourism (in order to maximise economic benefits) and therefore be more reluctant to regulate tourist numbers or to constrain the tourist industry.

The political and economic circumstances of each country may therefore have a major influence on the balance of tourist policies and management that each Park adopts. If controlling the impact of tourism on the natural environment is a main policy objective, Park authorities have many options as to how to achieve it:

1 By educating the tourist to behave in an environmentally sensitive way (through information, interpretation and wardening/ranger services).

2 By changing the type of tourist visiting the Park – this can be done by maintaining (or creating) conditions that attract the desired (i.e. the environmentally aware) type of tourist. Dedicated nature tourists, who are more likely to be environmentally sensitive, can be encouraged and casual tourists deterred by deliberately keeping access difficult, long and uncomfortable (e.g., by leaving roads unsealed) and by providing minimal facilities.

3 By curbing total visitor numbers (i.e. intervening directly in the tourist market). This can be done by a variety of management methods:

(*a*) by issuing a limited number of visitor access permits;

(*b*) by issuing permits for potentially damaging activities, limiting numbers, locations, times, etc, of the activity;

(*c*) by introducing permit, licence and tendering systems for tour operators to control their numbers, the number of their passengers, routes and locations to which they have access;

(*d*) through pricing – raising the cost of access/entry fees/accommodation.

4 By protecting particular sensitive areas of the Park by zoning. Each zone has a different level of accessibility, intensity of use and management input. The control of the spatial distribution of tourists within the Park also allows the Park to provide for a range of tourist experiences, covering the whole spectrum of tourist opportunities (Butler and Waldbrook, 1991), from the real wilderness through to an environment in which the casual nature tourist would feel comfortable.

5 By protecting particular sites from the direct impact of tourism by paving roads, surfacing paths, providing raised walkways or duckboards, protecting sites by railings, signs or enclosures, providing viewing platforms, etc. These methods

lead to the 'hardening' of the natural environment by introducing non-natural and urban style elements. These management techniques can increase the capacity of the site to accept tourist use, but inevitably change its character.

Park authorities thus have the potential to influence the course of the cycle of tourist development in their protected areas. The particular policy objectives and the combination of management techniques chosen to achieve them will vary from Park to Park. The resources allocated to the Park to implement the chosen policies, and therefore their effectiveness, will again vary and will depend on each government's view of the national importance of the Park and their commitment to conservation.

REFERENCES AND FURTHER READING

Those texts marked with an asterisk are particularly recommended for further reading.

Boo, E (1990) *Ecotourism: the potentials and pitfalls*, World Wide Fund for Nature.

Buckley, R and Parnell, J (1990) 'Environmental impacts of tourism and recreation in National Parks and conservation areas', *Journal of Tourism Studies*, Vol. 1, No. 1.

Burton, R C J (1974) 'The recreational carrying capacity of the countryside', Keele University Library, Occasional Paper No. 11.

Butler, R W and Waldbrook, L A (1991) 'A new planning tool: the tourism opportunity spectrum', *Journal of Tourism Studies*, Vol. 2, No. 1, pp. 2–14.

Eagles, P F J (1992) 'The travel motivations of Canadian ecotourists', *Journal of Travel Research*, Vol. 31, No. 2 pp. 3–7.

*Edington, J and Edington, A (1986) *Ecology, Recreation and Tourism*, Cambridge University Press.

Farrell, B H and Runyan, D (1991) 'Ecology and tourism', *Annals of Tourism Research*, Vol. 18, pp. 26–40.

Hall, C M (1991) *Introduction to Tourism in Australia – Impacts, Planning and Development*, Longman Cheshire, Melbourne.

Hammitt, W E and Patterson, M E (1991) 'Coping behaviour to avoid visitor encounters – its relationship to wildland privacy', *Journal of Leisure Research*, Vol. 23, No. 3, pp. 225–37.

Jenner, P and Smith, C (1992) '*The Tourism Industry and the Environment*, The Economist Intelligence Unit, Special Report, No. 2453.

Keller, C P (1987) 'Stages of peripheral tourism development in Canada's North West Territories', *Tourism Management*, Vol. 8, No. 1 pp. 20–32.

Laarman, J G and Perdue, R R (1989) 'Science tourism in Costa Rica', *Annals of Tourism Research*, Vol. 16, pp. 20–215.

Lindberg, K (1991) 'Policies for maximising nature tourism's ecological and economic benefits', *World Resources Institute*.

*Lindberg, K and Hawkins, D E (1993) *Ecotourism: a Guide for Planners and Managers*, The Ecotourism Society.

*Mathieson, A and Wall, G (1982) *Tourism: Economic, Physical and Social Impacts*, Longman.

*Ryan, C (1991) *Recreational Tourism – a Social Science Perspective*, Routledge.

Tourism Management (1993), Vol. 14, No. 2, April, (case studies of ecotourism in Antarctica, Micronesia, Zakynthos, Michaelmas Cay on Great Barrier Reef).

Valentine, P S (1992) 'Nature-based tourism' in Weiler, B, and Hall, C M (Eds), *Special Interest Tourism*, Belhaven.

Valentine, P S (1993) 'Ecotourism and nature conservation – a definition with some recent developments in Micronesia', *Tourism Management*, Vol. 14, No. 2, pp. 107–15.

*Whelan, T (Ed) (1991) *Nature Tourism*, Island Press.

QUESTIONS AND DISCUSSION POINTS

1 What is the difference between wilderness tourists, dedicated nature tourists and rural tourists? Is it possible for the same person to be all three?

2 In what ways can National Parks resolve the conflict between conserving the ecology of their Parks and allowing tourists access to them?

3 To what extent is it true that wilderness tourists are the ones who begin the cycle of destination development?

ASSIGNMENTS

1 You work for a National Park. The Park includes wilderness areas of coastal coral reefs, inland wetlands and dry savannah habitats within its boundaries. Your job is to produce a code of behaviour to guide, encourage and educate tourists to behave in a way that will minimise their impact on the Park's environment. Choose *one* of the three habitats and write a first draft of the code of behaviour (i.e. the 'do's' and 'don'ts') for visitors who use that part of the Park.

2 A remote coastal wilderness area with abundant and spectacular wildlife is located in one of the world's less developed countries where tourism is an important source of foreign exchange. The wilderness area is accessible by very rough unsealed (dirt/gravel) roads which are impassable in the wet season. The region is visited by a small number of independent tourists and a few four-wheel drive tour operators that cater for international nature based tourists. The tour operators are concerned about the wear and tear on their vehicles and the long periods of time that the area is inaccessible and have complained to the government about the state of the roads.

The government is now proposing to seal the main access road. This has caused a lot of controversy – with local people, the tourist industry, the government and international conservationists – who all have different opinions as to whether the road improvements should go ahead. You are an expert on tourism and the environment and have been invited by the editor of a major daily paper to write a short article presenting a balanced view of the arguments for and against the proposed road development. The editor has asked you to make a point of spelling out the possible long term implications of the proposed development.

Write the first draft of your article.

The use of historic resources for tourism

LEARNING OBJECTIVES

After reading this chapter you should be able to

- distinguish between heritage and historic tourism
- assess the size of the market for historic tourism
- be aware of some of the land use changes that occur in historic cities, independently of tourism development
- understand the evolution of the tourist quarter of a historic city
- assess the tourism management options available to the planners and managers of historic cities.

INTRODUCTION

Historic resources include the buildings, ancient monuments and artifacts that a country inherits from previous generations. Spatially, they may consist of single attractions (e.g. a stately home or archaeological site) dispersed in an isolated rural setting; clusters of buildings creating an attractive street scene or urban landscape in villages, towns or cities; or they may consist of collections of historic items assembled at a particular location (e.g. in museums). Historic tourism is not synonymous with heritage tourism, but it is a major element of heritage tourism. The term 'heritage tourism' has come to mean the tourist use of not only buildings and historic monuments, but also the landscape, natural history, art and culture of a country – in fact the use of any resource that is passed from one generation to another. In this respect, the concept of a 'heritage' resource is not particularly useful, as by definition everything that exists now (including a theme park, casino or Centre Parc) has the potential to become a heritage resource to the next generation. It has been suggested (Yale, 1991) that the term has been introduced more as a fashionable marketing concept, capturing as it does an image of nostalgia, agreed cultural values, patriotism and homeliness,

and replacing the rather dry, boring image of a dead 'historic' resource. However, this book has chosen to discuss historic resources separately, dividing them from landscape and wildlife resources (see Chapters 4, 9 and 10) and cultural resources (in Chapter 6 and 12). This is because there are not only significant differences in the spatial patterns of tourist development associated with each resource, but also because the range of legislative frameworks, management techniques and policy issues associated with the tourist use of each type of heritage resource is quite different. There are also small but quite distinct specialised (special interest) markets for each type of heritage resource, although it is acknowledged that the mass market is less selective. There is a large overlap in the mass markets for different types of heritage attractions and many tourists will enjoy a wide range of sightseeing experiences such as historic, cultural, landscape or artistic during a single vacation or even as part of a predominantly sun, sea and sand holiday.

THE MARKET FOR HISTORIC TOURISM

In spite of the possible difficulties of marketing 'historic' resources, there is no doubt that historic features hold a big appeal for the mass market. In 1987 in the UK there were 1072 historic buildings recorded by the English Tourist Board and British Tourist Authority as tourist attractions, which together attracted 55 million visitors; by 1989 this had risen to 69.6 million visits. But demand is strongly concentrated on particular attractions, with 23 per cent of visits concentrated on 3 per cent of the attractions. Figure 11.1 shows the list of UK historic attractions that drew over half a million visits each in 1989.

It is obviously much more difficult to estimate the numbers of tourists visiting a historic town but it is thought that places such as Windsor, Cambridge, York and Norwich each attract about 3 million tourists each year, while Stratford-upon-Avon, Bath and Oxford receive between 1 to $2\frac{1}{2}$ million visitors a year.

Although it is clearly a mass market, further analysis (e.g. Prentice, 1993) indicates that people visiting these sorts of attractions are more likely to be well educated and be drawn from white collar social backgrounds (i.e. to be non-manual workers or their families). The higher income professional and managerial types are particularly likely to be found in the visitor population while manual workers and their families are very much less likely to find historic attractions appealing. The demand thus appears to come mainly from the mid-centric to allocentric range of Plog's classification of tourists (*see* Chapter 7). The fact that in 1988 29 per cent of those visiting UK historic properties and 20 per cent of those visiting museums and art galleries were from abroad, reinforces the view that historic and cultural attractions are important to the 'wanderlusters' and cultural tourists (*see* Chapter 6). The authenticity of the historic resource will have a differing degree of importance to different sections of the market. The 'special interest' historian or extreme allocentric tourist may expect the resource to be left in its authentic state – that is, to be unrestored, to be the genuine original article. The heritage industry on the other hand represents, interprets and packages history in a way that appeals to the mass tourist, for example, by restoring buildings or artifacts by replacing damaged or adding missing parts, or by creating living museums or historic theme parks for the re-enactment of the past by people dressed in historic costume. Such re-creations of the past may be selective or may distort history by presenting to

---

Historic Buildings

With over 1 million visits, 1989
Westminster Abbey
St Paul's Cathedral
York Minster
Tower of London
Canterbury Cathedral
Edinburgh Castle

With 500 000 to 1 million visits, 1989
Roman Baths and Pump Room, Bath
State Apartments, Windsor Castle
Chester Cathedral
Stonehenge
Warwick Castle
Shakespeare's birthplace
Buckfast Abbey
King's College Chapel, Cambridge
Hampton Court Palace
Leeds Castle, Kent
Blenheim Palace
Tower Bridge
Beaulieu

Museums

With over 1 million visits, 1989
British Museum
Natural History Museum
Science Museum
Glasgow Art Gallery and Museum

With 500 000 to 1 million visits, 1989
Jorvik Viking Centre, York
National Museum of Photography, Bradford
Nottingham Castle Museum
National Motor Museum, Beaulieu

Fig. 11.1 Most popular UK historic attractions, 1989

the tourist only the image that is saleable and entertaining, that the tourist wants to see.

The degree of authenticity of a historic resource will also depend on the motivation and sources of finance of its owner or manager as well as on market demands. In the UK, properties owned by the Government or the National Trust (whose main objective is the preservation of the building) are more likely to be maintained in their authentic condition. Historic resources are expensive to maintain as the natural process of weathering and decay will gradually consume them (see Chapter 5). Even to maintain the construction in authentic conditions means protecting it from these forces, halting deterioration and preventing further decay. The maintenance of state-owned historic buildings is funded from public funds and does not rely solely on admission fees for upkeep. The National Trust obtains its funds from endowments and donations, as well as membership and admission fees. There is, therefore, a little less pressure on such owners to add money-making attractions over and above the normal facilities that tourists require on the historic site, so authenticity is more easily retained. Privately-owned historic buildings are a different matter. While grants from public funds are available for the upkeep of listed buildings in the UK, their maintenance remains the financial responsibility of the owner. Money-making attractions added to the site may be seen as a necessary evil to earn income to help cover the running costs of the building, or they may be seen as a business opportunity. Although listed building status seeks to control alterations to historic buildings, authenticity is generally at greater risk.

CLASSIFICATION AND SPATIAL DISTRIBUTION OF HISTORIC RESOURCES

Historic attractions include a very wide range of different types of features, and they can be grouped (or classified) in many different ways. Emphasis on the physical character of the resource gives a fourfold classification:

1 **Buildings or ruins of buildings,** such as stately homes, artisan's houses, churches and abbeys, castles, mills, factories etc. These can occur singly or in groups.

2 **Historic places where historic events occurred,** such as battles, religious, political or mythical events, but where no physical relics of the event are left at the site, for example, battlefields.

3 **Archaeological sites,** such as monuments or other constructions made by man, but not in the form of buildings (e.g. burial sites, ancient field systems, stone circles, fortifications, railways, inclined planes, mines etc).

4 **Collections of objects taken from a variety of sites and assembled at another location,** i.e. museums of all sorts. These can also include outdoor museums where, for example, industrial machinery or buildings have been removed from the original location and reconstructed together on the museum site (for example, Blists Hill at Ironbridge Gorge).

Prentice (1993) offers a different classification that is based on the original function of the historic resource, so his categories include:

1 Science based attractions (e.g. science museums).

2 Historic resources associated with primary production (i.e. mining, fishing, agriculture), for example, the Big Pit, Grimsby and other museums of rural life.

3 Craft centres using technologies of the past (e.g. weaving using water power).

4 Attractions concerned with the manufacturing industry (e.g. Gladstone Pottery Museum).

5 Transport (e.g. steam railways, canals, motor vehicles, dockyards).

6 Socio-cultural resources (e.g. domestic houses, museums of social history, costumes, toys, furnishings, etc).

7 Features associated with historic persons (e.g. Shakespeare's birth place, Brontë country etc).

8 Stately and historic homes.

9 Religious sites (churches, abbeys, temples, mosques, shrines, etc).

10 Military features (castles, battlefields, defensive walls).

11 Genocide monuments associated with mass killings of populations (e.g. Auschwitz).

12 Towns and townscapes in groups of buildings in an urban setting.

13 Villages and hamlets of pre-20th century architecture.

14 Seaside resorts of past eras.

Chapter 5 discusses the factors that help explain the current locations of historic resources on a world scale, i.e., factors associated with:

(a) the distribution of territory held by past civilisations; and

(b) the conditions that allow historic features to survive to the present day.

Within this broad generalisation there are more fine grained patterns of distribution of specific types of historical resource within a particular country or cultural territory. For example, fortifications and defensive settlements will be concentrated in the colonial zones of past civilisations or on boundaries between the territories of different groups, for example Hadrian's Wall and the Great Wall of China marked outer boundaries of the Roman and Chinese empires respectively, while in the UK, medieval castles abound in Wales and the Welsh borders (reflecting periods of conflict and colonisation of Wales by the English) and on Britain's south coast (reflecting past power struggles between England and both France and Spain). Industrial archaeological sites will be concentrated at the sources of the power or minerals that were important at each stage of technological development, while transport routes (e.g. old railways and canals) will often be found linking these old industrial sites with the ports or centres of population of the time (e.g. Morwelham Quay, Ironbridge canals).

However, from the point of view of understanding and explaining the current patterns of tourist use and development of historic resources, this chapter has suggested that other factors are more important. These include:

1 the policies and motivation of the site owners;
2 the intrinsic attraction (size, preservation etc) of the site;
3 but, most importantly from the locational point of view, whether they occur singly, in small groups in isolated inaccessible rural locations, or in clusters in existing settlements.

HISTORIC RESOURCES AND THE DESTINATION LIFE CYCLE

Dispersed resources

These are resources that are located in places generally unrelated to modern settlement and communication patterns. Tourists' motivation must

therefore be quite strong to make the journey to such sites, so the intrinsic qualities of the resource must be high in order to attract them. Prentice (1993) suggests that tourists have a hierarchy of preferences (a 'shopping list' of attractions). They visit the most preferred site first and then those lower down the list later in the holiday or on repeat visits to the same location. This mirrors the behaviour of countryside visitors, the most beautiful and dramatic sites being the 'honeypots' which are at the top of the majority of visitors' 'shopping lists'. This behaviour fuels the development process that leads to the evolution of a hierarchy of sites with differing levels of attraction, accessibility, levels and character of tourist use. Indeed, isolated historic sites in attractive rural settings form an integral part of the network of countryside attractions, alongside the beauty spots and natural features. The process and pressures for their development is similar to that of landscape attractions (*see* Chapter 9) but the motivations of the owners of historic sites and the policy response to their development may be quite different.

Possible cycle of development of dispersed sites

Stage 1
Historic resource is authentic and may be quite inaccessible. First tourists are special interest historians travelling independently. Tourist facilities – none.

Stage 2
Tourists Numbers increase particularly at the most dramatic sites.
Facilities Some pressure for the incremental addition of tourist facilities (particularly at the most attractive sites), for example, improved access and car parking provided by property or land owner.

Stage 3
Tourists Increase in number and length of season increases. Change of type from special interest to general countryside visitor.
Facilities Private owners of historic properties recognise the contribution tourism can make to the cost of the upkeep of buildings and begin to charge for access and also wish to promote the resource to increase income.

Stage 4
Tourists Sites tend to become less authentic. Growth in number of tourists accelerates and the

explorers/special interest visitors who require authenticity visit other sites (lower in the hierarchy, or in a different undeveloped region).

Facilities The upper hierarchy sites begin to change, with commercial facilities and attractions being added to the historical resource, for example, toilets, restaurants, gift shops and activities such as carriage rides, safari parks, special events. Private owners of lower hierarchy sites begin to promote their sites.

Stage 5

Tourists Mass tourism (upper hierarchy sites visited by coach groups) but predominantly mid-centric (as psychocentric types generally not attracted to historic or rural sites).

Facilities Increased density of sites and more choice for tourist. More sites offering historic, countryside and entertainment experiences, such as the interpretation and re-enactment of historic events, the restoration and operation of industrial archaeological features such as steam railways and waterwheels, the development of historic trails in the countryside. New attractions created, for example, open-air museums, and modern reconstructions of historic features may be created away from the original site. Improvement of access and associated tourist facilities (accommodation etc).

Thus, the process leads to the incremental clustering of additional reconstructed historical and non-historical attractions at the isolated historic site in order to increase its mass appeal (and provide the tourist with a 'complete' day out not just an historic experience). There is more incentive for site owners to develop and market their property on isolated locations in order to push their site up the 'shopping list' and provide a stronger motivation for the tourist.

Very small isolated historic settlements can develop in a very similar way. Ashworth and Tunbridge (1990) liken the tourist promotion of some of the small, rurally located, monofunctional tourist–historic settlements to that of theme parks. History, culture and education are the main 'themes', with fun and entertainment being very important but secondary. They quote examples of such settlements being 'enhanced' (e.g. Williamsburg, USA) by the removal of later buildings and the rebuilding of the originals, or even totally reconstructed on site (e.g. Louisbourg, Canada).

The sites are marketed and enhanced with interpretation, staff in period costume and other attractions, making them functionally similar to theme parks. Essentially, these developments are demand-led – although some conservation might occur without tourism, they would not be developed in this style without tourist demand. Because of this there is perhaps a greater likelihood that the cycle of tourist development (described in Chapter 7) will proceed in these cases. Historic 'theme park' type sites and open air museums may face phases of stagnation and decline in the future without the constant renewal of attractions and active marketing. Johnson and Thomas (1991) suggest that this is already the case with some rural/folk open-air museums.

HISTORIC RESOURCES GROUPED IN SETTLEMENTS – HISTORIC TOWNS AND CITIES

Single outstanding historic buildings do sometimes occur as individual attractions in a city, isolated in a matrix of modern development, where comprehensive redevelopment has swept away their original context. But the nature of urban change more often leads to buildings being replaced one by one over a long period of time. Thus, the oldest part of the settlement will retain its original street pattern and sometimes a proportion of its original structures, with buildings from later periods scattered amongst them. Historic resources tend therefore to occur in clusters. The higher the proportion of old buildings the greater the historical character and attraction of the townscape will be. The most outstanding buildings may form the focus of tourist attention but the overall character of the streetscene in which they are set is also an important part of the tourist experience. Individually each of the other buildings in the street may be of lesser interest, but together they create the atmosphere of the past. In the early post-war years in Britain, conservation policies were targeted on preserving just the outstanding buildings but in the last two decades there has been a much greater recognition of the need to conserve not only the outstanding buildings such as cathedrals, market halls and main public build-

ings, etc, but also the character of their urban setting. Conservation policies have now been
extended to protect significant groups of buildings
or historic areas of the city, in the form of 'conservation areas', where each single building may not
be of great historic or architectural significance but
where together they make up an area of distinct
historic character. These may be city centres but
also include older residential or industrial zones.
The economic and political reasons why clusters of
old buildings survive together in towns and cities
are discussed in Chapter 5. Essentially their survival depended on the shift of development
pressure over the centuries to other places. Effective planning control systems have only been in
operation in the UK since the Second World War,
so conservation policies have only been available
to protect such resources from the most recent
post-war development pressures. Apart from the
abandoned 'ghost towns' (see Chapter 5), most settlements still fulfil a variety of urban functions,
even those that have been bypassed by modern
expansion and industrial development. They meet
the social, leisure, entertainment and economic
(e.g. shopping and banking) needs of their residents and these functions may be spread
throughout the city's core, not solely in the historic
quarters. Tourists may be attracted by these other
qualities of the settlement as much as to its historic
features and visitors will use these facilities as well
as visit the historic attractions. So the essential spatial differences between isolated rural clusters and
urban historic attractions are:

1 The city location may provide a wide range of
other tourist attractions within a small physical
area so that the historic significance of the place
may be just one of a collection of factors drawing
tourists to the site. In contrast, isolated rural historic sites depend solely on their own individual
qualities to attract tourists.
2 At rural sites the pressure of tourist development is concentrated on the individual sites which
each seek to fulfil as wide a range of tourist needs
as possible, whilst in urban areas the other tourist
services can be spread throughout the surrounding parts of the settlement and are not necessarily
focused in and around the historic feature itself.

Except in seaside resorts (see Chapter 8),
tourism is only one part of the normal economy of

most cities, so the impact of tourist development is
more easily absorbed in most urban areas, where it
is more diffused and less obvious than in resorts
and in many more rural regions, particularly the
remote rural regions. The cycle of tourist development in historic towns and cities is therefore
grafted onto other urban processes and is only one
part of urban change. It does not have quite the
dramatic consequences as it does in single purpose
resort settlements, so the process can be divided
into two parts:

(a) the cycle of urban change that creates the
historic resource in the first place;
(b) the cycle of tourist development of that historic resource.

Ashworth and Tunbridge (1990) propose a model
of the evolution of the historic city (see Fig 11.2).

Stage 1
The original city is established in pre-modern
times. The city provides a whole range of urban
functions, for example:

- defence – city walls, city gates, castles, forts
- ecclesiastical – cathedrals, churches, temples,
  mosques
- residential – from palaces to artisans' houses
- commercial – market halls, market places,
  guildhalls, bazaars and so on.

Stage 2
Some city growth occurs on a variable scale
(depending on the political and economic factors
noted in Chapter 5). Sometimes growth is minimal
(e.g. Aigue Morte in the South of France) or small
scale (e.g. Wells in the UK), and sometimes on a
much larger scale (e.g. Chester or York). The
resulting spatial pattern is basically one of concen-
tric zones of development, decreasing in age
towards the outskirts of the city. The original city
retains its range of functions.

Stage 3
The historic centre and CBD partially separate.

(a) Firstly the historic 'original city' is preserved from major redevelopment (though a few
individual buildings in it may be altered or
replaced). This in the past has been due to inertia,
that is the lack of pressure for redevelopment
and/or the original functions of the old buildings

being retained. In modern times deliberate policies for conservation and preservation may contain and restrain development pressures, or divert them elsewhere.

(*b*) The CBD (Central Business District where the modern urban functions of retailing, commerce and administration occur) partially relocates by shifting away from its original location in the historic core into adjacent newer parts of the inner city or city centre where some new development can occur. This may be partly a result of the con-servation policies preventing redevelopment in the old city but also due to the combination of the high cost of redevelopment and the historic buildings being physically unsuited and too expensive to adapt to modern use. The narrow streets are inaccessible to modern vehicles while the internal spaces in the buildings are too small or inconvenient for modern offices, homes or shops. Also, new commercial uses may be inhibited by the high cost of meeting modern health, fire and safety standards in such old buildings. These processes

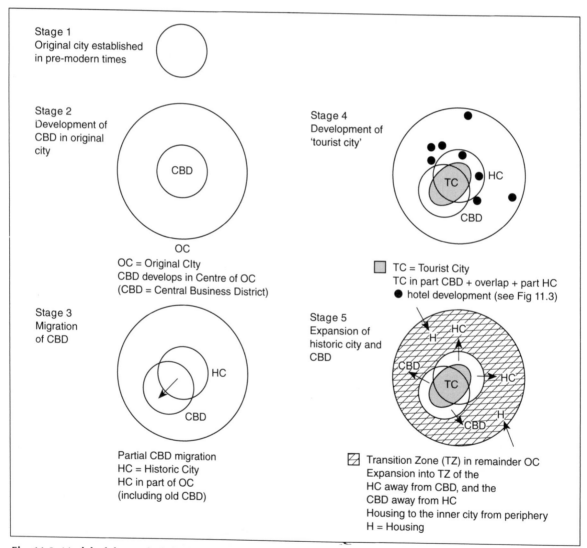

Fig. 11.2 Model of the evolution of the historic city
(*Source*: After Ashworth and Tunbridge, 1990)

result in the partial separation of the historic city and the functioning CBD and possibly to the decay and blight of the historic core, in the 'discarded' zone.

As the new CBD becomes fully established, some parts of the old city find new functions and parts retain their CBD status as the old city (the 'historic city') is conserved, restored and its environment upgraded. These changes occur as a result of deliberate conservation policies and of 'gentrification' as blighted properties fall in value and re-use becomes an economically viable proposition once more.

Ashworth and Tunbridge thus outline the processes by which the tourist resource (i.e. a conserved historic quarter of a city) is created. Their analysis continues by suggesting further stages of the model of the way in which tourism (as a new function) is grafted on to the historic city.

Stage 4

The development of the tourist city. The tourist functions include the normal range of tourist services:

1 Leisure shopping, including shopping associated with the historic character of the city, such as crafts and antiques.
2 Catering.
3 Nightlife and entertainment.
4 Other attractions including cultural attractions, such as opera, art galleries, etc, that appeal to the predominantly higher educational status historic property visitor.
5 Hotels and other accommodation.

It should be noted that most of these services (excluding hotels) will be used by the city residents as well as by tourists. Ashworth and Tunbridge conclude from empirical evidence that these services (again excluding hotels) tend to cluster together in a central zone that overlaps part of both the modern CBD and the historic centre. This zone is called the 'Tourist City'. At the same time the hotels and tourist accommodation tend to be found in a variety of suitable zones in the rest of the city (*see* Fig 11.3), mainly outside the CBD, tourist city and historic city centre, namely:

1 in traditional locations near the market or city gates of the historic city; or

2 around the main access routes and nodes: (*a*) near the railway station; (*b*) along main access roads; (*c*) on motorway and air transport interchanges on the city periphery (generally large modern hotels); or
3 in the CBD/historic city overlap (generally large modern hotels on inner city sites that have been allowed to be redeveloped); or
4 in gentrified and quality residential areas of the inner city (mostly medium-sized hotels).

Thus, it is suggested that the cycle of urban development can be extended into this fourth stage, which is characterised by the development of this 'tourist city', partly located in the CBD and partly in the historic city and the parallel development of clusters of hotels in other locations outside the city centre (as described above). The first 'historic' tourists will not necessarily be the 'explorers', as the range of urban facilities meeting midcentrics' needs already exist (for existing business and VFR tourists) and are part of normal urban life.

Stage 5

The expansion of the tourist city.
1 The final stage of the cycle sees the tourist city expanding both into the historic core and into the modern CBD, with an increase in the number and choice of tourist facilities and the creation of new tourist attractions (both historic and non-historic) and an intensification of tourist use, as numbers of tourists increase.
2 An expansion of the historic city into the oldest parts of the adjacent inner city but in the opposite direction to the CBD where new development has already occurred. This happens as conservation action is extended into now valued but previously blighted or redundant inner city zones. 'New' historic attractions are created in the form of restored townscapes (e.g. old industrial areas or waterfronts).
3 The CBD expands in the opposite direction.
4 Other parts of the inner city are gentrified and residential land uses return to the inner city as its environment is improved.

The question remains as to whether the final stages of the tourist resort cycle, i.e. stagnation and decline (*see* Chapter 7) will apply to historic cities. As most historic cities and towns are multi-functional before tourism develops, it would seem unlikely because, firstly, their economies are already

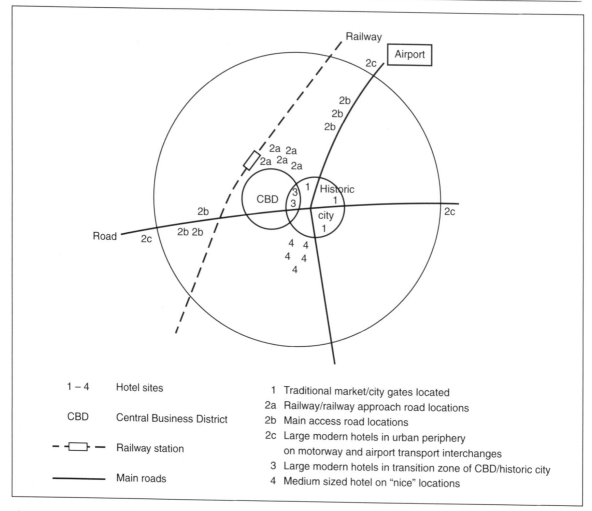

Fig. 11.3 Urban hotel locations
(*Source*: After Ashworth and Tunbridge, 1990)

diversified and tourism is only one of their business functions, and secondly, their tourist services (restaurants, attractions and hotels) already fulfil the needs of both residents and other types of tourist (e.g. business tourists). Thirdly, tight conservation policies may be able to control the overdevelopment of the historic resource itself, by regulating the pace and type of tourist development allowed in the historic core. This is done in the interests of both tourists and residents alike. The tourist appeal of the site and the quality of the tourist experience can be maintained by active tourist management in the historic city and the impacts of the tourists on the resource can be controlled.

THE IMPACTS OF TOURISM AND THEIR MANAGEMENT IN HISTORIC TOWNS

In addition to the effect tourism has on land use and the process of change in the city centre, the influx of tourists in historic cities can have two main environmental impacts:

1 Wear and tear on the physical fabric of the sites and buildings themselves.
2 Disruption of transport and patterns of pedestrian movement.

Large numbers of tourists can cause considerable damage to paths, floors and stairways just by walking through a site or building. Parts of buildings such as statues or railings can be worn away by constant touching. Inevitably tourists also bring litter and dirt. The conditions required by tourists (i.e. comfortable temperatures, humidities and light conditions) may not be consistent with the ideal environment for the preservation of the historic feature itself (for example, too much humidity or light can accelerate the decay of fabrics, books or paintings). The policy and management response will depend on the degree of authenticity and integrity required. If authenticity is important, managers may limit tourist numbers (by pricing, introducing quotas, or by limiting opening times) to a level of acceptable impact, or physically protect the resource from tourist impacts (e.g. by fencing off attractions, or providing protective coverings for surfaces). At the other extreme, managers might replace features with a modern copy when the original is worn out, or even provide a replica of the original feature elsewhere. Visitors can then be diverted to sites where their impact can be tolerated. This is perhaps more important in rural areas where visitor damage can threaten the archaeological excavation potential of the site and where spare land is available nearby.

Congestion is much more of a problem in the urban context. Twenty per cent of all visitors to British historical towns travel by coach, and the majority by car. The narrow streets of historic towns are not designed for modern vehicles, but tourist traffic seeks to penetrate as close as possible to the historic core. Tourist vehicles may be mixed with the normal business and commercial traffic in the CBD or with the residential traffic in the inner city. The solution to these problems lies with the urban planning or managing authority, not with the owners of the historical sites. In the CBD and historic core, traffic flow can be controlled through traffic management measures (lights, one-way streets, speed, weight and parking restrictions etc), but providing enough parking space in a densely developed city centre is often a major problem. There is often just not enough open space available for car and coach parking close to the historic core and conservation policies may preclude the clearing of sites; if open sites are available, their value is often too high for use as car parks, unless multi-storey car parks can be used by both workers and

shoppers in midweek and by tourists at weekends. Otherwise, towns may opt for 'park and ride' schemes, whereby large car parks are provided on open land near the edge of the settlement with frequent public transport services taking groups of visitors into the centre, effectively reducing the number of vehicles making the journey into the town centre (this has been done in Oxford, Bath and York). This solution is obviously inappropriate for coach parties; the problem here is one of routing coaches into the centre to drop off tourists as close as possible to the historic attractions and then directing the empty coach to wait in a peripheral coach park (as happens in York). This depends on the cooperation of both the tour operator and tourist to keep to timed pick up and drop off schedules in order to limit congestion at these critical inner city locations.

The gathering of large numbers of tourists on foot (for example, guided tours or queues at the entrances of buildings) can also cause major problems of congestion in the narrow streets of historic cities. The exclusion of wheeled traffic from critical areas (i.e. by creating pedestrian precincts) can ease the problem and provide a more attractive environment for the tourist. Again the implementation of such schemes depends on the design, planning and management skills of the public authority. Pedestrian flows can be influenced by the provision of information and good signposting. Some cities (e.g. Exeter) have developed historic trails that attempt to interest, inform and entertain the tourist but also to spread pedestrians more evenly through the inner city and attract them to the less well-known and less congested sites and buildings.

It is clear that public authorities have a very important role to play in the planning and management of tourism in the historic city centre. Local politicians' attitudes towards tourism will depend on their perception of the conflicts of interest between visitors and residents. Their policies will be coloured by the balance between the real financial cost of tourism and conservation to the public authority weighted against the perceived benefits to the town and its economy. Different public bodies, such as Local Planning Authorities and Tourist Boards, may be responsible for marketing and planning for tourism and this can lead to policy conflicts. The division of responsibility within a Local Authority (e.g. for traffic management, conservation and planning) may also lead to policy ambiguities and inconsistencies of priority. It is clear that the management of tourism in historic settlements can only be effective if there is coordination between:

1 the public policies and actions which conserve the historic resource and regulate land use change in the city centre (i.e. policies which regulate the progress of the cycle of development of the tourist–historic city, *see* pages 113–15); and
2 the promotion and marketing of the historic destination – a process driven by the interests of the private sector.

In the USA this is achieved by town centre management schemes which seek to coordinate the policies and action of the public and private sectors. Similar policy issues face the planners and managers of tourism in historic cities and it is difficult to separate the socio-economic impact of historic tourism from that of general urban tourism. The complex issues of the social and economic costs and benefits of urban tourism, and the city's public response are more fully discussed in Chapter 13.

REFERENCES AND FURTHER READING

Those texts marked with an asterisk are particularly recommended for further reading.

Ashworth, G J and Tunbridge, J E (1990) *The Tourist–Historic City*, Belhaven.
*De Bres, K (1994) 'Cowtowns or cathedral precincts? Two models for contemporary urban tourism', *Area*, Vol. 26, No. 1, pp.57–67.
*English Tourist Board (1991) *Maintaining the Balance*, Report of the Historic Towns working group.
*Glasson, J (1994) 'Oxford: a heritage city under pressure', *Tourism Management*, Vol. 15, No. 2, pp. 137–44.
Johnson, P and Thomas, B (1991) 'The comparative analysis of tourist activities' in Cooper, C (Ed) *Progress in Tourism, Recreation and Hospitality Management*, Vol. 3, Belhaven.
Johnson, P and Thomas, B (1992) *Tourism, Museums and the Local Economy*, Edward Elgar Publishing.
Prentice, R (1993) *Tourism and Heritage Attractions*, Routledge.
Yale, P (1991) *From Tourist Attractions to Heritage Tourism*, Elm Publications.

QUESTIONS AND DISCUSSION POINTS

1 How does the tourist development of historic sites in the countryside differ from that of historic attractions located in the city centres?

2 Why might the local politicians of a historic town be less keen to support policies to promote and maintain tourism than their equivalents in a seaside resort?

3 How important is it to maintain the 'authenticity' of a historic attraction when it is being developed and promoted for tourism?

ASSIGNMENT

Assess the historic resources and tourism issues in your nearest historic town.

Design a historic town trail for tourists that will help solve some of the tourism problems in the town (e.g. spread congestion, improve interpretation facilities etc).

CHAPTER 12

The use of cultural resources for tourism

LEARNING OBJECTIVES

After reading this chapter you should be able to
- **distinguish between ethnic and cultural tourism**
- **assess the size of the market for ethnic tourism**
- **be aware of some of the cultural changes that occur in non-western societies independently of tourism development**
- **assess the significance of cultural changes associated with ethnic tourism**
- **be aware of the complexity of the political context in which policies for cultural tourism are made.**

INTRODUCTION

Chapter 6 has described the character and spatial distribution of a range of resources that can be termed 'cultural' resources. These include the arts and entertainment facilities of modern western society that are found in many westernised resorts and most western cities. Because of their predominantly urban location and because they are used in association with other urban tourist resources, they are discussed more fully in Chapter 13 (on Urban Tourism). This chapter will concentrate on the other type of 'cultural' resource, that is, the way of life, customs, values and behaviour of the people of a country, as expressed in their religion, dress, cuisine, architecture and crafts etc. Cultural tourism depends on the differences between cultures. Most international tourists come from the relatively more affluent westernised capitalist economies of the world (*see* Chapter 15), countries that can be defined as the world's 'economic core'. There is a huge exchange of tourists between these westernised countries and there are regional cultural differences (language, cuisine etc) between them (for example, between northern and southern Europe and between Europe and North America) that may make important contributions to holiday experiences. But the similarities between the western developed countries are greater than the differences – most are secular or Christian, most are highly urbanised industrialised societies, where the influence of the family and other collectivities is declining, where important roles are being taken by 'modernising elites' and where greater autonomy of the individual is highly valued. The movement of tourists between modern western countries will have social and economic (rather than cultural) impacts on each host community, although some cultural impacts of tourism may be experienced in western countries where regional differences between tourist and host are greatest (e.g. between northern Europeans and Greek islanders, *see* Tsartas, 1992). Both the significance of the cultural element of the holiday experience and the potential for great cultural impacts on the host community will increase as western tourists venture into the non-westernised countries of the world's economic periphery (*see* Chapter 15). Harrison (1992) refers to these countries as the 'less developed' countries of the world, rather than 'Third World', 'developing' or 'underdeveloped' societies. In these countries factors such as traditional values, non-Christian religions and sometimes non-capitalist forms of economic organisation contribute to their cultural differentiation from modern western societies.

Chapter 6 notes that tourism specifically based on these special cultural resources might be termed 'ethnic' tourism, in order to distinguish this special interest market from general 'cultural' tourism. General cultural tourism sees an unusual culture as an important part of the tourist experience but more as a backdrop to general tourist activities than as the primary focus of the holiday itself. It is the local colour, festivals and costumes that attract cultural tourists, rather than specific interest in cultural practices (Wood, 1984). This chapter will discuss the market, impacts, processes of change and policy options for these two types of cultural tourism.

It should be noted that some writers refer to cultural tourism as also including the tourist use of a culture's historic and landscape resources – this has some validity as the nature of living cultures is inevitably bound up with their past and the land use landscape is a product of their way of life (both past and present). These resources are part of the destination's attraction to both the general tourist and the special interest tourist, but for the reasons explained in Chapter 11, historic and landscape resources are discussed elsewhere. This chapter chooses to concentrate on living cultures and their artistic expression and defines ethnic and cultural tourism as that which uses living cultures as the resource.

CULTURAL AND ETHNIC TOURISM

Ethnic tourism depends on first-hand experiences with the practices of another culture (Wood, 1984) and it is assumed that ethnic tourists want authentic experiences of exotic cultures. In practice, the market for the genuinely authentic experience is small – Cohen (1989) reports that only a handful of the early tourist to the hilltribes of Thailand were the original 'drifter' types (see Chapter 7) who lived with the tribal people for extended periods of time, eating their food and working with them in the fields. In the 1970s and early 1980s the typical trekkers were young travellers with little money on extended trips, wanting to avoid anything 'touristic', seeking unspoilt 'tribes', 'real adventure' and prepared to 'rough it'. In reality, Cohen reports, these young people were not prepared for the hardships of the living conditions and food of the

tribes (i.e. the authentic lifestyle of the cultures) and 'the trekkers in fact travelled in a "mini-environmental bubble" provided by the jungle company through its guides and tribal hosts' (Cohen, 1989).

A more recent study by Dearden and Harron (1992) of hilltribe trekkers between 1989 and 1990 showed them to be young (average age 28 years), highly educated, mainly professionals, teachers or students, on an extended world trip (average length six months) and travelling independently. Virtually all were from Europe, North America, or Australia/New Zealand (i.e. affluent countries of the world's economic core). The market for Australian Aboriginal cultural tourism is similar – highly educated, white collar and above average income.

The primary motivation for ethnic tourism is the cultural interaction between tourist and host (see Figs 12.1 and 12.2). Dearden and Harron conclude that the hilltribe trekkers believed that budget travel would put them in touch with local people and therefore they would be more likely to have 'authentic' experiences than mainstream tourists. They put the hilltribes as their primary motivation for trekking (followed by scenery,

Fig. 12.1 Interaction between host and guest: Thai hill village children

Fig. 12.2 Interaction between host and guest: Masai village people in Kenya

market for ethnic tourism is difficult to establish. Dearden and Harron (1992) report over 100 000 trekkers visiting the hilltribes of north Thailand in 1989/90. It has been estimated that 10 per cent of Mexico's tourists are cultural tourists (Van den Berghe, 1992). Bali, another destination mainly promoted on its cultural tourism, received about 700 000 foreign tourists in 1989 (a mixture of package tour, high-spending luxury tourists and individual budget tourists). However, surfing and beach activities are also major resources in Bali and it would be unwise to assume these were all cultural tourists, even though Bali markets itself mainly as a cultural tourist destination.

IMPACTS OF CULTURAL AND ETHNIC TOURISM

Living cultures are inevitably always changing. 'Westernisation' is just one force for change. For example, the Thai hilltribes have been greatly influenced by the action of the central Thai government, while in Bali (a province of Indonesia),

getting away from the city and seeking new experiences), but interestingly when asked about their visit after the treks were completed, seeing the hilltribes ranked only third. The whole experience and particularly the river rafting adventure activity ranked higher (*see* Fig 12.3). The size of the

Fig. 12.3 River rafting on hill village trek

Balinese culture and Balinese identity are being redefined in terms of their contribution to Indonesian national culture (i.e. 'Indonesianisation'). Thus, some ethnic groups are under pressure from their governments to conform to a more 'national' and less regionally different ethnic identity. Interaction between ethnic groups in the destination region may cause as much cultural change as the interaction with western economic and cultural forces or western tourists. Tourism may in fact be used by the parties involved to help achieve their own political and cultural objectives (e.g. in Bali – see Wood, 1984). Tourism is only one of a complex set of forces for change and it should be seen as one part of the process. The importance of the other (non-tourist) factors causing cultural change may have been underestimated by some anthropologists because some of the early ethnic tourism research projects were 'snapshot' studies completed at one point in time which therefore failed to put tourist changes into the context of longer term social and political change.

The cultural and social changes that have been attributed to tourism include:

1 Changes in the structure and values of society.

(a) Changes in social, political and economic structures, for example the creation of new institutions for the economic and/or political control of tourism (tourist boards, village councils, pressure groups, transnational companies, business associations).

(b) Changes in values and behaviour. The 'demonstration effect' of tourists is assumed to be a major influence for change. Whether tourism causes the change, or merely accelerates changes already underway is a matter of debate (Smith, 1993). The younger generation of the host community copies the behaviour and adopts the values of the western tourists they see. This then leads to changes in family relationships and the evolution of new criteria for social status. The power and influence of village elders may thus be eroded. Similarly, tourism is assumed to be instrumental in the replacement of moral values and interpersonal relationships by money values and commercial relationships.

These changes are related to tourism firstly, as an economic activity and secondly, as a means of exposing the ethnic group to other norms and values. In both cases it can be argued that, although tourism undoubtedly does have major impacts, other forms of economic activity (such as mineral development and extraction) and other forms of exposure to different cultural values (e.g. through the media – TV, radio) may have comparable or greater impacts. So it must be recognised that tourism is only one part of this process of change and should not be viewed in isolation.

2 Changes in the performance of artistic, religious or traditional practices.

(a) Material art. The presence of tourism changes ethnic arts into 'tourist arts' (i.e. arts and crafts produced by artisans belonging to ethnic groups intended ultimately for sale to an external audience – Cohen, 1992). These are artistic products that were originally made for religious or practical (or some other) use but are now made for sale to tourists, thus changing the meaning of the product to the maker. The form of the art (colours, patterns used), the way it is made (e.g. by machine instead of by hand) and the materials it is made from may also be changed to suit the tourist market. Once a product is popular, its very production may change (e.g. from being crafted by the ethnic group to being manufactured by outsiders, who make cheaper copies by mass production).

(b) Non-material art – the performing of ceremonies, ritual customs, festivals or events. Such events were traditionally associated with an achievement of a purpose for the ethnic group: the Sri Lankan 'devil dance' was originally performed to heal and exorcise (Simpson, 1993), the Tahitian (and Fijian) fire walking ceremony to obtain favours from the gods at a time when food was scarce (Zeppell, 1992). Their performance for the entertainment of tourists (for monetary gain) fundamentally changes their meaning for the performers. Only rarely is it possible for tourists to travel to the original location at the time dictated by the ritual in order to see the authentic activity performed for its original meaning (Sofield, 1991), but even here the presence of tourists may change its nature.

Material and non-material arts are thus 'commoditised' – changed from being produced for their cultural meaning to being commodities produced for sale. Again Cohen (1992) confirms that, through this type of process, tourism may change and sometimes destroy local cultures, but he states that ethnic arts 'were historically in a process of permanent though often slow, change' under the impact of internal forces and external contacts (i.e. the same forces bringing about social, behavioural and economic change). Tourism once again may not be the sole force of change, though Cohen does indicate that tourism greatly speeds up the process. The 'commoditisation' of arts and rituals (i.e. their performance or production for money) inevitably leads to a reduction in their authenticity (in that their original meaning is gone). Their authenticity (in terms of their outward appearance) may also be reduced in that, for example, dances may be modified or changed to become more appealing or entertaining to the tourist, or designs and colours of craft products changed to become more saleable. But if Cohen's view that

ethnic arts are always in process of change is accepted, then it is virtually impossible to define what was the original or authentic version of an artistic product. Therefore, if tourists are motivated by a wish to view or purchase the 'authentic' article, authenticity is as much a product of their perception (i.e. what they think of and accept as being authentic) as the article itself.

CYCLES OF TOURISM AND CULTURAL DEVELOPMENT AND CHANGE

The cycles of tourist development (*see* Chapter 7) take account of the social and economic impacts of tourism, so it might be assumed that these models (for example, Butler's) will apply unmodified to ethnic and cultural resources. Indeed the theories of tourist development produced specifically by

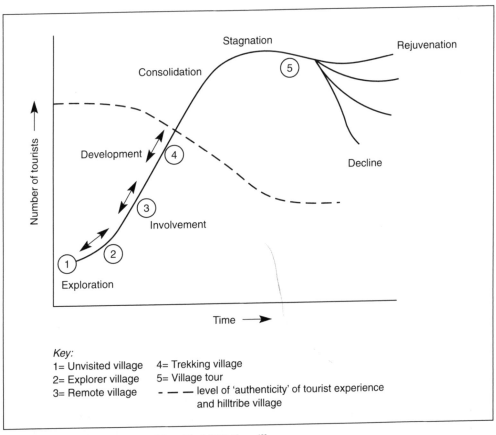

Fig. 12.4 Application of Butler's model to Thai hilltribe villages
(*Source*: After Butler, 1980 and Dearden, 1991)

anthropologists (*see* Wilson, 1993) show many consistencies with these general models, suggesting greater cultural change with increasing levels of tourism. Empirical evidence from the Thai hill-tribes (Cohen, 1989, Dearden, 1991 and 1994) confirms the postulated change in type of tourist from drifter to individual budget traveller to organised group ('mass') tourist, each accepting less 'authentic' experiences. Dearden (1991 and 1994) applies the Butler model to hilltribe trekking and relates the growth of trekking to changes in village tour organisation and with a reduction in the 'authenticity' of the encounter (*see* Fig 12.4). These changes go hand in hand with the progressive spatial spread of tourism to more and more villages. However, in the Seychelles, Wilson (1993) observes two qualitatively different types of tourism (typical of the first and final stages of the models) occurring at the same time (though in different islands in the group). He concludes that the critical factors affecting this qualitative variation were the scale of development and the control over development.

The use of these tourism development models suggests that tourism is the main cause of cultural (and other) changes. Wilson (1993), Wood (1993) and Harrison (1992) make the point that tourism is only one of the forces for social economic and cultural change.

POLICIES FOR ETHNIC AND CULTURAL TOURISM

Policies for this type of tourism are much more contentious and controversial than for other types of tourism, mainly because the resource itself is a people, who may have their own views and could participate in the policy-making process. The second reason why it is a contentious policy area is that policies for tourism (as a form of economic development) are inevitably bound up with general policies for economic development and the economic relationships between the affluent westernised countries and the less developed countries. Tourism often brings the very rich face to face with the very poor; this highlights the differences in wealth of the host and guest nations and the difference in power and status, and makes tourism at once a political, social, economic and moral issue. The moral issue raised by ethnic and cultural tourism is whether the cultural changes observed (whether as a result of tourism or not) are good or bad and who should make this judgement. The political issue raised is who should make decisions about ethnic and cultural tourism development and how should the decisions be made. Ethnic groups may not hold great economic or political power within their own countries and because they may wish to express their own identity through their special cultural practices, they may be encouraged by their national governments to conform to the national identity or even be suppressed within their own country. So, their potential for participating in political decision making may be limited. Political structures in the less developed countries may favour the interests of elite groups and not ethnic minorities, while the economic position of these countries (e.g. debts to western banks) may dictate development policies that do not favour ethnic minorities and which may accelerate cultural change. Wood (1984) notes that the relationship between governments and their local ethnic groups is complex; tourism alters the nature of politics and is also becoming a contentious issue in itself, particularly when governments impose tourism development without consultation.

Many writers on the cultural impacts of tourism and cultural tourist policies assume that:

1 the erosion of traditions is a bad trend and that cultural diversity is good; and
2 that achieving self-determination for the ethnic group will achieve the protection of tradition and maintain cultural diversity (even though Sofield (1991) warns that this may not necessarily be the case).

Traditionally, people can only make their own decisions and implement them if the political and legal frameworks of their countries make this possible (i.e. if they hold some sort of power). This generally means that opportunities for the control of tourism must be in the hands of the indigenous people and that tourism should be community driven (by 'bottom up' development). But Sofield (1991) notes that there must also be some input of policies and legislation from government (i.e. a 'top down' approach) to enable this to happen (i.e. to protect the community from commercial forces). This cooperation has happened in some cases, for example in Vanuatu (Sofield, 1991) and in Australia, where Aboriginal land rights (through land ownership and participation in National Park management) have given Aboriginals the opportunity to have considerable control over policies for the successful promotion of constraint of tourism on their land and the opportunity to become directly involved in controlling the nature of cultural tourism through their own tour operations and other commercial ventures (which with a few exceptions, they have generally chosen not to do) (Altman, 1989). The Australian Commonwealth Government has provided the legislative framework for the former and some state governments (for example, the Northern Territory) have been trying to support and encourage the latter.

It is clear that the impact of cultural and ethnic tourism is a complicated issue and that the general tourist destination development model greatly oversimplifies the situation, in that it does not take account of the other forces for change going on in a society. The policy-making framework is complex as well, because the 'resource' (i.e. the ethnic group) may be a participant in the process. Finally, policies for cultural and ethnic tourism in the non-westernised world cannot be separated from policies for 'development' as a whole.

REFERENCES AND FURTHER READING

Those texts marked with an asterisk are particularly recommended for further reading.

Altman, J (1989) 'Tourism dilemmas for Aboriginal Australians', *Annals of Tourism Research*, Vol. 16, pp. 456–76.

Cohen, E (1989) 'Primitive and remote – hill tribe trekking in Thailand', *Annals of Tourism Research*, Vol. 16, pp. 30–61.

Cohen, E (1992) 'Tourist arts', in Cooper, C P and Lockwood, A (Eds) *Progress in Tourism, Recreation and Hospitality Management*, Vol. 4, Belhaven.

Dearden, P and Harron, S (1992) 'Tourism and the hill-tribes of Thailand' in Weiler, B and Hall, C M (Eds) *Special Interest Tourism*, Belhaven.

Dearden, P (1991) 'Tourism and sustainable development in Northern Thailand', in *Geographical Review*, October, Vol. 81, No. 4, pp. 400–13.

Dearden, P (1994) 'Alternative tourism and adaptive change', *Annals of Tourism Research*, Vol. 21, pp. 81–102.

Harrison, D (1992) 'International tourism and the less developed countries – the background', in Harrison, D (Ed) *Tourism in Less Developed Countries*, Belhaven Press.

*Hitchcock, M, King, V T and Parnwell, M J G (1993) *Tourism in South East Asia*, Routledge.

*Lea, J (1988) *Tourism and Development in the Third World*, Routledge.

*Mathieson, A and Wall, G (1982) *Tourism – Economic, Physical and Social Impacts*, Longman.

Simpson, B (1993) 'Tourism and tradition from healing to heritage', *Annals of Tourism Research*, Vol. 20, pp. 164–81.

*Singh, T V, Theuns, H L and Go, F M (1989) *Towards Appropriate Tourism: the Case of Developing Countries*, Frankfurt: Peter Lang.

*Smith, V L (Ed) (1989) *Hosts and Guests – the Anthropology of Tourism*, Philadelphia: University of Pennyslvania Press.

Smith, V L (1993) 'Demonstration effect' in Khan, M A, Olsen, M D and Var, T (Eds) *VNR's Encyclopedia of Hospitality and Tourism*, New York: Van Nostrand Reinhold, pp. 629–35.

Sofield, T H B (1991) 'Sustainable ethnic tourism in the South Pacific – some principles', *Journal of Tourism Studies*, Vol. 2, No. 1, May, pp. 56–72.

Tsartas, P (1992) 'Socio-economic impacts of tourism on two Greek isles', *Annals of Tourism Research*, Vol. 19, pp. 516–33.

Van den Berghe, P L (1992) 'Tourism and the ethnic division of labour', *Annals of Tourism Research*, Vol. 19, pp. 234–49.

*Van den Berghe, P L (1993) 'Cultural impact of tourism' in Khan, M A, Olsen, M D and Var, T (Eds) *VNR's Encyclopedia of Hospitality and Tourism*, New York: Van Nostrand Reinhold, pp. 619–28.

Wilson, D (1993) 'Time and tides in the anthropology of tourism', in Hitchcock, M, King, V T and Parnwell, M J G (Eds) *Tourism in South East Asia*, Routledge.

Wood, R E (1984) 'Ethnic tourism, the state and cultural change in South East Asia', *Annals of Tourism Research*, Vol. 11, No. 3, pp. 353–74.

Wood, R E (1993) 'Tourism, culture and the sociology of development', in Hitchcock, M, King, V T and Parnwell, M J G (Eds), *Tourism in South East Asia*, Routledge.

Zeppell, H (1992) 'The festival of Pacific arts – an emerging special interest tourism event', in Weiler, B and Hall, C M (Eds), *Special Interest Tourism*, Belhaven.

QUESTIONS AND DISCUSSION POINTS

1 Much research on cultural and ethnic tourism focuses on the effects the tourist has on local cultures. Is it only a one-way process, or are tourists also influenced by the cultures they visit? If so, in what ways might they be influenced?

2 How do you think you would react if tourists from another planet in outer space came to your country as ethnic tourists to watch everyday events here (e.g. discos, weddings, funerals, etc) and perhaps even observed us taking our domestic holidays at our own seaside resorts?

3 Who do you think should make the decisions as to whether or not the ethnic resources of a less developed country should be promoted for tourism?

ASSIGNMENT

Review some of the current brochures of the special interest tours offered by outbound tour operators. Apart from trips to see the hilltribes of Thailand, can you identify any other trips that could be classified as ethnic tourism? If yes, which cultures do they visit and in which parts of the world? What sort of cultural experiences do they offer?

CHAPTER 13

The use of urban resources for tourism

After reading this chapter you should be able to
- distinguish between urban recreation and urban tourism
- identify the likely location of tourist quarters in the city
- be aware of the economic, social and environmental impact of urban tourism and urban tourist development
- understand the reasons why policies for urban tourist development are promoted in many of the older industrial cities.

INTRODUCTION

Urban tourism is tourism that takes place in towns and cities where the historic heritage is not the main attraction, even though the settlement may have some buildings pre-dating the industrial revolution. Urban tourism includes a wide range of activities and experiences from sightseeing, visiting cultural attractions (e.g. art galleries, concerts, opera, shows, museums etc), attending special events, leisure shopping, eating out and drinking, meeting people (e.g. friends and relatives), dancing and so on. Different visitors will select different combinations of these activities. Business tourism is another equally important element of urban tourism. These activities are mainly based on manmade resources (*see* Chapter 6), facilities that are used for recreation by urban residents as well as tourists. Because of this difficulty of separating leisure use from tourist use, there has been relatively little research on urban tourism, although much policy and planning effort has been put into promoting and developing urban tourism in recent years (i.e. since the mid-1980s). This has been because many urban planners and politicians have perceived the development of tourism to be a mechanism for the regeneration of declining inner city areas. Both cultural policy and tourism development (with its associated job creation potential) have been used as tools to solve some of these urban development problems. So,

once again, tourism policy must be seen in the context of other social and economic problems and policies. This chapter will start by identifying the urban tourist (as far as current research allows) and their motivation and behaviour. The chapter then discusses the spatial location of that tourist activity (as it differs from the tourist–historic city). This will be put in the context of patterns of urban change since 1980; the impacts of tourism and the policies for urban tourism will also be described.

THE URBAN TOURIST AND THE MARKET FOR URBAN TOURISM

The urban tourist is someone who lives outside a town or city but travels to that city for leisure purposes (they may be resident in the country or more likely in another town or city). A strict definition of tourism would confine the definition only to those who spend at least one night staying in the destination city. They may stay in tourist accommodation, or with friends or relatives. Many people would think of day visitors as tourists too. This would distinguish the 'tourist' from the city's residents who travel into the centre of their own town for leisure purposes (i.e. recreationists as opposed to tourists), and from those residents who use the 'tourist' facilities incidentally as part of a visit to the city centre that is mainly for other purposes (e.g. functional shopping, work, business etc). Little research has been done on the distinction between the urban tourist and urban recreationist. Surveys between 1982 and 1985 of several Dutch cities (Devanter, Kampen, Zwolle, S'Hertogenbosch and Dordrecht) (Jansen-Verbeker, 1986) suggest that on an average day one third of visitors came from beyond the city region and could be defined as tourists. More recent survey data from the UK confirms this finding: in provincial British cities between a quarter and a third of all visitors came from outside the local region (Law, 1992). They tended to be relatively infrequent visitors: 60 per cent said they came less than once in three months, more were men, and young people were relatively better represented in the tourist population. Families with children were less likely to visit cities as tourists, while slightly more tourists were highly educated than the recreationist, non-tourist visitor. Tourists tended to stay in the city centre longer than other visitors and spent more than recreationists (particularly in pubs, bars and restaurants).

According to Jansen-Verbeker the motivations of tourists and recreationists also differ. The tourist comes to the city primarily for 'a day out' (29 per cent of the sample of tourists in Dutch towns put this as the main reason for the visit), followed by shopping, professional motivations and visiting family and friends. Only 9 per cent of the tourists came primarily for sightseeing, and only 1 per cent mainly to visit museums, although 26 per cent of the tourists did actually go sightseeing and 10 per cent visited a museum. However, the most frequent tourist activities were eating out, walking around and shopping (with 50 per cent or more of the sample participating in each activity). The recreationist visits the city centre specifically for shopping and eating out.

LOCATION OF TOURISM WITHIN THE CITY

Jansen-Verbeker makes the distinction between the 'primary', 'secondary' and 'conditional' elements of the inner city as a tourist product.

The primary elements attract the tourists and consist of:

1 The leisure setting.

(a) The pleasant environment of the city centre which is made up of attractive architecture and interesting street patterns, squares, art objects, parks and green spaces, the industrial heritage, canals, rivers and harbours, historic features which add small-scale diversity. These characteristics may be spread throughout the city but Chapter 11 suggests that the oldest and most historic features will be near the city centre.

(b) The socio cultural setting which includes the language, local customs, way of life and general liveliness of the city. This will be concentrated where the natives of the city congregate. The most intensive commercial cultural and leisure activity of any city tends to be concentrated in and around its CBD.

These two sets of characteristics (the physical and socio-cultural settings) are free to the tourist, or publicly provided for citizen and tourist alike.

2 The activity place. These are the buildings or facilities in which particular tourist activities (i.e. cultural and entertainment activities) take place. They include theatres, museums, galleries, cinemas, casinos, bingo halls and so on. Some are publicly provided and some are commercial. In the past there has been a tradition of free access to public cultural facilities but in the UK this is now increasingly being replaced by a more commercial style of management. These facilities again tend to be clustered in or near the CBD, sometimes in 'cultural districts' adjacent to the CBD.

3 Secondary elements. These are not the main features attracting tourists to the city but are essential components of the tourist visit. They include all forms of catering facilities as well as a diverse range of shopping facilities (from specialist shops to malls and outdoor street markets). They are provided entirely by the commercial sector. Regular restaurants tend to be concentrated in the CBD while other food outlets (e.g. fast food, pizza parlours etc) are scattered more widely through the urban area (Smith, 1983).

4 Conditional elements. These are the parts of the tourist infrastructure that are necessary before the primary and secondary elements can be utilised. The conditional elements therefore include accessibility, parking facilities, sign posts and tourist information services. The information services may be located at transport nodes encircling the inner city (e.g. bus and railway stations, park and ride car parks, etc), but otherwise these services tend to be located as close as possible to the main tourist resources in the inner city.

It should be noted that tourist accommodation is the one service that tends to be concentrated in clusters in critical locations throughout the city, but generally outside the central area (*see* Fig 11.3, page 116). Apart from the historical resources (*see* Chapter 11), all these tourist resources are modern and manmade, so their location depends on man's contemporary economic, social and political decision making (Getz, 1993). It has been noted that many urban tourist functions are located in and around the CBD as a result of cumulative economic decision making. (Smith notes that some businesses have their own confidential definitions of ideal locations that presumably maximise sales.) The evolution and development of new tourist quarters in the inner city involve the creation of new resources and this is generally the outcome of public policy-making.

IMPACTS OF URBAN TOURIST DEVELOPMENTS

Studies of the impacts of urban tourism can be of four different types:

1 Studies of economic impacts of tourism in general (i.e. the capacity of tourism to generate jobs, the costs of generating tourism jobs, the income produced, its distribution and the scale of the multiplier effect). There have been many academic and policy related studies of this type (*see* Pearce, 1989).
2 Policy orientated studies of the particular specific impact of individual tourist developments (or types of development) mainly in terms of their economic impact, their ability to attract tourists and their impact on a city's image. Studies of this type have been carried out on attractions, conventions and conference centres, the arts, sport, special events and museums (*see* Law, 1992). However, from the discussion above it is clear that it is very difficult to separate out one element from the range of attractions and facilities used by the urban tourist.

3 Academic studies of the social impact of tourism on the city's residents, for example, on their perception of tourism and their attitudes to it.
4 Studies of the environmental impact of urban tourism developments.

The economic impacts of tourism

Tourists' impact on local economies is made via the money they spend in the tourist destination (in this case, the city). The money they spend (for example, in a shop or hotel) is used to pay the hotel or shop staff, to buy supplies and so on. This money is 're-spent' by others (i.e. the hotel and shop staff, the business' suppliers etc). This re-spending of money (which creates additional incomes to others) is called the 'multiplier effect'. The tourist multiplier can be defined as 'the number by which initial tourist expenditure must be multiplied in order to obtain the total cumulative income effect for a specified period' – Mathieson and Wall, 1982. These multipliers are generally calculated according to the type of accommodation used by each type of tourist. The main relevance for urban tourism is that hotel and guesthouse guests generate amongst the highest multipliers (and therefore benefit the local economy most), while daytrippers and those visiting friends and relatives generate much lower levels of multipliers and income generated. In terms of job creation, many studies confirm that tourism (particularly urban tourism) generates mainly female, low paid, part-time and non-union work. However, it is less frequently seasonal in the urban context; for example, only 12 per cent of the jobs created by tourism in Merseyside in 1985 (a total of 5500 jobs) were seasonal, but 49 per cent were part-time female jobs and only 17 per cent were for full-time males (Vaughan, 1990).

The impacts of specific types of tourist attractions or facilities

The results of these studies are difficult to compare; the different methods of calculating economic and job impacts make different assumptions and do not necessarily provide comparable data. A common theme is that in the UK many such developments are publicly grant-aided and are subsidised and many run at a financial loss. But the estimates of their ability to attract new tourists to a city, combined with their job creation and wider economic multiplier effects, justifies their development, even though these estimates may be rather general. It is claimed, for example, that conference and convention facilities attract delegates who spend two and a half times per day more than the average tourist. In Florida, USA, the city of Orlando attracted 1.67 million conference delegates in 1989, who contributed $1.044 billion to the local economy. Braun (1992) traces the multiplier effects of this spending throughout the different sectors of the local economy. The impact in the leading US convention cities (New York, Dallas and Chicago – each with over 2 million convention attendances) would be correspondingly greater. The jobs directly created by each facility is quite small (e.g. 125 jobs in the Birmingham National Exhibition Centre, and 62 in Manchester's GMEX), but it is maintained that the total job impact is many times greater (over 2000 in Birmingham). The arts and sports events also have measurable economic impacts (Myerscough, 1988) and do attract tourists; it is estimated that 37–40 per cent of theatre audiences are tourists and many tour operators make block bookings of successful West End musical shows to sell as part of short break London packages. Particular arts and sporting 'hallmark' events (*see* Chapter 6) are also significant: the Edinburgh Festival attracted 600 000 visitors to the city in the late 1980s, while Australia's defence of the Americas Cup yacht race (1986–7) attracted an additional 700 000 international tourists to the country. Adelaide's Grand Prix, although run at an operating loss of Aus $1–2.6 million, brought in an extra $20m to South Australia (Burgan and Mules, 1992). However, the event did not directly generate extra employment – only overtime for those already in jobs. Many other types of development have been studied (e.g. museums by Johnson and Thomas, 1992, and a range of inner city facilities by the Polytechnic of Central London, 1990). It is clear, however, that hallmark events and arts/cultural tourist facilities have a significant impact on non-residents' perception of a city. The 1988 Winter Olympics in Calgary dramatically increased levels of awareness of the venue both in the USA and Europe and changed the image of the city. But this awareness gradually declines after the event (Ritchie and Smith, 1991). Permanent new arts and sports facilities in a city may particularly influence businesses in their choice of business location. A combination of special events and new facilities appear to have good effects, for example in Glasgow, where the development and promotion of new facilities along with arts and special events led to its designation as European City of Culture in 1990, which has significantly changed its image from a negative perception of violence, slums and dereliction to a cultural city that is an attractive tourist destination (Hughes and Boyle, 1992).

The social impacts of urban tourism and attitudes of residents to the impacts of tourism development

Many studies of the impact of tourism on residents have been carried out in small rural settlements, coastal resorts, or where there is a significant cultural difference between tourist and resident. These studies (as summarised by Pearce, 1989) suggest a variety of reactions to tourism, some positive and some negative; for example, in some cases those who had business links with tourism showed a more positive attitude than other residents and some negative responses declined with distance between the tourist zone and residents' home area etc. However, these studies have been carried out in locations where 'the tourist' is reasonably easy to identify and residents can target their feelings towards a visible and identifiable group of people. This is much more difficult in the urban context, as 'the tourist' is less easy to identify: many big cities have resident communities from different ethnic and overseas backgrounds and non-locals may come to cities for other purposes besides recreational tourism, while in many cities (except the historic towns), the tourists will be overwhelmingly outnumbered by residents in the city centre. In the urban context it is perhaps more likely that local attitudes to tourism will be voiced in the political arena in terms of support or opposition to the creation of new urban images and the allocation of resources to tourism development rather than being directed at the tourists themselves (e.g. Hughes and Boyle, 1992, Critcher, 1992, Menzies, 1992). Where specific attitude surveys of urban residents have been carried out, they tend to concentrate again on attitudes to development and 'tourism' in general, rather than to the tourists. Such studies have been completed in Liverpool, Manchester and Chepstow (Polytechnic of Central London, 1990 and Jackson and Bruce, 1992). They have shown a generally favourable local attitude both to specific projects and to tourism in general.

Studies of the physical impacts of particular tourism developments

These studies tend to concentrate on the statistics of tourist developments, their impact on the city's circulation system (for example traffic, pedestrian crowding) and the nuisance effects (for example noise, litter, crime) associated with urban tourism. The Polytechnic of Central London (1990) studied 20 grant-aided urban tourism developments (ranging from Manchester's GMEX exhibition hall, to urban industrial museums, sports facilities, waterfront redevelopments and tourist accommodation). These schemes resulted in the reclamation of a total of 40 hectares of derelict land and refurbishment of 85 700 m² of buildings. In other countries, examples include the redevelopment of a 25-acre area blighted by urban decay into a cultural district in midtown Boston (with 10 theatres, 8 new galleries and a total of 400 000 sq feet of art space being built or renovated). Dockland redevelopment schemes cover much larger areas of over 200 acres (e.g. Baltimore, Bristol, London). Such surveys are often linked to statistics of the number of tourists drawn to the new developments.

POLICIES FOR URBAN TOURISM

The resources for urban tourism are all manmade and many are provided by the public sector, e.g. Jansen-Verbeker's primary element of the urban tourist resource (the physical leisure setting and the activity places) and the conditional elements (the transport, parking, information services etc). The development of urban tourism in the major cities (at least those that lack an extensive medieval historic core) is less likely to be demand-led and is less likely to evolve gradually as tourism use grows. The growth of urban tourism depends more on the conscious policy decisions of the public authorities in cities to create and promote new

tourist resources. This normally involves very large public investments in a fairly high risk industry. Nevertheless, many cities in the westernised world (particularly in the UK and the USA) have taken this course. Public expenditure by local authorities on tourist developments can never be justified on the grounds of providing a public service (as public expenditure on leisure facilities might be) because, by definition, the tourism service is provided primarily for the residents of another city and not for the local residents who are paying for it. The public investment must be justified in terms of benefits to the local population. Thus, the decision by a city to invest in tourist attractions and infrastructure is bound up with other aspects of urban planning policy: tourism is seen mainly as a solution to other urban problems and not as an isolated issue.

URBAN CHANGE AND TOURISM POLICIES

As cities grow older, their economic and physical structure changes, leading to social, physical and economic problems. Tourism development is sometimes proposed as part of the solution to these problems. In the older cities of the industrialised western countries these problems include the following:

1 The closure of old industrial manufacturing, warehouse and transport businesses ('deindustrialisation'). Some industries relocate (in new premises using new processes), either to other places in the city, or to other regions of the country, or they may even migrate to another part of the world in search of cheaper labour. This leads to a reduced demand for labour in the old city: in Manchester jobs fell from 365 000 in 1971 to 299 000 in 1981, while Sheffield lost 75 000 manufacturing jobs between 1971 and 1984.

2 The lack of new job opportunities leads to increased unemployment of blue collar workers (particularly concentrated in the inner city). In the early 1990s, white collar workers have also faced redundancy and unemployment. In Manchester in 1981 there were 27 000 looking for work, while in Sheffield unemployment averaged 14 per cent; in some parts of the inner city it reached 25 per cent.

3 Migration of population away from the inner city, leading to a declining population (e.g. Manchester's inner city population fell from 620 000 in 1951 to 297 000 in 1981).

These changes combine to create some large areas of dereliction in the inner city (e.g. old industrial areas, docks etc) which coincide with pockets of social disadvantage. The 'inner city' here is defined as the ring of oldest urban development surrounding the CBD and the old historic centre (if one exists). This zone also includes the oldest housing of the city; some housing may have been restored, conserved and 'gentrified' and occupied by the middle class, but it frequently remains poorly maintained and showing the characteristics of urban decay. Other parts of the inner city zone consist of old industrial premises often dating from the

heyday of western industrial production (for example, the Victorian period). The spatial coincidence of physical dereliction with pockets of social problems defines certain inner city areas as 'problem areas' to which public authorities are expected to respond.

Programmes for 'urban regeneration' supported by both local and central government have been set up to tackle these problems; the aims include fostering enterprise and business activities in order to provide new job opportunities, improving housing and solving inner city social problems, improving the image of the city as a whole and the physical environment of the inner city in particular by reusing old buildings and redeveloping derelict sites. It was assumed that improving the city's image was critical in attracting new business enterprise back into the city. The promotion of

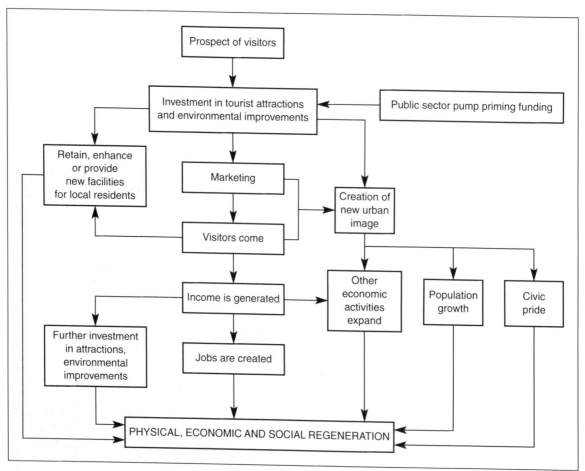

Fig. 13.1 The strategy of urban tourism
(*Source*: After Law, 1992)

tourism, perceived to be a major growth industry, particularly in the 1980s, was just one way of achieving some of these objectives. Law (1992) has summarised in Fig 13.1 the processes by which urban politicians and planners expected tourism to contribute to urban regeneration.

Different cities have selected different aspects of tourism as the focus of their development, for example Birmingham has concentrated on attracting the business tourist by investing in exhibition and conference centres and by capitalising on its location and transport links. Merseyside (in the Albert Dock development) has combined some cultural attractions with tourist shopping and business accommodation; while Manchester has combined conference tourism with cultural and urban heritage attractions. Other cities, for example Sheffield and Glasgow, have focused their tourism around sporting and cultural hallmark events with varying success. Bradford has also shown how imaginative promotion and marketing of existing attractions and the focusing on a very specific section of the market (in this case short breaks) can be effective even without massive public investment in new facilities.

Generally these developments were financed with substantial public expenditure, e.g. in Manchester about £140 million was spent on tourism capital projects in the 1980s. Many developments were joint private and public sector partnerships, with the private sector recouping their costs from the sale of housing and the renting of shop and office space in combined tourist and commercial developments. The various dockland and waterside redevelopment schemes were among the most ambitious, often managed by specially constituted Development Corporations, e.g. the London Dockland Development Corporation that is responsible for 20 km^2 of the redundant docks; and in Australia the Darling Harbour development in Sydney (on a 54 hectare site) is managed by the Darling Harbour Authority and its total development cost was Aus $2 billion (also a joint public/private venture, *see* Fig 13.2). These large scale schemes flourished in the 1980s; such developments are easier to initiate and finance in periods when property prices are rising and economic confidence is high.

Fig. 13.2 Darling Harbour, Sydney

There is no doubt that these developments have led to the physical rehabilitation of many hitherto derelict areas, transforming desolate urban landscapes into pleasant and attractive environments. The most successful have been in the areas of the inner city located close to the existing tourist city (*see* Chapter 11), i.e. close to those parts of the CBD that already provide many tourist attractions and services. Many of these developments now attract impressive numbers of tourists, for example Darling Harbour receives 20 million visitors a year, Albert Dock received three million in 1987, while the Granada Studios Tour in Manchester's Castlefield Urban Heritage Park attracted over half a million visitors in its first year. Jobs have been created (e.g. 900 in Albert Dock in the late 1980s, and an estimated 2500 in all of Manchester's inner city hotels and attractions), but this chapter has quoted evidence that the majority of jobs do not match the skills of the urban residents made redundant by the closure of industry. The cost per job (in terms of public money) is high, probably much higher than for other job-creating initiatives (Vaughan, 1990). Law (1990) concludes that for Manchester: 'tourism has so far only made a small contribution to urban regeneration in the inner city, both compared to other sectors and in relation to the needs of the area'. It has even been suggested that many local authorities have turned to tourism as a last resort, in the face of falling employment and a failure to attract 'high tech' industries (Hudson and Townsend, 1992).

The recession of the 1990s, sometimes combined with over-ambitious and over-optimistic project management during the development stage, has left some of these schemes in financial difficulties. The London docks, relying so much on associated residential and commercial property development for its financial success, have been particularly badly hit: the Butler's Wharf development, for example, went into receivership in 1990 (Menzies, 1992). Bad management in the development stages has left some authorities with huge debt burdens (e.g. Darling Harbour Authority – *see* Huxley, 1991). Such developments have also been criticised for not providing more for local people (e.g. low-cost housing). So, in terms of its contribution to urban regeneration, tourism has had some limited impact but at a relatively high cost; in terms of creating an improved environment and attractive new tourist resources in new tourist districts of the city, it has undoubtedly been very effective.

None of these newly created tourist districts have really been in existence long enough to assess whether or not their popularity with the tourist will decline; the application of the destination and product life cycle model (*see* Chapter 7) would suggest that continued marketing, updating and replacing or renewing of attractions will be necessary to maintain their viability. Studies of theme parks and open-air museums certainly suggest the life cycle model is applicable to this type of attraction. It has also been suggested (Huxley, 1991) that the proliferation of developments (particularly those that are not based on existing local culture or heritage) may reduce their attraction in the long run; the fact that the same multinational companies are involved in numerous developments in different parts of the world may lead to too great a repetition and duplication of a successful formula. In the end this may make the tourist quarters of the big cities too much alike and so reduce the essential 'uniqueness' of the tourist destination.

CONCLUSION

Urban tourist facilities fulfil the dual function of providing for the city's day-to-day leisure needs as well as for tourists; it is difficult to isolate the impacts attributable to tourism alone. Cities are multi-functional settlements and their development, growth and decay are not tied to the cycle of tourism development. Therefore, cities do not show the same characteristic pattern of cyclical tourism development as other destinations where tourism is a more significant land use and dominant economic activity. However, urban tourism policies are similar to those in other destinations in so far as tourism development is seen as a way of solving other (non-tourism related) social, economic and land use problems.

REFERENCES AND FURTHER READING

Those texts marked with an asterisk are particularly recommended for further reading.

Braun, B M (1992) 'The economic contribution of conventions: the case of Orlando, Florida', *Journal of Travel Research*, Vol. 31, Winter.

Brent Ritchie, J R and Smith, B H (1991) 'The impact of a mega-event on host region awareness: a longitudinal study', *Journal of Travel Research*, Vol. 30, No. 1, Summer.

Burgan, B and Mules, T (1992) 'Economic impacts of sporting events', *Annals of Tourism Research*, Vol. 19, pp. 700–10.

Critcher, C (1992) 'Sporting civic pride: Sheffield and the world student games' in Sugden, J and Knox, C (Eds) *Leisure in the 1990s – Rolling Back the Welfare State*, Leisure Studies Association, publication No. 46.

*Getz, D (1993) 'Planning for tourism business districts', *Annals of Tourism Research*, Vol. 20, pp. 583–600.

Hudson, R and Townsend, A (1992) 'Tourism employment and policy choices for local government' in Johnson, P and Thomas, B (Eds) *Perspectives in Tourism Policy*, Mansell.

Hughes, G and Boyle, M (1992) 'Place boosterism: political contention, leisure and culture in Glasgow' in Sugden, J and Knox, C (Eds) *Leisure in the 1990s – Rolling Back the Welfare State*, Leisure Studies Association, publication No. 46.

Huxley, M (1991) 'Making cities fun: Darling Harbour and the immobilisation of the spectacle' in Carroll, P Donohue, K, Mcgovern, M and McMillen, J (Eds) *Tourism in Australia*, Harcourt Brace Jovanovich.

Jackson, M and Bruce, D (1992) 'Monitoring and evaluating a tourism development programme: a study of Chepstow' in Johnson, P and Thomas, B (Eds) *Perspectives in Tourism Policy*, Mansell.

Jansen-Verbeker, M (1986) 'Inner city tourism: resources, tourists, promoters', *Annals of Tourism Research*, Vol. 13, pp. 79–100.

Johnson, P and Thomas, B (1992) *Tourism, Museums and the Local Economy*, Edward Elgar.

Law, C M (1992) 'Urban tourism and its contribution to economic regeneration', *Urban Studies*, Vol. 29, Nos. 3–4, pp. 599–618.

Law, C M (1993) *Urban Tourism: Attracting Visitors to Large Cities*, Mansell.

Mathieson, A and Wall, G (1982) *Tourism: Economic, Physical and Social Impacts*, Longman.

Menzies, M (1992) 'Tourism blueprint for Butler's Wharf', *Insights*, English Tourist Board.

Myerscough, J (1988) 'The economic importance of the arts in Britain', Policy Studies Institute, London.

Pearce, D D (1989) *Tourist Development*, Longman.

Polytechnic of Central London (1990) *Tourism and the Inner City: an Evaluation of the Impact of Grant-Assisted Tourism Projects*, HMSO.

Smith, S L J (1983) 'Restaurants and dining out – geography of a tourism business', *Annals of Tourism Research*, Vol. 10, pp. 515–49.

Vaughan, R (1990) 'Assessing the economic impact of tourism', in Hardy, S, Hart, T and Shaw, T (Eds) *The Role of Tourism in the Urban and Regional Economy*, Regional Studies Association.

QUESTIONS AND DISCUSSION POINTS

1 Why is urban tourism so difficult to study and why has so little research been done on urban tourism?

2 What are the different elements of the urban tourist product and who is responsible for providing and maintaining them?

3 Is tourist development the solution to problems of inner city decay?

ASSIGNMENT

You are a local councillor representing an inner city ward of one of the major cities of the UK. The city has high unemployment and there is some derelict land in your ward; it has some empty Victorian warehouses that are of considerable architectural interest. Your constituents currently use the open land in the derelict zone as a kick-about area as there are no local play spaces, playing pitches and few other local leisure facilities in the inner city.

A proposal has been put forward to redevelop the derelict land for a mixture of tourist and commercial uses; the proposal includes hotels, up-market shopping and leisure facilities and an industrial museum in the refurbished warehouses, a new (Wembley-sized) indoor hall/ arena, along with office space and executive housing. A small area of local housing will have to be demolished for the new development. The museum and arena need a major input of public money from the council for the scheme to be viable. A vote on the proposal will be taken at the next council meeting – your vote is crucial to decide whether or not the proposal goes ahead.

Will you vote in favour or against the proposal? Write notes for a speech you will give at your next local constituency meeting, explaining to your constituents why you voted in the way you did.

CHAPTER 14

Policies for tourism development and sustainable tourism

LEARNING OBJECTIVES

After reading this chapter you should be able to

- define some of the types of tourism that have been suggested as alternatives to mass tourism
- appreciate some of the ethical issues raised by mass tourism
- relate these types of tourism to the destination life cycle model
- understand the concept of 'sustainable development' and the nature of 'sustainable tourism'
- be aware of the conflicting objectives that government policies for tourism are seeking to acheive
- understand some of the problems facing governments who wish to limit the development of mass tourism.

INTRODUCTION

Tourism policies are statements of intent: they state the aims and objectives of the organisation and should include statements as to how those objectives will be achieved. In democracies very often policy statements are made in fairly generalised terms: governments represent a whole range of interest groups each of which may have different opinions about and vested interests in tourism development. Policy statements, therefore, often use rather vague terminology (that can be interpreted in many different ways). This is in order to offend as few interests as possible yet gain as much political acceptance from as wide a range of interest groups as possible (each of which interprets policy how it wishes) and to provide the widest scope for future action (that can be deemed consistent with policy) as circumstances change. Priorities between conflicting policies (e.g. between tourism and conservation) are resolved by the differential allocation of resources to the solution of each and the difference in vigour with which each policy is pursued. Government policies and action can, if the political

will exists, influence the amount and spatial location of tourism activity (e.g. Bhutan limits the total number of inbound international tourists to under 2000 per year, while the American government places limits on the numbers allowed into some National Parks). More often, government policies are much weaker and are just one factor amongst many others. Government can be on a national, regional or local level, representing the interests of different spatial combinations of the population, and there may be conflicts of interest between the different levels of government (e.g. a national tourism policy may be deemed to be in the interests of the population as a whole but may be against the interests of particular local communities or regions).

POLICY DILEMMAS

Previous chapters have underlined the fact that because the activity of 'tourism' involves travel away from home, tourist facilities provided in any location can never be used for tourism by the residents of that location (though some may be used for day-to-day leisure activities). The residents, by definition, can never benefit from the facilities in the way visiting tourists do even though the locals may be paying for them. Therefore, at the local level, tourism development must always be justified in terms of its other benefits to the community and it is consistently used to support and achieve other policy objectives. Tourism in general is justified in terms of its economic benefits (job creation, income generation, foreign exchange) (Baum, 1994), but different types of tourism are also used to support other policies, for example:

1 Urban tourism – cultural policies, physical regeneration of derelict urban areas;
2 Historic tourism – the conservation of historic resources;
3 Wildlife/nature-based tourism – to justify wildlife conservation measures;
4 Rural tourism – to support agricultural policy, stabilise population change, provide rural infrastructure (e.g. roads), landscape control.

Tourism policies, therefore, cannot be viewed in isolation, separated from general policies. They are an integral part of economic development, environmental conservation, agricultural and population policies. Governments are often tempted to overstate the positive aspects of tourism (i.e. the ways in which tourism can help achieve these various other objectives) and understate the environmental, social and cultural costs. The tourist industry itself, acting as a pressure group on governments, will very actively reinforce this tendency by 'marketing' tourism in the political arena (something that it is obviously very skilled in doing) in its attempts to influence political decision making in its favour. The policy dilemma that governments face is that having promoted or supported some tourist development (justified by its promised benefits in achieving other policy objectives), it is very difficult (in both practical and political terms) to control the growth of tourism when the social, environmental and political 'costs' become apparent, particularly if this occurs before the other policy objectives have been fully achieved. These 'costs' only become politically critical (i.e. so serious that pressure is put on governments such that they are politically unable to resist and must respond) once the destination life cycle (*see* Chapter 7) is well advanced.

The individual businesses that make up the 'tourist industry' have little interest in modifying their behaviour until the destination life cycle reaches its final stages (of stagnation or decline). Up to this stage the 'costs' have been borne by others and it is only when profits begin to fall that the industry itself will respond.

DEFINING THE PROBLEM

It is debatable whether the progress of the destination life cycle model is inevitable and that once tourism development starts it will inexorably grow. However, it is indisputable that cycles of change do occur, though the speed and character of the changes induced by tourism may not consistently follow the pattern described in the model, nor does the process always culminate in complete 'resort' development (*see* Chapters 8–13). The undesirable effects of tourism on the tourist resource, which increase as these changes unfold, have also been discussed in earlier chapters. It has generally been left to groups outside government or the tourist industry to draw attention to these problems. The research papers referred to at the end of Chapters 8–13 indicate the contribution made by academics (mainly university geographers, plus planners, sociologists and anthropologists but significantly few from Business Studies departments). These researchers have focused on identifying and understanding the scale and nature of the changes brought about by tourism on physical, biological, social and cultural resources and on the capacity of these resources to absorb tourist use. Many of these writers are in a position to conclude that non-tourist related economic activities have far greater impacts on the resources than tourism on its own. The ethical issues have been raised explicitly by a different section of society. A series of pressure groups have been set up since 1982 which have been concerned with the cultural impact of tourism, its political control and particularly the rights of local communities affected by tourism, specially those in the third world. These groups include: ECTWT (Economical Coalition on Third World Tourism, TW TEN (Third World Tourism European Network), Equations (Equitable Tourism Options), NAWET (North American Network for

Ethical Tourism), Tourism with Insight, and Tourism Concern (*see* Botterill, 1991).

Churchmen have a continuing interest in these issues and these groups not only raise the issues in the political arena but also campaign for and support the action of local communities. This is perhaps a trifle ironical in that many anthropologists cite the activity of missionaries in the third world as having far bigger and more dramatic effects on changing non-Christian cultures and practices and political power structures than tourism ever has. These groups have tended to promote the view that

1 Local communities should have more power to decide whether or not they want tourism development.
2 That they should have greater control over the distribution of the economic benefits of tourism.
3 That 'alternative' forms of tourism (i.e. alternative from mass tourism which is perceived to generate all the problems) should be encouraged.

This inevitably takes the debate into the realms of the ethics and politics of the economic relationship between first and third world countries (and of development policies in general) and the political power structures of the third world countries themselves.

This book will confine itself to discussing the debate as to whether there are any alternatives to mass tourism and, in the light of the destination life cycle model, what political action is necessary to implement them.

THE ALTERNATIVES TO MASS TOURISM

In the early 1990s, a bewildering array of different forms of tourism have been suggested as more desirable alternatives to mass tourism (Valentine, 1993). The desirable types of tourism that have some or all of the following characteristics are that:

1 The tourists behave differently to mass tourists.
2 They have different attitudes towards the resource they use compared to mass tourists.
3 The tourism is small scale (low numbers of tourists).
4 The local community (the hosts) have more control over the tourism.

These forms of tourism include:

Alternative tourism
Appropriate tourism
Community-based tourism
Ecotourism
Ethical tourism
Environmentally-friendly tourism
Green tourism
Responsible tourism
Sustainable tourism

Some of these appear to describe similar forms of tourism, but the next section provides definitions for each where the researchers have provided one.

Alternative tourism

This term does indeed seem to be all encompassing; the term has been referred to as being 'broad and vague' (Jarviluoma, 1992) or meaning 'almost anything to anyone' (Butler, 1990). Butler refers to it just as an alternative to mass tourism (implying that it is the opposite of mass tourism). Jarviluoma suggests it is 'small scale tourism developed by local people and based on local nature and culture'. Jones (1992) goes further, by summarising Krippendorf's conception of alternative tourism as 'independent, drifter travel by relatively small numbers of people to remote destinations, principally in the developing world'.

Butler (1990) notes that the assumptions behind the promotion of 'alternative' tourism are that it 'will have fewer and less severe negative effects on destination areas and their populations, without diminishing the positive economic effects, i.e. the best of all worlds'. Butler and Jarviluoma (among others) challenge these assumptions, pointing out that, for example, visitor–host interactions may be more intensive with small numbers and create more change than enclave mass tourism. This type of tourism is exactly the sort of tourism that begins the destination life cycle model and paves the way for mass tourism to develop in the new ('unspoiled') destination. In more emotive terms: 'voracious wolf in lamb's clothing, the sensitive traveller is the real perpetrator of the global spread of tourism and in this capacity must take responsibility for some of tourism's adverse impact' (Wheeler, 1992). The proponents of 'alternative' tourism give little indication of how such tourism could be managed to ensure the assumed benefit – perhaps they assume that by their own definition it needs no management or regulation.

Appropriate tourism

This term is used less widely. Where it has been defined (e.g. McIntosh and Goeldner, 1990), it is concerned with maintaining the host community's culture, identity and sense of place. It is 'tourism that actively aids in the perpetuation of an area's heritage – cultural, historical and natural' (McIntosh and Goeldner op. cit., p. 171). Characteristics of appropriate tourism are that:

1 The representatives of the indigenous population control, or have an equal voice in, the planning of interpretive programmes (this is done by interpretation training and planning).
2 Heritage is used as an conservation tool (i.e. is not exploitative or demeaning of the local population).
3 Tourists receive authentic heritage experiences.

The emphasis is, therefore, on the attitudes and behaviour of the host community, rather than the character and numbers of tourists. Indeed, it is suggested that this form of tourism can be used in both the mass tourism context and in areas that are just beginning to develop tourism. It is claimed that it is a form of sustainable tourism because it empowers local people to plan and interpret their own heritage in their own way and it is assumed that this helps perpetuate local life styles and values.

Community-based tourism

Community-based tourism is a form of tourist development decision making characterised by the participation of the local community in the decision-making process at an early stage. It has been called the 'community approach' and 'community-driven' tourism (Murphy, 1985 and 1988 and Prentice, 1993). It has been advocated in western democracies and widely debated and experimented with, for example, in the UK in the 1970s

in the context of education, housing and leisure planning. It has re-emerged to become a fashionable concept in tourism planning in the 1980s, both in the western democracies and as advocated for third world countries. This has been due to the recognition that the costs and benefits of tourism development are distributed very unequally between the local host population and 'outside' interests (e.g. national governments, multinational development companies), and that the local people often suffer more of the costs and experience less than their fair share of the benefits. Community tourism, where local people participate in decision making, is seen as a remedy to these perceived ills. The common assumptions behind the community approach are usually that

1 a unified view of what is locally acceptable can be found;
2 local communities will put a high preference on environmental quality when tourism development decisions are made.

The first assumption can be challenged in that, clearly, different members of a local population have very different interests in tourism and derive different costs and benefits from its development (see Chapter 7). The emergence of an identifiable 'local community' opinion on a particular development is much less likely to be achieved than a range of differing, often conflicting, views from different elements of the local population. Essentially, the expression of the 'local interest' depends on local politics and local power structures. Community-driven tourism planning may just expose community conflict rather than create consensus. The second assumption can also be challenged. Prentice (1993) concludes that in the North Pennines in the UK, local communities expressed an unambiguous preference for putting job creation associated with tourism development before environmental concerns. This was in an AONB (see Chapter 4) where the landscape conservation designation is made at the national level. This is a common situation in both the UK and internationally where local people may well resent the constraints imposed on them by nationally decided conservation measures.

Ecotourism

This is a term that has been used in several different ways (*see* Chapter 10), sometimes referring just to nature based tourism and sometimes (in a more value-laden way) to a particular form of non-degrading, non-damaging tourism that directly contributes to the continued protection and management of the natural resources used (*see* Valentine, 1993). It is experienced by 'environmentally and culturally sensitive' tourists who minimise their impact on the environment; thus ecotourism (used in this context) is characterised by both its contribution to conservation *and* the enjoyment of nature and by the assumption that 'enlightened travellers can even be a force for preservation' (Jenner and Smith, 1992). There are many different ways in which tourism can contribute to conservation:

1 By payment of fees for access to wildlife areas (e.g. National Parks). If the fees are paid directly to the managing authority the income generated can be used for conservation work in the area. Lindberg (1991) discusses the ethical pros and cons of this form of management and suggests multi-tier fee structures (e.g. low fees for residents and higher fees for foreigners). The justification for charging foreigners higher fees is that they do not pay taxes to support the park and do not bear the opportunity costs of not using the resources of the park for other economic activities (e.g. mineral extraction, agriculture or forestry). Lindberg points out that because many natural wildlife areas are scarce resources and each has its own special (if not unique) wildlife characteristics, the parks have, in effect, a monopoly power, and could raise park fees without loss of tourists to other parks or attractions. Lindberg also quotes evidence that some nature based tourists would be prepared to pay more. Other sources of income that can be paid direct to the managing authority might be taxes or levies on hotels near wildlife attractions (e.g. as in St Vincent and the Grenadines in the Caribbean), or by providing the visitor with more opportunities for spending (e.g. park visitor centres selling interpretive material, souvenirs etc).

2 The second way tourism can contribute to conservation is by channelling tourism income directly to local people to give them the incentive to adopt conservation measures, or inhibit them from exploitative forms of environmental use. This is done, for example, in Kenya where payments from tourism to the Masai 'compensate' them for the loss of grazing land to wild animals. In Micronesia a proposal has been made whereby local people will be required not to harvest birds, turtles, crabs or marine species from reefs on specific islets in return for capital and technical support to establish a small ecotourism venture (Valentine, 1993).

3 A third way in which ecotourism can support conservation is through the industry itself, with tour operators both educating tourists and modifying tourist behaviour (generally by example and by unobtrusive but effective psychological methods) and through the tour companies themselves voluntarily contributing to conservation research (e.g. Australia's Discovery Ecotours), or other direct conservation action (e.g. Canada's Wildland Adventures), or paying a fee or levy to the wildlife management authority. The potential role of tour operators also underlines one assumption on which ecotourism is based: that better informed and better educated tourists will behave in a way that will cause less impact on the environments they visit (e.g. by not collecting specimens, not leaving litter, by not using pollutants such as soap in natural water sources etc).

Ethical tourism

Ethics are concerned with moral questions and moral principles of right and wrong. Ethical tourism is tourism activity (by tourist, tour operator, government or any other 'actor' in the field of tourism) that conforms to a set of moral or ethical principles that might guide, for example the choice of type of holiday or its location, the way in which tour operators behave, or the sorts of tourism policies that governments produce (examples of these codes are listed by Wight, 1993). Governments may produce environmental guidelines for tourist developers (and planning systems may be capable of enforcing them by the granting of permission to develop only those conforming to the guidelines); such conditions may, for example, state that development should not degrade the environment, should minimise pollution, respect cultural features of the environment etc. Government departments and the tourist industry itself may produce guidelines for concessionaires, codes of conduct for tour operators, for example, the Tourist Industry Association of Canada's Code of Ethics for the Industry (1992) and the Australian Tourist Industry's code of environmental practice (1990). These include general statements of principle, from 'having regard for the environments in which they operate', to ensuring 'their natural ecosystems are not used beyond their sustainable capability by the activities of the tourism industry'. It is, of course, up to the operator and developer to assess whether or not their behaviour conforms to these principles. Codes of ethics have also been prepared for tourists, to try and influence their choice of holidays (for example, *The Good Tourist*, 1991) and their behaviour at the destination. These range from principles governing behaviour in other cultures to behaviour in natural environments. For example, Witty (1990) advises travellers to learn about the cultures they will visit, learn some of the language, respect local people and their religious customs, dress modestly, be aware of the impact of taking photos, be careful when bargaining to avoid economic exploitation and avoid exploiting local goodwill. The major environmental ethic presented to tourists is the simple message of 'taking nothing but photographs and leaving nothing but footprints', though this might be expanded to give more detailed advice on behaviour in the bush or countryside (e.g. the UK Countryside Commission's Country Code, or Western Australia's Department of Conservation and Land Management's Code of Ethics for recreational users of National Parks – *see* Dowling, 1991). These codes may be more accurately described as codes of conduct rather than ethical codes, but they do all reflect an underlying ethic of minimising tourism impact on the natural and cultural environment that it uses.

Green tourism

This appears to refer less to a type of tourism and more to its operation and image. It has been noted that products presented as 'green' or 'environmentally friendly' sell better (Wight, 1993). In the UK, the report *The Green Light* (produced jointly by the Countryside Commission, the English Tourist Board and the Rural Development Commission) exhorts tour operators to do an environmental audit of their operations to check whether they are using 'environmentally friendly' products (i.e. those which pollute less and consume less resources) and to support the local economy (by using local products and services). On the international scale, Green Flag International provides environmental audits for holidays, resorts and tour operators, according to their energy efficiency, waste disposal and recycling performance (*see* Wood and House, 1991). Elsewhere (Bramwell, 1990), the term 'green tourism' has been applied to a type of UK rural tourism that emphasises rural community development and community self-help, as well as environmental conservation.

Perhaps the greatest criticisms of these approaches are

1 That a 'green' image may only (rather cynically) be used by the industry to sell its products more effectively without any fundamental change in practice (Wight, 1993).
2 Environmental audits may divert attention away from more fundamental environmental issues; environmental audits may make the tourist feel good in that they are behaving in an environmentally responsible way by choosing the 'greenest' holiday. In practice, of course, this 'green' behaviour is cancelled out by the extra pollution and resources consumed by the travel itself (i.e. in the form of fuel consumed, etc). Genuinely 'green' behaviour would perhaps cut out luxury travel!

Responsible tourism

Some authors use this term in a very general, vague way, interchangeably with alternative/ appropriate/green tourism (Wheeller, 1991) to describe small scale, locally controlled, slow growth tourism that meets the needs of the individual, educated traveller. On the other hand, others (Hall, 1991) suggest that it describes the attitude of the tourist, rather than a type of tourism (although it follows that tourists behaving in a 'responsible' way may be more likely to favour the type of tourism described above). The 'responsible' tourist thus will

- learn about the destination and how the tourist can protect them
- respect the culture and privacy of the hosts
- abide by local laws and guidelines for environmental protection
- leave places as the tourist found them (or even in better condition)
- choose activities and tour operators that care for the environment
- actively contribute (in money or other ways) to protecting the environment.

This is a tourist who does more than just use environmentally-friendly products or choose the holiday with the 'greenest' image. It is a tourist who behaves in a responsible way according to the codes of ethics described above.

SUSTAINABLE TOURISM

All the types of tourism discussed so far (from 'alternative' to 'responsible' tourism) have been described as 'sustainable' tourism. The concept of sustainable development is another very vague term that can mean what the user wants it to mean. A widely accepted definition is that produced by the World Commission on Environment and Development in *Our Common Future* published in 1987 (generally known as the *Brundtland Report*): 'Sustainable development is development which meets the needs of the present without compromising the ability of future generations to meet their own needs'. In essence, sustainability is about limiting the rate of consumption of finite resources, regulating the use of renewable resources and reducing the production of harmful or wasteful emissions. A definition of sustainable tourism was put forward by Globe 90: 'meeting the needs of present tourists and hosts while protecting and enhancing opportunities for the future'.

So, sustainability as applied to tourism means regulating the use of tourist resources so that they are not consumed, depleted or polluted in such a way as to be unavailable for use by future generations of tourists. However, in Chapter 7 ways in which tourism modifies and produces cumulative changes in the environment are discussed: 'tourism in its development is essentially cyclical and that

unless specific steps are taken, tourist destination areas and resources will inevitably become over-used, unattractive and eventually experience declining use' (Butler, 1991). Thus, according to the theory of the destination life cycle, tourism inevitably 'consumes' (i.e. changes) the resource in such a way as to make it unusable for at least certain types of tourism in the future. It is clear that writers have assumed that 'appropriate/responsible' tourism is a form of tourism that causes least change to the tourist resource and is most likely to be sustainable. But this argument is countered by the observation that this type of tourism is typical of the forms of tourism that actually start or initiate the cycle of tourism development. The proliferation of this sort of tourism, far from sustaining the resource, might in fact accelerate its consumption.

However, Butler implies that 'specific steps', if taken, can change the cycle of development. These steps include:

1 Limiting tourist numbers before the impact of tourism begins to alter unacceptably the resource (i.e. alter it so much that the destination life cycle begins to progress) and/or limiting the places to which tourists have access in order to prevent the cycle starting in the first place. These constraints can only be imposed by governments. Butler notes that, according to his model, tourism development normally remains the responsibility of local government at the initial stages of the cycle and it has been shown that sometimes local people and local politics favour economic development and not environmental conservation. However, in the particular circumstances of the coincidence of interest between local indigenous communities and central government policy, backed up by strong central government control, both the political will and means of implementing the control of tourism access and numbers may exist. In these situations tourism may indeed be held at a 'sustainable' level, e.g. strong, central government was the enabling factor in Dominica, while in Vanuatu the wishes of local people coincided with central government policy; this, combined, with local control of tour operations and strong central government powers, allowed the strict control of tourism to Pentecost Island (Sofield, 1991). In Kadadu National Park (in

Northern Australia), a World Heritage site, tourism access and development is closely controlled by the majority representation of local traditional owners (Aborigines) on the Park's Board of Management and a Commonwealth Government with the political will to implement strict control policies even though they are unpopular with many visitors and some tour operators. These examples may be exceptional; local opinion on tourism development may often be divided and central government may therefore be politically unable to enforce the rather drastic measures (e.g. entry permits, prohibition of certain types of tourist etc) needed to control and restrict tourism. Pigram (1990) underlines the fact that political agreement between tourists, developers, environmental agencies and the local population is not easily obtained, particularly as a policy of sustainable tourism challenges established attitudes and modes of practice. In the absence of such agreement, strong central government action is required even more. Some authors (e.g. Wheeller, 1991) argue that addressing the issue of the huge volume of world tourism is the only way in which the problems of tourism impact will be satisfactorily dealt with. Other options may just divert attention away from the real problems and mislead the industry, policy makers and the tourists themselves into thinking that changing the nature of tourism (rather than controlling its numbers) is the solution.

2 It has been argued that a second way of inhibiting the progress of the cycle of destination development is to change the type of tourist visiting an area (from incipient mass tourism to a more enlightened and non-destructive form of tourism) (i.e. the 'alternative', 'responsible' tourism as defined earlier in this chapter). The fallacy of this argument lies in the fact that large numbers of even the most 'sensitive' and 'responsible' tourists will have a significant environmental and social impact, potentially over very extensive areas of the world. Once change is initiated, the cycle will progress, and tourism will not remain sustainable in this form (see Wheeller, 1991 and 1992, Butler, 1990 and 1991, Jones, 1992) although, as noted above, strong central government controls may be able to limit or at least constrain growth if the political will exists and the powers and resources to enforce the controls are available.

3 A third option put forward by Butler (1991) is education – of the tourist industry, governments, the tourist and the host population. He argues that the industry might modify its behaviour once it is realised that maintaining the quality of the common resource (the environment) is essential to maintain long term profitability. So far, some national, regional and international Tourist Associations have produced codes of ethics (see page 140) and support tour operator training and accreditation schemes. The sanctions available to ensure operators adhere to these codes of conduct are generally weak (e.g. refusal of Association membership which might, for example, deny access to marketing opportunities, but would not necessarily prevent an operator from continuing to trade). Decision makers in government certainly need to be informed, not only of the full range of impacts and benefits to be derived from tourism, but also (as tourism is generally part of a policy package focused on the achievement of other goals) its ability genuinely to contribute to these other objectives. Also, as governments face choices between tourism and other forms of development, they need information on the scale of the impacts and benefits of tourism compared to other types of economic activity (and, of course, compared to no development). It has been noted that for all its problems, the environmental impact of tourism may well be much less than that of other forms of environmental exploitation. Butler (1991) also notes the need for coordination between different levels and different branches of government – the latter being essential because tourism overlaps into so many other policy areas. It is clear that environmental education for the tourist may change attitudes and behaviour in the destination area. However, the mass 'sunluster' tourist may be unreceptive to such ideas and there is, of course, the danger that more environmentally-aware tourists (while forcing up standards of practice in the industry) might actually increase the demand for access to the currently untouched regions of the world and so exacerbate the problem. Environmental education of the residents of the host region is advocated on the basis that it may be possible to change the attitudes of those local populations that are currently liable to put economic development before the conservation of their local area.

CONCLUSION

Sustainable development and sustainable tourism are concepts that attract wide support. The concepts are so ill-defined that it is easy for all sections of the community to agree that they are desirable. Many writers have expressed great scepticism as to whether 'alternative' or 'responsible' tourism will be 'sustainable' in the long term. Real difficulties emerge when concepts of sustainability have to be translated into practical policies and action and only rarely does the political will exist to constrain tourism to 'sustainable' levels. Policies for tourism are normally closely tied to other economic, environmental, social and regional development issues and it cannot be studied in isolation from these other political realities.

REFERENCES AND FURTHER READING

Baum, T (1994) 'The development and implementation of national tourism policies', *Tourism Managment*, Vol. 15, No. 3, pp. 185–92.

Botterill, T D (1991) 'A new social movement: tourism concern, the first two years', *Leisure Studies*, Vol. 10, No. 3, pp. 203–17.

Bramwell, B (1990) 'Green tourism in the countryside', *Tourism Management*, Vol. 11, Dec, pp. 358–60.

Butler, R W (1990) 'Alternative tourism: pious hope or Trojan horse?', *Journal of Travel Research*, Vol. 28, No. 3, pp. 40–5.

Butler, R W (1991) 'Tourism, environment and sustainable development', *Environmental Conservation*, Vol. 18, No. 3, pp. 201–9.

Countryside Commission, English Tourist Board and Rural Development Commission (1992) *The Green Light*.

Dowling, R K (1991) 'The eco-ethics of tourism: guidelines for developers, operators and tourists', in Weiler, B (Ed) *Ecotourism – The Global Classroom*, Bureau of Tourism Research, Canberra.

Hall, C M (1991) *'An Introduction to Tourism in Australia'*, Longman Cheshire, Melbourne.

Jarviluoma, J (1992) 'Alternative tourism and the evolution of tourist areas', *Tourism Management*, Vol. 13, March, pp. 118–20.

Jenner and Smith (1992) *The Tourism Industry and the Environment*, Economist Intelligence Unit Special Report, No. 2453.

Jones, A (1992) 'Is there a real 'alternative' tourism?', *Tourism Management*, March, pp. 102–3.

Lindberg (1991) *Policies for Maximising Nature Tourism's Ecological and Economic Benefits*, World Resources Institute.

McIntosh, R W and Goeldner, C R (1990) *Tourism: Principles, Practices, Philosophies*, Wiley.

Murphy, P E (1988) 'Community driven tourism planning', *Tourism Management*, Vol. 9, pp. 96–104.

Pigram, J J (1990) 'Sustainable tourism – policy considerations', *Journal of Tourism Studies*, Vol. 1, No. 2, pp. 2–9.

Prentice, R (1993) 'Community-driven tourism planning and residents' preferences', *Tourism Management*, Vol. 14, No. 3, pp. 218–27.

*Smith, V L and Eadington, W R (Eds) (1992) *Tourism Alternatives*, Wiley.

Sofield, T H B (1991) 'Sustainable ethnic tourism in the South Pacific: some principles', *Journal of Tourism Studies*, Vol. 2, No. 1, May, pp. 56–72.

Valentine, P (1993) 'Ecotourism and nature conservation: a definition with some recent developments in Micronesia', *Tourism Management*, Vol. 14, April.

Wheeler, B (1991) 'Tourism's troubled times – responsible tourism is not the answer', *Tourism Management*, Vol. 12, June, pp. 91–6.

Wheeler, B (1992) 'Is progressive tourism appropriate?', *Tourism Management*, Vol. 13, March, pp. 104–5.

Wight, P (1993) 'Ecotourism: ethics or eco-sell?', *Journal of Travel Research*, Vol. 31, No. 3, pp. 3–9.

Witty, B (Ed) (1990) *Travel Wise and Be Welcome*, One World Travel.

Wood, K and House, S (1991) *The Good Tourist – a Worldwide Guide for the Green Traveller*, Mandarin.

QUESTIONS AND DISCUSSION POINTS

1 Why are government tourism policies often ambiguously worded?

2 Why are the so called 'alternative' forms of tourism thought to be more desirable than mass tourism?

3 What are the political difficulties facing a government that genuinely wishes to limit tourism development to a 'sustainable' level?

ASSIGNMENT

Obtain the latest tourism policies of your local authority (if it has any), or of a body such as the Countryside Commission, a National Park, or another local authority in a major tourist region.

Critically analyse the policies: are they clearly worded, what objectives do they seek to achieve, whose interests do they favour, are they 'sustainable'?

PART 2

General Patterns of World Tourism

INTRODUCTION

The first part of this book has focused on the nature of tourist resources; it has identified the many geographical resources that are used for tourism, their world distribution, their patterns of use and policy issues concerning their use.

The next part of this book concerns the tourists that use the resources: where they come from, the patterns of travel between their home and the tourist attraction and the world's regions that contain travel.

Chapter 15 begins by addressing the following questions:

1 Where do international tourists come from; i.e. which countries and regions of the world generate international tourism, and is there any clear spatial pattern of tourist generation in the world?
2 Why do these countries and regions generate tourism, i.e. what combination of social, economic and political circumstances leads to the development of international (and also domestic) tourism in a country?
3 Has the level of world tourism generation changed over time; i.e. has the performance of the world economy affected the generation of tourism on a world scale?

Chapter 15 addresses these questions and shows that tourist generation is particularly closely related to economic circumstances, and that tourist generation on a world scale is heavily concentrated in Europe, North America and, to a lesser extent, in the Pacific region.

Chapter 16 then considers world patterns of tourist travel. It seeks to answer the following questions:

1 How do transport systems evolve to link tourist generation regions with the attractions tourists wish to visit (i.e. their destinations)?
2 How are national, international and global tourist routes affected by the geographical characteristics of the earth?

3 How do tourists use these routes? Can we discern any general patterns of tourist travel between the tourist-generating and destination regions of the world?
4 Can the world be divided into coherent tourist regions on the basis of the distribution of tourist generation regions, the destination areas and the flows of tourists between them?

In general, transport routes and systems evolve (or are planned) to enable three main types of tourist movement to take place: a flow of tourists to the coast; a flow of tourists to and between urban areas; and a flow of tourists from the towns to the mountains and countryside. But on both the national and international scales, the overriding influence of the climate imposes a clear directional (i.e. towards the Equator) influence on these flows: tourists in the the Northern Hemisphere tend to travel south, while those in the Southern Hemisphere tend to travel north towards the warmer and sunnier climates. This, together with the evidence presented in Chapter 17 suggests that the world can be divided into four major tourist regions:

1 Europe and the Mediterranean basin;
2 North America, plus Mexico and the Caribbean;
3 East Asia and the Pacific; and
4 The remainder of the world's economic periphery (i.e. South America, Subsaharan Africa, South Asia and the Middle East).

These four functional tourist regions are clearly distinguishable in terms of tourist activity (both in overall volume and directional flow) but the regions are very large: they cut across the boundaries of the continents and overlap the division of the world into the economic core and periphery. In order to subdivide the world into more manageable geographical units, the remainder of this book is organised according to the more traditional units of the continents, rather than the four functional tourist regions of the world. However, this presentation should still allow the functional relationships between different parts of the world to become apparent.

CHAPTER 15

Tourist generation

LEARNING OBJECTIVES

After reading this chapter you should be able to
- list the factors necessary for tourist generation
- understand the relationship between the socio-economic development of a country and the development of its domestic and international tourism
- identify the economic core and periphery of the world
- locate the major world tourist-generating countries
- analyse and interpret economic data and tourism statistics to recognise the stage of economic and tourism development of a country
- understand the nature of the economic and tourism inter-relationships between countries of the world
- understand the factors influencing the growth of world tourism.

DETERMINANTS OF TOURIST DEMAND

Travel, whether it is within or between countries takes both time and money. Before anyone can take the decision to travel, first they must have time free of other commitments, available in long enough blocks and distributed at suitable times during the year.

Second, the individual needs money in order to utilise the time for tourism; for example, the unemployed may have plenty of time but be unable to travel widely because they cannot afford to. Their resources are used for items of greater priority (i.e. food, accommodation, clothing etc.) and they have little disposable income available. A country can only generate 'mass' tourism if time and affluence are coincidentally distributed throughout its population.

Third, political factors may constrain the individual's choice of destination, or even their freedom to travel at all. For example, governments, if motivated by economic pressures on their balance of payments, may impose limits on their citizens, perhaps curbing the amount of currency that may be spent abroad. This was experienced in Britain in the period between 1967 and 1969. On the other hand, governments may control travel more overtly for purely political reasons by limiting the individual's freedom of movement within or between countries.

These three factors – time, affluence and freedom of movement – are the necessary predisposing circumstances for tourism to take place, but even where they coincide travel will not occur unless the individual chooses to use their resources of time and money in this particular way. There may be different reasons (i.e. motivations) for travel:

1 **Religion** – an individual may wish to make a pilgrimage to a particular holy place, for instance Muslims may want to visit Mecca at least once in their lives, Hindus may desire to bathe in the Ganges, and Christians to visit Jerusalem.
2 **Business tourism** – people may be required to travel as part of their work to develop international trade, attend conferences and trade fairs, etc.
3 **Visiting friends and relatives** – immigration or jobs may lead people to settle in other countries; their friends and relatives may wish to visit them or the immigrants themselves may periodically wish to return to their old home to maintain social contact.
4 **Sport or cultural purposes** – a person may travel in order to take part in, or watch national or international cultural festivals or sporting events,

such as the Olympic Games, the World Cup, or the Cannes Film Festival.

5 Holiday travel – to take part in leisure pursuits in an 'away from home' environment. The motivation is generally that the leisure pursuit is more enjoyable away from home because, e.g. the **climate** may be better for that particular pursuit (be it sunbathing or skiing), or that travel is necessary to get to the **natural facilities** required for a given pursuit (for example, caves for potholing are located in limestone mountain regions) or the **customs** and **cuisine** are better or at least different from home, or finally, purely because travel to a particular country or resort is fashionable and tourists believe that they gain a certain sort of social acceptance or even social prestige from holiday travel. These motivations are a result of social attitudes, pressures and values of each society and the individual's response to them.

If these factors are important, one would expect to see different patterns of tourist generation in countries with different levels of economic development and affluence, and also in countries of different political, religious and social organisation.

ECONOMIC DEVELOPMENT AND THE GROWTH OF TOURISM

Time and money become more easily available to the individual in increasing quantities as a country's economy develops; the volume, type and distribution of tourism through the population changes in parallel with economic change. This process of social and economic change is best illustrated by outlining the changes that have occurred in the UK.

Social and economic change in the UK

The UK has taken around 250 years to change from an agricultural economy through a relatively well defined process of urbanisation and industrialisation and some would argue it has entered a 'post-industrial' phase of economic change. Other countries (such as those in Africa) may have only just embarked on this process, and others (e.g. Japan) have completed the transition much more quickly and in a very different way.

It is not suggested that the pattern of change shown by the UK is that necessarily followed by other countries but it does clearly illustrate the processes of social and economic change that have led to the growth of mass tourism, processes that can be identified in the current development of many countries of the world.

Medieval times to 1750 – a subsistence economy with leisure travel only for the elite

Before 1750, the UK economy was based on agriculture. Although some regions produced surpluses for export, the economy was essentially a self-sufficient economy, both nationally and regionally, with the majority of the population working very long hours on the land or as craftsmen associated with the agricultural industry.

Leisure for the majority consisted mainly as rest from toil, but life was not all work. Non-work time was devoted to socially structured activities such as religious holidays, festivals, and social occasions to celebrate festivities such as weddings, christenings, birthdays and others associated with the change of the seasons (harvest suppers, rituals to welcome spring, etc.). These activities took place at, or close to home. These occasions were, however, numerous: in the Middle Ages there were over one hundred public holidays.

Leisure in the modern sense was unknown to the general population and due to the physical difficulties of travel and the relative self-sufficiency of regions there was little motivation for the common person to travel. Only the few elite aristocracy and wealthy landed gentry, who derived enough income from their lands to support themselves and led lives of leisure, might have the motivation to travel. Before the days of modern hygiene and medicine in the UK, the wealthy travelled in search of health cures, and for social intercourse. The 'spa towns' grew up where pure, unpolluted springs of mineral water occurred, to provide accommodation for the visitors who travelled to 'take the waters' to improve their health, e.g. Bath.

The 'spas' developed a social life in the local assembly rooms, promenades, libraries and at balls 'designed to provide a concentrated urban emergence of frenetic socialising for a dispersed rural elite', an elite who 'out of season' lived on their country estates. It was not until 1752 that the use of sea water was first advocated on medical grounds.

During this pre-industrial period, culture and education were also the motivation for international travel. The young aristocracy were encouraged to travel across the Continent to Italy on the 'Grand Tour' to the city states where the cultural developments of the Renaissance were centred, e.g. Florence. Thus, domestic and international tourism was limited to a very small number of very wealthy people.

The Industrial Revolution 1750–1830: the 'loss of leisure' by the working population, but travel for the elite

As a response to the influence of Puritanism which made work a virtue and leisure an extravagant luxury, there had been a trend towards longer hours of work and fewer public holidays for the manual worker. In 1750 the Bank of England was shut on 47 days in the year, but by 1854 this was reduced to four days. These trends were reinforced by the changes of the nature of manual work with increasing industrialisation and factory work. Until the 1840s (not only in the UK but also in France and America) the average manual factory worker worked a 12-hour day (or 70-hour week). The process of industrialisation was paralleled by the rapid growth of insanitary and unhealthy urban areas, which provided very poor living conditions for the workers. The gap between the affluence and living standards of the rich and poor widened further, though some non-landed individuals who could profit from industrialisation became affluent and these 'nouveau riche' attempted to gain social acceptance and prestige by imitating the leisure habits of the aristocracy. Sea bathing (a logical extension of attempts to gain the supposed medicinal benefits of sea water), once adopted by royalty, became a fashion for everyone and by 1815 steamboat day-trips from London to North Kent coast were on offer.

The growth of domestic tourism 1830–1900

Pressure for the reform of work and urban living conditions came from both the socially motivated educated classes and from agitation by the industrial workers themselves.

In 1850 Parliament established a 50-hour week for women in the textile industry. The building industry adopted a 54-hour week in the 1870s and engineering in the 1880s. Shortening the working week created the Saturday half day holiday (while Sunday remained a sober Victorian Sabbath). Lloyds closed on Saturday afternoons in 1854, the Civil Service gained its Saturday half day holiday in the 1860s, followed by the textile operatives in 1874.

In the 19th century the annual summer holiday was also invented. It began informally with many workers taking time off work at their own risk and expense. In the north of England, however, where there was the most conflict over factory discipline, better holiday benefits were achieved. Factory owners began to acknowledge 'works weeks' as regularised weeks of holiday which were, in effect, traded in exchange for regular attendance at work. In certain industries, for example, the pottery industry in Stoke-on-Trent, works weeks are still observed. The 'potters holiday', in June, is a fortnight during which all the potteries shut down together.

However, in 1900 a holiday 'was taken for granted as a luxury which could be enjoyed at a certain level of income but which there was no special hardship in going without'. At the same time affluence began to both increase and spread throughout the population. The real national income quadrupled over the 19th century, and between 1860 and 1913 there was a 91 per cent rise in real wages, with the most rapid rise occurring in the 1870s and 1880s.

The pioneering of the railway age in the 19th century, made travel much easier and available to the masses, and the country now had a more affluent urban population with both time and the means available to travel. This led to the start of mass domestic day-trip tourism, with the first day excursion offered by railway companies running trips from London to Brighton in 1841.

The week's holiday by the sea also grew in popularity during this period of time. Blackpool, for example, developed very rapidly in the period 1840–1860 as the industrial workers holidayed by the sea in their works week.

International tourism was still limited to the affluent elite, though the motivations for travel were beginning to change. The Romantic Movement of 1840s onwards nurtured the appreciation of wild landscapes, and led to summer tourism to the mountains of Switzerland, while the need to explore and pioneer led to the development of Alpine climbing and of many geographical exploratory expeditions to more remote parts of the world as the British Empire widened.

The consolidation of the domestic tourist market and the beginnings of international tourism 1900–1950

The early years of this period saw the consolidation of domestic tourism. By 1911 it is estimated that 55 per cent of the population of England and Wales were taking day-trips to the seaside, and 20 per cent of the population were taking staying holidays on the coast.

The general trend towards greater affluence, more holidays and greater domestic tourism continued but was slowed down and punctuated by two world wars and the economic depression of the 1930s. By 1925 1½ million workers received holidays with pay and in 1938 the Holidays with Pay Act was passed. By 1945, 80 per cent of the population took paid holidays. This was reflected in the growth in use of the railway network for mass travel to the seaside for domestic summer holidays. It was the heyday of the seaside resorts.

International tourism also began to spread through a wider cross-section of the population, and winter sports holidays became fashionable. At home, the level of car ownership which was 109 000 in 1919 rose sharply to one million in 1930, and to two million in 1939, spreading the convenience of personal mobility through the population.

Growth of mass international tourism – 1950 to the present

This period is marked by the spread of affluence and leisure time through the whole population.

The decade of 1950 to 1960 was a period of post-war economic austerity and gradual recovery, and saw the transition to a more middle-class society well under way.

Holidays with pay became universal. By the 1960s 97 per cent of the population had two weeks' holiday with pay. By 1980 the vast majority had four weeks. There was a transfer of holiday travel from rail to road (car and coach). At the same time, car ownership was becoming much more widespread which quickly changed the nature of domestic tourist travel (see Fig 15.1). Access to flexible personal mobility allowed families more choice of holiday activity and destination, and railways and the seaside resorts began to decline in use.

High levels of car ownership also led to the development of new forms of holidays in the 1960s, such as camping and caravanning in new locations outside the traditional holiday resorts. International travel in the 1950s was mainly to France and Switzerland, reflecting the patterns set by the aristocracy in the previous century, but this period saw Spain becoming known first to the elite and then in the 1960s becoming the playground of the holiday masses with the expansion of air transport and holiday packages.

In the 1980s air travel became even more accessible to the general population, and the travel industry responded by providing package tours to farther flung destinations (e.g. Moscow, Morocco, The Gambia) and developing a widening net of long-haul tourist destinations. The elite responded by retreating to more distant or inaccessible parts of the world.

Patterns of domestic tourism have adjusted to these increasing levels of international tourism. The total number of main holidays in Britain has declined, leading to substantial loss of business by the traditional seaside holiday resorts, while second holidays and short breaks in Britain are on the increase.

	1950	1960	1962	1965	1968	1970	1980	1985	1987	1990	1992
Car	27	47	54	60	66	68	71	71	73	76	75
Bus/coach	27	21	18	21	16	15	12	14	14	12	11
Railway	47	30	26	21	14	13	13	10	8	7	8
Other	0	0	0	0	5	4	4	4	4	4	5

Fig. 15.1 Mode of transport to main holiday destinations in Britain
(*Source*: British National Travel Survey)

Phases in the evolution of international and domestic tourism

As exemplified by the UK experience, the process of economic development and the evolution of domestic and international tourism can be summarised as follows:

Phase 1 – a subsistence economy, society divided into peasants who have no leisure in the modern sense, and a small minority of the wealthy elite whose lives are totally leisure-orientated. This small element of the population participate in international tourism.

Phase 2 – the spread of wealth through the whole population through the processes of industrialisation, urbanisation, and institutionalisation of leisure time (in the form of holiday time from work). The development of mass domestic tourism and the provision of domestic tourist infrastructure to supply the needs of domestic tourists.

Continuation of international tourism by the small, but growing, affluent elite section of the population.

Phase 3 – increasing affluence throughout the whole population, leading to the growth of mass international tourism to nearby countries and a continuation of mass domestic tourism. The elite turn to long-haul destinations.

Phase 4 – high levels of affluence throughout the majority of the population. Diversification of mass international tourism to a greater variety of other countries. Increase in long-haul destinations and a corresponding change in domestic tourism in response to the loss of the mass main holidays to overseas competitors.

The two main factors regulating the nature and volume of tourism activity in a population are:

1 the **overall affluence** of a country (measured in terms of the Gross National Product per head of population); and

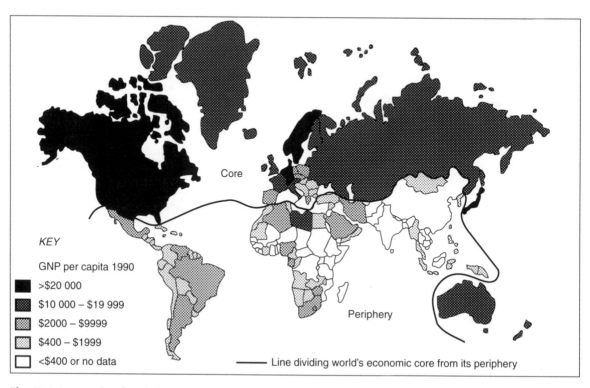

Fig. 15.2 International variations in Gross National Product per capita, 1990

2 the **social, political and economic structures and organisations** within a country that regulate the distribution of the country's wealth between the members of the population.

It might, therefore, be expected that the main tourist-generating areas of the world are those combining economic systems that generate high levels of wealth with social and political systems that allow the spread of wealth through the population as a whole.

WORLD DISTRIBUTION OF AFFLUENCE

Figure 15.2 shows international variations in the Gross National Product per capita for 1990, one of the most widely used international economic indicators. One interpretation of this world pattern would divide nations into:

1 The **affluent 'North'**, consisting of 'core' countries who play a dominant and active role in world trade – generally market-type economies which are large importers and exporters of goods, and exporters of capital.

2 The **poor 'South'**, consisting of the 'peripheral' countries whose economies are dependent on the core countries. The core countries are the source of their imports and are a destination for the products and exports of the peripheral countries.

Affluence and international tourism generation

The dominance of the 'core' or affluent 'North' in the generation of international tourism is illustrated in Fig 15.3.

This shows that roughly 93 per cent of world expenditure on international tourism is generated by the economic core. Examples of individual countries from the core show a close relationship between GNP per head and international tourist expenditure (*see* Fig 15.4).

Affluence and domestic tourism generation

Figure 15.5 shows that the economically advanced 'core' countries also have well developed domestic tourist markets, whereas some of the countries of the 'periphery' have hardly reached the stage of having even a significant level of domestic leisure travel.

International tourism expenditure 1991		
	(million US$)	(%)
The 'core'		
Europe	130 055	
North America	52 090	
East Asia and Pacific (including Japan and Australia)	45 748	
Total	227 893	92.84
The 'periphery'		
Africa	4 243	
Central/South America and Caribbean	8 418	
Middle East	3 681	
South Asia	1 245	
Total	17 587	7.17

Fig. 15.3 The generation of international tourism in the core and peripheral economies of the world (*Source*: WTO)

	International tourist expenditure 1991 ($m US)	GNP (US$ per head) 1990	Total population 1990 (million)
USA	39 418	21 700	249.9
Germany	31 650	22 730	63.2
Japan	23 983	25 430	123.6
UK	18 850	16 070	57.4
Italy	13 300	16 850	57.6
France	12 338	19 480	56.4
Canada	10 526	20 450	26.4
Netherlands	7 886	17 330	14.9
Austria	7 449	19 240	7.7
Sweden	6 104	23 680	8.6
Switzerland	5 682	32 790	6.6
Belgium	5 543	15 440	9.8
Norway	3 207	23 120	4.2

Fig. 15.4 International tourism expenditure by the world's most affluent 'core' countries (*Source*: WTO)

GNP per head 1990		Domestic nights (in all accommodation) per head of population 1990
Countries of the economic periphery		
Tanzania	120	0.029
Zaire	230	0.007
Senegal	710	0.009
Ivory Coast	730	0.035
Nicaragua	810 (1987)	0.006
Morocco	950	0.391
Syria	990	0.229
Turkey	1 620	0.122
Countries of the economic core		
Hungary	2 890	0.847
Czechoslovakia	3 140	1.621
Portugal	4 890	1.254
Spain	10 920	1.661
Belgium	15 440	2.434
Italy	16 850	2.904
Germany	22 730	3.709
Sweden	23 680	3.152
Switzerland	32 790	5.854

Fig. 15.5 Domestic tourist generation in 'core' and 'periphery' countries

VARIATIONS IN WORLD ECONOMIC ORGANISATION AND TOURIST GENERATION

It may be noted from Fig 15.2 that not all the countries with 'peripheral' economies have very low levels of GNP per head, for example, the average income per person in some of the oil exporting countries may be very high. Up to 1989 the World Bank divided the economies of the countries of the world into five types.

1 Industrial market economies – those that are in the main parliamentary democracies (e.g. all the members of OECD except Greece, Portugal and Turkey).

2 East European non-market economies – centrally planned economies which up until 1989

were all under totalitarian forms of government (for example, Albania, Bulgaria, Czechoslovakia, Hungary, Romania, USSR).

3 High income oil exporters – often Sheikdoms where wealth is concentrated in the hands of ruling families (e.g. Bahrain, Brunei, Libya, Oman, Qatar, Saudi Arabia, UAE).

4 Middle income developing countries with a 1990 GNP of over 400 US dollars per head. These have a variety of economic and political systems. These are sub-divided economically into:

(a) oil exporters (e.g. Algeria, Angola, Egypt, Indonesia, Iran, Mexico, Nigeria, Peru, Syria, Trinidad and Tobago, Tunisia, Venezuela etc.); and

(b) oil importers, such as Argentina, Greece, Israel, Portugal, Hong Kong, Singapore, and Yugoslavia which are major exporters of manufactures, plus countries that do not export manufactured goods.

5 Low income developing countries with GNP of less than 400 US dollars per head (e.g. Bangladesh, Cambodia, Chad, Haiti, Somalia, Sri Lanka, Zaire, etc.).

	International tourism expenditure (millions US dollars) 1984	% total world international tourism expenditure 1984
Industrial market economies	68 993	74.99
East European non-market economies	603	0.65
High income oil exporters	5 382	5.85
Middle income economies	16 042	17.43
Upper middle income	10 930	11.88
Low middle income	5 109	5.55
Low income economies	973	1.05
World total	93 144	100

Fig. 15.6 Types of world economies and international tourist generation

Region	1980 estimated million domestic tourist arrivals	% of world domestic tourist arrivals
Europe	1179.0	86.6
Americas	122.5	9.0
East Asia and Pacific	45.0	3.3
South Asia	6.0	0.4
Africa	4.7	0.3
Middle East	4.6	0.3

Fig. 15.7 World regional patterns of domestic tourist generation

The patterns of international tourism expenditure reflect the level of economic development and political organisation in these countries (*see* Fig 15.6). Although statistics concerning the development of domestic tourism are more fragmentary, in 1980 it was estimated that on a regional aggregate, the industrial market economies of Europe and America accounted for the vast majority of domestic tourist arrivals in the world (*see* Fig 15.7).

This confirms the fact that the most economically developed market economies of the world had reached the stage of having both a fully developed international and domestic tourist market, whereas the poorest countries of the world had yet to develop even a significant domestic market.

Thus, the characteristics of the tourist markets in the five types of economies classified by the World Bank may now be summarised as follows.

1 The industrial market economies. High values of GNP per head, wealth reasonably well spread over the whole population; well developed domestic tourism and substantial proportions taking holidays abroad (Phases 3 and 4 of the cycle of tourist market development) – *see* Fig 15.8.

Figure 15.8 shows that there is a close relationship between GNP and the proportion of the population taking any holiday away from home. As GNP reaches around 9–10 000 US dollars per head, 50 per cent or more of the population may be expected to take a holiday away from home, and as affluence increases further, the proportion of these holidaymakers that

	Departure rate 1990 (% of pop. taking at least 1 holiday of 4+ nights)	Place where holiday taken 1989 (%) Home	Abroad	GNP US dollars per head 1990
Switzerland	83	37	63	32 790
Sweden	80	45	55	23 680
Netherlands	70	42	58	17 330
Norway	70	55	45	23 120
Finland	70	55	45	26 070
West Germany	68	32	68	22 730
Denmark	66	38	63	22 090
Austria	60	30	70	19 240
UK	59	60	40	16 070
France	59	82	18	19 480
Italy	57	80	20	16 850
Belgium	56	33	67	15 440
Spain	53	90	10	10 920
Greece	52	90	10	6 000
Portugal	45	90	10	4 890

Fig. 15.8 Tourism in industrial market economies
(*Source*: TPR estimates)

go abroad increases to the point where it may even overtake the rate of domestic holiday taking (e.g. as in West Germany, Switzerland, Netherlands).

2 East European non-market economies (up to the 1989 revolutions). Middle–low income earnings measured in terms of GNP per head; wealth evenly spread through the population. Fairly well developed domestic tourism (e.g. 30–50 per cent of population taking holidays) but international travel tightly controlled and mainly between communist countries. Travel outside these countries limited to a political elite (for example, only just over five per cent of the Bulgarian population travelled abroad in 1985). (In Phase 2 of the cycle of development but further progress dependent on the removal of political constraints.)

3 High income oil exporters. These countries include those with the world's highest values of GNP per head, but wealth is generally concentrated in the hands of the few; though in some countries such as Saudi Arabia a new 'middle class' is developing. These countries have as yet no real domestic tourism, but generate small numbers of very high spending international tourists. (In Phase 1 of the cycle of tourist market development.)

4 Middle income developing countries. The more affluent countries of this group have a significant domestic tourist market at the upper level (e.g. Greece, Portugal, this may mean 40–50 per cent of the population taking a domestic holiday), and are just beginning to generate international tourists (up to ten per cent of the population). The lower income group, e.g. Syria, the Philippines, have only the beginnings of a domestic market with perhaps 2–12 per cent taking domestic holidays and have yet to generate any international tourists other than members of political or economic elites. (These countries illustrate the beginning of Phase 2 of tourist market development.)

5 Low income developing countries. This group includes the very poorest countries of the world. Virtually no domestic tourism occurs (other than perhaps limited travelling to visit relatives) and such economies generate little international tourism. (These countries illustrate Phase 1 of the cycle of tourist market development.)

The examples shown in Fig 15.5 on page 154 suggest that under one per cent of the total population take any form of domestic holiday.

Recent economic and political developments have changed this pattern to some extent, e.g. the East European non-market economies are in the process of a difficult transition towards market economies, patterns of oil production have changed a little, and world patterns of industrialisation are altering (with the development of the 'Tiger economies' of East and Southeast Asia, and the 'post-industrial' changes occurring in Europe). For the 1990s perhaps a more appropriate classification of the world's countries would divide them into the 'developing' and 'developed' economies. The 'developing' countries accounted for 14.65 per cent of the world's total tourism expenditure in 1991, while the 24 economically 'developed' countries of the OECD accounted for 83.7 per cent.

INTER-RELATIONSHIPS BETWEEN THE ECONOMIES OF THE WORLD

The world consists of over 170 countries all at different stages of economic change (or economic 'development') from highly affluent 'core' countries to the poorer peripheral countries; and all at a different phase of the development of tourism. It must be remembered that the countries of the world are closely interlinked and interdependent both in the economic sense and in terms of tourist movement.

Economic interdependence

The division of the world's economies into 'core' and 'peripheral' is based on one level of interdependence – core countries are dependent on peripheral countries for raw materials and to some extent for markets for their exports. The peripheral countries are very highly dependent on the core for capital investment and for imports, and peripheral economies will be crucially affected if the core countries change their requirements for raw materials.

A second level of interdependence relates to energy sources; all industrialised countries have increasing energy needs, and are dependent on their own or on world supplies of energy sources. The production of one of the world's main sources of energy (oil) is restricted to relatively few world locations and, thus, to relatively few countries (coal is both more widely spread and less easily transported). Therefore, the second level of economic interdependence relates to the role of oil in a country's economy, as to whether it is an oil importer or an oil exporter.

Because of these economic links, the performance of any country's economy (and, therefore, the growth of its affluence and its tourist generation capacity) cannot be considered in isolation and must be viewed in the context of the economic changes that occur throughout the world from time to time.

Interdependence of countries' tourism flows

By definition, a country that generates international tourism is economically linked to the countries which are the destinations of its tourists. The tourists of the generating country will spend money in the receiving country, and the economy of the destination may rely heavily on tourism for both the foreign income and the employment that international tourism brings. This may be particularly significant for the economically 'peripheral' countries that have few other economic resources. Any sudden changes in tourist flows between countries may, therefore, have significant economic consequences for these countries. Tourism receipts may be relatively less important to the more affluent and highly diversified 'core' economies, and any changes in tourism flows may have a less dramatic impact in these countries.

Tourism is highly sensitive to economic change. On a personal level it is likely to be one of the first items of expenditure to be cut down in times of economic hardship and will expand very rapidly (both in terms of numbers of people travelling and in terms of the amount of money they spend) when economic conditions improve. Changes in the level of economic activity in the world as a whole will inevitably have repercussions for the growth of tourism.

GROWTH OF WORLD TOURISM SINCE 1950

The total amount of international tourism in the world as a whole has been growing steadily since 1950. The same pattern of growth is shown whether tourism is measured in terms of international arrivals, tourism expenditure or tourism receipts.

When the number of arrivals is considered (*see* Fig 15.9), it can be seen that the increase in the total volume of tourism is accelerating. The average increase in numbers of arrivals per year ranged from five million a year in the early 1960s, to nine million a year by the early 1970s. This rose to nearly 13 million a year by the late 1970s and in the late 1980s the increase had grown to over 25 million arrivals per year. However, when the rate of increase is expressed in terms of the percentage

Year	International tourist arrivals (in millions)	Annual growth rate %
1950	25.3	–
1960	69.3	–
1961	75.3	8.6
1962	81.3	8.0
1963	90.0	10.7
1964	104.5	16.1
1965	112.7	7.8
1966	119.8	6.3
1967	129.5	8.1
1968	131.2	1.1
1969	143.5	9.3
1970	165.7	15.5
1971	178.8	7.8
1972	189.1	5.7
1973	198.9	5.1
1974	205.6	3.4
1975	222.9	8.0
1976	228.8	2.9
1977	249.2	8.9
1978	267.0	7.1
1979	283.0	6.0
1980	287.7	1.6
1981	289.7	0.7
1982	289.1	–0.2
1983	292.7	1.2
1984	320.1	9.3
1985	329.6	2.9
1986	340.8	3.3
1987	366.7	7.6
1988	393.8	8.6
1989	427.8	8.6
1990	455.5	6.4
1991	455.1	–0.1
1992	475.5	4.5
1993	500.1	(provisional)

Fig. 15.9 World tourism growth, 1950–1993
(*Source*: WTO)

increase of one year over the previous year, the rate of increase is shown to be much steadier: generally between four and eight per cent a year. Only rarely since 1950 has the rate of increase fallen below this band.

It has been demonstrated earlier in this chapter how tourist generation and the growth of tourism expenditure are related to economic development and how the economies of the countries of the world are interdependent. It is not surprising, therefore, that these temporary slowdowns in the rate of growth of world tourism have been related to major changes in the world economy.

1 The late 1960s. This brief check in world tourism growth coincided with the war in the Middle East and its economic consequences.

2 The mid-1970s. The pause in the growth of world tourism in 1974 and 1976 was triggered off by action taken by the oil producing and exporting countries (OPEC). The Group decided to both limit the production of oil and also raise its prices. This action had many economic implications. As far as world tourism was concerned the immediate effect was a sharp increase in the cost of travel (particularly air travel), to which tourists responded by cutting down on international travel. When the short-term impact of the price increases had been accommodated, the annual growth rate rose to 8.0 per cent in 1975. The short-term economic impact of the 'oil crisis' was a period of extremely rapid inflation in many of the world's economies, and this was reflected in the dramatic increase in total tourism receipts in the period 1977–80, but it also led to a second check in the annual growth rate of international arrivals in 1976.

3 The early 1980s. The virtual standstill in the growth of world tourism in the period 1981–3 can also be attributable to the economic implications of the oil crisis of almost ten years before. The economies of the countries of the world showed two longer-term responses to the increase in oil prices:

(*a*) The rapid inflation of the late 1970s led to a loss of purchasing power and a decrease in demand for goods and services; a general economic recession, and a decline in the rate of growth of the GNP.

(*b*) This led to widespread unemployment in many countries of the world and a reduction in

disposable income for many individuals; some people responded by cutting out international tourism altogether, others economised by going on shorter holidays and thus spending less money or choosing cheaper holiday locations. It can be noted that as in the two previous occasions, once the worst of the economic problems were over and both tourists and the travel trade had adjusted, there was once more a sudden sharp increase in the rate of growth in world tourist arrivals from −0.2 per cent in 1983 to +9.3 per cent in 1984.

Figure 15.10 summarises the impact of the oil crisis on both the world economy and on world tourist activity. The spatial impact of the recession has been uneven, with some countries and some regions of the world faring better than others. The oil producing countries were the initial beneficiaries of the economic upheavals of the 1970s and early 1980s, and their wealth increased

	Average annual growth rates (%)		
	Boom years 1960–73	Oil crisis years 1973–82	Recession and recovery years 1982–87
World economic indicators			
World industrialised nations' real production of goods and services (GNP)	5.0	2.1	3.1
World tourism indicators			
World international tourist arrivals	7.8	4.3	4.3
World scheduled airline traffic (recorded passenger miles)	13.0	6.9	6.3
World passenger car registrations	7.0	4.2	3.5

Fig. 15.10 The impact of the 1974 oil crisis on world tourism trends

dramatically. By 1981 Kuwait's GNP per head was US$19 200, while in Saudi Arabia it grew to US$14 075 per head. They were among the very few countries of the world whose tourism grew very rapidly during the period 1975–83, in terms of trips made, nights spent and in terms of travel expenditure (see Fig 15.11). Of the other countries of the world, the strongest and most affluent of the market economies (i.e. USA, West Germany, Japan, Norway, Switzerland) were least affected, but many of the weaker market economies saw a decline in international tourist activity, and the economically peripheral and the destination countries were hardest hit both from the change in the world economy and by the reduction of their revenues from tourism.

The recovery of 1987–90 saw a vigorous resumption in the growth of tourism.

4 The early 1990s. In 1991 the Middle East flared into war again, this time triggered off by conflict between two Arab states (Iraq and Kuwait) and the subsequent international intervention. The Gulf War had a world-wide impact on tourism in 1991, particularly on long-haul travel (with a drop of 35 per cent and 40 per cent in European, Western Hemisphere and Pacific long-haul travel in January and February when the conflict was at its peak). The destinations in or near the Middle East felt the greatest impact, both during the build-up of tension before the war and during the war: Jordan and Israel suffered a 30 per cent drop in tourist arrivals between August to November 1990, while numbers fell by 17 per cent in Egypt. In the early part of 1991, Jordan, Egypt and Cyprus saw further decreases in tourist arrivals. However some destinations in more distant parts of the world (e.g. in the Pacific) were hardly affected. The coincidence of the Gulf War of 1991 with another period of economic recession in the major world economies (US, Europe, Australia and Japan) led not only to this sharp decrease in arrivals in the countries near the Middle East but also to an overall drop in world tourism as a whole. There is also evidence of some slackening in demand for domestic tourism in some countries at the same time. However, growth in world tourist arrivals had resumed in 1992 (with an increase of 4.5 per cent in arrivals and 6.7 per cent in world tourist receipts over 1991).

The data for the first quarter of 1993 show that the continuing recession has caused outbound tourism from some of the major world economies to decline. For example, North American travel to many European destinations decreased, while outbound travel from Japan (to all destinations) was down by 6 per cent in the first few months of 1993. Some European countries showed a decrease in outbound tourism, though Germany seemed the most resilient in spite of the continuing economic problems caused by the costs of reunification. The regional impact of these changes varies. In North America and the Caribbean, tourism is buoyant as North American tourists opt for trips within the region and cut down on long-haul intercontinental travel. On the other hand in East Asia, those markets that rely fairly heavily on Japanese and American tourists (e.g. Korea and Taiwan) have been badly hit but otherwise tourism growth is still quite strong.

	Average growth rates % per annum 1975–83		
	Number of trips made	Number of nights spent abroad	Travel expenditure (excluding fares) at constant relative prices
Oil producing countries			
Kuwait	24.2	23.8	19.7
Saudi Arabia	18.9	17.5	11.6
Venezuela	17.5	15.4	14.4
Strongest market economies			
Switzerland	8.0	6.1	7.0
Norway	5.4	5.0	7.6
Japan	4.7	4.0	7.2
Netherlands	3.9	2.4	2.8
USA	2.9	1.7	3.5
West Germany	1.9	1.5	2.9
Weaker market economies			
Belgium/ Luxembourg	−0.3	−1.3	+0.1
Canada	−1.5	−2.8	−2.5
France	−0.6	−1.9	−0.7
Italy	−0.3	−1.2	+2.0
Mexico	−1.7	−2.9	+5.2

Fig. 15.11 The impact of the 1974 oil crisis on tourism in specific countries

CONCLUSION

This chapter has viewed the generation of tourism at a general level on a world scale, and has illustrated the relationship between the performance of the world's economy and the generation of international tourist travel. This relationship also holds good at the scale of the individual country.

A country's ability to generate tourism is related to its social, political and economic character, and this chapter suggests that each country goes through a clearly defined sequence of phases of tourist generation – from Phase 1 when only a tiny elite travel abroad, through Phases 2 and 3 when first mass domestic and then mass outbound (international) tourism develops, and through to Phase 4 when, finally, the proportion of the population travelling abroad is greater than that holidaying at home). These phases occur in parallel with economic and political change.

Different countries of the world are at different stages of economic development and tourist generation. The countries of the affluent economic core (mainly the continents of the Northern Hemisphere) currently generate the vast majority of the world's international and domestic tourists. Thus, tourist generation on a world scale is heavily concentrated in Europe, North America and, to a lesser extent, in the Pacific region. The countries of the economic periphery (essentially the poorer countries of South and Southeast Asia, Africa and Central and South America) play relatively little part in generating world international or domestic tourist travel.

FURTHER READING

World Tourism Organisation (1994) *Yearbook of Tourism Statistics*, 46th edn, Vols 1 and 2 (includes regional and country by country statistics up to and including 1992).

World Tourism Organisation (1994) *Compendium of Tourism Statistics*, 14th edn, (includes country by country summary statistics up to and including 1992).

World Tourism Organisation, *Travel and Tourism Barometer*. This is a quarterly publication with selected statistics for the year of publication.

QUESTIONS AND DISCUSSION POINTS

1 List the factors necessary for tourism to take place in a country. Is it possible to rank the factors in order of importance? If yes, on what basis have you assessed their relative importance? If not, why can the factors not be separated?

2 In which types of economy in the world would you expect the most rapid increase in:
(a) domestic tourism; and
(b) international tourism
to occur in the next few years and why?

3 What were the effects of the 1974 oil crisis on the development of world tourism? Have there been any more recent events that have had a similar effect?

ASSIGNMENTS

1 Research the economic, social and tourism history of a country other than the UK. To what extent does the development of its domestic and international tourism parallel that of the UK? What factors appear to have influenced the development of its tourism?

2 Study the data shown in Fig 15.1 on page 151. Is a bar chart or a graph the most appropriate method of plotting these data? When you have plotted the data, identify the period of time that saw the most rapid change in travel habits amongst British holidaymakers.

CHAPTER 16

Transport for tourism

LEARNING OBJECTIVES

After reading this chapter you should be able to
- understand the political and economic factors that influence the development of route systems and transport services
- be aware of the geographical factors that constrain transport networks
- be able to assess the suitability of different modes of transport for different client groups
- understand and be able to explain time differences and time zones
- locate the main European rail routes and European airports.

INTRODUCTION

A tourist cannot make use of tourist resources unless they are accessible: a transport system of some sort must link the tourists' home to their desired destination. The transport system consists of:

1 the **means of transport** (vehicles such as cars, trains, aircraft); and
2 the **network of routes** along which the vehicles travel (e.g. roads, railway tracks, air and sea lanes). The speed of travel of the vehicles along the network will govern journey times. At certain points these separate networks come together to provide interchange nodes where the traveller may change from one mode of transport to another.

Each form of transport will have different advantages in terms of speed, comfort, cost and convenience, and travellers will make appropriate choices between modes. On multi-mode journeys, the time taken to change modes at the transport nodes is perceived as part of the journey time. Therefore, improving the capacity and efficiency of the interchange facilities to handle passengers can make a significant contribution to the reduction of journey time.

PROVISION OF TRANSPORT NETWORKS ON LAND

Although circumstances vary from country to country, it is generally true that the public sector (i.e. central government or local authorities) provide most of the investment in road and rail networks. This has not always been the case, for example, the railways in Britain were originally provided by private companies during the industrial revolution, but the scale of investment in new motorways and high-speed rail tracks is now so great that private companies find it difficult to raise the capital.

Public sector provision

It is, therefore, the transport planning policies and decisions of world governments that are currently crucial in making destinations available to tourists. However, land transport networks are primarily designed to meet the needs of the commercial, industrial and commuter traffic that uses the network alongside the tourists. Only where tourism makes a significant real (or potential) contribution to a region or to a country's economy will the transport infrastructure be designed specifically to meet the needs of the holidaymaker. Governments also take the environmental impact of new road and rail developments into account and these considerations may have some influence on public investment decisions. Thus, the nature and geographical patterns of routes between tourist generating and destination areas depend not only on tourists' preferences and desires but also on the perceived balance of national costs and benefits and on the other political factors that influence governments' transport planning policies. At international level, the provision of through routes traversing more than one country will depend on the co-ordination of different national transport policies.

There are two processes by which public sector transport investment decisions are made; an incremental process by which a network is slowly adapted bit by bit in response to the needs of tourist and other traffic, and a comprehensive process by which a new transport network (or major new elements of the network) is designed in a co-ordinated way in conjunction with new tourist developments and constructed in a methodical manner to a clear plan. The incremental process could be summarised as follows:

1 tourists 'discover' and visit an area using roads designed for local economic needs;
2 the private sector responds by providing more accommodation and tourist attractions, and tourist numbers increase;
3 congestion builds up on the existing road network, particularly at nodes and settlements on the route;
4 piecemeal road improvements at the worst congestion points;
5 increased tourist (and non-tourist) traffic flows in response to gradually improving accessibility;
6 more congestion and eventual decision to add new roads (e.g. the motorways);
7 congestion of motorways; and
8 improvement of motorways.

Transport improvements have followed the growth of tourism. This process is well illustrated by the growth of tourism and improvement of the road network in southwest England. The region has always been one of the most popular holiday destinations in Britain, but road access to the peninsula has developed in a distinctly piecemeal fashion. Road improvements began with the construction of bypasses at bottlenecks and the

widening of other congested sections. Major feeder motorways (M4 and M5) linked the region to the main tourist generating areas before a distributor motorway (from Bristol into the southwest peninsula) had been constructed. The M5 was only later gradually extended to Exeter.

In contrast, the French planning system makes comprehensive planning much easier, and there have been several major integrated tourism developments.

Case study: Comprehensive planning in the Languedoc-Roussillon region of France

This region lies on the French Mediterranean coast, extending from the mouth of the Rhône westwards to the Spanish border. Before 1960 it was a backward, rural area with an ailing local economy and poor communications but with extensive underdeveloped sandy beaches. In the early 1960s, the French Government decided that the region should be developed, in order to stimulate and diversify the regional economy and to provide new tourist opportunities. A comprehensive plan was produced in 1964. Improving access and developing the tourist potential of the area were major elements of the plan but all aspects of the region's development were considered, including, for example, its agriculture, afforestation and wildlife conservation. The plan proposed five major concentrations of tourist accommodation, linked by expressways to a motorway located a little way inland. The additions and improvements to the local road network were conceived at the same time as the new tourist development, making the whole project a coherent, integrated unit. The original plan has progressively been implemented (though with some modifications in 1969 and 1972) in a systematic and orderly way, resulting in an increase in tourist bednights in the period 1968–79 from 16 million to 39 million, and an increase in visitors from 30 000 in 1961 to five million in 1990.

The process followed here is simply one of central government recognising the opportunity for tourist growth and taking the risk of making a major investment, followed by the systematic development and promotion of the scheme. In this case tourism growth has followed the process of development. Sustained tourist expansion does not always occur. The Italian Government tried to increase tourism in the extreme south of Italy by improving motorway access, but tourism has not grown as much as expected.

The modernisation and extension of rail networks is another area of public sector involvement. Again, the need to balance social and environmental considerations against commercial objectives makes public provision more appropriate, though in the 1980s in Britain the railway system was being prepared for privatisation. Europe has the densest rail network in the world, with over 140 000 km of track, built in the 19th century, on a radial pattern from the capital cities

to the frontiers. This network is currently being modernised.

A major programme of public investment in high-speed rail tracks is underway in the 1990s which will eventually result in a more co-ordinated international network of high-speed rail links in Northern Europe and a series of key routes to the Mediterranean (*see* Fig 16.1). By 1988 France had already completed their new high-speed line from Paris to Lyon, allowing TGVs (Train à Grande Vitesse) to run from Paris to Switzerland and the Côte d'Azur. Germany, too, is making major public investments in its rail system, with a specific aim of improving its north-south links.

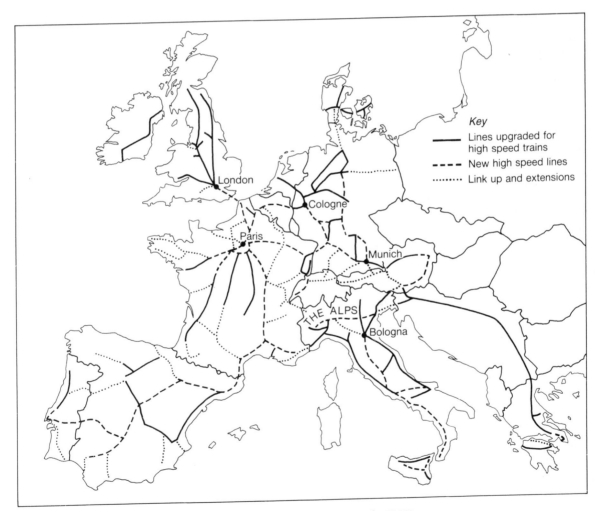

Fig. 16.1 European high-speed rail links (existing and planned network, 1989)

Private sector provision of land routes

The problems of raising enough capital and obtaining high enough returns quickly are so great that the private sector now plays relatively little part in the provision of roads and railway networks. Even though tolls are charged on many public road systems (for example, 3200 km of interstate highways in USA are toll facilities and tolls are also payable on many European motorways) the revenue is not sufficient to yield the profit required by private investors. Private companies do sometimes provide small scale tourist railways as attractions at the tourist destination (e.g. the Snowdon mountain railway) but their function is more to provide a leisure experience than a means of transport.

The influence of physical factors on road and rail networks

Surface transport routes often follow river valleys in order to take advantage of the relatively gentle gradients and level land on the valley floor. Very marshy or mountainous areas are the greatest barriers to land transport, but expensive engineering (e.g. viaducts, bridges, tunnels) can overcome most of these problems. In Europe the Alps and the Pyrénées are the major mountain barriers that obstruct the dominant north-south flow of tourists to the Mediterranean.

The major routes between France and Spain avoid the Pyrénées by skirting round the coast at either end of the mountain chain, but the Alps form a more intractable barrier and routes from Germany and Northern Europe to Italy and the former Yugoslavia are funnelled through a relatively small number of passes which are potential bottlenecks.

The approaches to the passes can be long and steep and in winter may be closed due to the weather (*see* Fig 16.2). In a few locations (e.g. Gt St Bernard Pass, St Gotthard Pass, and on the Chamonix-Courmayeur route at Mont Blanc) tunnels have been constructed that are passable during the winter but may occasionally need wheel chains on the approach roads in the worst of the snow.

Railways can climb at only very gentle gradients, and are much more limited in their choice of available routes through mountainous areas. In deeply dissected country, numerous bridges, viaducts, cuttings and tunnels are needed and are very expensive to build and maintain. The Alps still form a major barrier to the development of the European rail network, although rail links do cross the mountains, e.g. via the Lotschberg and Simplon rail tunnels. Major technical and financial

	Country	Height (m)	Maximum gradient	Winter conditions
Passes				
Gt St Bernard	Switzerland/Italy	2473	1 in 9	Usually closed Oct–June
Simplon	Switzerland/Italy	2005	1 in 9	Occasionally closed Nov–April
St Gotthard	Switzerland	2108	1 in 10	Usually closed Mid Oct–June
Splugen	Switzerland/Italy	2113	1 in 7½	Usually closed Nov–June
Brenner	Austria/Italy	1374	1 in 7	Usually open
Tunnels				
Gt St Bernard	Switzerland/Italy	1827		
Mont Blanc	France/Italy	1218		
St Gotthard	Switzerland	1157		

Fig. 16.2 Alpine passes and tunnels

problems must be overcome before such lines can be converted for high-speed trains.

Short stretches of water are generally more easily surmountable and can be crossed by bridges or tunnels for both road and rail transport. The Severn Bridge which carries the M4 from South Wales to Avon, has had an important effect on the economy of South Wales (including tourism) and has made the Pembrokeshire National Park and the beaches of the Gower Peninsula much more easily accessible from England. The level of traffic is so great that in 1993 a second Severn crossing is under construction, that will also link into the motorway system. However, the weather can also occasionally disrupt road traffic here, as the bridge may be closed for safety reasons, for example during spells of very windy weather. In this case, the railway link to South Wales passes under the Severn in a tunnel and avoids this climatic disadvantage.

The Channel Tunnel opened in 1994. It is one of the most ambitious engineering projects ever attempted, which aims to overcome the barrier of the sea crossing between England and France, and link the British road and rail systems with those of Europe. It is also one of the few major route developments which was planned to be financed by the private sector.

It is clear that networks of fixed routes on land evolve through the interplay of economic, political, physical and climatic factors, and generally depend on public investment. The interaction between governments' economic, transport and tourism policies has a crucial effect on the way in which routes are provided.

PROVISION OF TRANSPORT NETWORKS ON THE SEA AND IN THE AIR

Sea and air routes do not need to be constructed, and there are relatively few physical constraints on the movement of ships and planes. The sea and the air are freely available, and cost nothing to use; nevertheless, ships and aircraft may be required to follow specified air corridors and sea lanes for safety and environmental reasons. The direction and pattern of use of the lanes depend on the location of the transport interchanges (which are sea and airports) and the volume of traffic flows along the routes depends on demand for travel.

The operators will favour particular routes that are the most economic in terms of operating costs. Usually, the most economical route is the shortest. The shortest route between two places on the earth's surface is known as a 'great circle route'.

Great circle routes

The shortest route between Quito in Ecuador and Nairobi in Kenya is across the Atlantic along the line of the Equator. The shortest distance from London to Valencia (in Spain) is due south following the Greenwich meridian (0° longitude). The Equator and the Greenwich Meridian both divide the world into equal halves; lines such as the Equator that cut the world into two equal hemispheres are called Great Circles, and they can extend in any direction (east-west, north-south, north-west to south-east and so on). Using a globe, the course of the great circle route between any pair of places can easily be traced. But because of the distortions to shape and location caused by projecting the outlines of the world's continents from the curved surface of the globe onto a flat sheet of paper, a straight line drawn between two map locations is not necessarily a great circle route and may not be the shortest distance between them. Both ships and aircraft have the freedom to follow great circle routes.

Jet streams

Wind speeds can also affect operating costs of air travel, strong head wind by increasing fuel consumption and a tailwind reducing it. Aircraft generally fly at high altitudes (10 000+ metres) – well above the influence of surface winds.

In certain parts of the world there are winds of very high velocity blowing in the 10 000+ metre height zone. These are the jet streams, and the wind can reach speeds of over 400 km/hr, equal to the greatest speeds ever recorded at ground level. Aircraft can take advantage of the jet streams on some routes. The equatorial jet stream occurs at about 15 000 metres, and blows from the east across South Asia in the SW monsoon season. The sub-tropical jet stream occurs in a relatively narrow zone around the Poles between 12 000 and 15 000 m above the earth's surface and blows from the west, but it occurs in a relatively narrow zone

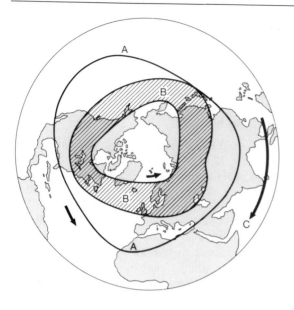

Key
A   Winter position of sub-tropical jet stream
B   Area of activity of the polar front jet stream
C   Equatorial jet stream
➤   Direction of jet streams

Fig. 16.3 Jet streams

around the Poles between 20° and 35° N and S.
The polar jet stream also blows round the Poles
from the west, at about 10 000 m and takes a variable path between latitudes 35° and 65° (*see* Fig
16.3). Where air routes coincide with the jet stream
bands, and the aircraft travels in the same direction as the jet stream, the journey time can be
substantially shortened.

Airport location

The site requirements of an airport are relatively
straightforward. It must have:

1 enough flat land with space for 3 000 metre runways and all the ancillary services and buildings;
2 no tall buildings or high land on the approaches;
3 a suitable local climate, i.e. with steady prevailing winds (as aircraft must take off into the wind),
little turbulence, or fog.

The problems of airport location stem more from
the incompatible needs to

1 be a long way from the urban population that
the airport serves in order to reduce the impact of
aircraft noise on the residents; and
2 be as close as possible to the city centre so that
the airport is accessible and the time advantages of
air travel are not squandered by a slow and inconvenient journey to the airport.

This will generate major conflicts in a densely populated area, such as the London region, where the
demand for more airport capacity is great, but
there is strong resistance by local residents to any
proposal for an additional airport in any specific
place. In London's case, proposals for a new airport at sites such as Maplin and Cublington were
each rejected in turn on environmental grounds,
and London still has no new international airport,
although Stansted is currently being expanded to
fill the gap.

However, a small airport catering specifically
for business travel has been located in inner
London itself. It is only environmentally acceptable because its use has been limited to a
particularly quiet short take-off and landing aircraft (the Dash –7) that can approach over the
Thames. An inner city airport would have been
unthinkable before this particular technical development. New airports are extremely costly to
build and once again investment on this scale has
normally come from the public sector.

Sea transport and port location

The age of long-distance sea passenger transport is
past. Ships are simply too slow to compete with
air transport over long distances. Britain is entering a period of port decline and many port
facilities, such as London, Bristol, Swansea,
Cardiff, are being redeveloped for leisure boating
and have completely lost their passenger and
freight transport function. The only passenger
ports that are thriving are ferry ports that cross
short stretches of water directly linking surface
routes on each shore.

Ferries usually keep to relatively sheltered
coastal waters, and are not subject to the full
rigours of the weather of the open oceans.

Nevertheless, winter conditions in the storm wave environments of the world (*see* Fig 3.3 on page 24) can be severe at times. Hovercraft and even ferry services from British ferry ports are occasionally disrupted.

PROVISION OF THE TRANSPORT SERVICE

Once a network of land, sea and air routes has been provided, competition between transport modes begins, and transport services develop. The private sector has a much more important role in providing transport services than in creating the infrastructure. Once a variety of services can be provided, the process of consumer choice begins and there is competition between transport modes and between the providers of services.

Travellers have varying requirements: the businessman needs quick reliable transport, preferably with space to work; the elderly need comfort; the student needs cheap travel, while the family with young children need a flexible and spacious travel mode that can adapt to the children's immediate needs. Modes of transport can be divided into independent means of travel (controlled by the individual tourist) and mass travel (where tourists travel together in groups to and from a common origin and destination).

	Independent	Mass
Cycle	X	
Car	X	
Coach		X
Train		X
Plane	*	X
Boat	*	X

* Boats and planes can be individual modes of transport for those who can afford one.

Fig. 16.4 Classification of modes of travel

Mass travel is less convenient as it usually involves at least one change of mode but it is normally cheaper than independent travel would be over the same distance.

Car travel

The tourist normally owns and controls this form of transport. The road network is extensive, and apart from toll routes, the motorist does not pay directly for the use of the system (payment is usually indirect via fuel or road tax). This provides car users with a unique level of freedom; they can control every aspect of their journey – its speed, duration, the route, the destination and the flexibility to change any of these at will during the journey itself. Finally, it is the only extensively used means of transport in which the traveller can complete the journey door to door without changing transport mode.

With all these advantages, it is not surprising that car transport is the dominant mode of travel for all world tourism. Road transport accounts for 77 per cent of all world international arrivals (particularly intra-regional travel) and in most developed countries, car transport similarly dominates the domestic tourist scene.

The main drawback of car travel to the tourist is the relatively low average speed of travel. Different countries have different speed limits, e.g. motorway speed limits are 100 kph in the Netherlands, 120 kph in Spain, and 130 kph in France and Germany. But average speeds are usually lower, and in congested conditions can be very low indeed (e.g. under 18 kph in Central London). The journey time and the fatigue experienced by the driver, as much as the cost of fuel, are the main constraints that limit the range of car-borne tourist traffic. For the European, 1 000 km appears to be a critical distance. Beyond this, too great a proportion of the holiday is taken up with getting to the destination and this tips the balance in favour of a faster, though in some respects a less convenient, form of mass transport.

Coach travel

As coaches use the same road networks, coach travel is almost as flexible as car travel in the choice of routes and destinations available, though the size and weight of the vehicle make some routes (particularly narrow scenic country lanes) and destinations (such as the streets of historic towns) inaccessible. The coach operator, therefore, can tailor the coach tour or scheduled service to the needs of the tourist. But the fact that coach travel is a form of mass transport immediately makes it less attractive to the user, though it is a relatively cheap form of transport; and scheduled services are mainly for non-car owners. Coach travel is ideally suited for two forms of tourist travel:

1 **circuit tours**; and
2 **transfer of mass tourists**, e.g. airport to hotel, airport to city centre.

Coach travel is generally the cheapest form of long-distance mass travel, but is, perhaps, the least comfortable.

Rail travel

Rail travel was the dominant form of mass public transport before the car age in the developed economies, and still remains the main travel mode in less developed countries, such as India. It is significant, however, that as affluence increases and car ownership extends through the population, rail travel declines. In spite of being a faster mode than the passenger car (the average speed of high-speed train services is 250 kph, though such trains are capable of 400 kph) its great limitation is the range of routes available. Train services are limited to the network of tracks, which usually form a radial pattern from the major conurbations, reflecting the spatial needs of freight, commuter and business traffic rather than holiday tourist flows.

It has been noted that railways are generally publicly owned and run, so the nature of the network, the cost (and level of subsidy) and type of service provided depends on government policy. France and Germany lead Europe in terms of investment in and subsidy of public transport and France is actually extending its range of high-speed train routes (TGVs). In France the use of the railway system (excluding the metros) has increased (in terms of passenger km) by 27 per cent between 1974 and 1984. In Britain, on the other hand, subsidies for public transport were gradually withdrawn during the 1980s, reinforcing the downward trend in tourist usage of trains.

Trains are on the decline as transcontinental passenger modes. The huge investment needed to

convert long-distance routes for high-speed trains is not justified by the current numbers of passengers. Canada is cutting its government funding for the railways and in 1989 services were cut by 50 per cent. The long-distance routes are disproportionately affected with the transCanada services falling from 14 to three a week. The 4500 km journey took over three days, and is no longer viable. In Australia a similar coast-to-coast journey of 4000 km (Sydney to Perth) takes nearly 66 hours, totally uncompetitive with air transport both in terms of time and cost, and even slower than the same journey by coach.

Rail travel is competitive with road and air transport in a relatively narrow distance band. Air transport begins to challenge rail on journeys of two hours duration or more, but rail is competitive on journeys up to 500 km in distance (and five hours in duration). It is thought that when the high-speed rail network in Europe is complete, rail transport will be competitive with air services on several intercity routes (*see* Fig 16.5).

Journey	Fastest time in 1990	Fastest time on completion of high-speed rail network
Brussels–Amsterdam	2hr 41 min	1hr 28 min
Frankfurt–Munich	3hr 46 min	3hr 00 min
Rome–Milan	4hr 05 min	3hr 05 min
Paris–Amsterdam	5hr 07 min	2hr 48 min
London–Paris	5hr 12 min	2hr 30 min
Barcelona–Madrid	6hr 13 min	3hr 00 min

Fig. 16.5 European intercity rail journeys

Air transport

A small proportion (12.5 per cent) of the world's tourists travel by air. Even though it is still only used by a minority of tourists, air transport has revolutionised the geographical pattern of world travel since 1960. Tourism has changed from a local to an intercontinental activity. It has created tourist industries in destinations hitherto untouched by the physical, social or economic impacts of tourism. In the mid-1950s the journey by ocean liner between Britain and Australia was measured in terms of weeks; in 1990 the same journey by air lasted less than 24 hours. The subsonic Jumbo Jet (the Boeing 747) flies at over 1000 k/h and supersonic aircraft can reach speeds of 1950 k/h. Concorde has cut the journey time between London and New York from about six hours to only three, making it possible for businesspeople to travel there and back in a day.

The speed and range of air travel gives rise to a problem for the traveller that no other form of transport causes. Air travel can take the tourist from one time zone of the world to another in a matter of hours, much faster than the body can cope with. It takes several days for the body's rhythms of waking and sleeping to adjust to a new pattern of day and night. The fatigue experienced during this period of adjustment is known as jet lag. It is most clearly felt when travelling to the opposite side of the world where the time difference between the tourists' home and their destination is the greatest.

Time zones

Pictures from outer space make it easy to visualise the world as a globe, spinning on its axis (one revolution being equal to a day) and orbiting round the sun (one complete circuit in one year). At any given moment, the part of the earth closest to the sun will be experiencing midday, and the point furthest away will be at midnight. Figure 16.6 shows the distribution of day and night when it is midday in London (which lies on the Greenwich Meridian 0° longitude). At this exact moment, the time in St Petersburg (30° E) is 14.00 hrs and in Tokyo (140° E) it is just after nine pm (and travellers from London to Japan must get used to a pattern of day and night which is almost the complete opposite to that to which their bodies are accustomed). In Toronto (80° W) it is just before seven in the morning. Each 15° of longitude experiences exactly one hour's difference in solar time. For convenience, the world has been divided into time zones roughly corresponding to each 15° longitude band, and each with generally one hour's difference in time between them (*see* Fig 16.7). The boundaries of the time zones follow lines of longitude closely, but may deviate where administrative boundaries lie close to that line (for example, in Africa the time zone boundary follows the Sudan/Ethiopia and Uganda/Zaire borders instead of the line of longitude, and in North America it deviates to follow some state boundaries). It is much more

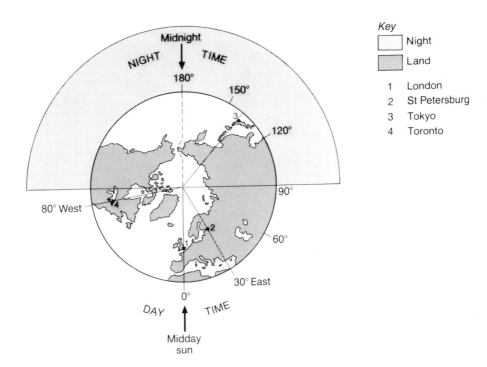

Fig. 16.6 World distribution of day and night (when it is midday in London)

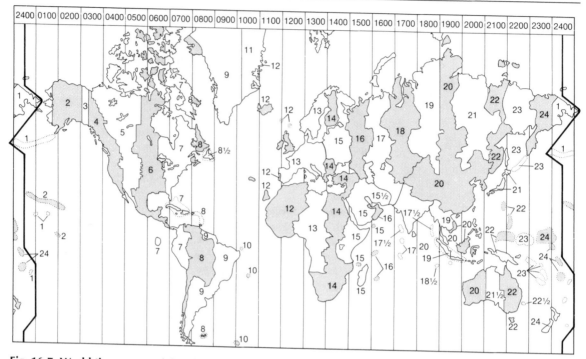

Fig. 16.7 World time zones (giving the time in hours, in each zone when it is midday in London)

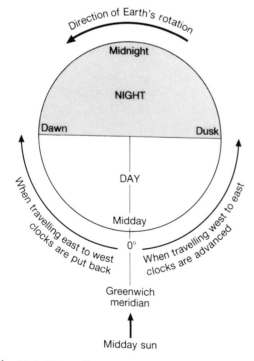

Fig. 16.8 Time adjustments around the world

convenient for one administrative unit to lie within one time zone.

As travellers go eastward and pass from one time zone to another they must adjust their watch one hour forward, and when they travel west, they must put their watches back one hour (*see* Fig 16.8). The only occasion when the whole world is experiencing the same day is when it is midday in London (*see* Figs 16.6, 16.7 and 16.8). From that moment the new day starts to sweep clockwise (westwards) round the world (*see* Figs 16.9 and 16.10). When travellers cross the International Date Line (180°) from east to west they will step ahead into the next day; when they cross it from west to east they move into the day before (*see* Fig 16.10).

The calendar on the Asian side of the international date line is always one day ahead of the American side. The location of the International Date Line was agreed in 1884. The line corresponds more or less with the 180° meridian, passing through the empty Pacific ocean. The occasional deviations in the line away from the 180° meridian allow some groups of Pacific islands to all lie in the zone of the same calendar day.

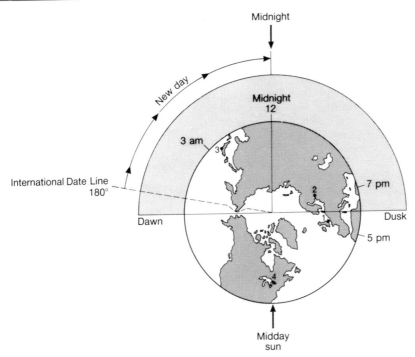

Fig. 16.9 Spread of a new day (west): dawn in the Pacific and midday in Toronto

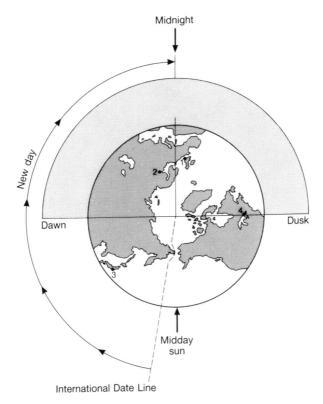

Fig. 16.10 Spread of a new day (east): midday in the Pacific and dusk in Toronto

EU airports listed by category

Category 1 Hub airports

Belgium:	Brussels-Zaventem
Denmark:	Copenhagen-Kastrup/Roskilde
Germany:	Frankfurt/Rhein-Main, Düsseldorf-Lohausen, Munich-Riem
Spain:	Palma-Mallorca, Madrid-Barajas, Malaga, Las Palmas
Greece:	Athens-Hellenikon, Salonica-Micra
France:	Paris-Charles de Gaulle/Orly
Ireland:	Dublin
Italy:	Rome-Fiumicino/Ciampino, Milan-Linate/Malpensa
Netherlands:	Amsterdam-Schiphol
Portugal:	Lisbon, Faro
UK:	London-Heathrow/Gatwick/Stansted, Luton

Category 2 Regional airports

Germany:	Hamburg-Fuhlsbüttel, Stuttgart-Echterdingen, Cologne/Bonn
Spain:	Tenerife-Sur, Barcelona, Ibiza, Alicante, Gerona
France:	Marseille-Marignane, Nice-Côte d'Azur, Lyon-Satolas, Basle-Mulhouse
Ireland:	Shannon
Italy:	Naples-Capodichino, Venice-Tessera, Catania-Fontanarossa
Luxembourg:	Luxembourg-Findel
Portugal:	Funchal, Oporto
UK:	Manchester-Ringway, Birmingham-Elmdon, Glasgow-Abbotsinch

Category 3

Includes all other airports officially open to international scheduled services.

Fig. 16.11 Europe's hub and spoke airports
(*Source*: European Commission)

Spatial distribution of air traffic

Most air traffic movements are concentrated in the more populated parts of the world, where there is the densest provision of airports serving that population.

Most countries have at least one major international airport capable of handling intercontinental traffic, and some of these have developed into major interchanges where many long-haul routes intersect, e.g. London, Frankfurt, Singapore and New York. London Heathrow handled over 34 million passengers in 1987. Frankfurt is Europe's second airport with 22 million. The smaller British regional airports (the runways of which may not be long enough to receive the jumbo jets) specialise in holiday charter flights or provide services into Heathrow (or Gatwick) to connect with the international flights. This pattern of 'hub' and 'spoke' airports is more firmly established in the USA, but Europe is also evolving this pattern

(*see* Fig 16.11). The bulk of international air traffic in Europe flows between the hubs, but as congestion increases, the secondary airports are beginning to take a more important role. Manchester, with 8.5 million passengers in 1987, was Europe's most important 'spoke' airport, followed by Barcelona and Hamburg. Many of the smaller airports have ambitious expansion plans, and the patterns and flows of air traffic may change and grow rapidly as total traffic increases and deregulation, plus the implementation of the Single European Act, take full effect.

SEA TRAVEL

It has been noted that the only major passenger transit role of sea transport is that of short sea (ferry) crossings in island nations, and local inner city ferry services for cities such as Venice and Sydney that have waterways in the heart of the urban area. In these cities, ferries provide both commuter and tourist transport. Ferries may be boats of traditional design, or hydrofoils where greater speed is required.

In general, boat travel has a greater leisure and tourism role than a transport role.

Cruising

Cruising is one of the forms of tourism in which the travel element is an integral and essential part of the holiday experience. The cruise ship is basically a floating hotel; passengers can enjoy the attractions of luxury hotel service while they are travelling between ports of call. The world market for cruising is quite small (3 to 3.5 million in 1987/88) but in style, cruising is essentially a form of mass tourism; while 800-berth vessels were cost-effective in the 1970s, the normal size in the 1980s was for 1500 berth vessels and in the late 1980s vessels double that size were being planned. These ships either leave from a home port, or in order to save days sailing to the cruise destinations, passengers may fly to the port of embarkation ('flycruises').

The main world locations of cruise activity are in the three island-studded, enclosed seas that by geographical accident are found in favourable subtropical or Mediterranean climatic regions and are also close to major tourist generation areas. These three seas are the Caribbean, the Mediterranean and the South China/Pacific, adjacent to the American, European and Australian/New Zealand/Japanese markets respectively. The more northerly coasts and enclosed seas, e.g. Alaska, China coast, Norwegian coast and Baltic are visited by cruise ships in the summer season but numbers are negligible compared to the three major regions. Cruising in the Mediterranean has been long established (for nearly 100 years) but the political difficulties of the Suez crisis in 1956/57 led to the temporary cancellation of Mediterranean cruises and both cruise ships and cruise businesses were transferred to the Caribbean.

Although the Mediterranean has partially recovered, the Caribbean has been the most important world region for cruising since the late 1950s. Initially ships departed from New York but from 1970 Miami took over as the leading Caribbean cruise port.

Not surprisingly, Caribbean cruising is completely dependent on the American market. American tourists are, however, also very important to the Mediterranean cruise business, which suffered a second major setback in 1985/86 after a Mediterranean cruise ship (the Achille Lauro) was attacked by Arab terrorists who killed an American tourist on board. American cruise visitors decreased from 75 000 pa before 1985 to virtually nil thereafter.

The main cruise circuits in the Mediterranean area are

1 The Western Mediterranean
2 Eastern Mediterranean/Aegean – Greek Islands (sometimes linked to the Holy Land and Egypt). Piraeus, Venice and Genoa are the most used start/finish points.
3 North Africa and the Canaries (a winter circuit).

The Pacific cruise business is geared to the Australian, New Zealand and recently developing Japanese markets, though some fly-cruise passengers come from North America and Europe. Trips to the islands of the South Pacific embark from Australian or New Zealand ports, but many of the cruises of the South China Sea start from Singapore or Hong Kong.

QUESTIONS AND DISCUSSION POINTS

1 What is a great circle route? Why is it normally advantageous for sea and air routes to follow them as closely as possible? Under what circumstances would boats and planes not follow them?

2 What is the most used mode of transport for tourism in the world? What advantages make it so popular?

3 Most major airports are located a considerable distance from their city centres, except in certain coastal cities. Why is this?

ASSIGNMENTS

1 A client has booked a trip to Australia through your travel agency. He has been given the following details of the journey (all local times):

Depart London Airport	on Monday	at 2235 hrs
Arrive Singapore	on Tuesday	at 2220 hrs
Depart Singapore	on Friday	at 0040 hrs
Arrive Cairns, Australia	on Friday	at 0900 hrs
Depart Cairns	on Friday	at 1030 hrs
Arrive Brisbane	on Friday	at 1250 hrs

The client is totally confused as to the length of time he will be travelling in the plane and the amount of time he will have at the stopover locations. Explain to him:

(a) the length of time he will be flying on each leg of the journey; and

(b) the length of time he has in Singapore (and how many *full* days of sightseeing he will have there).

2 A businesswoman books a return trip from London to San Francisco. Her schedule is as follows:

Outbound: Depart Heathrow 0900 hrs on Wednesday

Arrive San Francisco 1155 hrs on Wednesday

Meeting 1500 hrs on Wednesday in San Francisco

Return: Depart San Francisco 1720 hrs on Thursday

Arrive Heathrow ? (time to be calculated)

Meeting in London 1430 hrs on Friday. (*All local times*)

Her meeting in the United States is expected to last two to three hours. Advise the client on

(a) How much time she will have in the plane on the outbound journey to read her notes and prepare for the meeting;

(b) How much time she will have for sightseeing in San Francisco before she returns; and

(c) How long she will have to sleep on the plane on the return journey, and whether she will return in time for the London meeting.

CHAPTER 17

The growth and distribution of world tourism

LEARNING OBJECTIVES

After reading this chapter you should be able to
- list the factors that influence travel within and between countries
- locate the main world tourism generating and destination regions
- distinguish between inter- and intra-regional travel
- identify the four functional tourist regions of the world
- understand the logic of different subdivisions of the world into different tourist regions.

INTRODUCTION

The location of an affluent urban area alongside a region with attractive tourist resources, linked together by transport routes and networks, will trigger off the flow of tourists between them. The most powerful flows will be towards the most attractive, accessible and popular destinations.

These travel patterns occur on a domestic, international and inter-regional scale; various factors influence these directional flows of tourists.

FACTORS AFFECTING DOMESTIC TOURIST FLOWS

The directional flows of domestic tourists within a country will depend on the location of its natural resources and on the distribution of its population. However, each of the resources described in Chapters 2 to 6 generates a characteristic pattern of tourist travel.

1 A major wave of tourist travel flows outwards from the urban areas to the coast, often to the nearest (or most accessible) available coast, sometimes seemingly irrespective of its environmental quality (e.g. the residents of Manchester and Liverpool visit Blackpool, and the eastenders of

London traditionally travel to Southend-on-Sea). As Britain is an island, the flow to the coast is multi-directional from the cities, though with a general southerly bias towards the best combinations of climate and beaches.

2 A second, though far smaller, wave of tourists flows outwards from the cities towards the countryside and mountains. Again, in Britain this is fairly multi-directional, though this time with a bias towards the west (and northwest) towards the landscapes of upland Britain.

3 The third tide of tourist travel is in the opposite direction and represents the movement of rural and provincial residents into the conurbations for the cultural attractions and entertainments of the city centre.

4 The fourth stream of tourists takes place between the cities, representing travel by business and cultural tourists and people visiting friends and relatives. This interchange of tourists utilises the web of transport routes that evolved to meet the needs of commercial and industrial transport and the significant volumes of this element of tourist travel may be camouflaged by the even greater volumes of non-tourist traffic.

Superimposed on all these patterns of tourist movement is a general trend of travel towards better (i.e. warmer, sunnier or drier) climatic conditions. In Britain this results in a strong concentration of tourism in the south and southwest. Thus, in the Northern Hemisphere, the flow is essentially towards the south, and cultural, historic or landscape resources need to be of outstanding quality to draw tourists northwards against this tidal flow to the south. Of course, in the Southern Hemisphere, the pattern is reversed: in Australia and New Zealand, tourists tend to drift northwards for the better weather.

INTERNATIONAL TOURIST FLOWS

The same factors influence travel between countries, and, once again, climate appears to play a dominant role in shaping patterns of international travel.

Contrasts in climate would seem to be the most important factor that triggers off tourism worldwide. The main tourism generating areas are located in the northerly or mid latitudes that have cool and variable climates. The main tourist flows in both Europe and North America are north-south to the warmer and more reliable climates in the regions on their southerly borders (in Europe to the Mediterranean, and in North America to Florida and the Caribbean). The most clear-cut example of this type of travel is shown by the Scandinavians; in 1985 one quarter to one third of their travel outside the Scandinavian region is in the form of package holidays to the Canary Islands during the winter when hours of daylight (let alone hours of sunshine) in the northerly latitudes are very limited indeed.

Once again, it should be noted that in the Southern Hemisphere, the parallel trend is northwards. In Australia, for example, the residents of Melbourne and Sydney tend to travel north to the Queensland coast and beyond for their winter sun holidays, while New Zealanders may visit the Pacific islands to their north. On a world scale, therefore, the trek towards more favourable climates generates travel towards the Equator. However, in addition to the climate, other factors influence the direction, volume, mode and frequency of travel between countries. These are:

1 **Distance between countries**. The tourist flows between two countries are likely to be bigger, the closer together the two countries.
2 **Natural and manmade attractions**. Tourist travel will be triggered off between countries if one can provide the attractions (e.g. beaches, landscapes or historic resources) that the other country lacks.
3 **Communications**. Travel between countries will be encouraged where good transport infrastructures exist. Tourism will flourish particularly where travel between countries can take place without a change of mode of transport (e.g. entirely by car).
4 **Relative costs (cost of living and exchange rates)**. If two countries have significantly different costs of living, tourism flows will be encouraged from the more expensive country to the country with the lower cost of living.
5 **Cultural links**. Other things being equal, travel is more likely to occur between countries with some common cultural link (e.g. a common language or religion, shared political history).
6 **Political factors**. The long-term political stability of a country will make it a relatively more attractive destination both for investors in tourism and for the tourists themselves.

Distance

The majority of international tourist movements takes place between adjacent countries. Figure 17.1 lists some examples of countries in the world's economic core, showing the proportion of their international visitors that originate from countries with whom they have a common border.

As the distance a tourist travels increases, so the financial cost and the time taken for the journey tend to increase. The tourist must weigh these disadvantages of long-distance travel against the attraction of the far away destination. This 'friction of distance' may lead tourists to choose a similar type of destination that is closer to their home country in preference to the true long-haul destination, however attractive its character might appear to be.

Thus, the volume of tourist traffic will decrease with distance away from the tourist generating area. This relationship is known as the **distance-decay factor**.

Country	% international tourists from adjacent country/countries	Name(s) of adjacent country/countries
North America		
Canada	80.39	USA
USA	62.18	Canada, Mexico
Europe		
Austria	68.89	Germany, Italy, Switzerland, Hungary, former Yugoslavia, Czechoslovakia
Hungary	62.53	Former USSR, Yugoslavia and Czechoslovakia, Austria, Romania
France	55.25	Germany, Belgium, Spain, Italy, Switzerland

Fig. 17.1 Tourism between adjacent countries, 1991

Natural and manmade attractions

The lack of a particular type of attraction in a generating country may also trigger off significant flows of tourists to countries where those resources exist in abundance. For example, tourists from the Netherlands (appropriately known as the 'low countries' owing to the fact that most of the country lies below 200 metres, and much is below sea level) flock to Switzerland and Austria. The Alps are the second most important destination for Dutch travellers; 22 per cent of the Dutch visited France in 1990, followed by the Alps (Austria and Switzerland), with a 16 per cent share of Dutch holiday destinations abroad.

Germany has a very limited coastline in relation to its size, and the coast it has is in the north. This creates a strong demand among Germans for holidays in the coastal resorts of the Mediterranean countries. Britain's pageantry (particularly that associated with the Royal Family) attracts visitors from countries that lack such historic traditions or do not have monarchies.

Communications

Good transport links between countries are a prerequisite for the exchange of tourists between them. Where international borders cross land areas, road transport is the dominant mode of travel; road networks designed to meet local or industrial needs may predate tourist development and allow exploratory road travel by tourists (*see* Chapter 16). The Costa Brava in Spain was 'discovered' in this way by French visitors driving south across the border in the 1950s. It was only after the tourist potential of the costas was recognised that the roads were improved and airports built. Similarly, car-borne visitors driving from Europe towards Greece along the Adriatic highway found the attractions of the Yugoslavian coast worthy of more than a stopover visit.

Road transport is by far the dominant means of transport for tourism world-wide. Seventy seven per cent of world international arrivals are by road, and only 12.5 per cent by air, and 10.5 per cent for rail and boat together. In Europe, too, car transport dominates travel between countries (ranging from 60–80 per cent of visits). The same pattern holds for North America, where the bulk of international trips are by road; in 1987, 67 per cent of the visitors from USA to Canada went by road, and 66 per cent from Canada to USA.

Long-haul travel is on the other hand essentially airborne, and relies on either charter flights (purpose-designed for tourists and tailored to the short/medium-haul destinations for mass tourism) or scheduled flights. The networks and infrastructure of the scheduled flights are designed to meet the locational needs of commerce and business, linking urban and industrial centres rather than specifically the tourist generating regions with far-flung and less developed tourist destinations.

Relative costs

The relative purchasing power of the currency of a given country is a reflection of the strength of that country's economy and its standard of living. Prices to the consumer (and, therefore, to the tourist) will vary considerably between different countries. Travel will be inhibited to countries where consumer prices are relatively higher than in the home economy, while tourists will get better value for money if they travel to a country where consumer prices are lower than at home. Figure 17.2 shows the relative purchasing power of the pound in 1986 compared to other countries (values of the index above 100 indicate countries where goods were relatively more expensive than in UK, and below 100 indicates relative cheapness).

Country	Index
More expensive than UK	
Denmark	141
West Germany	127
France	119
Netherlands	115
Irish Republic	113
Belgium	110
Luxembourg	101
Less expensive than UK	
Italy	98
Spain	84
Greece	77
Portugal	68

Fig. 17.2 Relative purchasing power of the pound sterling, 1986

With changes in exchange rates, and varying inflation rates, the relative purchasing power of currencies will vary over time. For example, in terms of the pound's relative purchasing power, Italy became steadily less attractive to UK visitors over the period 1981–86, while the relative difference between Greece and UK remained the same over the whole period. Countries like Denmark and West Germany became increasingly expensive for British visitors.

	Index					
	1981	1982	1983	1984	1985	1986
Denmark	111	116	120	122	122	141
West Germany	102	106	115	115	111	127
Italy	72	75	83	86	85	98
Greece	73	78	78	79	74	77

Fig. 17.3 Relative purchasing power of the pound, 1981–1986

Such price differentials can strongly influence patterns of travel particularly where destinations are closely competitive, leading tourists to switch from one destination to the comparable but now somewhat cheaper alternative. However, changes in travel behaviour seem to take effect over a period of about one to three years after the change in relative prices.

Price differentials can also make destinations in the world's economic periphery very attractive to tourists from the economic core. The standard of living may be relatively much lower in the countries of the economic periphery, but costs of labour and costs of living are also low. If the countries of the periphery can overcome the economic problems of providing a tourist infrastructure at an acceptable standard, then the relative cheapness of holidays there may draw large numbers of tourists from the countries of the economic core. The zones of the economic periphery lying adjacent to the tourist generating regions of the world's economic core have certainly experienced an influx of tourists; for example, Mexico and the Caribbean (both on the fringe of the periphery) are major destinations for the North American market, while Turkey and North Africa (also on the fringe of the periphery) compete directly with countries of Southern Europe for the Mediterranean holiday trade. In the Pacific region, the countries of the periphery (e.g. Indonesia, Thailand and the economically under-developed islands of the Pacific) attract significant numbers of Australasians and Japanese.

Cultural links

There are three types of cultural links that influence travel between countries.

1 Countries with a shared cultural background are more likely to generate tourism between them. The Scandinavian countries share their Viking history, and between 31 and 38 per cent of their visitors come from other Nordic countries.

2 Patterns of immigration into a country will create cultural links between the receiving country and the immigrants' original homeland. The immigrants may wish to travel back to visit families left at home and vice versa, and the descendants of immigrants tend to be drawn to explore the countries where their ancestors once lived. The United States was peopled by immigrants, initially from Europe; from Britain, Germany and Ireland up to

1860, to which were added Scandinavians in the period 1860–1890, and Eastern and Southern Europeans from 1900–1914. In more recent years (since the 1960s) the immigrants have come mainly from Southeast Asia and Latin America. Apart from the slave trade, virtually no migrants came from Africa, and few from the Middle East. American overseas tourism appears to reflect these cultural links.

3 Past colonial links. Until their independence, many of the Third World countries were governed as colonies of European nations. The colonial power often imposed its language on the colony as well as its general style of education, culture, currency and political organisation. Some of these characteristics have been retained by the independent states even though the members of the colonial power have long since left. This may make the country an attractive destination for tourists from the original colonial power. The flow of tourists between France and its ex-colonies in French West Africa and North Africa illustrates this point. Similarly, there are significant flows of the Dutch to Surinam, the Belgians to Zaire and the British to former colonies in East Africa and Asia. These flows of tourists reflect the traces of the political geography of past eras.

Political factors

The current political geography of the world exerts a powerful control on tourist flows between countries.

Political conflict or co-operation between nations can inhibit or encourage tourism. Wars, terrorist campaigns or any form of political instability may immediately deter tourists temporarily or for a longer period of time. The memories and suspicions bred of past conflicts, and longer-term ethnic rivalries can also inhibit tourism between countries, e.g. India and Pakistan; Greece and Turkey – both pairs of adjacent countries with a long-term history of conflict reflected in a smaller than expected travel flow between them.

Countries may also erect financial and legal barriers to travel which may have profound effects upon international travel patterns. Until the 1989 upheavals in Eastern Europe, the travel restrictions imposed on both visitors and residents by the then communist countries reduced east-west travel in both directions to a mere trickle. Less drastic but still influential financial and legal barriers such as restrictions on foreign currency allowances, and access to visas may just as effectively control travel between certain countries (e.g. throughout the Central and South American countries).

On the other hand, political decisions may be made that facilitate and even encourage travel between countries or groups of countries. The Scandinavian countries have co-ordinated many of their laws and customs regulations, which allow virtually complete freedom of travel for Scandinavians between their countries. The Single European Act is designed to have the same effect on the EU.

All these factors will combine in different ways to shape and modify the overall patterns of world regional and inter-regional tourism. The flows of tourists between any specific pair of countries and, indeed, pairs of regions in the world will be a result of the interplay of these factors, although there must be the predisposing conditions for tourist generation in the one country, and tourist attractions (be they climatic, scenic, historic etc.) must exist in the other.

REGIONAL PATTERNS OF TOURISM

Chapter 15 located the tourist generating regions of the world as Europe, North America and parts of the Pacific (the world's economic 'core'). Chapters 2–6 located the main tourist resources of the world and showed that there are major concentrations of attractive resources in the Mediterranean basin, Central America and in the Caribbean. Chapter 16 and the first section of this chapter identified the factors that trigger off and encourage flows between any pair of tourist generating and destination areas. This next section will describe the overall world patterns of tourist arrivals at destinations that represent the outcome of this interplay of geographical factors, and on the basis of these patterns of tourism, the functional tourist regions of the world can be identified (*see* Fig 17.4).

The four functional tourist regions of the world are:

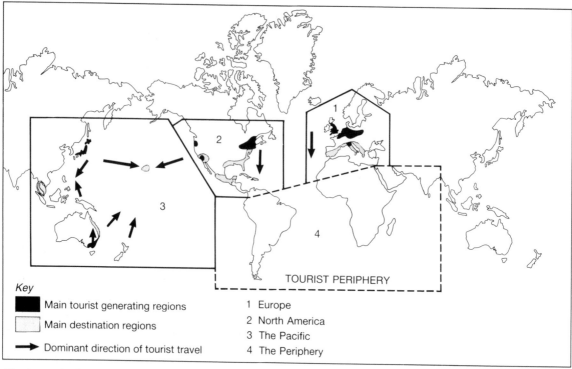

Key

◼ Main tourist generating regions

☐ Main destination regions

➡ Dominant direction of tourist travel

1 Europe
2 North America
3 The Pacific
4 The Periphery

Fig. 17.4 The four main tourist regions of the world

1 Europe and the Mediterranean: a region of high tourist activity with major tourist flows south to the coasts of the Mediterranean basin.

2 North America plus Mexico and the Caribbean: similar in many ways to Europe with dominant southerly flows of tourists to Florida, Mexico and the Caribbean.

3 East Asia and the Pacific: a region of much lower tourist activity but where tourism is growing very rapidly indeed. Due to the huge size of the Pacific Ocean, relatively few tourists travel right across it and the strongest tourist flows are around its edge – between the countries on the 'Pacific Rim' (again in a predominantly Equatorwards direction). A second flow takes place from these countries towards the centre of the Pacific, to island holiday destinations.

4 The remainder of the economic periphery: Subsaharan Africa, Central and South America, the Middle East and South Asia. The level of tourist activity is very low indeed due to factors such as political instability, inaccessibility, poverty and poor tourist infrastructure.

When tourist arrival data are grouped according to the World Tourist Organisation regions (*see* Fig 17.5), it is clear that Europe has always been the dominant international tourist destination of the world (the boundaries of these statistical regions are shown in Fig 17.6 on p 182).

Functionally Europe extends into the Mediterranean basin with all its wealth of tourist resources (climatic, coastal and cultural) and Spain, the south of France and Italy are the main Mediterranean destinations, with each country having over 25 million tourist arrivals in 1991, while another 15.5 million tourists filter into the eastern half of the Mediterranean and spread through Cyprus, Greece and, more recently, Turkey. The southern coast of the Mediterranean is much less popular. Up to 1987, North Africa was part of the European tourist region, as over 80 per cent of its visitors came from Europe and its destinations compete with other Mediterranean coastal resorts, but by 1991 the total number of Europeans visiting the north African coast had dropped to

Region	% world International arrivals							
	1950	1960	1970	1980	1985	1989	1990	1992
Europe	66.6	71.0	74.7	70.0	65.5	61.9	59.5	60.5
North America	24.6	21.4	16.1	12.5	11.8	13.4	15.7	21.5
Caribbean and Latin America	5.2	3.8	3.0	7.2	6.1	6.3	4.8	
Middle East	0.8	2.0	1.7	2.0	3.3	2.9	2.9	1.5
Africa	2.0	0.6	1.4	2.2	3.5	3.8	3.4	3.6
Asia/Australasia	0.8	1.2	3.1					
East Asia & Pacific				5.6	9.0	11.1	10.6	12.2
South Asia				0.6	0.8	0.7	0.8	0.7

Fig. 17.5 Evolution of regional patterns of world tourism
(*Source*: WTO)

just over two million representing only 29 per cent of all arrivals. African visitors had increased from 11 per cent to 67.8 per cent of all arrivals over the same period.

The second major functional tourist region of the world is North America (*see* Fig 17.4). While 61 per cent of world international arrivals were concentrated in Europe, only about 16 per cent were located in North America. However, these figures, with their emphasis on international travel, perhaps give a misleading impression of the overall scale of the dominance of Europe and distribution of tourist activity in the world. Both Europe and North America are regions with large, affluent and mobile populations (over 376 million in Europe, 245 million in USA); but because Europe is politically divided into many small countries, much of the tourist movement in the region is expressed as international travel. In contrast, the United States of America consists of 50 states (many of which are larger than most European countries) and interstate travel is recorded as domestic tourism: in 1988 US citizens made 1241 million person trips of over 160 km from home, of which 840 million were holiday trips, indicating a volume of tourist activity on the same scale as that in Europe.

It is the differences in the political history of the two regions – which has left Europe divided in many small independent political units, but resulted in the political unity of the USA – that gives rise to the apparently enormous difference in levels of tourism as shown by international tourist statistics. As in Europe, the main generating region of North America is in the north (particu-

larly between the Eastern Seaboard and the Great Lakes), while the major tourist resources lie to the south. The major destination regions are the states of Florida, Texas and Southern California, while Mexico and the Caribbean islands also attract very substantial numbers of Americans and Canadians. Thus, parts of Central America and the Caribbean are functionally part of the North American tourist region (*see* Fig 17.4).

Of the remaining regions of the world, the most significant in terms of international tourist arrivals is East Asia and the Pacific (*see* Fig 17.5). This region includes the economic 'core' countries of Japan, Australia and New Zealand (*see* Fig 15.2 on p 152), but also the rapidly industrialising 'tiger economies' of Taiwan, South Korea, Singapore and Hong Kong. The average growth rate of GDP of Asian countries throughout the worst of the recession of 1975–85 has been consistently of the order of five to seven per cent per annum – far outstripping the performance of the economies of the other 'non-core' countries of the world, and, indeed, far above the growth rates of many of the main core market economies too.

East Asia and the Pacific accounts for about 12 per cent of all world international tourist arrivals, and, not surprisingly, the region shows by far the highest growth rates of international tourism in the world. In 1984 and 1985 international tourism was growing by 11 per cent per annum; by 1987 this had increased to 15 per cent per annum and in 1988 had reached nearly 18 per cent per annum. This compares to annual growth rates of tourist arrivals of generally between five and seven per cent in Europe and America over the same period of time.

The generating and destination areas of the Pacific region are far more widely dispersed than in Europe or North America. Hawaii is the main destination and is located right in the centre of the Pacific, while the other significant destinations are scattered in an arc along the south and east sections of the 'Pacific Rim' (*see* Fig 17.4).

The remaining regions of the world (i.e. Central and South America, Subsaharan Africa and the Middle East, and South Asia) are similar in terms of their political instability, generally poor economic performance and low levels of tourist activity. This suggests that they might be considered together as the fourth functional tourist region of the world; a peripheral region, both in economic and tourist terms (*see* Fig 17.4). The continents of this region together account for barely 11 per cent of all international tourist arrivals, and their relative poverty generates little international travel from within their own regions. They are spatially separated from the main generating regions and depend on long-haul travel from the developed world for international arrivals.

Although the long-haul market is growing, it still accounts for a relatively small proportion of total world international travel.

Thus, the countries of these regions lie outside the spheres of influence of the three main tourist generating regions of the world's economic core. They are mostly in the first phase of tourist development (see Chapter 15), and few have even any significant domestic tourism, except perhaps for India, Brazil, Argentina and South Africa. They lack any tourist infrastructure, therefore, and their poverty denies them the resources to develop the necessary facilities for international tourism.

The general political instability of these regions also inhibits any coherent planning for tourist development, even though the foreign currency it would generate could benefit their ailing economies. Travel to the continents of the periphery is also inhibited by potential visitors' perceptions of them as prone to natural disasters, such as droughts, floods and famine, and prone to political disturbances, such as civil wars, border strife and coups. All these factors result in very

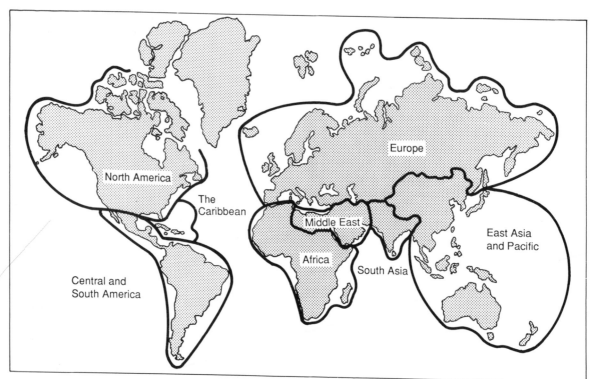

Fig. 17.6 World tourist regions

small numbers of international tourists in these peripheral destinations – less then five million in Subsaharan Africa, and two million in the Indian subcontinent, and six million in Latin America.

These fundamental problems are experienced in all the regions of the economic periphery but there are spatial variations. The main sub-regions of the periphery are shown on Fig 17.6 and consist of:

1 Subsaharan Africa which extends from the southern parts of the Sahara to the Cape of Good Hope.
2 The Middle East. Syria, Iran, Iraq, Saudi Arabia, the Gulf States.
3 The Indian Subcontinent and Indian Ocean
(*a*) Mainland countries: Myanmar, Bangladesh, the Himalayan states, India, Pakistan and Afghanistan.
(*b*) The Indian Ocean Islands, including Sri Lanka, the Seychelles, the Maldives, Mauritius, Madagascar.
4 Latin America
(*a*) Central America: Belize, Costa Rica, El Salvador, Guatemala, Honduras, Nicaragua and Panama.
(*b*) South America: the whole continent from Colombia to Argentina.

These general patterns of world tourism are shown more clearly in Fig 17.7 where the WTO regional statistics are regrouped to match the four functional tourist regions of the world.

These four functional tourist regions (Europe, North America, the Pacific region and the periphery) are relatively clearly separated tourist systems: most international travel takes place within these regions (i.e. as intra-regional travel) with the dominant flow of tourists towards the Equator within each separate region (*see* Fig 17.4). Up to 1980, about 80 per cent of all the world's international tourism was intra-regional. The remaining 20 per cent was long-haul inter-regional travel, mostly east-west travel between the three main generating regions (i.e. Europe, North America and the Pacific). During the 1980s the pause in the growth of world tourism (*see* Chapter 15) did not inhibit the expansion of long-haul travel, and by 1987 inter-regional travel accounted for between 30 and 40 per cent of arrivals in the three main tourist regions. At the same time, long-haul travel continued to develop in the tourist

Functional region	% world tourist arrivals	% world tourist receipts
Europe and Mediterranean basin Total	62.95	53.64
North Europe	5.56	8.89
C/E Europe	11.01	1.11
W Europe	24.84	23.40
S Europe & E Mediterranean	19.65	19.55
N Africa	1.89	0.69
North and Central America and Caribbean Total	19.26	25.12
N America	16.32	21.24
C America	0.45	0.39
Caribbean	2.49	3.49
E Asia and Pacific Total	11.84	15.43
The economic periphery Total	5.93	5.81
S America	2.16	2.47
Subsaharan Africa	1.59	1.07
Middle East	1.47	1.52
S Asia	0.71	0.75

Fig. 17.7 Functional tourist regions of the world. Regional pattern of world tourist arrivals and receipts (*Source*: WTO 1991)

regions of the economic periphery, for example, into Africa and South Asia.

Thus, the boundaries of the functional tourist regions are becoming more blurred with time as linkages between the regions strengthen. If these trends of increasing inter-regional travel continue, it may be more appropriate to divide the world into just three tourist zones: the economic core; the periphery and a transitional zone between (*see* Fig 17.8). With increasing east-west long-haul travel, the whole of the world's economic core may become one major interlocking tourist system. The adjacent edge of the world's economic periphery is essentially a destination zone for the generating regions of the core, receiving large numbers of tourists from the core. It represents, therefore, a transition zone, which is gradually expanding towards the heart of the economic periphery as new destinations are promoted. The remainder of the periphery still remains relatively isolated from the tourist systems of the core, with its tourism

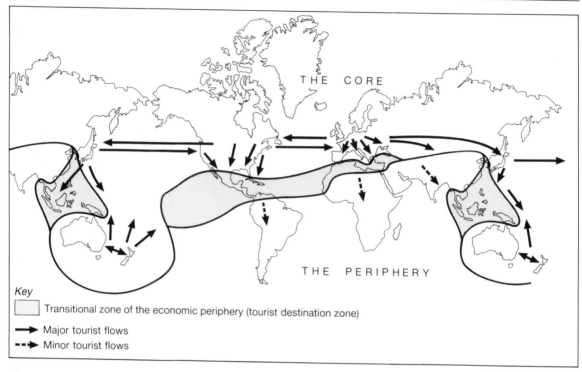

Fig. 17.8 'Core-periphery' tourist regions of the world

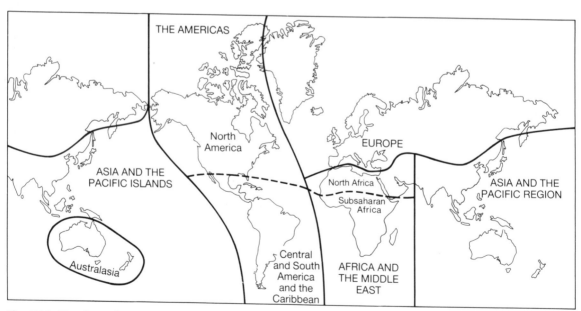

Fig. 17.9 'Continental' tourist regions of the world

depending on a small but growing band of long-haul travellers from the core, or on small, isolated pockets of tourist development (e.g. southern Brazil, South Africa) within its own borders.

It is clear that patterns of world tourism are evolving over time and that the boundaries of the tourist regions of the world are changing as long-haul tourism grows. The remainder of this book presents the information on individual countries on a different and perhaps less volatile basis. For convenience, therefore, the remaining chapters are organised around the traditional division of the world into continents which do not necessarily coincide with the functional tourist regions of the world (*see* Fig 17.9). It is hoped that this presentation will allow different approaches to the identification of tourist regions to be made and that it will not obscure the fundamental functional relationships between different parts of the world.

QUESTIONS AND DISCUSSION POINTS

1 What factors influence the direction and volume of tourist travel between two different countries of the world?

2 Referring to Fig 17.5 on p 181, describe how the regional pattern of world tourism changed between:
    (a) 1950 and 1970; and
    (b) 1970 and 1992
Explain the reasons for these changes.

3 On what basis can the world be divided into different tourist regions?

ASSIGNMENTS

1 You work for the British Tourist Authority (or an American or Australian equivalent – you may choose which one). Your job is to organise the international promotion of your country and to advise inbound tourist operators on their international advertising. Your department has recently expanded and you have appointed several new staff.

Prepare short briefing notes for the new members of staff, outlining the target areas for marketing your country in the next year. List the countries in your own region that will be targeted, and identify the other regions of the world (and the main countries within them) in which you will be actively promoting your country. Explain the reasons for this plan to your new staff.

2 Study the table below showing arrivals of foreign tourists at the Greek frontier in 1989. Suggest some possible explanations for this pattern of arrivals.

Country of origin	
Austria	3.1
Belgium	1.9
Cyprus	1.3
Denmark	3.7
Finland	3.0
France	5.6
FR Germany	19.4
Ireland	0.7
Italy	6.7
Netherlands	5.0
Norway	0.8
Spain	1.2
Sweden	3.1
Switzerland	1.6
Turkey	0.5
UK	19.1
USA	3.3
Yugoslavia	4.3
Rest of world	15.7

Table 17.1 Per cent of foreign tourist arrivals, 1989

PART 3

Patterns of Tourism in the World's Regions

SECTION 1

Europe

INTRODUCTION

This section of the book seeks to answer the following questions.

1 What is the distribution of tourist resources in Europe, and how are they used for tourism?
2 What is the tourist role of each European country; where are their resorts; who visits them and why?

Chapter 18 outlines the structure, climate and tourist resources of Europe and the broad flow of tourist travel within Europe. The established Mediterranean destinations of France, Italy and Spain are described in Chapters 19 to 21, while the evolving destinations in the eastern half of the Mediterranean coastlands (i.e. Greece, Turkey, Malta and Cyprus) are dealt with in Chapters 22 and 23. These Mediterranean destinations are in competition with the resorts along the North African coast. (The latter may be considered as part of the European tourist region but are discussed in Chapter 29.)

One of the major inland destinations of Europe is the Alpine mountain chain. The core of the mountains are in Switzerland and Austria and are discussed in Chapter 24, although the outer fringes of the Alps are dealt with in the chapters on France, Italy and Germany. The main tourist generating regions of Europe are discussed in Chapters 25 (Benelux and Germany), 27 (the UK and Ireland) and 28 (Scandinavia).

The tourist resources of Eastern Europe and Russia are described in Chapter 26. At the time of writing (1993), the economic and political geography of this part of Europe has undergone major changes and its undoubted tourist generating potential has yet to be fully realised.

CHAPTER 18

Europe

LEARNING OBJECTIVES

After reading this chapter you should be able to
- identify the main physical, climatic, cultural and political regions of Europe
- locate the most important tourist regions of Europe
- explain the relationship between Europe's structure, climate and resources and its pattern of tourism
- describe the general patterns of tourist routes and tourist movements within Europe
- explain the relationship between a country's European location and the mode of transport used by its tourists
- appreciate the influence of economic, political and cultural factors on the development of tourism within Europe.

INTRODUCTION

Europe is one of the world's most highly developed tourist regions, both in terms of levels of domestic tourism and in terms of international tourist activity, accounting for 61 per cent of all international tourists in 1991. When defined in terms of systems of tourist travel, the European region includes the UK, Scandinavia, mainland Europe and all the countries bordering the Mediterranean basin: this chapter will discuss European tourism on this basis. The patterns of tourism within each country and sub-region of the continent of Europe will be described in the following chapters, while the countries of North Africa and the Middle East that have a Mediterranean coast will be described in detail in Chapter 29. The patterns of tourist movement within Europe are influenced by physical factors on the one hand and by economic and political factors on the other.

PHYSICAL FACTORS INFLUENCING TOURIST FLOWS

The north of Europe is characterised by high concentrations of highly urbanised and industrial populations who live in cool temperate, highly variable climates. To the immediate south lies a comparatively undeveloped region with a climate that could be considered ideal for tourism encircling an enclosed sea: the Mediterranean.

This juxtaposition of regions of such contrasting character has led to the evolution of a massive twofold tidal flow of tourists. First, a north to south flow both on a national scale (reflected in the domestic tourism of each country) and on an international scale predominantly to the Mediterranean. Second, there is a major coastward flow, again internationally mainly to the Mediterranean but also at domestic levels to the available coastline within each national boundary.

These north to south coastward flows are seasonal, with the main summer peak but with a secondary less significant winter peak flow to the southernmost coasts only. Superimposed on these major flows are further resource-based tourist movements:

1 a double seasonal flow to the mountain regions of Europe in the summer for scenic tourism and in winter for winter sports; and
2 an all-season flow into the cities throughout Europe for cultural, historic and business tourism, and a complementary flow of local urban popula-

tions out of the cities to the tourist attractions in the cities' own region or hinterland.

These tourists travel along corridors that are partly constrained by physical barriers: southward road and rail flows are concentrated on routes through the mountain barriers such as the Rhône corridor in France and the main passes through the Alps. Once the coast is reached, the flow of tourists tends to be spread via routes running along the main tourist coasts (e.g. from Marseille, west along the Spanish coast to Alicante and Malaga and east to Livorno and beyond, and the N2 motorway running the length of the Italian Adriatic coast).

POLITICAL AND ECONOMIC FACTORS INFLUENCING TOURIST FLOWS

Chapter 17 has listed the economic and political factors that influence tourist flows between countries. In the past, of course, the major political divide was between the Western European democracies and the communist bloc of Eastern Europe, which inhibited travel into and out of the communist countries.

Evolving economic and political structures and affiliations are leading to new patterns of tourism in Europe. The political geography of Eastern Europe has been transformed since 1989: barriers to travel between the countries belonging to the European Community (the EC) have progressively been reduced, while movement of Scandinavians between Scandinavian countries is free of all restrictions.

Other historic political relationships may facilitate or inhibit the development of crossborder tourism, for example, the French outnumber other European arrivals in their ex-colonies of Algeria, Tunisia, and Senegal (originally the administrative centre for the whole of French West Africa) whereas longstanding conflicts (e.g. between Turkey and Greece) may still be reflected in low levels of travel between the countries.

PHYSICAL RESOURCES OF EUROPE

In very general terms, Europe can be divided into three main physical zones (*see* Fig 18.1), which are characterised by very different types of tourism. These regions are:

1 The Mediterranean basin – the focal point of the southward flow of summer tourists.
2 The mountain chains that form the east-west spine of central and southern Europe. This region is the magnet that draws the dual seasonal flow of summer scenic tourism and winter sport tourism. It is also the region that divides the Mediterranean basin from
3 The industrialised lowlands of the northwest margins and of continental Europe. This region is the focus of business tourism and the area that generates day tourism to the local coast and countryside.

Each of these regions will be discussed: the following sections will describe the physical resources that have some relevance for tourism.

The Mediterranean basin

Physical character

Figure 18.1 shows that the description 'basin' is very appropriate, as apart from in the southeast sector (Tunisia, Libya and Egypt), the Mediterranean sea is encircled by mountains and uplands, with generally only a narrow strip of coastal lowlands (the strip of land that has the true Mediterranean climate). This structure reinforces the factors that protect the marine environment of this enclosed sea, sheltering the Mediterranean from the influences of Atlantic weather and wave patterns.

Climate

The general characteristics of the Mediterranean type of climate make it ideal for tourism. The summers are hot (generally averaging over 21° C) yet the relative humidity is low enough to maintain a comfortable environment for many forms of tourism for most of the time. However, the daily temperature range is high (up to 11° C) with temperatures climbing to over 30° C at the hottest time of day (mid to late afternoon). This limits active pursuits during this 'siesta' period, although the diurnal temperature range at coastal resorts may be slightly less due to the moderating influence of the sea and the cooling effect of sea breezes. The sum-

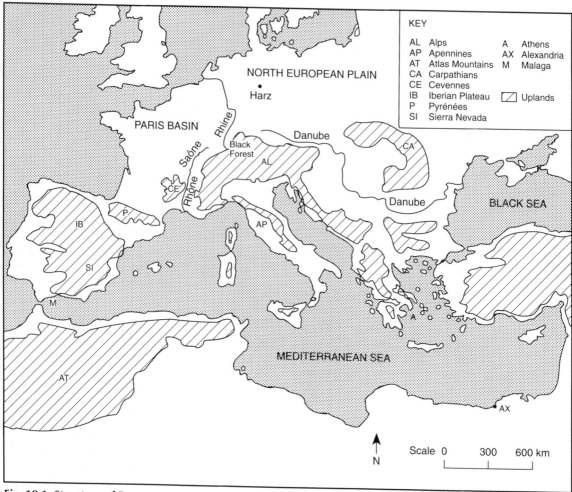

Fig. 18.1 Structure of Europe

mers are very sunny with cloudless skies through-out the sustained and reliable summer drought.

Even the winters have potential for tourism, as in many parts of the Mediterranean the temperatures in December and January rarely fall below 10° C and although the rainfall is concentrated in autumn or winter, it frequently occurs in intense bursts with clear, sunny skies in between. Much of the Mediterranean enjoys more than four hours' sunshine a day in December, and the greater part of the French and Spanish Mediterranean coast has less than ten rain days on average in January. Total amounts of rainfall range between 385 mm pa and 900 mm pa. The area that experiences this type of climate is shown in Fig 18.2.

It can be seen from the map that the Mediterranean basin extends over 3000 km east-west from the fringes of the Atlantic to the heart of the continental land masses of Asia, the Middle East and Africa, and extends roughly from latitude 31° N to 46° N, a north-south extent of more than 1500 km. Thus, within the broad climatic pattern described above, some variation in temperatures and rainfall is to be expected over so wide a region. The temperatures tend to increase not only to the south but also to the east of the Mediterranean basin. In summer the more land-locked eastern Mediterranean may be up to 2° C warmer than the western Mediterranean which is more open to the influences of the cooler, moister Atlantic weather systems.

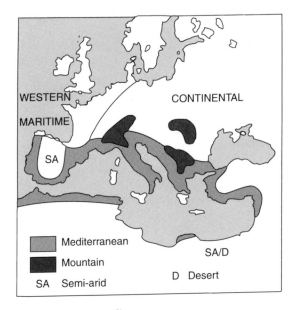

WESTERN

MARITIME

CONTINENTAL

SA

SA/D

D Desert

Mediterranean

Mountain

SA Semi-arid

Fig. 18.2 Europe's climates

The north-south temperature variations are more clear-cut; for example, the July average in Venice is 24.1° C, whereas in Djerba (on the North African coast) which is more or less due south of Venice, the summer average climbs to around 27° C.

The islands of the Mediterranean show a further variation in their patterns of temperature. The surrounding sea warms more slowly than land in the summer but retains its heat and, therefore, cools down more slowly in winter. This has the effect of marginally depressing the peak summer temperatures of the islands, but conversely it also has the effect of keeping the winter temperatures a little higher than those of the adjacent mainlands. The smaller the island, the more pronounced is this effect. Thus, some of the Mediterranean islands have important winter holiday trades (e.g. in 1988 Malta received 18 per cent of its visitors between November and February).

The second major variation in climate over the whole Mediterranean region concerns the distribution of rainfall. The total quantity of rainfall generally decreases to the east and south, whereas the length of the summer drought increases from two months in Marseille in the south of France, to three months (June–August) on the Spanish coast, six months (April–September) in Athens and the Greek islands,

and to nine months (February–October) in Alexandria. Not surprisingly, the total annual hours of sunshine increase across the Mediterranean in parallel with the increasing length of the summer drought (*see* Fig 18.3).

The Mediterranean type of climate thus has great tourist appeal and the whole coast of the Mediterranean basin enjoys its benefits, although Fig 18.2 shows that it is experienced on only a relatively narrow coastal zone. In the southern Mediterranean, the Mediterranean climate rapidly gives way inland to the deserts of continental Africa, while in the north and east the proximity of the European and Asian land masses causes the climate inland to become rapidly more extreme in temperatures. The mountain ranges in former Yugoslavia, the Apennines and the Alps all generate orographic rainfall, leading to sharp increases in rainfall inland away from the narrow Mediterranean coastal belt.

The Mediterranean coast and sea

The Mediterranean, as noted in Chapter 3, is one of the world's enclosed seas. Thus, the low tidal range (one metre at its very highest on the coast of Provence, South of France, and at the head of the Adriatic) combined with small waves (generally between 1 and 1.25 metres in height and seldom exceeding 2.75 metres in the winter storms) make tourism easy to provide and manage.

However, there are environmental problems arising from the fact that the sea is virtually completely enclosed, which may threaten the future of coastal tourism in the region. The Mediterranean Sea loses water from its surface due to intense

Place	Number of months' summer drought	Mean annual total hours sunshine	Mean annual total rainfall (mm)
French Mediterranean coast	2	2201	575
Malaga	3	2583	600
Athens	6	2737	396
Alexandria	9	3119	217

Fig. 18.3 Climatic variation in the Mediterranean

evaporation throughout the hot summer months; this is replaced by rivers, but more importantly, from inflow of sea water from the Atlantic through the Straits of Gibraltar. A little Mediterranean water flows out at sea floor level under the incoming current but this exchange of water is such that the Mediterranean water is completely exchanged only once in 75 years. Therefore, any pollution in the Mediterranean is relatively rapidly concentrated (by the evaporation) and only very slowly dispersed into the Atlantic.

There are about 350 million people living in the countries bordering the Mediterranean Sea, all discharging waste into the sea, either directly or via the main rivers such as the Po and Rhône which both flow from the main industrial areas. In summer, over 100 million tourists add to the problem. The waste includes some noxious industrial waste, but consists mainly of sewage runoff, which contains chemicals such as phosphates that plants need for their growth. The UN Environmental Programme shows that 85 per cent of urban effluent is discharged into the Mediterranean without previous treatment. In addition to this, it was estimated that in 1977 over one million tonnes of plant nutrients (from agricultural fertilisers washed from the fields into the rivers) were carried into the sea.

In particularly warm, still conditions the concentration of pollutants may build up in particular locations where the normal currents are slow to mix the sea and river water (e.g. at the head of the Adriatic). The surface water temperature in a normal August may reach 23–24° C; the combination of high water temperatures with the build-up of chemical pollutants many of which are in fact plant nutrients may trigger off the very rapid growth of small sea weeds and microscopic plants (algae) that float and multiply in the sea water by feeding on these dissolved plant nutrients. These 'algal blooms' were responsible for the green slime that developed in the sea off the Italian Adriatic resorts in the summer of 1989, and made sea bathing extremely unpleasant.

The other form of marine pollution that has an immediate effect on tourism is oil pollution. Very little of the Mediterranean is free of oil pollution as oil tankers regularly cross the sea from Suez and North Africa to the Atlantic. Over two million tonnes of crude oil a year are spilled into the Mediterranean during loading and unloading and tank cleaning operations.

Additional forms of pollution, for example from industrial processes, may be less immediately visible, but in the long run may have serious effects on health and thus inhibit tourists from bathing.

The mountain chains of Central and Southern Europe

Figure 18.1 shows that the mountain core of Europe consists of (east to west) the Pyrénées, the Cevennes (in the Massif Central), the Alps and the Carpathians. Three fingers of upland areas extend southward from this core into the Mediterranean region, namely the Iberian plateau with the Sierra Nevada of Andalucia forming its highest point, the Apennines that make up the spine of Italy and finally the chain of mountains that run north-west to south-east through former Yugoslavia, Albania, Bulgaria and Greece before being submerged to form the Greek Islands in the Aegean Sea. The Alps rise to over 4500 metres and dominate Southern Europe.

The core of the Alps consists of ancient mainly igneous rock, which when glaciated gives rise to jagged peaks and deep 'U' shaped valleys – dramatic landscapes of very high relative relief. The middle slopes may be wooded but towards the snow line the coniferous forest gives way to low growing vegetation adapted to conditions that are too cold for the growth of trees. The igneous Alps are flanked by and interspersed with mountains of limestone (e.g. the Jura, Dolomites, and further south the Dalmatian and Greek uplands), which in their southern extensions give rise to the typical limestone mountain or 'karst' scenery of dry valleys, rivers that disappear underground, extensive cave systems and barren mountain tops. Thus, the variety of mountain resources of Southern and Central Europe provide a wealth of choice for scenic and activity (i.e. climbing, walking, caving) holidays in summer in spite of the fact that the climate with its summer or autumn rainfall peak would appear to be less than ideal for tourism. It is, however, the winter climate that provides the second major tourist resource of these mountain regions. Even the southernmost extensions of the mountain systems have enough snow for the development of some winter sports centres, for example, in the Pyrénées the snow line descends to 1000 metres in mid-winter, and ski resorts have also been developed in the Sierra Nevada of Southern Spain and in the Apennines of the Italian peninsula. However, the major international winter sports centres are located in the mountain chains of continental Europe, where the continental high pressure system builds up and stabilises in winter, giving long spells of very cold, calm weather with clear skies and high amounts of sunshine. The effects of altitude and continentality thus combine to produce ideal conditions for the accumulation and maintenance of better quality snow over a longer winter season than in the more southerly mountain chains. The Alps are, therefore, the primary centre for international mountain tourism in Europe with many resorts that perform the dual function of providing for both summer scenic and winter sports tourism.

Further north in Europe, suitable snow cover does exist at progressively lower altitudes, e.g. in the Black Forest in Germany which rises to 1500 metres, the Harz (up to 1125 metres) and at 900 metres in the Cairngorms in Scotland. These regions, however, tend to cater for more localised domestic winter sports demand, as towards the north and western margins of Europe the climate becomes progressively windier and more variable (and thus less suitable for skiing) due to the increasing influence of depressions sweeping in from the Atlantic.

The lowlands of the north and west margins of continental Europe

The interior of continental Northern Europe has an extreme climate with very cold winters dropping below −30° C in January (e.g. Warsaw) and warm summers (19° C Warsaw, July) but the climate here suffers from a summer peak of rainfall associated with thundery, unstable weather conditions that develop over continental northern Europe. The rainfall peaks between May and August; Warsaw receives 87 mm rainfall in July alone. This reduces the tourist appeal of the climate of this part of Europe particularly in comparison to the adjacent Mediterranean climate.

It has been noted that the western margins of Europe experience an extremely variable climate dominated by the influence of cyclones moving northwest from the mid Atlantic over northwest France, Britain and Northern Europe. These depressions, caused by the process of mixing of moist Atlantic air with other air masses, bring cloudy weather with bursts of heavy rain, periods of freshening winds and showers, interspersed with spells of sunshine, all in quick succession. From time to time, however, the western margins of Europe may experience the sort of weather more typical of continental Europe – or indeed the Mediterranean – as the more stable air masses associated with these types of climate temporarily shift towards Britain. These can bring periods of intense cold weather in winter or conversely spells of hot, dry and sunny weather in summer, such as in the 'drought' years of 1976, 1989 and 1990 in the UK. It is the variability and unreliability of this type of climate that reduces its tourist appeal; it is virtually impossible to provide good long-term forecasts, so that tourists booking summer holidays in advance risk the chance of picking on a spell of wet or unsettled weather. In spite of this there is still a substantial flow of domestic tourism to the coasts of the countries of the 'western maritime' zone but increasingly this is of the short break, second holiday or day-trip type of tourism. Those who are able to take up international travel will be lured south to the reliable and predictably perfect summer weather of the Mediterranean region. Thus, the contrasts in the climate of Europe is one of the major factors which generates the north to south flow of tourists from Northern Europe to the Mediterranean coast.

PATTERNS OF TOURIST MOVEMENT IN EUROPE

There are two main concentrations of population in Europe: the first extends through the main industrial area of the Northern European lowlands stretching from Britain in the west through northern France, Benelux and Germany to the Czech and Slovak Republics and Poland in the east. The second (and the only major concentration of urban and industrial development south of the mountain spine of Europe) is located on the north Italian plain. These are the major tourist generating regions of Europe (*see* Fig 18.4).

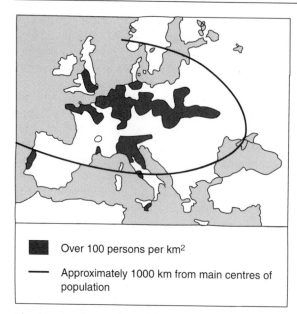

Over 100 persons per km²

Approximately 1000 km from main centres of population

Fig. 18.4 Major tourist generating areas of Europe

Car travel is the most important mode of tourist travel in Europe, dispersing tourists from these major population concentrations to the tourist receiving areas. Figure 18.5 shows domestic and international holiday travel habits and demonstrates the dominance of car travel to be a consistent pattern in most European countries, with the French at 81 per cent showing the highest rate of usage of the car.

Train travel only plays a significant part in countries such as Spain and Portugal which have lower than normal car ownership rates, or countries such as France with particularly good, fast inter-city rail services. Since 1986, the use of rail travel for tourism has declined significantly (to below 10 per cent in most countries by 1991). The notable exception was France, where 19 per cent of holiday trips now use the railway.

Predictably it is only countries which are wholly islands (e.g. Ireland) or which have much island territory (e.g. Greece and Denmark) that utilise boats to any great extent. These countries and those located in the periphery of Europe are the only countries to rely significantly on air transport for their main domestic and international holiday travel (e.g. UK, Netherlands, Luxembourg and Denmark to the north, and Greece on the southern periphery). However plane travel is on the increase throughout Europe, as increasing affluence encourages long-haul travel. By 1991 between 21 and 38 per cent of holiday trips in Germany, Netherlands, Luxembourg, Denmark, UK and Ireland were by plane. It is, however, road travel that dominates European holiday travel. In 1986, 68 per cent of all international and domestic holiday trips throughout Europe as a whole were made by car.

The main international flows of tourists from the main generating areas of Northern Europe are constrained by the mountain barrier to which they are

		Car	Coach	Train	Plane	Boat	Motorbike	
	France	81	7	15	6	2	2	Mediterranean territories (road and rail transport dominant)
	Portugal	76	16	17	3	3	1	
	Italy	73	11	15	5	5	2	
	Spain	70	12	16	5	2	–	
Northerly countries over 1000 km from most of the Mediterranean coast (air travel important)	Belgium	77	7	6	10	1	2	
	West Germany	61	7	16	17	3	1	
	Netherlands	70	14	8	14	5	6	
	Luxembourg	62	15	10	19	4	–	
	Denmark	59	4	14	18	11	3	Island countries (ferry travel important)
	UK	59	14	11	24	8	–	
	Ireland	51	6	11	31	18	1	
	Greece	78	0	4	13	25	1	

Fig. 18.5 Transport used by Europeans on holiday, 1986: per cent of residents' holiday trips (domestic and international) by mode of transport

attracted and through which they have to pass to reach the goal of the Mediterranean coast. Traffic is concentrated into the easiest north-south crossings of the Alps and considerable congestion may be experienced on the main routes at peak times.

The Rhône valley forms the major artery taking traffic via the Autoroute du Sol from the Paris region (and the western end of the Northern European conurbations) southwards round the western end of the Alps to the coasts of the western Mediterranean. The Rhine rift valley similarly forms a dominant north-south corridor of movement from the low countries and Germany to the northern slopes of the Alps. Here traffic either swings west to join the Rhône-Saône route southwards to the French or Spanish Mediterranean coasts or filters more directly south through the Alpine passes or tunnels into northern Italy for access to the Italian coast (and before 1989 the Dalmatian coast). Once the Mediterranean has been reached, tourists are dispersed via routes that hug the coast, keeping to the narrow strip of coastal lowlands (*see* Fig 18.6).

To the west, unbroken motorways run the length of the Spanish coast from the French border to Málaga, and to the east via the Côte d'Azur and North Italy. The western and Adriatic coasts of Italy are accessible from the Côte d'Azur and the north Italian plain (and the Adriatic highway ran along the length of the Dalmatian coast from Trieste to the Albanian border). Visitors can conveniently filter off these motorways directly into the coastal resort of their choice, though the proximity of major through routes running parallel to the coast may cause problems to local traffic, cutting off locals from the coast itself.

In spite of the convenient access by road to the Alpine and Mediterranean resorts, there is a limit to the distance and time that tourists are prepared to spend driving to their destinations. According to the Geneva-based International Touring Alliance, over 70 per cent of all leisure car trips in Europe are between 500 and 1000 km in length. Southern Spain, the toe of Italy, Greece and Turkey lie outside the 1000 km range of travel from the Northern European tourist generating area (*see* Fig 18.4). Significantly it is only Spain, Greece and Turkey of all the countries of mainland Europe that have a significant proportion of international tourist arrivals by air (*see* Fig 18.7), although, of course,

the tourist areas cut off from the tourist generating areas by sea, namely Britain, the Mediterranean islands and the countries of the North African coast also have a high proportion of incoming tourists arriving by air.

In those Mediterranean countries that rely on air transport for the bulk of their tourist arrivals, the developments for international tourists tend to be clustered in zones around the international airports, while in the countries of mainland Europe where car travel is the dominant mode of arrival, the tourist developments tend to be much more evenly spread through the attractive parts of each country.

General patterns of tourism in Europe

The Mediterranean basin is the dominant destination region of Europe with 113.2 million international arrivals to the coastal regions of the countries bordering the Mediterranean Sea in 1991. The greatest volume of mass tourism (118.0 million arrivals) is concentrated in the northwestern part of the Mediterranean (in France, Spain and Italy). The second important sub-region of the Mediterranean is the northeast section (Greece, former Yugoslavia, Turkey plus the islands of Malta and Cyprus) with 16.9 million arrivals. This sub-region has experienced two spurts of growth in tourist arrivals, firstly in the decade 1960–1970 when its share of Mediterranean arrivals jumped from 5.4 per cent to 11.6 per cent, and more recently in the period 1980–1985 when its market share rose from 13.9 per cent of all arrivals in the Mediterranean basin to 16.2 per cent (a growth rate of over 40 per cent, way above the growth rates of 13 to 18 per cent experienced in the other sub-regions of the Mediterranean). Since 1985, Cyprus and Turkey have continued to expand their tourism vigorously though not always at an even rate, but in the former Yugoslavia tourism has dropped from 7.8 million in 1990 to only 1.4 million in 1991 as a consequence of the civil war and distintegration of the country into smaller political units. The tourist flows to the African and extreme east coasts of the Mediterranean are negligible in comparison. In 1991, the southwest Mediterranean (i.e. the Islamic countries of Morocco, Algeria and Tunisia) received only 8.5 million arrivals and only 3.5 million visitors travelled to the southeast (i.e. Libya,

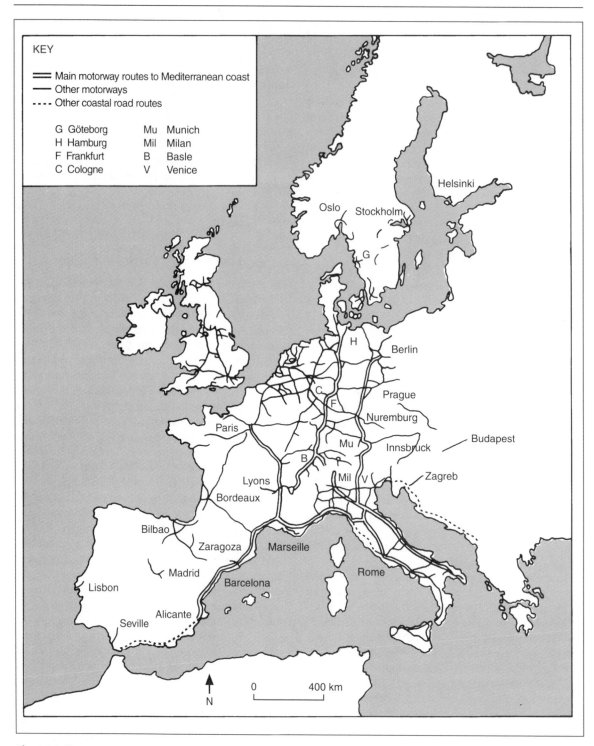

KEY

═══ Main motorway routes to Mediterranean coast
─── Other motorways
╌╌╌ Other coastal road routes

G Göteborg	Mu Munich
H Hamburg	Mil Milan
F Frankfurt	B Basle
C Cologne	V Venice

Helsinki

Oslo   Stockholm

G

H   Berlin

C   Prague

F   Nuremburg

Paris   Mu   Innsbruck   Budapest

B   Mil V   Zagreb

Lyons

Bordeaux

Bilbao

Zaragoza   Marseille

Madrid   Rome

Lisbon   Barcelona

Alicante

Seville

0   400 km

N

Fig. 18.6 European motorway routes

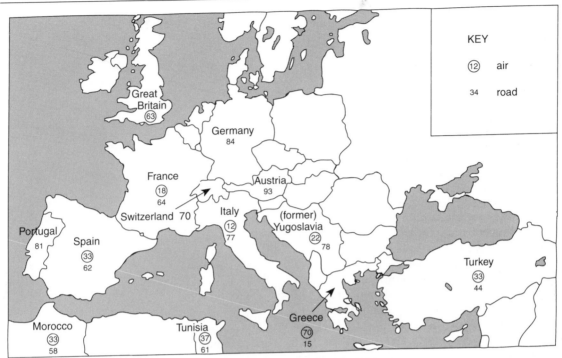

Fig. 18.7 European tourist arrivals: per cent arrivals by air and road, 1991

Egypt, Israel and Lebanon – countries where international conflict, civil wars and terrorist activity are currently occurring or have only relatively recently died down). In 1991 the region flared into war again, this time due to the Iraqi invasion of Kuwait, which affected tourism to Cyprus, Egypt, Jordan and Israel.

After the Mediterranean, Central Europe is the second most important tourist destination area with 56.9 million international arrivals in 1991. The Alps, of course, are a major attraction, with 31.7 million international visitors to Switzerland and Austria alone. Northern Europe received 25.3 million visitors.

Finally, Eastern Europe whose tourist resources consist mainly of the Carpathians (the eastern extension of the mountain chains of Southern Europe) and inland lakes and seas, such as Lake Balaton in Hungary and the Black Sea, received 43 million international tourists in 1988. This represented mainly travel between members of the communist bloc, as freedom of travel between Eastern and Western Europe was not possible before the upheavals in Eastern Europe in 1989.

The political changes in 1989 saw a dramatic (21.84 per cent) increase in tourism in the region, and tourist arrivals had reached 50.24 million in 1990. However, the economic problems associated with the revolutions combined with the world recession suggest that this growth may not be sustained.

POLITICAL AND CULTURAL FACTORS AND THEIR INFLUENCE ON PATTERNS OF TOURISM

The three main cultural and political regions of Europe are Western Europe, Muslim countries and the countries of Eastern Europe. Western Europe consists of Christian cultures, market economies and stable parliamentary democracies; and most countries of Western Europe are members of the EC, now known as the European Union (EU).

The European Community (EC)

Belgium	Italy
Denmark	Luxembourg
France	Netherlands
Germany	Portugal
Greece	Spain
Ireland	UK

Fig. 18.8 The twelve member states of the EC (1993)

There are relatively few constraints on travel between these countries, although until the end of 1992 and the full implementation of the Single European Act, there were still passport controls and differential rates of tax on goods necessitating customs controls. The Single European Act, or to give it its full title, 'The Single (Internal) Market of the European Community' defined the Single Market as 'an area without internal frontiers in which the free movement of goods, persons, services and capital is ensured'. As the Union evolves towards this situation, there will be changes in patterns of tourist movement throughout the member countries but the outcome may be simply an increase in total levels of tourism rather than its spatial redistribution. The overall effect may be simply to reinforce trends which are already well established.

The EU has, however, attempted to influence the spatial distribution of tourism more explicitly in two other ways. In 1986 the Community agreed to improve the seasonal and geographical distribution of tourism, by encouraging member countries to stagger holidays, to reduce congestion and also to promote social, rural and cultural tourism. More specifically member countries are invited not to encourage further tourist development in saturated areas, and to promote areas which have spare capacity.

The EU can aid the implementation of these policies directly through financial instruments such as the European Regional Development Fund, the ERDF, whose overall objective is to help correct imbalances in regional development, that is, to aid regions whose economic development is slow or declining. As tourism is one means of regional development and the ailing regions are likely to be those with spare capacity for tourism

and not suffering from tourist congestion, grant aid and financial assistance to tourism can fulfil both sets of objectives. Tourism projects accounted for 166 million ECU of ERDF expenditure in the period 1975–84. (N.B. 1 ECU in 1984 = £0.6013.)

	Million (ECU)
Belgium	6.71
Denmark	0.74
West Germany	13.02
Greece	7.73
France	4.33
Ireland	0.27
Italy	34.90
Luxembourg	1.59
Netherlands	2.38
UK	94.67
Total	166.38 m

Fig. 18.9 European Regional Development Fund – tourism grants, 1975–1984

Although the amounts of grant are small in the context of total (government and private sector) investment in tourism, these grants help support policies for the relocation of tourism.

The regions benefiting from this tourist investment were in the peripheral, mainly rural, regions of Europe (North and West Britain, the toe of Italy and the Greek Islands) or in certain depressed industrial areas of central Europe and in the Midlands and North of England.

From 1988 the Regional Fund was reformed; and priority was then given to regions whose economic development was lagging behind that of the community as a whole, to regions suffering from industrial decline, and to rural areas where alternatives to agricultural employment are needed. (*See* Lowyck and Wanhill, 1992). Between 1989 and 1993 48 300 million ECU were allocated to the achievement of these objectives, of which 2046.6 million ECU were allocated to tourism projects.

It has been suggested that these projects and other European environmental initiatives will result in an emphasis on tourism projects in the peripheral and rural areas rather than in the declining industrial regions of the EU.

Country	Million ECU
Italy	855.8
UK	237.9
Portugal	203.0
Ireland	188.6
France	184.0
Spain	182.0
Greece	166.7
Netherlands	19.1
Belgium	17.2
Germany	1.3

Fig. 18.10 Tourism-related assistance from Community Structural Funds, 1989–1993

The Eastern Bloc

Up to the autumn of 1989 the countries of Eastern Europe were all communist countries, with centrally planned economies but each country having differing levels of freedom of travel and of affiliation to the Soviet Union.

Yugoslavia was expelled from the communist bloc in 1948 and operated independently from the USSR, yet up to 1989 had retained communism as a means of government. The country was opened to western tourists in 1961. Albania is also a communist country independent of the USSR, but, in contrast to Yugoslavia, has been completely closed to Western travellers. There are signs, however, that Albania is starting to change and take in tourists. The rest of the communist world, which had been under the tight control of the USSR, has undergone profound changes as a consequence of the policy of *glasnost* introduced in the USSR, in 1986. In the autumn of 1989 the Warsaw Pact countries of East Germany, Poland, Czechoslovakia, Hungary, Bulgaria and Romania abandoned communism and started the process of transition to market economies and democratic forms of government. These countries up to 1989 had experienced severe controls on international travel by their citizens, and imposed strict controls on incoming Western travellers. Given longer term political stability the removal of these restrictions may eventually have very profound effects on patterns of tourism throughout

Europe, as new destinations are made available and accessible in Eastern Europe to Western travellers and a total population of over 110 million Eastern Europeans become more mobile to travel west as soon as their economic situation allows it.

However, further profound political changes have taken place in Eastern Europe since the revolutions of 1989. Firstly, East and West Germany were reunited during 1990 to become a single German state. In contrast the USSR has split up into a series of independent states and is facing a period of major political and economic readjustment. Czechoslovakia has also divided into two newly independent states (namely the Czech Republic and Slovakia). While these changes have occurred without conflict, the former Yugoslavia has broken up into civil war and in 1993 its political future was still not resolved. Its tourist industry has all but gone.

It is clear that the political, economic and social consequences of these changes are profound, and East Europe and the Balkans may still be facing a long period of instability and readjustment. A sustained period of political and economic stability is needed before new patterns of international tourism can evolve and become established.

The Islamic world

Islamic religious attitudes do not favour the promotion of Western-style sun, sea and sand tourism. Nevertheless, sporadic pockets of tourist development designed for the Western market have been established in the more politically stable countries of Morocco, Algeria and Tunisia although the association of Tunisia in 1985 with Palestinian terrorism has constrained further rapid development of tourism. The core of the political instability within the Islamic world centres on the long-running conflict between the Jewish State of Israel and the surrounding Arab/Islamic countries of Syria, Jordan, Lebanon, Saudi Arabia, Egypt and Libya. The conflict has existed since Israel was established in 1948 though the focus of the conflict has shifted. In the 1980s Egypt and Israel were not involved in conflict, whereas Lebanon had disintegrated into civil war. Thus, the potential for coastal and cultural tourism in this part of the region remains relatively undeveloped, and of all the countries in this region, Turkey is the most likely to undergo major changes in the near future. Although 95 per cent of Turks are Muslims, Turkey is an atheist State, and seems to identify itself more with the Western European style of economic and political organisation than those typical of the other Islamic countries. It is becoming politically more stable, and has expressed its desire to become integrated into Europe. In parallel with these changes, Turkey has been 'discovered' by Western tourists and in the 1980s it experienced the most rapid growth in international tourist arrivals in the whole European region. However, tourism to the Muslim countries of the southeast Mediterranean has been further disrupted by the 1991 Gulf War.

ECONOMIC FACTORS AND THEIR INFLUENCE ON PATTERNS OF TOURISM

Chapter 17 discussed the significance of differences in standards of living, exchange rates and relative costs in encouraging tourist flows between countries. Given the location of the major physical resources, and the political divisions within Europe, cost and price factors do influence specific destination choices. These factors have encouraged and reinforced the southward flow of tourists from the affluent Northern European countries to the relatively less developed economies in the south, for example, Spain, Portugal, Greece and Turkey. Cost factors also influence the distribution of tourists between these countries. The Economist Intelligence Unit estimates that over half the changes in the travel shares of competing Mediterranean destinations in the period 1980–1987 were due to changes in the relative cost of holidays in each destination. The success of the Northern European countries in adapting their economies to post-industrialisation, and the relative rates of economic development of the southern countries will, no doubt, influence the choice of specific geographical location of future tourist usage in the main destination regions of Europe.

FURTHER READING

Cooper, C P and Lockwood, A (Eds) (1994) *Progress in Tourism Recreation and Hospitality Management*, Vol. 5, Wiley.

Davidson, R (1992), *Tourism in Europe*, Pitman Publishing.

Lowyck, E and Wanhill, S (1992), 'Regional development and tourism within the European Community', in Cooper, C and Lockwood, A (Eds), *Progress in Tourism, Recreation and Hospitality Management*, Vol. 4, Belhaven.

Pompl, W and Lavery, P (1993) *Tourism in Europe: Structures and Developments*, CAB International.

QUESTIONS AND DISCUSSION POINTS

1 Study the figures in the following two tables. Which physical, political and economic factors help explain the pattern of tourist arrivals to Tunisia?

Nationality	Arrivals (000s)
French	411.6
German	330.5
British	124.4
Italian	58.7
Scandinavian	71.8
Swiss	34.0
Belgian	38.5
Dutch	46.0
Austrian	26.5
Spanish	17.1
Yugoslav	4.0
Luxembourg	2.4
Algerian	297.5
Libyan	3.9
Moroccan	6.7
USA	6.3
Canadian	2.4
Middle Eastern	22.4
African	5.8
Other	21.9
Total	1532.3

Table 18.1 Tourist arrivals in Tunisia, 1986

	By air	By sea	By road
European	1084.5	40.5	10.3
North African	42.4	2.7	263.0
Middle Eastern	21.7	0.2	0.7

Table 18.2 Tourist arrivals in Tunisia by mode of transport, 1986 (000s)

2 In what ways might the activities of the European Union influence the pattern of tourism in Europe?

3 A variety of reasons help to explain the movement of tourists between the countries of Europe. Some of these reasons are listed below. Can you rank them in order of importance? Are there any other factors that influence tourist flows that are not included here?
   - Distance between countries.
   - Differences in cost of living.
   - Convenient routes between countries.
   - Differences in climate between countries.

ASSIGNMENTS

1 Divide into groups of two.
   One of you works for a tour company based in London. Your chief executive is presenting a paper at an international conference in Genoa in Italy at Easter. He has asked you to make his travel arrangements for him. Outline the modes of transport and the routes that he might choose from. Recommend the route and mode that you think might best meet his travel needs. List the factors that influence your decision.

   The other member of the pair works in the AA Overseas Routes Unit. A party of students who share a car and are based at a college in South Wales also wish to attend the same conference, and have asked for your advice on how to get to Genoa. Outline the choice of routes open to them, and recommend a route that you think would be most suitable to them. List the factors that influenced your decision.

   As a pair, compare these two lists. Explain any similarities and differences in your lists.

2 You work for the European Union. You have just received two requests for grant aid for major tourist projects, one in Merseyside in the northwest of England, and the other from Sicily in southern Italy. The applications are for equal amounts of money. You only have enough money left in your budget this year to fund one of the projects.

   Identify the tourism and regional development objectives and policies of the EU. Make a reasoned recommendation of which project should be granted aid.

CHAPTER 19

France

LEARNING OBJECTIVES

After reading this chapter you should be able to

- assess the tourist potential of the climatic, landscape, historical and cultural resources of France
- distinguish the regional distribution of these geographical resources and their development and use for tourism
- demonstrate a knowledge of the main tourist resorts and tourist centres
- understand the role of France in the general pattern of European tourism
- be aware of the problems of seasonality and congestion in French tourist destinations and on the routes to them.

INTRODUCTION

France is characterised by a variety of tourist resources: different types of coast and climate, attractive, unspoilt rural areas, mountains, a wealth of historic and architectural sites and the cultural attractions of French nightlife and regional cuisine. With such a varied choice, it is

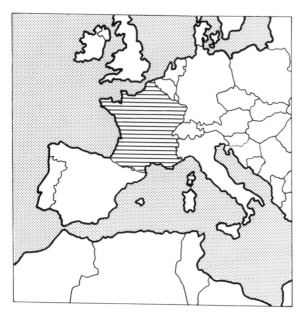

not surprising that the majority of the French take holidays in their own country. There is, however, a spatial imbalance between the distribution of the tourist resources and the location of the resident population: the greatest concentration of natural resources lie in the south of the country in upland and Mediterranean France while the most densely populated industrial areas of France are in the lowlands of the north and northeast, and around Lyon in central France.

The French domestic market is large, with an estimated 52 million holidays being taken in 1990, and is still very highly peaked in August. This inevitably leads to great congestion on the routes (the E1/A6 and N7) running south from Paris through Lyon via the Rhône Valley, to the Mediterranean coast at Marseille. The Côte d'Azur to the east of Marseille has long been the most popular holiday region for the French. Some of the other regions are relatively economically backward compared to the more densely populated and industrialised lowlands of northern France. The highly centralised French planning system has systematically developed certain rural regions for tourism, e.g. the Aquitaine, parts of the Central Massif and Languedoc-Roussillon, in order to encourage regional economic development. These projects have focused on the needs of the huge domestic market rather than those of foreign

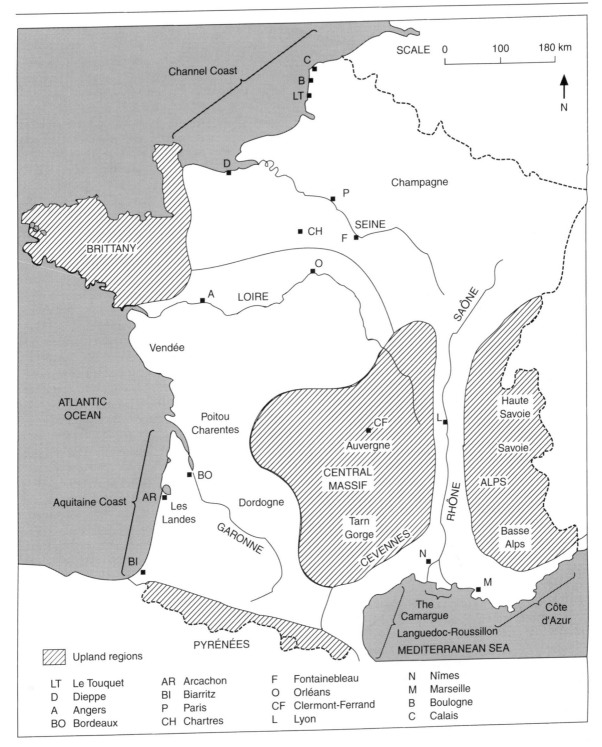

Fig. 19.1 Regions of France

tourists. Paris, the Côte d'Azur and the Alps are still the most popular destinations for the international visitor to France. 55.7 million foreign tourists visited France in 1991, making it the leading European international tourist destination.

Physically France can be divided into five tourist resource regions (*see* Fig 19.1):

1 The lowlands of the north and west (the Seine, Loire and Garonne basins).
2 The Channel and Atlantic coasts, including the Brittany peninsula. Both these two regions experience the variable western maritime climate.
3 Upland France. This consists of a series of uplands running from the Pyrénées in the south west, via the central Massif to the Alps and its associated ranges in the east. All these areas have the harsher climate characteristic of upland areas.
4 The Mediterranean coast.
5 The island of Corsica.

THE LOWLANDS OF NORTH AND WEST FRANCE

The Paris basin

This region consists of the Seine basin with the Paris conurbation (the Ile de France) at its centre. To the northeast of Paris, the open, flat landscapes of Picardy and the Nord rise gradually to the border with Belgium. To the east of Paris the lowlands give way to a series of scarps and vales, and then to the plateau of Lorraine. To the south, the Seine valley rises gradually into the gently rolling countryside of Burgundy. The chalk plateau of Normandy lies to the west of Paris. The countryside of the Paris basin is pleasant though unspectacular; it provides for the daily and weekend recreation of the city, rather than for tourist needs. International tourists tend to bypass the countryside of this region on their way south.

Paris itself is, of course, another matter. The Ile de France received 27 per cent of the foreign arrivals at French hotels (amounting to six million visitors) and 29 per cent of all foreign hotel bednights in 1990. The main historic and cultural attractions of Paris cluster along the banks of the Seine in a compact central area 4 km by 6 km. The

cathedral of Notre Dame is built on an island in the Seine itself, while the 'left bank' region (i.e. on your left as you look downstream towards the sea) is famous for its student life, its many museums and galleries (e.g. the Musée d'Orsay) and the Eiffel Tower. The right bank is dominated by a series of grand avenues planned by Haussman in the 1800s. These radiate out from the Arc de Triomphe. The most famous of these avenues is the Champs Elysées where many fashionable shops, cafes and commercial art galleries are located. It leads to the Place de la Concorde, the Tuileries Gardens and the Louvre, the most famous art gallery in Paris. More modern tourist attractions include Les Halles (a shopping complex built on the site of the old meat market) and the Pompidou Centre which has a permanent exhibition of 20th century art as well as space for temporary exhibitions. The fact that the attractions of Central Paris are mostly within easy walking distance of each other, and that the centre abounds with cafes, theatres, shops and nightlife makes it a popular destination for city breaks. It is also a very easily accessible city with two international airports (Charles de Gaulle 23 km from the city centre, and Orly, only 15 km out). Both are linked to the centre by bus and train. There are also attractions, both ancient and modern on the outskirts of Paris. For example, the Asterixland Theme Park (opened in 1989) which is located on the northern fringe within 40 km of the centre, and Disney World, which opened in 1992. This theme park is just part of the Euro Disney resort which includes hotels, golf courses and a complex of shops and restaurants. The Palace of Versailles, built in the 17th century, is located even closer to the city centre, on the southwestern edge of the city. Within an 80 km range of Paris there are additional attractions such as the Palace of Fontainebleau, Chartres Cathedral and the vineyards and caves of the Champagne region.

Paris also has an expanding range of exhibition and conference facilities. In 1990 it was the world's leading centre for international conferences and business tourism due to the combination of high quality facilities, city centre attractions and good accessibility.

The Charles de Gaulle airport will increase its importance as a rail, air and road communications hub as the European high-speed rail network is developed and the airport terminal capacity is increased.

The Loire valley

The Loire river rises in the central Massif, flows north towards Paris, and swings west at Orléans to reach the Atlantic at La Baule. The lowland landscape of the area, known as the Garden of France, is quietly attractive with agricultural land in the valley bottom and vineyards on the upper slopes. The historic resources are the major tourist attraction: over 120 châteaux are strung along the river, often sited on a prominent bluff or spur overlooking the valley. They range from defensive medieval castles through to renaissance residences to the classical houses of the 17th and 18th centuries. The main concentration of châteaux lies between Angers and Orléans. A significant number are now hotels, and many more have additional attractions: for example, Chambord (the largest château of the region) has a game reserve, the fortress-like Chaumont displays a range of horse-drawn vehicles, Villandry has superb formal gardens, and Saumur has a porcelain museum and a classical equitation centre.

The coastal lowlands of the Vendée and Poitou-Charentes link the Loire to the Aquitaine basin. They are a mixture of wooded lowlands, open plateau landscapes and moorland, making the transition from northern arable landscapes to the southern pastoral economy, and from the cool and variable north European weather to a sunnier and warmer western maritime climate.

The Garonne basin: the Aquitaine

There is a strong contrast in the landscapes and tourist attractions of the head waters, middle valley and coastal section of the Garonne basin. The sandy coastal lowlands of Les Landes are dominated by coniferous forests. The middle Garonne valley, the home of the Bordeaux wine, is an undulating rather monotonous landscape. These are rather low-key tourist areas, but the edges of the valley, e.g. in the Dordogne to the north of the river provide some more attractive landscapes. Most of the tourist facilities of the region are concentrated on the coast.

THE CHANNEL AND ATLANTIC COAST

Atlantic coast of Aquitaine

This stretch of coastline from Biarritz to the mouth of the Garonne has two geographical advantages favouring tourism and one disadvantage which until relatively recently has inhibited the development of its tourist potential. Of France's non-Mediterranean coast, this region has the advantage of the best climate for seaside tourism. Bordeaux has an August average temperature of 21° C and only 771 mm of rainfall a year (though the maximum is in July). Biarritz has 1231 hours of sunshine between April and September (compared to the French Mediterranean with 1800 hours). The region also has the advantage of a long (270 km) stretch of virtually unbroken sandy beach, backed by sand dunes. The drawback, however, is the relative inaccessibility of the beach. The dunes have caused the internal drainage to form shallow lagoons and marshes which are difficult to cross. The dunes (up to 10 km wide, and 100 m high) are an additional barrier and the Baie d'Arcachon is the only major natural gap through them.

A plan for the integrated tourist and rural development of the area was drawn up in 1967, and an inter-ministerial commission set up to coordinate the development, which was mainly financed and implemented by the private sector. The plan divided the coast into 16 sectors: nine zones to be developed for tourism (beach, lakeside and watersports activities), separated by seven 'green zones' where landscape and wildlife were to be conserved and measures taken to protect the fragile dune systems from recreational pressure. The development areas include the conservation of existing resorts such as Arcachon and Biarritz, the redevelopment and expansion of existing settlements (e.g. Lacanau where 22 000 new bed spaces, golf facilities and entertainment centres have been added, and Hossegor-Capbreton where there is now a 700-berth marina) and the creation of new resorts such as Moliets (*see* Fig 19.2). Facilities were developed and extended both on the coast and for water sports on the freshwater lakes behind the dune belt. The new accommodation was designed to meet the modern needs of the French domestic market. By 1982, 28 per cent of the bed spaces were in campsites; the serviced sector (guest houses and hotels) accounted for only just over 13 per cent of bed spaces, whereas 46 per cent were provided as second homes for French families.

Tourism in the region grew steadily since the development began. Hotel bednights remained fairly stable through the recession years of the 1980s while camping in the region continued to grow (from 13.4 million nights in 1982 to 15.6 million in 1987).

The Atlantic coast of the Loire and Brittany

Between the mouth of the Garonne and Nantes there are many seaside resorts both fashionable and for families, with good sandy beaches. But the climate becomes cooler and less sunny towards the north, and the region does not support mass tourism on the same scale as Aquitaine or the Mediterranean.

Brittany

The peninsula is similar structurally and physically to southwest England: the core of the region is infertile granite moorland but the effect of marine erosion on this type of rock creates a magnificent rugged coastline, consisting of bold cliffs and rocky headlands, with caves, stacks and cliffs, interspersed with coves and sheltered bays where fine sandy beaches and dune systems accumulate.

The isolation and backward economy of the region has led to long-term depopulation, though the area has a strongly independent cultural identity. The economy has depended on agriculture and fishing though attempts have been made to diversify the economy and living standards have slowly been rising.

Tourism is significant in the local economy, but it is a region that is declining in popularity. In 1983 the region received 9.1 per cent of French summer holidays, but in the period 1985–87 its total number of hotel bednights (French and foreign)

declined slightly, while the total number of camping bednights (French and foreign) dropped from 12.8 million in 1982 to 11.1 million in 1987. Of these, only about a quarter were overseas visitors (in the past, mainly from UK, and the Benelux countries). The climate and relatively isolated position of the peninsula may explain why the region's tourist industry is not growing. The climate is mild due to its maritime situation, but it is humid, drizzly and quite windy, with rain all year round, although total amounts of rain are fairly low (822 mm near Brest, and about 1180 mm on the inland moors). The summer average temperatures do not rise much above 17° C and Brest has 1190 hours sunshine between April and September. Thus, climatically the region is not able to compete with the Aquitaine, let alone the Mediterranean coast.

The Channel coast

This region also has the typical variable western maritime climate (770–1025 mm rainfall per annum, with average maximum temperatures in the range 18–20° C). There is a string of resorts along the coast (e.g. Dunkerque, Calais, Boulogne, Le Touquet and Deauville) catering for local demand from the Paris region and day-trip visitors from England. But this region also suffers from Mediterranean competition and shows the familiar problems of a declining serviced sector and outdated tourist infrastructure, just like the resorts on the English side of the Channel.

UPLAND FRANCE

The Pyrénées

The French–Spanish border runs east–west along the crest of this 400 km mountain chain. The mountains rise to over 3300 metres, but are only 50–80 km wide. The landscape is varied, with well wooded valleys, deep gorges, lakes and craggy mountains. The Pyrénées National Park connects with the Ordesa National Park on the Spanish side of the border. Thus, the landscape is an important tourist resource, but there is also enough winter snow to support ski resort development. The central Pyrénées normally have 100 days of snow cover at 1200 m and 170 days at 1800 m. A series of ski resorts have been developed: Font-Romeu, Aulus-les-Bains, Bagnères-de-Luchon and Superbagnères (a high altitude greenfield site) on the eastern section of the Pyrénées, and a second group of resorts on the northern edge of the National Park (including La Mongie, a modern resort, Barèges and the main centre at Cauterets – *see* Fig 19.2). In 1987, the Pyrénées had 10 per cent of total French ski lift capacity, and 13.5 per cent of the winter sport resort bed spaces. But it took only 8 per cent of the total market share. Another tourist resource of the area are the spas based on mineralised springs. This aspect of tourism is reflected in many of the place names like the spa town of Ax-les-Thermes and also places such as Aulus-les-Bains and Les Eaux-Bonnes.

The central Massif

This upland area (bounded by the 300 m contour) makes up one sixth of France. Its average height is 900 m but it rises to 1800 m in places. Its landscape is varied but the harsh climate inhibits the development of mass tourism. The major landscape resources are:

1 The Cevennes National Park, an area of monotonous granite moorlands which produce more dramatic landscapes on their eastern edge, where the mountains overlook the mouth of the Rhône Valley, and are deeply dissected by steep-sided ravines. From the summit of Mont Aigoual the land drops 1200 m in a distance of only six km.

2 The limestone plateaux and gorges of the Grande Causses area on the western edge of the Cevennes National Park. The river Tarn runs through a dramatic gorge here.

3 The puys of the central Auvergne. The term 'puys' refers to the 70 extinct volcanic cones that rise from above the plateau of the Auvergne. Some are regular craters with circular rims, some simply the remaining core of the volcano, standing out as precipitous towers of rock that are sometimes capped by a church or monastery. This scenery is found in the Puy de Dôme area of the Parc des Volcans d'Auvergne to the west of Clermont-Ferrand.

The climate of these uplands is variable, as it lies at the junction of Atlantic, continental and Mediterranean influences, but its height keeps temperatures low. Above 900 m, snow may lie between 30 and 100 days, and only three months a year are frost-free. Rainfall may reach over 2000 mm per annum, though the Mediterranean flanks are much drier. The region is economically backward, with a declining upland agriculture, and has long been considered France's most serious problem area. Integrated rural development schemes have been promoted since 1962 aimed at both improving the local economy and protecting the fragile landscape. In some areas (e.g. the inner zones of the Cevennes National Park) access is restricted and camping prohibited, but elsewhere tourism is promoted in three ways, by:

1 the support of rural landscape-based tourism;
2 the support of thermal spas (the central Massif has one third of all French spas) e.g. at Vichy;
3 the development of ski centres (e.g. Mont Dore). However, the snow cover and terrain cannot compete with the Alps or Pyrénées, and only two per cent of France's ski lifts are located here;
4 the creation of integrated holiday villages with a range of accommodation and sports facilities (e.g. swimming pools, boating and other activities).

In spite of these developments tourism in the region is still fairly low key. The core of the region (Auvergne and Limousin) received only about 5 per cent of French hotel bednights and 2.5 per cent of French and foreign camp bednights in 1987.

The French Alps

The southwest end of the Alpine chain is located in France (*see* Fig 19.2). The mountains drop from Mont Blanc (4807 m) in the north, through the Haute Savoie, the Savoie (around 3000 m) to the Basse Alps in Provence (2–3000 m) in the south. Although summer visitors outnumber winter sports tourists, the region is better known for its ski facilities. The average snowfall in the northern section is over 3 metres at 1500 m altitude but in the Basse Alps the average snow depth is only 2.5 m at the same altitude. The main season is

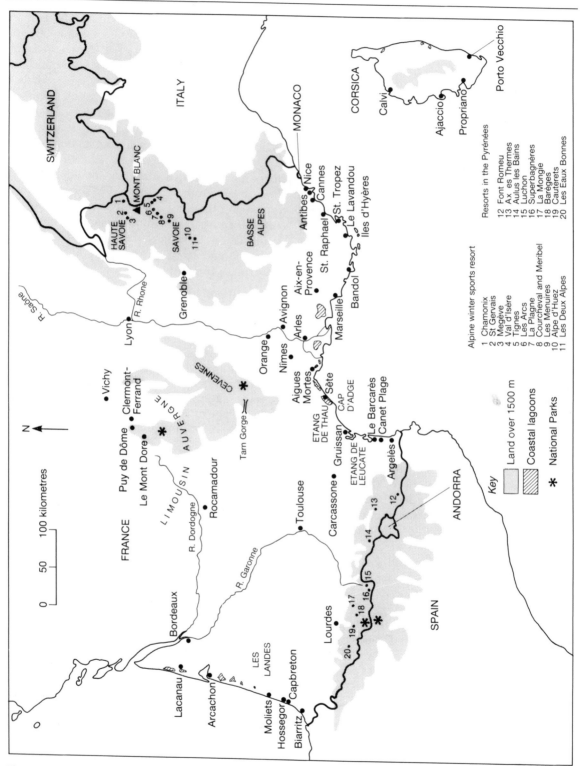

Fig. 19.2 Tourist resources of southern France

Key
- Land over 1500 m
- Coastal lagoons
- ✳ National Parks

Alpine winter sports resort
1 Chamonix
2 St Gervais
3 Megève
4 Val d'Isère
5 Tignes
6 Les Arcs
7 La Plagne
8 Courcheval and Meribel
9 Les Menuires
10 Alpe d'Huez
11 Les Deux Alpes

Resorts in the Pyrénées
12 Font Romeu
13 Ax es Thermes
14 Aulus les Bains
15 Luchon
16 Superbagnères
17 La Mongie
18 Baréges
19 Cauterets
20 Les Eaux Bonnes

February and March, but the season normally begins in early December and runs through to the end of April. Lower altitudes throughout the French Alps may get as much snow but it is more variable and the season is less reliable. If the effects of global warming continue to grow, the variability of snow cover at each end of the season is likely to increase.

The French Alps have been a winter sports centre since before the Second World War. The region now accounts for 82 per cent of all French ski lift capacity and over 480 km of ski piste. Eighty-one per cent of all winter sports holidays in France were located in the Alps. The original resorts, such as Chamonix and Megève were developed before 1939 and were based on existing climatic or thermal resorts. A second generation of resorts were based on expanded villages at higher altitude, e.g. Courcheval and La Plagne. These are large centres with over 30 000 bed spaces. Since the 1960s, high altitude greenfield sites have been developed for smaller modern purpose-built integrated ski centres. These have been located adjacent to new ski runs with the best slopes and reliable good quality snow. The traffic system segregates pedestrians, skiers and motor traffic; indoor sports facilities are included and the settlements are designed to cater for summer landscape, climbing and activity holidays as well as for winter sports.

The most significant of these centres (with up to 20 000 bed spaces) include: Morzine-Avoriaz and St Gervais in the Haute Savoie; and Les Arcs, Tignes, Méribel, Les Menuires, Alpe d'Huez and Les Deux Alpes in the Savoie region.

Like the other major regional tourist developments in France, the accommodation provided is geared more to the tastes of the domestic market than for overseas visitors. In 1988, 45 per cent of the bed spaces were in rented chalets or apartments and 30 per cent in second homes for the French. Only 11 per cent were in hotels.

THE MEDITERRANEAN COAST

This region receives more tourists than any other part of France. Its climate is the main attraction; it

	Average temperature °C	Average rainfall mm	Average relative humidity %
January	7	48	68
February	8	38	64
March	10	46	62
April	13	51	60
May	16	48	59
June	20	25	57
July	22	15	54
August	21	23	57
September	19	66	63
October	15	94	69
November	11	79	70
December	8	56	70

Total annual rainfall – 589 mm.
Total annual hours of sunshine – 2000 hours.
Average number of rainy days per annum – 100 days.

Fig. 19.3 Marseille's climate

has the most suitable weather for sun, sea and sand tourism of all the French coasts.

Due to its northwesterly location in the Mediterranean basin, the region has a shorter summer drought than, for example, Greece, and this reinforces the problems of seasonality that are characteristic of French tourist destinations.

The region also has much of cultural and historic interest. Well preserved ancient Roman buildings are found in the lower Rhône, for example, the Roman theatre and arch at Orange, the arena and Temple of Diana at Nîmes, and the Roman city at Arles. Medieval castles such as at Perpignon, walled cities (e.g. Carcassonne), cathedrals (e.g. Aix-en-Provence) and other buildings such as the 12th century bridge at Avignon are abundant throughout the area. Many of the famous artists of the 19th and 20th century lived and worked in the eastern part of the region, and are commemorated here. The Matisse Museum, Renoir's house and Picasso museums are located in the Antibes–Nice area, and Cézanne's home is in Aix-en-Provence. The living culture of folklore, carnivals and festivals (ancient and modern) add to the distinctive regional character. The dramatic landscapes of the Cevennes and the Basses Alpes provide the back drop to the region, but after the climate it is the coast that is the most important tourist resource of Mediterranean France. The coast can be divided into three zones (*see* Fig 19.1):

1 **The French Riviera**, from the Italian border to Marseille (the Côte d'Azur).
2 **The Camargue** (the delta at the mouth of the Rhône) between Marseille and Nîmes.
3 **The Languedoc-Roussillon coast** which runs from Nîmes to the Spanish border.

These areas are very different in their physical characteristics, and in the style of tourism that has been developed.

The French Riviera

This riviera consists (from east to west) of the coasts of the Départements of Alpes-Maritimes (the Côte d'Azur), Var, and Bouches du Rhône. The Alps protect the coast from cold winter and spring winds, e.g. the Mistral, that blow from the centre of the continent, so the coastal strip enjoys a mild winter climate that encourages some winter tourism. The coastal belt is narrow. The Côte d'Azur has many rocky promontories and cliffs interspersed with small bays and safe yachting harbours (e.g. Cannes). Most of the beaches are pebbly. From the very beginning of European tourism (from the Grand Tours of the 17th and 18th centuries) the Côte d'Azur has been a fashionable area, though it first became popular as a winter resort rather than for summer tourism. When the railway from Paris reached Nice in 1865 and sea bathing became popular, summer tourism grew rapidly, and the rich and famous bought land for their private villas and apartments and there is little land available for new development. The resorts are stylish and exclusive with luxurious grand hotels, nightlife and casinos (e.g. at Cannes and in the tiny independent state of Monaco). More recently, conference facilities have been added (e.g. at Nice in 1985). This section of coast is more or less at capacity. The coast of Var (stretching from St Raphaël to Bandol) has better sandy beaches (e.g. at St Tropez and the Iles d'Hyères); it has also been developed more recently and has facilities and accommodation for the mass market. Self-catering and camping resorts are located between St Tropez and St

Raphaël, and Le Lavandou is a new resort with a casino and all facilities (*see* Fig 19.2). There has been a huge increase in the development of self-catering apartments in the Côte d'Azur between 1986 and 1991 (from 3900 beds to 28 200 beds). They now account for 14 per cent of all the region's accommodation, and a further 18 000 beds were planned for the 1991–3 period. They are concentrated in the Cannes and Theoule regions. However, hotels still provide the bulk of the bed spaces of the region (45 per cent in 1991) while campsites are also important (providing 21 per cent of the bed spaces).

The French Riviera thus caters for all sections of the sun, sea and sand market, and in 1987 received a third of all France's camping bednights (French and foreign visitors) and about 14 per cent of the hotel bednights.

The Camargue

The lowlands of the Rhône delta occupy the 90 km stretch of coast between Marseille and Aigues-Mortes (south of Nîmes). It is a desolate, marshy area of inaccessible reed beds and shallow brackish lagoons. Wild white horses and bulls (reared for the bull rings in Provence) roam the marshlands, and wildlife such as duck, heron, flamingo, ibis and egret abound in a 15 000 ha nature reserve. The region caters only for very specialised tourism as the coast, with its shifting dunes and watercourses, is too unstable for coastal tourist development.

The Languedoc-Roussillon coast

Until the 1960s, this coast was hardly developed for tourism. The sweeping dune coastline is separated from the mainland by a series of marshy lowlands and shallow lagoons. The largest is the Etang de Thau, 20 by 13 km and 25 m at its deepest. The lagoons were infested with mosquitoes. In 1960 the French Government initiated the tourist development of the area by building access routes, clearing the swamps and eradicating the mosquitoes, as part of a coordinated regional development programme (*see* Chapter 16).

Tourist accommodation and facilities were concentrated in five centres (*see* Fig 19.2).

1 The northern group of resorts, which in 1990 contained 24 per cent of the tourist capacity of the region, is located on a 20 km stretch of sandy beach just to the south and west of the historic town of Aigues Mortes. Grau du Rois, Carnon and Palavas are older established resorts while Port Camargue and La Grande Motte are new developments. La Grande Motte is the biggest single resort on the Languedoc-Roussillon coast: it is famous for its group of pyramid shaped apartment blocks, and its large marina.

2 Thau. This group of resorts stretch along a 30 km length of sandy coast and provide 25 per cent of the region's bed capacity. They include the established resorts such as Sète, Mèze and Marseillon while Cap d'Adge is a new development. There are water sports provided on Thau lake.

3 Valras-Gruissan

4 Leucate-Barcarès. This group of resorts provides 22 per cent of the region's bed capacity, with marina developments at Baracarès.

5 Canet-Argelès. St Cyprien is one of the main centres in this group of resorts. It also has a marina and provides 13 per cent of the Languedoc-Roussillon coast's bed spaces.

Some of these centres were based on the original small resorts but others were completely new, developed in conjunction with a range of beach and water sports facilities (using both the lagoons and the sea). The tourist centres are separated by woodland and undeveloped nature reserves. The development is geared to the needs of the domestic market. By 1988, 63 per cent of the accommodation was in the form of second homes, while campsites provided another 26 per cent. The greatest attraction of the Languedoc-Roussillon region is the sun and sea (mentioned by 76 per cent of visitors) while sightseeing (28 per cent) and sports (23 per cent) were other important attractions. Tourism here is firmly based on outdoor activity: only 12 per cent mentioned nightlife as a significant attraction.

The region caters more for the domestic market than for international tourists: 88 per cent of the visitors in 1986 were French. By 1992 there were 54.1 million domestic nights. The foreign tourists came mainly from Belgium, Germany and The Netherlands. The region accounted for about ten per cent of all (domestic plus foreign) camping bednights in 1987, but only four per cent of foreign visitors' hotel bednights.

Corsica

Corsica is 170 km from the Côte d'Azur. It is the most mountainous of all the Mediterranean islands, with a variety of landscapes from Corsican pine forests to deep valleys and stony deserts. The east is low lying with lagoonal plains along the coast while the rest of the coast is a mixture of red cliffs and yellow sandy beaches. Being an island, its temperatures are a little less extreme than those on the nearby mainland (*see* Fig 19.4) though its summers are a little drier.

The island has fairly poor communications with the mainland (ferries operate from Marseille, Toulon and Nice), and very few tourists make the crossing. In 1987 only 137 000 French and 150 000 foreign visitors stayed on the island.

	August Max	Min	January Max	Min
Corsica (Ajaccio)	28	16	13	3
French Mediterranean coast (Nice)	31	15	18	0

Fig. 19.4 Comparison of temperatures on Corsica and on the French Mediterranean coast (average temperatures °C)

THE FRENCH DOMESTIC MARKET

Many of the new tourist developments in the regions of France have been designed with the domestic, rather than the international market in mind. The French domestic market is not typical of Western Europe as a whole. It is characterised by:

1 A much lower level of foreign tourism than most other Western European countries. In 1990 only 18 per cent of French holidays were taken outside France. This by definition means than 82 per cent of French tourism (which in 1991 was 53.7 million holiday trips) is accommodated in France itself.

2 A very pronounced peaking of holiday travel. The main French school holidays are in July and August with only short breaks at Christmas, in February and at Easter (*see* Fig 19.5).

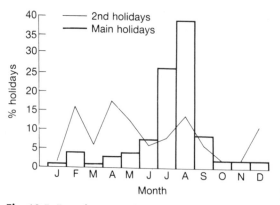

Fig. 19.5 French seasonality of holidaymaking

3 A strong reliance on the car as a means of holiday travel. Eighty-one per cent of all (domestic and foreign) holiday trips in France were by car.
4 A higher level of holiday taking among the urban population than among rural residents. In 1985 up to 83 per cent of Parisians took a holiday, and 64 per cent of the residents of the other major cities. Only 40 per cent of the rural population took a holiday. All these factors combine to create acute peak period congestion on the roads leading from the cities to the resorts and to overcrowding in the destination regions.

The French make little use of hotels for their city, coastal or rural domestic holidays, preferring rented apartments, camping, visiting friends and relatives or using their own second homes, though hotels are a little more popular for winter sports and touring holidays. There were 2.8 million second homes in France in 1990.

	%
Hotels	7
Visiting friends and relatives	29
Camping and caravans	18
Rented accommodation	18
Second homes (own and friends')	21
Holiday village	5

Fig. 19.6 Accommodation used by the French for domestic summer holidays, 1990
(*Source*: INSEE)

FRENCH HOLIDAY DESTINATIONS

About half of the French summer tourists make for the coast, and a quarter to the countryside. An additional 17 per cent favour the mountain regions. In winter the proportions change to 17 per cent to the coast for winter sun holidays, 28 per cent to the countryside and nearly 40 per cent to the mountains for winter sports. This pattern is reflected in the popularity of the destination regions of France for domestic tourism.

Geographical region and corresponding tourist statistical region	Number of arrivals at hotels and campsites (in millions) 1987
The Mediterranean coast (Côte d'Azur and Languedoc-Roussillon (1 and 2))	18.8
The Alps (Rhône/Alpes (3))	8.2
Paris (Ile de France (4))	5.9
Aquitaine (5)	5.5
Brittany (6)	4.5
Pyrénées (and part of central Massif (7))	3.8
The remainder of the central Massif (Auvergne and Limousin (8))	2.8

NB: The tourist statistical regions do not match perfectly with the physical regions (*see* Fig 19.8).

Fig. 19.7 Most popular regions of France for the French

French outbound travel

It has been noted that only a small proportion (18 per cent) of the French take their holidays abroad. The majority travel by road: only five per cent of the French take a package holiday, and only six per cent travel by plane. It is not surprising that the adjacent countries of Spain and Italy benefit most from French foreign summer holidays, these two countries together receiving 40 per cent of such trips. In 1991 Spain welcomed 8.79 million French tourists while Italy received 7.29 million. Long-haul destinations, such as USA, Asia in summer and Mexico, the French Caribbean

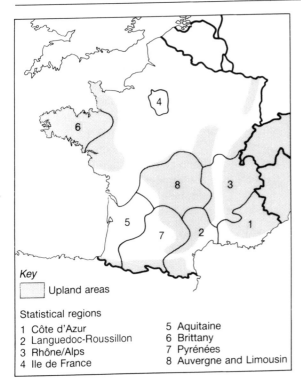

Key

Upland areas

Statistical regions
1 Côte d'Azur   5 Aquitaine
2 Languedoc-Roussillon   6 Brittany
3 Rhône/Alps   7 Pyrénées
4 Ile de France   8 Auvergne and Limousin

Fig. 19.8 Statistical and physical regions of France

islands and French Polynesia for winter sun holidays are increasing in popularity. However, Spain (including the Canaries) is still the most popular winter sun destination. The UK ranks second (behind Germany) as a destination for French business travel, and fifth in popularity as a summer holiday destination.

FOREIGN VISITORS TO FRANCE

The numbers of foreign visitors to France have grown steadily, from about 29 million in 1980 to over 55 million in 1991. Germany has always been France's main market and contributes about a quarter of all foreign visitors, while total numbers of Germans have increased from 8.4 million to 13.4 million over the decade. The UK has been one of France's other established markets but has grown more slowly. Numbers of Dutch tourists have hardly increased, so that the Netherlands has slipped from being France's 3rd ranking market in 1982 down to 6th (see Fig 19.9). The most rapidly growing markets are France's southern neighbours

(Spain and Italy) as they begin to develop thriving outbound tourism.

	1982		1991	
	Number (mill)	% market share	Number (mill)	% market share
Germany	8.40	25.1	13.47	24.2
Belgium	3.30	9.9	8.14	14.6
UK	6.01	18.0	7.17	12.9
Italy	2.00	6.0	6.88	12.4
Switzerland	3.21	9.6	5.02	9.0
Netherlands	3.88	11.6	3.44	6.2
Spain	0.89	2.7	2.84	5.1

Fig. 19.9 France inbound tourism, 1982–1991: international tourist arrivals at frontiers

The French Riviera is by far the most popular destination region (with about 35 million hotel and camping bednights in 1987) followed by Paris with 15.5 million hotel bednights alone, followed by the Alps, Aquitaine and Languedoc-Roussillon each with over six million hotel and camping bednights. Visiting friends' homes and rented accommodation are also popular forms of accommodation. The 'gîtes' are particularly popular with the UK market. They are self-catering holiday homes, often old farmhouses in the country, and in 1989 there were over 23 000 available.

CONCLUSION

It is evident that the less popular regions of France have the capacity and potential to take more tourists whereas the most popular regions such as the French Riviera are very congested at peak periods. There are signs, however, that the French might be prepared to change their traditional pattern of domestic holiday taking and spread the demands on facilities and accommodation over a longer summer season.

The opening of the Channel Tunnel will improve communications between UK and France, but it remains to be seen as to whether it will alter existing travel patterns or merely confirm the current flows.

FURTHER READING

Cockerell, N (1991) 'France', *International Tourism Reports*, No. 4, EIU, pp. 5–23.

Ghelardoni, P (1990) 'Tourism planning along the coast of Aquitaine' in Fabbri, P (Ed) *Recreational Uses of Coastal Areas*, pp. 191–7, Kluwer Academic Publishers.

Klemm, K (1992) 'Sustainable tourism development: Languedoc-Roussillon thirty years on', *Tourism Management*, Vol. 13, pp. 169–80.

QUESTIONS AND DISCUSSION POINTS

1 What distinguishes the French approach to the development of coastal and rural resources for tourism?

2 Rank the different sections of France's coastline in order of popularity and explain the reasons for the different levels of tourist use.

3 Why is France the leading tourist destination country in Europe?

ASSIGNMENTS

1 Mr & Mrs Driver live in Reading and are planning a three-week summer camping/caravan holiday in France, for themselves and their two children (aged 9 and 13). They have never driven on the Continent before and they are anxious to avoid the worst congested roads. They want a leisurely holiday away from the crowds but with plenty of outdoor activities for the children. They would like to see a variety of French historic attractions and regional cultures, but they also want to spend some time on the beach. Suggest a three-week itinerary for the family, specifying their route to and through France and a departure date that would avoid the worst congestion but also give them good weather.

2 You are the editor of a UK travel trade journal. You are planning an issue on the appeal of the UK to the French. Write a brief editorial note explaining the characteristics of the French holiday market and French holiday and travel tastes. Outline the difficulties that UK tour operators face when trying to market their tours and attractions to the French. Indicate the extent to which travel improvements between UK and France might affect the appeal of the UK to the French.

CHAPTER 20

Italy

LEARNING OBJECTIVES

After reading this chapter you should be able to
- assess the tourist potential of the climatic, landscape, historical and cultural resources of Italy
- distinguish the regional distribution of these geographical resources and their development and use for tourism
- demonstrate a knowledge of the main tourist resorts and tourist centres
- understand the role of Italy in the general pattern of European tourism.

INTRODUCTION

Tourism has been a well established industry in Italy for over one hundred years. The country has a huge diversity of tourist attractions ranging from its climate, coast, lakes and landscape, to its historic cities and winter sports resorts. These attractions draw in a high level of international tourist traffic, making Italy a leading world destination, with a peak of 60.2 million foreign arrivals

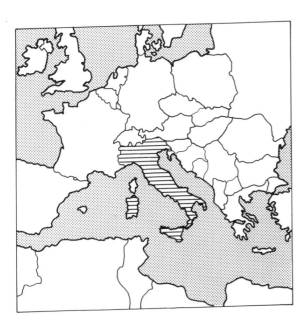

in 1990, including day-trippers, accounting for about 36 per cent of all the tourist arrivals in the Mediterranean region in 1991. Tourist arrivals held steady at 25 to 26 million between 1987 and 1991.

Tourism is, therefore, a major source of foreign currency for Italy and a major generator of jobs in the Italian economy, and the support for tourism is regarded as a high priority. However, northern Italy is one of the few highly developed industrial regions of the Mediterranean and the large domestic, urbanised population seeks to share the use of the national and cultural tourist resources with the international visitors. This leads to problems of congestion, over-use and deterioration of the quality of the resources, particularly in the north of Italy, whereas the tourist resources of the south remain relatively underdeveloped and underused.

PHYSICAL RESOURCES

Italy is naturally divided into four major physical units each with a different range of tourist resources and different climatic conditions (*see* Fig 20.1). The three main regions are from north to south:

1 the southern slopes of the Alps (northern Italy).
2 the north Italian plain, drained by the river Po which flows into the head of the Adriatic sea (Turin to Venice).

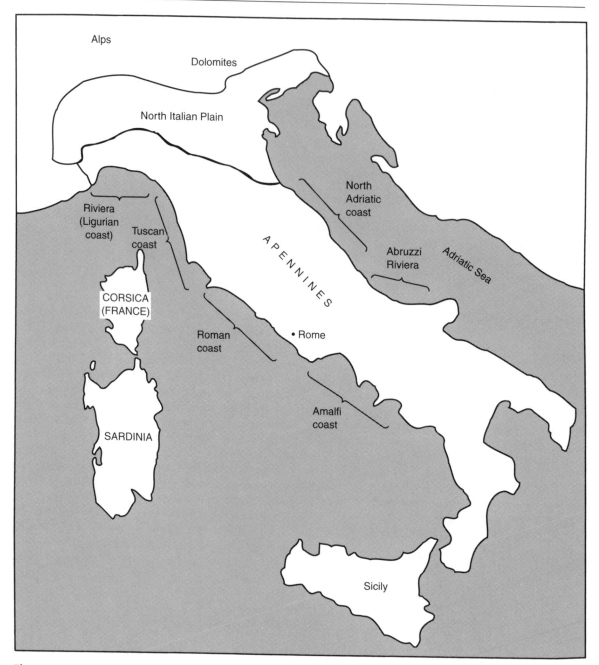

Fig. 20.1 Regions of Italy

3 The Apennines, a mountain range of lower altitude than the Alps, but forming the structural spine of peninsular Italy.

The fourth physical unit is
4 the coast and the surrounding seas.

The Italian Alps

Italy's share of the Alps consists of the south-facing slopes of the main Alpine peaks and the southerly pre-Alps which descend into the Po basin (*see* Fig 20.2). The area has the typical alpine climate with a summer precipitation maximum and cold, sunny winter conditions which allow the formation of good quality snow fields. However, the sheltered southerly aspect and the mass of the Swiss and Austrian Alps protect the Italian mountains from the coldest north winds which originate in the centre of Europe in winter. There are three subsections of the Italian Alps:

1 **West of Lake Maggiore**. Here, Italy's border with Switzerland and France follows the highest peaks and corresponds to the watershed between the Po to the east and the Rhône to the west. The mountains decrease in height from the spectacular sharp peaks of Mont Blanc (4807 m) in the north to Mt Argentera (3250 m) in the south, where they form the backdrop to the Italian Riviera of the Ligurian coast. The Gran Paradiso National Park, noted for its rare animals and plants, is situated close to the French border. The main skiing centres are concentrated in the Val d'Aosta region, made accessible via the routes that run up the valley from Turin to the Mont Blanc tunnel and the Little St Bernard pass (both to France) and to the Great St Bernard pass (to Switzerland). Although ski centres are extensively developed on the French side of the frontier, many French people visit the Val d'Aosta due to its accessibility and to the French speaking inhabitants. The main ski centres are Cervinia and Courmayeur.

2 **The central section: the Italian lakes**. This subregion is characterised by superb glacial landforms but the geology gives rise to fewer spectacular peaks (other than Ortles and Adamello). The distinctive tourist attraction is the series of lakes that lie in deep steep-sided 'U'shaped valleys gouged out by glaciers in the ice age. In this region the glaciers flowed from north to south (from the centre of the Alps), and left piles of moraines at the valley mouths as they melted. These moraines blocked the valleys and ponded back the lakes. The location of the lakes in sheltered south-facing valleys has given them an unusual climatic advantage and has led to their development as tourist resources. Temperatures here all year round but especially in winter are much higher than they normally should be; this is reflected in the vegetation of palms, citrus trees and olives which flourish here but are more typical of a southern, more truly Mediterranean, climate. A series of international resorts such as

Baveno on Lake Maggiore and Limone on Lake Garda have developed along the lake shores; 65 per cent of the bednights were taken up by foreign visitors in 1985, many of whom are Germans attracted to the motor boating. Elsewhere, the climate of the lakes region is more typical of the continental north with very cold winters and July temperatures climbing over 20° C. The summer rainfall peak tends to occur in sharp bursts often associated with continental thunderstorms.

3 **The eastern Alps: the Dolomites**. The landform consists of a mixture of resistant rock mixed with more easily eroded material which, through glacial action, produces a very dramatic mountain landscape with a series of spectacular sharp peaks (such as Marmolada), interspersed with tiny but extremely beautiful alpine lakes. The region is cut by the N–S valley of Val di Adige, which is followed by the motorway route from Verona to the Brenner pass. There are major concentrations of winter sports and summer scenery and climbing resorts in the Dolomites, e.g. Madonna di Campiglio (in Trentino), Val Senales (in Alto Adige) and Cortina d'Ampezzo (in Veneto). It is particularly accessible to and popular with German tourists, as this part of Italy is also German speaking, but it is also rapidly increasing in popularity in the domestic market. Foreign tourists congregate in the northern part of the region while domestic tourists favour the southern part (Trentino).

The north Italian plain

The Po basin is the industrial heart of Italy; it contains the major conurbation centred on Milan and its hinterland (*see* Fig 20.2). The region as a whole has over 22 million inhabitants. It is also a fertile agricultural area though subject to flooding in the lower reaches of the Po. The climate has continental overtones with quite extreme temperatures (in Milan the average January temperature drops to 1.9° C with over 100 days of frost, though the summer temperature rises to an average of 23.9° C in July). It is mainly a domestic tourist generating area but with the normal VFR and business tourism associated with developed urban areas. The Adriatic end of the region is, however, a major centre of Italy's cultural and historic tourism based on Venice, Padua and Verona, but also with fine architectural attractions in towns such as Bologna, Ferrara, Parma and Modena.

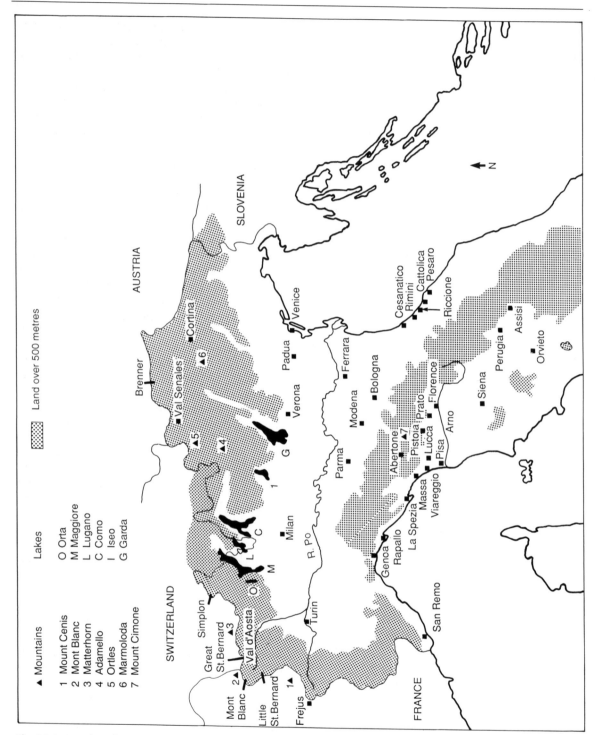

Fig. 20.2 North Italian plain

Venice

Venice is located on a low-lying island in the middle of a coastal lagoon that is separated from the sea by a line of sand dunes. The city owed its wealth to its role as a trading city state in Renaissance times. Many magnificent buildings (e.g. churches, palaces and squares) date from this period, while a profusion of artistic work was produced. The most famous landmarks are the Doges Palace, St Mark's Square and the Bridge of Sighs, but the whole city is of great beauty. However, its fabric is under threat of flooding, as the city settles into the soft silt on which it is built. The combination of heavy rain and high tides causes periodic flooding of the squares and buildings lining the canals in the winter. The prospect of even a slight rise in sea level (as a result of global warming) makes the outlook for the city less than optimistic in spite of the flood protection measures underway.

Like Florence and Rome, Venice is very rich in renaissance art treasures but it has a unique additional attraction. The medieval character of its winding alleyways, open piazzas and canal system is totally unspoilt. The only means of getting about the city is by boat or on foot, as there are no motor cars. This gives the tourist a unique experience of living in a pre-industrial city, although it can be very crowded with pedestrians in the peak season. At peak periods as many as 60 000 visitors a day arrive in the city – totalling five to six million a year (of which only about a fifth actually stay in Venice itself). Its medieval character, however, makes the city totally unsuitable for most economic activities other than tourism. The consequent problems of preserving the city have been discussed in Chapter 5.

The Apennines and peninsular Italy

The Apennines form the backbone of peninsular Italy. The mountain chain runs NW–SE for most of its 500 km length, until it reaches Sicily, where the orientation of the mountains changes abruptly to an E–W structure. It can be divided into three physical zones.

1 The North (located in Tuscany, Marche and Umbria (*see*** Fig 20.3).** This region is made up of unstable, softer, easily eroded rocks, reaching only 1669 m (Mt Magiorasca) to 2140 m (Mt Cimone).

Nevertheless, the climate is cold enough in winter to produce snow in enough quantity and quality to support ski centres for the domestic market, e.g. at Abertone (near Mt Cimone). The tourist development of this part of the Apennines is, however, focused on the urban areas fringing the more fertile Arno basin, with historic town centres such as Pisa, Lucca, Pistoia, Prata to the north and Siena (site of the Palio), Perugia (an ancient Etruscan city), Orvieto, Spoleto and Assisi to the south. But, of course, the main focus of cultural tourism in the region is in Florence.

The unspoilt city centre is full of 12th to 17th century buildings; the Uffizi Gallery contains one of the most outstanding art collections in the world, including famous paintings by Leonardo da Vinci, Botticelli and Michelangelo. The Accademia di Belle Arti houses the Michelangelo Statue of David, and other works of art abound in the churches and historic buildings.

For such a southerly, Mediterranean location, the climate of the Apennine chain is relatively harsh; most of the mountains receive more than 1200 mm rainfall a year, and on the higher peaks this reaches 2000 mm (even as far south as the mountains of Calabria). Only the islands of Sardinia and Sicily, the coastal lowlands and the heel of Italy have the typical long (three to four month) summer drought. The rainfall is, however, concentrated in autumn and winter and can be intense and violent, as demonstrated by the storms which caused the Arno to burst its banks and damage so much of Florence's art treasures in the mid-1960s. This relatively heavy rainfall is orographic in nature, caused by the Apennines blocking the path of west flowing moisture laden Atlantic air which penetrates into the Mediterranean basin in autumn and winter. Temperatures, however, are more characteristically Mediterranean, though the 'hot south' only truly begins south of Rome.

2 Central Apennines of Latium, the Abruzzi and Molise (*see*** Fig 20.3).** This region consists of some ranges of harder rock which give rise to the forest-clad mountains of Gran Sasso in the Abruzzi (2913 m). The 300 km^2 National Park here is noted for its landscape and wildlife, particularly for a species of bear unique to Italy. Elsewhere the landscape is one of pastoralism and thin forest but with many abandoned upland villages due to long-term

Fig. 20.3 Italy's regions

emigration to the north and to more local urban centres. International tourism is mainly confined to Rome, though modest winter sports (e.g. Terminillo), holiday resorts (catering for the domestic market) and unspoilt historic settlements are widely distributed.

Rome is a major historic, artistic and cultural centre, and is the site of the Vatican, the centre of the Roman Catholic faith. This busy, modern city also abounds with historic ruins, particularly from ancient Roman times, but it has many fine renaissance and baroque buildings too.

3 The deep south. Campania, Apulia, Basilicata, Calabria and Sicily (*see* Fig 20.3). The landscape is an attractive and varied one of well wooded, deeply dissected plateaux, mountain chains, and smaller steep-sided blocks with the bare, karst landscape typical of limestone areas at their summit. There is also evidence of recent volcanic activity, at present dormant at Vesuvius (Naples) but still active in Sicily (Mount Etna) and in the islands off Sicily (Stromboli, Vulcano and Lipari). Cultural tourism is centred on Naples (close to Pompeii and Herculanium) and Paestum, famous for its Greek temples.

The Mezzogiorno

This region as a whole remains unspoilt as it has been bypassed by the industrial revolution. The economy of the far south of Italy has long been underdeveloped, with the population suffering from high unemployment and a low standard of living. The region lacks industrial infrastructure, and has a backward agriculture on land suffering from erosion.

The regions of the south have experienced emigration for many years, resulting in abandoned agricultural land and deserted villages in the mountain areas. Since 1950 a special ministry, the Cassa per il Mezzogiorno, was given responsibility for promoting the development of the south. This has included the implementation of water management, reafforestation, some industrial development and provision of power and transport infrastructures so that now the Mezzogiorno is linked to the north by fast motorways. Although the bulk of the aid has gone into these developments, investment in tourism infrastructure has been encouraged by grants and loans in the hope that a well developed tourist industry would create suitable jobs and inject money into the local economy. The EC has also contributed to the cost of these projects (see Chapter 18). By the early 1980s 65 000 additional hotel rooms had been provided but these tended to be in large capital-intensive enterprises rather than in locally run establishments. Although much of the region contains much unspoilt mountain scenery and magnificent deserted beaches, in some places the local coastal scenery has sometimes been poorly managed: for example the proliferation of unplanned and uncontrolled second home development has spoilt some areas, whereas in others (e.g. Sicily) tourism has been developed near industrial zones in order to take advantage of the improved infrastructure. The number of tourists visiting the area remains low and is only slowly increasing. However, this is due as much to the peripheral location of the region as to the mismanagement of tourist development within it. The southern tip of peninsular Italy is well outside the 1000 km limit for car travel (see Chapter 18), and is thus too far for carborne travellers from the population centres of Northern Europe; it must, therefore, rely on air transport and compete with destinations such as Greece, Turkey and Spain which may be either environmentally more attractive to the potential visitor, or much more competitively priced.

Sicily is a mountainous island, whose interior is desert-like, whose relief is dominated by Mount Etna and whose population lives on the coast. It is rich in art and history, with, for example, Greek temples at Agrigento, Roman ruins at Syracuse, and a medieval castle at Catania, and has some good sandy beaches and resorts such as Palermo, Taormina and Cefalu. In spite of these resources, the island is underdeveloped for tourism, with less than four per cent of Italy's tourist arrivals.

Sardinia is another of Italy's Mediterranean islands which is visited by even fewer tourists. Much of its 1200 km coastline is still undeveloped, and is a sequence of white sandy beaches, cliffs and promontories. Its exposure to the British market during the 1990 World Cup football competition may make the island a little better known to potential tourists.

The coast

All the coastal lowlands have lower rainfall than the interior of Italy (under 800 mm) and experience the more characteristic Mediterranean climate, but the coast is relatively unevenly developed. It can be divided into sub-regions (see Fig 20.1) each with a different physical character and different balance of tourist development:

1 the Ligurian coast (between the French border and Pisa);
2 the Tuscan and Roman coasts (Pisa to Rome);
3 the Amalfi coast (Naples area);
4 the coast of the far south (Palermo to Lecce); and
5 the Adriatic (Lecce to Venice).

Ligurian coast – the Italian Riviera (see Fig 20.2)

This stretch of coast is backed by mountains, in the west by the Alps and eastern stretch (from Genoa to La Spezia) by the Apennines. The coast is characterised by cliffs, interspersed with sandy bays, though many of the shores are rather pebbly. Many of the bays form excellent yacht harbours such as Portofino and Rapallo. The coast is sheltered by the mountains, which protect the coast from cold continental air, keeping winter temperatures up. The January average temperature at Genoa is 8.4° C and frosts are hardly known; Diano Marina is one of the significant winter resorts. Land for tourist development is at a premium and many of the best sites have already been developed for tourist accommodation or private villas, since many settlements have been tourist resorts for over 150 years. The current pattern of tourism development is, however, varied, from classy 'up-market' resorts, e.g Portofino and Santa Margherita, and larger noisy centres of activity, e.g. Rapallo, to quieter fishing villages.

The Tuscan and Roman coasts

The crest of the Apennines moves inland, and wider coastal lowlands have developed in places. The alluvial plains are sometimes fringed by coastal dunes which produce fine, wide sandy beaches, for example Massa and Viareggio in the north and the beaches serving Rome in the south, e.g. Ostia, Terracina and Sperlonga.

The Amalfi coast

This stretch of coast varies in character from the lowlands north of Naples and the Gulf of Salerno, the islands of Ischia and Capri to the high cliffs south of Salerno. In the coves, sandy bays have been developed. This stretch of coast includes some famous resorts such as Capri, Sorrento, Positano and Ravello, but some are now very overcrowded or at capacity.

The coast of the south

The coast of the far south of Italy has the best climate for coastal tourism, very varied coastal landscape yet it remains relatively underdeveloped, with uncrowded beaches and unspoilt villages interspersed between small resorts such as Maratea. The climate of Sicily is even more conducive to coastal tourism, with under 700 mm rainfall per annum and July temperatures reaching 25.7° C. The south coast of the island has wide sandy beaches, while the islands off the north coast provide opportunities for underwater fishing, yet again the development of resorts and provision of bed spaces are limited.

The Adriatic coast

In the southern section from Pesaro to Foggia, the hilly coast is dominated by softer rock, eroded into low cliffs by the Adriatic. The main seaside resorts are relatively small (e.g. Guilianova, Silvi Marina, Francaville and Vasto). The Abruzzi coast is popular with Roman holidaymakers particularly for camping. The main modern, mass tourist development occurs on the short stretch of the northern Adriatic coast between Ravenna and Pesaro where the alluvial lowlands of the Po begin to open out, and the shallow Adriatic has accumulated extensive coastal dune systems, providing continuous, huge sandy beaches. With plentiful level coastal land for development of modern hotels, a string of modern international resorts have grown up to cater for the demands of mass tourism, for example Rimini, Riccione, Cattolica, Milano Marittima, and Cesanatico (see Fig 20.2). The resorts of the Italian Adriatic cater mainly for the domestic market (58 per cent of their arrivals). They expanded in the 1960s and 1970s, and have now passed the stage of 'maturity' described in Chapter 8, and they are now attracting fewer tourists. Several factors have contributed to this decline:

1 Italian outbound tourism is increasing, particularly since 1989, as foreign exchange controls have been finally lifted (tourism expenditure doubled between 1989 and 1990, from 6772 million US dollars to 13 826 million). This has led to a decline in demand for domestic seaside resorts.

2 The resorts are becoming less competitive with both other (southern) Italian resorts and newer resort areas elsewhere in the Mediterranean. The Adriatic resorts are less price competitive and also their accommodation stock has not adapted to modern demands (60 per cent of rooms are still in hotels and only 2.9 per cent are self-catering).

3 The Italian Adriatic coast also has suffered from serious marine pollution that became evident in the late 1980s. The River Po has a heavy burden of agricultural and sewage pollution; when dissolved in water these chemicals provide food for marine plants. The build-up of these plant nutrients led to a rapid 'bloom' of algae (seaweed) which made swimming unpleasant and led to an immediate and dramatic decline in tourism. The first patches of seaweed were seen in August 1988: in 1989 the growth began in late June and even earlier in 1990 (in May).

As a result of all these factors, foreign tourism in the Adriatic resorts fell dramatically between 1988 and 1990, particularly in the resorts of Rimini, Riccione and Catolica (from 184 800 arrivals in the peak month of July 1988, to 80 800 in July 1990). Domestic arrivals also dropped by between 9 per cent and 19 per cent in June and August 1989 but had more or less recovered by 1990. It has been suggested that an increase in the number of East Europeans visiting the region since 1989 has partly offset the decline.

The coast at the head of the Adriatic is dominated by coastal deposition of sand, but here the dunes and spits tend to enclose tidal or inland lagoons. The lagoons may inhibit tourist access but nevertheless the coast is extensively used at the resorts of Lido di Jesolo, Bibione and Caorle.

SPATIAL PATTERNS OF TOURISM

The bulk of Italy's tourist accommodation is concentrated in the four provinces of the north of the country: Trentino/Alto Adige, Veneto, Emilio Romagna and Toscano (*see* Fig 20.3). Here the location of mountain, coastal, cultural, social and business tourist resources coincide, and are most accessible to both the domestic and international markets. In 1990, 54 per cent of Italy's hotels were concentrated here (in contrast to only 11.6 per cent in the centre and 10.6 per cent in the south of Italy). Camping facilities are proportionally more important in Marche, Abruzzi and Latium,

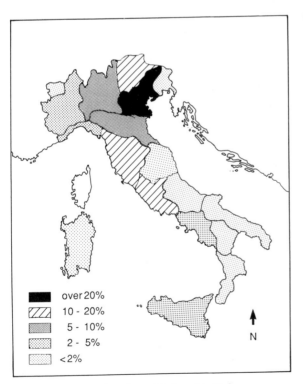

Fig. 20.4 International tourist travel in Italy (tourist nights)

over 20%
10 - 20%
5 - 10%
2 - 5%
<2%

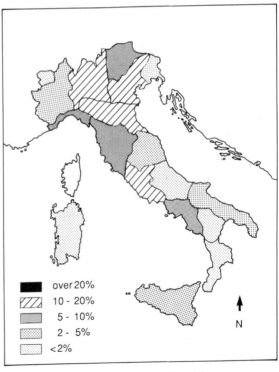

Fig. 20.5 Domestic tourist travel in Italy (tourist nights)

over 20%
10 - 20%
5 - 10%
2 - 5%
<2%

whereas rented accommodation plays a more significant role in the limited stock of bed spaces in Calabra and Apulia.

The spatial pattern of tourist arrivals and bednights mirrors this pattern, though there are some differences between the domestic and international patterns (*see* Figs 20.4 and 20.5). Domestic tourism tends to be relatively short-haul and predominantly within the tourist's region of residence, because the coasts of northern Italy have a good summer climate, the population tends to travel to their nearest coastal resorts instead of travelling further south. Thus, the most heavily populated regions of Emilio Romagna, Veneto, Toscano (all with local coastal resources) and Lombardia (with local scenic and winter sports resources) each receive about 8–13 per cent of the domestic market (1990). The international market (though still strongly concentrated in the north which receives 57.7 per cent of international nights) is especially focused on Veneto (20 per cent international arrivals 1990), but Toscano (centred on Florence) and Alto Adige (predominantly a winter sports region) both receive 13 per cent each; the Rome region ranks third with about 14 per cent of international arrivals. This reaffirms the fact that the Italian lakes, mountains and cultural resources are more popular with international tourists than with the residents. Forty-five per cent of foreign visitors chose Italy for artistic and historical attractions, 43 per cent for its climate, 27 per cent for its natural environment and, significantly, a third chose Italy for the possibility of combining several activities.

Conflicts between domestic and international tourists

The Italian domestic market is large; 39 million holidaymakers in 1991 compared to 20.2 million foreign visitors. Although there is not the massive road congestion due to the 'rush to the Mediterranean' coasts as there is in France, the Italian domestic market is similarly very strongly peaked in July and August. Sixty-five per cent of domestic coastal holidays and 51.5 per cent of all domestic and foreign bednights were taken in these two months in 1985. This leads to problems of congestion both in the cities and in the coastal

resorts. The peaking of holiday demand also creates the problem (for the tourist industry) of relatively low overall occupancy rates, the highest gross occupancy rates being 42 per cent in Lazio, 35.3 per cent in Tuscany, 32.1 per cent in Liguria and the lowest in the centre and far south (17.6 per cent in Abruzzi, 17.6 per cent in Basilicata, 19 per cent in Calabria).

INTERNATIONAL TOURISTS

The highest proportion of foreigners crossing the frontier into Italy in 1991 came from the adjacent countries of Switzerland, Germany, France and Austria. However, perhaps as many as half of these are day excursionists or in transit. The latter category would include car tourists from Central Europe travelling west through Italy to the coasts of France or Spain. Considering just the staying visitors, these come from a wide range of countries, reflecting the wide appeal of cultural tourism, but the German market dominates, particularly in the accessible Veneto and Alto Adige regions. Not only do more Germans visit Italy but they stay longer than any other nationality, when measured in terms of average length of stay at registered accommodation. It must be remembered though, that many long-haul travellers, for example from USA, Japan and even Northern Europe, may spend over a week in Italy but split the time between the three major cultural centres of Rome, Florence and Venice (thus depressing the average length of stay figures). Recent surveys showed that each nationality favours the particular elements of Italy's range of tourist attractions that complement their own domestic resources. Thus, over half of the visitors from land-locked Austria make their way to the Adriatic beaches, a quarter to the cities but only 10 per cent to the mountains. Fifty per cent of the French visit the cultural attractions of the cities and only a quarter go to the coast. The British tend to concentrate on the cultural attractions of Venice but also visit Emilio Romagna, Toscano and Campania.

According to WTO, tourist arrivals in Italy have grown very little (from 25.7 million in 1987 to 26.8 million in 1991), but all other indices of tourism in Italy have shown a sharp decline between 1990 and 1991 (much greater than the

	Number of arrivals at frontiers		Number of arrivals at registered tourist accommodation	Arrivals at registered tourist accommodation	Total bednights
	%	(million)	(million)	(%)	(%)
Germany	17.9	9.2	6.5	32.2	41.8
France	17.7	9.1	1.9	9.7	7.1
USA	2.2	1.1	1.4	7.0	4.4
UK	3.3	1.7	1.2	6.0	6.0
Austria	10.9	5.5	1.1	5.6	6.2
Switzerland	19.9	10.2	1.0	5.3	5.9
Spain	1.1	0.6	0.8	4.1	2.2
Netherlands	2.9	1.5	0.5	2.8	3.6
Japan	1.0	0.5	0.6	3.1	1.5
Belgium	1.8	0.9	0.4	2.3	2.8
Eastern Europe	3.7	1.9	0.8	3.9	
Total		51.3	20.28		86.74 million

Fig. 20.6 Overall pattern of international tourism to Italy, 1991
(*Source*: WTO)

average decline for Europe as a whole): frontier arrivals were down by 14.8 per cent, and arrivals at hotels by 4.7 per cent.

Virtually all Italy's foreign markets showed a decrease except for the small but rapidly expanding number of tourists coming from Eastern Europe (frontier arrivals up 12 per cent, East European tourist nights up 45.6 per cent and arrivals in accommodation up by nearly 32 per cent).

ITALIAN OUTBOUND TOURISM

A relatively small number of Italians take their holidays outside their country. In 1985 it was estimated that three million trips of four nights or more were taken by Italians abroad, compared to a domestic market of 36.3 million arrivals in 1984. The varied nature of Italy's resources means that most tourist tastes can be met at home. Nevertheless, the Italians' increasing purchasing power generated by an improving economy, coupled with the relaxation of exchange controls has recently led to a very rapid growth of foreign travel to 14.7 million trips in 1991. Tourism expenditure increased from 4536 million US dollars in 1987 to 13 826 million in 1990, doubling between 1989 and 1990 when exchange controls were finally lifted. The distribution of trips is shown in Fig 20.7.

Destination	1991 (million arrivals)
France	6.889
Spain	1.767
Greece	0.517
UK	0.714
Germany	0.808
Switzerland	0.659
Austria	1.044

Fig. 20.7 Italy: outbound tourism
(*Source*: WTO)

The distances travelled are generally short (nearly 50 per cent travelled less than 500 km) but the proportion of longer-haul travellers to countries other than those adjacent to Italy is rapidly growing. In 1982 24 per cent travelled over 1000 km, whereas in 1985 this had grown to 32 per cent.

CONCLUSION

In terms of the evolution of its own domestic and outbound tourism, Italy is in the early stages of the third phase of development (*see* Chapter 15). At this stage, mass outbound tourism becomes widespread, following the establishment of a mass domestic market in Phase 2. If Italy conforms to the pattern set out in Chapter 15, then growth in domestic tourism may slow down (as outbound tourism grows). This may ease some of the problems of increasing congestion in Italian resorts. It is unlikely that international tourism to Italy's coastal resorts will expand greatly due to the strong price competition from other Mediterranean destinations. On the other hand, the quality and range of Italy's historic and cultural attractions are unique and they will inevitably maintain their attractiveness to international travellers. The challenge of conserving the historical cities and managing their visitors is ever present.

FURTHER READING

Becheri, E (1991) 'Rimini and Co – the end of a legend? Dealing with the algae effect', *Tourism Management*, Vol. 12, September, pp. 229–35.

Bywater, M (1991) 'Prospects for Mediterranean beach resorts – an Italian case study', *Travel and Tourism Analyst*, No. 5, pp. 75–89.

Bywater, M (1993) 'Italy', *EIU International Tourism Reports* No. 4, pp. 4–26.

QUESTIONS AND DISCUSSION POINTS

1 Italy's tourist product is very varied. Is there any evidence available to suggest which of its resources (beaches, landscapes, historic or climatic) are the most popular?

2 Do you think Italy is well placed to withstand competition from recently developing Mediterranean destinations such as Greece and Turkey?

3 Why do you think the attempts to develop tourism in the far south of Italy have not met with great success?

ASSIGNMENTS

1 You work for a tour company that specialises in city break holidays in Europe for the UK market. You have been asked to update and rewrite their brochure for Italy. Select at least four cities with potential for city breaks and assemble notes on their history, historical and cultural resources, their location, accessibility and climate. Suggest the client groups that might find these cities attractive, and indicate the seasons (and specific months of the year) during which time these tours might be most successful. Prepare a draft of the text of the new brochure for one of these cities.

2 A 48-year-old widow is planning a two-week holiday in Italy with her 19-year-old daughter. She is interested in landscape painting and art in general but also enjoys relaxing on the beach. Her daughter is more interested in meeting other young people. They cannot agree on a venue and have come to your travel agency for advice on which parts of the Italian coast might meet their needs and to see if you can suggest a resort that they both might enjoy. Prepare some notes that might help them arrive at a decision.

CHAPTER 21

The Iberian peninsula: Spain and Portugal

LEARNING OBJECTIVES

After reading this chapter you should be able to

- assess the tourist potential of the climatic, landscape, historical and cultural resources of Spain and Portugal
- distinguish the regional distribution of these geographical resources and their development and use for tourism
- demonstrate a knowledge of the main tourist resorts and tourist centres
- understand the role of Spain and Portugal in the general pattern of European tourism
- be aware of some of the problems of over-development on the Spanish coasts
- locate and explain the particular tourist appeal of Spain and Portugal's island territories.

INTRODUCTION

Spain is the focus of Mediterranean mass coastal tourism, and is one of the world's leading destinations. Tourism to Spain has grown rapidly in the post war era from under three million in the 1950s to 34.3 million in 1990. Tourist development is strongly concentrated on Spain's Mediterranean coast and Mediterranean island possessions, for example, the Balearic islands. The Atlantic coast of the Iberian peninsula is relatively undeveloped for tourism: Portugal received only 8.6 million foreign tourists. The greatest concentration of tourism on Iberia's Atlantic coast is in the Algarve in the south of Portugal. The hot, arid plateaux of the interior of the peninsula attract relatively few tourists in spite of their historic and cultural attractions. Both Spain and Portugal possess islands in the Atlantic off the coast of West Africa that are far enough south and, therefore, have mild enough winters to attract visitors for winter

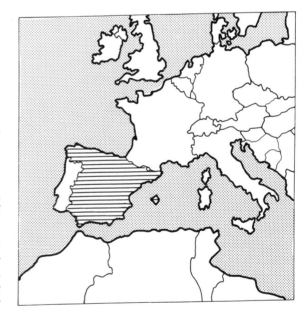

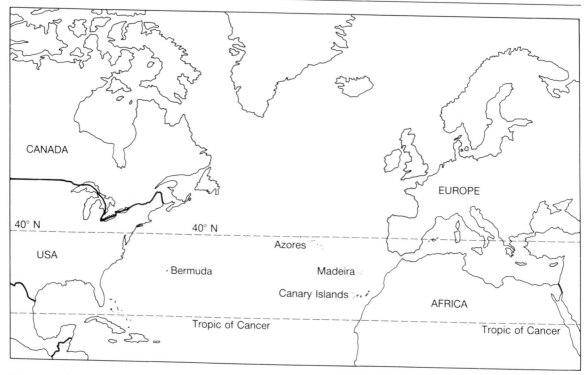

Fig. 21.1 The Atlantic islands

sun holidays. Madeira (32° N) belongs to Portugal, while the Canary Islands (28° S) are part of Spain (*see* Fig 21.1).

GROWTH OF TOURISM IN SPAIN

Spain was virtually unknown as a tourist destination in the period between the First and Second World Wars. The country was poor and the economy was further disrupted by its civil war of 1936–1939. Meanwhile, Italy, the Côte d'Azur and the Alps were prospering as Europe's main resort areas. In the early 1950s the first wave of carborne tourists from France explored the Costa Brava, found the climate attractive, the beaches deserted and the cost of living low. Tourism grew steadily from 1.26 million in 1952 to 4.19 million in 1959. The Spanish Government recognised the contribution tourism could make to its economy and encouraged tourist development in a variety of ways, for example, with loans for the construction of hotels.

In 1959 the economy was opened up for foreign investment, and the peseta was devalued, making Spain an even more attractive destination compared to the Riviera of France and Italy. The private sector in Spain responded very rapidly, and in the early 1960s new hotels, villas and apartments were built all along Spain's Mediterranean coast in a rather uncoordinated and unplanned manner. The volume of tourism quadrupled from six million in 1960 to 24 million in 1970. The expansion of air transport accelerated this growth by opening up Spain to the Northern European market, particularly Britain, although in 1970, 63 per cent of Spain's visitors still came across the border by car causing congestion on the coastal routes (particularly in July and August). Tourism had a significant effect on the Spanish economy, creating jobs (half a million in the mid-1960s and one million by 1975) and generating foreign earnings. Tourism accounted for a quarter of the value of Spain's exports in 1975. Not surprisingly, the Spanish Government continued to support tourism, although the accelerating and uncontrolled growth led to the destruction of forests and loss of environmental quality and to problems of tourists arriving to find hotel developments incomplete and with poor infrastructure. The continued concentration of development on the Mediterranean led to a shift in the distribution of the Spanish population away from the interior towards the costas and the Balearic Islands. By the mid-1970s, when the growth of tourism was checked slightly, Spain already had an extensive stock of large modern hotels tailor-made for the needs of the mass market. Exchange rates still made Spain an attractive destination for the British. In spite of the recession, tourism resumed its growth, and the industry continued to cater for mass tourists from the middle and lower class social groups. The growing prosperity of the Spanish, political changes in their country (for example the re-establishment of democracy and their entry into the EC in 1986) and the over-development and congestion on the coast and the bad behaviour of some visitors has led to some conflicts between tourists and residents.

In spite of this, however, tourism became even more important to the economy: it employed 11 per cent of the labour force, contributing 33.4 per cent of the value of Spain's exports in 1989, and 9 per cent of GDP. In the five years 1988–92 the total number of inbound tourists has stagnated at between 34 and 35 million each year. Most of Spain's main European markets held steady (e.g. France, Germany, Netherlands and Italy) between 1988 and 1990 with growth resuming in 1991 and 1992. The major exception to this pattern was the UK market – visitor numbers dropped dramatically from 7.6 million in 1988 to 6.1 million in 1991 (see Fig 21.2). It was assumed that this was due to the combined effects of the recession and competition from other budget destinations, bad publicity given to rowdy tourists (British 'lager louts') and the growing awareness of the environmental problems of many of the older Spanish coastal resorts. These resorts were showing many of the characteristics of the phase of decline in the destination life cycle (see Chapter 8), with problems of congestion, pollution, struggling hotel businesses with falling occupancy rates, and restructuring of the accommodation stock towards self-catering. The resorts that depend heavily on the UK market responded in several ways: by improving the local environment (with tree planting, traffic management, limiting 'happy hours', hotel refurbishment schemes, cleaning streets and beaches, and building new seafronts etc.), by providing and promoting new attractions, by going up-market and by targeting other markets. The Balearics, Benidorm, Salou and Torremolinos have either implemented or have plans to carry out such improvements (see Pollard and Rodriguez (1993), Morgan (1991), McGeehan (1993)). The year 1992 provided Spain with a unique opportunity to change its image. The coincidence of the Olympic Games in Barcelona, Expo '92 in Seville and Madrid being the 1992 European City of Culture drew attention to the country's culture and city destinations.

At the same time the Spanish Tourist Office put £1.9 million in UK into promoting the attractions of inland Spain. These events brought not only more tourists but also a different clientele to Spain in 1992 (e.g. a gradual increase of independent rather than package visitors from UK). The growth in tourism in 1992 appears to have been sustained into the early months of 1993. It remains to be seen whether or not the new wave of international tourists will continue to patronise the coastal resorts or favour these newly promoted Spanish destinations. In the meantime, the resorts on the Spanish costas are benefiting from the growing domestic tourist market: Spain's GNP per capita has grown rapidly in recent years, from US$ 4890 in 1986 to US$ 10 920 per head (1990) and holiday taking has increased from 41 per cent to 53.4 per cent of the population in the two decades up to 1990. The Spanish domestic market as a whole generated 22.7 million visits to Spanish hotels and campsites (accounting for 68 million nights) in 1991. This is increasingly concentrated on the Mediterranean coast: in 1991 it is estimated that there were 12.48 million Spanish arrivals at registered accommodation in the Mediterranean regions of Spain. The single resort of Benidorm attracted 3.2 per cent of all Spanish domestic tourism while Palma de Majorca drew another 3 per cent.

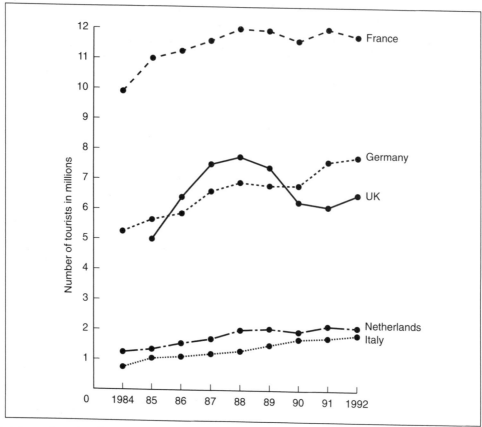

Fig. 21.2 Inbound tourism from Spain's main markets, 1984–1992
(*Source*: WTO)

THE TOURIST REGIONS OF SPAIN

Spain can be divided into two broad tourist regions: the coast and the interior, the former very heavily used for sun, sea and sand tourism, and the latter hardly visited although it abounds with cultural and historic attractions. The landscapes and climate of the interior make it a less varied and less attractive tourist destination than the interior of France.

The interior

Most of the Iberian peninsula is over 500 m. It consists of a high plateau with flat, monotonous skylines, divided into basins by east-west mountain chains that stand out above the plateau surface (*see* Fig 21.3). It has a hot semi-arid climate and maximum temperatures rise to over 30° C in Madrid in mid-summer. The uplands consist of dry, dusty ridges and rolling plains, but where irrigation is possible the valleys are green and fertile.

A semicircular rim of mountains frame the plateau on its northern, eastern and southern edges. These ranges are known as the Cantabrian and Iberian mountains and the Sierra Nevada (in Andalucia). The plateau gradually drops in height from these mountains to its western edge in Portugal. The plateau is cut into two basins by the Central Sierras running east and west across its middle.

The Cantabrian mountains

These run parallel to Spain's north coast, and they drop sharply to the Atlantic to form a steep, cliffed coastline. Turbulent rivers have cut deep valleys in their northern flanks. Some of the rivers (e.g. the Mino) are suitable for rafting and canoeing. The valleys are steep – often dropping over 2500 m in a distance of 1632 km. The hillsides are green and lush as the region lies in the path of moist Atlantic weather systems. The region is being promoted as 'Green Spain' with a focus on outdoor activities (walking, game shooting, horse riding, fishing, and also skiing in winter).

The region has its own distinctive cultural resources. In Galicia (at its western end) there are many medieval monasteries, religious houses and chapels associated with the 'way of St James', the Christian pilgrims' route to the town of Santiago de Compostela. The Altimira caves, famous for their 15 000 year old paintings of bison, are located southwest of Santander. The Basque country with its unique language and independent traditions lies to the eastern end of the region.

The Iberian mountains and the Central Sierras

The Iberian mountains form a more diffuse upland block at the eastern edge of the plateau of central Spain, while the granite mass of the Central Sierras rises to over 1400 m. The landscapes are much drier and more barren.

The basins and plateaux to the south of the Central Sierras have a hot semi-arid climate, and maximum temperatures rise to over 30° C in Madrid in mid-summer. The only part of the interior that receives any significant tourism is Madrid (the political and cultural capital). It is both a historic and modern industrial city of three million people. Over ten per cent of domestic tourism is centred here. Foreign visitors may come for business tourism but also for cultural tourism. The city

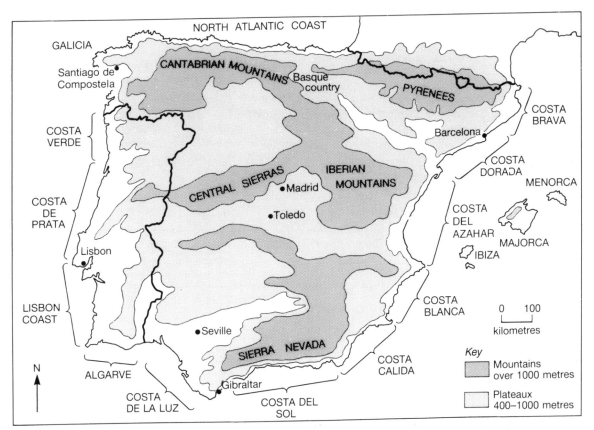

Fig. 21.3 Regions of Spain and Portugal

is the home of the Prado Museum, one of the world's most famous art galleries, with particularly fine collections of Spanish, Flemish and Italian paintings. The city has many more museums, galleries, cultural and historic attractions, spanning the centuries from the old medieval core of 'old Madrid', the grand 17th century square (the Plaza Mayor) and cathedral, to the huge 18th century Royal Palace. The town of Toledo (60 km to the south of Madrid) is another major cultural and historic attraction. It was a regional capital from Roman times (218 BC– AD 300), during the rule of the Visigoths and during the following period when Spain was ruled by invading Arabs (the Moors) who introduced Muslim culture and architecture in the period AD 712–1035. When Christianity was re-established, Toledo became the wealthy capital of the Kingdom of Castille until Madrid replaced it as capital in 1561. Thus modern development has been diverted away from Toledo, so it has survived virtually intact, and its narrow, winding streets, free of wheeled traffic, retain their medieval character. It is one of Europe's finest unspoilt medieval towns, even on par with Venice. There are many other historic sites in the region. El Escorial is famous for its monastery–palace and burial place for Spanish royalty. Avila, a walled medieval town and Segovia, with its castle, Roman aqueduct and cathedral, both lie to the northwest of Madrid, while Burgos which has another magnificent cathedral is further north.

The Sierra Nevada mountains of Andalucia

These form the southern rim of the plateau, and include Spain's highest peaks (over 3400 m).

The ranges extend over 125 km inland to the Guadalquivir valley, but are highest in the south and drop steeply to the Mediterranean coast, forming the backdrop to the Costa del Sol, and protecting it from any cold northerly weather influences. The mountains are rounded, smooth domes but in places their flanks are deeply dissected by spectacular valleys and gorges. Snow lies between November and May (above 2000 m), allowing winter sports developments, e.g. at Prada Llano 34 km south-east of Granada. The eastern end of the mountain chain (inland of the Costa Cálida between Almeria and Cartagena) is very hot and dry with a treeless and desolate pink and ochre landscape of gorges, badlands and rolling plateaux.

Andalucia has a long history with many of the settlements in the Guadalquivir valley having Roman origins. But it owes much of its particular cultural and architectural character to Moorish influence. The Islamic Moors arrived in Gibraltar (its name derived from the Moorish name Djebel al Tarik) in AD 711, and ruled most of Spain for several centuries, their occupation of Andalucia coming to an end in 1492 when Granada finally fell to the Christians. The region is rich in Moorish architecture such as the Grand Mosque (La Mezquita) in Córdoba, and the Alhambra Palace, a 13th–14th century fortified palace built of pink stone, in Granada. Seville is famed for its bullfighting and its April Fair when flamenco dress, music and dancing underline the special culture and character of the region. Seville also has many beautiful and historic buildings (e.g. the Alcazar – the fortified palace of the Moorish kings; the huge Gothic cathedral, and the Giralda tower).

The Pyrénées

The only other inland location that attracts foreign tourists in any significant numbers is the Pyrénées.

	Foreign tourists using hotels %	All accommodation %
Balearic islands	40.7	22.6
Canary Islands	17.7	18.4
The Mediterranean Coast:		
Northern section (Catalonia/Costa Brava)	15.2	20.6
Middle section (Valencia)	8.3	16.2
Southern section (Andalucia/Costa del Sol)	11.7	13.2
All the rest of Spain	6.4	9.0

Fig. 21.4 Distribution of foreign tourism in Spain, 1986

	Ave temp °C	Rainfall mm	RH %	Average sun hours per day
January	8.7	35	68	5
February	10.3	38	65	6
March	11.4	44	68	6
April	14.0	46	66	7
May	17.2	33	66	8
June	20.8	33	64	9
July	24.0	27	65	10
August	24.1	38	69	9
September	21.6	34	73	7
October	17.1	72	71	6
November	12.9	44	70	5
December	9.3	28	67	4

Fig. 21.5 Barcelona's climate

The Spanish side of the mountain range has similar landscapes to the French side (*see* Chapter 19). This area is visited for both summer and winter sports holidays (some resorts offer skiing for up to six months of the year). The main ski resorts are Baqueira Beret and La Molina-Supermolina.

However, Spain is synonymous with sun, sea and sand holidays, and foreign tourism is highly concentrated on a few coastal regions (*see* Fig 21.4).

The Mediterranean coast

The Costa Brava

This is the stretch of coast running from the French border to Blanes, 60 km northeast of Barcelona. Its climate is similar to that of Barcelona (*see* Fig 21.5). 'Costa Brava' means 'wild coast'. It is wild in that the scenery is rugged. The coast is spectacular, with cliffed headlands alternating with small

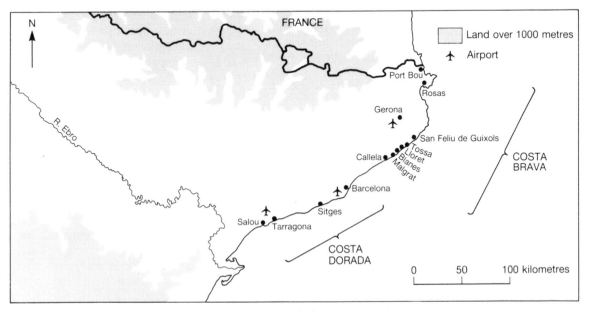

Fig. 21.6 Costas Dorada and Brava

sandy beaches in the coves and bays backed by steeply sloping hills. Some relatively quiet beaches may be found, but it is generally very intensively developed for tourism (see Fig 21.6). The large modern resorts consist of multistorey hotels and apartments and are very crowded (e.g. Lloret de Mar and S'Agaro). Some remain relatively unspoilt, for example Tossa (which was originally a Roman city with 12th century walls). Many of the original settlements were fishing villages that have been expanded by the addition of hotels, villas and apartments, e.g. Rosas and Estartit. All these resorts plus major centres like San Feliu and Blanes, are dominated by tour operators providing package tours mainly for the British and German markets (see Fig 21.7). Elsewhere, the development consists of sprawling settlements offering villa and campsite accommodation, catering for the independent and individual tourist. The number of villas built as second homes is growing rapidly, particularly on the steep hillsides overlooking the sea. The region has over 25 per cent of all Spain's campsites and these cater particularly for the French who drive the short distance across the border along the A17 motorway to the Costa Brava. Longer distance travellers arrive via the international airport at Barcelona or the more local Gerona airport which was opened in 1967.

Origin of visitors	% of all foreign visitors to hotels
West Germany	35.3
France	17.6
UK	12.1
North America	2.5
Other	32.5

Fig. 21.7 Foreign visitors to the Costa Brava, 1986

The Costa Dorada

This is the stretch of coastline south from Barcelona to Tarragona (see Fig 21.6). It has fine sandy beaches and has a gentler landscape than the cliffed and rocky Costa Brava. The motorway and railway run close to the coast, often cutting off the beach from the settlements inland. Tarragona has many well preserved Roman buildings and retains much of its original Roman plan. In 1984 the province of Tarragona had 14 per cent of Spain's campsite bed spaces, with a total of 51 000, but only 2.5 per cent of Spain's hotel bed spaces. The province is thus providing accommodation to appeal to French taste. Hotel visitors are more likely to come from Britain or Germany. Catalonia as a whole (the combined Costa Brava and Costa Dorada regions) has 49 per cent of all Spain's campsite accommodation in 1990, reflecting the needs of the nearby French market. Catalonia is also estimated to have 450 000 second homes (mostly owned by French or Germans).

Costa del Azahar

This extends from Viñaroz over 180 km south to Cap de la Nao (see Fig 21.3). It is an unbroken strip of lowland, again flanked by the motorway and railway. The coast is fringed by pine-clad dunes and long, sandy beaches, which are sometimes cut off from the mainland by lagoons, and hotels are scattered along the coast with no really large resorts. The region has only two per cent of Spain's accommodation but again the majority (three fifths) is in the form of campsites and apartments to cater primarily for the French market.

The Costa Blanca (The White Coast)

This runs from Cap de la Nao to Alicante (see Fig 21.8). The coastal plain is interrupted by the northern ridges of the Andalucian mountains as they run into the sea. In the northern section, white cliffs are interspersed with white shingle and sand beaches, but south of Altea the coast levels out and there are larger beaches of fine, white sand, for example Benidorm has two major beaches, one 3.2 kms long and the other of 1.6 kms. To the south, the beaches become a little more pebbly. The biggest and best beaches have all been developed since the 1960s, and the majority of the accommodation is in hotels. It is dominated by English-speaking visitors (the British make up 21 per cent of all foreign hotel visitors and 11 per cent are North Americans). Only about six per cent of hotel visitors come from France and Germany. Benidorm is the largest resort and it caters for this market well, with British food available, and a wide range of entertainments (e.g. bingo, entertainment parks, discos, nightclubs, and a selection of land and water sports). The region has also

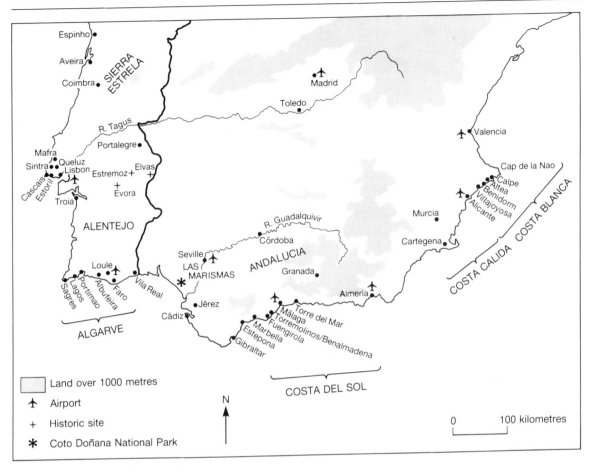

Fig. 21.8 Costas of southern Spain

been popular for the development of foreign-owned second homes (villas or apartments) which are used by the owners firstly as holiday homes and then as retirement homes. In 1986 there were about half a million along this stretch of coast, of which about a third are British-owned and a quarter are German.

The southernmost section (the coast of Murcia, south of Alicante) is sometimes known as the Costa Cálida. Here the coastal lowlands disappear as the mountains meet the sea. It has few resorts and can be extremely hot and dry in the summer.

The Costa del Sol

This coast runs from Almeria to Gibraltar (*see* Fig 21.8) and is backed by the mountains of the Sierra Nevada which rise to 3440 metres. It has many fine beaches, and the climate is appreciably warmer

and sunnier than the Costa Brava. Average temperatures reach 26° C in July and August in Málaga, and the summer drought is complete between June and August (15 mm only). Almeria averages over 10 hours of sunshine a day for four months (May to August). The region is densely populated and has a substantially urbanised or suburban tourist landscape. Nearly 70 per cent of the accommodation is in the form of hotels and apartments and the region is swamped by budget-priced packages, though there are some luxury hotels, and many foreign-owned second homes. The main resorts – Torremolinos, Benalmádena Costa, Fuengirola, Marbella and Estapona – are linked to the airport at Malaga by the coastal road. Again, the hotels of the area are most popular with the English-speaking visitors (17.5 per cent of hotel visitors come from UK and 10.8 per cent from North America).

	Area km²	% of land area of the archipelago	% of coast-line of the archipelago	% hotel bednights 1985	Airport	Flight time from London
Majorca	3660	73	45	80.9	Palma	2 hrs 15 min
Menorca	686	14	23	5.4	Mahon	3 hrs 30 min
Ibiza	593	11	17	13.0		3 hrs 30 min
Formentera	94	<2	<15			

Fig. 21.9 The Balearic Islands

The Andalucian mountains inland from the coast contain a wide variety of tourist attractions but are not so popular as the coast.

The Atlantic coast of Spain

Although the main concentration of tourist development is along the Mediterranean coast, the Atlantic coast has great potential for development (see Fig 21.8). The Costa de la Luz runs from Gibraltar to the Portuguese border and consists of the lowlands at the mouth of the valley of the river Guadalquivir. Sand dunes extend along the coast, impeding the drainage of the river and creating extensive marshy areas inland (Las Marismas). This is designated as the Coto de Doñana National Park on account of its exceptional wildlife, but there may be conflicts between the need to conserve the wildlife and the pressures for the tourist development of this stretch of coast. Cádiz and Jérez (from where sherry originated) lie at the mouth of the valley; Seville and Córdoba are towns which have many Moorish buildings, such as the eighth century Mosque at Córdoba, and both are steeped in Andalucian culture (characterised by flamenco music and dancing, bullfighting and religious festivals).

The North Atlantic coast

The coastline has many fine beaches and is quite popular with Spanish domestic tourists but has very little international tourism. Because the coast is open to Atlantic weather the climate is cooler (with average summer temperatures below 20° C) and much wetter, with rainfall all year round, than

the Mediterranean coast of Spain. Sunshine hours average seven a day in mid-summer (compared to 12 hours in Almeria). The landscape is lusher and greener than the Mediterranean and the coast is largely undeveloped and uncrowded.

THE BALEARIC ISLANDS

This group of islands is in the Mediterranean, nearly 200 km south of Barcelona and 240 km due east of the Valencian coastline. The total area of the archipelago is 5014 km² and the coastline is 1240 km long. The largest of the islands is Majorca (see Figs 21.3 and 21.9) and is the main centre of tourist activity.

These islands are Spain's most important tourist area with 3.6 million foreign visitors in 1986. Nearly 20 per cent of all of Spain's tourist accommodation is located here, consisting mainly of hotels and apartments (29 per cent and 31 per cent respectively of Spain's total stock) but very few campsites. This selection of accommodation is tailored to the needs of the British and German markets. The islands rely heavily on the British market, which accounts for 32 per cent of all visits to hotels and over half the total number of visitors though the proportion varies from island to island (see Fig 21.10). The British connection with the islands is longstanding. The island of Menorca was occupied by the British between 1708 and 1802, and there is a substantial and well-integrated resident British community on the island and a considerable proportion of the 9000 plus second homes on the island are owned by British people who may eventually retire there and thus further add to the resident British community.

	% tourists to		
	Majorca	*Ibiza (incl visitors destined for Formentera)*	*Menorca*
UK	41.9	52.3	76.7
West Germany	28.9	29.1	14.4
France	6.0	0.6	–
Switzerland	3.5	2.3	1.3
Netherlands	3.0	3.3	2.0
Norway	3.2	0.3	1.2
Denmark	2.9	2.0	0.9
Italy	2.6	5.1	0.6
Sweden	2.3	0.3	1.6

Fig. 21.10 Foreign visitors to the Balearic Islands: tourists by nationality and island of arrival, 1986

These cultural and historical links with the islands are one explanation of their popularity with British tourists and their natural resources have reinforced the connection. The islands have a typical Mediterranean climate (*see* p 19, Chapter 2). The summer temperatures, which rise to 25° C in July and August, are intermediate between those of Barcelona (to the north) and Athens to the east. Their maritime location makes them a little less extreme, i.e. wetter and more humid than Athens in the summer, but slightly milder and drier in the winter, making them more attractive for winter visits. The coastline is varied, consisting of rocky cliffs, deep inlets, and good harbours interspersed with fine sandy beaches of different sizes and character. Some are large and heavily developed and commercialised, while others remain isolated and deserted. Tourism is dominated by sun, sea and sand package holidays, although the landscapes also have tourist potential. For example, in Majorca there is a band of rugged mountainous terrain in the northwest of the island, extending 16 km in from the coast (*see* Fig 21.11). Its highest peak rises to 1459 m. There are high, almost vertical cliffs where the mountains jut into the sea. The peaks occasionally get snow in winter but they protect the rest of the island from cold NW winds in winter. The land to the southeast of the mountains is lower and is covered with almond orchards which flower in February. It is formed of less resistant rock that has been eroded by the sea to form two wide bays where the island's best beaches are situated (at Palma in the south and Alcudia in the north). These are the most intensively developed, e.g. the 1.6 km Playa de Arenal, east of Palma, and are backed by multistorey hotels and apartments, with all the entertainments and facilities to suit British holiday tastes. The east coast of Majorca is made of limestone and has slightly fewer and rather smaller beaches in a series of coves between rocky headlands. The south coast is much more cliffed and is the least developed for tourism. Although their coastlines have a similar mix of cliffs, coves and sandy beaches, the other three islands are much less rugged than Majorca. The highest point in Menorca is only 357 m; Ibiza rises to just 475 m and Formentera is virtually flat. These islands have extensive pine woods, and have a more relaxed atmosphere than Majorca. Tourism is less intensively developed and there are fewer high-rise buildings. Ibiza and Menorca are accessible by air but Formentera can only be reached by ferry from Ibiza.

The islands plan to diversify their tourist product with the development of active sports facilities such as golf courses and yacht moorings. It is, however, the very success of the tourist industry in meeting the needs of the mass sun, sea, sand package market that has led to environmental and economic problems. Sixty per cent of the islands' GNP comes from the tourist industry.

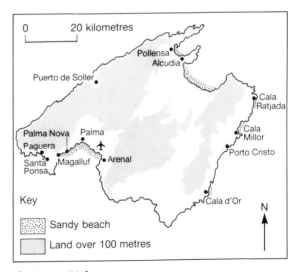

Fig. 21.11 Majorca

The economy of the islands is over-dependent on tourism, and relies too much on just the British and German markets which together account for 80 per cent of all visitors. The spending levels of British tourists are low, hotel profit margins have been declining and some new apartment developments have been badly built, threatening the beauty of the landscape. Majorca's season lasts from May to October with nearly 13 per cent of visitors coming in the winter months, yet only 40 per cent of its hotels are open in the off-season. The other islands have a far shorter summer season, with nearly 40 per cent of their visitors arriving in July and August, and negligible winter seasons. An additional pressure is for second home development (both for the developing domestic Spanish market and for foreigners). By 1981, numbers of second homes had risen to near two million. Flats and apartments are concentrated in the coastal and resort areas, but many small-holdings in the interior have been aquired by hobby farmers and are used mainly for holidays rather than for agriculture. These problems have led the Balearics Government to consider imposing much greater control on new development, and it plans to both diversify and upgrade the tourist product, and also to support the other industries of the islands (e.g. textiles in Ibiza, and leather and footwear in Minorca).

THE CANARY ISLANDS

These islands lie off the African coast well outside the Mediterranean basin, and the area has a sub-tropical climate (see Fig 21.1). The islands are considered in this chapter because they are politically and economically integrated with Spain. In terms of tourist perceptions, the islands are primarily a winter sun destination that compete with other longer-haul sub-tropical locations rather than with the Mediterranean.

The islands are ancient volcanoes, and some of the mountains are extinct craters. Many of the beaches are made of black sand derived from the volcanic deposits. Tenerife is the biggest of the islands with the highest mountain (Pico del Teide at 3718 m) and a huge extinct volcanic crater. Its main resort is Puerto de la Cruz. It has two international airports. Fuertaventura is the second biggest

island and has particularly good sandy beaches. Gran Canaria is next in size and has the other international airport (at Las Palmas). These islands (along with Gomera and La Palma) all have rugged landscapes and extinct volcanoes. Their settlements date back to the 16th and 17th centuries and many of the towns have attractive historic churches and castles. There is good duty free shopping and a wide choice of water sports. However, the winter climate and the coast are the main tourist resources, as the January maximum temperature can rise above 20° C and the winters are dry. The low rainfall and high visitor populations, however, lead to problems of water supply and an expensive desalination plant is required to obtain supplies from seawater. The most easterly island of the group (Lanzarote) is the flattest and driest, and has some eerie barren volcanic landscapes. In 1989 over 1.4 million visitors arrived on Tenerife and a similar number on the island of Las Palmas. Most of these visitors were from the UK or Germany, who stay in hotels and apartments.

DOMESTIC TOURISM IN SPAIN

The coastal resorts of Spain cater for the domestic market as well as international visitors, but do not suffer from such intense congestion as in France or Italy where international and domestic demands coincide. This is because the Spanish domestic market is small by Western European standards. However, as the economy develops, domestic tourism is gradually growing. By 1990, 53.4 per cent of Spaniards took a holiday, and the proportion of holidaymakers travelling abroad has increased from 7.6 per cent in 1988 to 10 per cent in 1990. Thus, Spain appears to be in Phase 2 of the evolution of its own domestic and outbound tourism (see p 152, Chapter 15). Domestic tourists generally stayed in cheaper accommodation (approximately 27 per cent with friends or relatives and only 29 per cent in serviced accommodation). So, again, domestic tourists do not yet compete directly with international visitors. However, more Spaniards are now visiting the Mediterranean resorts, particularly on the Costa Blanca where Benidorm is now the leading domestic holiday destination. The province of Valencia receives 15.7 per cent of all domestic main holidays. Andalucia and Catalonia are the next most popular domestic holiday regions (*see* Fig 21.12).

	%
Valencia	15.7
Andalucia	15.4
Catalonia	13.9
Galicia	6.6
Canary Islands	6.1
Balearics	5.5
Aragon	4.1
Castille-Leon	3.6
Madrid	2.9

Fig. 21.12 Main holiday region visited by Spanish tourists, 1990

This growth in domestic tourism has compensated a little for the downturn in UK tourism between 1988 and 1991 on the Costa Brava, Costa Blanca and Costa del Sol. The fact that domestic tourism is strongly peaked in August (the Spaniards, like the French, have a tradition of taking one long holiday in August) may lead to temporary conflicts of interest between domestic and international tourists. Fifty-seven per cent of all domestic holidays were to the coast but relatively few Spaniards visited the Balearics or the Canary Islands. The Costa del Azahar, Costa Blanca and Andalucia were the most popular destinations overall, but Spain's Atlantic coast is relatively more popular with domestic than international visitors: a total of 11 per cent of domestic tourists visited Galicia and Cantabria, and Santander is the third most important domestic resort.

Spanish outbound tourism

Outbound tourism is as yet little developed, and shows the following characteristics of an immature but rapidly growing market.

1 Numbers are low. However outbound tourism to adjacent countries (i.e. France and Portugal) is growing fast. Only 2.5 million Spaniards visited Portugal in 1986 but by 1991 this had climbed to 4.1 million. Spanish tourism to France more than doubled over the same period (from one million in 1986 to 2.8 million in 1991). Outbound tourism to more distant parts of Europe (e.g. UK and Italy) has grown much more slowly, and has even decreased slightly since 1989 or 1990.

2 Numbers of outbound tourists are growing rapidly. Growth rates (even in the recession of the 1980s) were in the range of 30 to 57 per cent to Portugal, Greece, Morocco, Turkey and Tunisia (all the relatively cheaper Mediterranean destinations). Lower growth rates were recorded for Spanish visitors to the relatively expensive destinations such as France, Italy and UK.

3 Few Spaniards travel by plane. Ninety per cent of Spanish outbound tourists left Spain by car, and only 7.5 per cent went to longer-haul destinations by plane. Coach travel is important and package coach tours abroad are popular. The majority of trips are fairly short, i.e. to adjacent countries. Much of the genuine long-haul air travel is still business tourism (40.7 per cent of Spanish visitors to Canada and 44.5 per cent to Japan were business travellers).

PORTUGAL

The country can be divided by the Tagus into two climatic regions; the north, dominated by cooler, moist Atlantic weather and the south where the climate and vegetation are more Mediterranean in character.

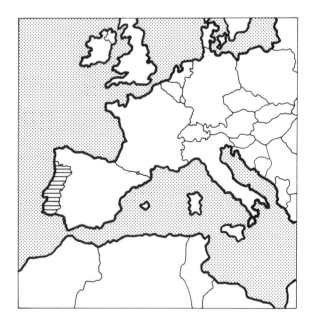

The north coast of Portugal (the Costa Verde) averages 1270 mm rainfall a year, while on the windward (west-facing) slopes of the mountains inland, the total may reach over 2500 mm a year. Lisbon (on the Tagus estuary) has 708 mm a year and two months (July and August) of drought. Faro, on Portugal's southern coast, has only 453 mm a year with a three-month dry period. In the south average maximum temperatures rise to 28° C in the summer drought, while Lisbon's average midsummer temperature is around 22° C. Physically the country is divided into:

1 **the uplands and plateaux**
   (a) the mountains of the north (Minho and Tras os Montes). These are located inland of the Costa Verde;
   (b) the plateaux of Beira and Alentejo (the edge of the Spanish Meseta). The Beira plateau is located inland of the Costa de Prata, while Alentejo is east of the Lisbon coast.
2 **the lowlands**
   (a) the coastal lowlands and plains
   (b) the Tagus valley.

The uplands

The mountains of the north rise to 780 m in Minho, and the Tras os Montes to over 1500 m. The landscapes are interesting rather than dramatic. The unspoiled, rugged granite uplands of Minho are well wooded with maritime pines and offer opportunities for walking and climbing, while the Tras os Montes is a monotonous treeless plateau dissected by deep valleys. The Beira plateau has more tree cover (pine and chestnut) and rises southwards to the more striking landscapes of the Estrela mountains. The rolling Alentejo plateau (rising to only 400 m) is a richer, arable agricultural landscape.

These regions form Portugal's interior, and tend to be dry and hot in the summer, as the plateaux rise to merge into the Meseta across the Spanish border. There are many unspoilt historic settlements, e.g. Estramoz and Portalegre, and the fortified hill towns along the border are of particular interest. These date from the 12th century and many, such as Elvas, have impressive medieval fortifications. Evora is another 12th century town that became Portugal's second most important city in the 17th century and has much magnificent architecture of the period. It is now a World Heritage site.

In spite of these attractions these parts of Portugal are hardly visited by international tourists, with less than two per cent of Portugal's foreign visitors.

The coast

The coast is the main tourist resource, and it can be divided into four zones (*see* Fig 21.3).

1 **The Costa Verde (the Green Coast).** The coast is green with forests and lush vegetation but the rainfall that supports the vegetation limits the tourism. The coastal plain is between 1.6 and 8 km wide and extends into the Douro valley inland of Oporto. The valley sides are terraced vineyards where the port wine is produced. There is a cluster of resorts with good sandy beaches around Oporto but the region attracted only 11.4 per cent of Portugal's total tourist bednights in 1990 and 7.1 per cent of foreign tourists.
2 **Costa de Prata (the Silver Coast).** This extends from Espinho (just south of Oporto) to Estremadura. The coast is flat, fringed with mobile sand dunes which have ponded back the River Vouga to form saltmarshes and lagoons at Aveiro.

These are now drained by a maze of canals and Aveiro has been likened to Venice and its surrounding countryside to Holland. The town had been a significant fishing port in the 16th century before the river mouth became choked with sand.

The most important historic town inland is Coimbra, Portugal's third largest city with one of Europe's oldest universities (dating from the 16th century). Elsewhere along the coast there are long sandy beaches but the resorts are quite small and are more spread out. The climate is more Atlantic than Mediterranean and the region attracted 11 per cent of Portugal's tourist bednights in 1990, but only 5.2 per cent of foreign visitors. These northern coasts cater mostly for the growing domestic market.

3 **The Lisbon coast (Costa Lisboa and Costa Dourada).** This is in the climatic transition zone towards a more Mediterranean climate. The coast is low lying with long beaches, some of which are more intensively developed both for staying visitors and day-trippers from Lisbon, e.g. Cascais,

Estoril, which has a casino, nightlife and a range of land-based sports, and Troia which is a modern tourist beach complex of hotels, restaurants, nightclubs, golf and watersports facilities. Lisbon itself has an excellent natural harbour and the site has been settled since pre-Roman times. Its cathedral dates from the 12th century and its Moorish quarter from the medieval period. But its wealth expanded with Portugal's overseas trade and the city was added to and partly rebuilt in the 17th and 18th centuries. It is still a thriving commercial and business centre: it attracts many domestic and international business tourists, but also all year round short-stay cultural visitors. The average length of stay is low at two to eight days for international visitors, but the visitors are high spenders and there is a good stock of up-market accommodation (over 40 per cent of all Portugal's five-star hotel rooms are in Lisbon). Elsewhere in the region there are also good camping facilities.

There are a number of historical sites inland that are accessible from Lisbon, such as Sintra, Queluz and Mafra. Much of the countryside inland of the Lisbon and Dourada coasts is forested with cork oak trees and is a centre of cork production. This region with its varied cultural and coastal attractions took 27 per cent of Portugal's bednights and drew its international tourists from a wide variety of generating countries.

4 The Algarve. This stretch of the southern coast of Portugal dominates Portugal's tourist industry, taking 40 per cent of bednights, and attracts most of the country's foreign tourists. It faces the Atlantic (*see* Fig 21.8) but because of its southerly aspect is relatively sheltered from Atlantic depressions. It has a long, warm and dry summer with virtually no rainfall June–August. Summer maximum temperatures rise to 28° C, though the average temperatures are lower than the Mediterranean. Nevertheless, it is well developed for coastal tourism. The beaches are extensive and sandy. The western section (from Faro to Sagres) is continuously developed with little land left for new development. High rise hotels, villas and apartments line the coast with particularly large concentrations of hotels in Portimao, and apartments in Albufeira and Loulé. The greatest number of campsites is at Lagos and Villa Real (at either end of the coast). The accommodation stock is dominated by budget quality facilities to meet the needs of the relatively low spending British pack-

age visitors. This, plus the overdeveloped and unplanned nature of the resorts and the speed with which they were developed, has led to some deterioration of environmental quality.

In 1992 the Government approved a £200 million scheme to refurbish the Algarve's hotel stock, and a strategic plan for the region was to be drawn up in an attempt to restore the region's tourist image.

With over half of the international arrivals, the Algarve is by far the most popular region of Portugal among foreign visitors. The economy of the region relies particularly heavily on the British market. British holidaymakers accounted for 51 per cent of all the nights in hotels, boarding houses and apartments, and most British visitors (73.4 per cent) came on package tours. Faro is the Algarve's international airport, and the primary gateway for package tourists. Spanish day-trippers come across the border by road.

MADEIRA

Portugal also possesses a sub-tropical Atlantic island located 650 km west off the Moroccan coast (*see* Fig 21.1). Madeira is 57 km east-west, and 22 km north-south. Two thirds of its territory is mountainous and the coast is precipitous, with mainly shingle or boulder beaches. Its climate is its main resource (*see* Fig 21.13).

	Av temp °C	Rainfall (mm)	Peak months for Non-Iberian tourist arrivals	Arrivals from Spain and Portugal
Jan	15	86		
Feb	15	91		
March	15.4	86	*	
April	16	51	*	
May	18	28		
June	19.2	10		
July	21	2		
Aug	22	2		*
Sept	21	30		
Oct	20	102		
Nov	18	119	*	
Dec	16	81		

Fig. 21.13 Funchal's climate and seasonality of tourism

The island has mild winters and warm, dry summers. The relatively dry climate, the growing local and tourist demands and the small catchment area of the island have led to problems of water supply. The best season is April to June but Madeira does have all year round tourism. This is made up of two distinct groups of tourists with contrasting seasonal patterns of demand.

Visitors from Spain and Portugal come to the island for their summer holiday, so there is a pronounced peaking of Iberian visitors in August. Other visitors from Europe, and particularly from Scandinavia, see the island more as a winter sun destination and there is a double peak of these visitors: the months of March/April and November each record over 25 000 non-Iberian visitors, while in summer (May to August) these visitor arrivals drop to around 15 000 a month. Northern European visitors prefer to travel to other resorts in the Mediterranean with better beaches during these summer months. When these patterns are superimposed it is clear that, in spite of the attractive climate in late spring, May is the month the island receives fewest tourists.

Madeira depends heavily on the British and German markets, which together account for about a third of the island's visitors, with another 17 per cent from Scandinavian countries.

The island has had historical connections with Great Britain, associated with the trade in Madeira wine. In the 18th century the wine merchants built their mansions on the islands and let them for the winter season. Modern tourism on the island did not expand until the airport was built at Funchal in the 1960s, but the topography has constrained tourist growth. The island is short of flat coastal land suitable for tourist development, including an airport. Madeira was originally served by air via the military base on the neighbouring small island of Porto Santo but this was an unsatisfactory arrangement and Funchal airport was built in the 1960s, but required major engineering work to create a long enough runway. In spite of these problems, Madeira is Portugal's third most important tourist region (after the Algarve and Lisbon regions) for international tourists, and it has 14 per cent of Portugal's hotel beds.

THE AZORES

This is a group of nine islands (the largest, Sao Miguel, being a little bigger than Madeira) located in the Atlantic 1500 km west of Lisbon, further north than Madeira. Consequently their climate is a little wetter, windier and cooler than Madeira, and tour operators perceive them to be summer destinations only. International tourism has hardly been developed, due to their limited accessibility by air. The majority (70 per cent) of the visitors are domestic tourists from mainland Portugal who come on internal Portuguese flights. The average length of stay of visitors to the islands is short (only three days), and the total number of visitors is around 100 000 a year (representing only 1.8 per cent of Portuguese domestic tourism and 0.6 per cent of Portugal's foreign visitors in 1990).

DOMESTIC AND INTERNATIONAL TOURISM IN PORTUGAL

The domestic market is as yet small: only 26–30 per cent of the 11 million population have taken annual holidays away from home since 1979. In 1986, only eight per cent went abroad. The regional pattern of domestic tourism is a little different from that of international, with the northern coastal regions having more appeal for the Portuguese (see Fig 21.14).

Region	Foreign %	Portuguese %
Costa Verde	4.3	15.8
Costa de Prata	3.5	13.4
Lisbon Coast	21.1	28.7
'Mountains' (incl North and Beira Plateau)	0.7	9.7
'Plains' (incl Alentejo Plateau)	1.0	6.0
Algarve	51.1	16.7
Madeira	17.6	6.3
Azores	0.7	3.4

Fig. 21.14 Distribution of tourists, 1986

The volume of tourism in Portugal

Portugal receives around 19.6 million frontier arrivals a year, but this includes a large number of day visitors from Spain, and only 8.6 million were classed as tourists in 1991. Under four million foreign visitors arrived at registered tourist accommodation.

Tourists from	Tourist arrivals at Portugal's frontier (%)
Spain	47.5
UK	13.4
France	7.7
Germany	9.1
Netherlands	3.8
USA	1.7
Italy	2.9

Fig. 21.15 Tourist arrivals at Portugal's frontiers, 1991

International tourism is growing rapidly in Portugal, at an average rate of 11 per cent during the 1980s and early 1990s. It has a particular importance for the British market, offering package tours to a near Mediterranean environment at very competitive prices.

CONCLUSION

Although the size of the tourist industry of Spain and Portugal is very different, the two countries show significant similarities. Tourist development in both countries is heavily concentrated in relatively small regions, where the sheer volume of tourist numbers and the level of development may be beginning to reduce the quality of the holiday experience. Yet in other parts of each country, tourism is hardly developed: both have empty stretches of Atlantic coast and an abundance of inland cultural resources.

Both countries also have rapidly growing domestic markets, and both are beginning to expand their outbound tourism.

FURTHER READING

Cockerell, N (1993) 'Portugal', *EIU International Tourist Reports*, No. 1, pp.23–42

Edwards, J (1992) 'The role of and attitudes towards tourism planning in Portugal', paper presented at *Tourism in Europe – the 1992 conference.*

McGeehan, A (1993) 'Spain – on the verge of a new golden age?', *Travel Agency*, February, pp. 27–29.

Morgan, M (1991) 'Dressing up to survive – marketing Majorca anew', *Tourism Management*, Vol. 12, March, pp.15–20.

Pollard, J and Rodriguez, R D (1993) 'Tourism and Torremolinos – recession or reaction to environment?', *Tourism Management*, Vol. 14, August, pp. 247–58.

Steward, T A (1990) 'Spain', *EIU International Tourism Reports*, No. 4, pp.5–25.

Steward, T A (1992) 'Spain Outbound', *Travel and Tourism Analyst*, No. 2.

QUESTIONS AND DISCUSSION POINTS

1 To what extent is it true that the combination of climate, coast and accessibility explains the spatial distribution of tourism in Spain and Portugal?

2 It has been suggested that over-development and environmental problems have led the Spanish 'costas' into crisis. Do you consider this to be true – if so, what should be done to overcome the problems?

3 Do you expect Spain to increase or decrease its share of Mediterranean coastal holidays in the future? Explain the reasoning behind your answer.

ASSIGNMENTS

1 You work in a travel agent that serves an inner city area. A young couple come in. They have never been abroad before and have saved up for their first holiday in Spain but they are muddled about where the various 'costas' are and what each 'costa' is like. Briefly explain to them where each of the Spanish 'costas' is located and what characteristics typify each one. Suggest at least one resort in each of the 'costas' that the young couple might like to choose for their holiday.

2 You work in the planning and development section of a major tour operator. The company sells a wide range of different types of holiday including cultural, activity and special interest holidays but currently has no tours of these types in Spain or

Portugal. You have been asked by the chief executive to assess the potential of inland Spain and Portugal for one of these types of holiday. Write a brief report:

(a) locating and describing the chief resources for either cultural, activity or special interest holidays;

(b) identifying any constraints imposed by climate, lack of infrastructure, difficulties of accessibility etc. on the development of such tours; and

(c) making recommendations as to which destinations/regions might be worth promoting.

CHAPTER 22

The Balkan region: Albania, Greece and the former Yugoslavia

LEARNING OBJECTIVES

After reading this chapter you should be able to

- assess the tourist potential of the climatic, landscape, historical and cultural resources of Albania, Greece and the former Yugoslavia
- distinguish the regional distribution of these geographical resources and their development and use for tourism
- demonstrate a knowledge of the main tourist resorts and tourist centres
- understand the role of Albania and Greece in the general pattern of European tourism
- be aware of the impact of political events on the development of tourism.

INTRODUCTION

Political instability and political changes have dictated the evolution of tourism in this part of the Mediterranean for decades. Although the earliest forms of tourism were established on the Istrian peninsula before 1900, modern mass tourism had to wait for certain political changes to occur: under President Tito in the former Yugoslavia, tourism began from 1965 (when freedom of movement was first allowed in the original Communist state). In Greece mass tourism took off after 1974 when the country made the transition from a military dictatorship to democracy.

Tourism in both countries grew rapidly during the 1970s and 1980s. The peak year for tourism in the region was 1988 when 16.9 million tourists visited former Yugoslavia and Greece (9.0 m to Yugoslavia and 7.9 m to Greece). Virtually no tourists were allowed to go to Albania at the time because Albania was a particularly isolated and closed Communist country during the 'Cold War' era (between the Second World War and the revolutions of 1989, see Chapter 26). In 1990 the country was just beginning to allow some very limited and highly controlled Western tourism.

The new attitudes after the revolutions in the other countries of the now ex-Communist block began to seep into Albania.

Since 1990, political instability in the Balkan region has increased dramatically with the political break–up and civil war in the former Yugoslavia.

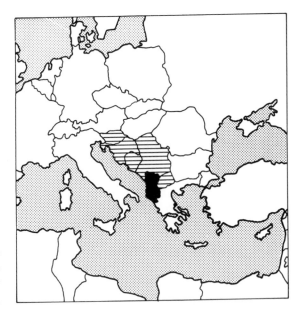

However, it was not so much the Communist revolutions that brought this about – it was more directly a result of increasing internal political tensions within ex-Yugoslavia that came back to the surface after the death of President Tito in 1980. Under Tito's form of Communist dictatorship, differences between the Yugoslav republics and their ethnic groups were held under control. After his death the constitution of Yugoslavia proved unable to cope with the internal tensions and conflicts of interest. After a decade of gradually worsening economic and internal political difficulties, Yugoslavia finally broke up into Slovenia, Croatia, Bosnia–Hercegovina, 'Macedonia' and the remnants of the former Yugoslavia (consisting of Serbia, Vojvodina and Montenegro). The collapse of communism in late 1990 was the final event that triggered off these changes. The disintegration of Yugoslavia was accompanied by sporadic fighting in Slovenia in 1991 but a more sustained war broke out between Croatia and Serbia, and a brutal civil war (between Serbs, Croats and Muslims) in Bosnia in 1992 and 1993. These wars have (from 1991) effectively ended tourism for the present in the territory of former Yugoslavia: at the time of writing the problems have not yet been resolved but the war has been contained within the boundaries of the former Yugoslavia.

Meanwhile tourism in Greece has continued to grow, but Greece is strongly opposed to the international recognition of a state called Macedonia as it is feared that this might trigger off political problems in the neighbouring Greek province which is also called Macedonia. The Greeks are thus very wary of any political developments that might cause the conflicts generated in the former Yugoslavia to spill over into Greek territory. Given a politically stable future, Greece may well benefit from Yugoslavia's loss: the Yugoslav market of nine million Mediterranean-bound tourists will be redistributed among the other Mediterranean destinations. In the short term this appears to be the case: in 1992 Greek tourism showed an 18 per cent increase over 1991 to a total of 9.75 million, its highest to date.

THE FORMER YUGOSLAVIA

Introduction

The former Yugoslavia was a federation of six republics. During 1991–2 these split up into five separate states:

1 Slovenia. This proclaimed itself an independent republic on 8 October 1991 and was fully recognised internationally in January 1992, with relatively little fighting. Its capital is Ljubljana; it has an area of 20 251 km^2, and a total population of 1.9 million.

2 Croatia. This republic also proclaimed itself independent and was recognised by the EC in January 1992 and accepted into the UN in May 1992. Prolonged fighting between Serbs and Croats has led to 30 per cent of its territory being under Serb control in early 1992. The Croatian capital is Zagreb. Its area is 56 538 km^2, and it has a population of 4.6 million.

3 Bosnia–Hercegovina. This republic also declared its independence in April 1992 but it was effectively partitioned between Serbia and Croatia: in 1992 Serbia controlled 65 per cent of its territory and Croatia 25 per cent, while the Muslim community was concentrated in isolated pockets. At the time of writing, civil war was still in progress and no political settlement had yet been achieved.

4 Federal Republic of Yugoslavia. This country was established in April 1992 and is made up of the territory of Serbia and Montenegro (including Vojvodina and Kosovo). Its capital is Belgrade. At the time of writing it was subject to UN economic sanctions banning commercial transactions and air links with other countries.

5 'Macedonia'. The former Yugoslavian state of Macedonia (capital, Skopje) was not recognised internationally (by either the EC or the UN) at the time of writing. 'Macedonia' has not been recognised as its official name.

The region has a wide range of natural resources for tourism, but international tourism was very strongly focused on the coast. However, it is the climate and scenery that were the main attractions rather than the beaches: most of the coast is rocky or shingly, but it enjoys a particularly sunny Mediterranean climate. In comparison to other Mediterranean destinations the country attracted a higher proportion of older, childless couples from higher socio-economic groups, rather than young couples or families with young children. Only 12 per cent of its visitors in 1986 were under 24 years of age.

Although Yugoslavia was in competition with destinations such as Spain, it thus offered a slightly different product and attracted a more specialised market.

Physical resources

The former Yugoslavia is predominantly a mountainous region of remote and unspoilt scenery; and can be divided into four main physical regions (*see* Fig 22.1):

1 the Adriatic Coast;
2 the limestone mountain chain that runs parallel to the coast down the length of the country
3 the Slovenian section of the Alps
4 the inland plains of the Danube and Sava.

The Adriatic coast

The coastal zone consists of a very narrow belt of land (only 1 to 60 km wide) that enjoys a true Mediterranean climate. In Split, the July and August temperatures hover around 25° C and although there is no complete summer drought, the climate is particularly sunny. Split enjoys an average of 2658 hours of sunshine a year, with 115 completely cloudless days and only 102 rain days a year. The coast is rugged and rises quickly inland to bleak bare mountain slopes. Most of the beaches are rocky or shingly as they are made of limestone, a rock which does not yield a sandy sediment. There are no big wide sandy beaches like the ones found on the Italian side of the Adriatic. The Dalmatian coast is fringed by 1000 islands, which are the submerged crests of limestone ridges running parallel to the mountain chain inland. Many are small and uninhabited.

The greatest concentration of resorts is on the coast of the Istrian peninsula (*see* Fig 22.1). The larger resorts, including Umag, Porec, Rovinj and Opatija, each had over one million foreign tourist nights in 1985. Centres such as Vrsar, Pula and Rabac each had half a million nights. Most of the resorts' modern hotels are grafted on to older settlements such as small medieval towns, e.g. Umag, fishing villages, such as Porec, or even older settlements. The town of Pula was a Roman military and administrative centre in the second century BC, and still possesses major Roman monuments such as the Amphitheatre, and the Temple of Augustus. On the other hand, Medulin and Rabac are essentially modern developments attached to small villages. These resorts (now in independent Croatia) were still open in 1992.

Tourists from Northern Europe reach the Istrian resorts via the airports at Pula and Ljubljana further inland, but the majority, from Germany and Italy, come by road. In fact, Istria is so close to the Italian border that most of the resorts offer coach or hydrofoil daytrips to Venice.

The Dalmatian coast between Opatija and Split was much less intensively developed, with a series of smaller more widely spaced resorts. The coast further south has been the focus of much fighting and much of the infrastructure has suffered, even the historic cities such as Dubrovnik. The climate is particularly sunny and there are some bigger beaches of coarse sand in Montenegro. The potential for tourism remains, but political circumstances prevent its development as yet. Most of the region's coastal resources are now located in the new state of Croatia.

The mountain spine

The mountain chain that backs the coast extends to 60–100 km inland, and averages 600 m in height, though substantial areas reach 1500 m. The mountains, running parallel to the coast in a NW-SE direction, lie at right angles to the prevailing winds and receive much more rainfall (totals of over 2500 mm) than the coast. The temperatures are lower, and the weather is quite harsh in winter as the climate is continental rather than Mediterranean. The mountains are made of limestone and have the typical 'karst' landscape of underground rivers, cave systems (e.g. at Postojna) and dry valleys. Thus, although the climate is wet, there is little surface water and the mountains appear dry and barren. Further inland, the geology changes, and rivers flow on the surface. Here the uplands are clothed with forests and pastures which provide a more attractive mountain landscape. The Plitvice National Park lies on the edge of the limestone zone, and consists of a series of 16 lakes linked by cascades and waterfalls, set in beech, spruce and fir forests. The central section of the uplands lie in Bosnia, at the focus of the civil war in 1992. No tourism is possible until peace is restored.

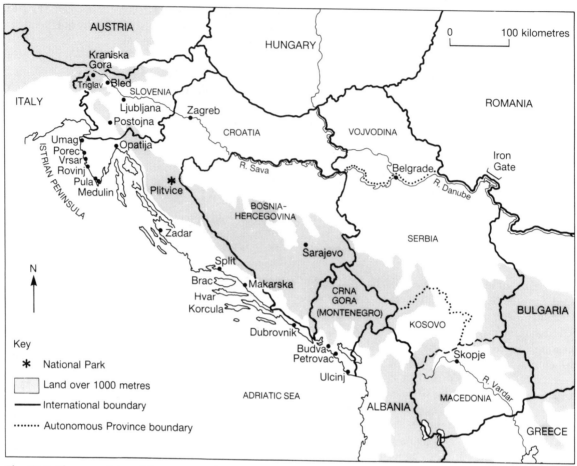

Fig. 22.1 The new states of former Yugoslavia

The Yugoslav Alps

A small section of the European Alps extends into Slovenia. Triglav is the highest peak (2863 m). The jagged peaks and flat-bottomed valleys create a much more dramatic mountain landscape than the limestone mountains further south. The lower slopes of the Slovenian Alps are forested, merging into alpine pastures above the tree line. Lakeside resorts such as Bled and Bohinj have similar climatic advantages to the Italian lakes – the average July temperature at Bled is 21° C. These resorts were popular in summer. Kranjska Gora was both a summer and winter sports resort, and ski facilities had also been developed at Planica. The lower cost and less crowded facilities made them very competitive with the winter sports resorts in Switzerland, Austria and Italy.

The inland plains

The northeasterly corner of former Yugoslavia consists of the monotonous plains of the Danube. These plains merge into the expanses of the Hungarian plains to the north. The climate is continental, with cold winters down to minus 0.2° C in Belgrade, and warm summers averaging 22.7° C in July. The interior is also relatively dry; the capital of the Federal Republic of Yugoslavia, Belgrade, has only 687 mm rainfall a year. Belgrade is the commercial and communications centre of the interior. The modern city has grown around a historic core, but it is mainly a centre for cultural, commercial and business tourism. Most of this territory is part of Serbia.

Conclusions

The distribution of tourist resources between the former Yugoslavia Republics

The majority of the coastal and climatic tourist resources of the former Yugoslavia lie within the officially recognised boundaries of Croatia (as of 1993) while Slovenia has the Alpine lake and mountain territory. The cultural, architectural and historic resources of much of the rest of the former Yugoslavia have been badly damaged by the war, along with the tourism infrastructure. The economies of all five republics have also been greatly disrupted and will take a long time to recover.

The current relative political stability of Slovenia may mean that this region may lead the reconstruction of the tourist industry. However, at the time of writing the war between Croats, Serbs and Muslims has not been resolved, and even if a political settlement were to be achieved quickly, there will inevitably be a very lengthy period of political readjustment, economic restructuring and physical rebuilding of the infrastructure before tourism could resume. It will also take some time for both tourists and tour operators to regain their confidence in the region. So in the short and medium term, the region cannot be considered as a functioning tourist destination.

ALBANIA

This Communist country has been politically and economically isolated from the West for many years, but in 1990 it was cautiously beginning to open up to Western travellers.

The country is physically and climatically similar to former Yugoslavia and Greece, as it occupies the stretch of coastal territory between them. The coastal plain varies in width, reaching 50 km inland in places (considerably wider than the coast strip of Croatia), and has more sandy beaches. Inland the well-forested mountains rise to over 2500 m. Three large lakes (Shkodres, Ohrid and Prespan) lie on the borders in the mountain region. Resorts do exist, for example there are beach hotels south of Durres, and Pogradec is a resort on Lake Ohrid (*see* Fig 22.2), but the cultural and historic resources have great potential for tourism. The

local people still wear traditional dress in the rural areas and there are few cars. Historic towns range from the picturesque museum towns of Gjirokaster and Berat, with their 14th century citadels, to the ancient ruins of Butrint (dating from the fourth and third centuries BC). In short, the country has great potential for tourism if the political situation allowed it to develop. Individual tourists and Americans have not been admitted to the country for many years although limited package tours are available. In 1990 tourism was still at the pioneering stage in Albania, as Albania was the last of the European Communist countries to challenge Communism and consider moving towards a more open society.

GREECE

Introduction

Although Greece has been the focus of small-scale historical and cultural tourism for many years, mass tourism is a more recent phenomenon. The trickle of post-war cultural tourists (mainly from the USA) was checked in 1967 when there was a coup d'état and a military dictatorship took over the government. This inhibited the growth of mass tourism at a time when it was developing rapidly elsewhere in the Mediterranean. It was not

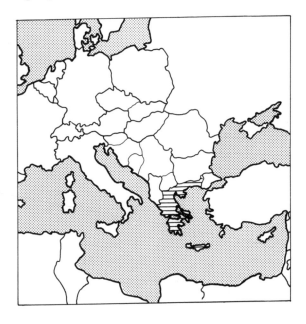

until 1974, when the country returned to democratic rule, that there was a sustained growth of tourist numbers. Since then sun-loving tourists have flooded into Greece, particularly to the islands: Greece was seen as an attractive, unspoilt and competitively priced alternative to the increasingly congested Spanish resorts.

The climate and island beaches are now the country's main tourist resource rather than the ruins of ancient cities and temples of classical Greece. Although Greece relies heavily on the British and German markets, the country does attract a wide range of different types of tourist from a large number of European countries. It is thus better placed than Yugoslavia was to benefit from the resumption in growth of European mass tourism that started in the 1980s. Moreover, the country was politically and economically more stable than Yugoslavia in the 1980s. The Greek tourist industry is as yet still relatively small (9.7 million visitors in 1992) but is still growing and is capable of adapting to new demands and changing tourist tastes.

Fig. 22.2 Tourist resouces of Greece and Albania

Greece's physical resources for tourism

Eighty per cent of Greek territory is mountainous. The limestone mountains that run NW–SE parallel to the coastline through Yugoslavia and Albania continue into peninsular Greece, and form its backbone. They gradually become lower from the north of Greece towards the south, and the islands are the submerged peaks of the mountain chain as it subsides into the Aegean sea. The coastline is broken by gulfs and inlets. The surface area of the country is only 131 994 square km but it has an exceptionally long coastline of 15 320 km. The island and coastal territories of Greece enjoy a typical Mediterranean climate with a long summer drought and average July temperatures everywhere over 27° C. All parts have at least 2300 hours of sunshine a year, and some islands receive over 3000 hours annually. The mountainous west is much wetter and the north of Greece has a more continental climate.

Greece can be divided into four mainland regions and five groups of islands (*see* Fig 22.3):

1 Mainland Greece
 (*a*) Northern Greece (Macedonia, Thessalonica, Khalkidiki, Kavalla and Thrace);
 (*b*) Central Greece (Epiros, Thessaly and Central Greece);

 (*c*) Athens region (Attica and Euboea); and
 (*d*) The Peloponnese.
2 The Islands
 (*a*) Ionian islands (including Corfu);
 (*b*) Cyclades;
 (*c*) Sporades;
 (*d*) Dodecanese (including Rhodes);
 (*e*) Crete.

Mainland Greece

Northern Greece

This strip of land consists of the southernmost extension of the Carpathian mountains, and the lowlands of the Vardar and Nestos rivers which flow southwards into Greece from across the Yugoslav and Bulgarian borders. The coast possesses many good sandy beaches, and the Khalkidiki region was being developed for mass tourism for the nearby Yugoslavian market, and for package tourists coming in via Thessalonica airport. However, the Yugoslavian market declined in the late 1980s due to that country's severe economic and its subsequent political problems, and northern Greece is being marketed more actively in other countries. The countryside is green and well wooded, and the mountains of Macedonia are particularly beautiful. It is rich in archaeological sites, but is still quiet and unspoilt, and the region accounted for 11 per cent of foreign overnight stays in 1986. Nearly half the accommodation is in the form of campsites and rented rooms.

Central Greece

The Pindos mountain range forms the central backbone of Greece and divides Epiros (in the west) from the lowlands of Thessaly to the east (*see* Fig 22.2). The limestone mountains themselves are stony and sparsely vegetated in spite of the higher rainfall on their west-facing slopes. Much of Epiros is, however, thickly wooded, and the land drops away to the Ionian coast where there is a mixture of good sandy beaches, estuaries and lagoons. Thessaly is also a fertile agricultural region, overlooked in the north by Mount Olympus (the home of the immortal gods of classical Greece). One of the most dramatic historical sites of the region, however, dates from Byzantine times. A series of sheer-sided rock columns rise

Fig. 22.3 Regions of Greece

from the plain to the northwest of Larissa. Monasteries have been built on top of each of 24 pinnacles. They date from the 4th to the 15th centuries, and the monastic community is known as Meteora. Central Greece is as yet relatively little used by tourists, and in 1989, central Greece and Thessaly received 4.5 per cent of the country's total foreign overnight stays, and Epiros only 0.5 per cent. These areas are more popular with domestic tourists than with foreign visitors, with about 20 per cent of domestic hotel nights in 1989.

Athens and the surrounding region

The capital, Athens, is a major tourist destination, taking 14 per cent of the country's overnight stays by foreigners, and has 17 per cent of the stock of hotel beds. It is easily accessible via the international airport, and its port (Piraeus) links it by ferry to most of the islands. It is a modern, industrial and increasingly polluted city but is dominated by the Acropolis perched on its rocky promontory overlooking the city. There are remains from every period of Greek history here, and the old town (the Plaka) spreads around the foot of the Acropolis. The modern city provides modern, luxury shopping, restaurants and nightlife. The whole of the coastline of the peninsula running southeast of Athens is well developed for tourism. The 70 km stretch of coast that extends from Piraeus to Cape Sounion is called the Apollo Beach. A series of resorts along the coastline provide beach tourism and for water sports, and a variety of accommodation (from rented rooms to modern luxury hotels) is available. The east coast of Attica (Cape Sounion north to Oropou) is similarly fairly intensively developed (*see* Fig 22.2). Athens and its region has declined in popularity as other parts of Greece have been opened up. The island of Euboea (Evia) lies to the north of Athens. It is linked to the mainland by road and ferry and provides a greater variety of busy resorts and unspoilt villages with quiet beaches. The landscape is also attractive, with wooded mountains and varied lowlands, but this region too suffered a decline in tourist nights in the 1980s. The region abounds in archaeological sites. Delphi is one of the most beautiful of the ancient Greek sites, and is located inland, 176 km northwest of Athens. It was built

on the southern slopes of Mount Parnassus, overlooking the coast. During the day it is busy with coach trips from Athens.

The Peloponnese

This is a large peninsula linked to mainland Greece by a narrow neck of land (six km wide) at Corinth. The core of the peninsula is a barren limestone plateau with mountains up to 2400 m high. It is scattered with archaeological sites such as Mycenae and Tiryns (dating from the 14th century BC), Epidavros (site of the well preserved Greek theatre), Olympia (the site of the original Olympic Games) and the ruined Byzantine city of Mistras. The west coast has some big sandy beaches but is relatively undeveloped for tourism. The east coast (linked to Athens by both road and ferry) is a series of bays, beaches and rocky promontories. The region receives about eight per cent of the country's tourism and is increasing in popularity. However, the adjacent islands of Aegina, Hydra and Spetse were promoted for tourism early and are visited by day-trippers from Athens. They contain 5.5 per cent of Greek holiday accommodation stock, but like the other old established tourist regions of mainland Greece, are losing tourists (with a drop of over half a million visitors between 1981 and 1986).

The Greek islands

About 60 per cent of Greek tourist nights occur on the islands. Island tourism appears to be of two contrasting types: certain islands are extensively developed for package tours, for example Corfu, Crete and Rhodes, and others cater for independent visitors travelling from island to island. There also appears to be some regional specialisation in that certain nationalities favour particular islands, e.g. the British concentrate on Corfu, the Germans in northern Crete and the Scandinavians in Rhodes. The islands can be divided into five groups.

1 The Ionian islands. This group includes Corfu, Levkas, Cephallonia, Ithaca and Zante (Zakinthos), and is located off the wetter west coast of mainland Greece. Corfu is green and well vegetated and has many beautiful beaches. The town of Corfu has retained its medieval character; the Venetians occupied the island in the 16th and 17th centuries and fortified the town between 1553 and 1558.

The island has 6.5 per cent of the total stock of Greek hotel beds and received nearly 9.8 per cent of all tourist bednights to Greece in 1989. It meets the needs of the package tour market.

Corfu caters primarily for the UK market: 27 per cent of all UK visitors to Greece stay in Corfu while no more than eight per cent of any other country's visitors stay there. The international airport at Corfu receives visitors from Northern Europe. The other islands of the group are less intensively developed but share Corfu's wooded green character and its abundance of medieval (rather than classical Greek) buildings. Zante also has an airport and the other islands are linked to the mainland by ferry. Accommodation is biased towards camping and rented rooms (60 per cent of the stock of rooms on these islands).

2 The Cyclades. This group of islands spreads over the Aegean Sea to the southeast of Athens. The islands are wild, rocky and barren, some of which show the remnants of decaying volcanic activity, for example Santorini is the eroded crater of an extinct volcano, and hot springs are found on Kythnos and Kimolos. The landscapes of the islands are characterised by barren hillsides, olive groves and vineyards, unspoilt sandy beaches, churches and chapels, square whitewashed cottages and windmills. Historic remains are abundant. Delos was a sacred island (supposedly the birthplace of the God Apollo) in ancient Greek times and is covered in ruins of temples and monuments. One of the most splendid Byzantine churches dating from the fifth century AD is found in Paros, and Byzantine paintings exist in many of the smaller churches in Naxos. In the medieval period Venetian castles were built on islands such as Paros and Andros. Most of the islands are accessible by boat from Athens. Tourism is generally small-scale and many of the islands and their beaches are quiet and unspoilt. The Cyclades as a whole received two per cent of all Greek tourist overnight stays in 1990 but have six per cent of the total stock of Greek holiday accommodation, 56 per cent of which is in the form of campsites and rented rooms: only four per cent of the bedspaces are in hotels. However, Milos, Poros, Santorini and Mykonos are accessible by air. Mykonos is the

biggest tourist centre and has a more cosmopolitan atmosphere, particularly popular with the gay community. It has 75 per cent of the total tourist nights spent in the Cyclades.

3 The Sporades and the Aegean islands. The Sporades (Magnesia) lie off the east coast of Thessally and the Aegean islands (Lemnos, Lesbos, Chios and Samos) are larger islands in the eastern Aegean close to the Turkish coast.

The Sporades are more fertile and green than the Cyclades. Their coasts are a mixture of rocky promontories, coves and sandy beaches, many of which are most easily accessible by boat. The islands are increasing in popularity and there is active nightlife with clubs, discos and tavernas. There are few big hotels, and the accommodation again is mainly small guest houses, rented rooms and campsites. The bigger Aegean islands are connected to Athens by air as well as by boat. They have abundant pine woods and olive groves, and also many good sandy beaches, though some are pebbly. Lesbos and Chios have many medieval castles dating from the 9th to the 15th centuries. Like the Cyclades, these islands have around six per cent of Greek tourist accommodation but receive only three per cent of total overnight tourist stays.

4 The Dodecanese. This group of 12 islands is to the southeast of Athens, and is close to the Turkish coast. The islands provide contrasting tourist attractions from the big hotels and sophistication of the busy islands of Rhodes and Kos to the smaller, quiet and less developed islands of Tilos, Halki, Astipalea and Kassos.

Rhodes is the biggest tourist centre of Greece. It took 22 per cent of foreign overnight tourist stays in 1990, and has ten per cent of the country's tourist accommodation much of which is in the form of hotel bed spaces. It is increasingly popular and, even through the recession of the 1980s, tourist nights increased by nearly three million. The island has an international airport and is well suited for the package tour market. It is one of the best developed islands in the Mediterranean and provides nightlife, casinos, watersports and sightseeing trips. The island is scenically not particularly outstanding but its beaches and climate (suitable for winter and summer tourism) are its main resources. The average temperature in January is 16° C and rises to 29° C in July. Rhodes is particularly favoured by Germans and 21 per cent of all German visitors to Greece stay there. A similar proportion of Austrian and Swiss tourists go there. The Scandinavians also favour this part of Greece (46 per cent of Swedish visitors to Greece, 56 per cent of the Norwegians and 31 per cent of Danes prefer Rhodes). This island is not so popular with the UK market: only 16 per cent of the UK visitors to Greece stay in Rhodes.

5 Crete. Crete is the third major tourist centre in Greece (of similar scale to Athens and Rhodes). It is the most southerly of the Greek islands, and among the hottest, both in summer and winter. The island has varied and attractive scenery (the mountains, with deep valleys and dramatic gorges, rise to over 2400 m) and a coastline of cliffs and rocky promontories interspersed with good sandy beaches. Although the climate, coast and scenery are its main attractions, Crete has a wealth of archaeological remains. It was the centre of Minoan culture from 2600–1100 BC and there are many remains of their palaces and tombs. The Romans and Byzantines (AD 395-823) also left many buildings and the castles of the medieval Venetian occupation are superimposed on more ancient settlements. The greatest concentration of tourist development (with hotels and modern facilities) is on the northern coast of the island: Hiraklion is the biggest centre with plenty of nightlife and the nearby international airport to attract package tourists. Crete as a whole has nearly 11 per cent of Greek tourist accommodation with an emphasis on hotel accommodation rather than rented rooms or campsites. In 1990 a quarter of all Greece's foreign overnight tourist stays were spent in Crete. The island is also particularly popular in the German and Dutch markets.

Conclusion: Greece

Greece offers a very varied tourist product, and attracts visitors from many different countries. It is a country for the young and active tourist (70 per cent are between 16 and 40 years old). The British market is of increasing importance to the Greek tourist industry, increasing from 14 per cent of arrivals in 1971 to 22 per cent in 1992, and it is now the country's main market (*see* Fig 22.4). Although the numbers of Americans visiting Greece is slowly

increasing, its share of the market has dropped from a quarter in 1971 to around seven per cent in the late 1980s and dropped to less than 3 per cent in the 1990s.

	Number (thousands)	%	Growth 1991/92
UK	2154	22.1	+28.7%
Germany	1944	19.9	+24.6%
Italy	622	6.4	+20.7%
The Netherlands	546	5.6	+21.7%
France	542	5.6	
Austria	345	3.5	
Sweden	314	3.2	
Denmark	281	2.9	
USA	278	2.8	
Belgium/Luxembourg	225	2.3	
Scandinavia (Norway, Sweden, Finland)	581	6.0	
Cruise passengers	424	4.4	
Others	–	–	
Total	9756	100%	

Growth 1991–2 = 18%

Fig. 22.4 Tourist arrivals in Greece, 1992
(*Source*: Greece Tourism Organisation)

This was partly a response to terrorist activity (a TWA aeroplane was hijacked at Athens airport in 1985, and Athens has a continuing reputation for poor airport security), and to the Gulf War. The Americans are among the few nationalities that visit Greece mainly for its antiquities, although 35 per cent of the Japanese, 25 per cent of Italians and 41 per cent of Spanish mentioned the historic resources as reasons for visiting Greece. However, the majority are attracted by the climate, this being particularly true of the British market (62 per cent of the British visited for the climate and only three per cent for the historic resources of the country). It has been noted that different nationalities congregate in the particular regions and islands which appear to specialise in meeting their needs, with the Spanish and Americans concentrating on Athens and the British, Germans and Scandinavians on particular islands. On the other hand, younger backpackers of all nationalities participate in 'island hopping' holidays so as to travel through many different parts of Greece. The French, too, do not appear to frequent the popular centres: although 19 per cent of French tourist nights were spent in Athens, 49 per cent were spent outside the main popular centres. Italian visitors to Greece also showed the same pattern of tourism.

QUESTIONS AND DISCUSSION POINTS

1 In 1990, great political changes were underway in Yugoslavia and Albania. How have these changes affected international tourism to these countries?

2 Tourism is heavily concentrated in four regions of Greece (Corfu, Crete, Rhodes and the Athens area). Rank the other regions of Greece in order of their tourist potential.

3 Is the growth of tourism in Greece likely to be a greater threat to the tourist industry of Spain or to that of Italy?

ASSIGNMENT

You work in a travel agency and the following people have enquired about tours to Greece:

(a) A middle-aged, middle-class, childless couple of limited means, who are looking for a seven-day seaside holiday.

(b) A group of students who plan to go backpacking for at least four weeks in their summer vacation.

(c) A couple who are in their early thirties and they have two children aged four and seven. They usually go to Spain for two weeks but fancy something a bit different this year.

(d) A newly retired couple (one was a dentist, the other a school teacher). They have both been to Athens before and they want a stimulating but physically relaxing holiday to celebrate their retirement. They can be away from home for up to three weeks.

Select appropriate resorts/itineraries for each group and suggest the best time of year that each client might take their holiday.

CHAPTER 23

Turkey, Cyprus and Malta

LEARNING OBJECTIVES

After reading this chapter you should be able to
- assess the tourist potential of the climatic, landscape, historical and cultural resources of Turkey, Cyprus and Malta
- distinguish the regional distribution of these geographical resources and their development and use for tourism
- demonstrate a knowledge of the main tourist resorts and tourist centres
- understand the role of Turkey, Cyprus and Malta in the general pattern of European tourism
- be aware of the influence political and cultural factors have on the nature and location of tourism.

INTRODUCTION

Tourism in this part of the Mediterranean basin is still on a small scale compared to the tourist industries of Spain, France or Italy. Turkey, with 7.0 million visitors in 1992 is the leading destination of the eastern Mediterranean. The countries of the region have suitable coastal and climatic resources to meet the growing and changing demands of Western tourism but political and cultural factors have dictated the scale, location and development of Western-style tourism in each country.

Tourism to Cyprus began early (in the 1960s) but was totally disrupted by later political events. On the other hand, Turkey's tourism could not begin until its internal political environment became more favourable during the early 1980s but it is rapidly growing. Turkey's tourism has dramatically increased from 3.7 million in 1988 to 7.07 million in 1992. Tourism in Cyprus has also shown very strong growth over the same period (from 1.1 million to 1.9 million tourists) while Malta's development has been consistent but steadier.

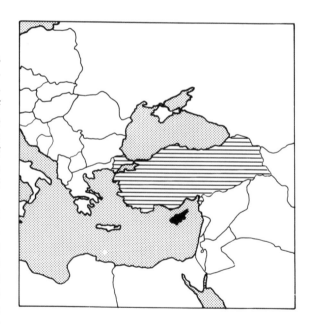

TURKEY

The development of international tourism in Turkey is a recent phenomenon, as the country was only opened to mass tourism from 1982. Turkey's tourism began to grow (from a base of 1.3 million in 1982) at 29 per cent per annum to an estimated 3.5 million foreign arrivals in 1988. This rapid expansion was triggered off by two factors:

1 the achievement of **internal political stability** and the installation of a government that welcomed the economic benefits of tourism.

2 a **receptive Western European market** that was ready to explore more exotic and unspoilt destinations further afield for sun, sea and sand holidays, combined with the overdevelopment of some of the traditional Mediterranean destinations (particularly in Spain and Italy).

The political and economic background

Ninety-seven per cent of Turkey's population are Muslims, although the social structures of the Islamic state were abolished in the 1920s and it is now a secular state. Islamic fundamentalism has not so far inhibited the country's move towards Westernisation, although the Government is beginning to put more emphasis on religion.

Turkey was disrupted by internal political instability and conflict through the 1970s and this culminated in a military coup in 1980/81. A period of Westernisation and democratisation of the Turkish Government and the economy followed, and civilian rule was established in the elections of 1983. The new government was committed to further political and economic reform; the country applied for EC membership and sought closer links with Europe, and although the 1990s began with both internal political problems and wars in Turkey's neighbouring countries, these processes still continue. Eastern Turkey has common borders with Georgia, Armenia, Azerbaijan and the Kurdish regions of Iraq, all territories that have experienced interethnic conflicts and political problems in the early 1990s. Turkey itself has had interethnic problems in its own Kurdish region in the southeast of the country. Turkey was of crucial strategic importance in the 1991 Gulf War although its troops were not directly involved in Iraq. Western tourists stayed away from Turkey in 1991 (tourism from West and Northern Europe dropped by one third that year) but the country benefited from an equally dramatic increase in visitors from Central

and Eastern Europe that year, so that in spite of the war, Turkey's tourism actually increased by 2.38 per cent in 1991. Turkey's main resort areas are concentrated on the west and southwest coasts (at the opposite end of the country from the political problem areas) so in spite of these other uncertainties, Western tourism has resumed its growth in the years since the Gulf War. The Turkish Government is committed to the promotion of tourism for its economic and employment benefits. In 1988 foreign tourism yielded over US $2 billion, representing about 20 per cent of total exports in 1986/7. The country is increasingly dependent on tourism: by 1990 receipts had grown to US $ 3.4 billion, making up 25 per cent of its exports. The Government has offered incentives to investors in the tourism sector, and has encouraged the construction of tourist installations, for example by providing loans and investment subsidies, certain customs and tax exemptions, reduced gas, water and electricity prices etc. In response to those measures, the accommodation capacity rose 86 per cent between 1983 and 1989; growth has continued at the same rate up to 1991 when accommodation capacity reached 196 900 bed spaces. Foreign investment in the Turkish tourist industry has also taken place. However, the speed of the new development has led to some of the problems experienced in Spain in the 1960s, i.e. uncontrolled, environmentally poor quality development, incomplete hotels and construction in progress at resorts and inadequate roads, power and water shortages. Marine pollution (from industry, agriculture and sewage) is an increasing problem (e.g. at Antalya and Izmir). Other undesirable environmental impacts due to tourism include threats to marine species (loggerhead turtles, monk seals), to natural features (e.g. at Pamukkale) and to historic resources (e.g. at Side). The government has responded by giving higher priority to conservation issues in its tourism policies and plans; mechanisms exist whereby the tourism incentives can be restricted to those developments that are in harmony with the environment. However, the OECD has urged Turkey to further integrate its environmental and economic policies to improve the implementation of existing environmental policy, and strengthen its enforcement of and investment in pollution control measures.

TURKEY'S PHYSICAL RESOURCES FOR TOURISM

Ninety-seven per cent of Turkey is physically part of Asia, and only three per cent (the lowlands of Thrace on the west side of the Dardanelles) is part of Europe.

The coast

Turkey has a coastline of about 8000 km, with plenty of beaches, though there are few really long stretches of sand. Almost everywhere the coast is backed by spectacular mountain scenery. The coast is divided into four main areas (*see* Fig 23.1):

1 The Black Sea coast
2 The coast of Thrace and the Sea of Marmara
3 The Aegean coast
4 The Mediterranean coast.

Most of the modern resorts that cater for the package tourist are located on the southern half of the Aegean coast (between Izmir and Marmaris) and the western section of Turkey's Mediterranean coast (from Marmaris to Alanya). These resorts are served by the three airports at Izmir (Adnan Mendres), Dalaman and Antalya.

The holiday resorts evolved in the 1960s and 1970s for the Turkish domestic market (as Turks were not then allowed to travel abroad because of tight exchange controls). Hence, they have a good supply of apartments, pensions and small hotels. Larger hotels catering for the new Western package-tour market were grafted on to these existing resorts.

The Aegean coast

The main attractions on the northern half of this coast are the historic sites of Troy and Pergamon. Along the 'Olive coast' (as the stretch from Lesbos to Izmir is known) there are some small resorts with villas and apartments such as Foca, set along a coast of coves and bays. Some beaches are only accessible by boat. Izmir is a modern city, and an important port, but has many hotels. Between Izmir and Kusadasi many of the bays are filled with high density, low-grade holiday townships and holiday homes with beach access. Many of these homes lack basic services (water, power, sanitation) and were built by local speculators for the domestic market.

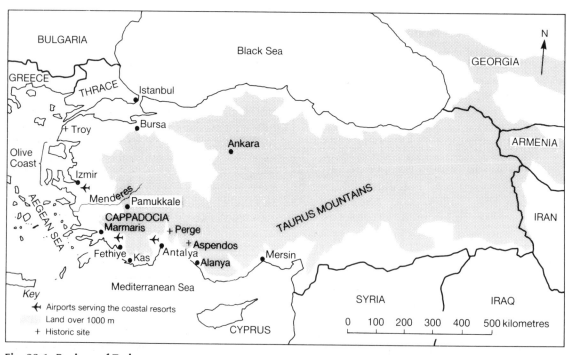

Fig. 23.1 Regions of Turkey

Better quality development designed for the international tourist has been grafted on to towns such as Kusadasi and Bodrum. Kusadasi is another port town, a lively resort that functions as a centre for trips to the ancient Greek and Roman city of Ephesus, founded in the 13th century BC. Ephesus has very well preserved ruins and is perhaps the most outstanding of the ancient Greek sites along this part of the Aegean coast. It attracts over one million visitors a year. Prienne, Miletus and Didyma are also important ancient Greek coastal sites which also receive substantial numbers of visitors (100–200 000 per annum) (*see* Fig 22.2).

Bodrum is a second major tourist centre, and the harbour is dominated by the 15th century Crusader Castle. Accommodation is primarily apartments, pensions, and small hotels, and some of the new building has suffered from the speed of development. Marmaris has a longer sand and shingle beach, set in a deep fjord-like inlet, and has some larger hotels.

In 1987, the Aegean coast ranked second in Turkey in its accommodation capacity with 26 000 beds but this stock will rise to over 77 000 beds when all those planned and under construction are complete.

The Mediterranean coast

This is sometimes known as the 'Turquoise coast'. The major resorts along this stretch of coast include Fethiye, Kas, Antalya, Side and Alanya (*see* Fig 23.1). The bigger hotels are concentrated in Alanya and Antalya, and this region will become the leading concentration of accommodation when all proposed developments are complete to provide 82 000 beds.

There are many historical sites in the region, for example, one of the best Roman stadiums is at Perge, and there is an outstandingly well preserved Greek theatre (dating from the second century AD) at Aspendos, which receives 250 000 visitors a year. The coast from Alanya to the Syrian border is less accessible and hardly developed for Western tourism: between Alanya and Mersin the mountainous coast provides spectacular scenery and has great tourist potential. There are historic sites of all dates (Paleolithic, Hittite, Roman, Byzantine and Crusader) reflecting the region's location in the centre of the ancient world and its successive colonisation by most of the ancient civilisations (*see* Chapter 6).

The coasts of Thrace and Marmara

In the late 1980s, the region had the greatest accommodation capacity of all Turkey's regions, (with 36 500 bed spaces) but will soon be overtaken by developments along the Aegean and Mediterranean coasts. The Thracian side of the sea of Marmara is rolling countryside, and the south coast is more mountainous and forested with some good sandy beaches. The resorts cater mainly for the domestic market, for example Erdeck and a new luxury resort being developed at the readily accessible site of Klassis.

However, Istanbul is the major centre of the region, and was Turkey's capital in Roman and Byzantine times and during the Ottoman Empire which was at its peak in the mid-16th century. The city has many splendid historical buildings such as the Topkapi Museum (once the residential palace of the Ottoman emperors), mosques, and the Byzantine church of St Sophia. The major attractions receive 1.5 to 2 million visitors a year. Istanbul is thus a centre of cultural tourism but also has a significant level of business tourism, although Ankara has now superseded Istanbul as the country's capital. Istanbul airport is one of the main gateways into the country – one of three Turkish airports with scheduled international services.

The Black Sea coast

This region has good weather, but is much more variable than the Aegean and Mediterranean climates, and is thus relatively less attractive as a location for beach tourism. The coast is mountainous and dramatic and there are some good sandy beaches, but the resorts are small and the accommodation rather basic – mainly country inns developed for the domestic Turkish market in the 1950s, 1960s and mid-1970s. The scale of tourism and speed of development are very much lower here than on Turkey's southern and eastern coasts. (Only 3500 bed spaces existed in 1987.)

The interior

Central Anatolia

The Anatolia peninsula is a vast high plateau (mostly 1–2000 m high) with a mixture of agricultural and forest landscapes. Two of the country's national parks are visited by overland coach trips. These are Pamukkale and Goreme (in Cappadocia).

Pamukkale, inland due east of Kusadasi, covers the scarp on the side of the Menderes valley. Warm springs saturated in calcium compounds issue from the rock and deposit pure white calcite as the spring water flows over terraces from pool to pool. Tourists bathe in the warm pools, but there is a danger that they will cause erosion damage to the terraces. The landscape of the Goreme valley is very different. The rock here is soft, volcanic material which has been eroded into fretted ravines, cones, chimneys and pinnacles (many surmounted by caps of slightly harder rock). The strangeness of the environment is emphasised by the fact that cave dwellings, churches and rock cities have been carved into the rock. These dwellings date from 400 BC including early Christian monastic settlements. Some of the rock carved dwellings are still inhabited, as at Soganli, but most have been evacuated due to the danger of rockfalls as the natural process of erosion continues. The Cappadocian region is relatively inaccessible but still attracts 500 000 visitors a year. The Anatolian mountains are high enough for good winter snow cover and several of the more accessible locations have been developed for skiing, for example, Bursa which serves the Istanbul region in the north, and Saklikent (48 km north of Antalya) in the south. There is enough snow here in spring (March and April) to combine skiing with beach holidays at Antalya (where the Mediterranean Sea is warm enough for bathing at this time of year). Most of the ski resorts cater for domestic tourists but there is significant potential for international tourism too.

Eastern Anatolia

The interior has a continental climate with great extremes of temperature (25° C in July down to minus 6° C and minus 18° C in January at Kars) and a summer rainfall maximum. The region is inaccessible and very rarely visited by foreign tourists, but it has desolately beautiful landscapes and scattered historic towns. There has been some political and ethnic unrest in the region between Turks and Kurds. Turkey has some common borders with Iraq and Iran, and the region suffered some disruption in the aftermath of the Gulf War.

Communications

An inadequate transport system is one of the factors limiting the spread of tourism through the country: the motorway system is improving, though there are many narrow, unsealed roads; there are good bus services between the main cities. Due to the distance factor and the lack of good road access from Europe, most foreign tourists arrive by air, so the coastal tourist developments are mainly serviced accommodation and are limited to sites easily accessible from the existing airports. There are very few campsites, as so few tourists come by car. The only major land border crossings occur in the east, with visitors from Syria, Iran and other Middle Eastern countries. There is very little ferry traffic from Greece into Turkey, the poor communications perhaps reflecting the long-standing poor political relations between the two countries. Some opinion in Turkey would favour the development of new airports at Bodrum to serve the Aegean coast better, and another charter airport on the east Mediterranean (between Antalya and Mersin) to encourage the opening up of this stretch of coast.

INBOUND TOURISM

Statistics on tourism in Turkey are patchy. It is estimated that about 2.9 million foreigners visited Turkey in 1987, plus 1.25 to 1.5 million expatriate Turks returning for holidays.

	Nights spent in all registered accommodation (%)
Germany	40.9
France	11.9
Austria	7.5
Scandinavia	6.0
Benelux	5.5
UK	4.9
Italy	4.0
Switzerland	2.9
USA	2.6
Total	13.2 million

Fig. 23.2 Foreign visitors to Turkey, 1990

The resident population of Turkey is around 50 million and it was estimated that the domestic market was between 2.6 million and six million in 1987. The domestic market generated eight million bed-nights in 1991, while 2.9 million Turkish citizens travelled abroad in 1992.

CYPRUS

Cyprus is the third largest island in the Mediterranean, after Sicily and Sardinia, with an area of 9216 km^2 (*see* Fig 23.3). It has a typical Mediterranean climate, but its easterly location gives it a prolonged hot dry season, and temperatures rise to 30° C between mid-May and mid-September. The winter, however, is more changeable, with periods of disturbed weather lasting several days as depressions pass over the island from west to east, but the weather stays mild (around 16° C on average) so the island is promoted as both a winter and summer destination. The island's north coast is rocky and is backed by the limestone Pentadactylos mountains which rise to 1000 m. The south coast has more sandy beaches interspersed with small coves. Coral Bay (west of Paphos) and Ayia Napa (on the southeast coast) are the largest and most popular beaches. Ayia Napa was a small fishing village and its development began with a scattering of large hotels along its coast, but within ten years it has grown into a mature urban resort, complete with a recreation business district. The main settlements (Paphos, Limassol and Larnaca) also cater for beach tourism but have additional cultural attractions, e.g. Roman remains (at Paphos and Limassol), Crusader Castles (e.g. Kolossi Castle also in the Limassol area), and abundant old churches and monasteries in the rural villages. The Akamas peninsula is an unspoilt nature reserve, and the Troodos mountains (rising to 1900 m) provide opportunities for walking and horse-riding activity holidays. Platres is the main mountain resort. Cyprus thus has all the resources of climate, coast and landscape to make it an ideal all year

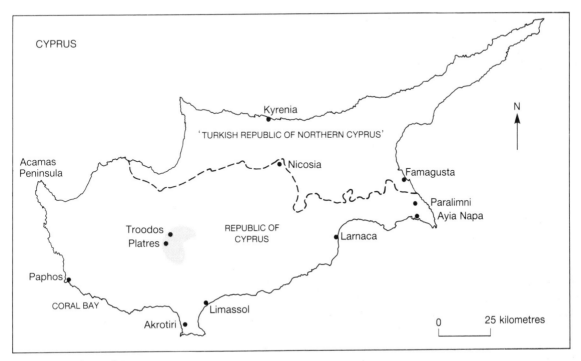

Fig. 23.3 Regions of Cyprus

round tourist location: tourist arrivals to the whole island reached nearly two million in 1992, but the development of tourism in Cyprus has been strongly influenced by political events.

The island's population is made up of Cypriots of both Greek and Turkish origin. It was a British colony up to its independence in 1960, and Britain still retains a military base at Akrotiri. Violence associated with the independence campaign and the ensuing political problems slowed down the early development of tourism in the 1960s when some other Mediterranean destinations were beginning to expand. Tourism grew more rapidly in the next decade, increasing from 25 700 in 1960 to a thriving 274 100 in 1973. Much of this expansion took place in the north of the island, with 65 per cent of the bed spaces concentrated in the two north coast resorts of Famagusta and Kyrenia.

In 1974 the tourist industry in Cyprus was disrupted by political events: a coup d'état occurred, and the Turkish army invaded the island. After a brief period of warfare a *de facto* partition of the island took place: the northern part of the island (37 per cent of the territory) was taken over by Turkish forces, and the south remained a contracted Republic of Cyprus (*see* Fig 23.3). Major population movements followed, with Greek Cypriots living in the north moving south. Many were hotel owners who abandoned their properties and businesses in the north coast resorts. In parallel, Turkish Cypriots living in the south moved into the northern Turkish-controlled part of the island. While this readjustment was taking place, tourism to the island slumped in 1975 to only 47 000 visitors. The political situation has since stabilised and in 1983 the northern territory was unilaterally declared the Turkish Republic of North Cyprus, but it is not recognised by the international community and no other governments have consulates there. In 1990 there were still tight border controls: visitors to north Cyprus are not allowed south, and tourists in the south are only allowed north for day-trips (in daylight hours). The International Hotel Association advised professional bodies in tourism not to cooperate with North Cyprus and the north is only accessible by air via Turkey (Istanbul or Izmir).

These political events have led to a complete change in the nature and location of the tourist industry in Cyprus: in 1990 the south has replaced the north as the major centre of the tourist industry with just over one million arrivals in 1988, while the scale of tourism in the north (230 000 visitors 1988) has not yet reached the volume of 1973.

TOURISM IN THE REPUBLIC OF CYPRUS (SOUTHERN CYPRUS)

After partition in 1974, the south was left with virtually no facilities but a trained, experienced personnel and a potentially loyal clientele. The accommodation stock in the south was located in Nicosia and the hill resorts in the Troodos mountains: very little was on the coast. Nicosia airport, which had served the whole island, was in Turkish-occupied Cyprus, and Cyprus Airways was left with no aircraft or airport. Air access was limited to the military bases until a replacement airport was swiftly constructed at Larnaca. Because of the importance of tourism to the economy, the Government strongly supported the rebuilding of the tourist industry with state loans for new hotel building, support for Cyprus Airways, and provision of further training and tourism infrastructure. Almost all the new development in the south has been at coastal sites. Limassol and Larnaca were the first towns to be developed for tourism in the 1970s whereas the expansion of Paphos did not begin until the mid-1980s (after the opening of the new airport in 1984). The most recent development has been concentrated in two coastal zones: south of Paphos (along the coast to Coral Bay) and in the Ayia Napa-Paralimni region. Forty-six per cent of hotel bed spaces and 42 per cent of apartment bed spaces that were under construction at the beginning of 1992 were located at Paphos (and similarly 20 per cent of hotel bed spaces and 35 per cent of apartment capacity were being built at Paralimni).

Limassol has been the largest resort in Cyprus for a long time and has steadily grown to a bed capacity of 15 172 in 1992, but the growth of Ayia Napa has been even faster so that in 1992 it replaced Limassol as the island's leading tourist centre (with a capacity of 15 487 beds) (*see* Fig 23.4).

Region	% bed spaces (hotels and apartments)	% tourist nights
Nicosia	0.32	3.00
Limassol	22.63	25.92
Larnaca	14.05	14.19
Ayia Napa	22.60 ⎫ Famagusta	38.39
Paralimni	15.34 ⎭	
Paphos	19.29	18.03
Hill stations	0.27	0.44

(Total beds: 62 910)   **(Total nights:** 7.966 million)

Fig. 23.4 Cyprus: regional distribution of foreign tourism, 1991
(*Source*: Cyprus Tourist Organisation)

The speed and urgency of this reconstruction have led to some poor quality development, for example ribbon development, incomplete building, poor infrastructure such as unfinished roads and lack of sewage, and this has spoilt some locations, as witnessed by the unsightly seafront at Limassol. But tighter controls on development were introduced in 1983 to improve the quality of provision and to encourage investment in entertainments, attractions and basic infrastructure to complement the expansion of tourist accommodation.

The Cyprus Government has tried to promote the island as an upmarket prestige destination in order to attract the higher spending visitor and until recently has restricted charters to the island. By 1985, 27 per cent of the new accommodation completed (and 41 per cent of hotel construction in progress) was in the four- and five-star category: of the rest, the balance has been in favour of apartments rather than one- to three-star hotels. This pattern has been maintained into the 1990s, so that by 1990, 46 per cent of all the hotel bed spaces were four- or five-star quality. Efforts are being made to diversify the island's tourist product by promoting conference, cultural tourism and the hill resorts in addition to beach tourism. However, these still remain very small elements of its total tourism, with 40 500 conference delegates in 1989, and only 3 per cent of foreign arrivals (generating 34 000 foreign overnight stays) in the hill resorts in 1991. In the 1980s the prices were higher in Cyprus relative to some other mass-market Mediterranean destina-

tions, and Cyprus has not wanted to enter into the mass market. Nevertheless in 1986, restrictions on charter regulations were eased, allowing some UK operators to introduce charter flights from the UK regional airports. By 1990 charter flights brought 51 per cent of the island's tourists and made up 45 per cent of the airline traffic. In the same year 82 per cent of UK visitors were on inclusive tours.

Inbound tourism

The rapid growth of tourism to Cyprus has been a significant feature of Mediterranean tourism in the late 1980s and early 1990s. It is the only European country to have sustained tourist growth at over 10 per cent per annum during this period (excluding the Gulf War year of 1991). Total tourist numbers have grown from 949 000 in 1987 to nearly two million in 1992 (showing a 27 per cent increase in arrivals over the pre Gulf War year of 1990).

Cyprus relies heavily on the UK market – about one third of all visitors came from UK in 1987. In spite of the Gulf War, the number of UK visitors doubled (from 0.5 million to 1.08 million) between 1989 and 1992, and UK visitors now account for 54 per cent of arrivals. Scandinavian tourism to Cyprus grew steadily in the early 1980s to total around 20 000 per annum (accounting for 21 per cent of arrivals in 1987) but by 1992 their market share had dropped to ten per cent. Other Northern Europeans, e.g. Germans, Irish, Austrians and Swiss (i.e. from areas of poorer climate) form the balance. However, 87 000 Lebanese visited Cyprus in 1989, Cyprus being a geographically close refuge from their own political problems, and a substantial number of Greeks also came, reflecting the political and cultural links between Greece and the Greek Cypriot parts of the island.

TOURISM IN NORTHERN CYPRUS

In 1975, the north of Cyprus was faced with the reverse of the situation in the south: the north had a plentiful stock of coastal accommodation, but with few experienced staff to run the hotels and no established market. The revival of the tourist industry has been slow. Tourist arrivals crept to 113 000 by 1978 but the world recession hit tourism in the north of the island badly, due mainly to the fact that north Cyprus relies very heavily on the Turkish market, and the lean years of 1978–84 correlated with a slump in Turkish arrivals. By 1988, 80 per cent of arrivals still came from Turkey. The accommodation stock (dating from the 1960s) met neither the needs of the Turkish market (who stay mainly with friends or in the cheaper accommodation) nor that of the potential West European market. The non-Turkish market is gradually recovering, with the UK and German market (10.6 per cent and 13.3 per cent of arrivals in hotels respectively) slowly increasing in importance.

In 1987, a more co-ordinated plan for the development and promotion of tourism was set up with incentives for both local and foreign investors, for example, low rents of state land, tax concessions for the first ten years of operation, repatriation of profits for foreign investors). This has encouraged new hotel development, with an increase of about 2500 beds within a year. Most of the new development was in the four- and five-star category, and located in the old established coastal tourist areas (the Kyrenia coast and the north of Famagusta). The standstill in tourist development between 1975 and 1987 has meant that North Cyprus has not suffered from the sort of over-development and poor quality environment that has been typical of some of the other Mediterranean mass destinations. Given better communications, it still has great potential to meet modern tourist needs, though it has to prove its ability to attract the West European market.

MALTA

The islands of Malta and Gozo are tiny (316 km^2) and together they are smaller even than the Balearic island of Ibiza. Malta's location (93 km south of Sicily and 290 km north of the North African coast) gives it a latitude as southerly as Crete or Cyprus, and it is therefore among the most southerly tourist destinations in the Mediterranean. The summer temperatures are high in spite of the moderating effect of the surrounding sea, but the heat is tempered by cooling sea breezes. Between June and September temperatures range from minima of 18–29° C to maxima of 33–36° C. Annual rainfall is only 670 mm, and the summer season (April–September) is dry. Winter temperatures do not drop below 10° C and daily sunshine totals average five or six hours from

November to February. The islands attracted one million tourists in 1992. Like the Balearics, they rely very heavily on the UK market which provides nearly two thirds of their visitors. The links with the UK date from 1800 when British occupation began but tourist links continued after the islands became an independent republic in 1964. The number of Germans visiting the islands has more than doubled between 1987 and 1992 and they now make up 15 per cent of Malta's tourists. The climate, coast and landscape are the main tourist resources. The islands are low, gently undulating limestone plateaux, with the terraced hillsides giving the landscape a distinctive character. The south and east coasts are good for watersports in the sheltered inlets that are drowned valleys. The west coast is more cliffed and craggy and has a few sandy beaches. Tourism in the islands grew rapidly in the 1970s (20–30 per cent growth per annum) and led to some problems of poor quality development and water shortages. Malta had the image of a low cost volume charter destination. Its overreliance on the UK market led to problems in the recession of the 1980s. Non-UK European visitors declined in the early years of the recession (the late 1970s) but this did not hit the UK market until 1981–84 when the numbers of British visitors fell by half. At the same time the Maltese economy became stronger, making the island less competitive for the British market. The island has also targeted other markets (e.g. Germany and East Europe) with some success, and has attempted to diversify into sport and special interest holidays. At the same time the Maltese Government has invested in environmental and infrastructure improvements (e.g. beach cleaning and new airport terminal facilities). Malta has been promoting its winter and off season tourism. Winter trade has steadily increased from 16 per cent to 19 per cent of arrivals between 1987 and 1992 while the shoulder months (of March to June, and October) attracted 44.6 per cent of arrivals by 1992. Accommodation has been improved to meet modern needs; self-catering bed spaces have increased fivefold between 1979 and 1989. Apartments and holiday complexes have also grown significantly, but more recently new development has been limited to four- and five-star grade accommodation in order to attract more high yield tourism.

FURTHER READING

Cooper, C and Ozdil, I (1992), 'From mass to "responsible" tourism: the Turkish experience', *Tourism Management*, Vol. 13, December, pp. 377–86.

EIU (1992), 'Cyprus', *EIU International Tourism Reports*, No. 2, pp. 43–64.

Ioannides, D (1992), 'Tourism development agents: the Cypriot resort cycle', *Annals of Tourism Research*, Vol. 19, pp. 711–31.

O'Reilly, N (1993) 'Turkey', *International Tourism Reports*, No. 3, pp. 77–97.

QUESTIONS AND DISCUSSION POINTS

1 With reference to the development of tourism in Turkey, Cyprus and Malta, discuss the influence of history, religion and political affiliations on the location, nature and development of modern tourism.

2 What competitive advantages and disadvantages does the tourist industry in Cyprus (or Malta) experience in comparison with other Mediterranean island destinations?

3 To what extent does the development of tourism in Turkey in the late 1980s parallel that in Spain in the early 1960s?

ASSIGNMENTS

1 You are the tourism specialist in a planning consultancy. The Turkish Government has commissioned your firm to prepare a report advising them of the dangers of rapid and unplanned coastal tourist developments and the alternative approaches to tourist development that the Government might adopt. Your brief is to write a report:

(*a*) outlining the current level and distribution of tourism in Turkey;

(*b*) assessing the environmental problems that tourist development has caused to date;

(*c*) with reference to the experience of other European countries (e.g. Spain), predicting the possible long-term effects (on the environment, on tourists themselves and on tourist businesses) of uncontrolled expansion and growth of tourist developments; and

(*d*) indicating the choices open to the Turkish Government concerning the type of tourism it wished to encourage and ways of avoiding the problems associated with the rapid expansion of tourism.

THE MEDITERRANEAN AS A WHOLE (CHAPTERS 19–23)

2 You work for a company called 'Two by Two' that specialises in two centre holidays in the Mediterranean for the UK market. These holidays consist of one week in an attractive inland landscape setting and one week on the coast. Your current range of holidays does not seem to be holding its popularity and the company is concerned that the centres chosen are not ideal. Therefore, the directors of the company have asked you to prepare a report outlining the features that the UK visitor finds most attractive in inland landscapes and in coastal locations. The report should also identify at least one pair of locations (towns or small regions of countries) in the Mediterranean that exhibit these ideal characteristics as closely as possible. The two locations must, of course, also display climates suitable for sun, sea and sand and activity holidays respectively. The centres must be easily accessible from Britain and close to each other.

Your report should present evidence for your conclusions and a full justification of your choice of centres.

3 Your company designs special interest cruises in the Mediterranean. The chief executive has been approached by two groups requesting quotes for special cruises.

(*a*) The head of history at a sixth form college has asked the company to suggest an itinerary for a fly-cruise illustrating the pre-Christian history of the Mediterranean, but in order to explain the history clearly to the children he has asked if the cruise could visit sites of historical interest in their correct historical sequence (i.e. the oldest first and the more recent last). Is it possible to construct an itinerary that meets this criterion? School finances dictate that the cruise cannot be more than ten days.

(*b*) A group of wine and cookery clubs have asked for a Mediterranean fly-cruise illustrating the best of the regional variations in wine and cuisine for the connoisseur. The itinerary must also include plenty of time to relax or to participate in active pursuits. Draw up a draft itinerary for discussion with the club representatives.

CHAPTER 24

The Alps: Austria and Switzerland

LEARNING OBJECTIVES

After reading this chapter you should be able to
- assess the tourist potential of the climatic, landscape, historical and cultural resources of Austria and Switzerland
- distinguish between the regional distribution of these geographical resources and their development and use for tourism
- demonstrate a knowledge of the main tourist resorts and tourist centres
- understand the role of Austria and Switzerland in the general pattern of European tourism
- be aware of regional variations in the development of winter sports resorts throughout the whole alpine chain
- understand the problems and opportunities afforded by the double tourist season in many alpine resorts.

INTRODUCTION

The Alps are the dominant mountain range in Europe. The core of the range runs almost east-west, but they curve southwards at their western end and drop down towards the sea to form the mountains backing the French and Italian rivieras. At their eastern end they gradually decrease in height until they are separated from the Carpathians by the widening valley of the Danube. Most of the Alps fall within Swiss and Austrian territory, but the southern section is divided between France and Italy, while the northern slopes just overlap into Germany; the far southeast extends into Slovenia. Most of the tourist developments are concentrated in the High Alps, which form the spine of the mountain chain and run from France, through Switzerland and into western Austria (*see* Fig 24.1). The landscapes and landforms are the major tourist resource: the flat-floored, steep-sided valleys rise to craggy peaks, producing dramatic landscapes of sometimes 1200 metres relative relief, and steep slopes suitable for ski runs. The mountain climate is characterised by cold, sunny winters but cool, wet and cloudy summers. This climatic regime enables the region to be developed for winter sports, while summer tourism takes place in spite of the less than ideal summer weather. Nevertheless, the volume of summer tourism is much greater than the winter sports trade measured either in terms of visitor numbers or in tourist nights.

There is, however, some significant regional variation in the nature of tourism and tourist developments throughout the Alps. In the western Alps the tourist centres are bigger (some over 40 000 beds), and many (for example in France) are purpose-built high altitude tourist settlements completely separate from the original villages.

While the French resorts cater primarily for their own domestic market, the tourist centres in central and eastern Switzerland and in west Austria are generally on a smaller scale, often consisting of small hotels and other accommodation units integrated into traditional valley villages. European travellers have significant regional preferences. Both Austria and Switzerland rely heavily on the German market but far more Germans visit Austria; the French prefer their own resorts but those who do cross into Italy, stay in the Alps of west Italy, while German visitors to Italy congregate in the Alto Adige. Dutch visitors clearly prefer

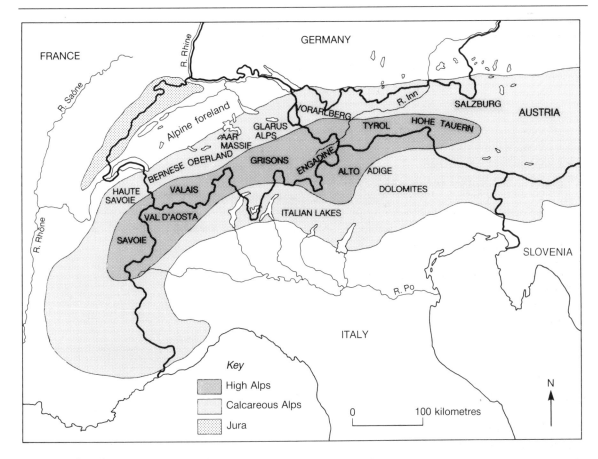

Fig. 24.1 The Alps

Austria to Switzerland while Belgians visit the two countries in roughly equal numbers. British and Italians show a preference for Austria. These patterns of tourist movement relate as much to historic factors, common languages and road communication routes as well as economic factors.

THE STRUCTURE AND LANDSCAPES OF THE ALPS

The High Alps form the core of the mountain chain but they are one of four physical regions, each of which has a different landscape character:

1 the High Alps;
2 the Calcareous Alps;
3 the Alpine Foreland and piedmont lakes; and
4 the Jura.

The High Alps

These mountains are made of resistant crystalline rocks which form the highest peaks, e.g. the needle-like peaks of the Aguille Rouges (3650 m), the pyramidal peak of the Matterhorn (4477 m) or sometimes more rounded summits (e.g. Mont Blanc 6087 m). The slopes are often very steep (frequently over 40°) and screes readily form. Some of the highest regions (over 2750 m) retain permanent snow and ice and some glaciers flow from these icefields. The longest glacier is 32 km long but most have retreated in the last century, and global warming might prolong this trend. The landscape is deeply dissected by wide U-shaped valleys gouged out by glaciers in the last Ice Age. The flat valley floors are cultivated, while forests clothe the valley sides. Above the tree line (at about 2000 m) alpine meadow plants can grow and are seasonally grazed. These are the classic Alpine meadows that provide a profusion of flowers such as anemones, gentians, saffrons, crocuses and edelweiss, in the spring, though the growing season is short (only 6–13 weeks). Above 2000 m it is too cold for plant growth and the meadows merge into high altitude rocky wastes.

The landscapes thus have an attractive mixture of farmed and wild landscapes with forests everywhere an important element. They also have extremely high relative relief with dramatic and craggy skylines. Sometimes there are small lakes in the valleys. All these characteristics combine to give an ideal and very attractive landscape for tourism (*see* Chapter 4). In winter the High Alps normally receive over seven metres of snow, which lies for up to six months. Snowfall is heavy everywhere above 1375 metres. The region thus has the resources for winter sports too.

The Calcareous Alps

These limestone mountains flank the High Alps to both north and south. On the north side they form the Bernese Oberland (dominated by the Jungfrau and Eiger) which merge eastwards into the northern ranges of the Tyrol, while on the southern flanks they make up the Dolomites (which run into Italy).

The landscapes range from tabular masses with dramatic white cliffs, scarps and terraced slopes, to frayed skylines with sharp peaks. Where the limestone rock is particularly soluble they produce the classic karst landscapes of gorges, caverns, underground rivers and high-level, stony, desert-like landscapes devoid of surface drainage. Some of the ranges are high enough to retain icefields and glaciers (e.g. in the Bernese Oberland). Again, the landscape and climate provide the ideal resources for both summer and winter tourism.

The Alpine Foreland

This extends to the north of the central core of the mountains, and is made up of softer rock which creates a varied landscape of relatively low dissected hills and less deeply cut valleys. There are many examples of glacial deposits, i.e. where the glaciers of the Ice Age spilled out from the High Alps. The region is fertile farmland, and is more densely populated than the High Alps. The major landscape features and tourist resources are the string of 'piedmont' lakes that are located at the foot of the Calcareous Alps (e.g. Lakes Geneva and Thun and Lake Lucerne).

The Jura

This mountain range is much lower than the Alps. It lies on the outer (north westerly) edge of the Alpine Foreland. The French/Swiss border follows the SW–NE trend of the mountain ridges and valleys. The landscape is not so dramatic as the Alps, though some of the rivers flow in deep gorges where they have cut across the ridges.

CLIMATE

The characteristics of mountain climates have already been described in Chapter 2. The Alps have a continental climate (i.e. of cold, dry winters and unsettled, mild summers) but modified by altitude. A major area of high pressure builds up over Central Europe in winter giving the sunny, dry, still weather so suitable for winter sports, though fog may form in these conditions over the Alpine Foreland. In spring the high pressure system breaks down and depressions crossing the Mediterranean may coalesce with those tracking over Northern Europe to create an area of low pressure north of the Alps. Under these conditions local winds may suddenly develop like the warm, dry Föhn wind that blows from the south. It is often funnelled along the courses of N-S valleys. It is particularly common in spring and causes very rapid snow melt and a danger of avalanches. Sometimes the wind causes violent squalls over the piedmont lakes on the north flanks of the Alps.

The highest rainfall occurs in the summer when afternoon thunderstorms may occur. Precipitation increases everywhere with altitude but the west-facing (windward) slopes get twice as much as leeward slopes at the same height. Some sheltered spots may be very dry, for example the upper

Rhône valley (in the Swiss Canton of Valais) which is in the rain shadow of the Mont Blanc massif, and receives only 609 mm precipitation. It is so dry in summer that the crops need irrigation. On the other hand, exposed west-facing slopes may get over 2450 mm a year. Snow lies longer at the higher altitudes but this again is modified by aspect: the south-facing slopes are sunnier but snow cover is less prolonged than on the colder north-facing slopes which are often in deep shadow all day. The valleys in the High Alps experience a high diurnal range of temperature in winter. The air warms up in the daytime, but at night the heavy cold air drains into the valley bottoms and the temperature drops sharply. This fact, combined with the effect of aspect on sunshine, has led to valley settlements (and tourist accommodation) being located on the sides of valleys on south-facing slopes.

There are some general regional patterns of variation in the climate. The western Alps, which are more exposed to depressions from the Atlantic and Mediterranean are wetter and slightly milder than the eastern end of the mountain chain. The climate becomes steadily more continental from west to east. In eastern Austria the summers are quite hot and rainy, while the winters are very cold indeed.

AGRICULTURE AND THE DEVELOPMENT OF TOURISM IN THE ALPS

The physical environment of the Alps does not favour agriculture, but it was the main industry of the mountain region. The original settlements evolved to meet the needs of a peasant agricultural population. Alpine agriculture is very labour-intensive and farms were relatively small, with an average size of about six hectares in 1960. Agriculture has become increasingly marginal and unprofitable, leading to outmigration of the young and depopulation of the remoter valleys. Tourism has always been seen as a means of supplementing incomes and providing employment in these problem areas, and the Swiss and Austrian governments have supported tourism

for this very reason. Alpine tourism began by farming families letting rooms to tourists and combining tourism with agriculture, and this initiated the tradition in both countries of small scale family-run tourist businesses though few are combined with farming now.

The first tourists to the Alps came to Switzerland to see the landscape in summer. In the early 19th century, a wealthy, foreign elite (especially the English) visited the lakes to enjoy the scenery. In Chopin's time, Interlaken was just a row of hotels but he noted (with some annoyance) that 'every other person was English'. The British also popularised mountaineering holidays, and resorts such as Chamonix and Zermatt developed as climbing centres. With the arrival of the railway in the Alps in the 1870s, tourism expanded further, and thermal spas such as St Moritz and Bad Ischl became fashionable. Although skiing was introduced from Norway in the 1870s and skating from Holland in the following decade, summer visitors dominated Alpine tourism until the 1920s, when the first Winter Olympics were held in Chamonix in 1924. Ski facilities began to spread, particularly in Switzerland, and the first French resorts (Alpe D'Huez, Tignes and Val D'Isère) were established in this phase of rapid growth. Although skiing centres still catered for a small wealthy elite, winter tourism accounted for as much as 14 per cent of overnight stays in the Tyrol by 1924, and while British visitors dominated the Swiss industry at the time, most of Austria's pre-war visitors came from east and southeastern Europe. The economic depression, the Second World War and its political aftermath completely disrupted these travel patterns. Switzerland (still relying on a Western European clientele and having been neutral in the War) recovered quickly with a rapid expansion of tourist accommodation outside the established centres; in 1950 Switzerland still dominated Alpine tourism while Austria was rebuilding her tourist industry. This was done with great speed and success and by 1955 Austria had overtaken Switzerland as the premier Alpine tourist region (*see* Fig 24.2) while France rapidly developed its own resorts from 1960 onwards.

| Million tourist bednights (domestic and foreign) | | | |
| | Switzerland | | Austria |
	in hotels	in all accom	in all accom
1934	12	–	–
1945	14	–	–
1950–51	–	–	19
1955–56	20	–	31.6
1960–61	–	–	50.7
1965–66	29	–	70
1970–71	–	–	96.5
1975–76	31	–	105.0
1980–81	–	79.1	121.3
1985–86	34	74.9	113.3
1989	–	–	124.5
1991	–	77.9	–
1992	–	–	130.3

Fig. 24.2 The growth of tourism in Austria and Switzerland, 1934–1992

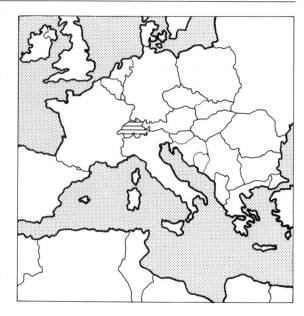

Tourism in both countries appears to have stagnated in the 1980s, partly due to the recession and competition from other destinations, but also because countries have been relatively slow in modernising and changing their accommodation stock to meet modern needs (for example for self-catering and high quality hotel accommodation). The fact that tourist businesses are small, and have limited access to capital for such modernisation, has also constrained expansion. In both countries, summer landscape-based tourism has shown the greatest decline while winter sports holidays are still growing steadily. A series of mild winters with late and poor quality snow in the late 1980s has caused further problems. If this trend is a foretaste of the effects of global warming (rather than just a short-term climate swing) then the ski resorts may have to face shorter and more unreliable seasons in the future.

SWITZERLAND

Switzerland's territory covers most of the central section of the Alps. The country includes parts of the four main physical regions of the Alps, each of which have different landscape and tourist characteristics. These are:

1 **The High Alps** – the Cantons (i.e. the administrative areas) of Valais, Tessin and Grisons in the far south of Switzerland;
2 **the Calcareous Alps** – the southern parts of the regions of Berne, Central Switzerland and Eastern Switzerland, and divided from the High Alps by the Rhône and Rhine valleys;
3 **The Alpine Foreland** – most of the remainder of Switzerland (including the main lakes);
4 **The Jura** – in the northwest of Switzerland the border with France follows the crest of these mountains.

The mountain resorts, the lakes and the cultural centres in the big cities are Switzerland's main tourist attractions (*see* Fig 24.7).

The High Alps

The characteristic landscapes of the High Alps have been described above. The region is divided into three sections: Valais; Tessin (Ticino); and Graubunden (the Grisons).

Valais

This region consists of the wide valley of the river Rhône, and the mountain block known as the Pennine Alps which increases in altitude towards the south to the peaks of the Matterhorn and Mount Rosa (Switzerland's highest mountain at 4634 m).

The Swiss/Italian border follows the crests of the mountains, but this massif forms an impenetrable barrier to communications, though there are passes that carry cross border routes around the west (the Great St Bernard) and the east (the Simplon) which end the mountain block (*see* Fig 16.2 on p 164). The mountains are high enough to retain permanent snow and ice fields, and summer skiing is possible on the glacier plateau, which is at 3500 m on the ridge between the Matterhorn and Mount Rosa. These icefields can be reached by ski lifts from Zermatt, an old established climbing and

skiing resort. The main skiing season here runs from early December to mid-April, and the centre has a variety of skiing and non-skiing activities as well as nightlife. The other main ski developments of the Pennine Alps are based on Saas-Fee; Verbier, a large, modern and mainly self-catering resort with good facilities for beginners through to more experienced skiers, and the quieter family centres around Champéry (*see* Fig 24.3).

The Rhône valley forms the northern boundary of the Pennine Alps. It is a wide structural trench which is followed by the river Rhône as it flows westwards from its source in the Rhône glacier (located just north of Gletsch). The valley is also followed by the

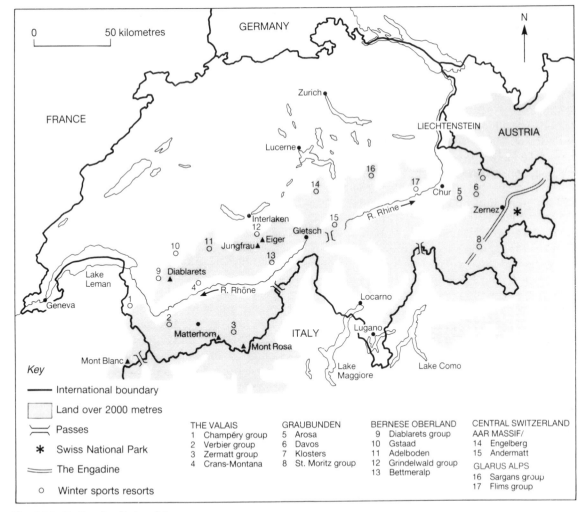

Fig. 24.3 Switzerland's tourist areas

main road and rail arteries between the Swiss Alps and France: the French influence is reflected in the fact that the region is partly French-speaking. The valley is sheltered from rain-bearing westerly winds by the Pennine Alps, and it enjoys a particularly dry and sunny climate, suitable for vineyards, peach and apricot orchards. The Crans-Montana development is situated on the dry and sunny south-facing slope of the valley. This is one of the biggest Alpine tourist resorts in Switzerland with a mixture of substantial hotels, self-catering apartments and plenty of nightlife. In the Valais area as a whole, 87 per cent of the beds are self-catering, and the region accounts for 15 million bednights. Domestic visitors match the numbers of foreign tourists.

Tessin (Ticino)

This part of Switzerland looks towards Italy: it is Italian speaking, and its southerly aspect and latitude give it a milder climate and a slightly more Mediterranean character than the northern Alps. A major transalpine route runs through the region linking Zurich (via Andermatt and the St Gotthard Pass) to the valley that runs south through Tessin to the head of Lake Maggiore and the north Italian plain. The High Alps are less massive in Tessin, reaching only just over 3000 m. The landscape has less densely forested hillsides, with extensive beech and sweet chestnut woods as well as the characteristically alpine coniferous forests. In the south it is mild enough for peaches, citrus fruit and vines to flourish. The far south of the province (in the Lake Maggiore and Lake Lugano region) is physically part of the Italian Lakes region, and has a similar pattern of essentially summer tourism based on the lakeside resorts such as Locarno, Lugano and Ascona. In 1986 Tessin was the fourth ranking Swiss Canton in terms of supply of bed spaces, but it attracted only five million bednights (a third of the number in Valais, Grisons and Berne). Self-catering accommodation forms three-quarters of the stock of bed spaces. The majority of visitors are foreign tourists as the domestic market takes up only 35 per cent of the total bednights.

Graubunden (the Grisons)

This is a high, rugged isolated mountain region. The valley bottoms do not fall below 1100 m while most of the mountains are over 3000 m high, and some have permanent snow fields and glaciers. It is a major summer tourism region but there are also clusters of relatively high altitude ski resorts, for example, Davos is at 1564 m and Arosa at 1700 m, and the ski season is consequently a little longer than at the resorts in the west. In the Grisons the season runs from the beginning of December to the end of April. Chur is the hub for a cluster of resorts including Klosters (a quiet, expensive and exclusive resort), Davos (originally a health resort and now a well established ski centre but with few facilities for young people) and Arosa (a modern resort located on a sunny SW facing valley shoulder with a wide range of ski and non-skiing facilities) (*see* Fig 24.3).

The Grisons mountains are cut by a confusion of 150 valleys: the biggest valley is the Engadine, a major trench up to a mile wide which cuts through the mountains from SW to NE, i.e. from the head of Lake Como northeast to the Austrian border. For most of its length it is drained by the River Inn which flows NE into Austria, and eventually to the Danube. St Moritz is situated in the upper Engadine Valley where a series of small lakes adds to the attraction of the scenery. The valley sides are covered with juniper scrub and pine, larch and birch forests. The wide, flat valley floor is cultivated meadow land. St Moritz was originally a health spa, based on the local mineral springs, but is now a large and expensive ski resort. It has all facilities and nightlife, but there are smaller and quieter resorts in the valley, e.g. Celerina and Zuoz. Below Zernez the Inn passes through a narrow gorge before emerging into the wider Lower Engadine valley. The landscape here is outstanding, making the region important for summer tourism as well as winter sports. The spectacular scenery of the Swiss National Park lies to the SE of Zernez and it has a wealth of alpine wildlife, such as ibex, chamois, deer and marmots.

After Valais, the Grisons has Switzerland's second biggest concentration of bed spaces, and receives roughly the same number (15 million) of visitor nights. Seventy-five per cent of the stock is self-catering accommodation. In the hotel sector, winter tourism bednights just outnumber summer bednights.

The Calcareous Alps and the Pre Alps

The landscape of the limestone Alps is significantly different from the High Alps (*see* p 272).

The region is split into three tourist regions:

1 The Bernese Oberland. This is in the south of the Canton of Berne. It is one of the most intensive tourist regions in Switzerland because it is the most easily accessible of the major mountain blocks. The Rhône valley allows access from the south and west, while on its northern flanks, routes penetrate deeply into the mountains up the series of parallel glacial trenches that run N-S towards the higher peaks.

The crest of the mountain range runs parallel to the Rhône valley, from the sheer rock faces of the Diablerets (in the SW) to the peaks of the Jungfrau and Eiger (in the NW) that tower over Interlaken. The 17 km long Aletsch glacier descends from the southern flanks of the Jungfrau massif. Most of the resorts in the western half of the range are quiet, good for families and suited to all levels of ski skills. One exception is Gstaad which is fashionable, expensive and glamorous. The resorts in the easily accessible valley to the south of Interlaken, such as Grindelwald, Wengen, Murren and Lauterbrunnen, are highly developed for summer tourism as well as winter sports.

The general pattern of tourism is similar to that of Valais: three-quarters of the stock of bed spaces are self-catering (though only half the bednights). The Berne Canton as a whole receives about 15 million tourist nights, half of which are generated by the domestic market and half by foreign visitors.

2 The Aar Massif of central Switzerland. This is located between Lake Lucerne and Andermatt, and is divided from the Glarus Alps by the Reuss valley which carries the N–S route from Zurich to Andermatt (and via Tessin to Italy). The valley is spectacular, particularly in the Scholleren gorge. The main resorts are grouped around Andermatt, with its lively nightlife, and Engelberg.

3 The Glarus Alps. Tourism here is on a relatively small scale compared to the Bernese Oberland. The main centres are at Flims and Sargans, and are quiet, with good ski facilities.

The Alpine Foreland

This is a lower region, with more gentle rolling landscapes. But a series of piedmont lakes lies at the foot of the high mountains, at the junction of the Alpine Foreland and the Calcareous Alps. These lakes with their backdrop of dramatic mountain landscapes make ideal locations for summer tourism, and many lakeside resorts have been developed, such as Interlaken and Wilderswil between Lakes Thun and Brienzer, and Lucerne and Weggis on Lake Lucerne. Lakes Leman, Zurich and Constance are in slightly gentler landscape settings. Zurich is Switzerland's second city and is a centre of banking and business, so attracts business rather than holiday tourism. Geneva (on Lake Leman) is also an international centre and is the site of the headquarters of many international organisations mainly due to Switzerland's neutrality and stable economy. Geneva, therefore, attracts many foreign visitors (both holiday and non-holidaymakers), and relies more heavily on hotel accommodation than the rest of Switzerland. Zurich and Geneva each attract around five million tourist bednights. Foreign tourists accounted for 75 per cent and 82 per cent respectively of the cities' bednights in 1991.

The Jura

The landscapes in this region are attractive but not as spectacular as the main Alpine chain, nor is the snow season so prolonged. The Jura is the least visited part of Switzerland, and mainly caters for the domestic market. It is, however, the centre for watchmaking, one of Switzerland's traditional industries. In 1991 it attracted only 2.2 per cent of all Switzerland's hotel stays (domestic and foreign).

THE VOLUME OF TOURISM IN SWITZERLAND

Tourists in Switzerland are of four types:

1 Domestic tourists;
2 Foreign staying visitors;
3 Foreign day visitors who are based in another country and make a day-trip into Switzerland and

return to their original starting point; 1991 estimates suggest that 44.6 million cars entered the country on one-day excursions; and

4 Direct transit visitors. These are visitors passing through the country on their way from their home to another holiday destination – essentially north Europeans on their way to the Mediterranean. In 1991 it was reported that 10 per cent of coach traffic and 6 per cent of private cars entering Switzerland were in transit.

As Switzerland does not collect statistics on border arrivals it is difficult to assess the size of the different markets. Swiss tourism statistics are based on arrivals at different types of accommodation. Fig 24.4 shows that a high proportion of the country's bed spaces are self-catering (particularly apartments). Almost 60 per cent of foreign overnight stays are in the hotel sector, while 62 per cent of domestic tourism is in self-catering accommodation.

Domestic tourists

Switzerland's population is around 6.6 million and, as shown in Chapter 15 (*see* Fig 15.8 on page 155), is an affluent population with a high propensity for holiday taking. Figure 15.8 would suggest a domestic market of around 2.3 million people. More reliable bednight data show the domestic market is substantial, generating 39 million bednights in 1991, and accounts for 53 per cent of all tourist bednights in Switzerland. The majority of

these (62 per cent) were in self-catering accommodation (chalets, apartments, campsites). The large stock of apartments have been built largely in response to the demands of the domestic market.

International staying visitors

Estimates suggest that international arrivals have stabilised at between 11.5 and 12 million in the mid-1980s but grew slowly to 13.2 million arrivals by 1990. Other available statistics suggest that foreign arrivals at hotels have not changed much over this period (hovering between 7.0 million and 7.9 million between 1987 and 1992). Foreign bednights in all accommodation has shown some slow growth (from 34.4 m nights in 1988 to 36.9 m in 1991).

In the mid-1980s international visitors responded to the recession by reducing the length of their visit to Switzerland rather than cutting it out. Lengths of stay are quite short as Switzerland is a relatively expensive destination due to the strength of the Swiss franc against other European currencies in the 1980s. The Germans, Dutch and Belgians tended to stay longest (with average stays of over five days) but these visitors favour the use of the cheaper self-catering accommodation rather than hotels. As most come by car they are mobile and independent and can take advantage of self-catering facilities. Intercontinental travellers (from USA and Japan) showed the shortest stays in 1985 (2.2 and 1.8 days respectively) and virtually all stayed in hotels.

Accommodation type (1)	Total bed spaces	%	Foreign bednights (millions)	%	Domestic bednights (millions)	%
Hotels	267 400	23.7	20.4	50.9	14.9	37.7
Apartments	360 000*	31.9	11.0	31.8	13.5	34.2
Campsites	264 900	23.5	2.7	7.7	5.5	14.0
Group Accommodation	226 600	20.1	2.0	5.8	5.1	13.0
Youth hostels	7 890	0.7	0.5	1.5	0.3	0.9
Totals	1 126 790	100 %	34.5 m	100 %	39.4 m	100 %

(1) Excluding health establishments and some other forms of accommodation.
* Underestimate. Total may be 480 000 (Swiss Tourism Office)

Fig. 24.4 Structure of Swiss tourism, 1990/91
(*Source*: Swiss Federal Statistics Office)

British and French visitors showed an intermediate pattern (averaging around four days in Switzerland, with the majority staying in hotels).

The relative stagnation of Switzerland's international tourist trade may be due to competition with new Mediterranean package summer destinations and the opening up of less developed rural and coastal summer destinations in the long-haul sector. It is also a reflection of the maturity of the Swiss tourist industry, its limited potential for growth and its relatively high costs (about 55 per cent of visitors perceived local prices to be rather high or very high).

Day visitors and transit visitors

Very little information is available on these types of visitors. Estimates suggest that in 1991, Switzerland attracted about 98 million day visitors and roughly seven million transit visitors. Roughly one third of the day trippers come from Germany, one third from Italy and one fifth from France.

Origins of international visitors

Figure 24.5 shows that Switzerland relies very heavily on the German market. Apart from that, the country attracts visitors from a wide range of both northern and southern European countries, reflecting the special nature of Switzerland's resources. No other European country (other than Austria and the Scandinavian territories) has mountain scenery or winter sports resources of the scale and quality of Switzerland. Austria and Scandinavia on the other hand have an abundance of snow and mountains and make a negligible contribution to Switzerland's international visitors.

Seasonality of tourism

Although landscape tourism is declining in popularity in Switzerland, the summer is still the busiest time of year. In 1991 57 per cent of domestic and international tourist nights were in summer. This pattern is more marked when international visitors are considered alone: in 1987 20 per cent of international bednights were at the height of the winter season while about 33 per cent were at the summer peak. Winter tourism (both domestic and international) is, however, continuing to expand. The hotel sector has a relatively steady trade all year (at around three million nights a month), but it is the self-catering sector that absorbs the seasonal peaks. In February this sector accommodates five million bednights, and 7.5 million nights in August, but demand drops back to under a million in the off-peak months of May, November and December. Thus, in spite of all year round tourism, some sectors experience very low occupancy rates.

	Bednights in hotels (million)	Total bednights in all accommodation (million)	Total bednights %
Germany	6.96	16.12	43.60
Netherlands	0.89	3.38	9.14
UK	1.84	2.54	6.87
France	1.54	2.50	6.78
Belgium	0.92	2.04	5.54
Italy	1.40	1.99	5.39
USA*	1.57*	1.77	4.80
Japan**	0.72**	0.75	2.00
Spain	0.46	0.71	1.92
Austria	0.41	0.58	1.57

* a reduction of 37% from previous year ⎱ both due to
** a reduction of 11% from previous year ⎰ Gulf War

Fig. 24.5 Foreign tourist nights in Switzerland, 1991

	1985 domestic & international bednights (%)	1987 foreign bednights (%)
January	8.78	9.7
February	10.89	7.8
March	10.46	11.6
April	8.03	10.2
May	4.40	4.6
June	6.60	7.2
July	14.40	12.5
August	15.99	17.0
September	8.70	8.6
October	6.14	5.0
November	2.19	2.2
December	3.33	3.7

Fig. 24.6 Switzerland's seasonal pattern of tourism

Regional patterns of tourism

The high mountain regions dominate Switzerland's tourism. The Cantons of Valais, Graubunden and Berne each had about 15 million tourist nights in 1986, with the latter Canton being the most popular region for foreign tourists (*see* Fig 24.8). The rural regions of Tessin and Vaud, and the cities of Zurich and Geneva each only had between four to five million nights each, while the other parts of Switzerland had very low levels of tourism. The hotel sector is only one element of the total accommodation stock but the spatial distribution of hotel nights also underlines the popularity of the mountain areas (*see* Fig 24.7).

	% all hotel bednights	Share of domestic and foreign tourism in each type of destination	
		% hotel bednights	
		domestic	foreign
Mountain resorts	39	45	55
Lakeside zones	21	40	60
Big cities	17	22	78
Other areas	23	55	45
	100%		

Fig. 24.7 Swiss tourist attractions, 1991

Tourism in the economy

The Swiss have a high propensity to travel and are relatively high spenders on outbound tourism: in 1984 they made 6.2 million trips abroad, spending 37.5 million nights out of Switzerland. Sixty per

cent of these (and 56 per cent of trips) were to European Mediterranean countries to enjoy the coastal resources that Switzerland lacks. In 1991 they spent 9.8 bn Swiss francs, but international tourism to Switzerland yielded 12.7 bn Swiss francs

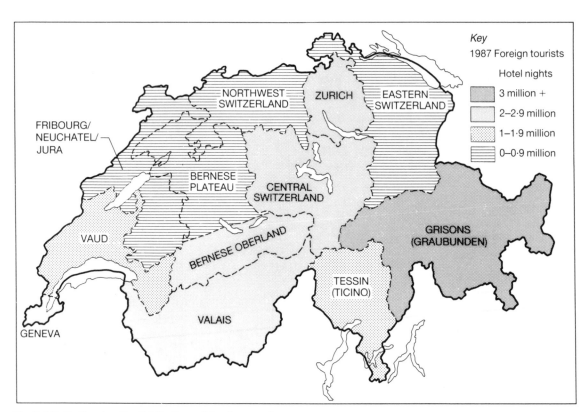

Fig. 24.8 Switzerland's distribution of foreign tourism

in receipts, so Switzerland has a favourable balance of tourist trade of 2.9 bn Swiss francs. International tourism is very important to Switzerland's economy, providing eight per cent of the national income and employment for 14 per cent of the population in the early 1980s. Tourism has been promoted by the Swiss Government because it is the only economic alternative to agriculture in the mountain regions, although it does create problems in the sensitive alpine environment and has caused some disruption to local communities.

AUSTRIA

Austria is twice as big as Switzerland but the two countries each have about the same area covered by the Alps – roughly 8000 square miles of mountain territory in each country. Austria's tourism is very strongly concentrated in its Alpine region, and the total volume of its tourist industry is much greater than that of Switzerland. The Austrian Alpine regions receive roughly twice as many visitors and tourist nights as the Swiss Alps.

The scenery and resources of the Alpine regions of the two countries are similar (*see* pp 269–70 for an overall description of the Alps) though it has been noted that the climate of the Austrian Alps is a little more extreme (slightly dryer, but colder in winter and warmer in summer) than the Swiss section.

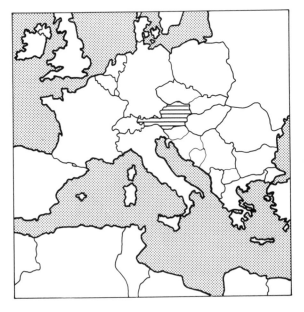

Location of Austria in relation to the structural units of the Alps

The spine of the Alps runs eastwards from Switzerland into Austria. The Austrian–Italian border follows the crest line of the High Alps to the south (*see* Fig 24.1). The northern slopes of the Alps fill the territory of the Austrian provinces of Vorarlberg, the Tyrol and Salzburg.

The River Inn (which flows from the Engadine on the Swiss border in the west) cuts these provinces in half, and the river valley separates the High Alps to the South from the Calcareous Alps and Pre Alps to the North.

The Alps gradually decrease in height as they drop away into central Austria. As in Switzerland and Italy, there are strings of lakes at the foot of the mountains, although they are on a smaller scale in Austria. These lakes form the Salzkammergut lake district on the northern flanks of the Austrian Alps and the lakes of the Drau Valley in Carinthia to the south.

The north and east of Austria (the provinces of Upper and Lower Austria, and Bergenland) belong to different physical regions, i.e. to the Danube valley and the southern edge of the Bohemian mountains and the edge of the Hungarian lowlands.

In summary, the physical regions of Austria are as follows:

1 The High Alps; and
2 The Calcareous Alps – the provinces of Vorarlberg, Tyrol and Salzburg;
3 The remainder of the Alps, the Alpine Foreland and piedmont lakes – the provinces of Carinthia, Styria and the southern parts of Lower and Upper Austria;
4 The Danube Valley; and
5 The Bohemian Massif – Lower and Upper Austria;
6 The edge of the Hungarian basin – Bergenland.

The High Alps and Calcareous Alps

Vorarlberg Province. The north and west of the province borders the Rhine and Lake Constance, and has a milder climate than the rest of the Austrian Alps. The mountains rise gradually towards the Tyrol, but are traversed by an important W–E routeway that follows the Arlberg pass and a tunnel carries the Paris-Vienna railway into the Inn valley. This route links Germany (via the upper Rhine valley) to the Austrian Tyrol, making this part of Austria relatively accessible to the German market.

The Tyrol. The most dramatic Tyrolean mountain scenery is in the south of the province, in the High Alps. The mountains are rugged and massive, with glaciers and pyramidal peaks and are cut by great glacial trenches running north into the Inn Valley. Resorts such as Ishgl, Obergurgl, and Mayrhofen lie in the upper reaches of such valleys (*see* Fig 24.9).

Ishgl and Galtur in the Patznauner valley are unsophisticated, traditional centres with good facilities for families. Winter tourism accounts for more than 65 per cent of tourist nights. Obergurgl, Hochgurgl and Solden are in the Otztal valley. Obergurgl has some large hotels (50–100 rooms) but it is a traditional and friendly resort with a long skiing season from early December to the end of April. It is visited for both summer and winter tourism. Hochgurgl is a small, purpose-built ski resort built on the French style, i.e. separate from original settlements. Solden is more isolated but is located on a sunny south-facing slope. Solden is the most popular winter sports resort in Austria (with 1.45 million nights in 1992). It is also patronised by

summer visitors, although winter visitors outnumber summer tourists in the Otztal region of the Tyrol as a whole. It is one of the most intensive tourist areas of Austria, with over one million overnight stays (excluding camping) in 1985. Mayrhofen in the Ziller valley is a gregarious, lively resort with some nightlife, and is the most popular resort with British visitors. It has summer skiing for experienced skiers on the Hintertux Glacier and is also promoted for walking and summer sports. Other resorts in the same valley offer skiing for all standards. The valley has tourism all year round and is another intensively visited area, with over one million tourist nights in 1985.

Another of these major N–S orientated glacial troughs is used by a major N–S route (via the Brenner pass) linking Austria with Italy. Thus, the Inn valley, at the heart of the Austrian Tyrol, is at a crossroads of major E–W and N–S routes through the Alps, making this part of the Alps readily accessible. Routes to the north also make it easily accessible from the German city of Munich (via the Inn Valley).

Innsbruck is strategically sited where these routes cross, and the site has been inhabited since Roman times. The old city was established in 1180,

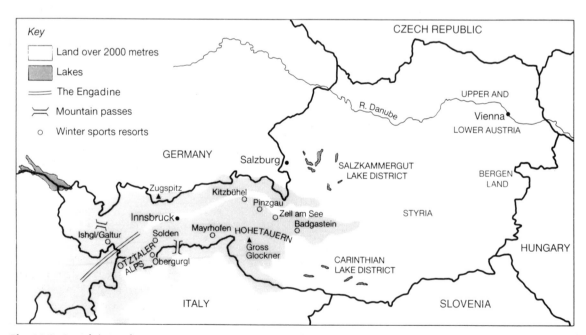

Fig. 24.9 Austria's tourist areas

and there are many medieval streets and buildings. There are also good ski facilities, including the Olympic course, used in the 1964 and 1976 Winter Olympics, and at Igls there are bobsleigh events. The area received 1.4 m tourist bednights in 1985.

The Calcareous Alps to the north of the Inn Valley give a different landscape of white, craggy rockfaces and screes above dark green forested slopes. These landscapes form the backdrop to unspoilt resorts such as Ellmau, Söll and Westendorf which are all summer and winter resorts. The Kitzbühel area is also in this section of the Alps (*see* Fig 24.9). This cluster of resorts includes Kirchberg, a big, international resort with some larger hotels (up to 100 rooms), varied skiing and lively nightlife. This valley also has tourism all year round and is a major centre of the region (over one million visitor nights in 1985). Seefeld (near Innsbruck) is the most popular summer destination for the British market, while Saalbach-Hinterglemm (near Kitzbuhel) is another significant summer tourism centre. This resort is the most popular all year round tourist centre in the High Alps (with a total of two million bednights in 1992).

The valley of the Upper Inn is a continuation of the Swiss Engadine, but the valley changes in character and widens into a very broad, flatbottomed trench below Innsbruck. Major routes follow the valley northwards towards Germany through a gap in the Calcareous Alps.

Salzburg Province. The Hohe Tauern is a massive block of High Alps that lies south of the Inn, to the south of Salzburg province. The mountains, which are part of the crystalline Alps, extend further into the province of East Tyrol. The range includes Austria's highest peaks (e.g. the Gross Glockner rising over 3700 m) and offers opportunities for summer skiing on high level glaciers. The mountains form one of the most visited areas of Austria, with tourism spread evenly throughout the region: mixed summer and winter tourism occurs on the western half, for example in the Pinzgau area near the spectacular Krimml waterfalls, but winter tourism is more important east of Badgastein (another major centre with over one million visitor nights).

The Alpine Foreland and piedmont lakes. The landscape is more subdued and less dramatic than the High Alps and receives relatively few visitors. The exception is the city of Salzburg, in the far north of its province. It is a tourist centre in its own right (with 1.4 million tourist nights in 1985). It has splendid architecture, is famed as being the home of Mozart and is the location of an important music festival. The Salzkammergut lake district straddles the Salzburg–Upper Austria border. The lakes are set in low forest-clad mountains and the lakeside resorts, e.g. St Gilgen, St Wolfgang and Strobl on Lake Wolfgang, cater for summer tourism which is concentrated in July and August. Austria's summer tourism has been declining in the 1980s, and areas such as the Salzkammergut and Carinthian lake districts have been hardest hit.

The remaining regions of Austria attract relatively few staying foreign tourists, though the east is experiencing an increase in the already high level of day-tripping. Vienna is the only major focus of tourism. The site has been settled since medieval times and St Stephen's Cathedral dates from 1258. Vienna retains some narrow streets reminiscent of its medieval past but the city reached its peak in the 18th century as the centre of the Hapsburg Empire.

Hofburg was the town residence of the Hapsburgs while the palace of Schonbrunn (a palace on the scale of Versailles) was their other residence. The Spanish Riding School, where the white Lipizzaner stallions perform dressage displays to music, still retains the classical methods of horse training of the period.

Vienna is still the capital and cultural centre of Austria. The many museums, including the Kunsthistorisches Museum (the museum of fine art), and the Vienna State Opera reflect its continuing association with the arts.

It ranks fourth in the league of European city tourism (after London, Paris and Rome), and in 1992, received 6.9 million overnight stays.

THE VOLUME OF TOURISM IN AUSTRIA

Like Switzerland and other countries that have many land border crossings, Austria does not collect data on foreign frontier arrivals. However, estimates suggest that in 1985 the total number of foreign arrivals was of the order of 130 million (of which 93 per cent came by road). Eighty per cent of all arrivals were holidaymakers, five per cent business tourists, two per cent shoppers and 13 per cent people visiting friends and relatives. These tourists fall into the same four categories as do those to Switzerland (*see* p 275), i.e.:

(*a*) Foreign staying visitors;
(*b*) Foreign day visitors; and
(*c*) Direct transit visitors.

Rough estimates indicate that about 50 million arrivals were day visitors, mainly from Germany, 15 million staying visitors (also predominantly from Germany) and the very high number of 50 million were direct transit holidaymakers on their way from Northern Europe to the Mediterranean coast. This reflects the location of Austria in relation to Europe's tourist generation and destination regions, and the fact that good N-S and E-W routes can be found through the Alps in Austria. Austria's road system is good, and it has no tolls, though the peak summer loads do cause bottlenecks in parts in July and August.

The political changes in Eastern Europe that began in 1989 may eventually allow countries such as Hungary, Poland and the Czech and Slovak Republics to develop outbound tourism. Austria might be expected to benefit from an increase in day shopping trips. In 1992 there were half a million East European border arrivals, which were mostly day trippers.

Domestic tourism

Austria's tourism is more accurately measured by arrivals and bednights at registered tourist accommodation. In 1992, 99.7 million bednights were generated by foreign visitors and about 30.6 million from the domestic market. Although Austria's population at about 7.8 million is larger than Switzerland's, Austrians have a much lower propensity to travel, both internationally or at home. This has had an indirect effect on the structure of accommodation that left Austria at a competitive disadvantage in the late 1980s. In the past, the small domestic market has favoured the use of private rented rooms rather than self-catering accommodation, and Austria lacks the enormous stock of self-catering apartments that Switzerland

now has. Self-catering accommodation is now rapidly expanding in Austria in response to changing international demand but by 1985 it still only made up six per cent of the total accommodation stock, but grew to 11.8 per cent by 1991.

Domestic tourism originates mainly from Vienna and is heavily concentrated in the east of Austria. Only 30 per cent of domestic tourists visit the Alpine western provinces.

Outbound tourism

Outbound tourism is slowly growing (to 2.6 million holidays abroad in 1990). Given Austria's own natural resources, it is not surprising that nearly 50 per cent of these were to seaside destinations and only four per cent to hiking, mountaineering or winter sport destinations. The trouble in former Yugoslavia has greatly disrupted Austrians' traditional pattern of holidaymaking: the Croatian Adriatic coast was a favoured destination (attracting 18 per cent of Austrian holidaymakers in 1988 but only two per cent in 1991). The pollution of the Italian Adriatic resorts probably inhibited travel to the Italian coast in the late 1980s (*see* Chapter 20). Surveys show a reduction in leisure trips to Italy (from 28 per cent to 19 per cent of Austrian travellers) between 1987 and 1990 but the political uncertainties of 1991 made Italy a more attractive destination once more (taking 30 per cent of outbound travel in 1991). Spain and Portugal are other Mediterranean destinations that became more popular with Austrians in 1991, as travel to Turkey was disrupted by the Gulf War.

International staying visitors

Although the total number of staying visitors to Austria at 19.09 million in 1992 is much higher than the number visiting Switzerland, the two countries share a similar general pattern of tourism: the numbers of staying visitors to Austria stabilised in the 1980s, but the average length of stay has declined (e.g. from 6.5 nights in 1981 to 5.5 nights in 1992). Summer tourism is declining, while winter sports holidays are still expanding (from 30 per cent of all tourist nights in 1975 to 41 per cent in 1988). The winter season is more important for The Netherlands and UK markets. Fifty-six per cent and 50 per cent (respectively) of Dutch and British bednights in Austria were in winter. Austria is now Europe's leading winter sports destination.

As shown in the following table, Austria relies even more heavily on the German market than does Switzerland.

	Foreign tourist arrivals (%)	Bednights at all accommodation (%)
Germany	55.8	64.87
Netherlands	6.7	9.02
Italy	6.3	3.61
UK	3.9	4.07
Switzerland	3.9	3.12
France	3.8	2.85
USA	3.2	1.52
Belgium	2.4	3.02
Sweden	1.5	1.35
E Europe	3.0	1.60
Total number of arrivals (mill) 19.09		**Total number of bednights (mill)** 99.75

Fig. 24.10 Austria: foreign tourist arrivals, 1992

While Germany contributes more than half the number of visitors, 78 per cent of Austria's bednights come from just three markets – German, Dutch and British – and Austria's tourist industry must, therefore, be very dependent on the health of the economy in these three countries. The growing Italian market is of increasing importance to Austria: Italian bednights in Austria have shot up from 1.6 million in 1987 to 3.6 million in 1992.

Spatial pattern of tourism

It has been noted that international tourism is very strongly concentrated in the mountains in the west: 70 per cent of Austria's visitors stayed in the provinces of Tyrol, Salzburg and Vorarlberg in 1992. The distribution of the accommodation stock mirrors this problem (*see* Fig 24.11).

Seasonality

Like Switzerland, Austria has a double peak of tourism through the year, but Austria's peaking is more marked than in Switzerland, and Austria's smaller domestic market does not even out demand to the same extent.

Province	% foreign bednights	% domestic bednights	% all bednights (domestic & foreign)
The High Alps	**70.4 %**	**30.3 %**	
Tyrol	43.0	9.8	35.2
Salzburg	19.5	17.8	19.1
Vorarlberg	7.9	2.7	6.7
The rest of Austria	**29.6 %**	**69.7 %**	
Carinthia	12.3	17.1	13.4
Styria	3.7	18.9	7.3
Upper Austria	4.2	13.1	6.3
Lower Austria	2.3	13.1	4.8
Bergenland	0.8	4.6	1.7
Vienna	6.0	2.6	5.3
Total bednights (mill)	99.75	30.65	130.41

Fig. 24.11 Regional distribution of tourism in Austria, 1992 (bednights in all accommodation)

	% of bednights at registered accommodation	
	International	Domestic
January	9.1	7.1
February	10.3	11.1
March	8.9	8.7
April	4.8	5.7
May	4.2	6.4
June	8.4	8.6
July	17.3	14.6
August	18.2	16.3
September	8.9	8.8
October	3.2	5.1
November	1.1	3.2
December	5.6	4.4

Fig. 24.12 Seasonality of domestic and international tourism in Austria, 1985

The summer peak of demand is high (nearly 20 million bednights in August 1985). The high season in winter is February (nearly 12 million bednights). In spite of the double tourist season, occupancy rates are still quite low (24.1 per cent in 1985).

CONCLUSION

Swiss and Austrian territory covers the heart of the Alps and alpine tourism is concentrated here but the French, German, Italian and Slovenian sections of the Alps have significant winter and summer tourism too, each with its own special character. Each country meets the winter sports needs of many of its domestic tourists but each has a slightly different niche in the international market. As the popularity of winter sports increases, all will face the problems of regulating the growing impact of skiing on the delicate alpine ecosystem (perhaps the greatest problems being experienced in the high level resorts that provide skiing to the door). All countries too share the problem of a declining summer market, and managing the sometimes incompatible demands for more ski developments

with the need to conserve the landscape for the summer visitor.

FURTHER READING

Austria
Hamilton, G (1993) 'Austria', *EIU International Tourism Reports*, No. 2, pp. 40–57.
Hamilton, G (1993) 'Austria Outbound', *EIU Travel and Tourism Analyst*, No. 1, pp. 31–50.

Switzerland
Cockerell, N (1991) 'Switzerland', *EIU International Tourism Reports*, No. 1, pp. 5–17.
Cockerell, N (1994) 'The international ski market in Europe', *EIU Travel and Tourism Analyst*, No. 3, pp. 34–55.

QUESTIONS AND DISCUSSION POINTS

1 List the major physical regions of Switzerland *or* of Austria. Identify the dominant type of tourism associated with each region.

2 The development and organisation of winter sports tourism in Switzerland is different from that of Austria. Describe these differences and explain how and why they have occurred.

3 A double (i.e. winter and summer) tourist season would be seen as an advantage to many tourist destinations. Why is it sometimes perceived as a problem in Austria and Switzerland?

ASSIGNMENT

You work in a travel agency in Birmingham and customers are beginning to think about their bookings for winter sports holidays. The following people come in asking for your advice on suitable European winter sports resorts that might meet their needs:

(*a*) A teacher who will be taking a school party (of 30 11–12 year olds, mostly beginners) on a winter ski holiday.

(*b*) A family of four. The mother is an experienced skier while her husband is a keen sportsman but has never skied. Their two children, aged 11 and 14, have both started learning to ski on artificial ski slopes in the UK. The whole family is also keen on many other indoor and outdoor sports.

(*c*) Two single businesswomen in the 28–35 age group who are both experienced skiers.

Make notes for each group of clients, selecting suitable resorts, suggesting the best time of the season they might go and the best routes and means of transport they should take.

CHAPTER 25

Central Europe: Benelux and Germany

LEARNING OBJECTIVES

After reading this chapter you should be able to
- assess the tourist potential of the climatic, landscape, historical and cultural resources of Benelux and Germany
- distinguish the regional distribution of these geographical resources and their development and use for tourism
- demonstrate a knowledge of the main tourist resorts and tourist centres
- understand the role of Benelux and Germany in the general pattern of European tourism
- be aware of the impact of changing economic and political circumstances on patterns of tourism.

INTRODUCTION

Four countries (Belgium, The Netherlands, Luxembourg and Germany) form the heart of the tourist generating region of Europe. Physically, these countries, plus the five Eastern European states, make up the non-Mediterranean core of mainland Europe (*see* Fig 18.1 on p 192). Benelux and Germany consist of three major physical units.

1 The Northern European plain. A low-lying undulating region, where features of glacial deposition dominate the landscape. The plain extends from Belgium, The Netherlands, through north Germany to northern Poland.
2 The Northern European uplands. Flat topped uplands which are tilted and rise gradually from the Harz and the Ardennes in the north to the foothills of the Alps in the south. They give rise to gently rolling forested landscapes, which become more dramatic where the uplands have been cut by broad valleys, or eaten into by more deeply incised valleys. These uplands extend through the territories of Luxembourg, southern Belgium and southern Germany.
3 The Alps. The mountain chain essentially runs east-west. The Alps make up only a very small part of German territory.

The combined population of Belgium, Holland, Luxembourg and Germany was over 105 million in 1991. It is a major tourist generating region as the population has a relatively high standard of living. The countries abound with unspoilt towns and other cultural and historic resources, but are poorly endowed with coasts and climate for mass beach tourism. The 'low' countries also lack mountainous territory. Together these factors generate a very special pattern of both inbound and outbound tourism (inbound tourism mainly to the historic towns and cities and outbound tourism to destinations that complement the domestic natural resources). However, the reunification of Germany in 1990 marked the end of one political era and heralded a period of profound political and economic change: new patterns of tourism may evolve in response to these changes.

BENELUX

The three countries of Benelux are small, but densely populated (*see* Fig 25.1). Together, their area is less than a third (but their total population is nearly one half) of that of the UK.

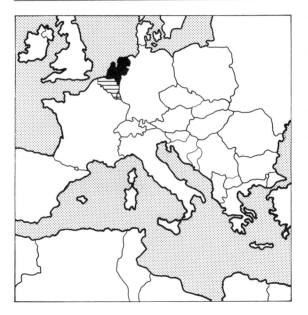

All three countries are relatively affluent. The Dutch and Luxembourgers have high propensities to travel (at 58 per cent) and, because of the small size of their countries, a high proportion (63 per cent) of this travel is to foreign countries. Most domestic destinations are within a few hours' drive. In comparison, the Belgians tend to stay at home: only 40 per cent of their population take holidays away from home, although 56 per cent of these trips were to foreign destinations. The natural resources of all three countries are easily accessible for day leisure trips and are intensively used by both domestic day-trippers and by day excursionists who cross the border from neighbouring countries.

The landscapes have a very individual character but are subdued. The climate is slightly drier than

Country	Area in km²	1990/91 population (million)	Population density (persons per km²)
The Netherlands	33 938	15.06	444.0
Belgium	30 513	9.97	327.0
Luxembourg	2 586	0.38	148.0

Fig. 25.1 Benelux population

that of UK or northern France but is still a far from ideal tourist environment. It is not surprising, therefore, that most international tourism to the Benelux countries is urban-based.

CLIMATE

The region has a western maritime type of climate, and lies in the path of frequent North Atlantic depressions, giving mild changeable windy weather. Variations of climate within the region are related to the topography. The climate becomes cooler and wetter as the land rises towards the south of Belgium and into Luxembourg, while the strength of the wind is particularly noticeable in Holland's flat exposed landscape. The summers tend to be drier and warmer than in the UK, particularly away from the coast: in Holland the rainfall decreases from 820 mm per annum on the coast to only 560 mm inland. But summer rainfall is still frequent enough to limit the country's potential as an international destination.

THE PHYSICAL REGIONS OF BENELUX

The countries are also known as the 'Low Countries' which aptly reflects their generally subdued relief and low altitude: much of The Netherlands is actually below sea level (*see* Fig 25.2). There are three physical regions:

1 The coastal sand dune belt. The coastline of The Netherlands and Belgium is sandy throughout its whole length and is backed by a belt of massive sand dunes, which average 6–12 m high (but sometimes rise to 60 m) and may extend 2–4 km inland. The dune belt is breached only by the Rhine delta. Elsewhere, they protect the low plains from inundation by the sea. Belgium's coast is almost continuously developed for seaside resorts, and the central Dutch coast is heavily used for day-tripping from the nearby Amsterdam and Rotterdam conurbations.

2 The inland plains. These were originally marshy areas but were progressively drained to create very fertile agricultural land. In The Netherlands' drainage channels, canals and lakes

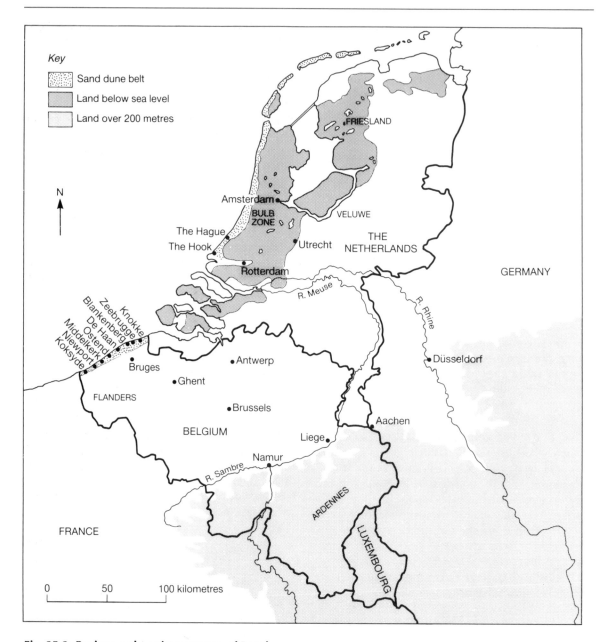

Fig. 25.2 Regions and tourist resources of Benelux

were created and windmills used to pump the water out and later land was even reclaimed from the sea. As the land dried out it shrank below sea level and dykes and sea defences were built to keep the sea out. All these features combine to create the distinctive 'polder' landscape of The Netherlands.

The landscape thus has a very special quality but is exceptionally flat and is not greatly valued for tourism except where the bulbfields (located between Leiden and Den Helder) add colour and interest. However, it is an ideal setting for cycling which is very popular in The Netherlands, and the waterways are extensively used for boating. The Netherlands has 883 marinas, mostly in the Friesland lake district and around Amsterdam and Rotterdam. Most of the historic towns of Belgium and The Netherlands are located in this lowland zone.

The interior of The Netherlands has a slightly more varied topography. It is a gentle landscape of undulating heathland and woodland – quite different from the flat, intensively cultivated landscape of the coastal lowlands.

Two of The Netherlands' three National Parks are located in this zone. The Veluwe (in the south) is particularly popular.

3 The Ardennes. These mountains are located in southern Belgium and Luxembourg. They rise to 450–600 m and consist of attractively wooded rounded mountains with a variety of rivers and lakes. Their climate is on the raw side (*see* Fig 2.1 on page 7), with persistently cloudy weather, over 850 mm of rainfall a year and up to 120 frost days per annum.

THE CHARACTER OF TOURISM IN THE NETHERLANDS

The domestic market

In 1990 Dutch people took 14.6 million holidays at home. The length of these holidays averaged seven days, and the vast majority were self-catering.

There are many campsites, particularly in the west of The Netherlands. Another form of self-catering holidays has recently become popular. The firm, Center Parcs, operate high quality self-catering complexes with a range of all weather/all year round sports and leisure facilities. They had seven sites in The Netherlands which attracted 1.5 million visitors in 1986, and an additional two sites in Belgium. Their sites consist of 120–160 hectares of woodland and water features. Self-catering bungalows, with high quality facilities and a range of indoor entertainments (e.g. TV and video) are set in the woodland, grouped around a central complex. This is dominated by a large indoor fun pool (with an artificial sub-tropical climate), shopping, dining and additional sports facilities. These may include tennis, squash, bowling alleys, windsurfing, canoeing and cycling. The company has also opened similar ventures in Germany, France and the UK (in Sherwood Forest and at Longleat).

In contrast to most European domestic markets, the Dutch tend to prefer inland locations. The two coastal provinces (of N and S Holland that include most of the sand dune belt) receive only 15.5 per cent of all nights. Gelderland (which includes the Veluwe) takes 27.7 per cent of campsite nights while the interior south has a third and the rest of The Netherlands' interior a quarter.

The explanation of this unusual distribution is twofold:

1 the coastal districts are very crowded: they accommodate half the country's population at densities of 634 people per km^2. Dutch holidaymakers like to escape to less urbanised environments for their holidays; and
2 the population living near the coast use it for daily and weekend recreation and therefore seek less familiar landscapes and activities for their domestic holidays.

Dutch outbound travel

In 1990 it was estimated that the Dutch took 9.0 million holidays abroad, and again, seaside destinations were not the most popular. In spite of its high relative costs. Germany attracted 14 per cent of Dutch travellers, but France was the most popular individual destination, where the Central Massif and the French Alps were the most popular. Austria and Switzerland accounted for an additional 16 per cent of Dutch foreign holidays. The contrast in landscape and the opportunity for winter sports activity would appear to be major factors accounting for these Dutch travel patterns. The remaining coastal Mediterranean countries take only 26 per cent of Dutch visits abroad.

Foreign holidays by the Dutch tend to be quite long (17 days' average stay), mostly in self-catering accommodation (57 per cent of all holidaymakers) and most travel by car (59 per cent).

Foreign tourism to The Netherlands

The small size of The Netherlands encourages day visits rather than staying visitors. In 1985 it was estimated that 21 million foreigners made cross-border shopping trips into The Netherlands while an additional 13 million visitors made day leisure excursions across the frontier. The pattern of foreign staying holidays also reflects the small size of the country. Overseas visitors stay only 2.8 days (average in 1990) and come mainly for business trips or city breaks. Business tourism accounts for half the hotel nights in The Netherlands, and is concentrated in the heavily populated regions of North and South Holland and Utrecht (i.e. primarily in Amsterdam, The Hague and Rotterdam, Europe's main port).

Foreign holidays, on the other hand, are focused on Amsterdam. The city is built around an extensive canal system and has many 17th century buildings. It is a cosmopolitan city with sophisticated nightlife, and used to be known as Europe's 'sex capital'. Amsterdam's Schiphol airport is a major European communications centre: it is Europe's fifth largest airport, with 19 million passengers, 66 per cent of whom travel to other parts of Europe. The Netherlands is also traversed by important Northern European road routes, while Rotterdam is Europe's biggest port. It is, therefore, not surprising that an estimated five million direct transit tourists pass through the country each year.

	% arrivals at registered accommodation
Germany	35.4
UK	14.2
USA	7.0
France	6.3
Belgium	6.0
Italy	5.3
Total number = 5.8 million	

Fig. 25.3 Origin of staying visitors to The Netherlands, 1991

TOURISM IN BELGIUM

The Belgian domestic market

After fluctuating around 19–21 million in the 1970s and early 1980s, it was estimated that the domestic market in Belgium reached 23.9 million visitor nights in 1990. Fifty-nine per cent of these were in coastal locations, such as the traditional resorts of Ostend, Knokke and Blankenberg and were strong-

ly peaked in July and August (*see* Fig 25.2). Belgium has a short coastline in relation to its size, so that most of its population does not have the routine daily contact with the sea and waterways as do the Dutch. The lure of the sea coast thus appears to be much greater for the Belgians. However, the Belgians share the Dutch preference for self-catering accommodation: in the summer of 1985, 28 per cent of domestic coastal visitor nights were in campsites and 50 per cent in other forms of self-catering facilities, such as flats, villas, or apartments. After the coast, the next most popular domestic destination was the Ardennes mountains, with six per cent of all summer domestic tourist nights.

Foreign visitors to Belgium

In 1992, Belgium received 3.2 million tourists. Foreign visitors to registered accommodation generated 12.17 million nights in 1991, mainly from adjacent countries – Fig 25.4 indicates their origin.

	% nights
Netherlands	35.9
Germany	16.9
UK	10.3
France	9.9
USA	4.1
Italy	3.0
Spain	1.9

Fig. 25.4 Foreign visitor nights at Belgian registered tourist accommodation, 1991

Belgium's attractions do not draw people from far afield (apart from Americans who include Belgium on their European tour). The average length of stay is short (under two days) but the visitor population is made up of several types of tourist:

1 **Businesspeople and bureaucrats**, who stay very short periods in the more expensive hotels in Brussels, Belgium's capital, which is the headquarters of the EC, NATO and of many multinational companies.
2 **City break visitors** to Brussels and the 'heritage towns' of lowland Belgium. There are at least nine towns with extensive and well-preserved medieval

quarters, with Antwerp, Bruges and Ghent being the most popular. These three towns took 85 per cent of the urban visitor nights outside Brussels.

Bruges is an unspoilt medieval city (*see* Chapter 5) built around a network of canals. Its narrow winding streets, picturesque old gabled buildings and hump-backed bridges give it a special character, sometimes likened to Venice. It contains many medieval buildings, for example the Belfry and Cloth Hall dating from 1248, the Town Hall from 1376 and many 12th and 13th century churches. The city also has several museums including the Groeninge museum which houses many fine works of art.

Ghent has also retained its medieval centre. The Castle was built in 1180 but Ghent Belfry and Cloth Hall date from 1300 and 1452 respectively. St Bravos Cathedral, built in the 15th century, houses many fine works of art of the period. The city is also famed for its flower show and flower pageants. Antwerp's main square dates from the 16th century; its huge gothic cathedral is outstanding among its many fine churches and chapels.

Brussels, Belgium's capital, also retains some medieval buildings but the main central square (Grand Place) is the main focus of the city. It was rebuilt in 1696, and is flanked by the gothic-style Town Hall, the Maison du Roi, and the Guild Houses.

The medieval cities form the main attractions for visitors from the USA, Italy, Spain and Switzerland, while the Germans and British share their interest equally between the coast and the historic towns.

3 Holidaymakers who stay longer, mainly in self-catering accommodation and on the coast. Twenty-nine per cent of foreign visitor nights were to coastal locations, which were particularly attractive to the French, Germans and British visitors. The Dutch once again favoured inland destinations: 65 per cent of Dutch visitors to Belgium went to the countryside, particularly the Ardennes.

4 Day excursionists, who visit Belgium for shopping or day leisure trips. In 1985 it was estimated that Belgium received 15 million cross-border day visitors.

5 Transit tourists. Like The Netherlands, Belgium is strategically located on the European route network. Routes between the Paris basin and north Germany pass through Belgian territory, while ports, such as Ostend and Zeebrugge, receive ferry

traffic from the UK. It is estimated that seven million direct transit visitors passed through the country in 1985.

Outbound tourism from Belgium

France was the main destination for Belgian visitors with just over six million arrivals in 1989. Mediterranean destinations (Spain and Italy) were next in popularity while the Alps came third. There are thus striking similarities between the pattern of foreign travel of the Dutch and Belgians (although it has been noted that the Belgian market is smaller). Very few Dutch and Belgians stay in each other's countries, perhaps due to their mutual lack of outstanding physical tourist resources, their small size and the ease of day-tripping between them.

LUXEMBOURG

The total number of tourists to Luxembourg is small in European terms (only 760 000 staying visitors in 1988 and an estimated two million day visitors) but they are crucial to the economy of this tiny country. Tourism is Luxembourg's third most important industry, and the country relies very heavily on Belgium and The Netherlands, who together generate 72.6 per cent of all foreign visitor nights in Luxembourg. Much of the tourism is business-orientated (Luxembourg city is the headquarters of the EC bank and many other foreign banks) but some tourists visit Luxembourg's share of the Ardennes mountains.

The total population of Luxembourg is about 366 000. It generates about one quarter of a million tourist trips abroad each year, most to neighbouring countries.

GERMANY

Germany has been divided since the end of the Second World War. West Germany (or, officially, the Federal Republic of Germany) became a Western-style democracy. Its economy and currency has become one of the strongest in the world, so that the economic recession in the 1980s had less impact on Germany than on many other Western

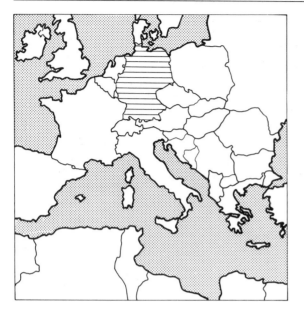

countries. Its continued economic growth made it an expensive country for foreigners to visit but gives its residents high spending power abroad. With an affluent population of over 61 million, it is a major tourist generating country.

East Germany (or the German Democratic Republic) was absorbed into the Communist bloc and its economic performance fell far behind that of West Germany. Travel between East and West Germany was gradually restricted until the building of the Berlin Wall in 1961 brought it finally to a complete halt. East German tourists were, therefore, limited to destinations within the Communist bloc. It was not until the era of 'glasnost' and 'perestroika' in the USSR and the collapse of Communism in 1989 that the borders were reopened, and the process of reunification began.

Full reunification was completed in October 1990, followed by a period of economic and political readjustment. The short-term economic impact of reunification has been most dramatic in Germany's eastern provinces (the former East Germany). The new valuation of their currency immediately increased affluence in the east in the short term but on the other hand many industrial and manufacturing businesses closed down as they were unable to compete with more efficient enterprises in the western German provinces. This led to a sharp increase in redundancies in the former East Germany and a slight decrease in real net

household incomes in 1991. The cost of supporting this unemployment has been borne mainly by the richer population of the western part of Germany: the economic consequences have been tax rises, higher inflation and cuts in Government expenditure, and a slow down in the growth of disposable incomes in 1991 for West Germans. The longer-term economic and political consequences of reunification remain to be seen: the period of readjustment may be far from over yet. The short-term effects of these changes on patterns of tourism in Germany are as yet difficult to discern as comparable pre- and post-1990 statistics are not available. It is suggested that immediately after reunification there was a sharp but temporary increase in travel from former east to west Germany but once the need to visit friends and relatives was fulfilled, East Germans have turned increasingly to foreign travel (again to fulfil demands that had been frustrated for so many years by communist travel restrictions).

In 1990 only about 25 per cent of East Germans travelled abroad but in 1991 this sharply increased to 45 per cent. However, the worsening economic situation in the eastern provinces may explain the fact that this fell back to 40 per cent in 1992.

The residents of the western provinces of Germany also took the opportunity to travel into formerly forbidden territory and domestic travel into the eastern provinces has increased, a trend that has been sustained into the early 1990s. Foreign travel generated by West Germans appears to have declined a little in the early 1990s, again perhaps an indication of the relative worsening of the economic position of the western part of Germany.

The overall effect of this has been in the short term a steadying of the growth of outbound travel from Germany: the drop in West Germans' outbound travel has been balanced by the increase in foreign travel from the eastern provinces. However, even with these setbacks the German economy is still very strong and the country remains one of the world's major tourist generators.

GERMANY'S PHYSICAL RESOURCES

Germany can be divided into five main physical regions (see Fig 25.5):

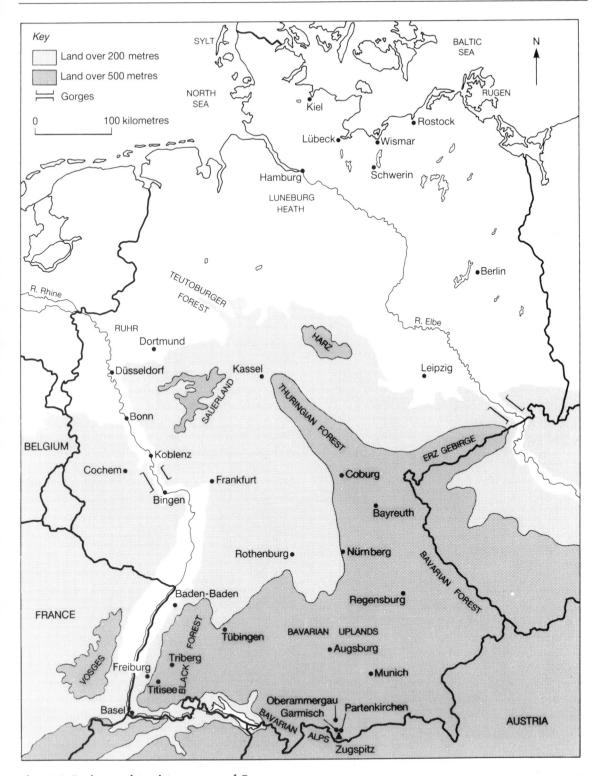

Fig. 25.5 Regions and tourist resources of Germany

1 the coast;
2 a section of the North European plain;
3 the central uplands, including the Harz mountains in the north and the Black Forest in the south;
4 the Bavarian Alps; and
5 The Rhine Valley, including the Rhine Gorge.

The coast

Germany has a short coastline in relation to its size. The North Sea coast is fringed with low sand dunes and gently sloping mud flats. The climate is cool, with a summer average of 15–17° C, and humid. On the island of Sylt the dunes are much bigger and the beaches more sandy, and in spite of the climate, a popular seaside resort has grown up which caters mainly for the domestic market. The coastline is broken by three estuaries which provide opportunities for sailing. The port of Hamburg is sited on the Elbe estuary. The Baltic coast is a more attractive and varied, though subdued, coastline, consisting of bays, inlets, sand bars and spits, low cliffs and drowned moraines (which give a fretted and broken coastline such as on Rügen island). The self-catering holiday centres of the Baltic coast put it among the top six most popular domestic holiday regions of western Germany, but it is bypassed by international visitors.

The resorts of Poel Island (offshore of Wismar) and Rostock are also crowded and popular seaside resorts for the east German domestic market. Kiel is a major ferry port which links Germany with the Scandinavian countries across the Baltic sea.

The North European plain

The landscape here is one of subdued relief, with rolling sandy heaths (e.g. Lüneburg) on the higher land and lakes in the hollows. The lakes become more frequent towards the east. The picturesque town of Schwerin is located on one of these lakes. The region attracts few holidaymakers, however, as the lowlands of the Nordrhein-Westphalia region are heavily industrialised (for example in the Ruhr region) and are the focus of business tourism only.

The central uplands

These varied broken uplands are most heavily used for tourism on their northern section (close to the heavily populated industrial regions of Germany) and on their southernmost edge.

The northern block includes the attractive scenery of the Sauerland, Teutoburger forest and the Harz mountains. All are popular domestic tourist destinations. The Sauerland borders the industrial area; it rises to just over 900 m and is a mixture of forests, rivers and lakes, with many caves. The Teutoburger hills are much lower, consisting of parallel forested scarps running into the north German plain. Again, their accessibility from industrial Germany explains their popularity, rather than any exceptional quality of their scenery. The isolated block of the Harz mountains rises to over 1250 m and has heavy winter snowfall which warrants the development of winter sports resorts. The northern edge of the Harz is steep with rocky cliffs, but the mountain tops are rounded with subdued relief. In places this high moorland is cut by deep forested valleys. The Thuringian Forest to the south of the Harz is a long, steep-sided ridge, also eaten into by deeply incised valleys. It has an even colder winter climate, with considerable winter snowfall. The ridge continues eastward into the highly dissected forest plateau of the Erzgebirge, which is bounded by a precipitous scarp on its SE side. This northern section of the central uplands is bounded by the Rhine Gorge to the west, and the Elbe Gorge to the east (on the Czech-German frontier). The Elbe gorge is located in a region known as 'Saxon Switzerland'. The Elbe has eroded the sandstone rock into craggy landscapes that are almost desert- and canyon-like, and has cut a dramatic deep cliffed gorge (200 m deep) through this landscape.

The southern half of Germany's central uplands includes two main tourist regions: the Black Forest and the Bavarian Forest (*see* Fig 25.5). The Black Forest is the second most important tourist area for both the foreign and domestic markets, taking 15 per cent of all tourist bednights in 1990. It is a highly dissected plateau rising to 1635 m in the south, bounded by steep slopes to its south and west. The landscape is a mixture of dramatic, deep valleys, forest, open moorland and mountain pastures. There are many holiday resorts with a variety of self-catering and family accommodation. Baden-Baden is a well established spa town, whose reputation was based on hot mineralised springs. There are many other spa towns in the area, while Triberg and the lakeside resort at Titisee are also tourist centres. Freiburg is a quaint university town with a gothic cathedral dating from the twelfth century. Tübingen lies to the west of the Black Forest and is an outstanding example of a well preserved medieval town. The Bavarian Forest is an area with a similar landscape, though perhaps more heavily wooded and not attaining the heights of the Black Forest. This region is also famous for the Wagner Festival held at Bayreuth, and for the unspoilt medieval towns such as Regensburg.

The Bavarian uplands and plateaux lie between the Black Forest and the Bavarian Forest. This region also has many historic and cultural centres set in attractive landscapes, including Rothenberg, an unspoilt medieval town encircled by its original city walls and Augsburg, which has buildings dating from the ninth to the 18th centuries. Munich is the capital of Bavaria and is a major cultural centre, but is also famous for its beers celebrated at the Oktoberfest, and also for the Fasching carnival.

Germany is famed for ancient towns that have been bypassed by modern development, and attractive examples can be found throughout the central uplands in southern Germany, for example Heidelberg.

The Bavarian Alps

The far south of Germany just reaches the first ranges of the Alps, and the German-Austrian border runs along the crest of the Calcareous Alps. The Zugspitz is the highest peak in Germany at 2968 m, and winter sports resorts, such as Garmisch and Partenkirchen are located nearby. Oberammergau, location of the Passion Play that is held once every ten years, is also sited in this area (*see* Fig 25.5). Bavaria as a whole (i.e. the Alps and the uplands) is the most popular tourist region in Germany for both domestic and overseas visitors, with 28.8 per cent of all tourist bednights in 1990.

The Rhine Valley

The Rhine flows north from the Alps along a wide, flat-floored north-south trench from Basel to Frankfurt. The Black Forest rises to the east while the Vosges mountains flank the river on the French side of the valley. Between Frankfurt and Bonn, the valley becomes much narrower where the river has cut a steep-sided gorge through the surrounding

uplands. The most dramatic landscape is between Koblenz and Bingen (*see* Fig 25.5). South-facing slopes are terraced for vineyards and the ruins of medieval castles are perched on crags above the river. River cruises along the Rhine have been popular for many years, but the region is more popular with foreign tourists than the domestic market.

Boppard and Rudesheim are the most popular resorts that form the focal point of many Rhine cruises. They are located in the most dramatic gorge section of the Rhine. Some cruises also visit Cochem on the Moselle. These resorts are characterised by steep narrow streets sloping down to riverside promenades, and by many lively wine taverns.

As well as being an important tourist resource, the Rhine Valley is a very important route carrying tourist traffic from the industrial areas of the Ruhr south to the Alps and beyond.

Up to 1990, inbound tourism has been concentrated on the Rhineland, the Black Forest and Bavarian Alps. Changes in the regional distribution of tourism following reunification will take time to become established. The short-term effect has been an increase in domestic day excursions across the old border in both directions. In 1990 there was a chronic shortage of international standard hotel accommodation in former East German territory, and staying tourism (apart from VFR travel) cannot increase until the new tourist infrastructure is provided. Meanwhile a transitional phase is expected, characterised by day-trips to the east from hotels based in former West German border towns (such as Lübeck, Coburg and Kassel).

TOURISM IN GERMANY

(N.B. pre-1990 statistics relate to West Germany only.) It is estimated that foreign and domestic tourists generated a minimum of 255 million tourist nights in registered tourist accommodation in Germany in 1990. The domestic market accounted for 86 per cent (220 million) of these, but it is not growing fast – it grew from 11.2 million holidays in 1985 to only 12.6 million in 1988). This is because each year more Germans travel abroad (20.9 million in 1985 to 28.6 million in 1989), although outbound travel is reported to have dropped to 24 million in 1992. Germans have always preferred to stay in hotels, boarding houses or inns but recent-

	Bednights in registered accommodation (%)	Purpose of visit %			
		Holidays	VFR	Business	Transit
Netherlands	19.4	–	–	–	
USA	14.7	37	20	20	
UK	8.8	31	25	37	
France	4.8	29	25	46	
Denmark	4.6	47	13	4	32
Switzerland	4.5	41	28	31	
Italy	4.3	–	–	–	
Sweden	4.0	36	17	6	34
Belgium	3.6	54	25	9	12
Australia	3.4	–	–	–	
Japan	3.4	40	14	36	

Fig. 25.6 Foreign visitors to West Germany, 1987

ly self-catering accommodation has become a little more popular, with much of this new capacity being located in Bavaria.

Figure 25.6 shows that in 1987, West Germany attracted a large number of visitors from a wide range of countries for many different purposes, but that the average length of stay was estimated as only four nights. A fairly low proportion came for holidays, reflecting the high cost of travel to a country with a strong currency and high standard of living. A surprisingly high proportion visited friends and relatives (particularly from USA and UK, perhaps partly associated with the stationing of NATO troops in West Germany). A high proportion of visitors from UK, France, Switzerland

and Japan were on business trips: many international trade fairs and conferences take place in Germany, for example, at Hannover, Hamburg, Düsseldorf, Cologne, Stuttgart and Munich, and it is estimated that the business travel market is expanding faster than the holiday trade. About a third of the visitors from Scandinavia were in transit, on their way south.

However, many transit visitors do not stay overnight in the country. Figure 25.7 gives an estimate of the breakdown of border arrivals in 1985. The huge number of transit travellers underlines Germany's strategic location on routes to France, the Alps and the Mediterranean. The number of day-trippers (particularly shoppers) from Eastern Europe (e.g. the former East Germany and Poland) rose very rapidly in 1989.

	Estimated number of visits (million)
Tourist arrivals	28
Excursionists (i.e. day visits on leisure or shopping trips)	100
Direct transit travellers (i.e. passing through without stopping)	70

Fig. 25.7 Estimated border arrivals of foreign tourists to West Germany, 1985

Outbound tourism from Germany

Outbound tourism from west Germany has grown steadily through the worst of the recession. However, the proportion of West Germans taking holidays and the proportion of these holidays taken abroad is increasing (*see* Fig 25.8). Also an increasing proportion of holidays are package trips and more are by plane to more distant destinations.

West Germans are the world's second biggest spenders (after USA) on travel and tourism,

	1970	1975	1980	1985	1988	1992
% population taking a holiday	42	56	58	57	65	71
% taking holidays abroad	53	54	60	66	68	70
% taking holidays by car	61	61	59	60	59	55
% taking holidays by plane	8	12	16	18	20	26
% taking package tours	17	18	26	34	38	39

Note: Figures for 1970–88 refer to West Germany only.

Fig. 25.8 Growth of tourism in Germany

accounting for about 13 per cent of total travel expenditure worldwide in 1991. The tourist industries of many European countries rely very heavily on the West German outbound market.

The Mediterranean has been the most popular destination for West Germans for many years (accounting for at least 44 per cent of their foreign holiday visits in 1988). Italy is the most easily accessible Mediterranean destination that Germans can reach by road. Spain is, however, rapidly increasing in popularity, and in 1989, was as popular a destination as Italy but it appears to be losing its appeal with the environmentally conscious West German

	1982 (million)	Holiday visits 1985 (million)	1989 (million)	1989 (%)
Italy	3.6	3.9	4.8	16.7
Spain	3.2	3.5	4.9	17.1
Austria	3.3	3.2	4.3	15.0
France	1.6	1.7	2.4	8.3
former Yugoslavia	1.2	1.8	1.5	5.2
Greece	0.6	0.9	1.2	4.1
Switzerland	0.6	0.8	1.0	3.4
Turkey	–	–	1.0	3.4
Netherlands	0.7	0.6	1.1	3.8
Denmark	0.7	0.7	0.9	3.1
Scandinavia	0.2	0.5	0.6	2.0
UK	0.3	0.4	0.6	2.0
Outside Europe	1.4	1.5	3.5	12.2

Fig. 25.9 German outbound tourism (west Germans)

market (showing a 20 per cent drop in German arrivals between 1985 and 1989). The Alps (Austria and Switzerland) account for 18.4 per cent of German foreign holiday trips and Scandinavia 5.1 per cent (*see* Fig 25.9).

The trends shown in Figure 25.9 may change significantly in response to the economic and political changes in Germany itself. The years 1990 (the year of unification in Germany and of the break-up of Yugoslavia) and 1991 (the Gulf War) both disrupted the established patterns of German outbound travel. The available figures for 1992 and 1993 indicate a resumed increase in German arrivals in many destinations: Spain, Portugal and (after 1991) Turkey and Cyprus showed significant gains, as did many long-haul destinations. German long-haul travel continued to expand even through the crises of 1990 and 1991. Most of these trips are to the United States but numbers fluctuate according to the relative strengths of the dollar and Deutschmark. The Far East is the second most important destination region, with a high proportion of business travellers to countries such as Japan and Singapore. However, Thailand attracted nearly 100 000 German visitors in 1985, most of whom were holiday tourists. Other popular long-haul holiday destinations include Sri Lanka, the Maldives, Kenya, Singapore and Hong Kong.

The growth of German arrivals to most of these destinations was also in double figures during the early part of 1993.

CONCLUSION

Just as the divide between East and West Germany has been removed, so the political divide between the countries of Central and Eastern Europe has also been lifted. The two regions should no longer be considered in isolation. The physical units of Benelux and Germany extend eastwards and they share many ethnic and historic characteristics with Eastern Europe. Up to 1990 the two regions operated as two separate tourist areas. The Eastern European countries had well established domestic tourist markets but very limited international tourism except some travel between them (particularly to the better coast and climates to the south of the then Communist bloc).

Benelux and Germany were integrated into the tourist flows of Western Europe with strong coastward and southerly tourist flows to other European and Mediterranean countries. The possibility of east–west travel may create new patterns of tourism to be superimposed on these predominantly north–south tourist flows. It is likely that the relative economic performance (rather than the political affiliations) of the countries of Central and Eastern Europe may play the more significant role in shaping these new travel patterns. The new patterns of domestic travel evolving within the boundaries of the now united Germany may be mirrored in changing patterns of international tourism.

FURTHER READING

Belgium

Cockerell, N (1993) 'Belgium and Luxembourg', *EIU International Tourism Reports*, No. 3, pp. 4–28.

Germany

Agel, P (1994) 'Germany', *EIU International Tourism Reports*, No. 2, pp. 21–40.

Cockerell, N (1993) 'Germany Outbound' *EIU Travel and Tourism Analyst*, No. 2, pp. 19–34.

Godau, A (1991) 'Tourism policy in the new Germany' *Tourism Management*, Vol. 12, June, pp. 145–50.

Luxembourg

Smith, R V (1992) 'Tourism's role in the economy and landscape of Luxembourg', *Tourism Management*, Vol. 13, December, pp. 423–7.

The Netherlands

Bywater, M (1994) 'Netherlands', *EIU International Tourism Reports*, No. 1, pp. 45–64.

QUESTIONS AND DISCUSSION POINTS

1 What effect has the reunification of Germany had on patterns of German tourism?

2 How does the physical nature of The Netherlands appear to influence the pattern of Dutch domestic and outbound tourism?

3 Belgium has been described as being located at the 'crossroads of Europe'. In what ways does its inbound tourism reflect this strategic location in Europe?

ASSIGNMENTS

1 You are a travel journalist. Write a short article for the travel column of a Sunday newspaper on the range of special interest holidays in the Benelux countries.

2 You work for the British Tourist Authority. The Authority is planning a survey of German visitors to Britain to find out the appeal of Britain to the Germans, the characteristics of their visits and expenditure, and their satisfaction with their visit to Britain. The survey results will be used: (*a*) in a marketing drive in Germany; and (*b*) to help design policies to increase British attractions to the Germans. Write a briefing paper for the head of the research team on the nature of the German outbound market at present and design a draft questionnaire for the survey and suggest when and where the interviews might be carried out.

CHAPTER 26

Eastern Europe and the CIS

LEARNING OBJECTIVES

After reading this chapter you should be able to
- assess the tourist potential of the climatic, landscape, historical and cultural resources of the Eastern European countries and the CIS
- be aware of the profound political and economic changes taking place in Eastern Europe and the CIS and their implications for the development of domestic, inbound and outbound tourism in each country.

INTRODUCTION

Eastern Europe is an easterly extension of the non-Mediterranean core of Europe, and it is made up of the territories of Poland, the Czech and Slovak Republics, Hungary, Bulgaria and Romania, and the Baltic States.

Physically they are made up of:

1 An easterly extension of the Northern European plain (running into north Poland and the Baltic States).

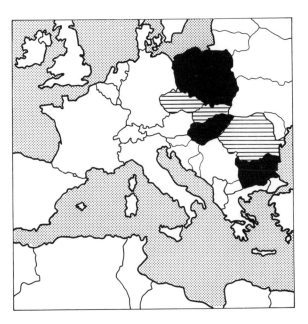

2 An easterly extension of the Northern European uplands.

3 The Carpathian mountains (which extend into the Slovak Republic and Romania from the easterly end of the Alps).

4 The plains of the Danube. The Danube flows from the Alps, southeastwards to the Black Sea. Its lower valley is cut into two sections (by the southern tongue of the Carpathians). The first part of the valley consists of the wide open, rolling plains of Hungary, while the other is located in southern Romania.

5 The Balkan mountains of Bulgaria. These two fingers of uplands run east-west from the Dalmatian mountains towards the Black Sea.

The countries of this region were part of the Communist bloc. The series of revolutions in 1989 and 1990 removed their Communist regimes and they began the difficult political and economic transition from centrally planned to market economies. Before 1990 they had formed the political buffer between Western Europe and the USSR. The Soviet Union's vast territory stretched almost halfway round the world from the Baltic Sea to the Pacific (through virtually 170° of longitude). It consisted of 15 republics, of which the Republic of Russia itself is by far the largest. The political geography of the region is continuing to evolve. In 1990 and 1991 the three Baltic republics of Latvia, Lithuania and Estonia became fully independent, and the remaining 12 republics of the former USSR became the Commonwealth of Independent States in December 1991.

Meanwhile demands for greater autonomy in parts of Czechoslovakia led to the peaceful separation of the country into two independent states, the Czech Republic and the Slovak Republic. The split formally came into operation from 1 January 1993.

Up to 1990 the USSR and the Eastern European countries had significant domestic tourism (the Communist regimes providing for workers' holidays) and some international travel was allowed between them (and to other Communist countries of the world) though information about their tourist industries was not always easily accessible. However, since 1990, the rapid changes under way in their economies have caused their populations some hardship in the short and medium term. Inflation has gathered pace, reaching peak rates of 700 per cent p.a. in Poland, 100 per cent in Romania and 1028 per cent in Bulgaria between 1990 and 1992; while GDP has declined (e.g. by over 11 per cent in Poland in 1990, 9 per cent in Hungary in 1991, 35 per cent in Czechoslovakia in 1991/92 and 10 per cent in Bulgaria). Economic forecasters anticipate some improvement in the mid-1990s. In spite of their economic problems, all the former Communist countries responded to the lifting of travel restrictions with an immediate surge of outbound tourism, in 1989 and 1990. Since then this flow has steadied in some countries (e.g. the CIS and Romania) while travel out of Poland has continued to grow.

New patterns of tourism (both domestic and outbound) are in the process of evolving in the region and it will take time for these trends to emerge and stabilise while these countries go through the difficult period of political and economic restructuring.

POLAND

Poland has the largest population of all the Eastern European countries at 38.1 million in 1990. It is one of the most heavily industrialised, but its industrial technology is outdated and its infrastructure is poor. The manufacturing and mining industries provide 28.4 per cent of Poland's jobs. Before the fall of communism the country was the major generator of outbound tourism, as Poles had relative freedom of travel in the 1970s. Inbound and outbound tourism both showed huge increases in 1989 itself but since then economic problems have damped down this growth. In Poland unemployment has grown to two million in 1992. GDP stood at US $3810 per head in 1993 but had fallen each year from 1989 to 1992 and the standard of living has dropped by 30 per cent. However, the private sector is growing fast and forecasters expect an improvement in the economy from the mid-1990s. In the short term these economic problems have led to a decline in the travel propensity of the Polish population (in 1990 53 per cent of the population travelled at home or abroad, while in 1991 this had dropped to 49 per cent). The domestic tourist market decreased from 47 per cent of the population to 44 per cent, but outbound holiday travel has still grown.

It is estimated that there were six million outbound trips (involving staying at least one night abroad) in 1990 and eight million in 1991 though outbound tourists spent very little. Day excursions abroad leapt from under ten million in 1988 to an estimated 13 million in 1989, but appear to have grown little since then, in fact outbound border crossings (for all purposes) dropped from 22 million in 1990 to 20.8 million in 1991. It is thought that in 1991, about a quarter of Poles travelling abroad went to shop or look for work.

The rapid inflation (still at 80 per cent in 1991) has pushed up prices in the country, and made a relatively cheap destination rather more expensive for the inbound tourist. However, foreign arrivals in Poland have continued to grow; the numbers of staying visitors grew slowly from 3.4 million in 1990, to 3.8 million in 1991 and four million in 1992. These economic factors have less effect on day trippers, and the number of day visitors has rocketed from less than eight million in 1989, to over 30 million in 1991. Thus the economic situation has greatly influenced the volume and development of inbound and outbound tourism since the fall of communism.

The spatial patterns of tourism into and out of Poland have also changed (*see* Figs 26.1 and 26.2).

	1988 %	1991 %
West Germany	11.0 ⎫	
East Germany	21.8 ⎭	44
USSR/CIS	17.7	7
Czechoslovakia	19.0	14
Hungary	8.0	9
Bulgaria	6.2	–
Holland	0.03	6
France	0.1	5
Italy	0.11	3
Belgium	–	3
Rest of world	16.1	18.0
Total number est.	10 mill	20.8 mill

Fig. 26.1 Poland outbound travel

	1988	1991
Western Europe (excluding Germany)	619	1 299
West Germany	522 ⎫	
East Germany	1 081 ⎭	20 885
USSR/CIS	1 739	7 545
Czechoslovakia	1 417	6 101
Hungary	567	179
Rest of Europe	72	358
Rest of world	178	478
Total	6.195 mill	36.845 mill

Fig. 26.2 Poland inbound frontier arrivals ('000)
(*Source*: WTO)

There have been huge increases in cross-border travel from Germany, CIS and Czechoslovakia into Poland between 1988 and 1991 while travel from other Western European countries has doubled but is at a much more modest level as yet. Outbound travel is more heavily concentrated on Germany than before, though travel to other Western European countries has grown very strongly. CIS and Czechoslovakia in particular have lost their market share. A huge proportion of the travel (in both directions) is for shopping, business and visiting friends and relatives, and will therefore be based on the towns in the most heavily urbanised parts of the countries concerned. Nevertheless,

Poland has many natural and cultural resources for tourism which may form the focus of holiday-based tourism in future. The shortage of Western-standard hotels and the reliance of many inbound tourists on friends, relatives and on camping for accommodation all indicate the lack of a developed tourist infrastructure in most of its tourist regions.

Poland's tourist regions

The Baltic sea coast

The Baltic sea is one of the world's enclosed sea environments (*see* Chapter 3) and has a very low tidal range, and rarely experiences large storm waves. The 524 km of the Polish coast is, therefore, one of marine deposition, and is characterised by the accumulation of sand dunes, spits and narrow sand bars all along the coast. These cut off lagoons on their landward side. Locally the waters are heavily polluted, e.g. at Gdansk, but elsewhere the broad sandy beaches are heavily used for domestic tourists, particularly at the beach resorts of Swinoujscie (for Stettin), Kolobrzeg, Ustka, Leba, Hel and Sopot (the local resort for Gdansk) (*see* Fig 26.3). Although it meets domestic needs, the region has climatic limitations and is unlikely to attract large numbers of international visitors: the July average temperature is only 17.7° C, at Swinoujscie, and the summer months of June, July and August are the wettest, although the annual total is fairly low at 627 mm and decreases eastwards. However, its proximity to the Scandinavian market may encourage more visitors from Norway and Sweden, particularly as there are good summer ferry connections into Gdansk and Swinoujscie.

Gdansk has rebuilt its historic centre but is better known now as the birthplace of Solidarity. It is also a major port, business and ship-building centre.

In 1991, 13.4 per cent of Poland's overseas visitors came to this region.

The northern plains of Poland

Poland's share of the north European plain is studded with shallow lakes, which formed in the hollows between glacial moraines deposited in the last ice age. Poland has more lakes than any other European country (except Finland). The well-wooded Mazurian lake district is the best known region, with picturesque landscapes of lakes nestling between the steep-sided but low hills. The area is used for camping, walking, and boating activities. 8.9 per cent of Poland's foreign tourists visited this region in 1991. The plains south of the lake zones are featureless and open with few trees. Warsaw, Poland's capital since 1596, is sited on the southern edge of these plains. Its historic centre is a World Heritage site (see Chapter 5) and has been rebuilt and completely restored after being severely damaged in the Second World War. Warsaw and the densely populated central zone of Poland received around 60 per cent of overseas visitors in 1991. As a high proportion of inbound tourism is business tourism and visiting friends and relatives it is not surprising that such tourism is concentrated in the more urbanised and industrial areas of Poland rather than the holiday zones.

The hills and mountains of southern Poland

The plains rise gradually southwest to the tilted block of the Sudeten hills, which are dominated by Krkonose. The mountains are used by large numbers of Polish day-trippers from the nearby Silesian industrial region.

SE Poland and the Carpathians

This region is rich in natural and historic tourist resources and it attracted nearly 12 per cent of overseas visitors in 1991. Again, the plains rise gradually south until they reach the ridge of the Beskid Mountains near the Polish–Czech and Slovak borders. The main ranges of the Carpathian mountains lie beyond the Beskids. The highest group is the Tatra mountains (in the 217 km^2 national park); they are glaciated granite and limestone mountains with dramatic alpine landscapes; and prolonged winter snow cover. Zakopane is a busy all year round resort catering for walkers and climbers in summer and skiers in the winter season (December to March). The historic city of Krakow is 100 km north of the Tatras. It has been a university town since 1364 and flourished in medieval times as it was sited on the crossing points of important trade routes. It has the largest medieval square in Europe

and has many churches, museums and art galleries; the town escaped destruction in the Second World War and is listed by UNESCO among the top 12 art cities of the world. Nearby are cultural attractions of a different kind; for example the Wieliczka Saltmines, which have been worked for 5500 years, are 13 km east of Krakow (see Fig 26.3). They contain many intricate religious statues carved out of the salt: some date from medieval times.

The sombre site of Oswiecim (Auschwitz) lies 54 km to the west of Krakow. The Auschwitz and Birkenau concentration camps are now museums and memorials. The Ojcow National Park is 22 km north of Krakow; it has a landscape of forested valleys, cliffs and caves. Czestochowa is a little further north again, where the Jasna Gora monastery is a place of Christian pilgrimage for the Poles. All the sites are busy with visitors, from all over Poland, but particularly from the nearby industrial regions. Krakow, the saltmines and Auschwitz are World Heritage sites, and the combination of resources in the Krakow region may well also appeal to the Western European tourist market.

The Bieszczady Mountains National Park is located in the far southeast corner of Poland. This, too, is a World Heritage site: like all Polish National Parks, it is subject to policies of environmental protection, but it is still used for summer hiking and winter cross-country skiing.

FORMER CZECHOSLOVAKIA

Czechoslovakia divided into two separate countries as of 1 January 1993. The western half of the country (the Bohemian Massif) became the Czech Republic while the eastern half (an upland area dominated by the Tatra Mountains) became the Slovak Republic. The border more or less follows the Odra-Moravia corridor, a belt of open rolling countryside which carries important N-S routes which link the industrial region of Poland to Austria and Hungary. It is also former Czechoslovakia's main industrial region (see Fig 26.3).

Czechoslovakia had the biggest and best organised tourist industry of the Eastern European countries. It had a good network of hotels and campsites throughout the country. Before 1989

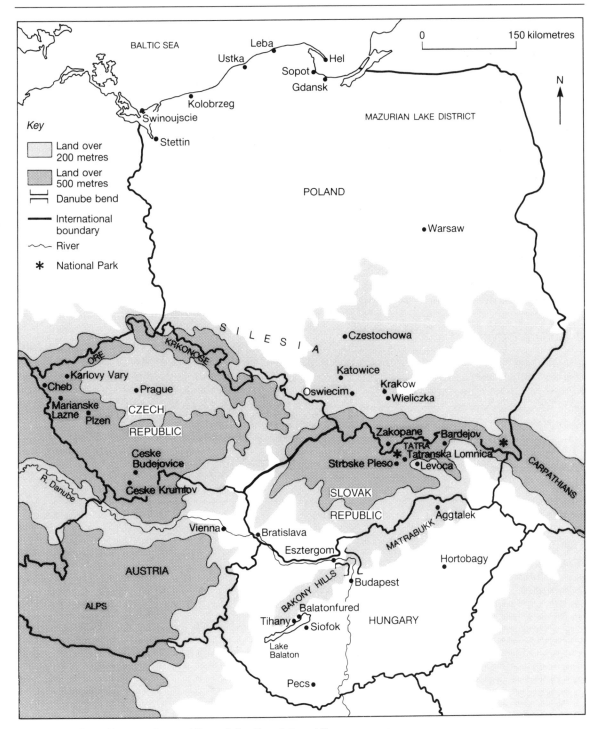

Fig. 26.3 Poland, the Czech Republic and the Slovak Republic

Czechoslovakia had the biggest inbound tourist industry of all the East European Communist states, with 24.6 million arrivals, though the vast majority of these came from Czechoslovakia's communist neighbours (*see* Fig 26.5) and most of them were classified as excursionists. The non-Communist visitors showed completely the opposite pattern of behaviour. Eighty-two per cent were staying visitors rather than excursionists, and most travelled for pleasure (though 17 per cent came for business reasons).

Czechoslovakia was also a heavily industrialised state, whose industry was based on the burning of low quality coal in large quantities which caused widespread environmental pollution. Czechoslovakia's extensive forests have thus been badly affected by acid rain. Nevertheless, it was among the most affluent of the Eastern European countries, with a relatively low national foreign debt. It was perhaps better placed to weather the difficulties of economic restructuring, and with a population of 15.5 million, had the potential to generate significant outbound tourism, particularly as it is a mountainous landlocked country lacking any major resources for water-based tourism. In 1988, outbound tourism had grown to 7.25 million but most was to other communist countries (*see* Fig 26.4), and a third were day-trippers. The most popular destinations were the adjacent countries of Hungary, East Germany and Poland, while most Western travel was to West Germany or Austria. Most travel to the West was for business trips, and the numbers travelling were very small.

After the fall of communism, Czechoslovakia's economy fared badly, with a 15 per cent drop in real GDP in 1991, from a value of 3140 US dollars per head in 1990. In spite of these economic prob-

lems, travel into and out of Czechoslovakia showed huge increases between 1989 and 1991. Outbound tourism, for example, grew from 8.5 million border crossings in 1989 to 20.6 million in 1990 and 39.6 million in 1991, though the majority were day-trippers who spent very little money abroad. Although the numbers of trips increased so dramatically between 1990 and 1991, the total tourist expenditure by Czechs dropped from 636 million US dollars to 393 million, a clear indication of the country's economic problems.

Three-quarters of the trips were to Western destinations and the most favoured Western European destinations were still Germany and Austria but with hugely increased numbers of visitors (15.3m and 14.1 m respectively). The number of Czechoslovakian visitors to Poland also grew substantially between 1990 and 1991 (from 1.3 m to 6.1 m) while outbound trips to Hungary hardly increased at all (at around 3.8 m).

Inbound tourism has also been transformed since 1988: the volume of travel has more than doubled (*see* Fig 26.5). Visitors from the combined territories of Germany still make up about 41 per cent of Czechoslovakia's visitors, while the number of Poles has doubled and Austria's market share has increased dramatically from 1.2 per cent to 11.5 per cent. Border crossings from Hungary into Czechoslovakia have, on the other hand, decreased substantially.

	1988	market share (%)	1991	market share (%)
Frontier arrivals* from:				
West Germany	619	2.5 ⎫	26 634	41.1
East Germany	9395	38.2 ⎭		
Hungary	6387	25.9	3709	5.7
Poland	4774	19.4	8546	13.1
Austria	316	1.2	7506	11.5
Others				
Total	24.59 mill		64.80 mill	

* includes day-trippers

Fig. 26.5 Czechoslovakian inbound tourism: number of frontier arrivals ('000s)

	1988	(% to West)	1991	(% to West)
Excursionist	2.34	0.7%	est 33.6 ⎫	
Staying visitor	4.91	(13.7%)	est 6.0 ⎭	75%
Total	7.25		39.6	

Fig. 26.4 Czechoslovakian outbound tourism (millions)

From 1993, the tourist statistics will reflect the division of former Czechoslovakia. The Czech Republic with a population of about 10.3 million may be expected to generate the greater amount of outbound tourism. Up to 1993, more foreign investment in tourism infrastructure had occurred in this part of former Czechoslovakia. However, the two new Republics face a further period of economic and political readjustment, which may slow down the rate of foreign investment.

Czech Republic

The country has an area of 78 864 km^2 (about a quarter of the size of the British Isles) with a population of 10.3 million in 1990. The capital is Prague. The city lies at the centre of the country, in a bowl, the rim of which is formed by a series of mountain ridges (*see* Fig 26.3). The Polish–Czech Republic border follows the crestline of the Krkonose (or Giant) mountains. These have rounded tops and are cut by forested valleys and receive heavy snowfall in winter. Harrachov is an old established ski centre. This and other resorts are promoted for both winter and summer tourism.

The German–Czech border follows first the Krusne Hory (Ore) mountains and then the ridge of the Bohemian forest (the Sumava mountains). All these forests have been particularly badly affected by acid rain. Prague is a major European art centre with a wealth of buildings of architectural and historic interest, including an area of medieval castles along the hilltops above the river Moldau. There is also a major art and music festival held in Prague in Spring.

Apart from Prague, most of the other tourist attractions lie around the edge of the region, just inside the mountain rim. There are smaller unspoilt medieval towns at Cheb, Ceske Budejovice and Cesky Krumlov. In the west there are a series of spa towns: Karlovy Vary (Carlsbad) is a Victorian-style spa town, based on 12 hot mineral springs, and Marianske Lazne which also expanded in the 19th century, has 140 mineral springs. The industrial city of Plzen is nearby, and is famous as the home of the pilsner beer brewery.

The summer tourist season runs from May to October. The hottest month (July) reaches a temperature of 19° C in Prague, but June, July and August are the wettest months of the year. The winters are cold and dry, and average January temperatures fall to minus 21° C at Karlovy Vary and Ceske Budejovice. Snowfall is light except in the mountain regions.

Slovak Republic

This new country is small (only 49 035 km^2), with a population of 5.3 million in 1990. Its capital is Bratislava. The Tatra mountains form the core of the country (*see* Fig 26.3). The triangular peaks rise to 2655 m and are massive and craggy. The lower slopes are densely forested, while alpine vegetation survives above 1800 m. The 50 000 km^2 Tatra National Park provides a refuge for chamois, wildcats, lynxes, bears and wolves. The highest peaks hold permanent snow, and snow lies for about seven months above 750 m. Precipitation is highest in summer, but the clear dry winter weather allows annual sunshine totals to reach 2000 hours. Resorts such as Stary Smokovec and Tatranska Lomnica function as both winter and summer resorts, while Strbske Pleso and Novy Smokovec are also promoted as health resorts. Ridges from the High Tatras run southwest, while the low Tatras lie due south. These mountains' tops tend to be more rounded and less scenically dramatic, except where limestone outcrops, to produce the splintered and craggy skylines characteristic of the Calcareous Alps, and caverns with stalactites and stalagmites below ground. In addition to the natural attraction of the region, there are unspoilt medieval towns such as Levoca and Bardejov.

HUNGARY

Hungary has a population of 10.7 million and a GDP in 1990 of US $ 2780 per head. Since the fall of communism the Hungarian economy too has gone through several bad years with high inflation and falls in GDP in both 1990 and 1991, but economic forecasters expect resumed growth from 1993. The country is thought to be the most economically and politically stable of the Eastern European region and its programme of economic reform (begun in 1968) is more advanced than those of its neighbours. Even before 1989 its tourist industry was well established (the second biggest in Eastern Europe after Czechoslovakia) and it was a popular holiday destination for Czechs, Poles and East Germans. However, it has actively encouraged Western tourists for sometime, particularly from the mid-1980s when Western tourists (mainly from Austria and West Germany) passed the total of two million a year. Another 1.4 million Western visitors travelled into Hungary on day trips.

By 1988, nearly 30 per cent of Hungary's visitors came from non-communist countries. The total number of frontier arrivals from all sources reached 17.9 million in that year. Foreign arrivals more than doubled immediately after the 1989 revolutions (to a peak of 37.6 million in 1990). Most of these new visitors came from Austria, Germany, Yugoslavia and Romania (*see* Fig 26.6). Eastern European arrivals dropped sharply in 1991 resulting in a drop in total numbers to 33.2 million, but Western tourism to Hungary continued its strong growth that year in spite of the international political situation.

	1988	1991
Austria	3.8	5.8
Czechoslovakia	3.5	3.8
Poland	2.8	2.5
E Germany	1.6 }	4.0
W Germany	1.2 }	
Yugoslavia	2.0	5.1
USSR	0.7	1.2
Romania	0.2	6.8
Italy	0.2	0.4
Netherlands	0.1	0.2
Turkey	–	0.9
Rest of world	1.86	2.56
Total	17.96 m*	33.26 m**

*(of which 10.5 m were staying visitors)
**(of which 20.8 m were staying visitors)

Fig. 26.6 Hungary inbound frontier arrivals (millions)
(*Source*: WTO)

Outbound travel by Hungarians to the West also grew steadily in the 1980s in the run-up to the revolutions of 1989, reaching one million in 1987. The total level of outbound tourism to all destina-

tions doubled between 1985 and 1988 (*see* Fig 26.7) but has climbed only slowly since then. This is in particular contrast to the situation in Poland and Czechoslovakia. The slow growth is partly due to the fact that foreign travel by Hungarians was already better established before 1989 so there was less pent-up demand, but is also a result of the strict foreign currency controls imposed by the Hungarian Government since 1990. Tourism expenditure on foreign travel by Hungarians was cut by half between 1989 and 1991.

	Inbound frontier arrivals	Outbound frontier crossings	
1985	15.1	5.5	
1988	17.9	10.7 of which	4.0m to Czechoslovakia
			2.7m to Austria
			1.0m to Romania
			0.7m to Yugoslavia
1990	37.6	13.5	
1991	33.2	14.3 of which	7.4m to Austria
			3.5m to Czechoslovakia
			0.8m to Romania
			1.8m to Yugoslavia
			0.8m to Germany

Fig. 26.7 Hungary tourism, 1985–1991 (millions)

So for various reasons, the political changes of 1989 did not have quite the same explosive effect on travel patterns into and out of Hungary as they did elsewhere in Eastern Europe.

Tourist resources

It is perhaps surprising that Hungary established such a thriving tourist industry before 1989, as it has no coastline and no outstanding landscape resources, though it does possess a huge inland lake and a wealth of cultural and historic attractions. Most of Hungary is in one physical unit: the oval expanse of the flat Pannonian plains. Its climate is typically continental; dry cold winters and warm summers with thundery outbreaks of heavy rain. Being lower and further south, the summers are a little warmer (generally reaching 21–22° C in July) than the more northerly countries of Eastern Europe.

Hungary can be split into two tourist regions: the north and the south.

Northern Hungary

This part includes most of Hungary's hill land. A ridge of uplands runs SW–NE parallel to Hungary's northern frontier. They reach just over 1000 m in the Matra-Bukk range, NE of Budapest. Limestone outcrops near the Czech border and there is a 22 km long complex of impressive scenic caves at Aggtalek. Vines are cultivated on the southern slopes of the hills and Eger, a historic city full of Baroque palaces and churches, is at the centre of the 'Bulls Blood' red wine district.

The Danube cuts a sinuous course through this range of hills north of Budapest. This 'Danube Bend' region is scenically attractive and historically important. The hills overlooking the Danube's course were old strategic sites, controlling routes north towards Vienna. Many medieval castles and palaces were built on the heights above the river, for example at the historic Esztergom and Visegrad, and the castle area of Budapest itself. The capital is made up of two original settlements – Buda is the older medieval part while Pest is the commercial centre. Budapest has been called the Paris of Eastern Europe: it is a lively, cultured city with opera, theatres and plenty of nightlife. Short cruises are available from Budapest and river boats link the capital with the towns upstream.

The Bakony Hills run southwestwards from Budapest. Lake Balaton is located at the southern foot of the range. The lake is 77 km long and is the biggest freshwater lake in Europe and is land-locked Hungary's most important tourist resource. The lake has sandy beaches and is quite shallow, with an average depth of three metres. It is warm enough in the summer season (June to mid-September) for bathing and sailing and a series of resorts have grown up, for example at Siofok, Balatonfured and Tihany. There are campsites, hotels, holiday cottages and workers' hostels around the lake.

Southern Hungary

The rest of Hungary consists of rolling cultivated lowlands and to the east the vast level grasslands of the 'Puszta' where nomadic herdsmen raise cattle and sheep. Pecs is a large historical city in the south, while Hortobagy with its fairs and horseshows is the centre of the livestock region.

ROMANIA

The 1989 revolution in Romania was more turbulent, and in spite of the execution of the dictator Ceausescu, the break with communism and the pre-revolutionary regime appears less clear-cut than in the other Eastern European countries. The economic difficulties are greater and the process of economic, political and social readjustment may be painful for the 23 million residents. Inflation has reached 100 per cent p.a. and output fell by 13 per cent in 1991, and GDP was only 1640 US dollars in 1990.

The country has a range of coastal and inland resources to meet domestic needs, and it may be some time before Romania generates outbound tourists in any numbers. Expenditure on foreign travel is very low indeed (only 114 million US dollars in 1991) but has grown every year since 1987. Information on outbound travel is sparse but it appears that most outbound trips are to Hungary (9.01 million reported in 1990) followed by Bulgaria (1.8 million) and Turkey (0.5 million in 1991). If Romanian outbound travel follows the pattern set by other East European countries, it is reasonable to assume that a high percentage of these trips are day visits.

Before the revolution, international tourist arrivals were few, just 3.5 million staying visitors and under one million day visitors. This was partly due to the political situation, although Romania was one of the few communist bloc countries to promote sun-sea-sand package tours for the Western European market along the Black Sea coast. Frontier arrivals reached 6.5 million in 1990 but most visitors were from Eastern European countries, mainly the former USSR (2.1 million) and Hungary (0.9 million). Only about 13 per cent of the arrivals came from the rest of Europe.

The country is only a little smaller than the United Kingdom, and its centre is an upland plateau. The U-shaped Carpathian mountain chain stands out above the tablelands, and continues north across the border through the Ukraine and into the Slovak Republic. The uplands are framed by flat plains on its other three sides. The country's tourist resources are scattered throughout these regions (*see* Fig 26.8).

The Carpathians and uplands of Transylvania

The forested northern Carpathians are relatively inaccessible but the monasteries in the Bukovina region are fortified and their churches are extensively painted with 16th century frescos, for example at Sucevita, Moldovita and Voronet. The central plateau of Transylvania is also a remote and unspoilt rural area and as yet has little tourist infrastructure. There are perfectly preserved medieval towns such as Sighisoara at its centre.

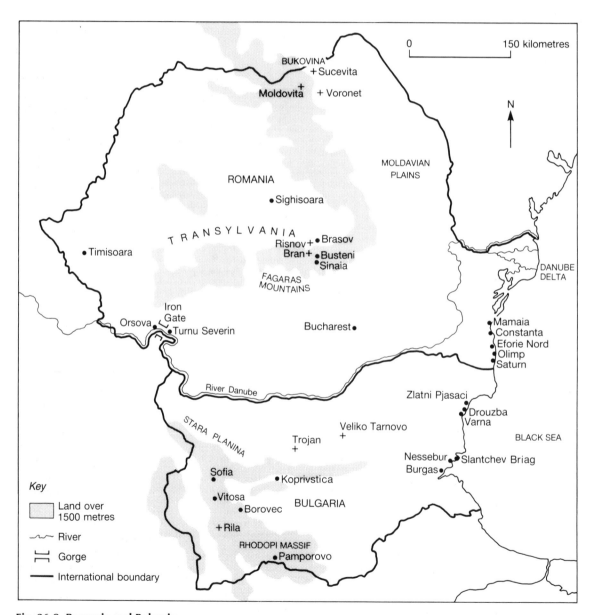

Fig. 26.8 Romania and Bulgaria

The higher mountains, e.g. the Bucegi and Fagaras which rise over 2500 m in the southern Carpathians have been better developed for hiking and winter sports and are extensively used by the domestic and East European markets. Sinaia and Busteni are the main winter sports centres for the Bucegi mountains and the cable cars link with marked trails for summer hiking. Brasov (which has a medieval centre) is another popular tourist destination. The Fagaras mountains are even more popular for hiking, but the summers are cool and the mountain climate can be wet. The best months for hiking are August and September, while snow cover for winter sports lasts from November to April. Risnov and Bran Castles (both dating from the 14th century) are situated in the foothills of these mountains. Bran is promoted as Dracula's castle but the much less accessible ruined castle, Poienari Citadel, further west is thought to be the real fortress of Vlad Tepes on whom the Dracula legend may be based.

The far western tip of the Carpathians almost meets the Yugoslavian mountains. The Danube, which marks the Romania-Yugoslavia border, has cut a deep gorge as it flows between the two mountain blocks. Between Orsova and Turnu Severin the narrow gorge is known as the Iron Gate; however, the river has been dammed for a hydro-electricity scheme, and there is now a lake where the river used to thunder through.

The plains

1 The western plains are a continuation of the Hungarian plains. Timisoara is the gateway to Romania for overland routes from Western Europe (via the Danube valley from West Germany, Austria and Budapest in Hungary). The region has few tourist attractions.

2 The Wallachian plains. The lower Danube valley is a landscape of gently undulating open farmed countryside. It has a fairly dry climate (Bucharest, Romania's capital, has 579 mm per annum). The capital has interesting churches and parts of the old town of Bucharest remain but many historic buildings have been demolished during city centre redevelopment in the Ceausescu era. However, there is some evidence of conservation: 297 rural buildings have been assembled as an outdoor village museum in one of the city's parks. The Danube delta is a wetland area of con-

siderable wildlife interest. Two hundred and fifty species of birds inhabit the marshy areas, while tourist boats take visitors along the main channel of the delta system.

3 The Moldavian plains form a gently sloping plateau to the east of the Carpathians. It is basically an agricultural area with extensive vineyards and some orchards, but there are few tourist features.

The Black Sea coast

The Black Sea is an entirely enclosed tideless sea, where summer temperatures rise to averages of 21 to 23° C. South of the Danube delta, the coast is gently sloping with soft, white, sandy beaches. The old established resort of Mamaia caters specially for Western European package holiday visitors. The string of resorts south of Constanta (Saturn, Venus, Aurora, Jupiter, Neptune and Olimp) were designed to cater for East European workers and in the 1980s were frequented by large numbers of East Germans and Czechs as well as Romanians. They have a range of accommodation from hotels to campsites. Eforie Nord is also a spa where black mud from nearby Lake Techirghiol is used for curative mud baths.

BULGARIA

Before 1989 Bulgaria had a relatively small, but economically important, foreign tourist trade. It received fewer staying visitors than Romania but a relatively high proportion (nine to twelve per cent) came from the West, bringing much needed foreign exchange. However, the industry relied mainly on the Eastern European holiday market: nearly 60 per cent of its 1.5 million holiday and VFR visitors came from Eastern European countries in 1991 (particularly Romania, Poland and the CIS). In 1992 this market virtually disappeared as a result of both the withdrawal of state subsidies for this form of tourism and the economic problems in these former communist countries. Bulgaria now has the same economic problems as the rest of Eastern Europe, with an over-reliance on outdated heavy industry and a shortage of consumer goods. The country has experienced hyperinflation between 1990 and 1992. Few Bulgarians were allowed to travel abroad before 1989, and economic forces will constrain their ability to use their new freedom of international movement. Expenditure on foreign travel is very low and has not increased in the 1990s. It is estimated that only 1.5 to 2 million Bulgarians travelled abroad each year since 1990. Bulgaria's own varied tourist resources may continue to meet most domestic needs as well as changing international demand. The country has a wide range of historic, landscape and coastal resources, located in two main tourist regions – the mountains and the Black Sea coast (*see* Fig 26.8).

The mountains

The Balkan mountains (the Stara Planina)

This round-topped, forested ridge rises to over 2300 m and is over 600 km long. It runs from east to west across the northern half of Bulgaria. The northern flanks of the ridge are gently sloping but the southern face is steep, dropping sharply to the 'Valley of the Roses', where 70 per cent of the world's rose oil is produced. The roses bloom between late May and early June. There are many historic settlements in the region, for example Veliko Tarnovo, Bulgaria's capital from 1186 to 1393, the monasteries dating from 1600 at Trojan, and an open air museum of Bulgarian history at the village of Koprivstica.

Sofia, the modern capital, lies on a plateau between the Stara Planina and the mountains of Southern Bulgaria (the Rhodopi massif). The city is strategically located on the crossing of routes connecting the Adriatic with the Black Sea, and Turkey with central and northern Europe (via Belgrade and Hungary). Indeed, a high proportion of Bulgaria's 3.2 million day visitor arrivals are Turks travelling by road across Bulgaria to work in Western Europe. Sofia is a cultural and historic city, but local heavy industry makes it one of the most polluted parts of Bulgaria.

The Rhodopi massif

Most of this plateau lies over 2000 m, but the highest peaks reach 3000 m. In places the landscape is similar to the Alps, with bare rocky peaks rising above heavily forested slopes. The edges of the massif are deeply incised by steep, wooded valleys. Snow may lie all year round on the higher

north-facing slopes, and there is plentiful winter snow cover for the development of ski resorts, notably at Vitosa (to meet Sofia's local needs), Borovec (an upmarket resort) and Pamporovo (designed for package tourists).

The summers are cool but the Rila mountains were extensively used by East Germans for summer hiking before 1989. There are also many historic monasteries in these mountains, such as Rila and Batchkovo, where Bulgarian Christianity survived during Turkish colonisation of the country between the 14th and 19th centuries.

The Black Sea coast

Bulgaria has a mostly sandy coastline of about 370 km with some very large sandy beaches. The summer climate is warm (reaching 22.8° C in July at Burgas) but rainfall peaks in June and December though totals are quite low (500–600 mm per annum). Although Burgas is roughly on the same latitude as Dubrovnik, its more continental location means that the winters are cold (January averages 2.0° C at Burgas and 1.7° C at Varna), which rules out the possibility of any winter coastal tourism. The summer season runs from June to September and the resorts are busy, although not as crowded as Romania's 60 km or so of sandy Black Sea coast. The main concentrations of hotels are at the resorts of Zlatni Pjasaci (known as 'Golden Sands'), Drouzbha, and Slantchev Briag ('Sunny Beach') where British and German package tourists are accommodated. Varna and Nessebur are historic towns that also function as resorts. Other resorts provide a range of bungalow, private room and campsite accommodation extensively used by the Czech, Polish, East German and Bulgarian holidaymaker before 1989. Sixty per cent of all Bulgaria's tourist accommodation is on the coast.

THE COMMONWEALTH OF INDEPENDENT STATES (FORMERLY THE UNION OF SOVIET SOCIALIST REPUBLICS)

The former USSR is a vast area of 22.4 million km^2 and spans a considerable range of climatic zones from the arctic conditions and tundra of the north to the extremes of the continental interior. Its landscapes and cultural resources are equally varied. In 1991 it had a population of 290 million made up of many ethnic groups and nationalities, including Russians, Ukrainians, Uzbecks, White Russians and the Turkish peoples of central Asia. Up to 1990 these were organised into 15 Socialist republics, by far the biggest of which is the Russian Federation, covering 76 per cent of the area of USSR, and containing Moscow, Leningrad (now St Petersburg), Rostov and the River Volga. Figure 26.9 shows the full list of the republics (*see also* Fig 26.10).

In 1991 the Baltic Republics (of Estonia, Latvia and Lithuania) split away from the USSR and became fully independent democratic nations. The remaining 12 republics also opted out of the USSR, effectively ending communist rule. They have all become independent countries with individual membership of the UN but in December 1991, they quickly regrouped to form the Commonwealth of Independent States. The CIS deals mainly with economic co-operation, military and defence issues common to all 12 states; each state is developing its own separate tourist industry and some are setting up new national airlines.

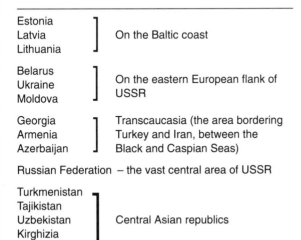

Fig. 26.9 Republics of the USSR as of 1990

The republics have faced profound political changes (from a soviet socialist system to more democratic rule) and fundamental economic restructuring (from centrally planned to more market orientated systems). These stresses combined with the ending of communist rule have uncovered nationalism, ethnic rivalries and tensions that had been suppressed in the past. These have resulted in ethnic conflict in some republics, for example in Azerbaijan and Georgia, and widespread political instability elsewhere. The economy of the CIS as a whole is in great difficulties and the rouble is very weak. Even so, some parts of the CIS have appreciably higher GDP per head than the other East European states. The Russian Federation and Ukraine (with GDP of 4610 and 3680 US dollars per head respectively in 1990) have the highest level of economic development potential and may be expected to generate most outbound tourism. The economic potential of the Central Asian states (Uzbeckistan, Turkmenistan, Kazakhstan and Tajikistan) is the weakest.

New patterns of inbound and outbound tourism will take some time to stabilise. Inbound tourism is constrained by the location and availability of Western-standard accommodation and infrastructure. The CIS has an uncertain future and the 1990s will inevitably see a long period of political readjustment and, perhaps, instability which may deter tourism.

Up to 1989, international tourism to Russia was centrally controlled and special facilities, e.g. hotels, special shops, were provided for the exclusive use of incoming visitors in selected destinations. By 1989, however, 147 centres had these facilities and were open to foreigners. By 1992 only six per cent of the CIS was still closed to foreigners, so new international-standard tourist facilities are needed in many new locations. In 1992 there was a severe shortage of accommodation in the main centres (e.g. Moscow and St Petersburg). Special facilities have to be provided for foreign tourists because the domestic market relies mainly on dachas (weekend wooden summer houses in the countryside near the cities), 'Sanatoria' and camping for its holiday accommodation, none of which can be easily adapted for use by international visitors. From 1987 to 1991 foreign investment in hotels in the CIS was limited to joint ventures with Soviet organisations. Since the formation of the CIS foreign companies may operate independently. Given political and economic stability, this may speed up the provision of tourist accommodation.

Fig. 26.10 The Baltic States and the CIS

To date, most of the new projects have been based in Moscow or St Petersburg.

Communications are generally poor, particularly the roads, as only six per cent of the population own cars. Most of the domestic resort areas are tied to public transport routes.

Although the CIS has a large domestic tourist market, the infrastructure is not suitable for international visitors. It remains to be seen whether the domestic market will eventually demand more Western-style tourism, or whether separate facilities in specific locations will continue to be set aside for foreign travellers. If the latter course is taken, then the choice of location of these invest-

ments will continue to regulate the spatial patterns of international tourism in CIS.

In 1990 there were five main destination areas (*see* Figs 26.11 and 26.12):

1 Moscow and the River Volga (in the Russian Federation);

2 St Petersburg (formerly Leningrad) (in the Russian Federation);

3 Kiev and Odessa (in Ukraine);

4 the Black Sea resorts (mostly in the Russian Federation); and

5 the eastern Black Sea and the Caucasus (Georgia, Armenia and Azerbaijan).

Fig. 26.11 Tourist resources of the western CIS

These are all located in the most accessible westerly part of the CIS, and represent only a fraction of the possible attractions of the region. Even the most westerly parts, e.g. Kiev and Odessa (*see* Fig 26.13) have a continental climate, with very cold winters and warm to hot summers but with a summer peak of rainfall. The climate will always be a constraint and the inbound tourist season is inevitably going to be quite short. The climate becomes more extreme nearer the centre of the CIS, so Moscow's winters are even colder and minimum temperatures may drop to minus 16° C, though the summers are almost as warm as Kiev's.

The cities of Moscow and St Petersburg (called Leningrad during the Soviet era) are the main destinations for foreign tourists. They are both located in the Russian Federation. Moscow is the capital of the Russian Federation and the hub of CIS politics (although Minsk is the official capital of the CIS). The main tourist attraction of the city is the Kremlin and Red Square. The Kremlin is a 64-acre site on the banks of the river Moskva – the site is enclosed by defensive fortress walls built in the 15th century. Inside the Kremlin there is a mixture of old and modern buildings. These include the

	Number hotel beds	% of beds	% foreign visitors (1990)	Main cities visited by foreign visitors (% foreign tourists) (1990)	
Russian Federation	31 819	58	71.7	Moscow	35.6
				St Petersburg	22.9
				Sochi	7.4
Ukraine	10 974	20	15.8	Kiev	6.4
				Yalta	6.0
Georgia	3 003	5.5	2.1	Tblisi	1.2
Armenia	1 888	3.4	0.4		
Uzbekistan	1 873	3.4	2.2		
Azerbaijan	1 609	2.9	0.2		
Belarus	1 518	2.8	1.7	Minsk	1.3
Moldova	777	1.4	1.5	Kishinev	1.5
Tajikistan	498	0.9	0.2		
Kazakhstan	417	0.7	0.4		
Kirghizia	203	0.3	0.4		
Turkmenistan			0.1		
Total	54 579				

Fig. 26.12 Regional distribution of tourism, 1991
(*Source*: USSR State Commission for Foreign Tourism)

14th century Grand Palace of the Czars, the golden-domed belfry and the 15th century cathedral. Red Square is located just outside the walls of the Kremlin, on its northeast side. The famous St Basil's Cathedral (with its colourful cluster of onion-shaped domes) is at the southern end of the square. This cathedral dates from 1555. However, much of the modern architecture in Moscow is drab and grey. St Petersburg in contrast has many elegant buildings (many reconstructed after damage in the Second World War) and is a major cultural centre. It was originally built by Peter the Great in 1703. The baroque Winter Palace and the Hermitage (which houses one of the greatest collections of Western paintings in the world, originally the Tsars' private collection) are major tourist attractions, but there are many other features of interest (e.g. the Summer Palace), cultural attractions (e.g. galleries and museums) and cathedrals. The city is known as the 'Venice of the North' as it is built on 44 islands in the river Neva, and has many canals.

The development of inbound and outbound tourism in the USSR/CIS

1 Soviet (pre-glasnost) period, 1981–6. Tourism was strictly controlled by the Soviet authorities and the flow of tourism in and out of the country was small and showed little growth, staying at

about 3.5 to 4.3 million frontier arrivals a year, and 2.3 to 2.8 million outbound tourists per annum. Over this period the number of non-communist visitors gradually decreased from 1.7 million to 1.4 million. Most came from Finland. In contrast arrivals from the other East European communist countries slowly grew (from 1.5 million to 2.7 million); the main sources were East Germany, Poland and Czechoslovakia.

2 Period of glasnost and transition 1986–9. During this period inbound tourism grew much more rapidly each year (by 21 per cent, 14 per cent and 29 per cent) to a peak of 7.75 million in 1989: two-thirds of the arrivals continued to come from other communist countries, but Poland was overwhelmingly the main source. Western tourism increased sharply to two million in 1987 but has since hovered between 1.7 and 2.1 million. Finland continues to be the main market, followed by Germany, but there was a significant increase in the numbers of Italians, Swedes and Americans travelling to USSR. Outbound tourism grew a little as the political changes gathered pace, until in 1989 outbound travellers outnumbered arrivals.

3 After 1989. The increased freedom of travel for residents of the Eastern European countries after 1989 diverted them away from the Soviet Union. The internal political problems within the USSR (as it made the transition into the CIS) coupled with the international crises of 1991 also meant that the number of Western tourists declined (by

	Kiev (central Ukraine)		Odessa (northern Black Sea)		Moscow (western Russia)	
	Av. temp (°C)	Rainfall (mm)	Av. Temp (°C)	Rainfall (mm)	Av. Temp (°C)	Rainfall (mm)
January	− 6.0	28	− 4.0	23	−11.0	28
February	− 4.9	20	− 2.0	18	− 9.3	23
March	− 0.5	38	1.6	28	− 4.4	30
April	7.0	43	9.0	28	3.3	38
May	14.0	43	15.0	33	11.5	48
June	18.0	61	20.0	58	16.5	51
July	19.2	76	23.0	53	19.0	71
August	18.1	61	21.4	30	17.0	74
September	14.0	43	16.5	35	11.0	56
October	8.0	43	11.0	28	4.4	35
November	1.0	38	5.0	40	− 2.2	41
December	− 4.4	38	− 0.5	33	− 8.2	38

Fig. 26.13 Climates of the western CIS

11 per cent) between 1990 and 1991. Consequently, the overall level of inbound tourism dropped in 1990 and 1991 (to a total of 6.8 million to the CIS in 1991). In contrast the growth of outbound tourism gathered pace until in 1991 10.8 million residents of the CIS travelled abroad.

THE BALTIC STATES: LATVIA, ESTONIA AND LITHUANIA

These three countries became independent of the Soviet Union in 1991. They are all small (roughly one-quarter to one-fifth of the size of the UK) and their total population was just over eight million in 1991. Their tourist resources include attractive forest, lake and coastal landscapes (e.g. in Estonia) seaside resorts (in Latvia) and the capital cities of all three countries are significant historic towns. Although these capitals attracted a small proportion of the USSR's inbound tourists in 1990, it remains to be seen whether they develop into significant tourist destinations for the other Scandinavian or North European countries.

CONCLUSION

The countries of Eastern Europe and the CIS had well-established domestic and international tourist industries before the profound political changes that occurred between 1989 and 1991. However, tourism under communist rule was politically controlled in terms of the numbers of citizens allowed to travel and the destinations they were permitted to visit. Essentially, outbound tourism was limited to destinations within the then communist bloc, behind the 'iron curtain' that divided communist Eastern Europe from Western Europe.

Hungary was the first of the countries to ease restrictions on outbound travel between 1985 and 1988 (in the period up to the fall of communism in the revolutions of 1989). Consequently, Hungary had a well-established pattern of outbound tourism to non-communist destinations by 1988, and many other East Europeans travelled to the West via Hungary during this period.

When communism was abandoned by the Eastern European countries in 1989, outbound tourism (particularly in the form of day-trips)

increased very sharply. More East Europeans visited adjacent Western countries (particularly Germany and Austria) but fewer were inclined to go to the previously well-visited resorts of the then USSR on the Black Sea coast (in Romania and Bulgaria). Inbound Western tourism to East European countries has also increased but not at the same phenomenal rate as the outbound tourism. Western travel has been inhibited by the lack of Western-standard accommodation and the relatively undeveloped tourist infrastructure of the East European destinations.

Outbound tourism from some East European countries (e.g. Poland and Hungary) has slowed down since 1990, due to the growing economic problems these countries face. Hungary has imposed currency controls which significantly reduced foreign travel by Hungarians in 1991. The economies of the ex-communist bloc may take some time to recover, and it may be some years before the countries are rich enough to sustain high levels of outbound holiday travel. However, given political stability and improving economies, the pattern of outbound tourism may be expected to follow the normal pattern of development, with an initial period of travel to adjacent countries, followed by the evolution of a more resource based pattern of tourism.

The tourist resources of the countries of Eastern Europe and the CIS are very varied. The region covers many different cultural and climatic zones. They present great opportunities for cultural, landscape and special interest holidays. But (like Central Europe) they have very little coastline and a continental climate with very cold winters. Countries such as Belgium, Holland and Germany have access to a limited section of the North Sea Coast, while Germany and Poland and the Baltic States have short stretches of Baltic Sea coasts: neither coasts are climatically suited to coastal tourism. Bulgaria and Romania have short sections of coastline bordering the Black Sea which is further south and, therefore, warmer than the Baltic or North Seas but not as favourable as the Mediterranean. It would not be surprising if the Eastern European countries and the adjacent CIS republics eventually generated high demand for sun, sea and sand destinations with a Mediterranean quality climate. The Benelux countries and Germany certainly do (*see*

Chapter 25), but political and economic conditions in the ex-communist countries of Eastern Europe have not allowed such demand to be expressed in the past. The political constraints are now essentially removed: a sustained period of political stability and improving economies is needed to trigger off these larger scale changes in travel patterns.

Up to 1990, international tourism to both Central and Eastern European countries has been based on their landscape and cultural resources. However, mass international holiday destinations are confined to the Alps. The Carpathians in Eastern Europe are much lower than the Alps (rising to 2655 m) but their interior continental location gives them prolonged snow cover, though it would be surprising if they developed a tourist industry on the scale of that of the Alps. The first wave of international tourists to flow into Eastern Europe were business, city break/cultural and VFR tourists particularly from the nearby affluent Central European countries. Changes to a more resource based pattern will depend primarily on the speed with which the tourist infrastructure can be extended and improved to meet the needs of international tourists, and on continued political and economic stability in the region.

FURTHER READING

Hall, D (1991) *'Tourism and Economic Development in Eastern Europe and the Soviet Union'*, Belhaven.

Harrison, D (1993) 'Bulgarian tourism', *Annals of Tourism Research*, Vol. 20, pp. 519–34.

Hunt, J (1992) 'Poland', *EIU International Tourism Reports*, No. 2, pp. 65–89.

Hunt, J (1992) 'Eastern Europe outbound', *EIU Travel and Tourism Analyst*, No. 5, pp. 23–43.

Hunt, J (1993) 'Bulgaria', EIU *International Tourism Reports*, pp. 21–39.

Hunt, J (1993) 'Foreign Investment in Eastern Europe Travel Industry', *EIU Travel and Tourism Analyst*, No. 3, pp. 65–85.

Hunt, J (1993) 'Latvia, Lithuania and Estonia',

International Tourism Reports, No. 4, pp. 71–88.

Kerpel, E (1990) 'Tourism in Eastern Europe and the Soviet Union', *EIU Special Report*, No. 2042.

Smeral, E (1993) 'Emerging Eastern European tourism markets', *Tourism Management*, Vol. 14, No. 6, pp. 411–18.

Trnkova, O (1992) 'Tourism and the environment in Czechoslovakia', *Tourism in Europe – the 1992 Conference*.

Williams, R (1992) 'Investment prospects in the hotel sector in the Commonwealth of Independent States', *EIU Travel and Tourism Analyst*, No. 4, pp. 66–83.

Williams, R (1992) 'CIS', *EIU International Tourism Reports*.

QUESTIONS AND DISCUSSION POINTS

1 Discuss the economic and political consequences of the 1989 upheavals in Eastern Europe. How have they affected the development of tourism in these countries?

2 What further economic and political changes must take place before Eastern Europe generates international tourists on the same scale as that of the core of Western Europe?

3 Which destinations in Eastern Europe might have most appeal to the Western European market and why?

ASSIGNMENT

You work for the government of one of the Eastern European countries (specify which one). You have been sent to an international conference in Britain on 'New Opportunities for Tourism in Europe'. Your government has been given 15 minutes of the conference programme time for you to make a brief presentation to the delegates on the attractions and opportunities for tourism in your country. You have also been allocated some exhibition space in the foyer of the conference hall. Prepare notes for your presentation and write the information packs for the exhibition.

CHAPTER 27

United Kingdom and Ireland

LEARNING OBJECTIVES

After reading this chapter you should be able to

- assess the tourist potential of the climatic, landscape, historical and cultural resources of the United Kingdom and Ireland
- distinguish the regional distribution of these geographical resources and their development and use for tourism
- demonstrate a knowledge of the main tourist resorts and tourist centres
- understand the role of the United Kingdom and Ireland in the general pattern of European tourism
- be aware of the dynamics of domestic demand and outbound tourism and the implications for established domestic tourist resorts and destinations.

INTRODUCTION: UNITED KINGDOM

The United Kingdom comprises England, Scotland, Wales, Northern Ireland, plus the Channel Isles and the Isle of Man. This area is the geographical base on which international tourism statistics are collected. On the other hand, domestic tourism statistics relate

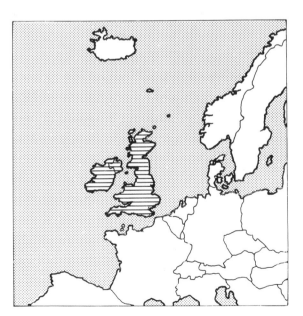

only to Great Britain (defined as just England, Scotland and Wales). Great Britain has a long established domestic market that has developed over more than a hundred years (*see* Chapter 15).

The basic geographical pattern of the infrastructure for domestic tourism, e.g. seafronts, piers, hotels, road and rail communications, was established by the 1960s. Most holiday facilities were concentrated in the south of England (along the south coast, and into the southwest peninsula) where the best combinations of temperature and sunshine are to be found. The coastal holiday developments in other regions were clustered near the densely populated industrial regions of the north, serving both their holiday and day-trip needs, e.g. Blackpool for the northwest, the north Wales coast for Merseyside and Birmingham, and Scarborough for the northeast.

This pattern of development once again reflects the characteristic pattern of national southward tourist flows (to the south and southwest) and regional coastward flows to the nearest accessible seaside (*see* Chapters 17 and 18). Since the growth of mass tourism overseas, there has been a shift in the nature of domestic tourism. In spite of the economic problems of the 1970s and 1980s, an increasing number of British people have holidayed abroad, to take advantage of the hotter, sunnier and more reliable climates of, first the Mediterranean, and now increasingly other destinations further afield. The old British seaside resorts have been unable to compete with the climate, cost and often more modern accommodation and better service offered by overseas destinations. The number of traditional family summer holidays of one or two weeks taken in Britain has fallen, leaving the British resorts to cater for those who do not wish to or are unable to holiday abroad. However, the nature of domestic tourist demand changed dramatically in the 1970s and 1980s with new demands for more varied types of holidays, self-catering holidays, shorter additional holidays and business tourism. At the same time, higher standards of accommodation, service and environmental quality are expected. While overseas destinations can develop rapidly to meet new needs, the domestic scene has been slower to adapt: the older holiday regions have a strong interest in maintaining old patterns of holidaymaking as they have so much (in terms of jobs and capital) invested in the existing infrastructure. Massive investment is needed to modify, update and add to facilities in order to compensate for their climatic disadvantage, and not all resorts have the prospects of a sufficient volume of trade to justify this new investment. The existing undeveloped coast is jealously guarded from new development by conservation policies, so coastal sites for modern developments are extremely limited. On the other hand, new tourist developments have been encouraged where they can meet other social and environmental needs, for example in the rejuvenation of inner city areas, in supporting the economy of ailing agricultural regions or in redundant docklands.

The domestic tourist industry has thus been going through a painful period of response and adaptation to the new demands generated by the changing structure of the domestic market. The response has been incremental – encouraged by the Government but led by the initiatives of individual companies. Although optimistic forecasts are made, it remains to be seen whether domestic short breaks and business tourism will grow enough to sustain the domestic market. Increasing affluence and improved accessibility to the Continent in the 1990s may accelerate the growth of overseas travel by the British.

International tourism to Britain is on a comparatively small scale (in terms of trips made) though of almost the same monetary value (in terms of expenditure) as the domestic market. It is far more geographically confined: overseas tourists are attracted by the historic and cultural resources of the country. They congregate in the urban areas of London, Stratford, Oxford and Cambridge and a handful of other historic towns, while international business tourism is also confined to the conurbations. Very few overseas visitors go to Britain's coast or countryside.

THE CHANGING STRUCTURE OF THE UK DOMESTIC MARKET

Population growth and structure

The population of the UK was 57.2 million in 1989. Government population projections anticipate modest growth to 59 million by the year 2000, and to stabilise around 59 to 60 million for the following 25 years.

Changes in the pattern of holidaymaking

Prospects for the growth of the tourist industry, therefore, depend on both changes in the population structure and changes in holidaymaking habits (i.e. the population taking more or longer holidays) rather than simply on population growth. For example, in 1985, 15.1 per cent of the population was 65 years or older (the highest proportion of elderly people of all EC countries), and with increasing life expectancy, the number of elderly is expected to grow, and if economic conditions allow their incomes to remain high, they may provide a new market of relatively affluent and leisured people who may wish to travel more than their predecessors did. Similarly the 45–59 year group will grow; a group with loosening family ties and plenty of disposable income, who are clearly potential overseas visitors. But this may be balanced by the projected decline in 20–24 year olds, who have always been keen foreign holiday takers. An increase in the 25–34 year old group, whose time and expenditure preoccupations are with family building, may lead to more emphasis on self-catering budget domestic holidays.

Evolution of patterns of holidaymaking

Holiday taking has grown substantially in the post-war period (*see* Fig 27.1). In 1973 it was estimated that British residents made 144 million tourist trips (including both domestic and foreign visits). The oil crisis of the mid-1970s and the recession of the 1980s retarded the growth of holiday taking, and it is only since the mid-1980s that the total number of trips has consistently exceeded the volume of 1973. However, the balance between domestic and foreign trips has shown a more consistent pattern of change.

Foreign holiday taking has steadily grown from five million trips in the 1960s (with only a minor check in the 1970s) to 33.8 million in 1992, while the domestic market has fluctuated mainly in the range of 123 to 132 million trips since 1980.

The domestic market

The total size of the domestic market regained its pre-oil crisis level in 1987. However, the total number of domestic holiday nights has decreased over this period, from 530 million in 1978 to 495 million in 1987, so the total size of the domestic market has shrunk a little. This is due to a structural change in the type of holiday taken. The traditional main (one or two week) family holiday in a British seaside resort has declined dramatically by 14 per cent between 1977 and 1987, and has shifted from serviced to self-catering. There has been a small increase in second holidays of four or more nights and in short break holidays (of one to three nights), but this growth has not been enough to offset the decline in traditional holidays (*see* Fig 27.2). Business tourism has however shown stronger growth, e.g. from 17 million to 20 million trips between 1978 and 1980 when domestic tourism as a whole was at its least buoyant.

Year	In Britain		Abroad	
	Million trips	Expenditure at 1987 prices (£m)	Million trips	Expenditure at 1987 prices (£m)
1970			8.0	
1971			9.4	
1972			10.6	
1973	132		11.7	
1974	114		10.7	
1975	117	2150	11.9	917
1976	121		11.5	
1977	121		11.5	
1978	119		13.4	
1979	118		15.4	
1980	130	4550	17.5	2738
1981	126		19.0	
1982	123		21.0	
1983	131		21.0	
1984	140		22.0	
1985	126	6325	22.0	4871
1986	128		25.0	
1987	132	6775	27.0	7255
1988			28.8	
1989			31.0	
1990			31.1	
1991			30.5	
1992			33.8	

Fig. 27.1 All tourism by British residents (for all purposes), 1970–1992

| | *Million trips* | | | |
	1976	1980	1986	1991
Main holidays 4+ nights	27	24	19 ⎫	
Additional holidays 4+ nights	11	13	13 ⎬	32
Short holidays 1–3 nights	30	32	32	26
Total trips	68	69	64	58

Fig. 27.2 Volume of British domestic holidays, 1976–1991

These changes in the structure of the market have had significant consequences in terms of accommodation used and led to a shift in the spatial location of tourism. The main holidays have used serviced accommodation less and less, leading to a conversion of hotels to other uses, e.g. flats, old people's homes. Some of the spare capacity in seaside hotels has been promoted for, and taken up by, the conference trade (business tourism) on weekdays, and by the short break market at weekends. But short break holidays on the whole use the same type of accommodation as the overall domestic market (e.g. only 17 per cent and 18 per cent respectively using hotels) though spatially short breaks are more likely to be taken by the seaside and in towns and less likely to be rurally based than main holidays (*see* Fig 27.3). Business tourism is more likely to use hotels and be located either in the seaside resorts for conferences, or in the major conurba-

	% of expenditure	(GB domestic tourism) 1986
Holidays		⎧ 5.5% short breaks (1–3 nights)
	50	⎨ 7.0% other short holidays
		⎩ 37.0% long holidays (4+ nights)
Holidays VFR	9	
VFR solely	8	
Business/ conferences	30	
Other	3	

Total expenditure 100 = £7150 m.

Fig. 27.4 Expenditure on domestic tourism

tions. Business and short break tourism are less peaked in demand than main holiday taking.

The economic impact of these different types of holiday are very different. Business tourists are the highest spenders while short breaks bring in least money (*see* Fig 27.4).

Location of holiday	Short breaks %	All holidays %
Seaside	42	37
Small town	14	14
Large town	14	11
London	9	5
Countryside	18	27
Not specified	5	5

Fig. 27.3 Destination of tourist nights in Britain in 1987

Day-tripping

Day-trips are not strictly included in the definition of tourism, but day-trippers visit the same range of attractions and compete with holidaymakers for road space at weekends and holiday times. There is evidence that levels of day-tripping hold up better than holidaymaking in periods of economic difficulty: when times get hard, people cut down or cut out their holidays but still visit the more local attractions on day-trips. Day-trippers spend significantly less on their visits than do tourists but can create significant management problems at tourist attractions. Day-tripping is much more responsive to changes in the weather than is tourism and in good weather outdoor attractions may be very busy but get negligible attendances in the rain. The overall level of day-tripping is difficult to measure accurately and estimates of the total volume vary. However, the 3327 tourist attractions that record accurate admission figures (which do not distinguish between tourists and day-trippers) counted 233 million visits in 1987.

OVERSEAS VISITORS TO THE UK

The number of overseas visitors to Britain grew steadily in the 1970s (in spite of the oil crisis) to a peak in 1977–9 at about 12.5 m. Numbers fell away in the worst of the economic recession in the early 1980s to a low of 11.4 million in 1981, since when the numbers of visits has gradually climbed again to 18.1 m visits in 1992 though the 1991 Gulf War led to a temporary decline (making 1991 a rather atypical year). The expenditure has also steadily climbed (from £2797 m in 1979 to £7630 m in 1992) in spite of the average length of stay of overseas visitors having fallen. In the 1980s, holidays made up around 43 per cent of all visits, business trips 21 per cent and holiday/VFR 18–21 per cent but as in the domestic market, business travel contributes more than its proportional share of income (29 per cent of income in 1987 but only 25 per cent of trips).

Nearly fifty-four per cent of Britain's overseas visitors came from EC countries in 1992, of whom 40 per cent came on holiday and 26 per cent on business trips (*see* Fig 27.5). The North American market has always been important, though Britain became less reliant on this market in the 1980s (*see* Fig 27.6). Overseas tourism to UK is basically business tourism, VFR and cultural tourism, so it is spatially highly concentrated on towns, and particularly concentrated on London, with 49 per cent of visits, 45 per cent of nights and 63 per cent of expenditure (*see* Fig 27.7).

1991	Trips (million)	Nights (million)	Expenditure (million £)
London	8.9	67.4	3799
SE England	1.9	17.8	538
E Anglia	0.9	8.2	248
Thames and Chiltern	1.3	11.4	364
S England	0.7	6.3	186
West Country	1.3	11.0	295
Heart of England	1.1	9.8	267
E Midlands	0.5	5.8	132
North West	0.9	5.0	242
Yorkshire and Humberside	0.8	7.1	178
Cumbria	0.2	1.2	34
Northumbria	0.3	3.2	93

Fig. 27.7 Regional distribution of overseas visitors to England

Visitors from	1973 %	1987 %	1992 %
North America	25.6	21.4	18.1
EC	46.3	49.2	54.0
Rest of Europe	10.9	9.7	9.5
Rest of world	15.8	18.1	18.2
Total no.	8.2 m	15.6 m	18.1 m

Fig. 27.5 Overseas visits to Great Britain

THE SPATIAL DISTRIBUTION OF TOURISM IN GREAT BRITAIN

Domestic holidays are strongly concentrated in England (*see* Fig 27.8). In 1991 77 per cent of domestic holidays of four nights or more were taken in England, 11 per cent in Wales and 12 per cent in Scotland: when short breaks are included the concentration in the South is even more marked.

Visitors from	1973 %	1987 %	1992 %
USA	31	18	15
Germany	10	10	12
France	9	13	14
Ireland	6	6	7
Netherlands	5	5	5
Belgium/Luxembourg	3	3	4
Australia	3	4	3
Italy	–	4	4
Spain			4
Canada			3
Japan			3

Fig. 27.6 Leading generators of foreign visitors to Great Britain

	Million trips	Expenditure (£ million)
England	58.3	5695
Scotland	5.6	900
Wales	6.6	770
N Ireland	0.9	95

Fig. 27.8 Holiday tourism in Britain by the British, 1991 (all holidays of one night or more)

This distribution reflects the two main factors of climate and population distribution. The westerly uplands of Scotland and Wales have a wealth of landscape and coastal resources but a wetter, cloudier, cool and unreliable climate. Second, the British population is concentrated in the southeast and (in spite of the relatively short distances between regions) most holidays are taken close to home.

The attractions and patterns of tourism will be described for each region in turn.

The distribution of tourism in England

There are 12 tourist regions in England (*see* Fig 27.9). Holiday tourism is strongly concentrated in the south: the three southern regions (S, SE and SW) account for nearly 40 per cent of all British holidays (*see* Fig 27.10), and have the warmest, driest and sunniest weather in Britain (*see* Figs 27.11 and 27.12). Only eight per cent of all holidays are taken in the two northernmost regions (Cumbria and Northumbria). These parts of England have cooler, wetter and cloudier weather and are also a long way north of the major concentrations of population (i.e. the main tourist generating areas). Very few holidays are taken in the land-locked regions of the Heart of England and Thames and Chiltern.

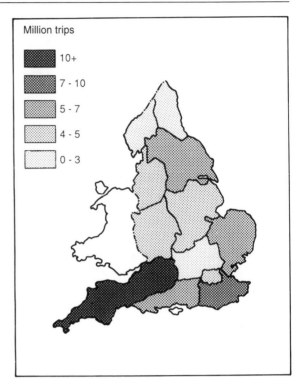

Fig. 27.10 Regional patterns of domestic holiday trips

Fig. 27.9 Britain's tourist regions

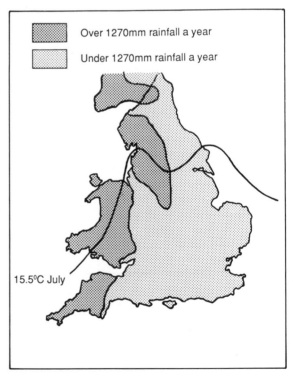

Fig. 27.11 Rainfall in England and Wales

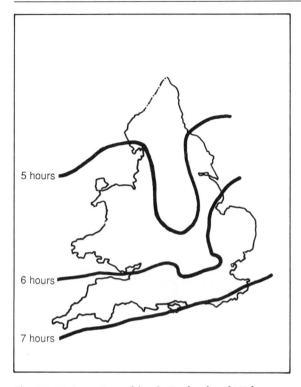

Fig. 27.12 August sunshine in England and Wales

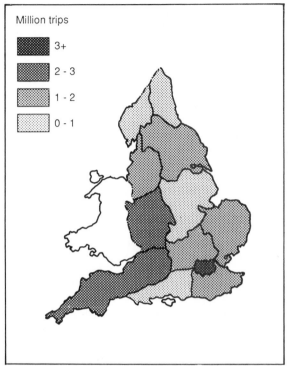

Fig. 27.14 Regional pattern of business tourism

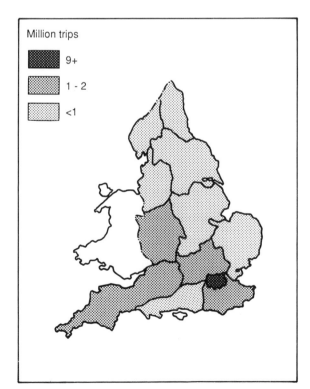

Fig. 27.13 Regional pattern of overseas tourism

It has been noted that overseas tourism shows a totally different spatial pattern (*see* Fig 27.13) with the emphasis on London and the South East, the inland regions of Thames and Chiltern (the location of Windsor and Oxford) and Heart of England (the location of Stratford-upon-Avon). However, the West Country does receive almost as many overseas visits as the Heart of England region.

Domestic business tourism shows a pattern halfway between these two extremes: London, Heart of England (site of the National Exhibition Centre in Birmingham) and the West Country (where conference facilities are located in many resorts) are the leading regions (*see* Fig 27.14). When all forms of tourism are amalgamated (including all domestic and foreign) and expressed in terms of nights spent in each region, London emerges as the leading destination (*see* Figs 27.15 and 27.16).

London is important as a location for overseas visits, for business tourism (domestic and international) and to a lesser extent for domestic holidays and short breaks. The West Country and the South East are the next most important regions: they

Rank Order	Region	Million tourist nights
1	London	103.0
2	West Country	92.7
3	South East	55.4
4	East Anglia	48.4
5	South	45.6
6	North West	45.6
7	Yorkshire and Humberside	38.4
8	Heart of England	36.4
9	Thames and Chiltern	34.0
10	East Midlands	31.5
11	Northumbria	19.0
12	Cumbria	13.9

Fig. 27.15 All British and overseas tourism to England, 1988

have a good mix of holiday, business and overseas tourism, but with domestic holidays being the most significant. Tourism is reasonably evenly spread amongst the other regions though the two most northerly regions (Cumbria and Northumbria) are the least visited and are consistently ranked lowest for all forms of tourism.

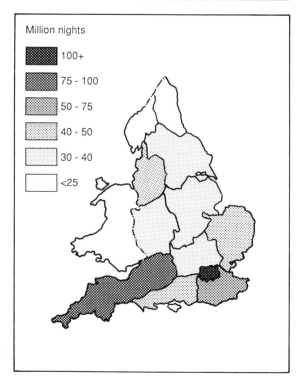

Fig. 27.16 All tourism

	Northumbria	Cumbria	Yorkshire and Humberside	NW	Destination regions Heart of England	East Midlands	Thames and Chiltern	London	SE	S	West Country	E Anglia
	%	%	%	%	%	%	%	%	%	%	%	%
Origin region												
Scotland	9	4	4	8	3	3	2	5	2	2	1	2
North	39	23	13	9	6	6	3	7	2	3	2	3
Yorkshire and Humberside	11	10	29	9	4	12	7	7	3	4	4	5
North West	7	25	9	32	5	7	4	9	4	5	6	4
East Midlands	4	7	6	5	5	25	6	5	5	6	6	10
West Midlands	8	6	7	8	32	7	8	10	6	7	12	5
East Anglia	1	2	2	2	2	4	3	3	2	3	2	14
South East	15	17	23	18	29	31	45	36	65	59	34	51
South West	3	4	4	5	8	5	15	11	7	12	27	4
Wales	1	2	2	4	5	2	5	6	3	3	6	1
	100	100	100	100	100	100	100	100	100	100	100	100
Total number of nights spent in each tourist region by British holidaymakers	11.7m	11.9m	28.1m	28.0m	19.9m	24.3m	13.1m	18.5m	23.9m	25.4m	68.5m	26.0m

Fig. 27.17 Regional patterns of domestic tourism, 1991
(*Source*: BTA)

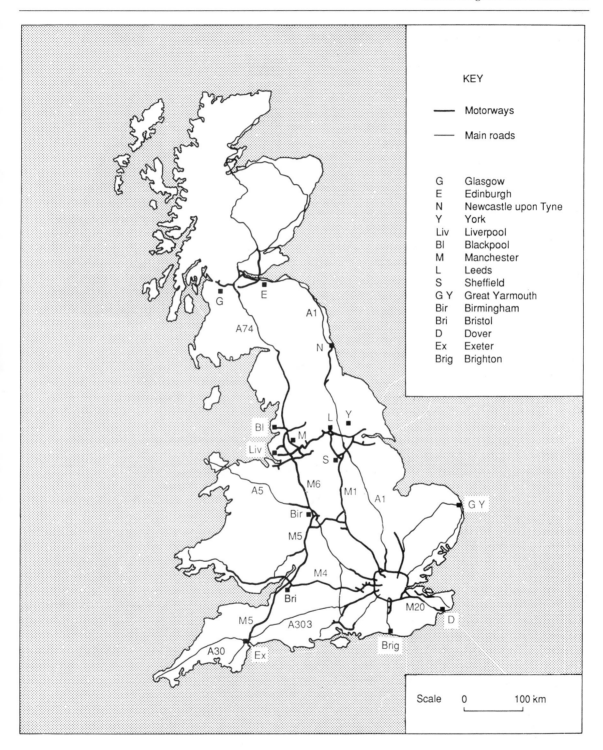

KEY

— Motorways

— Main roads

G	Glasgow
E	Edinburgh
N	Newcastle upon Tyne
Y	York
Liv	Liverpool
Bl	Blackpool
M	Manchester
L	Leeds
S	Sheffield
G Y	Great Yarmouth
Bir	Birmingham
Bri	Bristol
D	Dover
Ex	Exeter
Brig	Brighton

Scale 0   100 km

Fig. 27.18 Main road routes in UK

Thus, England appears to conform to the general pattern of tourist movement (the predominant flows being southward and coastward). However, a surprisingly high proportion of the British tourists stay within their own regions, or go to adjacent regions: travel distances are relatively short. Figure 27.17 shows the relationship between the regions that people visit and the regions in which those visitors live (i.e. each column shows the proportion of visitors to a given region that live in other regions). About a third of the visitors to the northern tourist regions live in that region; around a quarter of the visitors in the Midlands tourist regions live in the Midlands, while the South East is the dominant tourist generating region for the southern tourist regions.

Seventy per cent of Britain's population lives in the NW–SE band stretching from the South East, through the Midlands to the Merseyside and Manchester conurbations. The dominant radial communications patterns facilitate the southward flow of tourists (*see* Fig 27.18) towards London and the South East. It was not until the M5 was built and later extended to Exeter that travel from Manchester and Birmingham to the West Country was eased. This motorway, and the more recently constructed East–West links are the only significant elements of the network cutting across the radial pattern.

The regional road networks are also extremely radial, centred on the regional conurbations (e.g. Manchester, Birmingham, Bristol).

Regional patterns of tourism in England

London

1 Concentration of tourism in West and West Central (WC) London. In 1988 over 20 million tourists (British and overseas) and an estimated 40 million day trippers visited London. All but business travellers come for the historic buildings, cultural and traditional events, the shops, restau-

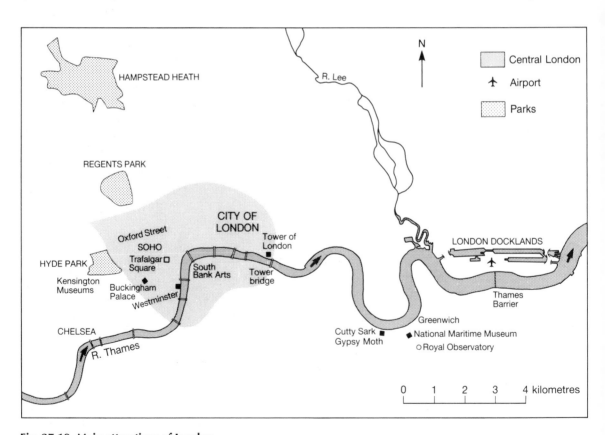

Fig. 27.19 Main attractions of London

rants, nightclubs and other entertainment. The vast majority of these attractions are located in the West of Central London (the 'West End') (*see* Figs 27.19 and 27.20) causing considerable congestion in the peak summer months. Although 68 per cent of British visitors stay with friends and relatives there is considerable pressure on hotel accommodation. British staying visitors are reasonably well spread through the year (the peak holiday months balanced by the growing short break market in spring and autumn) but the numbers are swelled in the summer by day-trippers and overseas visitors (*see* Fig 27.21), to a peak in July and August. During these months the most acute congestion can be expected in the middle of the day (12.30–3 pm). The congestion and conflicts between the needs of local communities and tourists have led some boroughs (such as Westminster) to limit new hotel developments. There is a growing shortage of hotel accommodation in London, made worse by Britain's housing policy in the second half of the 1980s when the budget hotels and bed and breakfast accommodation were used to house London's homeless (in 1988 11 000 spaces were thus taken up) and other budget accommodation has tended to trade up to more profitable four-star grade facilities.

	By British residents %	By overseas residents %
Trips started in:		
January–March	25	18
April–June	23	26
July–September	20	34
October–December	31	22
	100	100

Fig. 27.21 Seasonality of London's tourism (all staying visitors)

The focus of international tourism in the west of London is reinforced by the location of Heathrow on the western fringe. There is also a shortage of hotel accommodation close to the airport. Heathrow is the major international gateway into both Britain and Europe.

It is estimated that tourism generates nearly 200 000 jobs in London, and contributes £4700 m to London's economy. In order to meet the growing demand for tourism in London, and to sustain its economic benefits, there is an urgent need to resolve some of the environmental problems it causes, perhaps by spreading tourism more widely through Central London. Since the Greater London Council (London's strategic planning authority) was abolished in 1986, the London boroughs are responsible for promoting and controlling new developments, and they act primarily in the interests of their own residents. The London Tourist Board (which lacks any powers to enforce the implementation of its policies) has, however, taken the initiative to coordinate the policies of the boroughs and produced the Tourism Strategy for London in 1987. This provides the framework within which measures could be taken to spread tourism pressure and benefits more widely. However, the lack of an overall strategic planning authority and the current reliance on market forces may still lead to the over-concentration of tourism development in Central London.

	Million visits
Central London and West End	
British Museum	3.83
Westminster Abbey	3.25
National Gallery	3.22
Madam Tussaud's	2.70
Science Museum	2.43
Tate Gallery	1.58
Natural History Museum	1.36
London Zoo	1.32
(Plus Buckingham Palace, main shopping streets etc, that do not record attendances)	
West London	
Kew Gardens	1.18
Hampton Court	0.53
City of London, Docks & Greenwich	
Tower of London	2.18
Tower Bridge	0.53
St Paul's Cathedral	2.5 (est)
National Maritime Museum	0.7
Cutty Sark	0.4

Fig. 27.20 Attendances at leading London tourist attractions, 1988

2 Tourism in East Central London. There is a secondary concentration of tourist activity to the east of Central London. The City of London (the location of the stock market and the Bank of England) is the centre of business tourism, and St Paul's, the Tower of London, and Tower Bridge attract vast numbers of holidaymakers and day-trippers (*see* Fig 27.20). The slightly less popular attractions at Greenwich lie even further to the east (in LB Greenwich), and the old London Docks lie in the centre of this cluster of attractions. The city centre docks in many of Britain's city ports have become outdated, and port activity has either declined or relocated on new greenfield coastal port sites, e.g. Tilbury for London, Avonmouth for Bristol, where larger modern container dock facilities can be provided. The derelict city centre docks have been the site of active redevelopment in many cities and London is no exception. The London Dockland Development Corporation is the body responsible for rejuvenating an area of 20 km² (and over 88 km of waterfront) in London. Much of the redevelopment is for upmarket housing and commercial land uses but significant tourist developments have also occurred. Firstly, the docks have been linked to the City business area by the Docklands Light Railway, and the new London City Airport (built on the former quay between the Royal Albert and King George V docks at North Woolwich) links European destinations within a 600 km radius (principally Amsterdam, Brussels and Paris) of the City of London.

This improved transport infrastructure will, no doubt, encourage business tourism to this part of London, and new hotel developments in the docks are envisaged. There are also many opportunities to attract holiday tourists and day-trippers to this part of London through the conservation of historic buildings, and the development of the water sports potential and the other leisure opportunities of the docks. On the other hand, local communities would prefer to see the land developed for low cost housing to meet the needs of adjacent deprived inner city residents; and these developments remain the focus of local controversy.

The West Country

The southwest peninsula is Britain's second ranking tourist region after London (*see* Fig 27.15) in terms of tourist nights spent. It is essentially a rural region whose main resources are its mild climate, its inland countryside attractions, its sandy beaches and undeveloped coast.

Its main tourist function is as a holiday region (74 per cent of its British visitors and 52 per cent of its overseas tourists come on holiday in 1991, while under 17 per cent visit friends and relatives and only 6 per cent come on business trips). Tourism is highly peaked: 45 per cent of the region's British and overseas visitors come between July and September, when there is great congestion in the resorts and on the main access routes (the M5 and A30). The region has only one large resort – Torbay. Elsewhere the tourist accommodation is spread between the smaller resorts (such as Sidmouth, Dawlish, Teignmouth, Newquay, Minehead and Burnham-on-Sea), quaint old fishing villages, such as Clovelly and Polperro and more modern developments, such as caravan sites and new holiday villages. The south coast of the peninsula is a mixture of cliffs, sandy beaches and estuaries which provide good conditions for sailing. The north coast is more rugged, with rocky cliffs interspersed with small sandy coves and bays. Much of the coast is undeveloped. A large proportion is covered by the Heritage Coast designation (*see* Fig 4.13 on page 39) where landscape conservation policies take priority over tourist development and car access is strictly limited. Pedestrian access is encouraged and a long-distance footpath follows the whole length of the coast.

Inland, the rolling countryside provides an attractive backdrop to the many unspoilt historic villages, such as Lacock in Wiltshire, Selworthy in Somerset, towns, such as Dunster in Somerset, and the Roman and Georgian town of Bath in Avon, and historic monuments, for example Stonehenge in Wiltshire, Buckfast Abbey on the southeastern flanks of Dartmoor, and Wells Cathedral on the edge of the Mendips. The region's National Parks provide the biggest areas of open countryside: Dartmoor is characterised by large expanses of bleak, open moorland punctuated by dramatic rocky tors. Exmoor has a softer landscape: the moorland is limited to the crests of the hills which are cut by deep wooded valleys. Bodmin Moor, the Quantocks and the Mendip Hills provide smaller areas of open countryside. All these landscapes provide opportunities for walking, pony trekking, farm tourism and other rural activity holidays.

The past and present industries of the region have also been exploited for tourism, e.g. 19th century mineral workings have been restored at Morwellham Quay on the Tamar north of Plymouth, and several cider works throughout Devon and Somerset are open to visitors. In addition there is a range of man-made attractions, such as miniature railways, model villages, complexes such as Somerwest World at Minehead, the Tropicana Pleasure beach at Weston and the English Riviera Conference Centre at Torbay. Only a handful of these attractions receive more than half a million visitors a year, but the region is characterised by a huge variety of small attractions providing the tourist with a lot of choice. Most are located within easy reach of the coast where the tourist accommodation is concentrated. Because this adds to the pressures and congestion along the coast, many of the local authorities attempt to limit and restrain new tourist development in the coastal zone, while encouraging it in the remoter inland rural areas. At the same time the English Tourist Board and the local authorities are trying to promote the region and further diversify its tourist product (e.g. into conference and business tourism in the larger resorts). This is because the region relies so heavily on holiday tourism. The West Country has felt both the impact of the recession and the full effects of the shift from serviced accommodation to the rented and self-catering sectors in the late 1970s and early 1980s. For example, Torquay experienced a 22 per cent decline in tourist nights between 1977 and 1984. At the same time there was an 11.2 per cent decline in the use of serviced accommodation in Cornwall. The region is characterised by many small hotels (77 per cent had under ten bedrooms in 1991). These small businesses were hit particularly hard and there was a strong trend towards conversion either to elderly persons' homes or self-catering units.

The south coast (the South and South East tourist regions)

The coast of the south of England is different in character from that of the southwest. Southern England is essentially a lowland region with few cliffs, except where the chalk hills meet the coast at Dover, Beachy Head and in the Isle of Wight, and the limestone produces cliffs on the Purbeck coast of Dorset. The coast consists of a series of sandy and shingly beaches from Sheppey to Selsey, most of which were developed in the 19th century as traditional seaside resorts or more recently for commuter or retirement settlements.

The coast of the Solent (the channel between the Isle of Wight and the mainland) is less developed as it consists of a series of muddy marshes and estuaries, totally unsuited to beach tourism but the harbours are ideal for sailing and other boating activities. The countryside is not dramatic, although the North and South Downs, the heathlands of the Weald, and the woodland and heaths of the New Forest are very attractive and are heavily used by both tourists and day-trippers. Apart from the coast, the leading destinations of the region are Canterbury Cathedral and Thorpe Park (both with over one million visitors in 1988). The former is of great historic and architectural interest, while Thorpe Park is a modern theme park, developed from reclaimed gravel pits. It is very easily accessible, being close to the M25 on the southwest outskirts of London. Kent, Surrey and Sussex are very easily accessible from London and all the resorts and facilities here cater as much for day-trippers and commuters from London as for staying visitors. In spite of this, the traditional resorts have still experienced mixed fortunes. The larger resorts that have enough visitors to attract and justify new investment have diversified. Brighton has a 5000 seat conference centre and marina, while Deal and Eastbourne have new all-weather leisure facilities. Some of these resorts experienced an upturn in business in 1988 but the smaller resorts continue to decline.

A high proportion of the tourist traffic in the South East is transit traffic to and from the continent. The shortest and most heavily used ferry routes are from Dover and Folkestone to the ports of northern France and Belgium, but there are also ferries from Sheerness to Flushing (in Holland) and from Newhaven to Dieppe. Only four per cent of all the visitors travelling through Kent actually stay in the county: most traffic flows directly between the Channel ports and London (via the A2/M2 and A20/M20 routes). The completion of the Channel Tunnel will make cross-Channel day-tripping more attractive, and there have already been collaborative marketing exercises promoted by Kent County Council and Nord Regional

Council in France to encourage transfrontier tourism. However, it is anticipated that the region will still be ignored by most longer stay international tourists using the fixed link, who will continue to pass through rather than stay in Kent.

Air travellers show the same pattern of behaviour. London's second international airport, Gatwick, is located in Surrey. It handled 21.2 million passengers in 1989 (22 per cent of UK total air passengers) but most of these tourists head straight for London on arrival.

Transit traffic via Southampton is on a very much smaller scale. Hampshire and East Dorset rely much more on holiday tourism, although some centres in this part of the region have also attempted to expand and diversify into conference, short break and heritage tourism. Bournemouth, for example, has a 4000 seat conference centre, and Portsmouth is marketing its naval history and maritime connections. Nelson's flagship *Victory*, *HMS Warrior* (dating from 1860) and the recently recovered *Mary Rose* (Henry VIII's flagship) each attract over 300 000 visitors a year, and a new marina with its associated water-based leisure and conference facilities opened between 1986 and 1988.

East Anglia

This region, too, is mainly a lowland area with a low and gentle coastline. Most of the Essex coast is muddy and the estuaries form ideal locations for sailing rather than seaside tourism and there are a series of yachting centres on the Crouch, Blackwater and Stour estuaries. Harwich, at the mouth of the Stour is the main ferry port for Germany and Scandinavia. The good transport links with London mean that the resorts on the Essex coast (Southend, Clacton, Frinton and Walton) cater mainly for day-trippers. The coast becomes much sandier further north. Great Yarmouth has a huge sandy beach and is the biggest resort in East Anglia, with 2¼ million visitors to its pleasure beach in 1988. Inland from Great Yarmouth lie the waterways of the Norfolk Broads which are popular for boating holidays and all forms of water sports. The shallow inland waters are safe for even the most inexperienced yachtsmen. The management of the wildlife in the increasingly polluted wetland environment of the

Broads has caused concern for many years. The pollution comes from sewage effluent and agricultural run-off rather than from the impact of tourism. The Broads are now funded and managed in a way similar to the ten National Parks of England and Wales, though it is not a National Park by name (*see* Fig 4.13 on page 39). The total number of boats and their distribution is regulated in the interests of wildlife in order to minimise the impact of tourism on the Sites of Special Scientific Interest and National Nature Reserves.

The Midlands and North of England

Coastal resorts become relatively less important towards the north of England with a few notable exceptions. Blackpool is one of the most successful resorts in Britain in spite of its northerly location and its badly polluted coastal waters. It relies heavily on day-trippers from the adjacent conurbations. The Pleasure Beach at Blackpool is estimated to attract 6½ million visitors a year, but the resort has a wide variety of other indoor facilities (The Tower, the Sandcastle Centre and Louis Tussaud's Waxworks) and outdoor attractions (e.g. the Zoo and the Lights). The lights come on in the autumn and extend the season by many weeks. On the east coast, Scarborough (a spa town of the 18th century) is the main seaside centre. It undertook substantial investment in the late 1970s and early 1980s to update its facilities and expand its conference accommodation.

The countryside of northern England is more mountainous and dramatic than the lowlands of the south and southwest, and extensive areas of the uplands are designated as National Parks (see Fig 4.13). The North York Moors and Yorkshire Dales National Parks cater extensively for day-tripping and rural farm-based and activity holidays. The Peak District is the most heavily used of all the National Parks (with a lot of camping and caravanning) though permanent accommodation is strictly limited within the Park boundaries. Cumbria (whose main resource is the Lake District National Park) relies much more heavily on staying holidaymakers who are more likely to use hotels. The Northumbria National Park (the site of Hadrian's Wall) is the least visited of all the National Parks. It is the cultural and historic resources of these regions that lure visitors (particularly the overseas visitors) northwards. Cultural associations have made Stratford-upon-Avon (with Shakespeare) and Oxford (with the University) and to a lesser extent Grasmere (with Wordsworth) and Haworth (with the Brontës) such well known tourist destinations. Many overseas visitors also visit the historic cities of York and Chester. In 1988 York Minster (an 11th century Gothic cathedral) received 2.1 million, and the Yorvik Viking Centre 860 000 visitors.

The West Midlands and the conurbations of Yorkshire and Lancashire were the centres of the industrial revolution and saw the early growth of iron, steel, pottery, wool and cotton manufacturing. This industrial heritage is also being developed as the focus of urban tourism aimed at the short break market. The Ironbridge Gorge Museum (in Telford, Shropshire) was one of the first to conserve and promote industrial archaeology in 1971. Sites along the River Severn have since been restored and opened to the public, and the 42-acre open air museum at Blists Hill has been expanded. In 1988, the complex attracted over 400 000 visitors. The Black Country Museum in Dudley (Worcestershire) is a similar though more recent development, while the open air museum at Beamish (Newcastle upon Tyne) attracted 467 000 visitors. Bradford was among the first of the northern cities to develop an integrated package of attractions (including industrial archaeology, Asian cuisine, the Brontës, and the sites of popular TV serials) to generate tourism to what was thought of as an unlikely destination.

The other major northern cities have followed suit. Manchester has adapted derelict sites to new tourist uses: the GMex Centre, completed in 1986, is an exhibition and events arena developed from a converted train shed of the old Central Station. The Castlefield site in Manchester (designated in 1982 as Britain's first Urban Heritage Park) is a complex of new museums of science and industry, air and space, transport and electricity all converted from redundant buildings and linked to other attractions such as the Granada studios (where the TV set of *Coronation Street* is located) and remains of a Roman fort. Liverpool has also adapted its redundant dockland for new uses: the Albert Dock complex (consisting of shopping, catering and maritime museum facilities surrounding the dredged and cleaned dock basin) is estimated to attract 3½ million visitors a year.

Birmingham has capitalised on its central location and good road and air links to develop the National Exhibition Centre which now accounts for 30 per cent of UK exhibition space. The Midlands are also the location of Britain's most popular theme park (Alton Towers) and Britain's first 'Center Parc'.

SCOTLAND AND WALES

These two regions typify upland Britain. They are areas of mountain landscapes of moorland and forest with sparse populations and dramatic undeveloped coastlines. However, their northwesterly location leads to an unfavourable climate for tourism (cooler, cloudier and wetter than south and east Britain). They are more remote from the population centres of England. Only South Wales is easily accessible (via the M4) from London. Scotland is linked to the main road network by good trunk roads (e.g. A74 Carlisle–Glasgow and A696/A68 east coast route from Newcastle upon Tyne to Edinburgh) but access beyond Edinburgh and Glasgow into the Highlands is more difficult.

Scotland

The total volume of tourism in Scotland was 61 million bednights (1992). The majority of the holiday trips were generated by Scots (53 per cent) and 45 per cent from England. Foreign travellers accounted for 18 million bednights. Tourism is highly seasonal and concentrated during the better weather of July, August and September. Trip lengths are quite short (averaging under five nights). Main holidays are strongly concentrated in the Highlands but business, VFR and international tourism is more focused on the cities and population concentrations of the Central Lowlands. The Borders and Southern Uplands receive little tourism.

1 **The Central Lowlands**. This region consists of the Valleys of the Clyde, Forth and Tay, and is the most urban and industrialised region of Scotland, although most of the heavy industries are in decline. Edinburgh is a beautiful city and is the cultural and social centre of Scotland. Its dramatically sited 14th century castle is a major attraction, with the Royal Mile which links the Castle to the

Palace of Holyrood House. The latter is mainly 17th century but is associated with Mary Queen of Scots who was executed in 1587. The city also has a substantial and well-preserved Georgian area. The annual Arts Festival (The Edinburgh Festival) attracts many visitors from the South, but international visitors to Scotland also concentrate here. The Castle, the Royal Botanic Gardens and the Royal Scottish Museum (all located in Edinburgh) were among Scotland's leading attractions in 1988.

Glasgow, as European City of Culture in 1990, rivals Edinburgh as a centre of tourism, and the Burrell Collection was Scotland's leading attraction (with over one million visitors) in the late 1980s. Glasgow's art galleries and museums also attracted large numbers of tourists and the city is also the home of Scottish opera, theatre and orchestras.

There are many other urban attractions in the region. St Andrews has an attractive coastal location and is famous for its golf, University, Castle and Cathedral, while Glamis and Scone also have historical connections. The Magnum Leisure Centre at Irvine is a major attraction in the west of the region with over a million visitors in 1987. The industrial archaeology of the region has been less exploited than in England. New Lanark is a 200-year old cotton spinning village near Glasgow that has been restored and provided with tourist facilities. It is one of the most important industrial archaeological sites in the UK and has been nominated as a World Heritage site. Yet it received only 80 000 visitors in 1985. Whisky distilleries, such as Glenfiddich, which appear more associated with the image of Scotland, attracted twice as many visitors.

The countryside bordering the Central Lowlands is heavily used for tourism and day-tripping, particularly Loch Lomond and The Trossachs, the Queen Elizabeth and Argyll Forest Parks in the Grampians to the north of Glasgow.

2 The Highlands. The most outstanding, remote and unspoilt mountain and coastal scenery is located in the north and west of Scotland. It is an ancient landscape of rounded and worn down mountains which contrast strongly to the jagged peaks and precipitous slopes of the geologically younger mountain regions of the world such as the Alps, Rockies or Himalayas. The region is basically a dissected plateau which slopes down towards lower land on the east coast. The highest mountains are mostly on the western edge and lie in the path of rain-bearing winds from the southwest. These western mountains, therefore, have heavy rain (the core of the Highlands receives over 2500 mm and is the wettest part of the British Isles), but is relatively mild. The heaviest snowfall occurs in the Cairngorms (in the colder centre of northern Scotland). The range forms the highest land in the United Kingdom. They were estimated to receive around 200 000 visitors in the summer season of 1987. The scenery and remoteness are the most important qualities valued by walkers in the area. In winter the upper slopes keep enough snow to support a ski industry centred on Aviemore, but the high cost and unreliable climate make it a relatively unattractive destination for southerners compared to Alpine packages. The Cairngorms appear to cater for more local demand.

The west coast is rocky and deeply indented. The inlets (known as sea lochs) have a landscape reminiscent of fjords (though not on the dramatic scale of the Norwegian coast). There are many islands along the west coast; Skye is the most developed for tourism, although Mull, Jura, Islay and Arran are also popular. Many locations in the Highlands are also associated with Scotland's romantic history and folklore, for example Glencoe, Skye and Loch Ness.

The country is sparsely populated and the main industry for many of the small villages on the west coast is now tourism. Inverness is the main urban centre and gateway to the Highlands.

The offshore islands (the Outer Hebrides, Orkney and Shetland) are accessible by air and sea but are less frequently visited. The east coast of northern Scotland is drier and sunnier than the west but still averages less than five hours' sunshine per day in August, and July temperatures average between 13 and 14° C. This effectively rules out beach tourism on any significant scale in northern Scotland. Landscape and activity holidays (hill walking, skiing, fishing, golf and climbing) are climatically more appropriate.

3 The southern uplands. These uplands, like the Highlands, consist of the denuded remains of an ancient range of mountains; the landscapes consist of rounded hills and moorlands, forests and rolling agricultural landscapes in the lower areas. They serve the local leisure needs of the population of Scotland's Central Lowlands, but are largely bypassed by tourists from the south on their way to Glasgow, Edinburgh or the Highlands .

Wales

The more southerly location of Wales makes beach tourism possible. The coast receives only a little more rain than southwest England but the mountains inland generate orographic rainfall and totals increase rapidly inland to average over 1525 mm pa in the higher areas. The coastline averages 5.5–6.0 hours' sunshine a day in August compared to 6–7 hours in southwest England and the best beaches average between 14.5 and 16.5° C in July.

The Principality is much more accessible to the English market; its landscape, coast and historic resources are more heavily used by English visitors. The best beaches are located in the Gower peninsula (South Wales), the Pembrokeshire National Park (in the southwest of Wales), in the Isle of Anglesey and the Lleyn Peninsula in the northwest, and along the north Wales coast. The latter is close to the Merseyside conurbation and has a string of traditional resorts, e.g. Rhyll, Llandudno and Colwyn Bay. The Rhyll Suncentre is the leading attraction.

Much of the coast of Central Wales is cliffed and the beaches are inaccessible around Aberystwyth and Barmouth, which were both developed to cater for visitors from the Midlands conurbations. There are good surf beaches in the southwest-facing coves in South and West Wales. The undeveloped estuaries around the coast of Wales are ideal for boating activities and there is great pressure to develop them for marinas.

Wales has a wealth of historic resources, notably the medieval castles, such as Caernarfon, Conway, Chepstow, Pembroke, Harlech and Beaumaris. Heritage attractions based on Welsh industry and crafts have also been successfully promoted (such as the Llechwedd slate caverns in Snowdonia, and the Big Pit mining museum in South Wales). As in other parts of the UK, redundant docks in Swansea and Cardiff have been redeveloped for tourism and watersports. The landscapes of Wales are sparsely populated and unspoilt. Southwest Wales is subdued (the land is basically a dissected plateau) and more intensively cultivated than much of the rest of Wales. Even so, many holdings are small and of marginal profitability. Many farms and cottages are sold at relatively low prices and become second homes for the English, much to the annoyance of many of the local people.

The problem of rural depopulation and the replacement of locals by temporary residents is more acute in the more accessible but agricultural harsher environments of the Central Uplands, and particularly Snowdonia. These landscapes are scenically more attractive than southwest Wales and are much closer to the conurbations of the Midlands and Northwest England. Central Wales is mountainous with stretches of forest, remote rounded grassy uplands and deep valleys. The Elan Valley has been flooded and the reservoir lake adds interest but its fluctuating water level sometimes mars the landscape. Apart from the second-home owners, this part of Wales is generally bypassed by visitors who prefer the coast or the more dramatic landscapes of the Snowdonia National Park in North Wales. Gwynedd is Wales's major tourist region and has by far the greatest concentration of hotel bedspaces.

The Snowdonia region has an ideal combination of outstanding landscape, good beaches nearby, historical attractions (ranging from Harlech Castle to Criccieth (Lloyd George's birthplace) and from the Ffestiniog Railway to water-powered wool mills, weaving Welsh tapestry) and opportunities for activity holidays (e.g. pony trekking and climbing). For the less active, Snowdon's summit is accessible by the mountain railway.

The third National Park in Wales is the Brecon Beacons (adjacent to the heavily populated region of South Wales). Its inland location and less dramatic landscapes of rounded grassy mountains make it a less popular destination than Snowdonia. However, it is particularly noted for its activity holidays which include pony trekking, hill walking, lake sailing, canoeing and pot holing in the caves of the limestone region on the southern edge of the Park. The Park is also used for day visiting from the South Wales towns, and new opportunities for countryside recreation (e.g. Aberdare and Afan Argoed Country Parks) have been created in the reclaimed industrial valleys of South Wales between the towns and the Brecon Beacons.

THE REMAINDER OF THE UK

1 The Province of Northern Ireland has great tourist potential. It has miles of undeveloped coast and countryside, though it shares an unfavourably wet and cloudy climate with northern England. Political unrest and terrorist activity have effectively inhibited tourist developments since 1970.

2 The Isle of Man (located in the Irish Sea at a similar latitude) also has attractive landscape and coastal resources but its relative inaccessibility constrains tourist development.

3 The Channel Islands are located off the French coast, due south of west Dorset and consequently have a slight climatic advantage over most of the English coast. Between May and August maximum temperatures reach 20° C and sunshine averages eight or nine hours a day. The islands are accessible by both air and ferry. Development in the islands is strictly controlled and they offer quiet undeveloped coasts and an old-fashioned and relaxing pace of life. No cars are allowed on the smaller islands of Herm and Sark, and there is a maximum speed limit of 30 mph on Alderney.

UK OUTBOUND TOURISM

Travel abroad from the UK has grown rapidly since 1970, and the majority of the trips (68 per cent in 1991) were for holidays (*see* Fig 27.22). Although Britain has a wealth of attractive beaches and varied countryside, the weather is so unreliable that the British people prefer to travel abroad to a coast where sunshine is guaranteed. Visits abroad by the British substantially outnumber overseas trips to Britain; this pattern was also set in the 1970s and has been maintained into the 1990s.

Holidays taken by the British abroad are likely to be twice as long as domestic visits, and expenditure per trip is proportionally even higher: the average cost of a holiday of over four nights in Britain was £140 in 1992, while a comparable foreign holiday cost £547 including the cost of travel.

| | Overseas trips from the UK (1990) | |
	Summer season (million trips)	*Winter season* (million trips)
Visiting friends and relatives	2.3	1.6
Holidays	14.4	6.8
Business trips	2.4	2.3
Other (inc. shopping, educational, sporting etc.)	0.6	0.6
Total	**19.7 m**	**11.3 m**

Fig. 27.22 UK outbound tourism

However, cheap fares and a stronger pound have made foreign holidays relatively cheap in the late 1980s. A strong pound encourages the shift from domestic to overseas tourism, while also making Britain a less attractive destination for foreign visitors. At the end of the decade the combination of recession, the Gulf War and a less stable exchange rate had slowed down the growth of outbound tourism in terms of numbers of trips (declining from 31.03 million trips in 1989 to 30.5 in 1991). However, expenditure on foreign travel continued to grow even through the most difficult years (e.g. 1991); all indices of outbound tourism showed a recovery and further growth in 1992 and the early part of 1993.

Summer holidays overseas tend to be spread over a relatively long season in order to avoid the worst congestion at airports and at continental resorts. Three-quarters of these holidaymakers travel by air and 64 per cent of the trips are package tours. Hotels are the most favoured form of accommodation (often the larger modern hotels in the resorts). Spain, France and Greece are the most popular summer destinations (*see* Fig 27.23).

Beach holidays are the most important, with the majority of visitors to Spain, Greece, Portugal, Tunisia (and since 1987 Turkey) taking two-week coastal resort holidays. During the early 1980s Spain maintained its share of sun-sea-sand

Destination	'000 trips	Destination of British foreign holidays Million nights	% travel by air	% inclusive tours	Expenditure per night (£) excluding fares
Spain	4 393	57.9	92	70	19.1
France	2 419	27.4	16	45	18.7
Greece	1 606	21.4	99	84	20.1
Irish Republic	749	6.2	21	0	17.9
Italy	713	9.8	77	62	21.3
Portugal	604	8.4	98	66	20.9
Yugoslavia	588	7.2	–	–	–
West Germany	476	5.5	46	28	20.0
Total (incl other destinations)	15 058	214.1			

Fig. 27.23 UK summer holidays abroad, 1987

Destination	'000 trips	% inclusive tours	Main holiday type
Spain (incl Canary Is)	1945	71	Winter sun
Portugal (incl Madeira)	265	69	Winter sun
Greece	208	82	Winter sun
Austria	330	85	Winter sports
Switzerland	145	55	Winter sports
France	945	50	Winter sports/city breaks
Italy	221	73	Winter sports/city breaks
Irish Republic	410	0	Visiting friends/relatives
West Germany	258	22	Visiting friends/relatives and city breaks
Total (including other destinations)	6858		

Fig. 27.24 Winter season holidays abroad, 1987/88

holidays (at about 45 per cent of all beach holidays) but became markedly less popular at the end of the decade, with a decrease of over one million British visitors between 1987 and 1991, and its market share dropped from 23.9 per cent to 16.0 per cent. Greece and Yugoslavia rapidly became more popular, with an increase of 21 per cent and 24 per cent per annum respectively in their numbers of British visitors from 1983 to 1987, but the break-up of Yugoslavia has ended tourism to that part of the Adriatic. The impact of the Gulf War has meant that Turkey had gained relatively little of this market by 1992. On the other hand, UK tourism to Cyprus has grown dramatically from just over 300 000 in 1987 to 932 000 in 1992. The numbers of British travelling to France has

remained little changed during the 1980s, up to 1987, but it has become a significantly more popular destination with an increase from 5.03 million visits in 1988 to 7.8 million in 1992. It has now replaced Spain as the leading UK destination (with a 24.2 per cent market share in 1991). It provides a much wider range of holidays, from shopping trips, camping or caravan touring, rural farmhouse/gîtes holidays as well as beach tourism, which appeal to the more mobile and independent British holidaymaker. Visits to the Irish Republic and to Germany are predominantly visits to friends and relatives.

Winter holidays show a greater diversity of types of holiday and of destination. It is estimated that about 40 per cent of winter trips were to winter sun destinations, 15 per cent for winter sports, 15 per cent for city breaks and 18 per cent visiting friends and relatives.

Long-haul travel

A substantial proportion (43 per cent) of long-haul trips made by the British are to North America. The numbers flutuate from year to year depending on the relative strengths of the dollar and the pound. In 1987/88 there were 1.12 million trips, 729 000 (64 per cent) of which were summer season visits. A high proportion of these summer visits were for beach holidays: Miami is now a more important gateway into the USA than New York for British summer visitors. Summer tourism to the USA has grown very strongly in the late 1980s to 1.158 million trips in 1991 (a growth rate of 36.4 per cent between 1987 and 1991). Winter visitors also seek winter sun holidays, but around a third of all trips to North America are to visit friends and relatives. The average visit has decreased from 23–25 days to 18 days, and only about 18 per cent use inclusive tours. Long-haul travel to other parts of the world is much more evenly spread throughout the year (with over 700 000 trips in both the summer and winter seasons). As high a proportion as 37 per cent of the trips are to friends and relatives, for example in Australia, New Zealand, India and the Caribbean. However, 33 per cent of these long-haul trips are inclusive tours: a great variety of packages are now available, ranging from wildlife safaris in East Africa, trips down the Nile to see the Egyptian temples and tombs, cultural trips to Bali, Himalayan treks, and winter sun holidays to exotic destinations such as The Gambia, Thailand and the Caribbean. Most of these trips are high cost holidays, often over £2000 (1988 prices), but in spite of the costs, all long-haul travel is growing in popularity. Total trips have increased from 3.01 million in 1990 to 3.26 million in 1992.

REPUBLIC OF IRELAND

Ireland is the remaining outlying region of north-west Europe. It is relatively isolated from tourist resources and tourist markets of mainland Europe. Its extreme westerly Atlantic location puts it at an immediate climatic disadvantage when competing

	Ave temp °C	Rainfall mm
January	6.6	139
February	6.6	132
March	7.1	114
April	9.0	94
May	11.0	81
June	14.0	81
July	15.0	96
August	15.0	122
September	14.0	104
October	11.0	142
November	9.0	139
December	8.0	167

Fig. 27.25 Valentia's climate

for international tourists. The winters are mild but the summer weather is cool and is as variable as England, but it is always wetter (*see* Fig 27.25). Valentia is located in the extreme southwest of Ireland. Its climate is far from ideal but is typical of the southwest which is Ireland's leading tourist region (*see* Fig 27.26). However, the mild, moist climate does allow plant growth virtually all year round, making the landscapes particularly green.

The most attractive and popular scenic resources are in the west and southwest. The coast here is very indented with many bays and drowned valleys, for example in the Cork and Kerry region, and numerous offshore islands (e.g. Galway and Connemara). Ireland's mountains are also located in groups around the coast, e.g. the Twelve Pins in Connemara, the mountains of Kerry, and Wicklow just south of Dublin. Many of these landscapes are quite unspoilt and not very intensively used for tourism. The centre

	% of tourist revenue
Southwest	20.4 – includes Cork and Kerry
Dublin	22.6 – major cultural centre
West	14.6 – includes Connemara
Southeast	10.5 { the Wicklows and Dublin's hinterland
East	9.8
Northwest	9.3
Mid-West	12.6

Fig. 27.26 Spatial distribution of tourism in Ireland, 1991 (*Source*: Bord Failte)

of Ireland is an expanse of rather featureless flat or rolling landscapes, and is the least popular tourist region of Ireland (*see* Fig 27.26). It attracted only 6.5 per cent of tourist revenue in 1986.

The total volume of tourism to Ireland hovered around 2.5 million in the 1980s but reached 2.66 million in 1987 and 3.66 million in 1990. Its main market is the UK. Seventy per cent of its visitors came from England, Scotland, Wales plus Northern Ireland, but less than 36 per cent visited Ireland for their main holiday. Most (55 per cent) were visiting friends and relatives and 20 per cent came on business. Many Irish have emigrated over the years in response to Ireland's economic problems and lack of jobs, and it is these people, or their descendants who make up the bulk of Ireland's visitors. The spatial distribution of this type of tourism will depend more on the residence of the friends and relatives than the natural resources of the country, although many VFR trips are combined with holiday trips.

The Irish also emigrated to the USA in search of work, so the USA is the next most important source of Ireland's tourists. About 400 000 visitors from America spent time in Ireland in 1990. In the past these have had strong ties with Ireland; about 10 per cent of these were Irish natives, another 15 per cent had Irish parents and 51 per cent had some ethnic link to Ireland. The American tourists were the highest spending visitors to Ireland, and Ireland has been vigorously marketed in the USA. However, tourism from European countries to Ireland has grown rapidly in the second half of the 1980s, and maintained this expansion even through the difficult year of 1991. For example, French tourism increased from 95 000 in 1985 to 220 000 by 1991, Germany from 98 000 to 203 000 and Italy from 16 000 to 96 000 over the same period. In contrast North American travel to Ireland dropped by 20 per cent in 1991 (to a total of 321 000). In spite of the political differences between the Republic of Ireland and Northern Ireland the tourist boards of the two parts of Ireland have combined to market a joint Irish package to the Americans.

The 'troubles' in Northern Ireland began in 1969 and resulted in a drastic reduction of tourism from the UK to the Republic of Ireland, from which it has only recently started to recover. Nevertheless, there is a large volume of day-tripping from Northern Ireland to the Republic: in 1986 this was estimated to be 7.4 million.

FURTHER READING

Ireland

Hannigan, K (1994) 'A regional analysis of tourism growth in Ireland', *Regional Studies*, Vol. 28, No. 2, pp. 208–14.
McEniff, J (1991) 'Republic of Ireland', *EIU International Tourism Reports*, No. 4, pp. 24–45.
McEniff, J (1994) 'Republic of Ireland Outbound', *EIU Travel and Tourism Analyst*, No. 3, pp. 19–33.

UK

Beachey, A (1990) 'The UK longhaul market', *EIU Travel and Tourism Analyst*, No. 1, pp. 42–53.
BTA (1992) *Regional Fact Sheets*.
BTA (1993) *Digest of Tourist Statistics*, No. 17.
Buckley, P J and Klemm, M (1993) 'The decline of tourism in Northern Ireland', *Tourism Management*, Vol. 14, No. 3, pp. 184–94.
Edwards, A (1991) 'United Kingdom', *EIU International Tourism Reports*, No. 3, pp. 5–21.
Lavery, P (1993) 'UK Outbound', *EIU Travel and Tourism Analyst*, No. 3, pp. 20–34.
Littlejohn, D and Goulding, P (1994) 'Scotland', *EIU International Tourism Reports*, No. 2, pp. 62–81.

QUESTIONS AND DISCUSSION POINTS

1 Describe the trends in British domestic and outbound tourism. Do you expect these trends to continue?

2 What explanations can be put forward to explain the fact that a very high proportion of England's domestic tourists take holidays in the region where they live?

3 What geographical disadvantages does Britain experience when trying to attract European tourists? To what extent can good marketing overcome these disadvantages?

ASSIGNMENTS

1 (a) You are the tourism officer employed by the County Council of one of the English counties (you may specify which one). The districts in the county and the county itself have made financial contributions to a fund earmarked for a programme to jointly market the tourist attractions of

the county. The steering group has asked you to prepare and present a paper at their first meeting. It should identify the character of the county and its constituent districts and suggest a theme around which its attractions should be marketed. Be prepared to explain the reasons for your proposal at the meeting.

(b) *Several months later.* The steering group has decided on the theme, the target market/s, and the main media to be used (leaflets plus adverts and articles in the local/regional press). Again you have been asked to do some research and prepare a paper for the next meeting. Your brief this time is to investigate where the county's current tourists come from, and to suggest where the promotional material should be distributed (i.e. countrywide or targeting particular regions of the country, or indeed overseas). Again, you are expected to make a brief presentation to the meeting, explaining the reasons for your recommendations.

2 You work for a new UK-based tour company 'Culture Vultures' specialising in tours for inbound tourists to Britain's historic and cultural centres. The company acknowledges that it must include the most popular destinations in Britain but it is company policy to introduce some less well known, less crowded and less commercialised destinations in its tours where possible. Your chief executive has asked you to draw up itineraries suitable in length and choice of attractions for:

(a) Visitors from the USA;

(b) Japanese parties; and

(c) The German market.

3 You are responsible for organising the international conference on 'New Opportunities for Tourism in Europe'. You expect several hundred delegates to attend; you cannot miss the chance to demonstrate the best of the new developments in tourism in Britain to this international audience. You can do this by your choice of conference venue (to demonstrate the accessibility, convenience and suitability of Britain as a conference venue), and by organising two half-day trips from the venue to examples of new British attractions or tourist initiatives that represent the best of the new opportunities for tourism in Britain. These trips are part of the conference programme. Select a suitable conference venue, demonstrating its accessibility and the quality of its conference facilities and accommodation. Construct the itineraries for the two half-day trips, making sure they fulfil the above requirements and also give the delegates an enjoyable experience.

CHAPTER 28

Northwest Europe: Scandinavia

LEARNING OBJECTIVES

After reading this chapter you should be able to
- assess the tourist potential of the climatic, landscape, historical and cultural resources of Scandinavia
- distinguish the regional distribution of these geographical resources and their development and use for tourism
- demonstrate a knowledge of the main tourist resorts and tourist centres
- understand the role of Scandinavia in the general pattern of European tourism
- be aware of the constraints imposed on the development of tourism in Scandinavia by its climate and latitude
- be aware of the political and economic organisation of Scandinavian countries and the consequences for tourism within and between Scandinavian countries.

INTRODUCTION

The region consists of the countries of Norway, Sweden, Finland, Denmark and Iceland, a wide region of some variation but with a strong common cultural identity.

Scandinavia lies well to the northwest of the industrial and urban core of Europe; Copenhagen

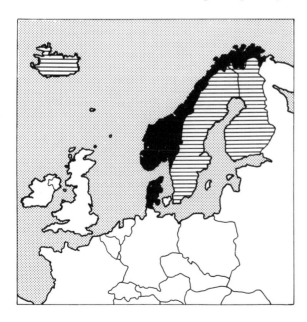

(Scandinavia's most southerly capital) lies at approximately the same latitude as Edinburgh, and one third of Scandinavian territory is north of the Arctic Circle. The influence of this northerly latitude on climate and tourism is profound. The region has long, harsh, dark winters with $19\frac{1}{2}$ hours of total darkness in December in Lappland. The summers are brief and cool, although they enjoy prolonged daylight ($18\frac{1}{2}$ hours in Stockholm in June).

The popular perceptions of the landscapes of Scandinavia are dominated by the images of dramatic fjords in Norway, the ice caps and volcanoes of Iceland, the lakes and forests of Finland and the quieter, agricultural landscapes of Denmark. These perceptions are partly based on fact but in reality there is a greater variety of landscape types in the region.

In spite of having dramatic and varied coasts and landscapes, which are sparsely populated and largely unspoilt, Scandinavia has few international tourists from outside its own boundaries, for which the unfavourable climate and short season are two explanations.

These environmental influences are reinforced by economic factors; Scandinavians enjoy a very high standard of living and thus show high propensities for travel (*see* Fig 28.1). But the countries are seen by other Europeans as expensive destinations when compared to the sunny and relatively cheap Mediterranean. On the other hand, Scandinavians show a strong tendency to travel to the resorts of Greece and Spain, particularly for winter sun holidays, as well as frequent travel between their respective countries.

CULTURAL UNITY

Scandinavia lay outside the influence of the ancient world of the Mediterranean: it was never incorporated into the Roman world; and it was remote from the main cultural centres of medieval Europe (*see* Chapter 5). Its cultural roots and cultural unity stem from the development of the Viking culture AD 800–1100, which spread from the Baltic region throughout Finland, Sweden, Norway and Denmark. Their seafaring, piratical and trading way of life led them to colonise the Faroe Islands between 820 and 900, Iceland and Greenland (877) and, around AD 1000, they reached North America. The core regions of Viking settlement, where most of the historic relics are situated, were the Helsinki coast of Finland, Stockholm and its hinterland, the islands and east coast of Denmark and pockets of colonisation round the Norwegian coast, for example Oslo, Bergen and Trondheim.

From Viking times to the 19th century, the political development of the region has been characterised by the development and expansion of power, stagnation and decline of various parts of Scandinavia – for example, Denmark was dominant in the 13–14th centuries, and Sweden from 1400 to 1800.

Due to its isolation and inaccessibility, the region was largely bypassed by the industrial revolution and the internal developments of the Scandinavian countries have not been greatly influenced from

outside. Nordic co-operation stems from 1856, though this did not become expressed in legal terms until 1962 (the Helsinki Agreement) whereby many of the laws of the countries have been harmonised. Citizens of Nordic countries do not need work permits and customs regulations are co-ordinated. Passports are not routinely checked which means that travel for Scandinavians between Scandinavian countries is very easy and the area is basically one whole domestic tourism unit.

Travel for Scandinavians between their countries is also made physically easier by co-operation in the planning, provision and management of the transport infrastructure. For example, the airlines of Denmark, Norway and Sweden were merged in 1951 to form the Scandinavian Airlines System (SAS). In the Öresund region (the channel between Copenhagen and Sweden) transport and urban planning is co-ordinated to provide good links and ease travel between Denmark and Sweden. There are four ferry routes across the sound which carry high volumes of passenger traffic (e.g. 21 million ferry passengers in 1982).

SCANDINAVIA AS A TOURIST GENERATING AREA

The region has a relatively small population – 22.9 million in 1991 (*see* Fig 28.1) but the Scandinavian countries are among the most affluent in the world.

They appear to owe their affluence to a healthy mining and manufacturing sector and the willingness of the workforce to retrain and acquire the new skills needed for a modern economy, although the economy was hit hard by the recession in the 1980s and early 1990s. In Sweden inflation broke into double figures in 1990 though the unemployment rate was still low.

	1990 GDP per head US dollars	1991 population (millions)	1989 holidays abroad	Holiday departure rate – 1991 (ests) (4 nights +)
Norway	23 120	4.2	45%	70%
Sweden	23 680	8.5	55%	80%
Denmark	20 090	5.1	63%	66%
Finland	26 070	4.9	45%	70%
Iceland	21 150	0.2	–	–

Fig. 28.1 Levels of affluence and tourist generation in Scandinavia

The population as a whole has a high level of holiday entitlement (five weeks plus) and holiday-making, but much use is made of rural and coastal second homes, located in the sparsely populated countryside not far from the cities. Thus, self-catering family holidays form the bulk of domestic tourism. The total volume of domestic tourism is shown in Fig 28.2.

Outdoor activities are particularly popular with the Scandinavians, for example over 70 per cent of Swedes take part in one or more active pursuits, such as swimming, boating, climbing, fishing and sledging, and 68 per cent go ski touring. Business travel is growing, particularly since 1982.

	Domestic nights in all accommodation (million)
Sweden	27.11
Norway	11.57
Denmark	13.33
Finland	10.26

Fig. 28.2 Domestic tourism – Scandinavia, 1990 (*Source*: WTO)

Because of the ease of travel for nationals within Scandinavia, comprehensive data on tourism between Scandinavian countries do not exist. However, Fig 28.7 would suggest that at least one third of the foreign arrivals are travellers from within Scandinavia, and the governments of Norway, Sweden, Denmark and Finland have encouraged their tourist boards to promote 'stay at home' Scandinavian holidaymaking. The cultural affinity between the countries reinforces the tendency to travel within Scandinavia and the harmonisation of laws and the co-operation between the countries makes it easy.

PHYSICAL AND CLIMATIC RESOURCES OF SCANDINAVIA

Physically, the region consists of a series of countries grouped round the enclosed Baltic Sea, plus two groups of North Atlantic islands (Iceland and the Faroes) which have climates and cultures in common with Baltic Scandinavia.

Baltic Scandinavia

Physically and climatically, the region can be split into three distinct sub-divisions.

1 The western fjord coast and Scandinavian mountains – a ridge that forms the backbone of the Norwegian–Swedish peninsula;
2 The lower lands surrounding the Baltic; and
3 Denmark.

The Scandinavian mountains and fjord coast

The highest part of the mountain chain hugs the west coast, with the two highest groups of peaks lying at opposite ends of the chain. In the far north, the mountains rise to just over 2100 m, while the middle section round Trondheim Fjord is a little lower. The highest peaks (2481 m) are found in the Jotunfjell mountains at the southern end of the chain.

During the last glaciation the thickest part of the Scandinavian ice cap was centred on these mountains. The immense erosive power of the ice gouged out deep steep-sided valleys as the ice cap spread and flowed outwards under the force of its own weight.

Peaks with typical alpine landscape of rocky ridges, sharp peaks and crests stand out above the valleys, creating a dramatic landscape with very high relative relief (up to 1500 m).

The lower sections of the glaciated valley systems were flooded by the sea after the ice cap melted, creating the classic fjord coastal landscape, fringed by a whole series of offshore skerries and islands. The narrowest and longest fjords are to be found on the coast of the southern half of the mountain chain. In the north they are a little wider, though they still create magnificent landscapes. The lower slopes of the mountains are clad in coniferous forests, with pockets of fertile farmland. The climate of the higher peaks and of the northern mountains is too cold for trees, which give way to open arctic and tundra vegetation.

Climatically the region is wet, windy, cloudy and short of sunshine, but the coast is not so cold in winter as the rest of Scandinavia. The mountains lie across the path of the prevailing westerly winds which bring comparatively mild moist Atlantic air onto the west coast (*see* Fig 28.3). This air rises over the mountains producing a great

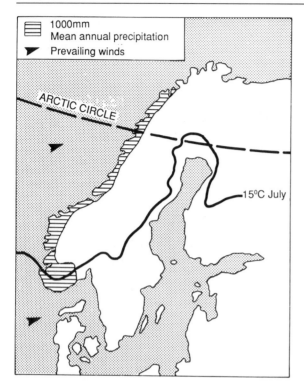

Fig. 28.3 July temperatures in Scandinavia

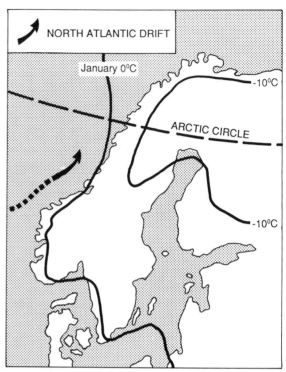

Fig. 28.4 January temperatures in Scandinavia

deal of turbulence, cloud and orographic precipitation (up to 2057 mm per annum in Bergen, and even 4000 mm in the northern snowfields) much of which falls as snow on the mountains in winter. The coast, however, is normally kept ice-free in winter due to the north atlantic drift (*see* Fig 28.4). The region receives the heaviest rainfall of the whole of Scandinavia.

The summer is also cool and cloudy, with average temperatures below 15° C in July.

Unfortunately, this region which has such superb coastal and landscape qualities lacks a climate suitable for mass tourism.

The lower lands surrounding the Baltic: the continental interior

The eastern flanks of the mountains drop away gradually to the lowlands fringing the Baltic. The mountains are cut by straighter glaciated NW–SE valleys, often with lakes in them, draining into the Baltic, or into the North Sea in southern Norway.

In sharp contrast to the mountains, the lowlands are characterised by very low relative relief (generally under 100 m); and due to the scouring action of the spreading ice sheets, they no longer have any clearly defined valleys. Water, therefore, cannot escape to the sea and floods the shallow depressions in the land surface to form the intricate and extensive lake systems, so characteristic of the Finnish lake district and of southern Sweden.

A band of distinctive 'fissure valley landscape' runs diagonally across southern Finland and southern Sweden. Here, the land surface is cut by a network of narrow steep-sided valleys and hollows, frequently lake-filled, interspersed with plateau-like blocks of often bare ice scoured rock.

At the coast, this landscape creates a very beautiful series of islands, for example in Southwest Finland, Åland and Stockholm, the latter stretch being much used by Stockholmers for summer holidays. On the west coast of Sweden there are greater accumulations of sand between the rocky stretches and this is again popular for domestic tourism and is known as Sweden's 'Golden Coast', (*see* Fig 28.5).

In spite of its northerly latitude, the summer climate of this part of Scandinavia is favourable for coastal tourism. It is both much drier and warmer than the west-facing fjord coast of Norway. As the westerly air flow passes over the mountain crest, the turbulence dies down, the winds drop and the now relatively dry air subsides into the Baltic region and the cloud melts away. Thus, on the east side of the Scandinavian mountains the rainfall totals are low and decrease from south to north (e.g. Gothenberg and Oslo in the south have 711 mm and 584 mm rainfall per annum respectively, while the north end of the Midnight Sun Coast (on the Gulf of Bothnia) has only about 317 mm). Although there is a summer (July/August) maximum, this falls in short, thundery outbursts that interrupt the generally sunny weather.

The combination of low cloud cover and high latitude (with long hours of daylight) gives high annual sunshine totals (over 2100 hours a year) and average summer temperatures climb to 18° C in southeast Finland in July and daily maxima may reach 25–30° C – near the temperatures reached in the Mediterranean. However, the summer season is short and winters are intensely cold; the Baltic and Gulf of Bothnia freeze over in winter.

Denmark

Denmark's landscape and coast are very different to those of the rest of Scandinavia. The gently undulating landscape is subdued; more than half the country is below 30 m, and around 70 per cent of the countryside consists of manmade agricultural landscapes. The coast is a more significant leisure resource, and the country has 7300 km of beaches. The west coast is fringed by a continuous 320 km stretch of sand dunes, which enclose lagoons on their landward side. The strong offshore currents sometimes make seabathing dangerous here and the coast is not extensively developed for tourism. The Baltic coast (on the east) and the islands provide a mixture of open bays, deep inlets and good beaches, providing ideal conditions for sailing and other water sports. The most developed section of the coast (the Danish 'riviera') lies between Copenhagen and Helsingor.

SPATIAL DISTRIBUTION OF TOURISM IN SCANDINAVIA

Norway

Oslo and its hinterland is the focus of Norway's domestic and international tourism. Oslo is the capital, and is the cultural and artistic centre of the country. It is, for example, the location of folk, maritime and whaling museums, and Viking remains and burial mounds are found locally. The hinterland of Oslo is also significant for domestic tourism. Nearly 30 per cent of Norway's stock of hotel beds (1991) were in the series of forested valleys which run from the flanks of the Dovrefjell, Jotunheim and Hardanger Plateau down to the Oslo fjord (Norway's Eastern Valleys, *see* Fig 28.5). The valleys are thus easily accessible from Oslo and provide for a wide variety of scenic and activity holidays. Winter and summer skiing activities are enjoyed at the resorts in the upper reaches of the valleys, e.g. at Tynset in the upper Glomma valley, and summer activities such as walking, riding and all water sports in the middle and lower sections of the valleys, e.g. at Kongsvinger, Elverum and Rena in the lower Glomma valley.

The other tourist regions are centred around Bergen in the Western Fjords, where nearly 10 per cent of hotel beds are located; the Telemark coast where bathing beaches are interspersed with rocky coasts and harbours (seven per cent hotel beds); and the Trondheim region (7.4 per cent beds) (*see* Fig 28.5).

Sweden

In Sweden, tourist activity is more widely spread. Stockholm and its hinterland is, of course, the main centre for both domestic and international tourists. In addition to the city nightlife, the region includes the archipelago of over 2000 islands just offshore, many of which are accessible by boat, and provide opportunities for scenic and water sports tourism. The Stockholm and Uppsala area receives nearly 17 per cent of domestic tourist nights (hotels and supplementary forms of accommodation), and 24 per cent of all foreign bednights in 1990. The next most popular region is the Golden Coast (*see* Fig 28.5) which includes a 400 km stretch of sandy coast with excellent beaches

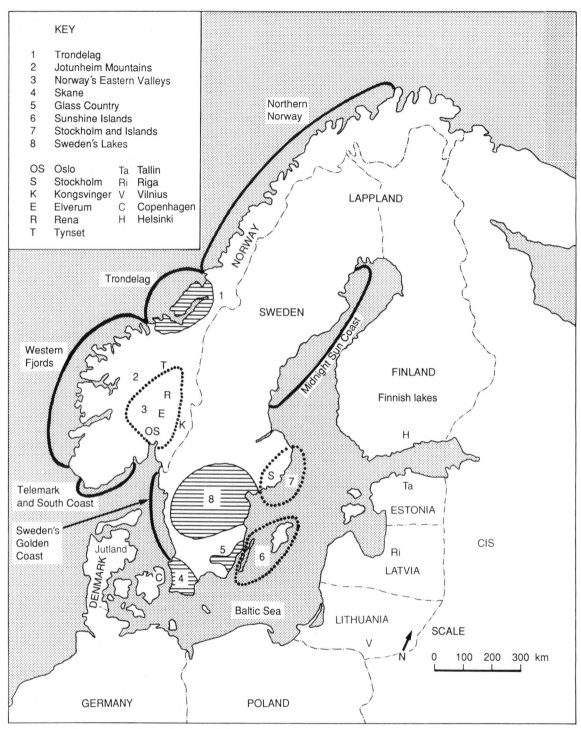

KEY

1 Trondelag
2 Jotunheim Mountains
3 Norway's Eastern Valleys
4 Skane
5 Glass Country
6 Sunshine Islands
7 Stockholm and Islands
8 Sweden's Lakes

OS Oslo   Ta Tallin
S Stockholm   Ri Riga
K Kongsvinger   V Vilnius
E Elverum   C Copenhagen
R Rena   H Helsinki
T Tynset

Fig. 28.5 Main tourist regions of Scandinavia

mixed with a variety of other coastal landscapes. It accounted for over 14 per cent of domestic tourism and 13.7 per cent of foreign bednights in 1990. The other three main tourist regions of Sweden – the Swedish lakes, the Glass Country (the centre of Swedish glass-making) and the Midnight Coast – are about equal in popularity with the domestic market, each taking about ten per cent of the domestic trade. The far north attracted 9.7 per cent of all foreign bednights in 1990, but proved more popular with Nordic visitors than tourists from the rest of the world.

Finland

Finland shows the same differences between international and domestic tourism as the other Scandinavian countries. International arrivals are strongly concentrated on the capital, Helsinki (with 38 per cent foreign bednights in 1992) at the expense of the rest of the country, whereas Helsinki accounted for only 7.3 per cent of domestic tourism. A third of domestic tourists makes for the inland lakeside venues throughout the Finnish lake district; international visitors tend to reach only the lakes just inland of Helsinki. A further third of domestic overnight stays are in the northern territories, i.e. Lappland and the Finnish Midnight Sun Coast, whereas only 15 per cent of international visitors venture so far north.

Tourism in all three countries is very strongly seasonal (*see* Fig 28.6).

Domestic tourism is also peaked in the summer season June–August but not so strongly, for example 30.8 per cent of Swedish domestic tourism is in July and 12.6 per cent in August. This inevitably leads to low overall occupancy rates, ranging from a low of 35.7 per cent for Swedish hotels in 1984 to a high of 53.2 per cent for Finland. A range of types of accommodation is available, from hotels, farmhouses, self-catering chalet villages and forest cabins, to well equipped camp sites.

About 60 per cent of travel in Scandinavia is by Scandinavians, and 40 per cent comes from outside the region. Non-Scandinavians rely mainly on the hotels, and the majority of these tourists come from the adjacent north European countries, but surprisingly large numbers come from North America. However, there was extensive immigration from Scandinavia to USA in the 19th century, and these cultural ties are still strong.

Scandinavian outbound travel

It has been noted that a high proportion of outbound travel from each of the Scandinavian countries is to other Scandinavian countries. The next most important group of destinations are the adjacent north European countries – mainly Germany but also France, UK and the newly accessible destinations of the Baltic States and Poland. In 1990, Germany was the most important destination for Danes, while Germany attracts 17.7 per cent of Sweden's non-Scandinavian outbound travel. However, the coastal and climatic resources of the Mediterranean are a powerful lure, and about 18 per cent of all Scandinavian outbound travel in 1991 was to the Mediterranean coastal regions of Spain (particularly the Canary Islands), Italy and Greece, while Cyprus and Turkey are growing in popularity.

Tourism in Denmark

Denmark's unexceptional physical resources do not make it a significant tourist destination on European terms. Nevertheless, the volume of its incoming tourism is on a par with that of Sweden or Finland. The majority of its visitors (36 per cent of bednights) are Scandinavians, but it relies heavily on the German market for 37 per cent of bednights. Its extensive coastline and its common border with Germany make it an attractive destination for German coastal tourists, and Germans account for 60 per cent of all camping bednights in Denmark. For other nationalities, it is the cultural

Overseas visitors	% Bednights		
	Finland (1989)	Norway (1984)	Sweden (1984)
April	8.0	3.8	2.6
May	7.7	6.1	3.8
June	10.3	15.4	11.6
July	13.2	21.0	39.7
August	10.6	17.9	22.5
September	8.7	7.6	4.9
October	7.7	3.8	3.5

Fig. 28.6 Seasonality of Scandinavia's tourism

	Foreign tourist nights (000s)			
	Denmark (all accom) 1992 (1991)	Finland (all accom) 1992	Norway 1992 (1991)	Sweden (all accom) 1991
Germany	4 496	476	850	(1 319)
UK	379	130	428	(275)
Netherlands	991	81	174	(321)
France	149	99	242	(164)
N America	322	152	351	(270)
Italy	231	89	–	(134)
Other Scandinavian total	3 912	816	1 471	2 158
made up of:				
Denmark		72	(701)	(519)
Finland	(233)		(118)	(556)
Norway	(1 062)	114		(1 083)
Sweden	(2 567)	630	(680)	
(Scandinavian %)	(34.1%)	(31.6%)	(34.4%)	(38.5%)
Total nights	11 456	2 586	4 275	5 600

(*NB*: figures in brackets are for 1991)

Fig. 28.7 International tourism in Scandinavia

and historical heritage of the country that is the main attraction (e.g. the old town of Ribe). It has many attractive villages and castles, and as it still has a constitutional monarchy, there are palaces and pageantry associated with the royal family. There are also several Viking museums, e.g. at Helsingor and Copenhagen. Copenhagen is the main focus of international tourism, attracting 28 per cent of foreign arrivals in 1990. Apart from its historic attractions, the city is famous for its breweries and for the Tivoli Gardens (a major and old established amusement and theme park which attracted 4.1 million visitors).

Legoland (close to Billund airport) is in the centre of Jutland. It is another popular theme park with over one million visitors in 1990. It is popular with the UK market.

ICELAND

Although Iceland is culturally part of Scandinavia and it shares a northerly latitude (just south of the Arctic Circle), it is physically nearer Greenland. Its isolation and character make it a very specialist destination, with only very few international visitors (only 143 459 in 1991).

The island stands astride the central ridge running down the length of the Atlantic Ocean, marking the zone where the ocean floor is splitting and spreading, as the continents of Europe and North America drift further apart. As the earth's crust split, molten rock escaped from the seabed which built up to form Iceland. As this process is still active, there are intermittent volcanic events on the island which have created a landscape of mountains, lava fields, geothermal springs, geysers and bubbling mud holes.

The older volcanic landforms have been modified by glaciation, and the mountains are blanketed with snow in winter. The coast has a fjord-type landscape, particularly in the northwest. Much of the island is uninhabited, with the majority of the 255 000 population concentrated in the capital, Reykjavik, or other small coastal settlements. Much of the island is untouched wilderness. Its particular appeal is its unpolluted environment, its landscape, geology and wildlife.

Its tourist season, in common with Norway, Sweden and Finland, is short, perhaps even shorter than countries with culturally based tourism, as access to the mountains is often by unsealed roads which are often impassable until well into the summer months. Accommodation in the remoter parts is basic (simple farmhouses, youth hostels or huts), although there are first class hotels in Reykjavik.

In 1991 31 per cent of Iceland's visitors came from other Scandinavian countries, 16 per cent from USA, 15 per cent from Germany and 10 per cent from the UK.

FURTHER READING

Bywater, M (1991) 'Sweden', *EIU International Tourism Reports*, No. 3, pp. 41–55.

Bywater, M (1992) 'Denmark', *EIU International Tourism Reports*, No. 1, pp. 32–51.

Cockerell, N (1991) 'Sweden outbound', *EIU Travel and Tourism Analyst*, No. 5, pp. 42–56.

EIU (1993) 'Norway', *EIU International Tourism Reports*, No. 3, pp. 55–76.

Weston, C (1991) 'Finland', *EIU International Tourism Reports*, No. 2, pp. 67–85.

QUESTIONS AND DISCUSSION POINTS

1 'The attractions of Norway and Sweden appeal to such a specialised market that these countries will never attract very large numbers of non-Scandinavian visitors.' Discuss whether you think this is a true or a false statement.

2 In 1985 it was estimated that Denmark received roughly 15 million day excursionists, five million direct transit travellers and only five million staying visitors. To what extent does Denmark's size and geographical location explain this pattern of inbound tourism?

3 List the most popular foreign holiday destinations of the Scandinavian market. Offer explanations for this pattern of outbound tourism from Scandinavia.

ASSIGNMENTS

1 A newly set up tour company called 'Scandal' specialises in tours for the UK market in Scandinavia. Currently they offer tours to the main urban centres (Copenhagen, Oslo and Stockholm). They have commissioned you as a consultant to write a short report outlining the geographical potential of the rest of Norway, Sweden and Denmark for tourism, the types of holidays that might take advantage of this potential, the seasons of the year in which such holidays might best be offered, and the potential market. Make recommendations as to how the company could develop a range of new tours to complement its city tours.

2 You work for a cruise company that is considering a plan to develop cruises in the Baltic. You have been asked to assess the geographical opportunities and constraints on such developments. Write a preliminary report:

(*a*) describing the climate of the Baltic and indicating the months during which cruises would be most attractive. Note any other constraints that might limit the operation of such cruises;

(*b*) listing the places of interest that could feature on the itineraries and the nature of their special interest;

(*c*) identifying the markets to whom such cruises might appeal; and

(*d*) recommending whether or not you think the company should go ahead with more detailed investigations and aim to develop such cruises.

Africa and the Middle East

INTRODUCTION

This section seeks to answer the following questions.

1 What is the volume, character and spatial pattern of tourist activity in the continent of Africa and the Middle East?
2 What is the role of the region in the general pattern of world tourism?
3 What and where are the region's tourist resources?
4 What are the long-term economic and political problems that inhibit the expansion of tourism in the region?

The whole of the region lies in the economic periphery of the world, and is characterised by generally low levels of tourism (poorly developed or non-existent domestic markets, and very limited in- and outbound international tourism). The region is beset with political and economic problems: many of its countries are politically unstable, and consequently the region has many recent or ongoing civil wars. There are also longstanding international disputes between certain countries in the region. Nevertheless, the region has outstanding tourist resources that are promoted for international tourism where local political circumstances allow.

The region falls into two zones, divided by the natural barrier of the Saharan and Arabian deserts. The northern part, described in Chapter 29, consists of the mainly Islamic countries of the Middle East and the countries bordering the east and south Mediterranean (from Syria to Morocco). Functionally, however, this part of Africa and the Middle East used to belong to the European tourist region, but growing intraregional travel means that this is no longer so clearly the case.

The other half of the continent, described in Chapter 30, lies south of the Sahara desert and is known as Subsaharan Africa. It extends roughly from latitude 15° N to the Cape of Good Hope; and also includes the islands off the African coast (in the western half of the Indian Ocean). In terms of its world tourist function, the region is truly peripheral.

CHAPTER 29

North Africa and the Middle East

LEARNING OBJECTIVES

After reading this chapter you should be able to
- assess the tourist potential of the climatic, coastal, landscape, historical and cultural resources of North Africa and the Middle East
- distinguish between the regional distribution of these geographical resources and their development and use for tourism
- demonstrate a knowledge of the main tourist resorts and tourist centres
- understand the role of the region in the general pattern of world and European tourism
- outline the political, religious and economic constraints on tourist development in the region.

INTRODUCTION

The region covered in this chapter consists of the part of Africa that lies north of the Sahara desert and the Middle East. Figure 29.2 shows that, with only two exceptions (Israel and Lebanon), the vast majority of the populations of each country are Muslims. The region forms the heart of the Islamic world, although Fig 29.2 also indicates that the majority of the world's population of Muslims live outside the region, in the countries of Turkey, CIS, Pakistan, India, Bangladesh, Indonesia and Nigeria.

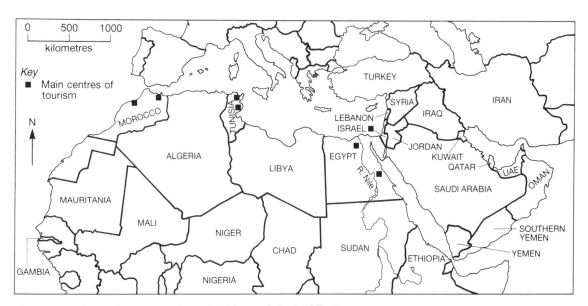

Fig. 29.1 Main tourist centres of North Africa and the Middle East

The predominant religion imposes some constraints on the development of Western-style tourism, but not in all the countries of North Africa and the Middle East. Western-style tourism in the region is on a small scale as yet, and is currently located in some of the countries making up the eastern and southern shores of the Mediterranean Sea (i.e. from Syria to Morocco). These countries possess coastal, climatic and cultural resources that have the potential to attract Western tourists. They lie in the sphere of influence of the European tourist market and can be considered as function-ally part of the European tourist system. In 1990 they received 10.5 million tourists.

On the other hand, tourism is hardly developed at all in the remainder of the Middle East (i.e. in Iran, Iraq, Saudi Arabia, Jordan, Yemen (north and south), Oman and the Gulf states). The total number of tourists to the region as a whole was estimated at only 6.9 million in 1988. The Gulf War has temporarily disrupted the pattern of tourism of the region but the established destinations appear to have recovered by 1992 (*see* fig 29.3).

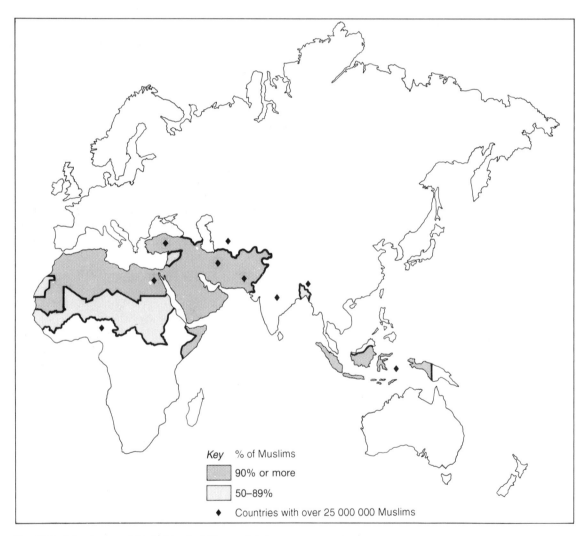

Fig. 29.2 Islamic countries in North Africa and Asia

Country	International tourist arrivals (000s)		
	1990	*1991*	*1992*
Egypt	2600	2209	3206
Israel	1111	943	1376
Jordan	2633	2227	

Fig. 29.3 Effect of the 1991 Gulf War on tourism – selected destinations in the Middle East

Jordan, Israel and Egypt experienced a 15 per cent drop in their tourism in 1991. Israel and Egypt recovered in 1992 with a 45 per cent increase.

TOURISM IN THE COUNTRIES BORDERING THE MEDITERRANEAN

As well as their Mediterranean coastal resources, these countries, Syria, Lebanon, Israel, Egypt, Libya, Tunisia, Algeria and Morocco, have climates ranging from Mediterranean through semi-arid to desert conditions (*see* Fig 18.2 on p 193). They also have a wealth of cultural and historic resources (*see* Chapter 5).

It is more the political situation that deters visitors from venturing to the region in any large numbers or investors from developing it extensively. Syria, for example, has little interest in Western-style tourism, although Latakia is a coastal resort catering for Arab visitors. Lebanon has been suffering from a violent civil war, and the longstanding hostility between Israel and the Arab states has still to be resolved though significant moves towards a settlement were made in 1993. Political problems within Israel have also reduced the country's attraction to Western visitors. Egypt, having played a mediating role in Middle East politics and having made peace with Israel, is better placed to take advantage of Western tourism, but to date, has directed tourism development inland or towards the Gulf of Aquaba and the Red Sea, rather than to its Mediterranean coast. However, Islamic fundamentalist guerrilla attacks on tourists in 1993 has hindered this development. Libya, being an Islamic fundamentalist state, does not welcome Western tourism.

Tunisia, Algeria and Morocco are physically closer to the European market and are politically a little more orientated towards Europe, and beach resorts have been promoted in Tunisia and Morocco. In practice, however, Western-style tourism has been limited to a relatively few locations in the region where and when political circumstances allow: in Tunisia, Morocco, Egypt and Israel.

In the latter two countries, it is mainly their cultural and historical features that draw international visitors to this inherently politically unstable region. Beach visits may be an added extra on tour itineraries but are not usually the primary purpose of the holiday though Israel marketed sun, sea and sand holidays in the 1980s which attracted less than 300 000 visitors in 1987 – mainly from Scandinavia (but also some from Germany, Switzerland and the Netherlands). Thus, Egypt and Israel are not strong competitors with other Mediterranean countries for the mass beach tourist market.

ISRAEL

Israel's cultural attractions are unique. The 'Holy Land' sites are of equal historical and religious significance to Jews and Christians alike, while Jerusalem itself is also of major religious importance to Muslims. Jerusalem is clearly the main tourist destination while Galilee (including Nazareth) and Bethlehem (the latter in the Israeli-occupied West Bank) are also much visited (*see* Fig 29.4). It is estimated that around 20 per cent of non-Jewish visitors come on a pilgrimage or specifically for religious purposes, while touring and sightseeing (including Holy Land Tours) are the main interest of 30 per cent of all visitors.

Israel, however, has many other sites of religious and historical interest which are sometimes included on tours, for example Acre (the site of a major Crusader stronghold), Jericho and the Dead Sea.

Tel Aviv, Israel's capital, is located on the Mediterranean coast and is the other major destination of the country. It has the twin attractions of both modern cultural facilities and fine sandy beaches. Natanya is another important Mediterranean beach resort that is a little more popular with the domestic market than with international visitors. The Red Sea resort of Elat in the far south of the country is much more frequently used by Israeli holidaymakers.

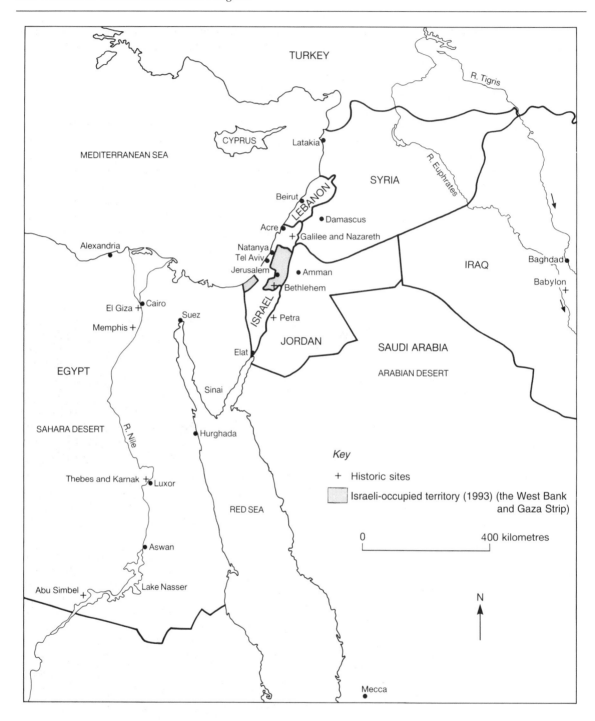

Fig. 29.4 The Middle East

Since 1980 Israel has attracted just over one million foreign visitors a year but its international tourism is greatly affected by political events and is influenced by media-generated perceptions of the scale of political unrest. The American market (which makes up around a quarter of Israel's foreign visitors) are particularly sensitive. Visitor numbers drop when violent events occur but tend to recover in time. Israel's international tourist industry will always be subject to these fluctuations until long-term political stability is established in the region. On the other hand, Israel has a substantial VFR component to its incoming foreign tourism (39 per cent of Jewish visitors and 22 per cent of all visitors). Israel has attracted Jewish immigrants from many parts of the world which generates a significant flow of people wishing to visit their friends and relatives now resident in Israel. These visitors may be less responsive to the political events.

EGYPT

Egypt's tourism is focused around the monuments, tombs, temples and settlements of the Pharaohs. These outstanding archaeological remains are located inland, along the Nile Valley from Cairo to above the Aswan Dam. Western-style coastal tourism (with its emphasis on sunbathing, bars and lively entertainment) does not fit easily into an Islamic culture though the Egyptians themselves do visit the seaside and there are crowded public beaches near Cairo. Western tourism is accepted at the most popular

Fig. 29.5 Valley of the Queens (near Valley of the Kings), Egypt

tourist cities but coastal bathing is not yet a major element of Egypt's tourist industry. However, the Government set up plans in the late 1980s to diversify its tourism product into sun, sea and sand (and conference) tourism. Like Israel, Egypt has access to the Red Sea as well as to the Mediterranean and most of the coastal tourist initiatives are located in Sinai or along the Red Sea coast further south. Here Hurghada is the main resort where there is good snorkelling. The fish are particularly abundant on the coral offshore. In 1990 seven tourist villages were under construction on the Red Sea for Western visitors.

In addition to the cultural constraints on tourism, the climate imposes some limits. The region has a hot desert (rather than a Mediterranean) climate and average temperatures reach 27° C in Cairo but 32° C inland, e.g. at Aswan. From June to August, daily maximum temperatures rise far higher, which Western tourists tend to find stressful, in spite of the low relative humidities. The peak seasons for Western tourism are spring and autumn (March to April and October). However, visitors from other Arab countries (i.e. 37 per cent of Egypt's total) are not deterred by the very high temperatures in mid-summer and most arrive in June, July and August. Such visitors sometimes find these high temperatures a little lower than those experienced in their own country, where summer averages may rise to 35° C.

Most cultural tours include Cairo for the Giza sphinx and the Pyramids, the museum with Tutankhamun's treasure, and Memphis. The other most important archaeological sites on the tourist itineraries, such as the Valley of the Kings and the Karnak Temples, are within reach of Luxor and Aswan on the mid-Nile. Tourists generally transfer from Cairo by air (or rail in winter), often picking up 4–6 day cruises which ply between Luxor and Aswan. By 1986 there were 82 cruise ships in operation, with new ships being added to the Nile fleet each year.

Egypt draws its tourists from all over the world: the USA, Sudan, Saudi Arabia, France, Germany, UK, Italy and Japan are the most important visitor generating countries. Since making peace with Israel in 1979, Egypt has been one of the more politically stable Middle Eastern countries and its total tourism has grown steadily in the 1990s. However, the 1985 Achille Lauro

hijack and bombing of Libya in 1986 led to a sharp (temporary) decrease in visitors from USA. This was more than compensated for by the growth in numbers from other sources, and the total number of all tourists continued to climb. In 1987 Egypt received 1.8 million non-Arab visitors. However, the events of the Gulf War in 1991 saw the total European and American component of Egypt's market drop to 0.8 million, though by 1992 it had recovered to 1.67 million. The internal political problems in 1993 have led to a further 30 per cent downturn in European tourism to Egypt in the first four months of 1993.

THE NORTH AFRICAN COAST

The Mahgreb, consisting of the countries of Tunisia, Algeria and Morocco, is the only significant centre of tourist development in the south of the Mediterranean. Even so, tourism is small scale: the three countries together account for around seven per cent of the total Mediterranean tourist trade. They are closer to the centres of population in Western Europe but their development for tourism perhaps relates more to their political past: all were formerly French colonies.

They, therefore, have cultural links with potential Western markets; European languages are spoken, and although the people of the Mahgreb are Muslims, Western visitors are more welcome. The countries also have a good basic infrastructure that was established in colonial times. The good road systems in Morocco for example are a valuable foundation for the development of tourism. However, the three countries have very different styles of tourist development. Tunisia specialises in mass beach tourism, Morocco in a varied product for prestige tourism, and Algeria is only recently becoming involved, and tourism here is still on a very small scale.

The Mahgreb

The Atlas mountains run SW–NE roughly parallel to the North African coast from Tangiers to Tunis (*see* Fig 29.6). They average 1–2000 metres, though the peaks rise to 4000 m. In the High Atlas in Morocco, land over 2500 m has snow for four to five months in the winter. The ranges that

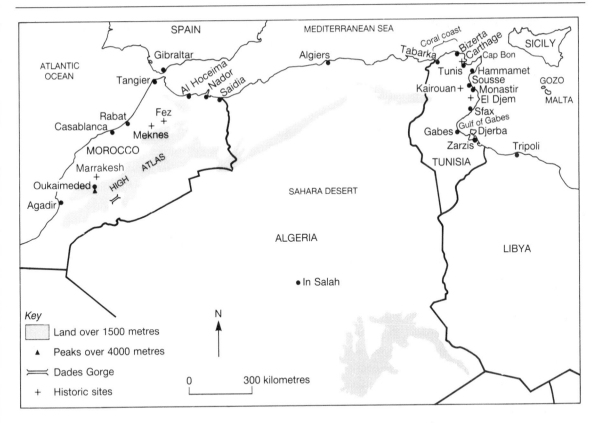

Fig. 29.6 Countries of the Mahgreb

back the coast are lower but are rugged, with deep gorges, scarped rocky coasts, and steep hillsides. Southern Tunisia is a different physical world, it consists of the level lands of the edge of the Sahara Desert with rock and sand dune deserts, low-lying salt lakes and scattered fertile oases, and which have a true hot desert climate. Here summer maxima climb to 40° C and the diurnal temperature range can be as high as 15° C. Once again, the Mediterranean climate is limited to the narrow coastal strip of the mountains, and Tunis has a monthly average of 26° C from June to September.

TUNISIA

Ninety per cent of Tunisia's tourism is coastal. The accommodation is concentrated in purpose-built holiday villages outside and separate from the major urban centres. The coast consists of three zones:

1 The north coast from the Algerian border to Cap Bon. The coast west of Bizerta is known as the Coral Coast. Coral grows underwater (though not in reef formation) and divers collect it for commercial use. The coast is slightly cooler and moister than Tunisia's desert coast and it has good beaches and coves between rocky outcrops, but it is relatively underdeveloped for tourism, though plans exist to develop a 10 000 hotel-bedspace resort at Tabarka near the airport.

Tunis itself caters for both foreign business as well as excursion tourism, and there are attractive beach resorts nearby. East of Tunis the coast is green with citrus groves, olive trees and vineyards. This whole section of coast had 16 per cent of Tunisia's bed spaces (mostly concentrated in Tunis) but only 11 per cent of bednights in 1990.

2 The west coast (The Sahel). This runs south from Cap Bon to Sfax and is the most intensively developed for beach tourism. There are three clusters of resorts around Hammamet, Sousse and

Sfax. The beaches are big, wide and sandy, while inland the countryside is a patchwork of olive groves, grainfields and sheep grazing. In 1990, the region had 62 per cent of Tunisia's bed spaces, but took 69 per cent of bednights. The stretch of coast between Monastir and Sfax was expanding its accommodation stock most rapidly of all Tunisia's tourist areas in the 1980s.

3 The Gulf of Gabes. The coasts of the Tunisian Sahara are flat, sandy and dry. Average summer temperatures in Djerba reach 28° C in August, and sea temperatures rise to over 25° C, while in winter the average air temperature is 11° C in January. The island of Djerba has big, sandy beaches with only few rocky patches. Most of the hotels are low-rise and are located on the island's east coast where there is a 20 km stretch of sandy beach. The climate allows year round tourism, although the high season runs from April to October. Winter tourism is being actively promoted and there is growth in off-season visits by Germans, British and Scandinavians. Here, as along the whole of Tunisia's coast, there are plentiful opportunities for water sports, such as fishing, scuba diving, sailing and water skiing. The mainland coast is dry, though Zarzis and Gabes are coastal oases and the resorts are surrounded by palm trees, and an almost tropical environment. The region as a whole has 18 per cent of Tunisia's bed spaces and 17 per cent of tourist nights in 1990.

4 The interior. Although the coast is Tunisia's main resource, there are many historic and cultural attractions. The pre-Roman civilisation at Carthage, the Roman amphitheatre at El Djem and the Muslim city of Kairouan, founded in AD 671 are all destinations of day-trips from the resorts. Day excursions also penetrate into the deserts and inland oases in the south, though there are only a handful of hotels located away from the coast.

Visitors to Tunisia

Tunisia relies heavily on the European mass market. In 1987, 83 per cent of the 1.8 million visitors came from Europe. Since then Tunisia's total tourist arrivals have grown to 3.2 million, but this has been due to an increase in regional travel (particularly from Algeria and Libya) rather than an increase in tourism from Europe. Up to the year of the Gulf War, European tourism had grown slowly from 1.5 million in 1987 to 1.7 million in 1990. During the Gulf War, Tunisia took a more pro-Iraqi line than some countries of the region, and inbound European tourism was cut by a third in 1991. Before the war nearly 79 per cent of European arrivals came by air, and half of these came by charter flights via Monastir airport which was purpose-built for the charter market. France ruled Tunisia as a colony from 1881 to 1956, and not surprisingly the majority of Tunisia's visitors came from France, although the German market is almost as important (and, since 1985 more important in terms of visitor nights in registered accommodation). By 1990 Germans just outnumbered French. Nearly 0.5 million Algerians crossed the border into Tunisia, while Britain remains the third most important non-Arab market when tourist numbers and nights spent are taken into account.

The number of Algerians and Libyans visiting Tunisia fluctuated in the 1980s due to:

(*a*) changing travel restrictions placed on Algerians by their own Government. Algerians visit for shopping trips and to visit friends and relatives; and

(*b*) the evolving diplomatic relations between Tunisia and Libya (the border was closed for a period between 1983 and 1987) but since the border was reopened, Libyans have also visited Tunisia for shopping trips and to visit friends and relatives (in 1988 the total number of Libyan tourists had increased to 1.2 million).

ALGERIA

Algeria was also a French colony, and was frequented by wealthy French and British tourists in the late 19th century. However, the country has not encouraged modern tourism, although it has similar resources of climate, coast and culture to Tunisia. Until recently, Algeria has had little economic incentive to promote tourism, as 95 per cent of its foreign income comes from the export of oil and gas. However, in the 1980s the economy faltered as the price of oil and gas gradually fell, and unemployment rose. The Algerian Government began to consider tourism as a means to solve these economic problems.

In 1987/8 the Government took a more positive approach, including measures to attract private investment alongside or in partnership with the Government, and undertook more serious marketing, for example by producing promotional literature in languages other than French. It remains to be seen whether these initiatives will be sustained by the Algerian Government and will attract investors, and indeed whether the Western European market will be prepared to come to Algeria.

In the past, Algeria's attempts to promote beach tourism have been rather half-hearted and have led to small, isolated developments well away from the urban areas. These create resorts of limited appeal which are difficult for the tour operators to promote.

In 1987, tourism was still on a small scale, with only 48 000 bed spaces and just three-quarters of a million visitors. Most of these were from France, and included mainly business tourism with few holidaymakers.

After 1987, the improving political relationships with Algeria's neighbours dramatically increased tourism from African countries (from 90 000 p.a. to over 400 000), and the total level of inbound tourism grew from 777 000 in 1987 to 1 136 900 in 1990. However, tourism from Europe over the same period increased from 163 000 to only 227 000. Algeria's new approach to tourism envisages a significant increase in accommodation capacity (planned to reach 129 000 beds by the year 2000).

MOROCCO

Morocco has 3000 km of coast, though much is west of the Straits of Gibraltar and faces the Atlantic rather than the Mediterranean. The Atlantic coast is the better developed for tourism and competes with the Mediterranean resorts though it is also a significant site for winter tourism.

	Number
Mediterranean coast	34 894
Atlantic coast – Centre	37 578
– South	29 243
Interior	13 385
Marrakesh	22 661

Fig. 29.7 Distribution of bed spaces in Morocco, 1990

The country's resources are varied, ranging from long, sandy beaches (at Agadir), desert and mountain landscapes, ski resorts in the High Atlas, and a wealth of historic cities. During the 1970s and 1980s, the Government encouraged upmarket tourism, although later it tried to encourage family-orientated mass tourism. The total volume of Morocco's tourism appears to relate to the price differences between Spain and Morocco.

Morocco's regional resources

1 The Mediterranean coast. The coastline is a mixture of creeks, bays, cliffs and sheltered beaches, with good opportunities for swimming and water sports. It is essentially undeveloped, apart from the relatively new resorts of Al Hoceima M'Diq and Restinga-Smir (all summer-only resorts). Nador and Saidia are longer established (*see* Fig 29.6). Attempts have been made to market these as competitive seaside resorts but in fact they declined in popularity in the mid-1980s. The cosmopolitan city of Tangiers (which has both Mediterranean and Atlantic beaches) lies opposite to Gibraltar and is the gateway for car and passenger ferry arrivals from Spain. It also has an international airport.

2 The Atlantic coast. The northern parts are rocky but have some good beaches, while the biggest sandy beaches are towards the south. Agadir has a superb eight km beach; it is a modern luxury resort, rebuilt as a holiday city after the old city was destroyed by a major earthquake in 1960. It has a range of accommodation from luxury high-rise hotels to self-catering, and golf, horse riding and tennis facilities in addition to water sports. South of Agadir (on the Sahara desert coast) there are long stretches of undeveloped white sandy beaches. The coast is on the same latitude as the Canary Islands (which are only 45 minutes away by air) and the Moroccan coast is similarly suited to winter tourism.

3 The interior. Morocco is the oldest Muslim kingdom in the world, and was independent until it became a French protectorate in 1912. The cities of Fez, Meknes and Marrakesh are sited on the western flanks of the Atlas and have all been the country's capital in the past (Rabat, on the coast, is the modern capital). The ancient city of Fez was founded in 808 AD, while Marrakesh has medieval alleyways and a wealth of ancient monuments, palaces and tombs, and Meknes was laid out in the 17th century. All form the focus of cultural tourism. Skiing has been developed in the mountains above Meknes, and at Oukaimeded which is only a half hour's drive from Marrakesh. The desert landscapes of the south have yet to be extensively developed for tourism, although the sand and rock deserts, oases and the dramatic gorges of the Dades and Todra have great potential.

Visitors to Morocco

In 1988, the country welcomed 2.8 million visitors. Excluding Moroccans who are resident abroad and who return to Morocco for holidays, the biggest share (26.8 per cent) come from France, reflecting Morocco's colonial past. Nearly 20 per cent come across the Straits of Gibraltar from Spain, while the UK and Germany each contribute around 11 per cent. The American market dropped away in the 1980s (from 100 000 in 1985 to just 38 000 in 1986) following the Achille Lauro hijack and was further hit by the Gulf War. On the other hand, better political relationships between Morocco and Algeria have allowed Algerians to visit Morocco in growing numbers for shopping trips. The number of Algerians visiting Morocco increased from 375 000 in 1988 to 1.4 million by 1990, and to over two million in 1991 while European tourists decreased from 1.3 million to 1.1 million over the same period. However, France, Spain and Germany remain Algeria's main European markets.

THE MIDDLE EAST

In spite of the high per capita incomes of Middle Eastern oil-exporting countries, they are included in the economic periphery of the world (*see* Fig 15.2 on p 152). Their capacity to generate outbound tourism is considerable but the potential of the region as a tourist destination is extremely limited, and, physically, the climate is a major constraint. The Arabian peninsula is a true desert with temperatures as high as the Sahara. Its vast and gently sloping plateau is a gravel surface with patches of sand dunes. Iraq's territory covers the valleys of the Tigris and Euphrates, and its climate is dry

(under 300 mm of rain per year) with extreme temperatures averaging 34° C in the summer, while the January average drops to 10° C. Iran's mountainous territory has a little more rain (up to 500 mm pa) but the altitude makes winters even colder. The natural environment is thus inhospitable. The countries have many historic and cultural resources, however (*see* Chapter 5) but none of the factors that might encourage Western inbound travel can operate in this part of the world – in fact, circumstances combine to reduce the likelihood of Western-style tourism.

First, the political circumstances of the region deters tourism, and the Iran-Iraq war of the 1980s and the more recent Gulf War have effectively put a stop to tourism development here. Second, the prevailing Islamic way of life does not find Western tourism acceptable, and there are increasing trends towards Islamic fundamentalism. Sharjah had begun to encourage stopover tourism in the early 1980s but local opposition (triggered off by concerns over the erosion of Islamic culture and traditions) led to Sharjah banning the sale of alcohol: this effectively stopped its inbound tourism. Third, the oil-rich countries of the region have no economic incentive to develop tourism for Western visitors, and Western travel to the Middle East (where it does exist) is essentially business tourism: Saudi Arabia does not even issue visas for pleasure travellers.

Thus, it is clear that the region is truly on the periphery of the Western world's tourism. However, the region is the focus of international travel for other groups of the world's population. Saudi Arabia is an important destination for Muslim pilgrims visiting Mecca. These travellers come from countries with large Muslim populations, notably Nigeria, Indonesia, Egypt, Yemen, Iran and Pakistan. It was estimated in the mid 1980s, for example, that about 2.5 million pilgrims arrived in Mecca each year, including 1.5 million from foreign countries.

CONCLUSION

North Africa and the Middle East have much to offer the tourist. Many of the region's countries have a very varied resource base, and could meet the needs of a wide range of tourist markets: they are located in the economic periphery but immediately next to the expanding European tourist region (*see* Chapter 17). However, cultural attitudes and political events have controlled the spread of European tourism into the region in the past. Any major political change in the Middle East will have profound economic and political consequences for most of these countries, due to their strategic location, and their political affiliations. This will no doubt continue to be the case until long-term political stability is established in the Middle Eastern region.

FURTHER READING

Balasubramanian, S (1993) 'United Arab Emirates', *International Tourism Reports*, No. 3, pp. 29–54.

Cockerell, N (1992) 'Jordan', *EIU International Tourism Reports,* No. 3, pp. 23–39.

EIU (1991) 'Egypt', *EIU International Tourism Reports*, No. 1, pp. 52–71.

Gant, R and Smith, J (1992) 'Tourism and National Development Planning in Tunisia', *Tourism Management*, Vol. 13, September, pp. 331–6.

Marks, J (1990) 'Algeria', *EIU International Tourism Reports*, No. 1, pp. 32–46.

Paul, B K and Rimmawi, H S (1992) 'Tourism in Saudi Arabia – Asir National Park', *Annals of Tourism Research*, Vol. 19, pp. 501–15.

Seekings, J (1992) 'Morocco', *EIU International Tourism Reports*, No. 3, pp. 40–57.

QUESTIONS AND DISCUSSION POINTS

1 In what ways do you think Western tourists should modify their behaviour in Islamic countries in order to avoid offending the local population?

2 To what extent do you agree with the proposition that Israel will always have a significant inbound tourist industry, irrespective of the political circumstances she finds herself in?

3 Locate, name and date the main historic resources of the region. Are all of them currently developed for tourism? If not, why not?

ASSIGNMENTS

1 You work for 'Meddy-Sun', a tour company that specialises in sun, sea and sand holidays in the Mediterranean for the North European mass market. The company's business in Spain and former Yugoslavia has declined and your chief executive is considering sites in the south and east Mediterranean for new tours to compensate for the poor performance of the existing range of tours to the north Mediterranean coast. He has asked you to prepare a report briefly reviewing the opportunities for the development of tours to the south and east Mediterranean coast from Syria to Morocco. He has specially asked you to:

(*a*) compare the suitability of the coasts and climates of each country;

(*b*) assess the risk factor – that is the political situation and each government's attitude to the promotion of Western tourism; and

(*c*) the accessibility of each country.

In your conclusion, list (in order of preference) three possible sites for new tours.

2 You work in the research department of a major world tour operator. You have been given a continuing brief to periodically update the chief executive on the current political situation in the Middle East and to advise him of the implications of the situation for the operations of the company. Write your annual review of the Middle East, outlining the current political situation, and drawing attention to any implications of recent developments there for the company's current or future operations.

CHAPTER 30

Subsaharan Africa

LEARNING OBJECTIVES

After reading this chapter, you should be able to
- assess the tourist potential of the climatic, landscape, wildlife and cultural resources of Subsaharan Africa
- outline the regional distribution of these geographical resources and their development and use for tourism
- understand the role of the region in the general pattern of world tourism
- outline the political and economic constraints on tourist development in the region.

INTRODUCTION

Subsaharan Africa includes all of Africa except the countries on the coast of the Mediterranean sea, and the heart of the Sahara desert itself (*see* Fig 30.1). Thus, Subsaharan Africa extends from latitude 15° N to the Cape of Good Hope at 35° S. The region is part of the world's economic periphery (*see* Chapter 15) and is similarly peripheral in terms of its world tourist function; it receives 1.6 per cent of the world's total international tourist arrivals (*see* Chapter 17). In 1991, 7.25 million tourists visited the region (*see* Fig 30.2). Its countries are mainly in the first phase of the development of tourism, i.e. they have yet to develop any significant domestic market, although a tiny but affluent elite may indulge in international travel (*see* Chapter 15). There are, therefore, few countries able to generate tourists within the region itself and the region contributes only 1.5 per cent of the world's total expenditure on outbound travel.

The region consists of three major physical units: the west coast; the major area of plateaux and uplands; and the offshore islands.

1 The west coast (from the Gambia to Congo) which is mostly coastal lowlands and river basins. There are good beaches in Gambia, Ivory Coast,

West Africa		Eastern Africa	
Benin	117	Burundi	109
Burkina Faso	46	Comoros	8
Gambia	101	Djibouti	47
Ghana	172	Ethiopia	82
Ivory Coast	200	Kenya	822
Mali	38	Madagascar	35
Niger	16	Malawi	132
Nigeria	190	Mauritius	301
Senegal	234	Réunion	186
Sierra Leone	98	Rwanda	43
Togo	103	Seychelles	90
		Somalia	46
Middle Africa		Sudan	–
Angola	46	Tanzania	187
Central Africa Rep	6	Uganda	50
Cameroon	115	Zambia	141
Chad	21	Zimbabwe	664
Congo	46		
Gabon	128	**South Africa**	
Tome	1	Botswana	412
Zaire	46	Lesotho	182
		Namibia	213
		South Africa	1710
		Swaziland	279

Total 7.25 million

Fig. 30.2 Tourist arrivals in Subsaharan Africa, 1991 (000s)
(*Source:* WTO)

Fig. 30.1 Subsaharan Africa

Key
Attractions
: Kalahari Desert
* National Parks
K Kruger
M Masai Mara
S Serengeti
○ Victoria Falls
● Great Zimbabwe

Togo and Ghana. The climate makes an abrupt transition from tropical on the edge of the Sahara (e.g. Banjul in the Gambia, *see* Fig 2.8, p 12) to true equatorial in Ghana. The tropical climates (with a clear dry season) have some European winter sun tourism, but most of the 1.3 million arrivals (1991) are generated within West Africa or are business tourists: only ten per cent of the top hotel arrivals are pleasure travellers.

2 The plateau lands and uplands. The rest of Africa is basically physically a tilted plateau with its highest areas in the east (over 2000 m in places), while it drops to about half that elevation in the west. In some areas the plateaux are deeply dissected.

Climatically the plateaux can be divided into three sections:

(*a*) the more mountainous arid 'Horn of Africa' (consisting of war-torn Ethiopia and Somalia), which received only 120 000 visitors in 1991.

(*b*) The Kalahari Desert on the southwest coast (Namibia and Botswana). The semi-arid lands of Botswana are within South Africa's tourist hinterland and the region had over 600 000 arrivals in 1991.

(c) The remainder of East and South Africa. The high plateaux are very extensive, but in East Africa they are cut by a series of N-S rift valleys, in which large lakes have formed. The valleys are bordered by old volcanic mountains, e.g. Kilimanjaro, creating an area of outstanding landscape. The region has a tropical climate (i.e. alternating dry and wet seasons), with two wet periods close to the Equator (October and April/May) merging into a more clearly defined dry period (June–August) and wet season to the south of the Equator. The altitude modifies the temperatures and January average temperatures vary between 19 and 22° C (depending on altitude and latitude) while in July they may fall to between 10 and 15° C. This is the climate that sustains the open tropical savanna grasslands and mixed forest and grass which can yield rich farmland, but when undisturbed supports the great herds of herbivores (zebra, wildebeeste, antelope, elephant and giraffe etc.) and their predators, that form the focus of wildlife tourism throughout the region (*see* Chapter 4). East Africa (Kenya, Uganda, Tanzania, Zimbabwe, Rwanda, Malawi and Zambia) received about two million visitors in 1991 but most tourism is concentrated in Kenya and Zimbabwe (*see* Fig 30.2).

South Africa, with its more advanced economy, is the only significant tourist generator of the region yet it also attracts inbound tourism. The late 1980s have been a period of profound political change in South Africa, and steady progress has been made towards ending apartheid and installing a new constitution, with majority rule finally achieved in 1994. This has made South Africa a more acceptable destination for many Western tourists: inbound tourism has grown at an accelerating rate since 1989. South Africa plus its neighbours, Lesotho and Swaziland, attracted about 2.1 million visitors by 1991.

3 The islands off the east coast of Africa (in the Indian Ocean). These include Madagascar, Réunion, the Seychelles and Mauritius. These islands cater for a total of around 612 000 upmarket international visitors seeking tropical island destinations.

CHARACTERISTICS OF TOURISM IN SUBSAHARAN AFRICA

Much of the region has a range of outstanding tourist resources (climate, landscape, wildlife and coastal). However, the political and economic environment has inhibited their development. Most countries of Subsaharan Africa have very low per capita GNP ranging from the poorest such as Ethiopia, Chad, Guinea Bissau, Malawi and Zaire, all with under 250 US dollars per head in 1990, through to the richest three, Botswana, Gabon and South Africa, with over 2000 US dollars per head.

Most of these countries rely on exports of a limited range of primary products to the developed world: for example Zambia exports copper; Nigeria exports palm oil; Kenya, tea and coffee; and Ivory Coast, coffee. These economies were crippled when world prices of these products fell in the 1980s and fuel prices rose; most countries have huge foreign debts and foreign exchange is needed to service the debts. Income from tourism would be a welcome source of foreign currency but their very poverty means that the infrastructure required for Western-style tourism is not available or cannot be maintained where it is provided: roads and communications are poor and there are few top quality hotels, with few experienced or qualified people able to manage the tourist businesses.

If the tourist infrastructure is provided by overseas investments the country risks losing the economic benefits: in the Gambia, for example, the airlines, hotels and tour operators are owned by foreign interests and the profits are taken out of the country. These difficulties generate an ambivalent attitude to tourism in some African governments, and may also raise doubts in the minds of potential Western tourists as to the morality of such development.

Other factors also inhibit the development of a tourist infrastructure. Many of the Subsaharan countries are politically unstable: wars and disputes siphon off scarce resources and rapid changes of regime disrupt attempts to plan tourist development. The region has experienced conflicts resulting from the process of decolonisation (with wars of independence waged against former colonial powers as occurred in Zimbabwe, Angola and Mozambique). The other sources of conflict in the region are interethnic disputes, often a result of ethnically inappropriate boundaries between countries. Political units established in colonial times disregarded the spatial pattern of ethnic territories, and border disputes between countries and civil wars generated by ethnic rivalries within them have been the result. There is almost a built-in element of political instability in the region, and since the 1960s there have been more than 20 major wars and 40 successful coups.

The region thus has a poor image overseas. The perceived dangers of political unrest, the extreme poverty and poor quality of the tourist infrastructure, combined with the danger of AIDS and other tropical diseases make it difficult for African countries to attract large numbers of tourists, and tourism is limited mainly to special interest travellers to pockets of relative stability in the continent.

WEST AFRICA

The Gambia and Senegal

The Gambia is a tiny country of 11 295 km^2 consisting of a thin strip of land on either side of the River Gambia. It has been politically stable since independence in 1970. Its land borders are entirely surrounded by the territory of Senegal. Both the Gambia and Senegal are former colonies of European countries (Senegal belonged to France, and the Gambia was a British colony). Both have a tropical climate, with a hot, dry season running from November to May and a summer wet season with heavy rainfall. Both function mainly as winter sun destinations for European tourists (46 per cent of the Gambia's air charter tourists arrive between December and February). Together they form the main holiday tourist region of West Africa. Their main tourist resources are their climate and the most developed stretches of coastline are the Petite Côte (80 km south of Dakar) in Senegal, the superb beaches in the Gambia just south of Banjul, and at Cap Skirring in the southern part of Senegal. Other attractions include the scenery and wildlife (mostly birds) along the Gambia River and in the south of Senegal, where there are several National Parks. The vegetation here is savanna grassland and scrub.

In the northern part of Senegal the landscape becomes drier as it merges into the Sahara Desert. Both countries have historic settlements and colonial fortifications associated with the slave trade. River trips up the Gambia are another attraction.

Tourism statistics for African countries are sometimes inconsistent but according to WTO, tourist arrivals to the Gambia have ranged between 86 000 and 100 000 a year between 1987 and 1991, while Senegal's tourist numbers have fluctuated between 234 000 and 259 000. Both are heavily dependent on their former colonial links for their tourists: 31 per cent of the Gambia's visitors came from UK in 1990, while in 1991 56 per cent of Senegal's tourists came from France. The Gambia (as a winter sun destination) also attracts the Swedes (7.7 per cent of visitors) and Germans (5.5 per cent) while Senegal attracts more Italians and Germans. In Senegal the facilities are mainly designed for the luxury end of the market (60 per cent of Senegal's accommodation is four- or five-star). There is a wider range of quality of hotels in the Gambia, which is beginning to attract younger and less affluent tourists amongst its charter market.

Tourism contributes about 10–15 per cent of the Gambia's GDP and is supported by the Gambian Government. However, a high proportion of the profits from tourism flow out of the country (it is estimated that Gambia retains only 23 per cent of the cost of each holiday) since most of the hotels are owned by foreign investors and the best paid jobs in the hotels are also filled by foreigners.

The rest of West and Central Africa

The tourist industries of these countries remain small, and are mainly based on business tourism (e.g. Nigeria) or small-scale winter sun tourism (e.g. Sierra Leone and Togo). The oil-producing countries of Gabon, Cameroon and Congo also had growing business tourism until the reduction in oil prices; Gabon has the potential for a beach based tourist industry but is a relatively expensive sun-sea-sand destination.

EAST AFRICA

Kenya and Zimbabwe dominate East Africa's tourism in terms of total numbers (*see* Fig 30.2) but Kenya remains the only country that attracts intercontinental visitors in any numbers: European tourists made up 57 per cent of its clientele in 1991, while Zimbabwe relies on its African neighbours (mainly South Africa and Zambia) for over 70 per cent of its tourists.

Kenya

Kenya consists of four main regions:

1 the tropical coast with a modified (hot and humid) equatorial climate, with coral reefs offshore, and good beaches of white sand. The coast was settled by Arab traders from the first century AD, and the distinctive Swahili culture developed along the coast as a result of the mixture of Arab and African people. The Swahili people inherit their religion (Islam) from this Arab influence.
2 the uplands in the southwest of the country. These consist of grassy plains and forested mountains that rise to 5200 m (Mt Kenya). The Aberdares is another of the mountain ranges. Some of the highest mountains are ancient volcanoes (some extinct and some semi-active).
3 a deep, wide rift valley that runs North–South through the west of Kenya, and bisects the upland area, creating magnificent landscapes. There are several large lakes (e.g. lakes Naivasha, Nakuru and Baringo) strung out along the valley bottom. Many of these are major wildlife habitats (e.g. for flamingo, hippo and crocodiles).

The rift valley and uplands of south and south-west Kenya support the most wildlife on the open grassy plains and forests. The wildlife is in competition with the nomadic people such as the Masai who graze goats and cattle on the open grassland ranges.

4 the lowlands of the east of Kenya. Much of this is semi-desert.

Kenya has been another of the more politically stable countries, although even here there was a coup attempt in 1983, and has been most successful in developing wildlife and beach tourism. These two types of tourism have slightly different seasonal rhythms.

The dry seasons (January and July–September) are the best for wildlife viewing as the drought draws the animals to the waterholes where the tourist lodges are built. The short rains in October/November do not deter visitors as this is the period when the animals gather in vast numbers in the Masai Mara for their annual migration. It is the period of the 'long rain' between March and May that is the 'low' season for wildlife tourism because the animals disperse from the waterholes (as other water sources become available), the unsealed roads make the safari drives difficult and the savanna grass grows tall and hides the animals. The low season for the beach resorts is longer as they are primarily winter sun attractions for the Northern Hemisphere market. Their peak occupancy rates are achieved between November and February. Only ten per cent of Kenya's bed capacity is in the wildlife parks but they have a much higher occupancy rate though with short average stays. Fifty-one per cent of the bed capacity is on the coast, and beach accommodation accounted for 26 per cent of the bednights in 1989. The main beach centres are Mombasa, Diani Beach and Malindi (where coral reefs grow offshore), while the Lake Nakuru, Tsavo, Amboseli, Aberdare, particularly the Masai Mara National Parks, are among the most popular wildlife areas, where the 'big five' (lion, leopard, elephant, buffalo and rhino) can be seen.

	Tourist arrivals (%)	Av temp °C Max	Av temp °C Min	No of raindays
Jan		25	12	5
Feb	29.9	26	13	6
Mar		24	14	11
April		24	14	16
May	19.4	22	13	17
June		21	12	9
July		21	11	6
Aug	24.8	21	11	7
Sept		24	11	6
Oct		24	13	8
Nov	25.9	23	13	15
Dec		23	13	11

Fig. 30.3 Nairobi's climate

Parks	('000 visitors)
Masai Mara	196.2
Lake Nakuru	167.4
Nairobi NP	155.2
Amboseli	140.4
Tsavo East	101.1
Tsavo West	96.8

Fig. 30.4 Visitors to Kenya's most popular National Parks, 1989

Most visitors come from Europe, particularly Germany and UK, and from the USA. However, the different nationalities show significantly different preferences for Kenya's resources. Tourists from USA are mainly interested in the wildlife and scenic attractions (Americans account for nearly 20 per cent of all the bednights in game lodges). The Germans are orientated towards the coast: 40 per cent of the bednights in the beach hotels were generated by German tourists. They tend to take shorter safaris and spend most of their time on the coast. The British market is rapidly becoming more interested in Kenyan beach holidays, but are still major participants in scenic and safari trips (or combine the two).

	% total
UK	17.29
Germany	15.5
Tanzania	11.5
Uganda	7.1
USA	6.68
Italy	4.90
France	4.85
Scandinavia	3.86
Switzerland	3.62
Other	26.7
	100%

Total number: 817 550 tourist arrivals

Fig. 30.5 Kenya tourist arrivals, 1991

In the early 1990s the Kenya Wildlife Service expressed concern that the loss of wildlife from poaching, the bad management and overuse of the most popular National Parks (*see* Fig 30.4) and Game Reserves is making them less attractive to the tourists. A decline in safari tourist numbers was anticipated (partly due to the tourist congestion in Kenya's Parks and partly due to growing competition from wildlife tourism that is increasingly available in other East African countries). The Wildlife Service proposed a scheme to limit the impact of tourism in the currently most popular parks and at the same time open up new areas and diversify into more special interest activities

(such as mountaineering, horse safaris, fishing etc.) while extending the system of sharing tourist revenues with the residents of the parks and adjacent areas.

There are also environmental problems facing the coastal resorts. The 40 000 annual visitors to the Malindi marine park are damaging the coral reefs, while beach tourism offends local Muslim populations. Other cultural impacts are considerable, with an increase in the number of prostitutes and beach boys.

Kenya's Nairobi airport is the main international gateway to East Africa.

Tanzania

Tanzania is located in East Africa directly to the south of Kenya. It shares many of Kenya's physical characteristics:

1 **Coastal plains** with a hot near-equatorial climate, with cultural influences from Arab traders and other past civilisations. The lowland plains are however much narrower than in Kenya. There are many beautiful and undeveloped beaches, with some coral reefs offshore.
2 **Inland highlands** with a tropical climate. North West Tanzania also has a double wet season (the long rains from March to May, and a second less distinct wet season in November/December), but a clear dry period June to October.

Most of the upland plateaux are 1–2000 m high and consist of open plains of savanna and bush, or semi-desert. Some higher mountains rise from the plateau: Mt Kilimanjaro in the north is the highest mountain in Africa. It rises to 5895 m and its peak is always snow covered. The Kenya Rift valley extends southwards into Tanzania and contains lakes Natron and Eyasi. The Olduvai Gorge (famous for its fossils) is located in the Rift valley. The southwest border of Tanzania follows a larger Rift valley system (in which the larger lakes Tanganyika and Nyasa are situated).
3 **The highlands** are also rich in **wildlife**. There are several National Parks along the border with Kenya: the Serengeti is a southern extension of the Masai Mara in Kenya. It is a huge area (33 660 km^2) of grassy plains with vast herds of wildebeest, zebra and gazelles. The Ngorongoro crater (the centre of a huge extinct volcano) holds one of

the biggest permanent concentrations of wildlife in Africa, with all year round game viewing. The country has many other national parks, forest reserves and game reserves. The Selous game reserve in the south is another huge area of abundant wildlife. The Serengeti, Ngorongoro and Selous are all designated as World Heritage sites (the only ones in East Africa).

In spite of having comparable (or even more spectacular) wildlife resources than Kenya, Tanzania's tourism is at a much lower level and the parks are much less intensively visited (*see* Fig 30.6). This is mainly due to political and economic factors. Tanzania started out to develop tourism in the late 1960s and early 1970s but the country opted for a socialist collectivist economic system in the 1970s, and this inhibited foreign investment. A combination of economic and political factors led to a period of general economic decline. A change in presidency in 1985 provided the opportunity for new economic policies; the private sector is once again being encouraged and a restructuring of the economy has begun. However, the country's tourist infrastructure is not well developed and it has generally poor roads (except between the main towns) and unreliable internal air connections, and poor-quality hotel accommodation. Fuel and other goods have been in short supply.

It is thus not surprising that Tanzania's tourism is still at a very small scale and most consists of short trips (average 3.5 nights) for wildlife viewing as an extension of a Kenyan safari. Many of the American and British tourists come from Kenya across the border by road for visits to Serengeti and Ngorongoro. This element of Tanzania's tourism is thus highly dependent on

	No of visitors (daily ave)	Total annual visitor days	Visitor density (no per '000 km²)
Ngorongoro	191	69 882	23
Manyara	95	34 576	296
Serengeti	68	24 920	5
Kilimanjaro	28	10 382	38

Fig. 30.6 Tourist use of Tanzania's main game areas, 1989

the health of the Kenyan safari industry, and on political relations with Kenya (the Tanzania border with Kenya was closed for some time and reopened only in 1983).

The other main element of Tanzanian safari tourism arrives by air from Nairobi to Arusha. Thus most of the safari tourism is concentrated in the northern parks and reserves. The coast is hardly developed for beach tourism as yet.

Tourism plays a small but growing role in the country's economy, and the numbers of tourists are slowly increasing (*see* Fig 30.7).

1983	54 000
1986	103 400
1989	137 900
1991	183 000

Fig. 30.7 Total numbers of foreign tourists to Tanzania
(*Source*: WTO)

Africa	39	(Main market: Kenya 18.6%)
Europe	36	(Main market: UK 7.6%)
Americas	22	(Main market: North America 22%)
Other	3	
	100%	

Total number : 183 000

Fig. 30.8 Tanzania: main markets, 1991 (per cent)

Uganda

Uganda's tourist industry was destroyed and the National Parks decimated during the Amin era (visitor numbers fell from 85 000 in 1971 to 12 700 in 1983) and tourism has hardly recovered, although facilities were being restored and tourism encouraged in the late 1980s.

Zimbabwe

Zimbabwe on the other hand has shown a stronger expansion since its independence in 1980, though most of its visitors came from South Africa or Zambia.

Most of the country is between 1000 and 2000 m in altitude: the highest mountain ranges (rising to 2592 m) follow Zimbabwe's eastern border, and the altitude gradually decreases westward to Lake Kariba on Zimbabwe's northwest border. This border follows the course of the Zambezi River. The Victoria Falls are on the Zambezi, west of Lake Kariba. The natural vegetation of much of the country is mixed woodland or open grassland (the High veld) providing excellent wildlife habitats where it is not in agricultural use. The Hwange, Matapos and Nyanga National Parks are of particular importance for both wildlife and tourism.

Climatically, this region has only one long wet season (from November to March) so the end of the dry season (in September) is the best time to see the greatest concentrations of wildlife at the waterholes. Many of the roads in the parks are impassable in the wet season (e.g. Mana Pools). However, tourism is not strongly peaked; there is a modest peak between July and October but South African visitors tend to come over Christmas and during the April and July school holiday periods, thus spreading the demand through the whole year.

Zimbabwe's tourism is highly dependent on its adjacent African neighbours (38 per cent coming from South Africa and 28 per cent from Zambia). Only 9.5 per cent came from Europe in 1991 (and these mostly from UK or Germany). However, the European tourists stay longer (average eight to 11 days) than visitors from surrounding African countries (two to five days) and are much higher spenders than the African tourists (although tourism is not a major component of the country's economy). The South African tourists are attracted mainly to Lake Kariba, while convention, domestic and VFR tourism is concentrated in the capital Harare. The intercontinental package tourists include Harare, Hwange Game Park and of course Victoria Falls on their itinerary. The Falls are a major attraction to the regional and domestic tourists too. The Great Zimbabwe ruins are a four-hour drive from Harare, and are also a major attraction. The 720-hectare site is the abandoned citadel of a civilisation that existed up to the 15th century. Many walls, enclosures and foundations of buildings survive.

SOUTHERN PART OF AFRICA

This part of Africa consists of Namibia, Botswana, South Africa and the small states of Lesotho and Swaziland that are largely surrounded by South African territory.

There have been major political changes in this part of the world in the late 1980s and early 1990s: South Africa made steady progress towards majority rule culminating in the election of Nelson Mandela as South Africa's first black president in 1994, and Namibia was granted independence in 1990. These changes have opened up destinations that have hitherto been unavailable to most tourists for political, ethical or safety reasons. These countries are as yet heavily dependent on interregional tourism but intercontinental travel (particularly to South Africa) is beginning to develop. Their main resources are once again their climatic, scenic and wildlife attractions. Namibia's Etosha and Namib Naukluft National Parks are her biggest, located in central and northern Namibia. Botswana's reserves are well managed and contain abundant wildlife. The swamps and wetlands of the Okavango delta are the main attraction here, while the Chobe Park has large elephant herds. The Chobe River acts as a focus for the animals' migration in the dry season. Both countries have opted to promote high value, low volume and low density tourism in order to control tourism pressure on sensitive ecosystems. In Botswana this will be done through licensing and regulation of operators. Both countries have well established wildlife conservation policies. Both wish to avoid mass tourism, while maximising tourism's contribution to their economies.

South Africa and its hinterland form a distinct tourist subregion. Until the late 1980s its policy of apartheid led to its international isolation, though holiday visitors from Europe increased sharply in 1987/88 in response to the beginnings of internal change within South Africa. The country has a good tourism infrastructure and a well established white domestic market while the black population's growing middle class is beginning to participate more widely in domestic tourism too. The Kruger National Park (near the Mozambique border) is probably Africa's most intensively used wildlife park with half a million visitors (and over one million bednights) in 1988, but South Africa has

To	Namibia % (1991)	Botswana % frontier arrivals (1991)		South Africa % tourists (1992)
From				
South Africa	62.9		46.7	
Other Africa	8.1		3.5	4.7
		Zimbabwe	37.2	14.4
		Zambia	3.1	0.9
		Botswana		8.5
		Lesotho		28.9
		Swaziland		15.2
		Namibia		6.6
Europe	26.2		7.2	14.4
of which:				
Germany	*13.9*		–	*3.3*
UK	*4.8*		*3.3*	*5.4*
Other	2.7		2.3	6.7
	100		100	100
Total number	213 000		899 000	2 703 191

Fig. 30.9 Tourist arrivals in southern Africa
(*Source*: WTO)

many other parks and game reserves. The country also has many good beaches while Cape Town and Durban are the main urban tourist centres. Seventy-nine per cent of South Africa's inbound tourists come from other African states while UK visitors dominate the overseas arrivals (*see* Fig 30.9).

The future of tourism in South Africa has been inextricably bound up with the process of political change in the country. The peaceful transition to majority rule may allow domestic and international tourism to blossom in the 1990s.

ISLANDS OFF SOUTHEASTERN AFRICA

Madagascar is the largest of the islands off the east coast of Africa but it is least developed for tourism, has few hotels and caters for special interest (including wildlife) holidays. Réunion, Mauritius and the Seychelles are the main island destinations. These are mostly mountainous, jungle-covered islands, but are fringed by unspoilt beaches and coral reefs. They are relatively expensive winter sun destinations for the European market, and tourist development is closely controlled in order to maintain its quality. Their high season is roughly November to January, but they do have a secondary peak in August when the climate is drier but cooler. The French make up nearly one third of the tourists travelling to Mauritius (up to 1810 it was a French possession) while the UK is the main market for the Seychelles. However, both countries have since diversified their markets (*see* Fig 30.10). The Seychelles are also noted for their wildlife. Their isolation has led to the evolution of many species of very rare plants and birds unique to the Seychelles, or even species limited to one island within the Seychelles group.

	Mauritius % 1992	Seychelles % 1991
Europe	**41.4**	**71.7**
of which:		
France	18.7	16.6
UK	7.5	16.5
Italy	4.5	16.8
Germany	7.6	10.3
Africa	**46.0**	**20.8**
of which:		
Réunion	27.9	–
S Africa	13.7	13.1
Asia	**6.1**	**4.2**
of which:		
India	3.2	
Other	**6.3**	**1.9**
	100%	100%
Total numbers	237 680	90 100

Fig. 30.10 Inbound tourism in Mauritius and the Seychelles
(*Source*: Mauritius Government Tourist Office/WTO)

CONCLUSION

Subsaharan Africa thus has a wealth of climatic, coastal and wildlife resources suitable for tourism, but its peripheral location, its poor economic circumstances and general conditions of political instability all inhibit its development for tourism and limit international tourism to but a few dispersed locations within the continent. However, the increasing demand for wildlife tourism, and the improving political situation led to some modest growth of tourism at the beginning of the 1990s.

FURTHER READING

Bachmann, P (1988) 'Tourism in Kenya – a basic need for whom?', *European University Studies Series* 10, Vol. 10, Peter Lang, Berne.

Beachey, A (1990) 'Malawi', *EIU International Tourism Reports*, No. 1, pp. 47–59.

Curry, S (1990) 'Tourism development in Tanzania', *Annals of Tourism Research*, Vol. 17, pp. 133–49.

Dieke, P (1991) 'Policies for tourism development in Kenya', *Annals of Tourism Research*, Vol. 18, pp. 269–94.

Dieke, P (1993) 'Tourism and development policy in the Gambia', *Annals of Tourism Research*, Vol. 20, pp. 423–49.

EIU (1990) 'Senegal and the Gambia', *EIU International Tourism Reports*, No. 3, pp. 49–66.

EIU (1991) 'Managing tourism and the environment – a Kenyan case study', *Travel and Tourism Analyst*, No. 2, pp. 78–87.

EIU (1991) 'Kenya', *EIU International Tourism Reports*, No. 2, pp. 49–66.

Fowdar, N (1991) 'Mauritius', *EIU International Tourism Reports*, No. 4, pp. 47–71.

Harrison, D (1992) 'Tradition, modernity and tourism in Swaziland', in Harrison, D (Ed) *'Tourism and the less developed countries'*, Belhaven.

Hawkins, P (1992) 'Zimbabwe', *EIU International Tourism Reports*, No. 3, pp. 5–22.

Matthews, G (1992) 'Tanzania', *EIU International Tourism Reports*, No. 2, pp. 6–25.

Matthews, G (1994) 'South Africa Outbound', *EIU Travel and Tourism Analyst*, No. 2, pp. 24–38.

Murphy, R (1992) 'Botswana and Namibia' *EIU International Tourism Reports*, No. 4, pp. 85–114.

QUESTIONS AND DISCUSSION POINTS

1 Can the expansion of international tourism in the poorer economies of Africa help develop those economies; or can tourism only be successfully promoted once the economy has been improved by other means?

2 Where are the main concentrations of international tourism in Subsaharan Africa? Do these locations share any characteristics (e.g. the nature of their resources, their economic or political conditions) in common?

3 Where are the current conflict zones in Subsaharan Africa? To what extent might these regions have tourist potential if they were politically stable?

ASSIGNMENTS

1 You work for a tour operator that specialises in worldwide wildlife holidays, but their only African destination at present is Kenya. You have been asked to prepare a report identifying other suitable destinations in Subsaharan Africa. Select

at least three other possible locations where new tours might be promoted; identify their wildlife interest and indicate the market to which they might appeal.

2 A small company specialising in adventure holidays is considering developing an 'Africa: coast to coast' safari. Is it possible to construct a coast to coast route across Subsaharan Africa (either east to west, or north to south) that

(a) avoids countries that are currently experiencing war or civil unrest; and

(b) includes some of the major sights of Africa? What would be the risks of undertaking such a business venture?

SECTION 3

The Americas

INTRODUCTION

This section of the book seeks to answer the following questions.

1 What and where are the main tourist attractions in the Americas?
2 Where are the main tourist generation regions located in relation to the tourist destinations? What is the pattern of flow of tourists between them?
3 To what extent do the patterns of tourism in the Americas parallel that of Europe and its adjacent regions?
4 What is the role of the Americas in the general pattern of world tourism?

The main tourist resources of North America (i.e. the USA and Canada) are described in Chapter 31. These countries belong to the world's economic core (*see* Chapter 15) and their affluent mobile populations are concentrated in the eastern half of North America, particularly in the northeast between the Great Lakes and the Eastern Seaboard.

The predominant flow of tourists is southwards to the better climates of Southern California, Texas and Florida within the USA, but also to Mexico and the Caribbean. These latter destinations, along with the rest of Central and South America are discussed in Chapters 32 and 33.

Most of Central and South America belongs to the world's economic periphery, and these countries are also peripheral in terms of their tourist function (*see* Chapter 17).

Many similarities exist between the pattern of tourism in the Americas and that of Europe and Africa: the most densely populated regions lie to the north, while Florida, Mexico and the Caribbean possess tourist resources that mirror those of the Mediterranean; the two regions fulfil a very similar tourist function in relation to the generation regions to their north. Likewise Africa and South America are regions with similar economic and political problems, and both are peripheral in terms of their tourist function, attracting very few international tourist arrivals.

CHAPTER 31

North America

LEARNING OBJECTIVES

After reading this chapter you should be able to
- **assess the tourist potential of the climatic, landscape, historical and cultural resources of Canada, and the USA**
- **distinguish between the regional distribution of these geographical resources and their development and use for tourism**
- **demonstrate a knowledge of the main tourist resorts and tourist centres**
- **understand the role of each country in the general pattern of North American tourism**
- **assess the similarities and differences between patterns of tourism in North America and Europe.**

INTRODUCTION

The continent is part of the world's economic 'core' (*see* Chapter 15) and is a huge, unbroken landmass of about 20 million sq km stretching from beyond the Arctic circle in the north to the region of the Tropic of Cancer in the south. Its climates range from polar to sub-tropical (*see* Fig 31.1), the best tourist climates being the Mediterranean type (on the west coast) and sub-tropical (to the south).

This region possesses an immense range of natural landscapes – deserts, mountains, lakes, plains and wetlands, but has a short coastline in relation to its size (*see* Fig 31.2).

The continent's territory is divided between only two countries: Canada and the USA. Its population (of about 277 million) is heavily concentrated in a pocket between the Great Lakes and the east coast. This is the highly urbanised and affluent economic core of the continent. But this region has a humid continental climate: long, hot, uncomfortably humid summers and intensely cold winters. Although the region meets some of its own tourist needs, this combination of factors generates a strong southerly flow of tourists down the east side of the continent to the sub-tropical coasts of Florida, Mexico and the Caribbean (*see* Fig 31.2).

The island states of the Caribbean and Mexico itself are more economically backward than USA and Canada, making them attractive destinations on account of the relatively low costs of living, but are at present low generators of tourists themselves (*see* Chapter 32). This general pattern of climate, economic development and tourist movement very closely parallels that of Europe. However, there are four significant differences between the characteristics of European and North American tourism.

1 The first difference relates to **spatial patterns of tourism**. North American tourist flows are not entirely N-S. In North America, there is a secondary population concentration on the Pacific Coast of the USA in the Mediterranean climatic zone which is cut off from the rest of USA by the Rockies. It is a very affluent region (California's 29 million population produces more than the whole UK economy). Its population generates very high levels of tourism within the region but it also attracts some visitors from the continent's economic core, generating a secondary significant westerly flow of tourists across the Rockies to the Pacific coast (*see* Fig 31.2) in addition to the southerly flow from Pacific Canada. The continent's most dramatic landscape features, e.g. the deserts and Rocky Mountains, are also located in the west. Twenty-six of the USA's 41 National Parks and 84.8 per cent of its public outdoor recreation land are located in its mountain and Pacific regions. This distribution of resources also generates a significant, though much smaller, westward drift of tourists to the inland deserts and mountains.

2 The other differences between the general patterns of European and North American tourism relate more to the **nature of tourism** rather than its spatial distribution.

The southerly flow of tourists down the east side of North America, although primarily a summer phenomenon, is a little less sharply seasonal than that of Europe. The climatic differences between North American tourist generating and destination regions are more extreme in winter than in most of Europe (i.e. the winters around New York and Toronto are colder while Miami and the Caribbean are warmer than the corresponding regions of Europe). This leads to stronger climatic

'push' and 'pull' factors which generate a much stronger winter sun holiday trade in North America, making destinations around the Gulf of Mexico (particularly Florida) virtually all year round destinations (*see* Chapter 2). In Europe most of the Mediterranean destinations are just not quite warm enough to sustain such high levels of winter sun trade: European winter sun seekers have to travel further afield to destinations outside Europe (such as the Canary Islands and the Gambia).

3 North American tourism differs most strikingly from European tourism in that **it lacks historic resources and cultural variety**. The native (Red Indian) population of the continent was nomadic and left few permanent features to mark their development, although Central America's ancient urban civilisations have left many historic sites. White colonisation of the continent dates from as late as the 17th century, and settlement only gradually spread westwards from what is now North America's economic core. Much of the continent with the exception of Mexico shares a common

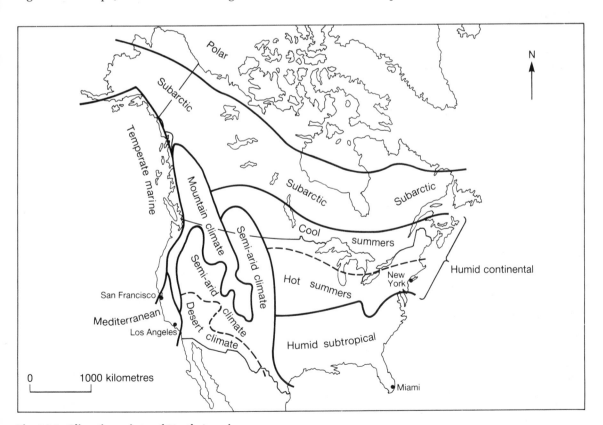

Fig. 31.1 Climatic regions of North America

Fig. 31.2 Regions and coastlines of North America

language and culture. Therefore, in contrast to most European cities, urban tourism in North America is based on the cities, climates, their modern culture and their manmade entertainment facilities, rather than their history, architecture or cultural variety. The relative lack of historic resources, and the strong cultural ties that still link it to Europe generate a substantial transatlantic flow of North American tourists to Europe. The modern cultural links between the two continents reinforce this trend.

4 The final difference between European and North American tourism is perhaps more apparent than real though it does have important consequences. The two main tourist generating

countries (USA and Canada) are both huge and, apart from their lack of historic towns, possess a great variety of tourist resources; they can each meet most of their needs for travel and tourism within their own borders. Therefore, **most of the tourist movements within the continent are registered as domestic rather than as international trips**. This contrasts sharply with the high level of international tourism in Europe (*see* Chapter 15). However, this does have important implications for the nature of tourism in Canada and the USA. Political constraints on tourist travel in North America hardly exist. There is a unity of travel infrastructure within each country which facilitates long distance travel: in 1990 the average domestic round trip in the USA was over 1500 km, and the population generated 884 million vacation trips of over 160 km. Although it may not be reflected as international tourism statistics, the volume of travel and tourism in North America is huge, and is strongly concentrated in three regions: the Pacific coast, the sub-tropical south and in the economic core of the Atlantic seaboard (*see* Fig 31.3). When tourism is measured in terms of receipts, Texas also appears as a significant tourist region.

THE UNITED STATES OF AMERICA

The economic core

Many parts of the USA have significant levels of tourism (*see* Fig 31.3) but tourist activity is strongly focused on three regions: Florida; California and its region; and the states of the northeast of the USA that form the country's economic core.

The northeast of the USA

Roughly 40 per cent of the population of the USA live in this region which is made up of the states of New York, Pennsylvania and Virginia, plus the smaller states of Maine, New Hampshire, Vermont, Massachusetts, Connecticut, Rhode Island, New Jersey, Delaware, Maryland and West Virginia. The population is concentrated on the coast in the great string of cities centred on New York (*see* Fig 31.4).

The industrial and heavily urbanised hinterland of New York extends inland as far as Chicago. This part of America is not only the major tourist generating region of the continent but is also the main domestic tourist destination region. Measured in terms of domestic tourist spending on trips over

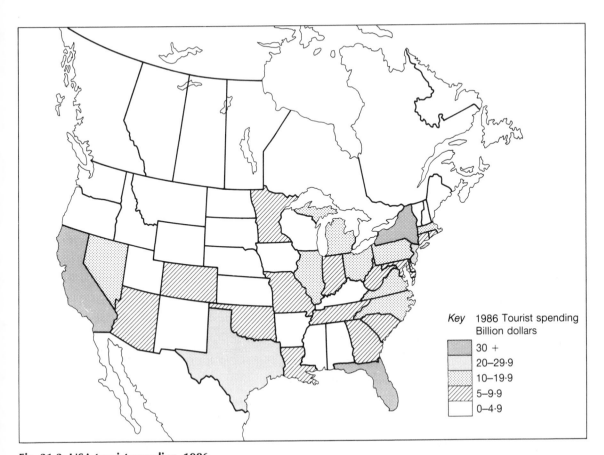

Fig. 31.3 USA tourist spending, 1986

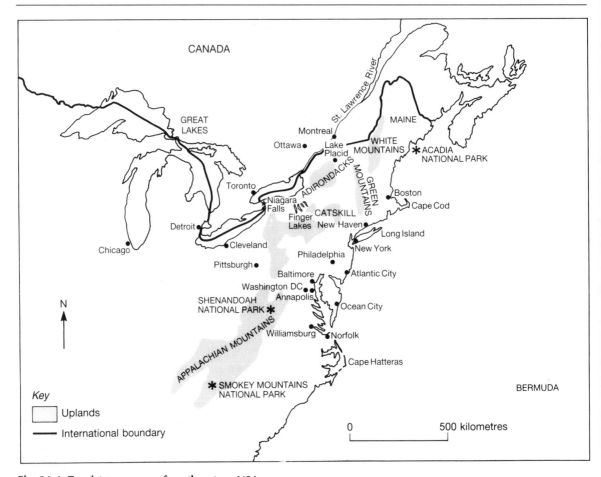

Fig. 31.4 Tourist resources of northeastern USA

40 km from home, this core area of the USA received 37.6 per cent of all domestic tourism in 1986. Of this regional total, two thirds of the tourist activity was focused on the three states around New York (New York State itself, plus New Jersey and Pennsylvania).

The popularity of the region as a tourist destination is due in part to the variety of its tourist resources. Its climate, though not ideal to live and work in, provides conditions for both summer coastal tourism and winter sports activity. Average summer (July/August) temperatures rise to 21 to 22° C on the coast and over 23° C inland, but there is a general peak in rainfall over these same months (223 mm at New Haven) and humidity is uncomfortably high for city life, though bearable on the beach. In winter, temperatures are generally below freezing from December to February with heavy snowfall, allowing winter sports to take place on the mountains inland. These rural areas also provide opportunities for hiking, camping, canoeing, hang-gliding and other outdoor sports in summer.

Although North America is short of historic resources, the best of them are in this region. The Pilgrim Fathers landed on these shores in 1620 and there are a few 17th century buildings remaining and some 18th century streets in the older cities. Finally, the region is a thriving centre of modern culture and business, epitomised by New York itself.

The coast

The sandy coast from Cape Hatteras to Cape Cod is fringed by sand bars or dunes for much of its length. Dangerous offshore currents inhibit its development for tourism round Cape Hatteras itself which is left as a wildlife refuge. Between Norfolk and Long Island there are safe, sandy beaches and a string of resorts, such as Virginia Beach, Ocean City, Wildwood and Atlantic City.

Atlantic City is one of the older resorts, and had suffered a decline in the face of competition from Florida and California, until casino gambling was legalised in 1977. By 1987 it was USA's fourth most popular city, with an estimated 31.8 million visitors and a gaming revenue of 2.73 billion dollars. Most of the casino arrivals came by road for day visits from a 160 km radius, and the resort (like many declining north European seaside resorts) is attempting to diversify into the conference trade and is also upgrading its airport to increase its catchment and attraction for staying visitors (both business visitors and casino arrivals). The sandy Atlantic beaches of Long Island and the access roads to them are very congested with day visitors from New York at the weekend, although some parts are exclusive haunts of the wealthy.

The coast north of Long Island becomes more indented and varied with opportunities for sailing (e.g. Newport, Rhode Island, and Martha's Vineyard) but again, many of the New York elite own second homes here in exclusive and expensive developments, with many private beaches. These are mixed between the more popular resorts. The coast of Maine is much more rocky and less intensively developed towards the north, although the Acadia National Park (on Mount Desert Island) is very crowded in July and August. Although it is small, it is the second most popular National Park in the USA and receives about four million visitors a year.

Bermuda is another coastal destination for the residents of this part of the USA. This group of islands is located 960 km east of Cape Hatteras in the Atlantic Ocean. Bermuda is roughly at the same latitude as Madeira and has a similar subtropical climate, although quite windy in winter. It is, therefore, mainly a summer destination (with a peak season between May and August). The English character of the islands (they are a British Dependency) and quiet setting appeal to the USA market, and 95 per cent of their half million visitors come from the USA.

Historic and cultural resources

Many of the USA's historic sites are in the coastal zone, where the first settlements and ports grew up (e.g. Boston) where early industry was established and where many important events of both the War of Independence and Civil War took place (e.g. at Valley Forge and Gettysburg near Philadelphia). Annapolis is a beautiful colonial town on the coast near Washington DC, while Williamsburg in Virginia is another restored colonial town. Many of the big cities are major modern cultural centres. Philadelphia is an important business centre, although it has recently declined as a conference venue due to competition from Baltimore, New York and Washington. Washington DC is the federal capital and attracts tourists to the White House and its important galleries and museums. It has broad avenues, classical-style buildings and is cleaner and greener than most American cities. In 1988 it attracted 19.6 m visitors (6.2 million of whom stayed in hotels and motels while 4.8 m were day-trippers; the rest visited friends or relatives). 1.62 million visitors were foreign arrivals and tourism is vital to the city's economy as visitor spending contributed 2.5 billion dollars in 1987 and only the Federal Government supplies the city with more jobs. It is a more important tourist destination than New York in terms of visitor numbers but not in terms of visitor spending. In 1987 New York City received an estimated 17.8 million visitors but they spent about 16.5 billion dollars on its theatre, cinema, museums, jazz clubs and other entertainments, and conference facilities. New York is still a major gateway for foreign visitors to the USA, and it took about a 14 per cent share of the country's foreign visitor expenditure.

Rural resources

The coast is backed by a series of uplands. The interior of Maine is remote, forested and studded with lakes and rivers that are good for white water rafting. Nearer the urban area, the White Mountains (rising to 2000 m) in New Hampshire are much more heavily used, for hiking in summer, for Fall Foliage Tours in the autumn (the state is 90 per cent forested) and skiing in winter.

New Hampshire attracted ten million visitors in 1987, 65 per cent of whom came in summer and autumn. The Green Mountains in Vermont are lower (up to nearly 1500 m) but are still well visited for both autumn colours (which are best at the end of September) and skiing (e.g. at Stowe). The Catskill Mountains in upstate New York have lost much of their traditional markets to newer attractions; the Adirondacks have good quality winter sports facilities (for example Lake Placid hosted the Winter Olympics in 1980), while the Hudson Valley and the Finger Lakes have attractive landscapes and extensive vineyards (*see* Fig 31.4). The most dramatic scenic attraction is, of course, the Niagara Falls. The Canadian side offers the better view and is more commercialised. The city of Niagara Falls on the US side attracted ten million visitors in 1987. The first ridges of the Appalachians rise in New Jersey and run SW, parallel to the coast; the Shenandoah National Park is only 128 km from Washington DC but remains a wilderness area. The Appalachians increase in height towards the south where the Great Smokey Mountains National Park is located. This is the most popular and heavily used of all the USA's National Parks and attracted 11 million visitors in 1987.

Florida

Florida is the size of England and Wales together. It is a low-lying region (its highest point is only 115 m above sea level), with a sub-tropical climate and all year round tourism (*see* Figs 2.15 and 2.16 on p 16). Winter and spring are the high seasons. The summers are wetter and more humid with a risk of hurricanes in August/September. It has a gentle sandy coastline and its flat interior is a mixture of cattle ranches, lakes, orange groves and swamps.

Florida's tourist industry began in about the 1870s when it was a winter holiday area. Many wealthy Americans have second (winter) homes here, but since the mid-1920s many more retired to the state, and its population is growing at three times the rate of the USA as a whole. The region now has a huge tourist industry; in 1987 it received 34 million out-of-state visitors. An almost equal number arrived by car as by air (*see* Fig 2.16). Its tourist receipts (from in- and out-of-state visitors) reached 40.2 billion dollars, providing

1.28 million jobs (23 per cent of the state's jobs). Apart from its climate, Florida's tourist resources are threefold: the beaches, manmade attractions and natural features (*see* Fig 31.5).

The coast

Much of the coast is fringed by offshore sand bars which are linked to the mainland by causeways crossing the enclosed lagoons, for example at Miami Beach and Fort Lauderdale which has 400 km of lagoons, rivers and canals on its landward side. The water is shallow and warms up quickly; it may reach a 30° C maximum temperature between June and September. On the Atlantic Coast there is a more or less continuous string of resorts from Miami Beach to Daytona Beach; all are busy but some have a particular character. Miami Beach is lined with multistorey hotels and is also a retirement centre. It is struggling to maintain its position as a leading resort but is diversifying into conference business and is becoming more popular with North European package tours. The wealthy elite moved north and many have property in Palm Beach, while the flat,

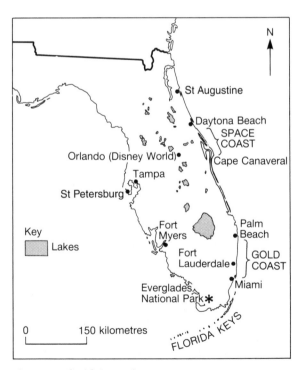

Fig. 31.5 Florida's tourist resources

hard sands of Daytona Beach are popular with holidaymakers from the New York region and students during the spring break. The beaches between Daytona and the state border are relatively quieter, though more heavily used by carborne visitors. On the Gulf Coast (the west coast) of the peninsula there are some of the state's best white, sandy beaches, e.g. between Fort Myers and St Petersburg (*see* Fig 31.5). The latter resort is also a major retirement centre.

Natural features

The far southern part of the peninsula is less developed. The Everglades National Park is a subtropical wetland, with abundant wildlife but is under threat from pollution and falling water levels. Winter is the best time to visit when it is drier and there are fewer mosquitoes. The tip of the peninsula is fringed by living coral reefs which form the basis for the marine Biscayne National Park. The Florida Keys are a chain of coral islands curving away from the peninsula but linked by a road, and the coral region provides good snorkelling.

The manmade attractions

Vast amounts of capital have been invested in manmade entertainments to augment Florida's natural attractions. The biggest attraction is Walt Disney World, 24 km south of Orlando. It is a huge complex of three theme parks (Magic Kingdom, The Epcot Center, and Disney MGM Studios Theme Park) plus two water parks (River Country and Typhoon Lagoon), an entertainment complex, hotels and conference centre. The Epcot Center (The Experimental Prototype Community of Tomorrow) alone cost one billion dollars. The whole complex covers 11 200 hectares and is estimated to attract 26 million visitors a year. There are many other smaller sports facilities and attractions, e.g. dolphinaria but the other major feature is the Space Center at Cape Canaveral. The central part of Florida (where these attractions are located) is equally popular with air and car visitors. A survey in 1990 showed that the manmade attractions were by far the most popular, with Disney World the most important (*see* Fig 31.6).

	% visitors
Disney World	32.7
Sea World	13.2
EPCOT center	10.7
Spaceport USA	10.0
Parks and Preserves	8.9
Everglades National Park	7.9

Fig. 31.6 Visits to attractions in Florida, 1990

Visitors to Florida

Visitors arrive in Florida by car and air in roughly equal numbers, although air arrivals are in the majority in winter (January–March), while car arrivals are slightly more numerous throughout the summer (*see* Fig 2.16 on page 16). The peninsula has a good road system and is linked to the interstate highway system. The car arrivals are more likely to stay in the north of Florida, which is the most accessible part by road, while the air arrivals frequent the areas round the airports, although many do hire cars on arrival. Thus, air arrivals heavily outnumber car arrivals on the Gulf Coast around Tampa airport, and particularly on the Gold Coast in the far south between Miami and West Palm Beach airports. However, these balance out and the total number of visitors in each region is fairly even; only the 'Space Coast' is relatively less popular (*see* Fig 31.5). Air and car arrivals show similar patterns of use of accommodation: most use hotels but about a third visit friends and relatives. Other forms of accommodation are hardly used. Florida has a huge and expanding stock of hotels but due to the non-seasonal nature of tourism, they have high occupancy rates (72.9 per cent in 1987). However, in spite of the heavy use of hotel accommodation, package tours are not popular with the domestic market (in the mid-1980s only 12 per cent of air arrivals were booked on a tour). The visitors know the region well as between 80 and 90 per cent have been before, and many have retired friends or relations living in Florida.

Transit tourists form a much smaller, though important, element of Florida's visitors. Miami is the main port of embarkation for Caribbean cruises and over a million passengers join their cruise ships here each year.

California

The state is the USA's leading tourist region, both in terms of number of trips and tourist expenditure (i.e. when domestic and international visitors are taken together). It is a long (1600 km) narrow (average 400 km wide) area of land. Some 91 per cent of its 28 million population live in cities, most of which are located on the coast, and 80 per cent of the population lives within 64 km of the sea. Much of the tourist trade depends on domestic day and weekend trips to the coast but it is still one of America's most important international tourist destinations. The state has a Mediterranean climate (*see* Chapter 2) and a varied coastline of sandy beaches, surf and cliffs, but it also has a wide range of inland resources (manmade, scenic and climatic), again all within easy travelling distance from the coastal conurbations. The physical regions of California run roughly N-S parallel to the coast and are:

1 **the coast**
2 **the coastal ranges** – rolling hills between 610-1220 m high
3 **the Central Valley**, a wide, flat-floored, intensively cultivated region
4 **the Sierra Nevada range** of the Rocky Mountains, which rise to 5000 m.

These landforms have been moulded by movements along fault lines in past geological times. Central Valley, Death Valley and Coachella Valley have not been eroded by rivers but have all been created by blocks of land dropping between rising mountain masses. Indeed, parts of Death Valley and Coachella Valley have dropped well below sea level. These processes have created spectacular landscapes of huge relative relief: the lowest point of Death Valley (–84 m) rises to the highest point in the main part of America (Mount Whitney at

4418 m) within 112 km. Although these landforms were created millions of years ago, intermittent movement still occurs along these fault lines, triggering off earthquakes and volcanic activity. San Francisco is sited on one of the major faults (the San Andreas Fault) and experienced a devastating earthquake in 1906. Its modern buildings are designed to withstand earth tremors and relatively little damage was done by the fairly severe earthquake that hit Santa Cruz (90 miles south of San Francisco) in October 1989. Mount Lassen, in its own National Park, is the most recently active volcanic peak in California (with eruptions between 1900 and 1921) but now it produces only sulphurous steam. In neighbouring Washington State, Mount St Helens (in the same mountain chain and related to the same fault line) erupted dramatically in 1980, and more sporadically since then. The Sierra Nevada mountains in California (which are the southern continuation of these mountains) currently have no active peaks.

The climate and tourist development

The state enjoys a Mediterranean climate on the coast but it is much modified by the presence of the mountains inland, and by other factors on the coast (*see* Fig 31.7).

The coast

The climate becomes hotter and drier towards the south of California.

1 **The north coast.** The coastal temperatures are depressed by the cold south-flowing California current (*see* Fig 31.8), which cools warm coastal air to produce frequent fog banks along the coast, particularly in the San Francisco region (Point Reyes, for example, has 1860 hours of fog a year),

		July Average temp °C	Jan Average temp °C	Annual Total rainfall mm
North Coast	(Eureka)	13.3	8.0	925
Central Coast	(San Francisco)	15.0	10.0	500
South Coast	(San Diego)	21.0	13.0	233

Fig. 31.7 Climates of the California coast

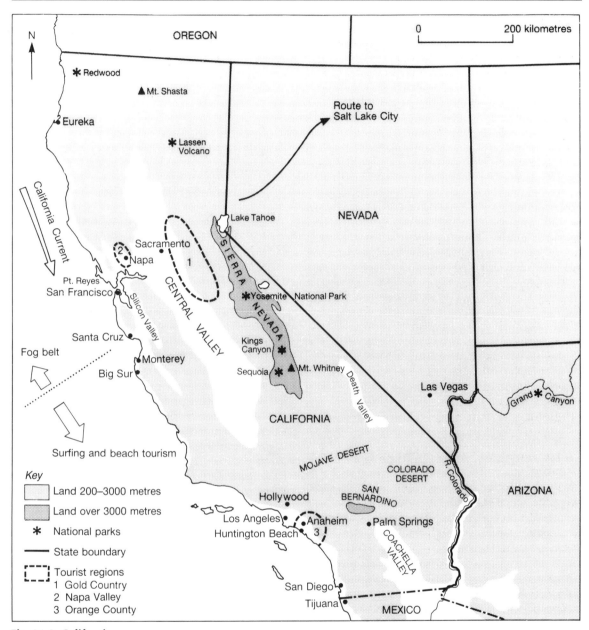

Fig. 31.8 California

but the 'fog belt' extends from Monterey north into Oregon. North of San Francisco the fog, cool offshore waters, heavy surf, and increasing rainfall make the beaches unattractive for swimming and much of the coast is undeveloped, though rugged and very beautiful. Landscape and wildlife are the main attractions and camping and hiking the main activities.

In the far north however, the Redwood National Park is a significant attraction, where giant redwood trees thrive in the moist coastal conditions and grow to 121 m tall and 6.6 m in diameter.

2 Central and southern coasts. Surfing and beach tourism starts in the Santa Cruz/Monterey area and intensifies southwards, and the beach resorts are often set among outstanding coastal scenery.

The main developments, however, are between Los Angeles and San Diego, where the climate is the hottest and the sea is warmer.

San Francisco attracted 12.8 million visitors but Los Angeles is the main centre of California's tourism and is the USA's most popular tourist city with 49.3 million visitors in 1987. It is an enormous, sprawling, suburban city linked by multi-lane freeways. Its attractions include Hollywood (with its tours of film studios and nightlife), Disneyland, seven theme parks and Knotts Berry Farm (another theme park with white-knuckle rides). Disneyland and Knotts Berry are located at Anaheim in Orange County but the area is functionally part of sprawling Los Angeles. Pacific coastlines receive ocean 'swell' waves (see Chapter 3) and Los Angeles' Huntington Beach is styled as the 'surfing capital of the world'. Further south, San Diego is also a major resort, attracting 32 million visitors in 1987. Tourism on the south California coast is very large scale, urban and beach-orientated.

The Central Valley

The Central Valley lies on the rain shadow of the coastal hills. California's main wine region is just inland of San Francisco in the Napa Valley where wine-tasting tours operate. The Central Valley proper is a flat, intensively cultivated landscape of irrigated crops. Its western slopes, where the valley rises to the foothills of the Sierra Nevada, were the site of the mid-19th century gold mining region that generated the 'gold rush' to California. The area is marketed to tourists as the 'Gold Country' (see Chapter 5).

The Central Valley gets drier towards the south where it rises to merge into the Mojave desert inland of Los Angeles. The San Bernardino mountains (which are high enough to provide enough snow for winter sports) separate the Mojave desert from the Coachella Valley. Palm Springs is located at the foot of this range where lowest winter temperatures reach 30° C. This desert resort is fashionable and expensive with many swimming pools and golf courses but many attractions close in the hottest summer months.

Death Valley is further inland and is in the complete rain shadow of the much higher Rockies (Sierra Nevada). It is also a no-go area in summer as it is even hotter: maximum temperatures can reach 53° C and averages 47° C in July. The coolest period is November to March and the best tourist season is spring when wild flowers are briefly in bloom.

The Sierra Nevada and the Rockies

These high mountains lie in the path of westerly rain-bearing winds. Precipitation is heavy and as most of it occurs in winter, at this altitude the rain turns into heavy snowfall (up to 1000 mm) on the west-facing slopes. The more northerly peaks, e.g. Mount Shasta, have permanent snow that generates glaciers. Lake Tahoe (which is easily accessible as it lies near the E-W route across the Rockies from San Francisco to Salt Lake City) is a major attraction. It has 6 m of snow but is also a very sunny location, and is a thriving ski resort in winter and a busy summer water sports and hiking centre.

Three of USA's oldest established National Parks, Yosemite, Sequoia and Kings Canyon attract substantial numbers of visitors. Yosemite has spectacular landscapes with sheer rock faces dropping 1000 m to a forested valley and is visited by three million people each year. Parts of the Park get very congested in July and August but the remoter parts remain quieter. Two other major Rocky Mountain tourist attractions lie across the State border but are accessible from Los Angeles. These are Las Vegas (in Nevada State) and a little further inland the Grand Canyon (in Arizona). Las Vegas is the commercial and neon-lit gambling city, full of casino hotels and entertainment. It attracted 16.2 million visitors in 1987, and they spent 8.6 billion dollars in the city. The Grand Canyon is further up the Colorado valley where the river has cut a spectacular 1500 m deep gorge in the flat plains of the Arizona desert. It is also a popular National Park, with 3.5 million visitors. Another short cross-border attraction is, of course, Tijuana, only a 15-minute journey into Mexico from San Diego. In 1987 42 million Americans crossed the border here, and 19 million spent time in the city.

Many of the other states in the USA have important tourist attractions; for example, Texas has Gulf Coast beaches, the Houston Space Center, theme parks, etc.; there are abundant outdoor recreational opportunities in the mountain states of Colorado, Utah, Wyoming, Idaho and Montana, while adventure cruises sail up the west coast to Alaska. However, the three main regions – California, Florida and the northeast of the USA – possess the greatest concentrations of tourist resources and attract by far the largest numbers of tourists.

VISTORS TO AND FROM THE USA

International visitors to the USA

A total of 42.7 million foreign visitors swelled the number of tourists in the USA in 1991. These visitors can be divided into two groups:

1 from neighbouring countries (i.e. Mexico and Canada). These made up 62 per cent of the total. Most Canadians were lured south to Florida, but New York, Hawaii and California were also important destinations. However, most Canadian and Mexican tourists to the USA arrived by overland routes (77 per cent of Canadians arrived by car). Overland Mexican arrivals tended to stay within the 40 km US border zone; only just one million penetrated further into the interior of the USA.
2 from overseas – literally. Of these overseas and intercontinental travellers, 47 per cent came from Europe (and of these the biggest share came from the UK with a total of 2.49 million); 31 per cent came from Asia, mostly from the USA's biggest overseas market, Japan. Two-thirds of the 3.3 million Japanese holidaymakers to US territory stayed in the Pacific Islands of Hawaii or Guam. Japanese visitors to the US mainland tended to come in groups, often combining business trips with sightseeing. On average overseas tourists visited two states during their trips (*see* Fig 31.9).

Twenty per cent of all overseas visitors entered USA via Los Angeles or San Francisco. California,

		% of all overseas tourists
1	California	37.1
2	New York	28.3
3	Florida	19.0
4	Hawaii	14.0
5	Washington DC	10.0

Fig. 31.9 Most popular destinations for overseas tourists to the USA, 1987

which faces the Pacific, has significant Asian immigrant communities and is also the major entry point for Asian visitors. It is also the country's major location of new high-tech industries that the Japanese are likely to visit (e.g. computers in Silicon Valley in San Francisco).

New York remains the primary point of entry (with 29 per cent of all overseas visitors first arriving there) and it is the major gateway for European visitors, though increasing numbers fly straight into Florida now that Orlando airport has increased the number of direct flights from abroad. Miami also received 11 per cent of all overseas arrivals direct.

The overall regional distribution of all foreign tourism in mainland USA in 1990 shows the main concentrations (with 17.9 per cent of arrivals) in the New York region (New York State, Pennsylvania, New Jersey, Maryland and Washington DC), Florida and the adjacent Atlantic coast states (18.5 per cent) and in the Pacific coast (19.5 per cent).

Outbound tourists from the USA

For a country of 250.8 million people, the USA generated the very low number of only roughly 52.8 million trips abroad in 1992, and the vast majority of these stayed in Canada (12 million) or Mexico (16 million staying visitors). However, huge numbers of Americans made day-trips across these borders – an estimated 23 million made a trip to Canada and over 50 million to Mexico in 1985. In 1992 25 per cent (13.6 million) of the outbound travellers made for Europe, with the UK and France the most popular destinations. Another 17 per cent stayed in the Far East while 10 per cent (5.2 million) holidayed in the Caribbean.

It is clear that the statistics relating to international movement in and out of the USA need to be interpreted with some care in order to get a clear picture of the real volume and direction of tourist flows. It must be remembered that the total of 52.8 million American overseas travellers may exclude visitors to the Pacific Island of Hawaii, the 50th state of the USA. American tourists to these islands are included in domestic tourist statistics.

American domestic tourism

It has been noted that the domestic tourist market is huge, a reflection of the country's size and population. However, Americans typically only receive two weeks' vacation a year so any long weekend (created by a Friday or Monday bank holiday) will generate high volumes of domestic travel. Thus it is not surprising that domestic holiday trips averaged only about four nights duration in 1990, and 51 per cent of the trips were of three nights or less. Thus a very high proportion of the domestic market can be classified as 'short breaks'. Most travel is by road: 80 per cent of trips are by car and only 15 per cent by air. Nevertheless, in 1990 Americans travelled long distances on vacation. Only 21 per cent of the trips were under 480 km while more than a quarter were over 1500 km. Beach and lakeside destinations are increasing in popularity, as are the mountains and National Parks, but city-based holidays are becoming less popular.

CANADA

Canada is another huge country and has a similar geographical pattern of physical regions and a similar distribution of population as the USA, but it has a very much smaller population (of only 26.5 million in 1990). Vast areas of Canada are sparsely populated and there are extensive tracts of untouched wilderness (see Fig 4.6 on p 33), with outstanding scenic attractions, and much undeveloped coast. However, its more northerly latitude means that the summer season is relatively short: in Vancouver (on the west coast) average temperatures reach over 16° C for only two months (July and August) and in St John's (on the east coast of Newfoundland) for August alone. Beach tourism thus has only limited development, and Canadians are drawn south to the better climates of the coastal resort areas of the USA or the winter sun resorts in Mexico and the Caribbean. Toronto, located in the heart of the most densely populated region of Canada, has longer summers with temperatures over 15° C from June to September.

In general terms, Canada's pattern of domestic tourist movement is broadly similar to that of the USA, with major concentration on destinations in the most densely populated eastern provinces of Ontario and Quebec, and a secondary focus on the Pacific Coast (in British Columbia and Alberta) in the west. Canadian outbound tourism to the USA is also strongly concentrated in the far east and west, particularly in the states just across the USA border (for example, to the states of New York, Maine and Michigan in the east, and to Washington in the west). The longer-haul travellers on the eastern seaboard travel south to Florida or the Caribbean, while those in the west are drawn to California or Mexico (see Fig 31.10). Canadians made about 18.9 million visits to the USA in 1991.

Eastern Canada: Ontario and Quebec

Ontario being the most southerly part of Canada has the warmest summers of the country: Toronto has four months averaging over 15° C and maximum temperatures can reach 26° C. It is the economic heart of the country with one-third of the country's population, and half its industrial resources. Ottawa (the capital) and Toronto are the main urban centres. Ottawa has a thriving cultural life with Canada's main museums and the National Arts Centre (a complex of theatres, concert halls and art gallery). Toronto is a more cosmopolitan city with good shopping, entertainment, cultural attractions and pleasant parks. The outstanding natural attraction in Ontario is the Niagara Falls, though there are two small National Parks (Georgian Bay Islands and Point Pelee) nearby in the south of the province.

Quebec is the French-speaking province with its own special cultural heritage and character. Montreal is the main urban centre and retains some of its historic past in the cobbled streets and old buildings of Vieux Montreal. The modern city and port that has enveloped the old centre is lively and cosmopolitan. Outside the urban areas the Laurentian mountains (a region of lakes, forests and mountains) are popular for camping, hiking and water sports in summer and skiing in winter. The Gaspé peninsula offers wildlife, forests and dramatic coastal landscapes (particularly at Percé).

	West coast		East coast	
Domestic	British Columbia	971	Ontario	1973
(value in million Canadian dollars 1984)	Alberta	855	Quebec	1006
			New York	2025
			Michigan	881
International	Washington	1358	Maine	660
(Number of trips by Canadians 1985)			Vermont	601
(000 trips)				
	California	660	Florida	1459
	Mexico	203	Bermuda and Caribbean	514

Fig. 31.10 Regional pattern of Canadian tourism

Western Canada: British Columbia and Alberta

British Columbia has Canada's best scenic, coastal and climatic resources. Its coastline is spectacular, with fjords, islands and some good sandy beaches backed by mountains rising to 4000 m. The far southwest of the province has a climate well suited to tourism with sunny, warm summers but mild winters. Vancouver is the main city, in a beautiful coastal setting. Vancouver Island is a focus of tourism with good coastal resorts, mountain landscapes and excellent fishing. There are several National Parks inland in the Rockies (such as Glacier National Park).

In Alberta, the Banff National Park is located in the higher ranges of the Rockies but on the drier eastern flanks. Its climate, dramatic mountain landscapes and hot mineral springs have led to the development of summer health and winter skiing tourism.

INTERNATIONAL TOURISM TO CANADA

Tourist arrivals in Canada have stagnated between 1987 and 1992, fluctuating between 14.8 million and 15.4 million a year. The number of American tourists is gradually declining (from 12.7 million in 1987 to 11.8 million in 1992). In the late 1980s the growth of the North East Asian market (primarily Japan and Hong Kong) kept numbers up, but since 1990 the number of Japanese arrivals has dropped too. The downward trend continued in the early months of 1993.

International tourism to Canada is also concentrated in the east (Quebec and Ontario with about ten million visits in 1986) and the west (British Columbia, four million). Eighty-two per cent of Canada's total inbound tourism in 1988 came across the border from the USA. The UK and France (reflecting VFR tourism), West Germany and Japan account for the bulk of the rest (with 3.4, 1.5, 1.7 and 2.1 per cent of arrivals respectively in 1988).

The vast majority of Canadian outbound tourism is to the USA. In contrast to inbound travel, Canadian outbound tourism to the USA is growing rapidly (from 12.4 million in 1987 to 18.9 million in 1991). Most visits (both staying and day-tripping) are to the northern states. But around 40 per cent of Canadian outbound travel is to sun (winter and summer) destinations in the southern USA, Mexico or the Caribbean. In 1988 just over one million trips were made to Northern Europe (mostly to UK), and around 38 per cent of these were VFR trips.

FURTHER READING

Ahmed, Z U (1992) 'Review of tourism in the USA', *Tourism Management*, Vol. 13, September, pp. 336–41.

Fockler, S (1991) 'United States of America', *EIU International Tourism Reports*, No. 2, pp. 26–47.

Loverseed, H (1992) 'The North American short breaks market', *EIU Travel and Tourism Analyst*, No.4, pp. 48–65.

Taylor, G (1991) 'Canada', *EIU International Tourism Reports*, No. 3, pp. 56–71.

Treitel, R (1991) 'The US domestic travel market', *EIU Travel and Tourism Analyst*, No. 6, pp. 63–76.

QUESTIONS AND DISCUSSION POINTS

1 What makes Florida such a successful all year round tourist destination?

2 Why is tourism in California concentrated so strongly in the south of the state?

3 To what extent is it true to say that Florida is the 'Spain' of North America?

ASSIGNMENTS

1 You work in a travel agency in London. A British couple, Mr and Mrs Smith are planning a visit to their aunt and uncle, Mr and Mrs Robson who live in Toronto, in the autumn. The Robsons are celebrating their silver wedding in November and the Smiths wish to arrange a one-week winter sun holiday for them (a 'second honeymoon') as a silver wedding present. The Smiths do not know much about North America or its region and have asked you to suggest some likely destinations that might suit their aunt and uncle (who are in their late 50s but like a bit of fun and enjoy sightseeing). Select at least two possible destinations and outline their main attractions, showing how they might appeal to Mr and Mrs Robson.

The Smiths will be visiting Toronto for three weeks but would like to spend another week or 10 days in Canada and the USA before they return to England. They want to see as much as possible but do not want to spend too much of their time travelling between destinations. They do not have to return via Toronto. Suggest an itinerary for them.

2 A young couple have won a two-week holiday in Florida in a prize draw, and they are very excited at the prospect of visiting the USA, but they are not sure that Florida is for them. They have the opportunity of taking the cash value of the prize and are thinking of doing that and spending the money on a holiday in another part of the USA. They are in their 20s and are active, outdoor people with a keen interest in wildlife and the environment, although they do like beach and watersports if the beach is not too crowded. They are very undecided as to what to do and have come to your travel agency to find out more about Florida and other destinations in the USA that might suit them better, before they choose to take the prize holiday or the money. Advise them on the attractions of Florida that they might enjoy and the aspects of it that they might dislike, and suggest other possible destinations in the USA that they might find more appealing. Would the cash value of the prize cover all the cost of these alternative destinations?

CHAPTER 32

Mexico and the Caribbean

LEARNING OBJECTIVES

After reading this chapter, you should be able to
- assess the tourist potential of the climatic, landscape, historical and cultural resources of Mexico and the Caribbean
- distinguish the regional distribution of these geographical resources and their development and use for tourism
- demonstrate a knowledge of the main tourist resorts and tourist centres
- understand the role of each region in the general pattern of world tourism
- assess the similarities and differences between the Caribbean and the Mediterranean as major world tourist destinations.

INTRODUCTION

Central America consists of the narrow strip of land that links the continents of North and South America. Mexico is the largest country of Central America and also its main tourist destination. The rest of Central America is split into seven small – and sometimes politically unstable – states (Belize, Costa Rica, El Salvador, Guatemala, Honduras, Nicaragua and Panama) which are covered in Chapter 33.

The southern coast of the United States and the coast of Central America form the northern and western boundary of an enclosed sea. The northern part of the sea is called the Gulf of Mexico and the southern half is the Caribbean Sea. The Florida peninsula, plus the arc of the Caribbean islands, mark the sea's eastern limit, while the South American coast completes the enclosure. As the whole region lies between the latitudes 10° N and 30° N, its climate is tropical, and many parts of the coast and islands are developed for beach tourism for the North American market. It is clear that this enclosed sea fulfils a similar tourist function (in relation to the industrial areas of North America) as the Mediterranean does for Northern Europe. In terms of the world's functional tourist regions

(see Chapter 17), Mexico and the Caribbean are as much part of the North American tourist system as the Mediterranean is part of Europe. On the other hand, the struggling economies of Mexico and the Caribbean states put them unequivocally in the world's economic periphery (see Chapter 15) and they generate few tourists themselves. However, as a tourist destination, they are far from peripheral: if Florida and the Gulf coast of the USA are included, the region attracted well in excess of 70 million staying tourists in the mid-1980s, making it the leading destination for the North American market.

MEXICO

Introduction

Mexico is a mountainous country: over half is above 1000 m. The structure of the Rocky Mountains continues south to form the spine of Mexico, but here the mountains are known as the Sierra Madre. They rise southwards to culminate in a series of volcanic peaks (of up to 6000 m) that surround the high-level plateau where Mexico City is located, at about 2300 m. The only extensive lowlands fringe the Gulf of Mexico and they widen out to form the bulk of the Yucatan peninsula. Mexico has a substantial population of 81 million which is heavily concentrated on the high plateau around Mexico City. The city's population is still growing very rapidly, and in 1989 was approaching 20 million.

However, Mexico has major economic problems, with an enormous foreign debt and a GNP per head of only 2490 US dollars. Hence, her large population generates relatively little domestic or international tourism (in 1992 about 38 million domestic visitors and 4.3 million tourist departures abroad), but Mexico has a wealth of tourist resources and the country functions mainly as a tourist destination for the United States.

Cultural resources

Mexico has a long history of Indian urban cultures that have left thousands of archaeological sites including temples, pyramids and palaces. The Mayans, Toltecs and Aztecs are but three of the six civilisations that existed at different times before Spanish colonisation (*see* Chapter 5). Three centuries of colonial rule (up to Mexico's independence in 1821) has added the Spanish dimension to language, culture and architecture. The fusion of Indian and Spanish architecture produced the 'Mexican colonial' style. A few towns that grew up in the colonial period and that still have many unspoilt buildings in this style are preserved as national monuments, where new building is forbidden. Taxco and San Miguel de Allende are two such towns, while cities where colonial and Indian remains occur together include Cholula, while Oaxaca has a more Indian emphasis. The Teotihuacan pyramids (56 km north of Mexico City) is one of the most important and most visited Aztec/pre-Aztec sites and dates from AD 400–800. All these cities form part of a group of historic sites located on the high plateau within reach of Mexico City, where the climate is dry, sunny and pleasant (*see* Fig 32.1).

A second group of Mayan and Toltec sites (also with temples and pyramids) is to be found in the humid tropical lowlands of the Yucatan, e.g. at Palenque, Uxmal and Chichen Itza. Mexican culture, ancient and modern is one of the country's important tourist resources, and tourists crossing the US-Mexico border experience a very abrupt change in culture.

Climatic and coastal resources

In contrast to the ancient Indian sites, the purpose-built seaside resorts are modern and American in style. These resorts are concentrated in the Yucatan (on the Gulf coast) but some are also scattered all along Mexico's Pacific coast. The climate of the northern part of the Pacific coast is very hot (up to 37° C) and dry all year round; in fact it is a continuation of the desert of southern California. Sea breezes moderate the temperatures, and allow all year round tourism. Loreto and Cabo San Lucas (on the Baja California peninsula) are two fairly small modern resorts, while the resort of La Paz is based on an older settlement. All these resorts are accessible by road from California. Further south along the Pacific coast, the climate is much wetter, until, south of the Tropic of Cancer, it becomes humid (75–80 per cent RH) with a pronounced wet season and temperatures that hover around 28° C all year. Acapulco, for example, has very heavy rain between June and September (over 250 mm each month) but December to April is a period of drought. It has a typical west margin tropical climate (*see* Chapter 2). Acapulco, and the other coastal resorts in this climate zone, function as winter sun resorts for the US market in the same way as the Gambia does for Europe. Acapulco's beach is lined with high rise hotels and with 16 700 hotel rooms (in 1991) it is Mexico's biggest coastal resort. All the other traditional resorts (including Vallarta and Mazatlan in the tropical zone) together provide another 28 536 hotel rooms (*see* Fig 32.1) and attracted over two million visitors in 1991.

Two major purpose-built coastal complexes are sited on the tropical Pacific coast. Ixtapa/ Zihuatanejo has a 25 km beach backed by high-rise hotels providing 4271 hotel rooms. A potentially much bigger development (that could expand to 27 000 rooms) is the Bay of Huatulco project, covering a 35 km stretch of coastline. Its first phase (providing 1400 hotel rooms) was officially opened in 1988, and land is allocated for an airport and many other facilities in the next phases. These planned resorts together attracted 0.75 million visitors in 1991.

On the north coast of Mexico (the Gulf coast) there are fewer resorts. Some of the coast is industrialised with offshore oil fields. There is, however, a cluster of purpose-built modern

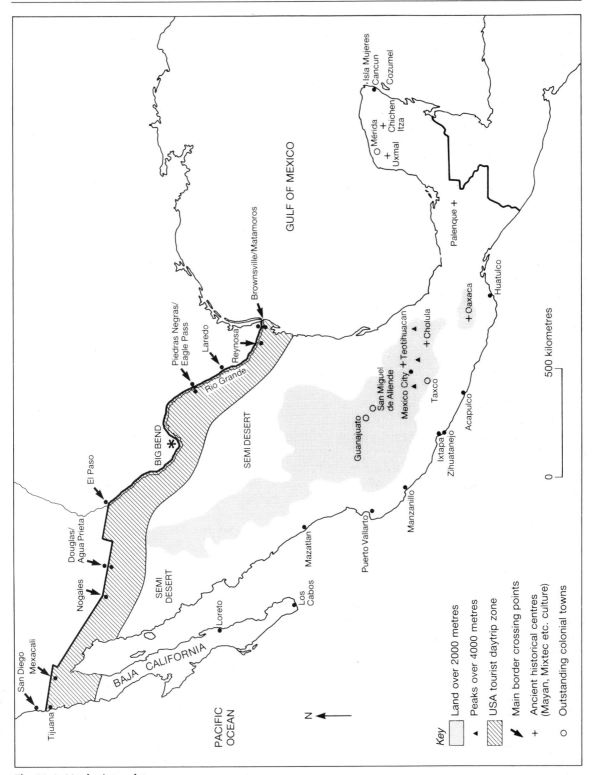

Fig. 32.1 Mexico's tourist resources

Key

Land over 2000 metres

▲ Peaks over 4000 metres

USA tourist daytrip zone

→ Main border crossing points

+ Ancient historical centres (Mayan, Mixtec etc. culture)

○ Outstanding colonial towns

GULF OF MEXICO

PACIFIC OCEAN

N

0   500 kilometres

Isla Mujeres
Cancun
Cozumel
Chichen Itza
Mérida
Uxmal
Palenque +
Huatulco
+ Oaxaca
Brownsville/Matamoros
Reynosa
Piedras Negras/ Eagle Pass
Laredo
Rio Grande
SEMI DESERT
+ Cholula
Mexico City + Teotihuacan
San Miguel de Allende
Taxco
Guanajuato
Acapulco
BIG BEND
El Paso
Ixtapa
Zihuatanejo
Manzanillo
Douglas/ Agua Prieta
Nogales
SEMI DESERT
Puerto Vallarta
Mazatlan
Loreto
Los Cabos
San Diego
Mexicali
BAJA CALIFORNIA
Tijuana

resorts on the tip of the Yucatan peninsula where the waters are clear and unpolluted, with good coral and excellent snorkelling, e.g. at Isla Mujeres, Cozumel and Cancun. Cancun was the first to be opened in the late 1970s, and had 17 990 hotel rooms by 1991. In 1991 it attracted 1.6 million visitors, but had suffered severe damage in September 1988 when the peninsula was struck by Hurricane Gilbert. Most of the resort was repaired in time for the 1989 season but all Caribbean resorts run the risk of being hit by a hurricane in the late summer.

The beach resorts and Mexico City itself are the most popular destinations. In terms of total numbers of visitors, the rank order of destinations is shown in Fig 32.2.

	Tourists staying 3 nights or more	Tourists staying at least 1 night	Day-trippers (excursionists)
1988	5.6	14.1	56.6
1989	6.1	14.9	58.1
1990	6.3	17.1	64.0
1991	6.3	16.5	64.5
1992	6.7	17.0	

Fig. 32.3 Mexico inbound tourism (in millions)
(*Source*: Mexican Ministry of Tourism/WTO)

1	Cancun
2	Mexico City
3	Acapulco
4	Merida (Yucatan)
5	Oaxaca
6	Cozumel
7	Puerto Vallarta
8	Los Cabos
9	Guadalajara
10	Manzanillo
11	The colonial cities
12	Ecotourism destination

Fig. 32.2 Mexico: rank order of destinations, 1992
(*Source*: Mexican Ministry of Tourism)

Patterns of tourist use

Mexico is very heavily dependent on the US market, which provides 89 per cent of its visitors. About four per cent come from Canada, and another few per cent from Europe. Visitor statistics distinguish between day-trippers (excursionists), tourists who stay at least one night, and staying visitors who spend more than three days in the country. Apart from 1991 there has been a steady growth in inbound tourism of all forms (*see* Fig 32.3).

The day-trippers are concentrated in the towns along the US-Mexico border, while staying visitors are of two types: beach tourists or cultural tourists who explore the interior.

1 The border zone (about 160 km into Mexico from US border). This area is heavily used by car-borne day trippers who cross into Mexico via the 12 main points of entry (*see* Fig 32.1). Mexican border towns tend to be highly commercialised, with souvenirs, gambling, prostitution and hustle, while officials on the US side of the border are vigilant for illegal Mexican immigrants. Tijuana is characteristic of this style of development. Towns a little further from the border are still busy and commercialised but retain a little more of their original Mexican character.

2 The interior and tropical coast. Here, tourism is geared more to the needs of staying visitors (who fly in) and the coastal resorts are clustered round their airports. Tourists rely on air transport because Mexico's highways vary in quality. Those focusing on Mexico City are good, and the highway running down Baja California peninsula is paved but narrow with few services. Elsewhere many roads are unsealed, and night-time driving is dangerous. Nevertheless 40 per cent of US visitors to the interior of Mexico arrive by car (mainly to Mexico City and its region), but the majority fly into the country. The pattern of air routes was reorganised in the late 1980s with the lifting of restrictions on charters and the liquidation of Mexico's domestic airline (Aero-Mexico). Mexico City remains the main international airport but there are over 25 smaller international airports which take flights direct from USA cities to the resorts (e.g. Miami–Cancun). New patterns of visitor movement will evolve as the air routes become stabilised once more.

Tourism is extremely important to Mexico's economy. It is now the second major source of foreign revenues and the biggest source of employment in the country. Its reliance on the US market is a problem and paradoxically US citizens are low-spending visitors (spending only 290 US dollars per head on average). This is because so many visit only for a day. Canadians and Europeans spend much more (on average 710 and 1150 dollars per head respectively in 1987) and Mexico is trying to attract more long-haul visitors for whom it is a relatively attractive destination. In the late 1980s, the weak peso made it 30 to 40 per cent cheaper than many competing destinations and it has a similar range of cultural, historic, coastal and climatic resources to destinations such as Thailand.

THE CARIBBEAN

Introduction

The Caribbean islands are strung along a 4000 km arc which sweeps eastwards from Florida to the Venezuelan coast. The islands surround the fairly shallow enclosed Caribbean Sea. The water is warm (24–29° C), clear and free of pollution, so that coral reefs fringe some of the islands, for example off the north coast of Jamaica and west of Andros in the Bahamas). The tropical climate is dominated by the easterly trade winds that blow at 5–20 knots from the mid-Atlantic towards Mexico. Temperatures are generally over 25° C but relative humidity is usually over 70 per cent, although conditions are made comfortable for tourism by the trade winds themselves and by daily land and sea breezes. Rainfall does occur all year round but the winter is generally drier (some islands do have a clear, dry winter season). The winds drop and relative humidity increases in the wet summer months, and the later summer may be disrupted by hurricanes which, over the course of 7–10 days, track from east to west across the Caribbean, before they peter out when they hit the coast of the Gulf of Mexico. Only the islands close to the South American coast are exempt from this danger.

	Average annual frequency (% of total hurricanes)
January	1
February	1
March	1
April	1
May	2
June	4
July	16
August	25
September	25
October	15
November	6
December	3

Fig. 32.4 Frequency of Caribbean hurricanes

The most catastrophic hurricanes appear to occur at the end of the wet season (in September), when wind speeds may exceed 170 mph, and the storms bring intense rain and high seas: any island lying in their path may experience very great damage, although there is usually a reasonable warning of their approach. Not surprisingly, the tourist high season in the Caribbean is in winter (40 per cent of the region's bednights are between January and April) but there is a secondary summer (July/August) peak in spite of the weather. May/June and September/October are the low months. The main attraction of the islands is their combination of climate and coastal resources: beach tourism dominates but most of the islands also offer a wide range of other water-based activities, such as fishing, snorkelling, diving, sailing and cruising. The region relies very heavily on the North American market – 82 per cent of its 11.3 million staying visitors came from America in 1991.

Regional variations

The distribution of visitors is not evenly spread throughout the region. There are variations between the islands in terms of:

1 their **physical character and relief**;
2 their **climate** (which is related to their relief);

		Tourist Arrivals 1991 (stayovers)	Cruise arrivals 1989
Northern Caribbean	The Bahamas	1 427 000	1 645 000
	Turks and Caicos	55 000	–
	Cuba	408 000	5 000
	Jamaica	845 000	444 000
	Cayman Islands	237 000	404 000
	Haiti	120 000	–
	Dominican Republic	1 321 000	100 000
	Puerto Rico	2 626 000	777 000
	US Virgin Islands	512 000	1 063 000
	British Virgin Islands	147 000	72 000
Eastern Caribbean	Anguilla	31 000	–
Leeward Islands and Windward	St Maarten	548 000	472 000
Islands (The Lesser Antilles)	Saba	24 000	–
	St Eustatius	19 000	–
	St Kitts-Nevis	84 000	72 000
	Antigua and Barbuda	197 000	208 000
	Montserrat	19 000	10 000
	Guadeloupe	303 000	86 000
	Dominica	46 000	6 000
	Martinique	315 000	368 000
	St Lucia	165 000	104 000
	St Vincent and Grenadines	52 000	50 000
	Barbados	394 000	337 000
	Grenada	92 000	120 000
Southern Caribbean	Trinidad and Tobago	220 000	21 000
	Bonaire	50 000	8 000
	Curaçao	206 000	125 000
	Aruba	501 000	70 000

Fig. 32.5 The Caribbean islands: tourist arrivals, 1989/1991

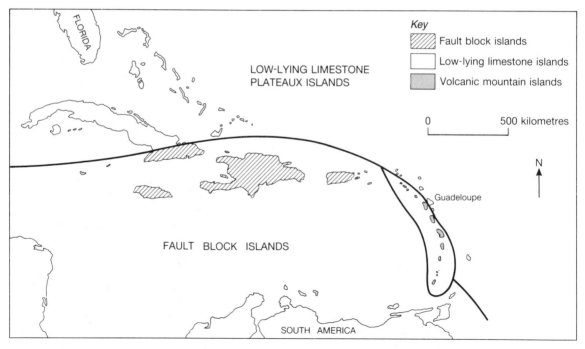

Fig. 32.6 Physical character of the Caribbean

3 their **colonial background**, political affiliations and economic organisation; and

4 their **accessibility** (which is related to their political backgrounds as well as their physical location).

Thus, these factors combine to make some islands very significant centres of tourism (with over a million arrivals) while others receive barely 10 000 visitors each year.

Variations in the physical character of the islands

There are three types of island (*see* Fig 32.6).

1 **Very flat low-lying limestone islands**, made of accumulations of coral debris or limestone sand. These occur on the outer side of the arc of islands, and include the Bahamas, Turks and Caicos, Anguilla, Barbuda, Antigua, the eastern half of Guadeloupe, Barbados, and Aruba, Curaçao and Bonaire in the south. Parts of Cuba are also very low-lying plains. These islands generally have the best sandy beaches, with the exception of Curaçao where at least two artificial beaches have been built. These islands also have the climatic advantage of having little rain (generally under 1200 mm per annum) with a very clear winter drought (*see* Fig 32.7).

	Annual rainfall (mm)
North Bahamas	
(Nassau)	1185
South Bahamas	
(Turks Is)	750
Central Caribbean	
(Anguilla)	762
(Antigua)	1251
South Caribbean	
(Bonaire)	512

Fig. 32.7 Rainfall in the flat limestone islands of the Caribbean

The climate does bring other problems. All these islands suffer a shortage of water, particularly when local populations are swelled by influxes of tourists. Nassau supplements its limited local supply with both desalinated seawater and water shipped in from the bigger Bahamian islands. The flat, desert-like landscapes, vegetated with thorn scrub and cactus, are not particularly attractive, and tourism in these islands is firmly focused on the beach and water sports.

2 **The volcanic islands**. These are mountainous islands with dramatic landscapes created by extinct or dormant volcanoes. The last major eruption was in 1902 when Mount Pelée (on Martinique) destroyed the town of St Pierre, but many mountains, for example on Dominica, Montserrat and Guadeloupe, still have hot springs, sulphur craters and active geysers. The volcanic mountains rise to 1500 m and have created the string of islands on the inner (western) side of the Leeward and Windward groups, extending from the tiny island of Saba in the north to Grenada in the south. Saba has been described as having a 'near vertical landscape, with lots of scenery but no beaches'. The group as a whole has a varied coastline with cliffs, coves and some good sandy beaches. St Kitts-Nevis, St Vincent and Montserrat have some beaches made of black volcanic sand, although Montserrat is one of the islands with rather few beaches, while St Martin has at least 32 white, sandy beaches. Heavy surf sometimes makes the windward sides of the islands less attractive, e.g. on the rocky east coasts of St Vincent and the Grenadines. These windward sides of the islands are also much wetter. The high mountains lie across the path of rain-bearing winds and generate very intense orographic rainfall, which increases with altitude, for example from 2000 mm at sea level to over 4500 mm on the mountain slopes. The rain comes in short, violent downpours but with clear sunshine in between. The west (leeward) sides of the islands are generally much drier as they sit in the rain shadows of the mountains. Most of the resorts and settlements are in such sheltered locations. The vegetation of these islands is much lusher than the flat, limestone islands, with tropical jungle in the wettest parts.

3 **Non-volcanic mountainous islands**. The Central Caribbean islands (Southern Cuba, Jamaica, Hispaniola, Puerto Rico and the Virgin Islands) are made of uplifted, flat blocks of rocks. They consist mainly of fairly high plateaux with mountain ridges running east-west which rise to over 3000 m in the Dominican Republic. In places the plateaux are deeply incised with narrow valleys, giving rise to attractive landscapes. Like the volcanic islands, their rainfall is fairly high but varies according to aspect. For example, the windward side of Jamaica receives 3328 mm per annum (at Port Antonio) while Kingston (in the lee of the hills) receives 870 mm (*see* Fig 2.6 on p 11).

Similarly on Puerto Rico, Humaçao on the exposed easterly end of the island gets 2121 mm per annum while Ponce has only 909 mm.

Variations in the islands' political, cultural and economic backgrounds

The islands are culturally varied, depending on their past colonial and present political affiliations. From the 16th century Spain, France, England, Denmark and Holland all established colonies in the Caribbean, and some islands changed hands during the competition for trade. America later acquired some islands, for example, it purchased the Virgin Islands from Denmark in 1917 and in the 20th century many of the British islands became independent. Each island's language,

architectural style, and political organisation is a result of its colonial background. The Cuban revolution of 1959 turned this island into a socialist state and cut it off from Western trade and from American tourism. Up to 1989, Americans, though not forbidden to travel to Cuba, were not allowed to spend US dollars there.

Fig 32.8 indicates the variety of cultural and political organisation in the Caribbean.

The remaining islands are mainly English-speaking British colonies or independent islands. The economies of most of the islands (except Trinidad) are highly dependent on tourism, and their governments are generally keen to promote tourism. Hence there is some competition between them to attract visitors. However, in many islands, the currency is closely linked to the US dollar and there is relatively little difference in price between them. Levels of use depend more on accessibility. The major exceptions are firstly Haiti and the Dominican Republic – both very poor countries with weak currencies that make them the cheapest Caribbean destinations and thus attractive to the US market, but their poverty and political instability has tended to inhibit potential US visitors and

Island	Political status	Official language	Currency
Bahamas	Independent	English	*
Cuba	Independent (socialist)	Spanish	Cuban peso
Jamaica	Independent	English	Jamaican dollar
Barbados	Independent	English	Barbados dollar
Trinidad	Independent	English	Trinidad/Tobago dollar
Haiti	Independent	French	Gourde
Dominican Republic	Independent	Spanish	Dominican peso
Puerto Rico	Commonwealth of USA (not an American state but Puerto Ricans are USA citizens)	Spanish	*
US Virgin Islands	Unincorporated US territory	English	*
UK Virgin Islands	British colony	English	*
St Martin } St Maarten }	One island, half French, half Dutch	French Dutch	French franc *
Guadeloupe } Martinique }	Both overseas departments of France	French French	French franc French franc
Curaçao	Netherlands' territory	Dutch	Guilder
Bonaire	Netherlands' territory	Dutch	Guilder
Aruba	Dutch in transition to independence	Dutch	Guilder

*(denotes US dollar is legal tender)

Fig. 32.8 Cultural and political background of selected Caribbean islands

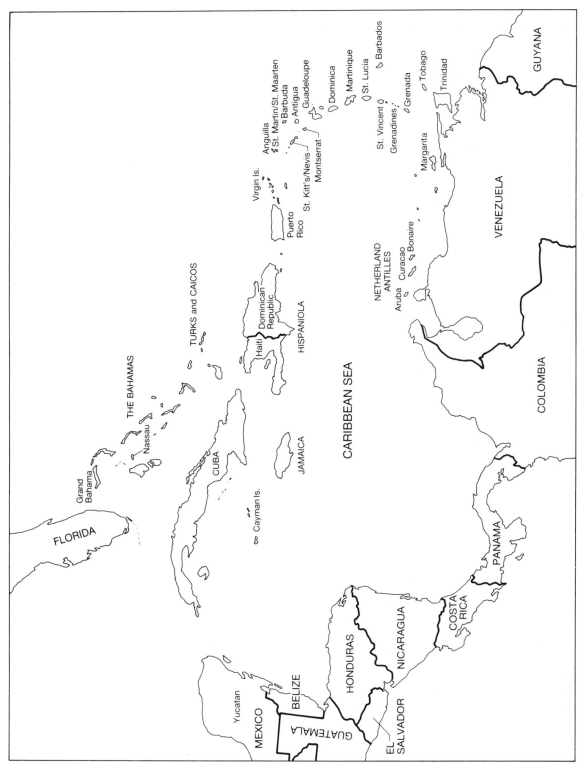

Fig. 32.9 Caribbean islands

constrain the growth of their tourist industry. Nevertheless 71 per cent of the 911 000 visitors to the Dominican Republic are from the USA.

The second exception are the colonial islands that have European currencies, which make them relatively more expensive for the North American market. Language differences may create another barrier and these islands tend to have relatively fewer visitors from the USA. On the other hand, Europeans visiting the Caribbean will be more likely to visit colonies of their own countries.

Distribution of tourism in the Caribbean

The general pattern of accessibility has led to a strong concentration of tourism in the northern half of the Caribbean (*see* Fig 32.9). Not only are the northern islands nearer to the North American markets but, apart from Cuba, all the other factors combine to make them the most attractive and accessible. Air routes reflect the political affiliations of islands, and these are also crucial in moulding the flow of tourists into the region.

The Bahamas are closest to the Florida market, and Miami is one of the region's most important links into the international air travel system but some of the more distant islands also have direct air links to other markets. Puerto Rico has flights from New York and other eastern seaboard airports, where the vast majority of its visitors come from. Puerto Rico is the main hub for the eastern Caribbean, but St Maarten also has direct flights from several US and European cities, while Guadeloupe and Martinique have direct connections to France (where more than half their visitors live) and Antigua and Barbados receive direct flights from UK.

These more accessible islands are the focus of tourism in the southern half of the Caribbean and also act as distributors for the smaller islands in the Windward and Leeward groups. Aruba, Curaçao and Bonaire are isolated from these groups of islands and have fairly low visitor numbers. Most of Aruba's tourists come from the USA but substantial numbers of Venezuelans visit Curaçao by ferry from the South American mainland.

Cruise traffic in the Caribbean

The south of the Caribbean is also isolated from the main centres of cruise activity (Miami and

Puerto Rico) which are all located in the north of the region. There are three types of cruises:

1 short one to four day cruises from Miami to the Bahamas, and from Puerto Rico to the US Virgin Islands;
2 one-week cruises from Miami to the northern Caribbean and Yucatan, and from San Juan (in Puerto Rico) to the south;
3 two-week cruises from Florida to the whole of the Caribbean. These are declining in popularity and the southernmost islands have lost substantial numbers of cruise arrivals.

Puerto Rico

Puerto Rico is the fourth biggest island in the Caribbean (after Cuba, Hispaniola and Jamaica), but it is the leading tourist destination (*see* Fig 32.5). It was originally a Spanish colony but was ceded to USA in 1898, so now it is very Americanised and both English and Spanish are widely spoken. The island has a central mountain range (rising to 1337 m) surrounded by coastal plains where sugar cane and pineapples are grown. In the north east of the island some of the original rainforest has survived and is designated as the El Yunque National Park. The island has good beaches and resorts (e.g. Luquilla Beach) and many coral reefs and keys. San Juan is the capital and is the main communications hub in the Caribbean – the international airport has frequent flights arriving from many European and American cities (e.g. Los Angeles, Chicago, Washington, Miami and New York) and to the other islands. San Juan is also one of the main cruise ports of the region and most of Puerto Rico's hotel accommodation is concentrated here. The old city of San Juan dates back to 1521 and has many restored Spanish colonial buildings, churches and forts. It is now designated as a National Historic zone. The modern town has plenty of nightlife, and several casinos.

Of Puerto Rico's 2.6 million tourists, 70 per cent come from the USA, a mixture of holiday makers and Puerto Rican emigrants returning to visit friends and relatives. Its accommodation stock reflects this. The island ranks only 4th in the Caribbean in terms of its number of hotel rooms, but it has 20 per cent of the Caribbean region's guest house rooms. Tourist numbers stabilised at about 1.5 million through the mid-1980s, but grew sharply in the late 1980s (for example by 20 per cent in 1987) to reach over 2 million by 1988. Growth has continued since then but at a slower rate.

The Bahamas

The Bahamas consists of over 700 small islands and islets spread out over 970 km of ocean between the Florida coast and Hispaniola; less than 22 of them are inhabited.

They have no rivers, so water is obtained from underground sources. The islands are lowlying and are mostly coral reefs with many white sandy beaches. The shallow waters are warm, clear and unpolluted and they are excellent for snorkelling, scuba diving, fishing and yacht cruising. The climate is a little cooler, drier and sunnier than many of the other Caribbean islands. The islands have only their sun, sea and sand as tourist resources but there are several types of tourism:

1 **Mass tourism**. The visitors come by air and are based in the developed resorts on New Providence and Grand Bahama Islands. These two islands receive 54 per cent and 31 per cent respectively of the Bahamas' staying (stopover) visitors (in 1991). The resorts have additional attractions such as shopping, entertainment and gambling.
2 **The undeveloped islands** (collectively known as the Family Islands) with little tourist infrastructure. These attract 15 per cent of Bahamas' stopover tourists.
3 **Cruise ship arrivals** which are limited to the main ports. Cruise ship arrivals easily outnumber the stopover tourists.

Whilst stopover tourism in the Bahamas grew rapidly in the 1960s (to reach over 1 million by 1970), it expanded only slowly in the 1980s to a peak of 1.57 million in 1989 and declined slightly to 1.42 million in 1991. The cruise ship business increased very rapidly in the 1980s, from 557 000 in 1980 to 2.02 million in 1990.

According to the Caribbean Hotel Association, the Bahamas have the largest concentration of hotel accommodation in the region in 1991.

The location of the Bahamas (only 60 miles off the Florida coast) has provided both advantages and disadvantages. The islands have been able to benefit from the trend towards shorter Caribbean cruises originating from Miami. The Bahamas are often the first port of call. On the other hand the islands rely almost exclusively on the US market (which contributed 82 per cent of visitors to the Bahamas in 1991). Stopover tourism is very sensitive to the state of the US economy and has declined when the US economy has been in recession. The majority of Bahamas' tourists come from the east of USA, from the north eastern 'core' area (Boston, New York, Philadelphia and Washington), and from the south (Miami, Atlanta and Charlotte region). The seasonal pattern of tourism in the Bahamas reflects the pattern of US holiday taking (rather than the weather) with spring (March/April) and summer (August) peaks; the islands are less of a winter sun destination than the rest of the Caribbean.

Dominican Republic

This country occupies the eastern part of the island of Hispaniola. The Dominican Republic is the second largest of the Caribbean states (after Cuba) but with a GNP per head of US $950 in 1990, only Haiti is poorer. Its tourism grew very rapidly from about half a million in the early 1980s to over 1.5 million by 1990. The country should not be confused with the island of Dominica, which is a small volcanic Caribbean island in the Windward Islands and has fewer than 50 000 visitors a year. The Dominican Republic is one of the fault block islands, so its interior has plateaux and mountains (rising to over 3000 m) but its main tourist attractions at present are its unspoilt beaches, e.g. around Puerto Plata and the Samana Peninsula, both on the country's north coast, and also on the south-east coast. The capital, Santo Domingo was founded in 1496 and the old part of the city has been conserved, but the new parts are lively, with discos, casinos and other entertainment.

Tourism development in the Dominican Republic has been of a different nature to that in many other Caribbean states; it began later, it was largely domestically financed and it caters for lower spending tourists, being one of the relatively cheaper Caribbean destinations. The development of tourism was triggered off by government investment, and the Dominican private sector (aided by tax incentives etc.) followed their lead. There has so far been relatively little foreign investment; in 1987, only 21 per cent of the hotel rooms were in foreign owned establishments. The scale of this development is reflected in the fact that, according to the Caribbean Hotel Association, the Dominican Republic had 13.4 per cent of all the hotel accommodation in the Caribbean in 1991 (only just behind the long established Bahamas). The country's infrastructure has not kept up with the pace of development and the rapid growth of tourist accommodation (e.g. the cruise port facilities are not up to the standards available in other Caribbean islands) and this appears now to be the limiting factor.

The 1991 recession hit the Dominican Republic hard, with a 13.8 per cent drop in tourist arrivals. Tourism development will no doubt remain crucial to the Dominican government. Tourism is the country's main foreign exchange earner and contributes 10 per cent of the country's GNP.

Jamaica

Jamaica is the third largest island in the Caribbean; it is 146 miles long and 51 miles wide and is located in the north of the Caribbean, only 1.5 hours' flying time from Miami. It has a wide range of tourist resources and attracted over 1 million tourists (stopover plus cruise ship arrivals) in 1991. Its tourism development has been restricted by political and image problems – there were scattered riots in the island in 1985; it was struck by Hurricane Gilbert in 1988; and has a reputation for drugs and drug-related violence. Its main attractions are its beaches, scenery and lively nightlife. The beaches are white and sandy and fringed by coral reefs on the north, where the main resorts are Montego Bay, Ocho Rios and Negril (on the east tip of the island). Most of Jamaica's hotel accommodation is concentrated in these three resorts there. About 80 per cent of tourists arrive via Montego Bay international airport. There are some black sand beaches on the south coast but these are less popular and there are fewer resorts there. Inland, the island is dominated by a mountain ridge rising from about 1000 m in the west to the Blue Mountains (2000 m) in the east. These limestone mountains are heavily forested, with caves and spectacular waterfalls.

In 1992, 62 per cent of Jamaica's 909 000 stopover tourists came from the USA, 11 per cent from Canada and another 10.6 per cent come from UK (holiday makers and emigrants returning to visit friends and relatives). In 1990 it attracted 385 000 cruise visitors.

Its tourism is well established, the island having been a fashionable winter destination for wealthy British (and Americans) in the 1950s. France suggests that tourist development is in its 'mature' stage.

Saint Maarten/St Martin

This tiny island is located in the northern part of the Leeward group of islands. Although it is so small, it received 548 038 tourists by air in 1991 and over half a million cruise arrivals in 1990, making it one of the leading Caribbean destinations. The island is politically split between the French (northern two-thirds) and Dutch (one-third of the island). The French sector is an overseas Département of France, though no passports are required by tourists travelling between the two sectors. Physically the island is split into a volcanic mountainous western section and a flat eastern peninsula. Most of the accommodation is in big luxury hotels that have lively entertainment, dancing and casinos, though the French part of the island is quieter. The climate, beaches and water based activities are the main physical attractions, though the town of Phillipsburg retains its Dutch colonial architecture and atmosphere and there are many duty free shops. Even though it is small, the island has an international airport with regular flights arriving from the USA and Europe and to other Caribbean islands. This partly explains the huge number of tourists. In 1991 48.7 per cent of the visitors came from the USA, but 20 per cent from France.

US Virgin Islands

The US Virgin Islands consist of a group of about 50 small islands, totalling 354 km². The three largest islands are St Croix, St Thomas and St John. They were Danish Colonies until the US Government purchased the islands in 1917. They lie 50 km east of Puerto Rico. These political and locational factors have led to their intensive use for tourism with over half a million stopover tourists in 1991 and an estimated 1.119 million cruise visitors in 1990. In 1992, 85 per cent of the visitors came from the USA. The islands are often the first port of call for cruises that begin in nearby Puerto Rico. Most cruises go to St Thomas (to Charlotte Amelie) but some also call at St Croix.

The islands' attractions centre on the beaches and watersports, including snorkelling, night diving and submarine trips to view the coral and marine life. Buck Island Reef (off St Croix) is an underwater National Park, while two-thirds of the small unspoilt island of St John is also a National Park. The Danish colonial towns of Christiansted and Charlotte Amelie retain much attractive 17th and 18th century architecture.

Cuba

Cuba is the largest of the Caribbean islands (with an area of 110 860 km^2). It is located only 145 km from the south of Florida, so is ideally located to accommodate the US market. Through the 1930s and up to 1959 the island did indeed function as the hub of Caribbean tourism. In 1957 it received 272 000 tourists, 87 per cent of whom came from the USA. Tourism was then based on prostitution and gambling, as well as beach tourism. However, political changes suddenly stopped Cuba's international tourist development – in 1959 Fidel Castro established a Communist state on the island, and relations with the USA became very hostile. Cuba enjoyed the support of the USSR but due to the political tension and various political crises international tourism dropped to only about 3–5000 visitors a year in the 1960s. The USA banned Americans from visiting Cuba and Cuba concentrated on developing its domestic tourism in the 1960s. Since then, although domestic tourism has remained a priority, the country has begun to encourage international tourism once more for economic reasons. By 1987, Cuba's economic situation was worsening as support from its Communist allies declined (as a result of the political changes leading to the revolutions in Eastern Europe). This led the Cuban government to reassess the role of international tourism in the economy, although the country did not participate in the process of modernisation and change that other socialist countries had embraced. Tourism was made a top economic priority, with the aim of increasing its number of tourists to half a million by 1992. Resources were set aside to update and refurbish existing hotels and the government encouraged joint ventures between the Cuban tourist development agency (Cubanacan) and foreign investors to build new hotels, facilities and resorts and upgrade the transport system.

At the end of 1985, 30 679 rooms were available for tourists, mainly located in Havana (32 per cent) and the main beach resort of Varadero (26.7 per cent). The plans of the late 1980s aimed to channel most of the new accommodation into Havana and the north coast resorts of Varadero (where the target is 30 000 new rooms by the year 2000), Santa Lucia and Guadalavaca. Cuba's tourist resources are typical of the Caribbean – the island has 289 recognised beaches, many coral reefs and keys (e.g. Cayo Largo) and many opportunities for water sports, although few of the resorts so far are equipped for more than a limited range of activities. Varadero is the main beach destination. In 1988, over 100 000 tourists visited the resort and it generated 33 per cent of Cuba's total foreign revenue from tourism that year. Cayo Largo attracted 2500 visitors. The island has attractive colonial towns (e.g. Old Havana and Trinidad, founded in 1514). Inland the mountains, forests, landscape and wildlife offer the possibility of adventure tourism (e.g. camping, trekking, caving, horse riding and climbing) and ecotourism; there are six national parks. Health tourism is another speciality. The country has relatively low-cost, high quality health care and some health care resorts are planned.

The political changes that have occurred in Cuba and elsewhere have led to drastic changes to the structure of its inbound tourism (*see* Fig 32.10). Before the 1959 revolution, the USA was the dominant market but the restrictions imposed by the USA on Americans travelling to Cuba has reduced their numbers to a mere trickle. On the other hand, package tours from Canada were started in the early 1970s and this has led to a growth of Canadian visitors, who have made up around 22 per cent of Cuba's tourists over the last decade. The socialist countries of Eastern Europe also contributed about 20 per cent of Cuba's inbound visitors up to 1985, but the political changes in Eastern Europe and their economic consequences reduced this to about 9 per cent by the early 1990s. In contrast, the proportion of western Europeans has increased from 17 per cent in 1981 to 40.77 per cent in 1990 (mainly from Germany and Spain).

	Number	Originating country			
		USA (%)	Canada (%)	Socialist States (%)	Germany (%)
1957	272 226	87			
1974	12 000				
1980	51 054	5.27	21.49	20.87	
1985	192 179	2.2	23.6	16.19	
1987	282 000	2.3	17.3	11.36	9.04
1989	314 000	3.9	23.0	13.06	21.0
1990	340 329	no info	21.8	8.8	17.48
1991	424 041	2.6	21.7	no info	no info

Fig. 32.10 Tourist arrivals to Cuba

More recently there have been significant increases in visitor arrivals from Latin America as new air connections are established.

Tourism to the remainder of the Caribbean islands

The varied physical character, colonial background and transport links make each island a unique destination with its own characteristic pattern of tourism. In general, the region relies heavily on the US market but it has been noted that certain islands depend on other very specific markets (e.g. 78 per cent of Guadeloupe's tourists come from France, 29 per cent of Curaçao's from the Netherlands, 22 per cent of tourists to Barbados come from the UK, while 22 per cent of Cuba's originate in Canada). Tourism arrivals to the region as a whole grew by 5–6 per cent in the late 1980s up to 1991. The Gulf War and the American economic recession led to a reduction of 1.15 per cent in 1991 but a significant number of Caribbean destinations saw a recovery in 1992 and the early months of 1993.

REFERENCES AND FURTHER READING

Mexico
Cockerell, N (1993) 'Mexico', *International Tourism Reports*, No.1, pp. 5–22.
Long, V H (1991) 'Government–industry–community interaction in tourism development in Mexico', in Sinclair, M T and Stabler, M J (Eds), *The Tourism Industry – an international anaylsis*, CAB International.

Caribbean
EIU (1992) 'The Bahamas', *International Tourism Reports*, No. 4, pp 36–53.
EIU (1993) 'Jamaica', *International Tourism Reports*, No. 4, pp. 27–49.
France, L (undated) 'An overview of tourism in the Caribbean', Centre for Travel and Tourism.
Gayle, D J and Goodrich, J N (1993) *Tourism marketing and Management in the Caribbean*, Routledge. (This book has useful chapters on Bahamas, Jamaica, Barbados, St Lucia, Trinidad and Cuba.)
Hall, D R (1992) 'Tourism development in Cuba', Chapter 8 in Harrison, D (Ed) '*Tourism in the less developed countries*', Belhaven.
Mather, S and Todd, G (1993) 'Tourism in the Caribbean', *EIU Special Report*, No. 455.
Riley, C W (1992) 'The Atlantic–Caribbean cruise industry', in Cooper, C (Ed) *Progress In Tourism*, Vol. 4.

QUESTIONS AND DISCUSSION POINTS

1 With reference to Fig 32.5, rank the top ten Caribbean destinations (in terms of tourist *plus* cruise arrivals). In which part of the Caribbean are the five most popular islands? What explanations can you put forward for this pattern of tourist use?

2 Discuss the relative significance of location, accessibility and colonial history in determining the volume and nationality of tourist arrivals to the Caribbean islands.

3 What geographical factors combine to make Mexico the leading international destination for American tourists?

ASSIGNMENT

You work for a cruise company based in Puerto Rico. Your existing 7 and 14-day cruises are declining in popularity. Your chief executive has asked you to review the cruise routes and draft three new itineraries (7 or 14 days in length focused around particular Caribbean themes). He has asked you to include one itinerary illustrating the theme of 'cultural variety in the Caribbean', and a second to demonstrate the wealth and variety of natural landscapes and environments to be found in the Caribbean.

Prepare a report, outlining and explaining these two itineraries. Include a third itinerary illustrating another theme of your own choice.

CHAPTER 33

Central and South America

LEARNING OBJECTIVES

After reading this chapter you should be able to
- assess the tourist potential of the climatic landscape, historical and cultural resources of Central and South America
- distinguish between the regional distribution of these resources and their development and use for tourism
- demonstrate a knowledge of the main tourist resorts and tourist centres
- understand the role of the region in the general pattern of world and American tourism
- outline the political constraints on the development of tourism in the region.

INTRODUCTION

Tourism in Central and South America is still on a small scale, accounting for only 0.45 per cent and 2.16 per cent of world arrivals respectively. Central and South America are not only part of the world's economic periphery but they are also physically distant from the world's main centres of population. Most of their tourism is intraregional, so they seem to function separately from the main world tourist system (and indeed quite separately from each other). This pattern of growth of tourism bears little relationship to worldwide trends and has more to do with local political and economic circumstances. Central and South America are notorious for their political and economic instability.

Central and South America form a huge and physically varied region, stretching from the rainforest in tropical latitudes north of the Equator in Central America, southwards through all the world's climatic zones to Cape Horn (at 55 °S), which is not far from the Antarctic. The continent possesses a wealth of tourist resources: beach and climatic resources attract tourists from within the region, but only those countries with outstanding historic, wildlife and cultural resources attract intercontinental travellers on any scale. The reef, rainforest and tropical wetland habitats are the main ecotourism resources, while the areas of Mayan and Inca settlements attract most cultural and historic tourism. Central America consists of seven small countries – Guatemala, Costa Rica, Panama, Belize, El Salvador, Honduras and Nicaragua. The smallest is 21 000 km^2 (just 8.6 per cent of the size of the UK) and the largest only 120 349 km^2 (49 per cent of UK) – *see* Fig 33.1. The total population of the region in 1990 was just over 29 million. Nearly 40 per cent of its 2.06 million tourists are generated within the region, while 34.7 per cent come from North America and 13.1 per cent from Europe. Only 8 per cent of its tourists come from South America.

South America, on the other hand, is a huge continent consisting of 12 countries (*see* Fig 33.2) including Brazil (the fifth largest country of the world). The region's population was 297.9 million in 1990, but with an average GNP per head of only just over US $ 2000 in 1988, it generates relatively little outbound tourism as yet. The region received only 9.818 million tourist arrivals in 1991, but 72 per cent of these were South Americans. Europeans constituted 14.5 per cent and North Americans 11.13 per cent of total arrivals, while less than 2% came from Central America. The two parts of Latin America thus function as fairly isolated tourist units: they exchange very few tourists and most of their arrivals come from within their own boundaries.

Country	Area (km²)	Number of tourists (000s)	North America %	Europe %	Central America %	South America %
Guatemala	108 889	513	31.3	18.2	43.1	4.1
Costa Rica	51 000	505	44.2	13.6	13.6	6.5
Panama	75 082	279	25.4	6.6	24.3	30.7
Belize	22 965	223	37.7	11.7	50.6	–
El Salvador	21 400	199	31.2	6.1	57.9	3.4
Honduras	112 088	198	34.4	8.9	49.9	3.7
Nicaragua	146 286	146	20.9	15.7	57.0	3.0

Fig. 33.1 Central America inbound tourism, 1991
(*Source*: WTO)

Country	Area (million km²)	Number of tourist arrivals (000s)	North America %	Europe %	Central America %	South America %
Argentina	2.76	2870	9.8	10.1	9.8	70.0
Uruguay	0.17	1510	1.3	2.9	–	78.1
Brazil	8.51	1352	14.3	25.1	0.3	54.4
Chile	0.75	1349	5.3	7.7	2.4	82.9
Colombia	1.14	857	18.8	6.3	–	–
Venezuela	0.91	598	29.1	42.5	1.2	15.7
Ecuador	0.27	365	21.2	16.1	2.0	57.4
Paraguay	0.40	361	7.6	11.5	6.0	72.7
Peru	1.28	232	23.0	35.3	1.2	31.6
Bolivia	1.08	221	14.5	34.9	1.4	44.5
Guyana	0.21	73	–	–	–	–
Suriname	0.16	30	–	–	–	–

Fig. 33.2 South America inbound tourism, 1991
(*Source*: WTO)

CENTRAL AMERICA

Central America is a relatively narrow strip of land linking the huge continents of North and South America, *see* Fig 33.3. At its narrowest point (in Panama) it is only 60 km wide. Most of its territory is rugged highlands, between 1000 and 2000 metres in height. The mountain chain that runs through the length of the region links the Mexican highlands to the Andes. The highest peaks rise to over 3000 m and some are active volcanoes. The most extensive lowlands are the marshy coastal plains of Belize, Honduras and Nicaragua, facing onto the shallow, calm and enclosed Caribbean Sea. The west coast faces the rollers of the open Pacific Ocean. There are good beaches on both coasts, though the Caribbean coast is fringed with a long coral reef. The Caribbean coast has a hot tropical climate with rain-bearing onshore winds all year round, though the summer months (May–October) are wetter. Sea level temperatures range from 20 to 30° C, and the natural vegetation is tropical rain forest. The mountains are cooler and a wide range of different wildlife habitats occur here as the climate changes rapidly with increasing altitude. On the west (Pacific) side of the mountains, the climate is drier with a clearly defined wet season (November–April) and heavy rain from May to October. The

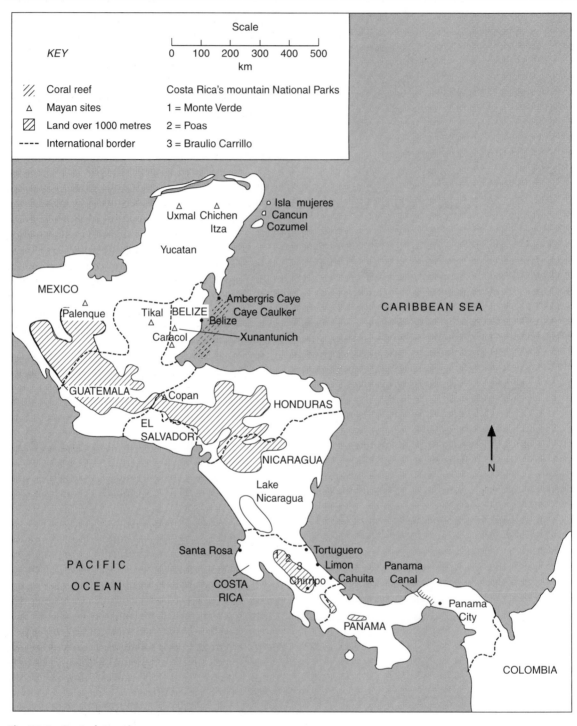

Scale

0	100	200	300	400	500

km

KEY

Coral reef

Mayan sites

Land over 1000 metres

International border

Costa Rica's mountain National Parks

1 = Monte Verde

2 = Poas

3 = Braulio Carrillo

Uxmal   Chichen
                   Itza

Isla mujeres

Cancun

Cozumel

Yucatan

MEXICO

Palenque

CARIBBEAN SEA

Tikal   BELIZE

Ambergris Caye

Caye Caulker

Belize

Caracol

Xunantunich

GUATEMALA

Copan

HONDURAS

EL
SALVADOR

NICARAGUA

Lake
Nicaragua

Santa Rosa

Tortuguero

PACIFIC

OCEAN

Limon

COSTA
RICA

Chirripo

Cahuita

Panama
Canal

PANAMA

Panama
City

COLOMBIA

N

Fig. 33.3   Central America

vegetation here is tropical savannah. The region has a rich cultural industry. The ancient Mayan empire flourished between 300 AD–800 AD and was based in present day Belize, Guatemala and Honduras, as well as extending into the Yucatan peninsula of Mexico (*see* Chapters 5 and 32). Many spectacular ruins of temples, step pyramids and other buildings still exist. The area was conquered by the Spanish in the seventeenth century, so the official language is Spanish in all Central American countries (except Belize which was a British colony and never came under Spanish rule). The countries became independent in the 1820s and 1830s but most (except Belize and Costa Rica) have had turbulent political histories in the 20th century, so tourism development is still on a very small scale.

Belize

Belize is one of the smallest countries in Central America, being only 22 965 km^2, and has one of the smallest populations in the world (194 000 in 1991), so it is very sparsely populated. Much of its natural environment remains unspoilt and untouched by human activity. It is a lowlying and mainly forested country. Its main tourist resource is the 185-km long coral barrier reef that runs parallel to its coast just offshore in the shallow Caribbean Sea. It is the second biggest coral barrier reef in the world (after Australia's Great Barrier Reef). The country's other main attractions are the wildlife and the impressive ancient ruined cities of the Mayan civilisation. Tourism in Belize is still at a small scale; it has grown from 88 000 visitors in 1986 to 222 779 in 1991 at an average growth rate of about 19 per cent per annum.

Coastal tourism

The coast of Belize is mainly swampy with mangroves, but there are some good sandy beaches amongst the lagoons and marshy areas. However, most sun and sea holidays are based on the coral islands (Cayes) offshore, where there is excellent subaqua diving, snorkelling, fishing, yachting and other water sports. Sixty per cent of Belize's tourists visit Ambergris Caye and 33 per cent to Caye Caulker, where the underwater caves are a particular attraction for divers. A third of all Belize's hotel bed spaces are located in hotels and

resorts on these two islands and 76 per cent of all Belize's hotels are located on the coast and cayes.

The government has attempted to limit the impact of tourism on the reef by designating some parts as marine and wildlife reserves and placing restrictions on the removal of coral and on fishing in some areas.

Wildlife tourism

A survey by the World Wide Fund for Nature in 1988 suggested that for 52 per cent of Belize's tourists natural history was one of their reasons for visiting the country, although only 8 per cent said it was their main reason. Obviously the marine wildlife of the reef is a major attraction, but the country also has a good system of inland National Parks and wildlife reserves that cover 40 per cent of its territory. The government has a strong commitment to environmental protection and to promoting only balanced and environmentally-sound tourism, and the practical implementation of these policies is improving. The main wildlife attractions of the National Parks are jaguars, howler monkeys, orchids and butterflies.

Historic attractions

The most important Mayan sites are near the Guatemalan border, at Xunantunich, Cahal Pech and Caracol, although the latter is still being excavated and is as yet rather inaccessible. Belize is cooperating with Guatemala, El Salvador, Mexico and Honduras to promote tourism based on the range of Mayan sites in the region. Tourists will be able to follow a circuit of sites (to be known as La Ruta Maya) through the five countries.

Belize's main tourist markets are North American. In 1991, just over a third of its tourists were fairly high spending visitors from the USA, and 3.6 per cent from Canada. However, it is thought that up to half its visitors are cross-border trippers from Mexico. The country's colonial history is reflected in the fact that as many as 5 per cent of its tourists are from the UK, even though in 1992 there were no direct flights from Europe (air access is usually via Houston or Miami).

The nature of the resources and environment of Belize clearly indicate that it would not be suited to mass tourism, but does have great potential for small scale environmentally-based tourism. The government has opted for a high value, low volume type of tourism in its development policy and is cautious in its approach to new resort development.

Guatemala, Honduras, El Salvador and Nicaragua

These four countries have histories of civil war, political instability and frequent coups, and although they have tourism potential, their tourist industries remain undeveloped as yet. Peace initiatives begun in the late 1980s are starting to improve the situation, but the political future is still somewhat uncertain. All the countries have a variety of resources, including volcanic mountains and lake landscapes, unspoilt beaches and offshore islands and old colonial architecture. There are also important Mayan sites, particularly Copan in Honduras and Tikal in Guatemala. Tikal ranks alongside Chichen Itza (in Mexico) as one of the most impressive Mayan sites in Central America. The ruins include tombs, temples and pyramids set amongst tropical forest. It is accessible by air from resorts in Mexico and cross-border travel is now easy. In 1991, El Salvador, Honduras and Nicaragua each attracted less than 200 000 visitors, mostly from other Central American countries. Guatemala received 513 000 visitors, but again nearly half came from Central America.

Costa Rica

In contrast to its neighbours, Costa Rica has had a generally peaceful history, with over a hundred years of democracy. In 1948 it even abolished its army. Its current president (Oscar Arias Sanchez) has been influential in attempts to bring peace to the region.

Costa Rica has some good beaches (e.g. South of Port Limon and at Cahuita) but relatively few significant historic resources, having been outside the Mayan sphere of influence and not having been heavily colonised by the Spanish. However, its location and topography mean that it has a wide variety of different types of wildlife habitat and a larger than normal range of species present. Although its natural environment is far from untouched (two-thirds of its rainforest have

been cleared, half of it since 1950, and clearance is continuing), the Costa Ricans are very aware of the value of their natural habitats and 20 per cent of the country has been designated as National Parks. However, the protection of these areas has caused conflicts of interest between local villages who traditionally have exploited the Parks' natural resources and the national conservation policies that seek to preserve them (see Place, 1991).

There is significant domestic tourism to these parks (over quarter of a million in 1989) and the government has vigorously promoted the country as an international ecotourism destination since the mid-1980s, as the poor economic situation of the country meant that foreign currency was desperately needed. During the 1980s, its inbound tourism hovered around 300–350 000, but since 1989 (when the political situation in neighbouring Nicaragua began to improve) it has suddenly increased, reaching 504 649 by 1991. This represents a growth rate of 14–16 per cent per annum. Thirty-four per cent of its tourists come from USA, 7 per cent from Canada, and 13.6 per cent from Europe. In the 1986/87 season, over a third of all tourists to Costa Rica said that ecotourism was their main reason for coming.

Ecotourism in Costa Rica

Because Costa Rica is situated on the landbridge between North and South America it has animal and plant species from both continents. It is located in tropical latitudes (8° to 11° North of the Equator) yet its highest mountain (Chirripo Grande) reaches 3820 m. The country is only 119–282 km wide, so the transect from the tropical climate at sea level to the peak of Chirripo Grande crosses a large number of climatic zones (and therefore ecological environments) in a very short distance. Because of these factors, the country has about 6000 kinds of flowering plants (including 1500 species of orchids), at least 825 species of birds and 237 species of mammals (including jaguars, tapirs and ocelots). The country has 24 National Parks: the Braulio Carrillo Park covers five kinds of forest, while the Monteverde Cloud Forest Reserve includes eight different ecological zones down the side of the Tilaran Mountain. The centre piece of the Poas National Park is a dormant volcano which has a hot water lake in its crater and has outstanding mountain scenery. The Santa Rosa Park on the Pacific coast is a forest and savannah habitat. On the Caribbean coast, the Cahuita Park is a coral reef, while the Tortuguero Park is a mixture of tropical rain forest, swamp, lagoons and beaches where the green sea turtle breeds. Many of the Parks have tourist facilities and lodges. In 1989, nearly 162 000 foreign tourists visited the parks (the Poas National Park being the most popular in the mid-1980s).

Panama

In 1991, Panama was the third most important tourist destination in Central America (*see* Fig 33.1) but its attraction lies more in its strategic significance than in its natural resources. The Panama Canal, linking the Caribbean Sea with the Pacific Ocean, is both an attraction in itself and also brings foreign visitors, along with the commercial shipping. It is a major centre for duty-free shopping, while Panama City is noted for its nightlife and gambling. However, the country does have many other attractions, from its colonial city architecture, its beaches, fiestas and sports. In contrast to Costa Rica, the country chooses to use its wildlife resources for big game hunting rather than for conservation and ecotourism. The species which are hunted include jaguar, puma, wild boar, ocelot, deer and peccary.

The country draws its tourists more from its local region than from the North American and European markets: only 22 per cent came from the USA and 6.6 per cent from Europe.

SOUTH AMERICA

Although South America is on the periphery of the world's tourism and economic systems, it is a little more affluent than the other regions of the world's economic periphery and generates much more intra-regional tourism than Africa or South Asia. In 1988 its poorest country, Bolivia, had a per capita GNP of US $ 470 while 12 of the 19 countries had GNPs of over US $ 1000 per head. The main tourist generators are Argentina, Brazil, Uruguay and Venezuela, all of whom had GNPs per head of more than US $ 2000 in 1988 (*see* Rizzotto, 1991). On the other hand, nearly all the

countries of Latin America have experienced very rapid inflation in the 1980s and have enormous foreign debts.

These South American countries also have a reputation of political instability: some countries still have military dictatorships while others are returning to democracy, but the region's long-standing reputation for violence (e.g. associated with cocaine trafficking in Colombia and terrorism in Peru) is hard to overcome. Indeed, most South American countries have been involved in some civil, border or general war since 1973. North American media coverage of these events is very important because the region is very dependent on the USA for its inter-regional visitors. About three quarters of a million North Americans travelled to South America in 1987.

Attractions and resources of South America

The continent is made up of three physical units (*see* Fig 33.4):

1 The Andes which run the whole length of the west coast of South America. The mountain chain splits and runs through Central America to merge into the Rockies.

2 Two major river basins (the Amazon and the River Parana) which drain into the Atlantic on the east coast.

3 A large area of plateaux and uplands separating the two river basins.

The continent spans a wide range of climate zones from the equatorial climate of the Amazon Basin to the cold temperate conditions of the far south of Argentina and Chile. The natural resources of the continent include the mountain scenery of the Andes, the tropical rainforest environment of the Amazon, spectacular waterfalls where the major rivers descend from the plateaux into the lowlands and good beaches on the coasts of Venezuela, Brazil and Argentina. However, the continent is too far from the major tourist generating regions to attract any appreciable inter-regional beach tourism, so some countries (e.g. Brazil and Ecuador) have begun to promote ecotourism as a way of attracting visitors from Europe and North America. The main attraction for inter-regional tourists however, is the culture of the Andes, the ruins of the Inca cities (particularly in Peru), and the Spanish colonial

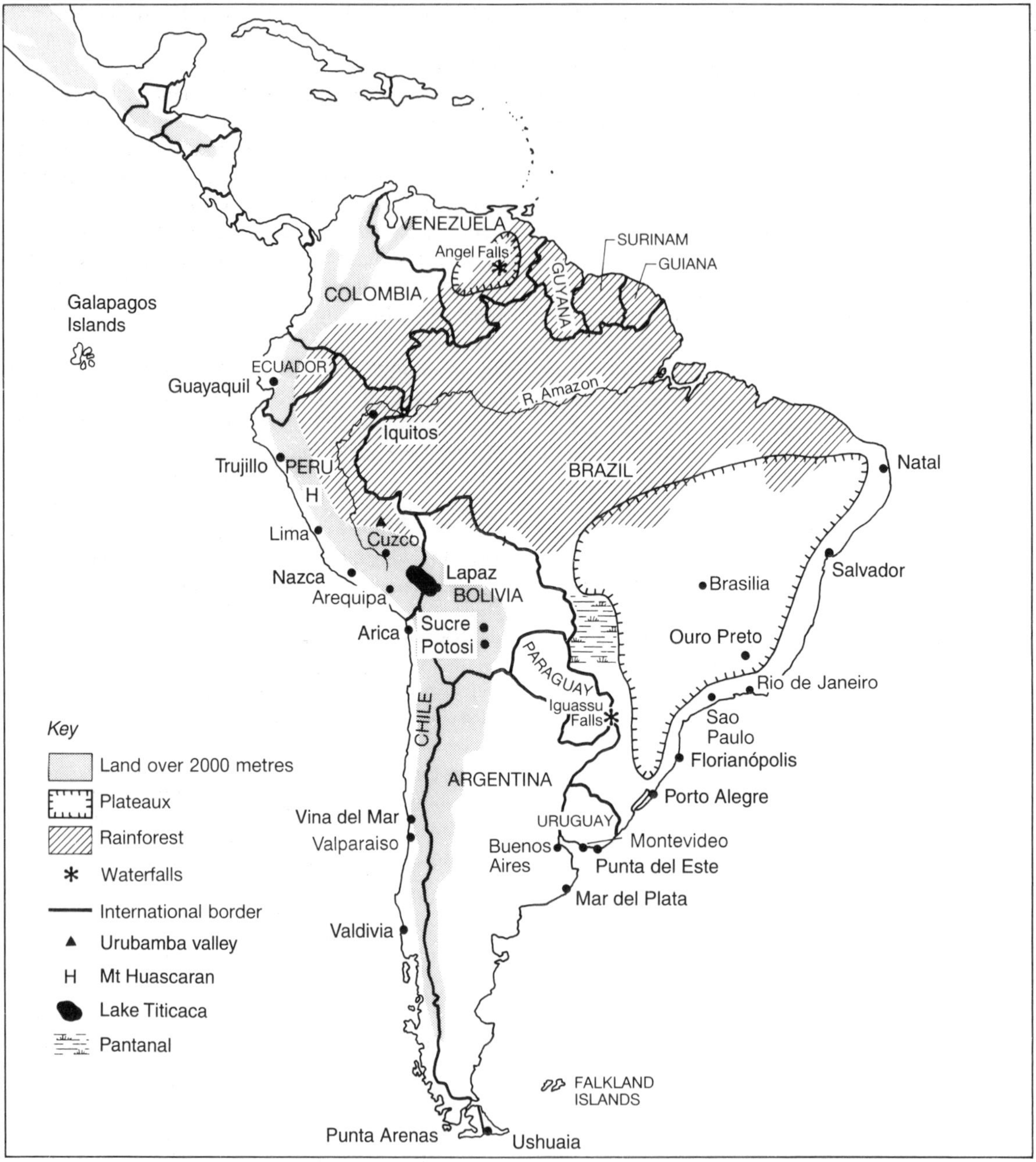

Fig. 33.4 Latin America's resources

architecture of many of the Andean cities that make South America unique.

It is those countries that combine the attractions of wildlife, scenery and Inca cultural resources (along with some beach and urban entertainment) that draw the highest proportions of their tourists from outside the region, namely Peru, Ecuador, Bolivia, Venezuela and Brazil (*see* Fig 33.2). Argentina, Chile, Uruguay, Colombia and Paraguay draw most of their tourists from their neighbouring

South American countries. Each of these countries also has a significant domestic market and reasonably well developed tourist infrastructure, but they form their own isolated tourist system, receiving a small proportion of their tourists from outside South America. The sheer distance of these destinations from the main Northern Hemisphere tourist-generating zones inhibits inter-regional travel to these countries. This reinforces the region's other disadvantages of poverty and political instability. Although special interest long-haul international tourism is growing on a world scale, this region may not be the first to benefit.

The countries of South America can thus be considered in three groups, each having a fairly distinct physical, historical and cultural character:

1 The Indian Andes: Ecuador, Peru and Bolivia. The High Andes form much of the territory of these three countries and roughly a quarter-to-a-half of their population is still made up of South American Indians, so they still possess a uniquely South American flavour to their modern culture. Most of the main Inca sites are also found in this part of the Andes. Although they have appeal for inter-continental travellers, tourism is still on a small scale – they received

only 8 per cent of all the tourist arrivals in the continent in 1991.

2 The countries of the south: Chile, Argentina, Uruguay and Paraguay. Apart from Paraguay, 85 per cent or more of the population of these countries is of European origin (the native Indians having been wiped out in colonial times). Although these countries are the focus of South America's tourism (receiving 62 per cent of all the tourist arrivals in the continent), they are so far distant from other tourist markets that 70 per cent or more of their inbound tourism is from adjacent South American countries.

3 The cosmopolitan countries of Brazil, Venezuela and Colombia. The population of this part of South America is very mixed: mestizo, European and people of many other ethnic origins. The character of tourism here is varied too, but with more emphasis on mainstream beach, landscape, urban and entertainment attractions. This region of South America attracted 29 per cent of its international tourist arrivals, and a significant proportion came from North America and Europe. The Guianas have very small tourist industries as yet.

Each of these three parts of South America thus also have significantly different patterns of inbound and outbound tourism (*see* Fig 33.5).

Country		1991 total number tourist arrivals (000s)	Inbound tourism (1991) percentage from			Outbound tourism (1988) percentage to		
			Other South American countries	North America	Europe	Other South American countries	North America	Europe
Ecuador		365	57.4	21.2	16.1	69.94	20.74	2.75
Peru	} 1	232	31.6	23.0	35.3	33.4	45.0	11.13
Bolivia		221	44.5	14.5	34.9	81.12	11.9	3.8
Argentina		2870	70	<9	10	74.91	8.06	14.8
Uruguay	} 2	1510	78	1	3	96.52	1.5	1.45
Chile		1349	83	5	8	82.63	11.1	4.87
Paraguay		361	73	8	11	96.26	2.2	1.00
Brazil		1352	54	14	25	24.4	25.1	45.63
Colombia		857	–	19	6	–	54.98	12.52
Venezuela	} 3	598	16	29	42	49.55	27.92	15.2
Guyana		73	–	–	–	–	–	–
Suriname		30	–	–	–	–	–	–

Fig. 33.5 The three tourist regions of South America
(*Source*: WTO and EIU)

Ecuador, Peru and Bolivia

These three countries have outstanding natural and cultural tourist resources, but their poverty, lack of infrastructure and political instability have inhibited the development of inter-regional tourism on a large scale. Their Indian population and culture are not particularly valued by South Americans of European or mestizo origin so they generate little intra-regional cultural tourism.

Historic and cultural resources

1 Pre-Colombian historic resources. These are resources predating Christopher Columbus' discovery of the Americas. South America's oldest civilisations were centred in Peru and spread north and south into Ecuador and Bolivia. The earliest civilisation which sprang up on the coast near Supe can be traced back to 2000 BC. At Chavin there are ruins of a fortress–temple complex dating from about 600 BC. This period was followed by the parallel development of the Nazca tribes in the south, and the Mochica in the north (between 150 and 800 AD). The Nazca lived in the coastal deserts south of Lima and were responsible for the Nazca lines (huge geometrical lines and outlines of birds and animals marked on the desert floor that are so big that they can only be properly seen from the air) and cemeteries, fortresses and aqueducts. It is thought that this civilisation was at its peak between 400–800 AD. The Mochica lived in the area around modern Trujillo, between 170–700 AD. They constructed the Pyramids of the Sun and Moon, the largest pre-Colombian structures in South America. They are similar to the Pyramids of Teotihuacan in Mexico but are made of adobe bricks rather than stone.

These coastal cultures gradually spread inland into the high Andes: their descendants are thought to have founded the Tihuanaco civilisation at the southern end of Lake Titicaca (in Bolivia) between 9th and 13th centuries. From the 11th century AD, the Chimu and Inca civilisations began. The Chimu ruled over 1000 km of the coastal zone north of Lima from Trujillo, to Guayaquil in Ecuador. The ruins of their main city are at Chan Chan, covering about 28 km^2 and consisting of palaces, temples, workshops, warehouses, irrigation canals, reservoirs and step pyramids.

The Inca civilisation began in the Urubamba valley in the Andes (near Cuzco). Their empire expanded to cover much of Peru and also parts of the Andes in Ecuador and Bolivia. They conquered the Chimu in the mid-1400s but were themselves conquered and their civilisation eventually destroyed by the Spanish between 1500 and 1600. The Incas founded many settlements using a unique method of building (without cement or mortar) by carving the building blocks to fit each other exactly. They also built paved roads linking the settlements and elaborate terraces and irrigation systems. Their gold and silver treasures and art works were plundered by Spanish and many Inca buildings destroyed (the stone was used to construct Spanish colonial towns) but some superb sites still remain (e.g. Machu Picchu). These are mainly centred in Peru, but some are in Ecuador and a few in Bolivia.

2 Spanish colonial rule. The Spanish founded many colonial towns in the region between 1500 and 1600 and some have survived almost intact with many churches, former mansions and narrow medieval streets. The Spanish brought Christianity to the region though the modern Indian population celebrate their fiestas with strong traces of their pre-Colombian pagan traditions.

Physical resources

The region consists of three physical and climatic regions:

1 The coast
2 The Andes
3 The tropical eastern flanks of the Andes and the upper Amazon basin.

The coast

The coastal plains are very narrow. The northern part (in Ecuador, north of Guayaquil) has a hot tropical climate with a wet summer season (January–April), but the sea is cold. The Humboldt current brings cold water from the far south of the Pacific (from the Antarctic) up the South American coast, so although there are good beaches along the whole length of the continent's west coast, international beach resorts are absent. Some parts of the coast also suffer from fog (e.g. at Lima) due to the warm air passing over the cold water (this situation parallels that of the Californian coast). In places the sea is very polluted. The coastal plains from Guayaquil southwards are deserts, though they are very fertile when irrigated.

The Sierra

The coastal plains quickly rise to the mountains of the High Andes. In Ecuador and Bolivia the mountain ranges are divided by a high valley or dry plateau (known as the Altiplano in Bolivia) where most of the Indian population lives (the average height is 3–4000 m). The peaks of the Andes rise to over 6000 m (e.g. Huascaran at 6768 m). Some, for example Cotopaxi (5896 m), are active volcanoes. The scenery is spectacular with glaciers and snow-capped peaks. The climate obviously becomes colder with altitude: at 2–3000 m the temperature can drop to near freezing at night but rises to just over 20°C in the day. However, the climate is quite dry so the mountains provide good conditions for trekking. The lack of oxygen in the thin air can bring on breathlessness and heart pounding, but some visitors may also suffer from the symptoms of mountain sickness (headache, dizziness, nausea etc.) until they acclimatise (over a period of about a week).

The eastern flanks of the Andes and the Amazon Basin

These areas are open to rainbearing winds and have heavy rainfall in the Southern Hemisphere summer (Nov–May). Temperatures rise as the Andes fall away towards the equatorial lowlands of the Amazon Basin. The transitional foothills (at altitudes between 600–1600 m) are known as the Oriente in Ecuador, the Montana in Peru, and Llanos in Bolivia. The natural vegetation is tropical or subtropical forest, and these regions are sparsely populated and mostly underdeveloped. The territory of each of the three countries extends far enough east to reach the genuine equatorial rainforest of the low-lying Amazon Basin with its high temperatures and year-round rainfall. The most extensive area is in Peru, in the region known as the Selza.

The three countries thus have much in common in terms of their cultural background and their physical characteristics. Their pattern of tourist development show similarities but there are some differences in each country's policy and approach.

Tourism in Ecuador

Ecuador is one of the more politically stable countries of South America. The country became independent of Spain in 1822 and it claimed the Galapagos Islands in 1832. The possession of these islands has allowed Ecuador's tourism to capitalise on the ecotourism market.

The islands (which are now a National Park) lie on the equator, 1000 km off Ecuador's Pacific coast. There are 13 main islands and many islets spread out over 3000 square miles of ocean. The islands are famous for their unique wildlife that has evolved in isolation; Charles Darwin visited the islands and what he saw there was instrumental in the development of his work on the origin of species.

The island's wildlife consists mainly of reptiles, birds and marine mammals, but many are unique to the island: 27 of the 56 resident bird species are only found on the islands and the giant tortoises are perhaps the islands' most famous species. Ecuador has successfully combined wildlife trips to the islands with cultural tourism on the mainland: a World Wide Fund for Nature survey in 1988 confirms this (*see* Fig 33.6).

The Galapagos Islands have been designated as a World Heritage Site; so, also, has Quito, the country's capital city. It is a very beautiful Spanish colonial city, situated high in the Andes. It has a wealth of colonial art, splendid churches, monasteries, cobbled streets and museums. It is the second

	% responses
Natural history	76
Sightseeing	49
Cultural history	38
Business	8

Note: adds up to over 100% because of multiple answers

Fig. 33.6 Main reasons for tourists visiting Ecuador, 1988
(*Source*: WWF)

most important tourist destination in Ecuador. However, there are many other cultural attractions in the Ecuadorean Andes, such as the native markets and crafts (particularly weaving), at Otavalo to the north of Quito, and the Inca site at Ingapirca in the south. It is the only surviving Inca site in Ecuador and consists of a complex of houses, courtyards, terraces, temples and fortifications.

The ecology of the mainland is also an important attraction. The Cotacachi–Cayapas reserve (where the Andean Plateau and coastal rainforest meet) is the most accessible being a 140 km drive from Quito, and it is the most visited. More recently, trekking in Ecuador's other mountain National Parks (e.g. to the volcanoes of Chimborazo and Cotopaxi which is also easily accessible from Quito) and excursions into the Amazon jungle (e.g. from Misahualli) have been combined with the tours of the Galapagos and Quito. These additional destinations are a minority interest as yet: only 5.5 per cent of all Ecuador's hotel rooms are located in the Oriente (which includes the Amazon jungle) – *see* Fig 33.7.

Although there is no detailed data on the spatial distribution of arrivals in Ecuador, EIU suggests

that the coastal zone caters mainly for South American visitors (mostly from Colombia and Peru). Foreign tourists outnumber nationals in the Galapagos, but about a third of the visitors to the Cotopaxi National Park are international tourists (*see* Fig 33.8).

Tourism in Peru

Peru was the centre of both the Inca and Spanish colonial empires. It abounds in ruins of Inca settlements and beautiful colonial towns, set in spectacular desert, mountain or jungle landscapes. Cultural and historic tourism is the focus of tourism here. However, Peru experiences several disadvantages that have limited the expansion of tourism:

1 Peru is a very poor country (GNP per head US $ 1140, 1990) and lacks the resources to develop its tourist infrastructure, particularly its transport system.
2 It has some political instability. The terrorist group (the Shining Path) has targeted tourists in the past. It was reported that the leaders of the group were captured in the early 1990s, but the situation was still very tense in 1993 with armed guards provided for tourists at many locations.
3 A recent cholera epidemic centred on Peru.
4 In common with all South American countries, tourists must beware of pickpockets, bag snatchers and thieves. Many cities (e.g. Lima) are dangerous.

These internal problems, linked with the Gulf crisis and world recession, have led to a significant decline in tourism to Peru in the early 1990s. In 1991 the total had dropped to 232 072 (from a peak of 359 281 in 1988).

	% of registered establishments	% of rooms
Coast	43.9	44.6
Sierra	45.6	48.3
Oriente	7.9	5.5
Galapagos	2.6	1.6

Fig. 33.7 Regional distribution of Ecuador's accommodation, 1990

	Number of national visitors	Percentage of national visitors	Number of foreign visitors	Percentage of foreign visitors	Total number of visitors
Cotacachi–Cayapas	69 276	81.49	15 726	18.51	85 005
Galapagos	17 236	41.84	23 956	58.16	41 192
Cotopaxi	27 462	67.32	13 330	32.68	40 792
Cayamba–Coca (in Amazon Sierra)	20 356	100.00	–	0	20 356
Cajas (Sierra)	14 395	96.33	548	3.67	14 943
Limoncocha (Amazon)	1 400	41.17	2 000	58.83	3 400

Fig. 33.8 Visitors to Ecuador's Reserves and National Parks

Cultural and historic attractions

1 Pre-Inca sites

The desert coastal plains have a number of important and impressive pre-Inca sites that are accessible to tourists, e.g. Chan Chan, Nazca, and inland there are other more inaccessible sites, e.g. Kuelap (a non-Inca fortress on the same scale as Machu Picchu), that are yet to be fully excavated and promoted for tourism.

2 Inca sites

The centre of the Inca empire was located at Cuzco and in the nearby Urubamba valley. Cuzco was a sacred city and the Inca capital in the 11th and 12th centuries. There were huge temples and fortresses here but most of the upper parts of the constructions were destroyed by the Spanish. However, the foundations remain, and many colonial churches and other buildings have Inca stonework in their foundations. Outside the city there are several Inca ruins that have not been built on, for example, the Sacsayhuaman fortress, which is only 4 km from Cuzco; it is a series of three walled platforms (360 m long) linked by flights of stairs built of huge blocks of stone (up to 9 x 5 m in size).

Cuzco was also a major Spanish colonial city although Lima became the Spanish colonial capital. It has many beautiful churches, with gold, silver and precious stones in the ornamentation (e.g. the cathedral and La Merced Church). Cuzco is the centre from which tourists visit the Urubamba valley, the sacred valley of the Incas. There are many Inca ruins here and the hillsides are terraced in places (remnants of the Inca agricultural and irrigation systems). A tourist train takes visitors into the valley where they can either join the Inca trail for a five-day trek (34–45 km) or continue the journey by train to reach Machu Picchu – known as the 'Lost City of the Incas'. The citadel of Machu Picchu was never discovered by the Spanish so was not destroyed and was abandoned at the fall of the Inca empire and overgrown by jungle vegetation. It was discovered in 1911 and was cleared and partly restored later. It is now designated as a Historic Sanctuary. The city consists of a 5 km^2 complex of agricultural areas, storage areas, cemeteries, temples, workshops and many other buildings. However, it is the setting of the city that makes the site so dramatic; it is perched on the summit of a narrow mountain crest at over 8000 feet, overlooking the Urubamba river. The Inca trail is a stone paved path constructed by the Incas linking the site into a network of routes focused on Cuzco. It is built with stone stairways and tunnels as it winds through the dramatic mountain scenery. Tourists can camp along the trail but trekkers need to be reasonably fit, as it is all above 2500 m and includes a climb of over 2000 m in the first 15 km. The best season for visiting Machu Picchu is May to September: the valley is on the wetter Amazon side (the River Urubamba is a tributary of the Amazon) and rain, cloud and mist are possible all year but the wetter season runs from October to April. There are other Inca trails and ruins on the Altiplano, but none so well preserved or in such a spectacular setting.

3 Spanish colonial cities

Cuzco (*see* above) is the most visited, but Arequipa is another town that has retained its colonial atmosphere. It was founded in 1540 and has many ornate old churches, mansions and a large nunnery (the Monasterio de Santa Catalina). Lima (the original colonial capital) was largely destroyed by an earthquake in 1946; it retains some colonial buildings but does not have the colonial atmosphere of the smaller cities and has little to attract the tourist.

4 The living culture

The Indians of the Altiplano have their own folk music and dancing. There are many folk markets and festivals (such as Inti Raymi held at Sacsayhuaman on 24th June). Tourists also visit the Indian villages on the floating islands of reeds on Lake Titicaca (at the Uros islands).

Other attractions

Peru has been promoting its landscape and natural features as additional attractions to its cultural and historic tourism. These fit well with the interests of the adventure market which chooses to visit the Inca ruins by walking the Inca trails. The Huascaran National Park covers the highest peaks of the Peruvian Andes. The park is a World Heritage Site and a Biosphere Reserve. Activities available here include trekking, climbing, glacier skiing and river rafting, as well as wildlife based tourism.

	Percentage N American visitors	Percentage European visitors	Percentage S Americans	All visitors
Cuzco	49.4	58.5	28.7	47.0
Arequipa	12.8	33.4	13.8	20.9
Puno (and Lake Titicaca)	11.8	33.2	6.8	18.4
Huaras (near Huarascan)	7.5	13.2	2.4	8.5
Iquitos	12.7	9.5	3.8	8.3

Fig. 33.9 Main tourist destinations in Peru, 1986

The Colca canyon is located near Arequipa. It is reputed to be the world's deepest canyon. Walking and horseriding treks, river rafting and canoeing are also being developed here. A nature reserve with spectacular marine wildlife is being promoted near Nazca. There is thus a clear pattern of adventure and environmental tourist resources being developed at suitable places physically near to or accessible from the major cultural sites. The exception, of course, is Iquitos – an isolated settlement in the Amazon, accessible only by plane or river boat, where rainforest and river trips, wildlife tours and adventure activities are promoted.

In spite of the difficulty of access, over 9 per cent of all European visitors and nearly 13 per cent of North American tourists visited Iquitos in 1986 (*see* Fig 33.9).

Visitors to Peru

The United States has been Peru's main market for a decade, with between 69 000 and 70 000 visitors a year between 1981 and 1989 (but dropping below 50 000 in 1990 and 1991). The USA accounts for around 20 per cent of all Peru's tourists. The former USSR has also made a major contribution to Peru's inbound tourism since 1989. Another 23 per cent of Peru's visitors come from its South American neighbours (Ecuador, Colombia, Brazil, Bolivia and Chile) while Argentina contributed 5.3 per cent of its tourists in 1991. Another quarter of Peru's tourists come from Europe, mostly from Germany, UK, Italy and Spain. Japan is Peru's only other significant market outside those regions (*see* Fig 33.10). It has been noted that the total number of tourists travelling to Peru has declined since 1989, with a particularly sharp drop of 26.7 per cent in 1990–91. This has been due to a drop in tourist arrivals from all Peru's markets.

	Percentage tourist arrivals
USA	19.79
Former USSR	9.42
Chile	6.32
Bolivia	5.61
Argentina	5.33
Germany	4.49
Colombia	3.91
Ecuador	3.72
UK	3.60
Italy	3.53
Spain	3.44
Japan	3.13
Others	
Total	100.00

Fig. 33.10 Peru's main markets, 1991
(*Source*: WTO)

Tourism in Bolivia

Bolivia has as wide a range of cultural and natural attractions as Ecuador and Peru, but political instability and economic problems which led to astoundingly high (over 8000 per cent) annual inflation rates in the early 1980s, have made it difficult for the government to promote tourism or invest in the infrastructure. Indeed, the government showed little interest in encouraging tourism, although the road network was improved in the early 1990s.

At present western tourism to Bolivia consists mainly of a brief addition to a visit to Peru, so only those attractions near the Peruvian border in the La Paz–Lake Titicaca region are visited on any scale. In 1986 the average length of stay of European visitors was 2.9 nights, only 3.4 nights for North Americans.

Tourist resources

The well-known Inca remains are on the Altiplano and the east-facing flanks of the Andes in the La Paz region. There are Inca ruins near Cochabamba, an Inca trail that is better preserved than that at Machu Picchu, running down towards the Amazon from Corioco and the remains of Inca temples of the islands of the Sun and Moon in Lake Titicaca itself (accessible from Copacobano). There are substantial pre-Inca ruins at Tihuanaco, 42 miles from La Paz. These date from about 800 AD.

Potosi and Sucre are splendid examples of medieval Spanish colonial towns. Potosi was the centre of the silver mining activities under Spanish rule but was virtually abandoned when the silver ran out. So the town was left unspoilt until tin and other minerals were mined there in modern times. The town (at 4070 m) is located even higher than La Paz, so the winter night temperatures fall well below freezing. Sucre (at an altitude of 2790 m) has a much milder climate and is another quiet and beautiful colonial town unspoilt by modern suburbs. It was founded in 1538. Both these towns are a long way south of La Paz and are visited by few tourists as yet. In 1986 only 5.6 per cent of Bolivia's foreign tourists went to Sucre and 4 per cent to Potosi. However, the majority visit La Paz, the capital. This is a modern city but has a historic city centre (dating from 16–18th centuries).

The lower valleys (known as the Yungas), that run down from the Andes towards the Amazon and the Amazon lowland itself, have great potential for ecotourism: the habitats vary from semi-tropical jungle, open savannah and forests to dense rainforest. The high Andes also abound in wildlife and opportunities for adventure tourism. This potential is as yet undeveloped, and most of Bolivia's tourism is cultural/historic tourism based on the country's Inca and colonial heritage.

Tourism trends

Tourism arrivals (at hotels and similar establishments) reached over 200 000 in 1978, but declined to a low point of only 133 169 in 1986. Over the next four years tourism recovered (at between 10 and 16 per cent per annum) and reached 220 902 by 1991 (*see* Fig 33.11).

Fig 33.12 shows that Bolivia's main markets have changed relatively little between the low

point in 1986 and the peak of 1991. The only major change has been a significant increase (in total numbers and percentage share) of visitors from Peru from 6.91 per cent in 1986 to 16.43 per cent in 1991.

Year	Number of visitors
1978	203 000
1979	159 415
1980	155 412
1981	155 600
1982	250 142
1983	175 900
1984	184 000
1985	*no information*
1986	133 169
1987	147 005
1988	167 512
1989	193 557
1990	217 071
1991	220 902

Fig. 33.11 Trends in inbound tourism to Bolivia

		Percentage of all visitors	
Origin of visitors		1986	1991
Regions:	Latin America	42.02	44.5
	North America	14.04	14.58
	Europe	36.44	34.92
	Other regions	7.49	5.95
Countries:	Argentina	13.25	10.60
	Brazil	8.92	6.02
	Peru	6.91	16.43
	Chile	6.77	6.20
	USA	11.55	11.62
	Germany	8.92	6.77
	France	5.62	3.97
	UK	4.09	4.60

Fig. 33.12 Bolivia's main markets
(Source: WTO)

Chile, Argentina, Uruguay and Paraguay

It has been noted on page 409 that these four countries make up a fairly self-contained tourist unit: between them, they provide between 50 and 70 per cent of each other's tourists. North America contributes no more than 9 per cent of the tourists to any of them and in spite of the fact that their population is essentially of European origin, European visitors nowhere make up no more than 11 per cent of their tourists.

Physical regions

The countries are made up of four structural regions that are aligned north–south, parallel to each other. These four regions each cross several climatic zones, so they are subdivided according to their climate. The four physical regions are:

1 **The Pacific coastal zone of Chile**
2 **The Andes**
3 **The east facing uplands that lie between the Andes and the Atlantic coast**
4 **The basin of the River Parana**

The Chilean coastal zone

In the north, the coast has a hot dry desert climate. Arica is a beach resort frequented by rich Bolivians, but it is a sparsely populated region. The central section has a Mediterranean climate and is also the most densely populated region of Chile. There are beach resorts catering for local (Chilean and Argentinian) tourists, for example at Vina del Mar near Valparaiso. However, its relative isolation from world markets and the fact that the sea is cold (the offshore current brings cold water from the cold Antarctic and far South Pacific) limits its potential to attract inter-regional markets. The climate south of Concepcion merges into a cool temperate regime, while the climate of the southernmost islands of Chile becomes subarctic tundra.

The Andes

The Chile–Argentina border follows the crest of the mountain chain, which gradually decreases in height from over 6600 m in the north to 2–3500 m in southern Chile. The scenery is spectacular. The 'Lake District' that straddles the border south of Valdivia is a mixture of semi-dormant volcanoes, forests, glaciers, snowcapped mountains and lakes. Several ski resorts have been developed, mainly on the east facing slopes of the Andes, but also some on the Chilean side. The season runs from May to September.

The Uplands

These are dry regions; some of Argentina's oldest and most attractive colonial cities (e.g. Cordoba, Tucuman and Salta) are in the northern section. The southern section (Patagonia) is a cold desert.

The Parana basin

The upper part of the system is called the Chaco. It covers most of Paraguay and the northern section of Argentina. It is a flat area of clay plains with many marshy regions. The coastal section of the river basin (eastern Argentina and all of Uruguay) is drier and consists of the open grassland of the Pampas where cattle ranching is the main agricultural system. The two countries' capitals (Buenos Aires and Montevideo) are located near the mouth of Parana on the Plate estuary.

There are many sandy stretches on the nearby Atlantic coastline and the climate has moderate rainfall all year and maximum temperatures in summer reach the high 20s°C. This makes them suitable for beach resort developments, e.g. at Punta del Este in Uruguay and Tigre and Mar del Plata in Argentina.

TOURISM TO THE ANTARCTIC

The Antarctic is a huge continent centred on the South Pole. It is snow and ice covered and is a harsh and inaccessible environment. Less than 2 per cent of the land is ice free. It has been called one of the world's last tourist frontiers. No country has legal sovereignty over any of the continent but many lay claim to parts of it. Argentina, Chile and Britain all claim the segment containing the Antarctic Peninsula, situated south of the Falkland Islands and close to Cape Horn. This is the most accessible part of Antarctica and has the least harsh climate. It has abundant wildlife and it can be reached by ship or plane from South America.

Most cruises to the Antarctic set out from Punta Arenas or Puerto Williams (in southernmost Chile) or Ushuaia (on the southern tip of Argentina). The crossing by ship takes 48 hours. The first tourists visited the continent in 1957/8 when Argentina and Chile ran four cruises to the South Shetland Islands (off the Antarctic Peninsula). There was growth in tourism in the early 1970s (numbers rose to over 1000 per annum) until the world oil crisis limited further expansion. However, the growth in ecotourism and adventure holidays in the late 1980s has stimulated a resumption of Antarctic cruise developments. Visitor numbers had grown to over 6000 in 1991/2. Most are thought to come from North America. There is concern about the impact of tourism and the need for its effective management in such a sensitive and fragile natural environment (*see* Hall, 1993).

BRAZIL, VENEZUELA, COLOMBIA AND THE GUIANAS

This huge area of South America consists of the territories of Colombia, Venezuela, the Guianas (all lying north of the Equator) and Brazil (which extends roughly from the Equator to the Tropic of Capricorn). The area is dominated by the Amazon basin, but has many other smaller and varied physical regions round its perimeter: the Guiana Highlands, the Orinoco basin and the Caribbean coast to the north, the Andes to the west, and the Mato Grosso (Brazilian Highlands) to the south and east. These regions have a wealth of natural tourist resources and many lively and beautiful cities, but its size makes it difficult to include all the highlights in one manageable tour. The region includes some of South America's more affluent countries; Brazil and Venezuela both have significant outbound tourism markets, each generating over a million outbound tourists and Colombia has the potential for rapid growth. In 1988 70 per cent of Brazil's and 43 per cent of Venezuela's (and 67.5 per cent of Colombia's) outbound tourism was destined for Europe or North America; they also receive significant proportions of their tourists from these other regions (*see* Fig 33.5). Thus these countries are much more fully integrated into the world's tourist system than are the other parts of South America.

Brazil

Brazil is one of the largest countries in the world (at 8 511 965 km^2), with a population of over 144 million. Two-thirds of the population are concentrated on the coast around São Paulo and Rio de Janeiro and on the north east coast (Salvador to Natal). The rest of the interior is very sparsely populated. In such a huge country, the transport infrastructure is critical for the development and spatial distribution of tourism. There is a reasonable road network but only 8 per cent of the roads are paved (sealed). Bus services link the main cities. Most of Brazil's South American visitors come by road; EIU suggests the majority of the 605 000 visitors from Argentina, Uruguay and Paraguay come on one-day shopping trips, but what information is available indicates that they mainly visit the cities and beach resorts of southern Brazil, between the border and Rio de Janeiro.

Brazil's population (with a GNP per head of US $ 2840 in 1990) generates a significant domestic tourist industry: in 1989, domestic tourists accounted for 84 per cent of the total 29.4 million room nights.

There are 170 commercial airports (including 16 international airports) and there are 4000 landing fields. Most non-South Americans arrive by air and 90 per cent come via São Paulo and Rio de Janeiro. This evidence suggests that domestic and international tourism is strongly concentrated on the coast in Brazil's south, south east and 'Golden coast' (north east) regions. Elsewhere, particularly in the remoter interior, tourism is likely to be limited to the areas easily accessible from the airports and airfields.

The coast and coastal areas

Rio de Janeiro is one of the most scenically beautiful cities in the world. It is located on a beautiful stretch of coastline, with many bays and splendid beaches (e.g. Copacabana and Ipanema) and an inland lagoon. The setting is made more unusual by the steep sided mountains, some craggy and some forested, which rise above the city's skyscrapers. The Sugar Loaf is the best known of these landmarks (rising to over 430 m), though the 775 m Corcovado (part of a 120 km^2 National Park in the heart of the city) is another symbol of Rio: it has the famous statue of Christ at its summit, overlooking the whole of the city. However, air pollution is a problem, and the views are sometimes masked by smog.

Rio is also famous for its carnival. The four day long pre-Lenten carnival is celebrated all over Brazil (in February or March), but is at its most spectacular here. Neighbourhood groups (known as Samba schools) compete against each other to prepare the best float for the grand parade, each with flamboyantly costumed singers, musicians and dancers. The theme of the parade is a different aspect of Brazilian history or folklore each year. The preparations for such a spectacular event carry on throughout the year, so tourists can often see the rehearsals even if they are not there for the carnival itself. Thefts and robberies are common, particularly at carnival time and on the beaches, though this is an ever-present problem all over South America. The city also has a growing reputation for sex tourism.

São Paulo is located inland and is the country's main business and cultural centre. It is the biggest city in South America and has a modern high-rise centre. It is a very cosmopolitan city, with lively night life and entertainment. South of São Paulo there are many beach resorts, particularly round Florianopolis (42 beaches), Camboiu, Santa Catarina Island, and further south on the coast of Porto Alegre (e.g. Torres). The climate here is more temperate than further north, with an average maximum of in the low 20s but the region has a rainier summer season.

The beaches of the north east are in a tropical zone, so temperatures do not fall much below 20° C. Winter is the wetter season here. There are many cities with beach resorts (e.g. Forteleza, Recife) all along this coast.

Inland resources

These consist of cities, sights and wildlife.

Mato Grosso

These are uplands of south and east Brazil. Brasilia, the capital, is a spacious, modern city with innovative modern architecture. However, it is located well away from the country's main centres of population and lacks the liveliness of established cities such as Rio. In complete contrast, there are old colonial towns such as the old mining town of Ouro Preto founded in 1711. It has many beautiful colonial mansions, baroque churches and gardens, with narrow cobbled streets. It is a national monument and a World Heritage Site.

In the southern section of the uplands is one of Brazil's outstanding natural features: the Iguassu waterfalls. The falls mark the border of Brazil, Paraguay and Argentina, at the meeting of the Parana and Iguassu rivers, where the rivers descend 60 m from the plateau into the lowlands of the Parana to flow south through Argentina. The falls can be visited from Argentina and Paraguay but intercontinental tourists generally see them as part of a tour of Brazil. The falls are as spectacular as Niagara or Victoria falls.

Wildlife tourism in the wetlands and rainforest

Brazil's huge territory covers semi-arid savannah, coastal and forest zones and there are 34 designated National Parks. However, ecotourism is mainly focused on the wetlands of the Pantanal and in the Amazon rainforests. The Pantanal covers 210 000 km^2: in the wet season (November–April) the area is flooded and species such as leopard, anteaters, snakes and alligators retreat to the remaining dry higher areas, but these tend to be in the interior and access is difficult. In the dry season the waters recede and the water birds congregate for nesting. There are 600 different species of birds.

The Amazon rainforest is also rich in species of plants, animals, birds and insects. River trips are available from Manaus and recently jungle lodges have been set up where 2- or 3-day packages are available which include photographic safaris, night jungle walks and canoe trips. In 1992, 38 ecotourism projects were being considered for development in the Amazon region. The best season climatically is July to October although tourists also come at Christmas. Currently the majority (65 per cent) of tourists to the Amazon come from Europe, and 19 per cent from North America.

Tourism problems in Brazil

Tourism to Brazil grew steadily in the 1980s from 1.147 million in 1982 to a peak of 1.934 million in 1986. Since then it has declined at an accelerating rate until 1990, to a low of 1.091 million. However, in 1991 there was a 23.9 per cent increase (to a total of 1.352 million). Thus tourism to Brazil has shown virtually the opposite of world trends. This has more to do with tourists' increasing perception of Brazil's problems of poor safety, poor public services, lack of promotion of tourism and poor transport, than with the world economy or world political events. Brazil now has a deficit on the tourism account (with the rapidly growing number of outbound Brazilian tourists spending more abroad than foreign tourists to Brazil); all these factors have led to an increase in promotion and an attempt to improve Brazil's tourist image.

Venezuela

The country is a land of physical contrasts. It has five physical regions, each providing very different landscapes and natural environments:

1 The Maracaibo basin. A large shallow lake enclosed by fingers of the Andean mountains, it is very hot, humid and windless and is the focus of Venezuela's oil industry.

2 The Cordillera de Merida. This mountain range is an extension of the Andes, with varied landscapes and some ski runs. The old colonial town of Merida is the main tourist centre here. It is located near the country's highest mountain and the town has the world's highest cable car (that reaches 4675 m above sea level). The views are excellent but are sometimes obscured by cloud in the wet season (June–December).

3 The Orinoco basin and the Llanos. The landscape is flat grassland, much of which floods in the winter rains. There is a lot of wildlife in the swamps near the rivers but the region is little used for tourism.

4 The Guiana Highlands. This plateau covers about half of Venezuela's territory. It has been eroded into many very steep-sided and inaccessible table top mountains and there are many dramatic waterfalls where rivers plunge over the plateau edge. The best landscapes are on Venezuela's eastern borders in the Gran Sabana. There are several National Parks and Reserves in this region: the best known is the 3 million hectare Canaima National Park. The highest waterfall in the world (the Angel Falls) is located in this park, where the Churum River plunges 979 m over the plateau edge.

5 The Coast. Venezuela has 4000 km of Caribbean coastline and most of Venezuela's tourism is beach tourism. There are luxury resorts and completely deserted stretches of sandy coastline and opportunities for water sports and diving (there are coral reefs around many of the offshore islands). Margarita is the biggest and most developed island, with resorts, hotels and duty-free shopping, but many undeveloped beaches, too.

The capital city, Caracas, is 16 km inland, spread out along a valley at the foot of Mount Avila (which separates the city from the sea). It was founded in 1567 but it is now an expanding busy modern city, although some of its historic centre has survived. It has plenty of nightlife.

Originating country	Number	Percentage
USA	120 261	20.13
Netherlands	51 629	8.62
Trinidad and Tobago	46 904	7.83
Germany	46 117	7.70
Colombia	37 611	6.28
Italy	36 045	6.02
Canada	47 079	7.86
Spain	31 771	5.30
France	31 320	5.23
UK	21 915	3.66
Others	N/A	N/A
Total	598 328	100%

Fig. 33.13 Venezuela tourist arrivals, 1991

Venezuela draws its tourists from a wide range of 'core' countries – *see* Fig 33.13. The North American market is mainly attracted for the beach tourism particularly during their cold winters. Tourism grew steadily in the late 1980s in spite of some internal political problems in 1989 and 1990. Growth continued into the 1990s, with a 14 per cent increase in arrivals in 1991.

Colombia

Colombia is a physically varied country in the tropical climate zone. It has all the resources for a thriving tourist industry and is better located to take advantage of North American and European markets than many other South American destinations. Its tourist arrivals had crept up to 857 000 by 1991, but its turbulent political history, its reputation for theft, mugging and kidnapping and its involvement in the international drugs trade has seriously inhibited the growth of tourism. The US mafia moved into the country in the 1970s and Medellin is the centre of the cocaine-producing region. The drugs cartel and a Colombian guerilla movement are together in conflict with the country's security forces. The Colombian government has been promoting its offshore Caribbean and Pacific islands as diving destinations, which may be perceived as being quite separate from the internal political situation. There are many mainland attractions that could be developed: the Andes provide spectacular scenery, there are attractive colonial towns such as Antioquia, Cartegena and Popayan, though the latter was severely damaged by an earthquake in 1983. Cartegena was fortified by the Spanish in the mid-16th century and the old city (inside the massive walls) retains much of its 16th-century character. The main site for Colombia's pre-conquest culture is San Agustin (now an Archaeological Park). There are large stone statues thought to date from the 6th to 13th centuries and manmade burial caves (with wall paintings) at Tierradentro.

At present, 72 per cent of Colombia's tourists come from other South American countries. In 1991, 154 062 (17.97 per cent) came from the USA and only 53 691 (6.26 per cent) from Europe.

The Guianas: Guyana, Suriname and French Guiana

These were British, Dutch and French colonies and have quite different population structures from the mainly American Indian and European countries of the rest of South America. In the Guianas, labour was imported from other colonies so there are Hindu (East) Indians, black people and even some Javanese and Chinese.

The countries consist mainly of swampy tropical coastal plains rising to the low plateaux and rolling hills of the lower eastern extension of the Guiana highlands. There are some spectacular waterfalls (e.g. Kaieteur falls) but the tourist resources are generally limited and tourism is not encouraged.

REFERENCES AND FURTHER READING

Those texts marked with an asterisk are particularly recommended for further reading.

Central America

* Chant, S (1992) 'Tourism in Latin America: perspectives from Mexico and Costa Rica' in Harrison, D (Ed) *Tourism in the Less Developed Countries*, Belhaven.

*Doggart, C (1993) 'Belize', *International Tourism Reports*, No. 2, pp. 4–20.

Place, S E (1991) 'Nature tourism and rural development in Tortuguero', *Annals of Tourism Research*, Vol. 18, pp. 186–201.

South America

*Doggart, C (1992) 'Ecuador', *International Tourism Reports*, No. 2, pp. 26–42.

*Doggart, C (1994) 'Tourism in Antarctica', *Annals of Tourism Research*, Special Issue, Vol. 21, No. 2.

Hall, C M (1993) 'Ecotourism in Antarctica and adjacent sub-Antarctic islands: development, impacts, management and prospects for the future', *Tourism Management*, Vol. 14, No. 2, pp. 117–22.

Rizzotto, R A (1991) 'South America outbound', *EIU Travel and Tourism Analyst*, No. 2, pp. 40–54.

Brazil

Rizzotto, RA (1992) 'Brazil', *International Tourism Reports*, No. 1, pp. 52–67.

Ruschmann, D M (1992) 'Ecological tourism in Brazil' *Tourism Management*, Vol. 13, March, pp. 125–28.

QUESTIONS AND DISCUSSION POINTS

1 Why do most South American countries attract so few tourists from outside the region?

2 In terms of the character of its tourism, should Central America be considered as part of the Caribbean, the North American, or part of the South American tourist region?

3 What problems does Brazil face in promoting itself as a destination for European tourists?

ASSIGNMENTS

1 An American professor of history living in New York State has just completed a book on the ancient cultures of Central America and the Andes. She wishes to go on a quick tour of the most important historic sites in order to take photographs which will illustrate the book. Construct an itinerary for her.

What is the shortest time in which she could complete the trip? Is she likely to encounter any climatic problems that might interfere with her photography, and if so, when?

2   A tour operator is interested in developing special interest tours to South and Central America and has asked you to prepare a short report updating him on the political developments in the region. Your brief is to assess the current political situation in the main trouble spots in the region and to advise the operator as to which parts of the region would be safe for tourism and which should be avoided in the short and medium term.

SECTION 4

Asia and the Pacific Region

This section of the book seeks to answer the following questions:

1 What characteristics make the Pacific region (as defined by WTO, *see* Chapter 17) the third most important region of the world?
2 What and where are the main tourist generating countries (actual and potential) in the region?
3 What and where are the major tourist destinations, and what are the patterns of tourist travel around the region?
4 How does South Asia relate to the Pacific region in terms of its tourist development and tourist flows?

INTRODUCTION: THE PACIFIC

The Pacific is a vast region extending through all the world's climatic zones (from arctic to equatorial). Its centre is empty ocean but almost 65 per cent of the world's population live in the countries bordering the Pacific (i.e. on the 'Pacific Rim'). With a total of about 54 million tourist arrivals, it is the world's third most important tourist region, after Europe and North America (*see* Chapters 15 and 17) and its tourism is growing faster than that of any other region of the world. The countries of the Pacific Rim are culturally varied and at different stages of economic development and contrasting affluence: some belong to the world's economic core and some to the periphery (*see* Fig 15.2 on p 152). Therefore, their ability and inclination to generate tourists differ as widely.

The affluent Westernised countries (USA, Australia, New Zealand) in practice generate relatively low numbers of international tourists in the region. The poor South American and war-torn Southeast Asian countries, such as Vietnam, Kampuchea and Laos, play virtually no part at all in tourism in the region as yet. In between, lie the developing Asian countries, e.g. South Korea and Taiwan, and the ex-colonies, such as Singapore and Malaysia, which generate modest but very rapidly growing numbers of tourists, while the population giants, Japan and China, have only relatively recently decided to end their isolation from the rest of the world. Since 1964 when Japan eased constraints on travel to and from her shores, outbound tourism has grown very rapidly to over ten million by 1990, and Japan is already the leading tourist generator in the region. This ten million represents only a small proportion of Japan's 123 million population. The potential exists, therefore, for further great increases in outbound tourism if the taste for foreign travel spreads throughout the Japanese population, and the rapid growth of Japanese outbound tourism is one of the factors fuelling the growth of tourism in the region as a whole. (Japanese investment in tourist development throughout the region is another important factor.) Hawaii is the major destination of the region. It is politically part of the USA, although it lies in the geographical centre of the Pacific region. Around 6.5 million tourists flocked to Hawaii's beaches in 1992, but the islands rely heavily on a handful of countries (specifically USA and Japan) for their visitors.

Thailand, on the other hand, attracts about five million but draws tourists from many Pacific nations as well as long-haul travellers from Europe. It has a much more varied resource base with beach, cultural and landscape attractions. Singapore and Hong Kong have less varied resources but their ex-colonial status is reflected in the high numbers of Europeans visiting them. Several other developing countries in the West Pacific also attract two to three million visitors but have more localised catchments (e.g. Japan and Korea). The volume of intra-regional travel is growing very strongly as political constraints and economic restrictions are eased in countries such as Taiwan and South Korea.

The vast size of the Pacific means that relatively few travellers cross its whole expanse (with those that do being mostly Americans and Japanese) though the romantic image of the Pacific does lure tourists from the rim into the more accessible of the mid-ocean archipelagoes. Most of the tourist movements in the region are N–S journeys along the Pacific coast of Asia, mainly between a series of fairly small countries scattered along the western edge of the region. A small number of tourists leak out of the region towards Europe (but well over one million Europeans arrive in the Pacific in exchange). A very few travel westward from the Pacific to South Asia or vice versa. South Asia looks towards Europe and North America for its tourists and is not really functionally part of the Pacific tourist system.

The Pacific region consists of three cultural and economic subdivisions, each of which has its own style of tourism.

1 Australasia (Australia and New Zealand). Australia and New Zealand are Western countries with strong domestic markets and international tourism that was limited to the nearest Pacific islands but is now rapidly extending to the rest of the Pacific region.

2 The Pacific islands, and Asian archipelagoes (the Pacific groups, Indonesia and Philippines). These are peopled by Asians or Polynesians; some are developed for Western-style beach tourism.

3 Mainland Asia and related islands. (The eastern cultures of the Asian 'Pacific Rim' (i.e. East and Southeast Asia).) This part of the region is characterised by rapidly growing travel between its own countries, and also by the development of cultural and beach tourism for the Western market.

SOUTH ASIA

This region has its own distinct pattern of tourism that has more in common with the 'peripheral' continents of Subsaharan Africa and South America.

Chapters 34 and 35 will describe tourism in Australasia, and the Pacific Islands while Chapters 36 and 37 deal with the countries of East and Southeast Asia where tourism is growing so rapidly. Finally Chapter 38 considers the potential of South Asia.

CHAPTER 34

Australia and New Zealand

LEARNING OBJECTIVES

After reading this chapter you should be able to
- assess the tourist potential of the climatic, landscape, historical and cultural resources of the region
- distinguish the regional distribution of these geographical resources and their development and use for tourism
- demonstrate a knowledge of the main tourist resorts and tourist centres
- understand the role of Australia and New Zealand in the general pattern of tourism in the Pacific region
- assess the attractions of Australia and New Zealand as long-haul destinations for the UK market.

INTRODUCTION

The two countries are physically very different from each other and are over 1900 km apart, but have similar colonial backgrounds and (in terms of the size of the Pacific region) they are near neighbours. Their physical resources complement each other, each providing what the other lacks.

This combination of factors has resulted in their tourist industries being very dependent on each other, and thus they form a distinct sub-region of the Pacific. But as the economies of the other Pacific countries have developed, Australia's tourism in particular has become more integrated with that of the region as a whole, and it is becoming less and less appropriate to consider these two countries in isolation from the rest of the Pacific region.

Political, economic and tourist links between Australasia and the rest of the Pacific have been strengthening: in the 1980s the number of Japanese (and other Asian) visitors travelling to Australia has dramatically increased. The Japanese are choosing to invest heavily in Australia's tourist infrastructure (particularly in north east Australia), while Australians are travelling more widely in the Pacific.

AUSTRALIA'S PHYSICAL CHARACTERISTICS

Australia is a huge continent (only a little smaller than the USA). The journey across Australia from north to south (e.g. Adelaide to Darwin) is 2623 km by air, and east–west (e.g. Sydney to Perth) is 3278 km. The population is small, only 17 million in 1990, and 86 per cent live in the urban areas which are concentrated on the east coast. Vast areas of the interior are very sparsely populated, the roads carry little traffic and there are extensive tracts of wilderness (see Chapter 4).

The main climatic, physical and tourist regions of the continent are as follows (see Fig 34.1):

1 the tropical north;
2 the sub-tropical east coast, and the Great Dividing Range;
3 the Mediterranean southwest; and
4 the desert and semi-desert of the centre.

The tropical north

The north coast has a wet tropical climate (see Fig 2.7 on p 12) with a clear, dry season between May and October. Darwin is the only settlement of any size in Australia's north (the 'Top End'), and it has an international airport. Kakadu National Park is the main attraction here: it is a World Heritage site on account of its landscape, aboriginal rock art and its wetland wildlife (e.g. crocodiles and many species of water birds). Accommodation in the Park is strictly controlled and access to the Park is by coach, car, four-wheel-drive and by boat. Adventure and activity holidays are popular.

The east coast

This can be divided into three tourist regions:

1 The north (Rockhampton to Cape York). Here the main attractions are the coastal rainforests, the Great Barrier Reef and the tropical climate (similar to Darwin). Its main tourist season is the dry, sunny Southern Hemisphere winter (Cairns' driest months are July to October). The Great Barrier

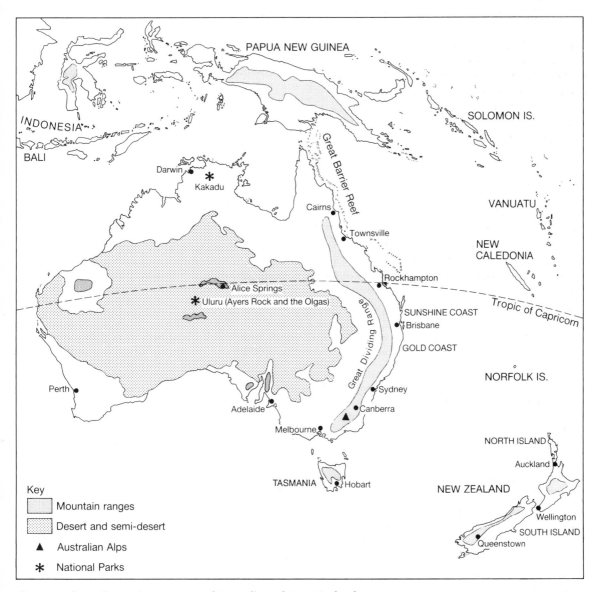

Fig. 34.1 The main tourist resources of Australia and New Zealand

Reef is an immense series of offshore coral reefs, cays and islands: it provides the best scuba diving, snorkelling and big game fishing area of the world, and the reef is closest to the shore in the Cairns–Port Douglas region. Day-trips (e.g. in big high-speed catamarans) operate from here and other coastal towns, while longer trips and diving expeditions are also available. In 1988 the world's first 'floating hotel' (a boat permanently moored on the reef) was anchored off Townsville. It is estimated that the half million visitors to the reef in 1986 generated 2.2 million visitor days' use of the reef. The tourist pressure on this vulnerable ecosystem is managed by the Great Barrier Reef Marine Park, who zone it for different levels of use (some areas being reserved for 'look, don't take' tourism where destructive activities such as reef walking, collecting and fishing are not allowed). The accommodation ranges from exclusive island resorts (e.g. Lizard Island, Bedarra Island) to modern international hotels in the major resorts (as at Cairns) through to backpackers' accommodation. The coast is backed by the Atherton Tablelands which are the northern part of the Great Dividing Range. There are several National Parks in the tropical rainforest (e.g. Bellenden Ker and Cape Tribulation), and the swift flowing rivers are ideal for white water rafting.

Long stretches of coast are completely undeveloped where they are designated as National Parks. Tourism here is essentially a dry season business. The intense rains and danger of poisonous jellyfish in the inshore waters in the Southern Hemisphere summer (December–March) limits the main tourist season to the months of May–October. Hence, during these months the north Queensland coast functions as a 'winter' resort for the population of Sydney and Melbourne but as a 'summer' destination for travellers from the Northern Hemisphere. It attracts relatively few overseas visitors but the upgrading of Cairns airport is encouraging direct flights from Japan, the USA and Europe, and Cairns is in fact a slightly shorter flying time from Tokyo than is Hawaii.

2 Brisbane region. Thus Brisbane is at the centre of the major holiday area for the population of south-east Australia. Although this part of the Queensland coast is visited all year round, it is primarily a winter sun destination. The high temperatures, humidity and rainfall in December–February make it a little less attractive in this season (*see* Fig 34.2).

The central stretch of coast is most intensively developed for beach tourism particularly along the Gold Coast (to the south of Brisbane) and the Sunshine Coast (to its north). The Gold Coast is a 40 km stretch of unbroken sandy beach and the development is typified by Surfers Paradise, where the beach is backed by high-rise hotels and apartment blocks, with a range of attractions such as casinos, seaworld, and theme parks in the vicinity.

The Gold Coast is served by Coolangatta Airport 27 km south of Brisbane, while the Sunshine Coast, to the north of Brisbane, is more accessible via Brisbane Airport. The Sunshine Coast is a little less intensively developed. Noosa, for example, is a quieter resort with smaller hotels, and is adjacent to a National Park. The resorts cater for all water sports, including surfing. Japanese interest is also increasing in this region, as it is along the whole of the Queensland coast. By 1988, the Japanese had bought up 70 per cent of land earmarked for development along Queensland's Gold Coast, and 800 million dollars had been invested in Queensland tourism projects. By 1987 only about 215 000 Japanese visited Australia but Japanese arrivals to Queensland are growing at twice the rate of Japanese travel to Hawaii.

3 Sydney–Melbourne region. This is where most of Australia's population is concentrated. The climate here has wetter winters and drier summers (*see* Fig 2.14 on p 16) and thus complements

	Summer season			Winter season			
	Dec	*Jan*	*Feb*	*June*	*July*	*Aug*	*Sept*
Ave max temp °C	29.1	29.4	28.9	20.8	20.3	21.8	24.0
Ave min temp °C	16.6	26.6	20.4	10.7	9.3	10.1	12.7
Rainfall (mm)	127	152	165	76	51	51	51

Fig. 34.2 Brisbane winter and summer climate

Brisbane's climate. Most summer coastal activities can take place here, and the local beaches cater for day-trips throughout the year and for summer tourism. There is good surfing though some beaches are dangerous due to offshore currents. The cities, however, are the main focus of tourism, particularly for international VFR tourists. Sydney is situated on the banks of a long branching inlet, spanned by the Harbour Bridge, so provides a beautiful setting for Australia's leading city of 3.5 million people. Ferry transport in the city forms an attractive alternative to the crowded roads. The architects of the Opera House also took advantage of the dramatic waterside site between the Bridge and the Botanic Gardens to create the now world-famous building.

Melbourne is Australia's second largest city, with a population of 3.0 million, and it has good restaurants, gardens and plenty of opportunity for land-based sports. The nearby coastline is cliffed, rugged and dramatic, and its landscape and wildlife (e.g. pelicans, seals and penguins) are particular attractions.

The Great Dividing Range is Australia's major mountain chain that hugs the east coast from Cairns to Melbourne. It reaches its highest point in the Snowy Mountains between Sydney and Melbourne and although the highest point, Mt Kosciusko, is only 2230 m, it is high enough for heavy winter snow. Ski resorts such as the village of Thredbo in the Kosciusko National Park provide for winter sports holidays. There are many other National Parks scattered along the length of the range, providing landscape, wilderness and activity holidays that can be combined with beach tourism based on the coastal settlements (for example, Lamington National Park near Brisbane and the Blue Mountains west of Sydney).

Australia's capital, Canberra, is also sited on a plateau high in the Great Dividing Range. This modern and spacious city is laid out round an attractive artificial lake and is surrounded by mountain ridges.

4 Tasmania. The island state of Tasmania is Australia's southernmost territory; its climate is cooler than the rest of Australia, with maximum temperatures reaching 21° C in summer and 11° C in winter. Rainfall is spread evenly throughout the year and is heaviest in the southwest of the island. Its farmed landscapes are more 'English' than much of Australia, though it also has tracts of untouched upland and wilderness, with dramatic waterfalls, gorges, mountains and lakes. The state capital, Hobart, is small with only 180 000 people, and also has a beautiful harbour setting. The island, however, is not a major tourist area.

The Mediterranean southwest of Australia

The west coast also spans a wide range of climatic zones but it is sheltered from rainbearing winds and is generally drier than the east coast, with long stretches of desert. The best tourist climate is in the small pocket of Mediterranean type climate around Perth. Average summer temperatures rise above 21° C (December–March) and rainfall is very low. In winter the rainfall increases and temperatures drop to 13° C. This is also the only population concentration on the west coast, but is very remote from the rest of Australia.

Its climate is not a powerful enough magnet to draw tourists the long distances from the Sydney and Melbourne beaches in summer, while Perth's winter climate cannot compete with the east coast winter sun resorts in Queensland. Southwest Australia is thus one of the few areas of the world with a Mediterranean climate that is not a major tourist region, in spite of its spectacular unspoilt beaches, excellent yachting facilities, desert landscapes, abundant spring wild flowers and inland historic mining towns.

The arid centre (the 'Red Centre')

Most of Australia's interior is hot desert, or arid zone land, with under 225 mm rainfall a year. There is little surface water, though underground sources can be tapped at the natural springs and waterholes or by artesian wells, so water shortage is not an overriding constraint on tourist development.

The landscape is dominated by open plains of very low relative relief and indeterminate internal drainage. Intermittently flowing seasonal rivers flow westward off the Great Dividing Range into salt lakes (e.g. Lake Eyre) in vast internal basins. Trees line these watercourses while elsewhere the desert is covered in tough tussocky grass or scrub. Further west, the desert is drier and is a mixture of stony plains, sand dunes and claypans. The landscape is red and dusty due to iron oxide deposits which coat the rock surface. The plains are interrupted in the geographical centre of Australia by a series of mountain ranges (e.g. the Macdonnell, Musgrave and Petermann Ranges). More isolated outcrops (remnants of very ancient mountains) are located in the basins between these ranges. Ayers Rock and Mt Olga in the Uluru National Park are the best known of these dramatic isolated rocks. Ayers Rock rises 370 m from the flat plain (*see* Fig 34.3); it is the major tourist attraction and is accessible from the nearby Yulara resort, a well-designed tourist centre which provides accommodation ranging from international standard hotels to open air camping. It has its own airstrip but most visitors come by air to Alice Springs and then transfer (by air or coach) to Yulara. The climate (*see* Fig 2.10 on p 13) is hot but does not inhibit tourism if visitors are careful.

PATTERNS OF TOURISM IN AUSTRALIA

Domestic tourism

Seventy-seven per cent of tourism demand (in terms of tourist nights) is generated by the domestic market, which has grown steadily in the 1980s by two to three per cent p.a. This represents a real increase in trip taking as the population has been growing at only 1.5 per cent over the same period. In the 1991/92 season Australian residents took 48 million trips from home. Most were summer (Dec/Jan) holidays on the beaches of the southeast, or winter holidays to the Queensland coast, with smaller numbers of ski trips to the Snowy Mountains or visits to the Red Centre. Only 8.5 per cent of domestic holiday trips involve air travel, a surprisingly low figure for such a huge continent but it reaffirms the fact that the population can meet most of its tourist needs relatively locally, particularly in the southeast of

Fig. 34.3 Ayers Rock (Uluru)

the country. Most travel is by road. Car travel is easy on the rural roads which are empty by European standards. Good intercity, long-distance coach services are also available between the cities of the southeast and to the Brisbane coast. The further flung resort areas – i.e. Darwin, Alice Springs, Cairns and Tasmania – rely much more heavily on air transport, and tourism in these locations was very badly hit by the prolonged domestic pilots' strike in 1989/90.

Inbound tourism

International tourists to Australia use the internal airlines far more extensively than do domestic tourists: 45 per cent of foreign visitors fly within Australia and over half visit more than one state: on average UK, Japanese and Americans visited 2.2 to 2.4 states. Even so, international tourism is heavily concentrated in the more populated southeast, particularly in New South Wales (and in Sydney). This pattern of tourism partly reflects the high VFR element (over 19 per cent of all foreign visitors stay with friends or relatives while this figure rises to 29 per cent of New Zealanders and 52 per cent of all UK tourists to Australia). Australia is essentially a winter destination for the Northern Hemisphere: 32 per cent of overseas visitors come between October and December, with UK visitors particularly concentrating on November and December

with a secondary peak in March. Climate, plus the family nature of the Christmas festivities, would appear to account for this pattern.

Australia is a long-haul destination for all markets and inbound tourism was badly hit by the world recession of the 1980s. After a period of rapid growth in the late 1970s tourist numbers stagnated between 1980 and 1985. The following seven years were marked by exceptionally rapid growth of inbound tourism triggered off by world economic recovery in the late 1980s which coincided with several hallmark events in Australia, i.e. the 1986 Americas Cup Yacht Race near Perth and the bicentennial celebrations and Brisbane's Expo, both in 1988. International tourism had more than doubled from 800 000 in 1979 to reach the two million mark in 1988, and 2.6 million in 1992.

The composition of Australia's international tourism has changed significantly over the same period. In 1979 Australia's tourism was very highly dependent on the New Zealand market which provided 34 per cent of its inbound tourists. Since then the numbers of tourists from other Pacific Rim countries have dramatically increased; for example Japanese tourists increased from 41 636 in 1979 to 352 000 in 1988, and over 600 000 by 1992 (*see* Fig 34.5). The number of tourists from other Asian countries also tripled.

Tourists from Asia now account for 42 per cent of Australia's inbound tourism, and New Zealand's share dropped from 24 per cent in 1988. This does not represent any decline in the popular-

State	% of all domestic nights	% of all foreign nights
New South Wales	30	33
Australian Capital Territory (i.e. Canberra)	2	3
Victoria	17	19
Queensland	27	25
South Australia	8	5
Western Australia	11	12
Tasmania	3	2
Northern Territory	2	3
Number of nights	216 million	61 million

Fig. 34.4 Spatial distribution of international and domestic tourism in Australia, 1992
(*Source*: Australian Bureau of Tourism Research)

	To Australia	%	To New Zealand	%
New Zealand	447 600	17	–	
Australia	–		363 642	34
Japan	629 900	24	128 962	12
Rest of Asia	473 200	18	113 260	10.7
UK	298 700	11	98 247	9.3
Rest of Europe	278 300	11	102 716	9.7
USA	262 900	10	131 357	12.4
Rest of world	212 700	8	117 497	11.1
Total arrivals	2 603 300		1 055 681	

Fig. 34.5 Inbound tourism to Australia and New Zealand, 1992

ity of Australia as a destination for New Zealanders. In fact the reverse is true. Australia is increasing its market share of the New Zealand outbound trade, and the number of New Zealanders visiting Australia has doubled through the 1980s. Rather, it represents the faster growth rates of tourism from the rest of the Pacific and the increasing integration of Australia – both politically and in its acceptance of Asian immigrants – with the rest of the Pacific region.

UK tourism to Australia has increased but at a much slower rate (from 114 000 to 298 000 between 1979 and 1992) and accounts for only 11 per cent of Australia's foreign visitors.

Outbound tourism

In 1987 only 1.6 million Australians travelled abroad. Its outbound tourism shares many characteristics with that of the USA: its own huge territory can meet most of its travel needs, while adjacent countries (in this case New Zealand) take the bulk of outbound travellers and significant numbers visit Europe, to visit friends and relations and for cultural tourism. However parallel with the changes in Australia's inbound tourism, Australians are travelling more widely to the Asian Pacific rim (e.g. Bali, Hong Kong, Thailand and Malaysia), rather than just to the nearest Pacific islands, such as Fiji and New Caledonia.

Destination	% Outbound tourists		
	1974	1984	1987
Asia	19.2	30.0	33.7
Oceania	35.1	29.8	25.7
Americas	8.1	12.3	13.3
Europe	32.6	26.5	25.2
Africa	0.9	1.2	1.3

Fig. 34.6 Australian outbound tourism, 1974–1987

NEW ZEALAND'S TOURIST REGIONS

This country consists of two islands (totalling about 267 000 km^2) of varied climate and landscape with the latter being its main tourist resource.

New Zealand's isolation and emphasis on landscape tourism result in a small (though economically important) tourist industry with about 1.05 million visitors in the 1991 season. The country has a population of only 3.4 million (in 1991), of whom 75 per cent live in North Island, and who generated 750 000 outbound trips in 1992. New Zealand's tourism is highly dependent on Australia, which is both the leading destination for New Zealand's outbound travellers but also the main source of New Zealand's tourist arrivals. Like Australia, however, the country is gradually becoming more integrated to the Pacific region.

North Island

1 Auckland peninsula. This is the largest area of lowland, the most densely populated and has the mildest climate of the whole of New Zealand. Auckland, like Sydney, has an east margin warm temperate climate. In the summer period (December–March) temperatures range between 14° C and 23° C, while the winter is cooler (7–14° C), with some rain all year round but a winter maximum and a total of 1650 mm p.a. On average, Auckland is a few degrees cooler than Sydney but with about the same amount of rainfall. North Island averages about 2000 hours' sunshine a year. The climate is pleasant and allows beach tourism in summer, but given its greater isolation from its markets it cannot compete with the other beach tourist destinations of the Pacific region. The landscapes of the Auckland peninsula are green and fertile and quite English in character, although there are also areas of vineyards. Auckland and the Bay of Islands are the main tourist attractions, and Auckland is one of the major international gateways. Foreign tourist trips are strongly concentrated in the north half of North Island.

2 The centre of North Island. The region has several volcanic mountains and still shows signs of volcanic activity and tourists can see geysers, hot springs and boiling mud pools at Rotorua, the centre of the thermal region. The nearby lakes of Rotorua and Taupo are also centres for water sports. New Zealand's native population, the Maoris, are of Polynesian origin and there is a Maori Village and Arts and Crafts Centre at

Rotorua which attracts many visitors. Rotorua's varied attractions make it the country's leading destination with 60 per cent of all holiday visitors.

The volcanic peak of Mt Ruapehu lies at the heart of North Island and the popular Tongariro National Park lies further south.

North Island as a whole attracted 55 per cent of overseas visits in 1990/91.

South Island

The Southern Alps dominate the Island, forming its spine. The mountains reach 3760 m and divide the wild, wet and rugged west coast (which receives up to 4000 mm rainfall per annum) from the sunnier and drier east. The climate is significantly cooler than North Island. In winter the mountains receive heavy snowfall and have excellent skiing conditions which attract many Australian tourists. The landscapes are spectacular, with glaciers such as the Fox and Franz Joseph glaciers and fjords, e.g. Milford Sound, on the southwest coast. The Tasman glacier provides all year round skiing. The Island has seven National Parks with many opportunities for outdoor activities, such as climbing, walking, canoe safaris, jet boating and white water rafting. Although much of the Island is rugged and mountainous, the road system is good, with little traffic; the attractions are accessible and distances between them fairly short. Independent car touring (and camper vanning) is the main travel mode, although bus/coach touring is also important. Queenstown (on Lake Wakatipu) is an old goldmining town but is within easy reach of the main scenic attractions of South Island, and it is the leading South Island tourist centre, although foreign tourism is spread throughout the Island.

The domestic market is three times as big as the inbound international market. Even though New Zealand has such a small population, it generated 42.7 million domestic tourist nights in 1989. Domestic tourism is much more strongly concentrated in North Island than international tourism, but is more evenly spread throughout the Island (though Auckland, Northland and the Bay of Plenty are the main destinations). Canterbury is the main focus of domestic tourism in South Island.

INBOUND AND OUTBOUND TOURISM

Most Australians visiting New Zealand come for holidays, although there is also a strong VFR and business element. More than half the visitors from UK come to visit friends and relatives. The growing Japanese and American elements of the inbound tourist market are dominated by holidaymakers.

Tourism by New Zealanders is becoming more outward looking. The outbound market grew rapidly in the late 1980s while domestic tourism was declining. Domestic nights and trips dropped in 1985, 1986 and 1987. North Islanders appear to be substituting trips to South Island by international travel to Australia and other more distant destinations, such as the USA and the UK. However, other Pacific destinations, e.g. Singapore, Japan and Hong Kong, are becoming increasingly popular. As with Australia, New Zealand is becoming more integrated into the Pacific region.

FURTHER READING

Bywater, M (1989) 'Australia outbound', *Travel and Tourism Analyst*, No. 1, pp. 37–51.

Bywater, M (1990) 'Australia', *EIU International Tourism Reports*, No.4, pp. 63–83.

Bywater, M (1990) 'New Zealand', *EIU International Tourism Reports*, No. 2, pp. 44–67.

Carroll, P, Donohue, K, McGovern, M and McMillen, J (1991) *Tourism in Australia*, Harcourt Brace Jovanovich, Sydney.

Chester, G (1993) 'Managing tourism to a seabird nesting island', *Tourism Management*, Vol. 14, No. 2, pp. 99–105.

Faulkner, H W (1990) 'Swings and roundabouts in Australian tourism', *Tourism Management*, Vol. 11, pp. 29–37.

Hall, C M (1992) *Introduction to tourism in Australia – impacts, planning and development*, Longman Cheshire, Melbourne.

Oppermann, M (1994) 'Regional aspects of tourism in New Zealand', *Regional Studies*, Vol. 28, No. 2, pp. 155–67.

Pearce, D (1993) 'Domestic tourist travel patterns in New Zealand', *GeoJournal*, Vol. 29, No. 3, pp. 225–32.

Wearing, S and Parsonson, R (1991) 'Rainforest tourism', *Tourism Management*, Vol. 12, September, pp. 236–244.

West, G R (1993) 'Economic significance of tourism in Queensland', *Annals of Tourism Research*, Vol. 20, pp. 490–504.

Westcott, G C (1991) 'Australia's distinctive national parks', *Environmental Conservation*, Vol. 18, No. 4, pp.331–40.

QUESTIONS AND DISCUSSION POINTS

1 New Zealand has always depended heavily on the Australian market for her international tourists. Is the relationship between Australia and New Zealand changing and, if so, how and why?

2 Why do you think the Perth region of Australia is relatively little developed for tourism (domestic or international), in spite of its favourable Mediterranean-type climate?

ASSIGNMENT

Three young friends have saved up to go to Australia together next year. They are all interested in wildlife, adventure and wilderness holidays and they wish to see as many of Australia's different natural environments as possible and to try as many different activities as possible.

Their list of places they want to visit includes Kosciusko National Park (the Snowy Mountains), Uluru (the Red Centre), Cape Tribulation (rainforest), the Great Barrier Reef, and Kakadu (for the wetlands). They can only take a month off work and they have to co-ordinate their leave. They have come to your travel agency for advice before they tell their employers when they want their holiday next year.

Is there any one month in the year when it would be suitable to visit all the National Parks on their list? If not, in which month would they be able to visit most of the Parks in comfort (and which ones would they have to leave out)? Advise them on the weather, road conditions and activities they could do at that time of year in each part. Also, suggest a route to and through Australia that would minimise internal travel distances.

CHAPTER 35

The Pacific Islands

LEARNING OBJECTIVES

After reading this chapter you should be able to
- **assess the potential of the climate, landscape and cultural resources of the region**
- **distinguish between the regional distribution of these geographical resources and their development for tourism**
- **demonstrate a knowledge of the main tourist destinations**
- **relate patterns of accessibility and colonial history to patterns of tourist use.**

INTRODUCTION

The huge scale of the Pacific region differentiates it from the other tourist regions of the world. The Pacific Ocean covers a quarter of the earth's surface. The Pacific 'Rim' that surrounds it is made up of the coasts of North, Central and South America to the east, and the dynamic economies of east and south east Asia to the west, and Australasia to the south west (*see* Fig 35.1). There is a significant movement of tourists between the countries of the Pacific Rim but relatively little travel across it. On the American side, the drift of tourists is mostly towards the Pacific coast and southwards along the Rim (*see* Chapter 31). On the Asian side there is a more complex interchange of tourists between the countries on the Rim. Political and economic factors appear to have the greatest influence on tourist travel patterns along the coasts of east and south east Asia at present (*see* Chapters 34 and 36) but tourists from the two more advanced economic regions (Australasia and Japan) show a marked drift of tourist travel towards the Equator. The size of the Pacific Ocean means that it is very expensive to travel across and it takes a long time, even with modern air transport (e.g. Los Angeles to Tokyo takes 10 hours, Santiago to Sydney, 19 hours). Destinations must possess very special qualities to tempt visitors from this distance. Only the most affluent holiday makers and business travellers are

likely to make the journey, and the volume of cross-Pacific travel is light.

The island states that are scattered across the vast expanse of the Pacific Ocean are physically very small and they have small populations: they generate little travel themselves. Their tourist role is to function as stopover destinations for cross-Pacific passengers or as tourist destinations in their own right.

THE PACIFIC ISLANDS

The islands can be grouped into five categories:

1 The Hawaiian islands, located on the Tropic of Cancer in the centre of the north Pacific; Hawaii is one of the states of the USA. They attract the most tourists (6.8 million in 1991) and are the main Pacific island destination, particularly for the North American market.

2 Micronesia. This group of islands are closest to the east asian coast of the Pacific Rim, extending from the Equator to 20° North (between Japan and the Philippines). Together they attracted 1.17 million tourists in 1991, mostly from Japan.

3 Melanesia. This string of islands is located off the north east coast of Australia and runs south east towards New Zealand. The majority of their 428 000 tourists come from Australasia. They also lie in tropical latitudes, between the Equator and 30° S.

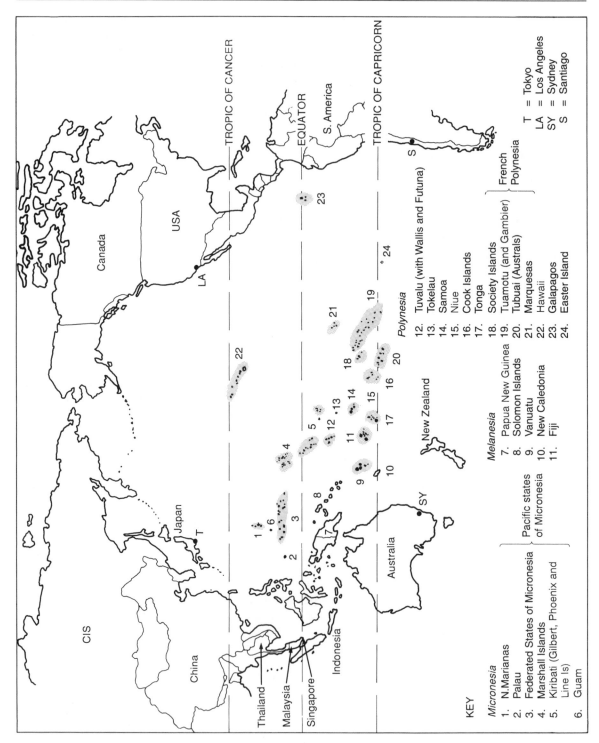

Fig. 35.1 The Pacific

4 Polynesia. These islands are widely scattered over the centre of the South Pacific, over an area between the Equator and the Tropic of Cancer and over a distance of more than 3000 miles east–west. They are the most isolated and remote tourist destinations in the Pacific and attracted a peak total of 298 000 visitors in 1989, but only just over a quarter of a million in the crisis year of 1991.

5 The isolated islands of the east Pacific. The Pacific basin is physically divided by the Pacific ridge, an area of shallower sea which runs from the Antarctic up towards the Mexico/California coast. Easter Island (which belongs to Chile) lies on this ridge and there are a few other islands between this ridge and the South American coast (e.g. the Galapagos which belong to Ecuador – *see* Chapter 33). There are a few other isolated small islands off the Chilean coast. This section of ocean makes up about a third of the Pacific but although it is mostly shallower than the eastern two thirds of the ocean, it has far fewer islands in it.

HAWAII

Hawaii is politically part of the USA, but it is a long way from the American mainland (San Francisco is 3840 km and five-to-six hours' flying time to the east). It is even more remote from the western edge of the ocean (Tokyo is 6160 km to the west). However, deregulation of the American air-lines has led to intense competition and airfares to Hawaii are relatively cheap, making it a popular tropical destination for both US and Japanese markets. The state of Hawaii consists of five main islands (*see* Fig 35.2). Hawaii is the name of the biggest island but it is relatively little used by tourists; the state capital, Honolulu, and most of the tourist activity, are centred on the island of Oahu, where the main international airport is situated. The island group is made up of the exposed tips of undersea volcanic mountains, which rise nearly 4500 m above sea level. Most of the volcanoes are dormant but Kilauea (on Hawaii Island) is still active and forms the centre piece of the Hawaii Volcanoes National Park.

The climate is subtropical with relatively little seasonal variation (*see* Chapter 2) and tourism also shows little seasonality. There is a slight but not very marked peak in June, July and August, though being in the same latitude as the Caribbean, late August and early September are the danger times for hurricanes. However, bad storms are quite unusual: Hurricane Iniki which hit Kauai in September, 1992 was the first hurricane the islands had experienced for ten years. The Hawaiian islands are in the same climatic situation as the volcanic islands of the east Caribbean: they sit in the path of the trade winds that blow from east to west. Like the Caribbean islands, the Hawaiian group have wet humid climates with very heavy rainfall on their eastern sides (which catch the torrential orographic rain), while the western ends of the islands are dry, sheltered and sunny. Honolulu (*see* Fig 2.9 on page 13 for climatic statistics) is in a sheltered site and has only 607 mm of rain a year. The exposed eastern slopes of Mount Waialeale on Kauai have an average of 12 344 mm per annum, and is among the wettest places on earth. With this amount of rainfall the mountain slopes are eroded into steep ridges and ravines clothed with lush green tropical vegetation. These landscapes are in sharp contrast to the bare black and brown rocky volcanic features and produce a varied and dramatic backdrop to the tourist beaches. Much of the coast, however, is cliffed and rugged. The islands' population is a blend of various ethnic groups (including Japanese, Chinese, Philippino, Black, Puerto Rican) plus the native Hawaiians. It is a multicul-

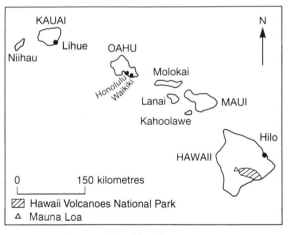

Fig. 35.2 The Hawaiian islands

tural destination, though museums, hula and Tahitian dance shows and Luau pig roast feasts demonstrate Polynesian culture. The majority (64.6 per cent) of tourists come from the US mainland and a high proportion of these from California and other west coast states; the average stay is 11 days. Twenty per cent of Hawaii's visitors come from Japan and, although they spend more per head, they stay only five days on average. Canada, Australia and Europe contribute roughly another four per cent each. The Americans tend to be repeat visitors and they show an increasing inclination to explore the less-developed islands after their first visit. Direct flights from the US mainland to Maui, for example, have encouraged this trend, and a quarter of the visitors to Hawaii now bypass Oahu altogether. Further expansion of Hawaii's tourist industry is likely to be focused on the spreading of tourism more widely throughout the islands. Hawaii is America's most popular tropical destination; it has an appealingly different local culture but the advantages of a common language,

currency and basic legal framework with the USA. Above all it has political stability. A weak dollar only serves to reinforce all these advantages.

Oahu

Oahu is the focus of Hawaii's tourism with over 5 million tourist arrivals in 1991 and over 50 per cent of all Hawaii's hotel rooms. The island's international flights come in to Honolulu airport, which is the communications hub for the other islands. There are frequent domestic flights to the other islands which are about 20–45 minutes' flying time away (but no ferry service as the islands are just too far apart to make this viable). Honolulu is the capital and is the biggest urban area on the islands. It is a lively modern city with many high rise buildings and multi-storey condominiums and hotels on the ocean front. Waikiki is the most famous beach, but it is quite small and crowded (*see* Fig 35.3). There is luxury shopping, and plenty of Japanese snack bars and eating

Fig. 35.3 Waikiki Beach

places. Most shops provide information in Japanese as well as English. The night life and entertainment are mostly American style, though there are plenty of popularised Polynesian events (e.g. Hula dancing and Luau, a modern version of a traditional Polynesian feast). The Polynesian Cultural Centre is located on the north shore of the island. It is a 42-acre park where there are reconstructions of traditional villages from Tahiti, Fiji, Tonga, Samoa, Hawaii, the Marquesas and Maori buildings (from New Zealand) and entertainments (pageants, revues and extravaganzas) but the culture is very highly commoditised and far from authentic (*see* Chapter 12). Other tourist attractions around the island include Pearl Harbour (where the Japanese attacked the US navy in 1941 and brought them into the Second World War), Diamond Head (a 760-feet high extinct volcanic crater at the east end of Honolulu, Waimea Falls Park, and pineapple plantations. The north shore of the island is much less developed and there are good surf beaches. There are plenty of opportunities for water sports (diving, snorkelling, surfing etc) all round the island.

Hawaii Big Island

This lies 120 miles south east of Oahu. Although at 4038 square miles it is the biggest island in the group, it has only 12.3 per cent of Hawaii's hotel rooms and 1.1 million tourists in 1991. It is dominated by the two volcanic mountains, Mauna Kea and Mauna Loa (both rising to over 4150 m). They are high enough to have snow cover at their summits in winter. Mauna Loa can be classified as an active volcano: the most recent lava flows date from 1950. However, the subsidiary crater of Kilauea is more active and spews out lava every few years. In 1991 a lava flow overran one of the palm-fringed, black sand beaches into the sea and created 80 hectares of new land. The eruptions are normally intermittent and quite mild, consisting of steam, gases, cinders and slow moving lava. The volcano is a National Park and an observatory, scenic drives, an interpretive centre and walking trails have been built around the main crater.

The island is much less densely populated than Oahu, although there are resorts all along the sheltered and drier west coast. However, although it is quite cliffed with few large beaches, there is good diving and watersports. There are airports on both the west (Kona) and east (Hilo) sides of the island, but Hilo is very wet. There is little development on the south shores which are threatened by lava flows (fire insurance for the buildings is not available!)

Maui (The Valley Isle)

Maui lies in the centre of the Hawaiian group, only a twenty-minute flight from Honolulu. It is 729 square miles in area with a population of a little over 100 000. It is rather more up-market, with many white sand beaches and more spacious and less densely developed resorts, hotels and condominiums scattered along the coast, e.g. at Kaanpali. The main development is on the drier, more sheltered west coast. There are many up-market sports, e.g. golf, sea fishing, hunting, sailing and horse riding, as well as the usual swimming, diving and snorkelling. The west half of the island is dominated by the dormant Haleakala volcano. The crater is still barren of vegetation but it is safe and stable, with cabins, camping and walking in the Haleakala National Park. The island is the second most important Hawaiian destination, with 25 per cent of the total accommodation stock and 2.2 million tourists in 1991.

Kauai (The Garden Isle)

This island is the most westerly of the group and its central mountain (Waialeale) is reputedly the wettest place on earth. The flanks of the mountain have lush green lowland landscapes of sugar cane fields and, before Hurricane Iniki, new coffee plantations, many golf courses and some very exclusive resort developments (e.g. near Lihue). The island's accommodation was badly damaged by Hurricane Iniki, but most hotels had been repaired and were beginning to reopen by May 1993. The island had 10.5 per cent of Hawaii's hotel rooms in 1992. The main scenic attraction is the Waimea Canyon, a dramatic 4000-feet deep trench cut into the volcanic deposits, and the nearby Hanapepe lookout which provides dramatic views when the clouds clear.

The other main islands, Molokai and Lanai, are much less developed at present, with only 0.45 per cent of the hotel rooms and they receive relatively few tourists.

Islands and archipelagoes	Number of islands	Total land area (km²)	Number of tourists 1991 (000s)
North Mariana Islands	14	457	430
Guam	1	549	729
Federated States of Micronesia (inc. Yap, Chuuk, Pohnpei and Kosrae)	607	700	8
Kiribati (inc. Kiribati, Phoenix and Line Islands)	33	861	3
Marshall Islands	1225	180	7
Palau	350	508	<10

Fig. 35.4 Micronesia

MICRONESIA

Micronesia is made up of five main groups of islands, plus Guam (*see* Fig 35.4).

North Mariana Islands

This string of mountainous volcanic islands stretches over 650 km of ocean. They are the closest Pacific islands to Japan (only just over 3 hours' flying time away). The islands have an international airport at Saipan with direct air connections to Japan. The islands are linked to Japan in another way: Japan was granted formal control over Saipan in 1920, but more recently the islands became trust territories of the USA. It is thus not surprising that 78 per cent of the islands' tourists come from Japan and another 18 per cent from the USA.

Tourism did not really take off until 1976, but growth was rapid up to 1980. Tourist numbers stagnated until 1985, when the islands entered another period of very rapid growth (19 per cent–35 per cent per annum) until 1991. Total visitor numbers more than doubled from 195 000 in 1987 to 430 000 in 1991. This paralleled Japan's policy on its own outbound tourism (*see* Chapter 36). Tourism is concentrated on the island of Saipan and a little spreads to Rota and Tinian, the two islands located between Saipan and Guam. Some tourists come to the North Marianas as part of a trip to nearby Guam (air taxi services are available from Guam to Rota and Saipan).

Guam

This is the most important island destination in the Pacific after Hawaii. It attracted 863 000 tourists in 1992. It is also one of the bigger islands with an area of 549 km². It is a hilly island with a dramatic cliffed coastline, but some sheltered sandy beaches on its west coast and coral reefs all around the island. The main resort area is Tumon Bay. The climate is hot tropical with a drier season December to March and a hotter (up to 33° C) wet season.

The island is now a self-governing territory of the USA, although it was briefly occupied by the Japanese during the Second World War. There is a US naval base on the island so there are good airport facilities and direct air services to USA, Australia and several parts of Japan. The island acts as a transport hub for surrounding islands.

Tourism to Guam grew rapidly in the early 1970s until the oil crisis checked development. Like the Marianas, rapid tourism growth resumed in the second half of the 1980s, when there was a major phase of Japanese-financed hotel and condominium development. The accommodation stock rose from 3018 rooms in 1986 to 4600 rooms in 1990 and plans existed in the early 1990s to increase this to 13 000 rooms. Guam relies very heavily on the Japanese market: like the Marianas, 78 per cent of its tourists come from there. They are attracted for honeymoons, short weekend breaks and also to visit the Second World War sites. Although Japanese honeymoons may be 6 or 7 days' long, the average length of stay in 1986 was only 3.6 days. The island's tourist industry is already feeling the effects of the recession in Japan: the numbers of Japanese tourists declined by between 17–31 per cent in the first few months of 1993. Seven per cent of Guam's tourists come from the USA.

Palau

Palau is located only 1000 km from the Philippines but receives less than 10 000 tourists a year. The group of islands stretches 650 km north–south and they include some rugged volcanic and limestone mountains while others are classic coral atolls. All are surrounded by a huge barrier reef, which is reputedly one of the best diving locations in the world. Koror, the capital, has an international airport but flights go via Guam. Most tourists come from Japan (50 per cent) or the USA (25 per cent). American visitors tend to be attracted by the diving, while the Japanese are general holiday makers.

Federated States of Micronesia and Kiribati

Physically, these are groups of tiny remote islands scattered over huge areas of ocean. A few are mountainous volcanic islands, e.g. Pohnpei, but most are low lying coral atolls: Chuuk is surrounded by a huge barrier reef. These have a very limited water supply and the vast majority are uninhabited. They are isolated in terms of transport, e.g. international flights to Pohnpei are via Guam (3 hours' flight away) or Honolulu, so it is not surprising that the islands' main markets are also Japan and the USA. Tourism is, as yet, very small scale, with a mixture of ecotourism and special interest diving trips, but there are proposals to develop capital-intensive hotel and golf resorts on Pohnpei and Kosrae.

Kiribati is another group of archipelagoes spread out over a huge area of ocean. Their inaccessibility and lack of major airport runway facilities limit their development even as special interest destinations. The majority of their 3000 visitors in 1991 were residents of Kiribati, Tuvalu or Nauru: only 15 per cent came from Australia, 13 per cent from the USA and 7 per cent from Japan.

Marshall Islands

These are mostly low lying coral atolls, spread out over 1 900 000 km² of ocean. They are so isolated that one of their main claims to fame has been as weapons and nuclear testing sites (e.g. on Kwajalein and Bikini Atolls). The capital is Majuro with a population of 12 000, where the international airport is located. International flights go via Honolulu and are expensive; the other islands have only a weekly service to Majuro. This makes them unsuitable for the predominantly short-stay Japanese market. High value, low intensity ecotourism is a possibility.

MELANESIA

This region consists of the following groups of islands (*see* Fig 35.5):

	Number of tourists (000s) 1991	Number of islands	Area km²
Fiji	259.3	320	18 272
New Caledonia	81		19 103
Vanuatu	40	80	11 880
Solomon Islands	11		29 785
Papua New Guinea	37	600+	461 690

Fig. 35.5 Melanesia

Fiji

The Fijian group of islands is the main destination of Melanesia. They are located 2000 km north of New Zealand and 4400 km south west of Hawaii. The main two islands, Viti Levu and Vanua Levu, are extinct volcanoes, so they are mountainous. The capital (Suva) and the international airport are on Viti Levu. The climate is tropical, but being south of the Equator, the hottest and wettest season is December to April.

March is the wettest month (with 14 inches of rainfall) and cyclones are also a danger towards the end of the wet season. The north west sides of the islands are the more sheltered from the rainbearing south easterly and easterly winds. Most of the hotel/resort complexes are on the leeward sides of the islands. In addition to the usual Pacific island attractions of deserted beaches, local culture, entertainment, snorkelling and swimming, there are 4–7 day cruises to the nearby smaller islands from Suva. Pacific cruises that visit other Melanesian island groups also call in at Fiji, but the numbers of visiting ships are quite small. Fiji is much more accessible by air than many south Pacific island groups: it is one of the main stopover destinations for cross-Pacific and round the world flights, and has good services to Australia and New Zealand. Because of these factors, it does not rely quite so heavily on one or two specific markets for its tourism as do most of the other Pacific islands (*see* Fig 35.6): its visitors come from Australasia, Japan, USA and Europe. Fiji has a major regional communications role: it is the main regional gateway and other Pacific island destinations depend on its intercontinental connections. The growth of tourism to Fiji has been steady rather than spectacular, and a whole series of events (some worldwide and some local) have slowed it down. The world energy crises led to drops of 11 per cent and 0.1 per cent in tourist numbers in 1975 and 1981 respectively, while the 1991 Gulf War reduced Fiji's tourist numbers by 7 per cent.

In the late 1980s local events also had a significant impact: cyclone damage had led to a decline in tourists in 1983; after this, visitor numbers began to increase in line with the trends in world tourism in the second half of the 1980s, but another local problem meant that Fiji failed to benefit fully from this trend. In 1987, political unrest in the island led to two coups, unfavourable publicity and a 26 per cent drop in arrivals that year (from 257 800 in 1986 to 189 900 in 1987).

The origin of the political problems lay in the island's colonial history and ethnic composition. Fiji was a British colony and Asian labour (mainly Indians) was brought in by the British to work on the sugar plantations about 100 years ago. The Indian community now outnumbers the local Fijian population and political control was passing into the hands of the Indian population. The Fijians responded by staging coups in the spring and autumn of 1987. As normality returned, tourism numbers had virtually recovered to the 1986 levels by 1989, but Fiji had missed the opportunity of attracting some of the foreign investment that was going into Pacific/Asian tourism at the time. Tourism is crucial to the islands' economy and the Fijian government has been very active in promoting the islands and restoring its image.

New Caledonia

The main island in this group is called Grande Terre; it is 50 km by 80 km and is mountainous, with a large coral reef around its shoreline. The capital is Noumea. This group of islands is closest of all the Melanesian countries to the main population centres of Australasia. It has a distinct European character. It is a French possession and has a very significant French element to its population. The islands have good air connections with Europe, Australasia, Japan and other parts of the world.

Tourism grew rapidly for ten years from 1974 to a peak of 91 500 visitors in 1984, in spite of the world economic problems of the period, but like Fiji, New Caledonia's internal political problems prevented it from benefiting from the expansion of

Islands	Total number of tourists (000s)	Percentage of tourists from				
		Australia	New Zealand	USA	Japan	Europe
Fiji	259	33	12	12	11	16
New Caledonia	81	21	12	1	31	19
Vanuatu	40	54	18	3	2	3
Papua New Guinea	37	41	5	13	5	16
Solomon Islands	11	37	14	9	6	12

Fig. 35.6 Melanesia inbound tourism, 1991

world tourism in the late 1980s. In 1985 the island suffered a series of political riots (described as a low intensity colonial war). Visitor numbers plummeted to 51 200 in 1985 and grew by only 10 000 over the next 3 years. By 1990, total numbers had crept up to 86 900 but the early 1990s saw tourism in decline once more. The islands used to rely heavily on the Australian market. In 1977 62 per cent of New Caledonia's tourists came from Australia or New Zealand. By 1980 this had dropped to 38 per cent, by 1987 to 29 per cent and to 21 per cent in 1992. Over the same period of time the Japanese have increased from less than 10 per cent to over 32 per cent of New Caledonia's visitors. Being a French colony, French tourists consistently make up another 19–21 per cent of the total. Club Méditerranée is established on the island. In addition to the staying tourists, the islands receive a substantial number of cruise visitors (over 40 000 per annum in the late 1980s).

Vanuatu

This archipelago consists of 80 islands occupied by 90 different tribes dispersed over 800 km of ocean. The main island is Port Vila where the airport and most hotels are located. Day trips to some of the other islands are available. The islands, resources include the typical mix of Pacific island destinations: beaches, diving, climate, watersports and landscapes. On Tanna island (towards the southern end of the archipelago) there is a volcano which is a significant attraction. However, traditional cultural values ('Kastom') are both a major resource and a constraint on tourism development. On Pentecost island (200 km north of Port Vila) small groups of tourists are allowed into the villages to witness the Pentecost Land Dive ceremony (Solfield, 1991 and *see* Chapters 6 and 12). In 1988 groups of 40 tourists were permitted at each of the eight ceremonies. In 1989, this was increased to 50 visitors but only four events took place. A locally controlled company organises the tour package and it is fully booked up to four years in advance. The authentic nature and local control of the event have singled it out as being a genuinely sustainable form of special interest ethnic tourism. The traditional nature of Vanuatu society has been a factor that has limited tourism as well as promoted it.

The traditional system of land tenure and indigenous land rights claims have hindered some tourist developments (de Burlo, 1989)

The fragmented nature of its society into many different island groups has also caused problems. In 1980 the islands became independent but this triggered off an armed rebellion by some of the tribes particularly from the island of Espiritu Santo in the north of the archipelago. Although things quickly returned to normal in the early 1980s, there was further political unrest in 1988. These events led to a decline in tourist numbers, which was accelerated by other problems: Ansett Airlines withdrew its services (between Vanuatu and Australia) from 1985 to 1987. As the tourist industry relied heavily on this direct air link and depended on the Australian market for about three-quarters of its tourists, this was a major setback to tourist growth at a period when world and regional tourism were growing rapidly. These problems were made even worse when a cyclone hit the islands in 1987 and damaged the hotel stock. The impacts of these events on tourist arrivals can be traced in Fig 35.7. The substantial number of cruise ship arrivals (75 700 in 1985) also rapidly dropped away in the following years. On the other hand, the table shows that tourist growth has been vigorous once these problems were resolved, with a substantial 14 per cent increase

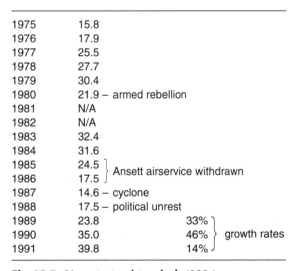

1975	15.8	
1976	17.9	
1977	25.5	
1978	27.7	
1979	30.4	
1980	21.9 – armed rebellion	
1981	N/A	
1982	N/A	
1983	32.4	
1984	31.6	
1985	24.5 ⎫ Ansett airservice withdrawn	
1986	17.5 ⎭	
1987	14.6 – cyclone	
1988	17.5 – political unrest	
1989	23.8	33% ⎫
1990	35.0	46% ⎬ growth rates
1991	39.8	14% ⎭

Fig. 35.7 Vanuatu tourist arrivals (000s)

even in the Gulf Crisis year of 1991. Nevertheless, the history of tourism in Vanuatu (as in Fiji and New Caledonia) emphasises the problems of isolation and inaccessibility faced by the South Pacific islands and the disproportionate effect of local political events reported in distant countries.

Papua New Guinea (PNG)

This country consists of over 600 islands, just 160 km north of Australia's north coast. The biggest area of PNG territory is the eastern half of New Guinea island (the western half is the Irian Jaya province of Indonesia (*see* Chapter 37). PNG became independent of Australia in 1975 but maintains close links with the country and over half its tourists come from Australasia. It has other economic resources (e.g. minerals such as gold and copper) besides tourism. Unlike many South Pacific island nations, it is not so dependent on tourism and has not always promoted tourism with much vigour, so visitor numbers are quite low. The natural resources of the region are such that it is more an adventure and ethnic tourism (i.e. a special interest) destination rather than a mass beach tourism location. The main island is mountainous with active volcanoes along its north coast which are fringed with mangrove swamps. The islands have a great variety of wildlife habitats and great species diversity. Some of the rivers are suitable for white water rafting for the adventurous and there are cruises for the less active. Jungle treks, caving (e.g. on the island of Bougainville), game fishing and diving are other adventure activities available in PNG. The tribal diversity of the territory is also promoted for ethnic tourism; each tribe has its own characteristic variation of local customs, style of architecture and crafts. Some village ceremonies are staged for tourists, although the 'sing-sings' (tribal gatherings) with dancing, singing and chanting may still be authentic.

Port Moresby is the capital. The international airport is nearby and over 90 per cent of PNG's visitors arrive via Port Moresby. Air links to Australia are good but are only slowly developing elsewhere, so most non-Australian tourists would have to travel via Australia, which adds to the length of the journey (in 1992 for example it would take two whole days to get there from

London). In 1989 it was linked to the key Pacific hub of Guam, but direct routes are an essential pre-requisite for any major expansion of its non-Australian markets. In the 1980s holiday makers accounted for under a third of all PNG's visitors. About 40 per cent were on business trips, while another 20 per cent were visiting friends and relatives (there are still many expatriate Australians living there).

Solomon Islands

This archipelago is situated between Papua New Guinea and Vanuatu, but its tourism is still on a very small scale. The development of tourism is constrained by poor international air connections, shortage of hotel capacity and lack of transport between the islands of the archipelago. Virtually all the hotel accommodation is located in the capital (Honiara). In 1991 just over 50 per cent of the 11 105 tourists were from Australasia, and only 9 per cent from the USA and 6 per cent from Japan.

POLYNESIA

Polynesia is made up of several groups of islands as illustrated in Fig 35.8.

	Number of islands	Area of land (km²)	Number of tourists 1991 (000s)
French Polynesia	130	4000	121
Cook Islands		240	40
Western Samoa	9	2934	39
American Samoa	7	197	37
Tonga	172	748	22
Tuvalu	9	25.9	1
Niue	1	260	1
Tokelau	3	12	
Wallis and Futuna		274	

Fig. 35.8 Polynesia

French Polynesia (Tahiti)

French Polynesia makes up the biggest total land area of the South Pacific island territories, but it is split between 130 islands spread over an area of ocean the size of Europe. They are grouped into five archipelagoes: the Society Islands (which include the island of Tahiti), the Tuamotu, the Marquesas, Gambiers and Australs. All except the Tuamotus are extinct volcanoes so they are mountainous with deeply eroded valleys; the high rainfall generates many streams and waterfalls. The coasts are a mixture of cliffs, lagoon and coral reefs which generate white sand beaches. Due to the islands' volcanic origin, some of the beaches (e.g. on Tahiti) are made of black sand. In contrast, the Tuamotu group of islands are mostly low lying coral atolls that are not developed for tourism. Over half of the population, and the tourism, is concentrated on Tahiti in the Society Islands, where the capital (Papeete) is located. The nearby islands of Moorea (90 minutes by ferry from Tahiti) and Bora Bora are the other more developed islands.

The islands are French territories and are economically part of France: this gives Tahiti's tourism some advantages in that French investment has provided a good local infrastructure and good international air connections. But it also makes Tahiti a relatively expensive Pacific island destination and it has been unable to compete with nearby developing Pacific island destinations since 1986. It received a peak of 161 200 visitors in 1986 but numbers have declined virutally every year to a low of 121 000 visitors in 1991. North America was Tahiti's main market in the 1980s, making up about half of its visitors. US visitors peaked at 98 641 in 1986. Since then the US market has dropped away. By 1991 only 35 772 Americans travelled to French Polynesia and they made up less than a third of all the islands' tourists. The only markets to have grown over this decade were the Japanese (from about 2000 visitors in the early 1980s to about 14 000 in 1991 due to improving air links) and some European markets (e.g. Germany and Italy). French visitors now make up 16 per cent of the visitor population.

Tourism is fairly well spread out through the year: American visitors tend to prefer October and November, the French between June and August, while Australasian numbers peak in December and January.

Cork Islands

This group is also a mixture of volcanic mountains and flat coral atolls. The main island Rarotonga is a steeply mountainous island with a narrow fringing coral reef. Its political links with New Zealand combined with good air services to Australia and New Zealand mean that Australasians dominate its inbound tourism. Up to the mid 1980s New Zealanders made up more than half the visitors, but since 1987 numbers have stabilised at around 14–15 000 a year, while other markets (notably the North American and European) have grown a little.

Western Samoa, American Samoa and Tonga

These island groups lie between Fiji and French Polynesia. Many of the visitors to Samoa are from other Pacific islands (30–70 per cent), while Tonga attracts more Australasians. As its islands are fairly close together it specialises in yacht cruises round its own archipelago, but the luxury South Pacific cruise market has declined sharply since the early 1980s. Tonga's cruise ship arrivals dropped from 49 500 in 1983 to just over 9000 in 1987.

Niue

This isolated island is physically different from many other Pacific island destinations. It is a coral atoll that has been up-lifted so its coast consists of mainly coral cliffs, caves and chasms. It has virtually no beaches. Its fringing reef provides good diving and snorkelling and it is a specialist destination. New Zealanders make up about 75–80 per cent of its tourists (its single air connection is with New Zealand). An airline dispute in 1988 halted its developing tourist industry, while a severe cyclone in February 1990 damaged much of its infrastructure.

REFERENCES AND FURTHER READING

Those texts marked with an asterisk are particularly recommended for further reading.

Cockerell, N (1993) 'Hawaii', *International Tourism Reports*, No. 4, pp. 50–70.

de Burlo, C (1989) 'Land alienation, land tenure and tourism in Vanuatu', *Geojournal*, Vol. 19, No. 3, pp. 317–21.

*Fletcher, J and Snee, H (1989) 'Tourism in the South Pacific islands', in Cooper, C (Ed) *Tourism, Recreation and Hospitality Research*, Vol. 1, Wiley.

*King, B and McVey, M (1994) 'Fiji', International Tourism Reports, No. 2, pp. 4–21.

Lockhart, D (1993) 'Tourism to Fiji: crumbs off a rich man's table?', *Geography*, Vol. 78, Part 3 July, pp. 318–23.

*Milne, S (1992) 'Tourism and development in South Pacific microstates', *Annals of Tourism Research*, Vol. 19, pp. 191–212.

Sofield, T H B (1991) 'Sustainable ethnic tourism in the South Pacific: some principles', *Journal of Tourism Studies*, Vol. 2, No. 1, May, pp. 56–72.

Valentine (1993) 'Eco-tourism and nature conservation: a definition with some recent developments in Micronesia', *Tourism Management*, Vol. 14, No.2.

QUESTIONS AND DISCUSSION POINTS

1 To what extent does the pattern of tourist development in the South Pacific depend on the policies and routings of the international airlines?

2 Theoretically, a region as isolated as the Pacific should have outstanding potential for ethnic and eco-tourism. Is this true of the Pacific island states?

3 Why, in spite of its physical isolation, is Hawaii such a successful tourist destination?

ASSIGNMENT

A young British couple come to your Travel Agency. They are getting married in early August and had considered booking their honeymoon in Oahu, Hawaii, as they like the idea of a Pacific island honeymoon. However, they are having second thoughts as they think Oahu may be too crowded. Select at least two other Pacific island destinations that may suit them (either in Hawaii or elsewhere in the Pacific). In order to help them come to a decision, indicate the similarities and differences in climate, resources, costs, accessibility and intensity of tourist development between your suggested destinations and Oahu.

CHAPTER 36

East Asia

LEARNING OBJECTIVES

After reading this chapter you should be able to

- assess the tourist potential of the climatic, landscape, historical and cultural resources of the region
- distinguish between the regional distribution of these geographical resources and their development and use for tourism
- demonstrate a knowledge of the main tourist resorts and tourist centres
- relate the political and economic development of the region to changing patterns of tourism
- assess the impact of Japanese tourism and investment in the region.

INTRODUCTION

This region includes China, Japan, Korea, Taiwan, Hong Kong and Macao (*see* Fig 36.1). It is physically dominated by China, a country of 9.6 million km^2 and a population in 1990 of 1139 million, but which is underdeveloped as a tourist country as yet. The dominant economy of East Asia is Japan. Even though it is beginning to feel the effects of the recession of the early 1990s, it is still one of the world's strongest economies. With an affluent population of 124 million, it is the main tourist generator of the region. A series of smaller countries lie between these two. They are the newly industrialised countries and colonies of South Korea, Taiwan, Hong Kong and Macao. They are among the rapidly developing so-called 'tiger economies' of the Pacific region. Their patterns of tourism have been more dependent on recent political changes in the region. These combined factors have led to the very rapid growth of tourism in East Asia in the late 1980s.

JAPAN

Introduction

Japan consists of a series of densely populated mountainous islands (of 377 835 km^2 in area),

mostly located between the latitudes 30 and 46° N: it has temperate-to-cool climates. Its world and regional tourist significance lies less in its size or physical resources but more in its population, history and economy. The success of Japanese manufacturing exports and the reluctance of the Japanese to import foreign goods has created a huge trade imbalance with many other countries. The Japanese government has seen the growth of Japanese tourist expenditure abroad as one way of redressing such imbalances. However, the history and culture of the country have not encouraged holidaymaking and foreign travel in the past. So, instead of having tourist policies focused on attracting overseas spending to their country, Japan has adopted policies that are almost the reverse and are actively encouraging the Japanese to travel abroad and spend money in other countries. This is more difficult than it may seem because social customs in Japan demand a very high commitment to work. Consequently the Japanese are reluctant to take time off work for travel, but attitudes are beginning to change and outbound travel is increasing. Japan's huge trading surplus also provides funds for overseas investment in tourism projects and real estate – the Japanese now own many hotels and resort developments throughout the Pacific region. Thus Japan

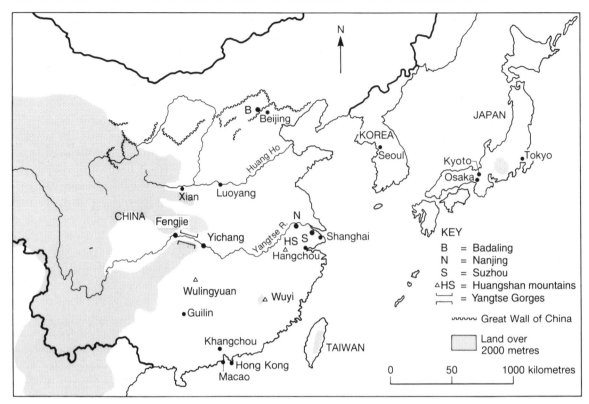

Fig. 36.1 East Asia

is having a double impact on the scale, development and location of tourism in the region – firstly, through the growth of outbound tourism and secondly through funding tourist development.

Work and leisure in Japan

The first way in which the government has sought to increase foreign travel is by making more leisure time available. This is a difficult task because the Japanese work extremely long hours and take little time off work: in 1987 the average yearly working hours were 2111, and workers receive an average of one week of annual vacation and an average of one day off each weekend. During the 1980s manufacturing workers' average hours increased from 2043 in 1975 to 2168 in 1987. Only 37 per cent of workers enjoy a two-day weekend. The reasons for these long hours of work are three fold:

1 There is a high amount of overtime work available because high economic growth has led to labour shortages and companies use overtime to respond quickly to changing economic demands.
2 Basic rates of pay are relatively low and so workers are encouraged to take overtime.
3 There is a strong sense of loyalty and duty to both the work team and to the company (which provides many benefits, such as housing, for workers). This, combined with institutional and cultural pressures for individual conformity, make it difficult for the Japanese to take time off. Any leave of over 4 consecutive days is considered long and in 1987 the average Japanese worker took only 50 per cent of their leave entitlement. One exception is the Japanese honeymoon, when a longer holiday of an average of 7.9 days and overseas travel is then accepted. Ninety-three per cent of the 700 000 couples getting married each year take their honeymoon overseas.

The Japanese government has been attempting to reduce working hours: the Labour Standard Law of 1988 aims to gradually reduce working hours from 48 to 40 hours a week by the mid

1990s, and to a 1800 hour working year. By way of example, the government grants its own employees 4 weeks' annual leave. These policies are having only mixed success as yet. Although the Japanese government reports that working hours are declining slowly (with the proportion of the workforce taking a two-day weekend increasing from 35 per cent to 37 per cent between 1987 and 1989), the average length of stay by Japanese tourists in overseas destinations has actually decreased from 8.8 days in 1985 to 8.0 days in 1990. If the government does achieve its objective of shortening the working year, it will have a dramatic effect on the time the Japanese have for travel. Average paid leave would increase from 8 to 20 days a year. The inclination of the Japanese to take their holiday entitlement may be changing. In 1990, 42 per cent of the population classified themselves as work orientated (i.e. they enjoyed leisure but work came first, or they were devoted to work) but the proportion of such work orientated people dropped to 15–20 per cent amongst teenagers. However, Dutton (1991) notes that these attitudes may change to conform to the predominant work ethic as the young people enter the workplace. The desire for leisure and overseas travel is undoubtedly growing. In 1987, 43 per cent of the Japanese said they would like to travel abroad, while a couple of years later this had increased to 63 per cent.

Government attempts to encourage overseas travel

The Japanese do not have a long tradition of overseas travel: outbound pleasure travel was severely restricted before 1964. Outbound travel increased rapidly to 2.2 million in 1973 but it stabilised at this level in the mid–late 1970s (due to the 1974 oil crisis). In the late 1970s and early 1980s it doubled again (to 4.6m in 1984). But this was still a very small proportion of the total population (about 3.8 per cent). In 1987 the government launched its 'Ten Million Programme' campaign aimed at increasing overseas travel to 10 million by 1991. The objectives of the campaign included

1 contributing to the economic growth of other countries, and
2 solving the imbalance of international payments between Japan and its trading partners.

The target was reached in 1990, with a total of 10.99 million outbound travellers (with growth rates of 23 per cent between 1986 and 1988 and 14–15 per cent in 1988–1990). The Gulf War in 1991 interrupted this pattern of growth, with a drop of 3.3 per cent to a total of 10.63 million outbound tourists for the year, but by 1992 the total had increased again to 11.79 million. Japanese spending abroad has shot up from US $ 10.76bn in 1987, to 22.5bn in 1989 and 35.39bn in 1992. The main economic impact of this has been felt in the Pacific region.

The main destinations in the Pacific region are Hong Kong, Korea, Singapore, Hawaii and mainland USA (each receiving over 1 million Japanese visitors), while Taiwan, China, Thailand, Guam and Australia each attract over half a million Japanese. The numbers of Japanese in all these destinations has roughly doubled since 1985 (*see* Fig 36.2). The most dramatic new market has been Japanese travel to Australia which has increased from 107 500 to 629 900 between 1985 and 1992. In contrast, tourism to Europe has been established for much longer. France now attracts over 1 million Japanese, while Germany, Italy and UK receive over half a million each.

In 1991 the government announced a follow up to the 'Ten Million Programme'. This new campaign, the 'Two Way Tourism 21' programme (the TWT21) puts equal emphasis on the promotion of inbound and outbound tourism for Japan in the 21st century. The world recession has slowed Japan's economic development and some of Japan's rural and older industrial regions need investment. The development of leisure and tourism projects in such locations has been seen as a way of boosting both domestic demand and encouraging inbound tourism. In 1987 the 'Resort Act' was passed, which enables the government to provide tax benefits and allowances to developers and for the government to provide the infrastructure for major domestic resort developments (e.g. marinas, ski resorts, hotels and golf courses). By the end of 1989, 646 approved projects in different parts of Japan were underway. All these factors together have led to a decrease in Japanese overseas tourism from September 1992. Outbound tourism was down (by between –2.6 per cent and –5.5 per cent) in each month of the last quarter of

Year	South Korea	Taiwan	China	Hong Kong	Singapore	Thailand	France	Hawaii	Guam	Australia
1985	638.9	615.5	470.4	635.7	377.6	221.4	470.2	855.0	301.6	107.5
1986	791.0	696.6	483.5	727.2	404.2	259.3	543.6	944.0	332.3	145.6
1987	893.5	807.7	577.7	1033.5	541.3	341.8	612.0	1161.0	412.6	215.5
1988	1124.1	917.1	591.9	1240.4	682.4	449.0	772.2	1216.7	493.5	352.3
1989	1379.5	962.1	358.8	1176.1	841.3	546.9	1256.7	1319.3	555.7	349.6
1990	1460.2	914.4	463.2	1331.6	971.6	635.5	1264.8	1439.7	637.5	479.9
1991	1455.0	825.9	640.8	1259.8	871.3	543.0	1016.7	1385.3	582.2	528.5
1992	1398.6	795.0	791.5	1324.3	1000.7	568.0	n/a	1637.0	676.6	629.9

Fig. 36.2 Japan outbound: the growth of Japanese tourism (000s)
(*Source*: WTO, PATA, National Tourist Offices)

1992 and this trend continued into the first quarter of 1993 (with a 6 per cent drop in outbound travel from Japan).

However, overseas investment in tourism projects has continued through government aid (Official Development Assistance), with loans for infrastructure development associated with resort development (e.g. in Malaysia, Thailand and Indonesia). This follows the major expansion of investment in Australia and other parts of the south Pacific in the late 1980s (Bywater, 1990). Private overseas investment has also expanded: 15.6 per cent of all Japanese overseas investment was in real estate and about a quarter of this was in hotels.

JAPAN AS A TOURIST DESTINATION: PHYSICAL AND TOURIST REGIONS

Physical character

Japan consists of four main islands: Hokkaido, Honshu, Shikoku and Kyushu, which lie between 30° and 46° N, but there are about 3000 minor islands off the coast; some of these make up the Ryukyu Islands which run south from Kyushu to Taiwan almost to the Tropic of Cancer (*see* Fig 36.3). Over three-quarters of the land is mountainous with many dormant volcanoes, hot springs and other signs of recent volcanic activity. The mountains form part of the 'Fiery Ring' that surrounds the Pacific Ocean, marking areas of instability of the earth's crust where the floor of the Pacific is being thrust underneath the continents of Asia to the east and the Americas to the

west. Japan is also prone to frequent earthquakes – another consequence of these movements of the earth's crust. Flat areas of land are few and far between. Most lowlands are scattered around the coast, or are located in river valleys or between the mountain ranges. The Tokyo Bay area is the most extensive lowland region; 77 per cent of Japan's population live in towns and cities located on these pockets of lowlands. The urbanised areas are therefore very densely developed and very congested. Similarly, the limited land that is suited for agriculture is very intensively farmed, with two crops a year where the climate allows. As Japan's territory extends over about 1400 miles (2250 km) north–south, the islands span several climatic zones. Hokkaido in the north has a humid continental climate, with cool summers, about 1000 mm precipitation, and cold winters with up to 4 months' snow cover. This gradually phases into temperate and humid subtropical climates (becoming warmer and wetter) towards the south. Tokyo has cold, dry, sunny winters (down to freezing from December to February). Summer temperatures in July and August range between 70°F (20°C) and 86°F (30°C), with wet and windy weather in September and October (the typhoon season). Temperatures climb even higher further south, while annual rainfall amounts increase to 2500 mm per annum. In spite of the beautiful forested mountain and lake landscapes and some areas of favourable climate, the main type of inbound tourism is cultural, historic and heritage tourism. There are numerous castles (residences of the shoguns – warlords of the 17th and 18th centuries), Shinto and buddhist temples and shrines, and palaces of the imperial family. The unique cul-

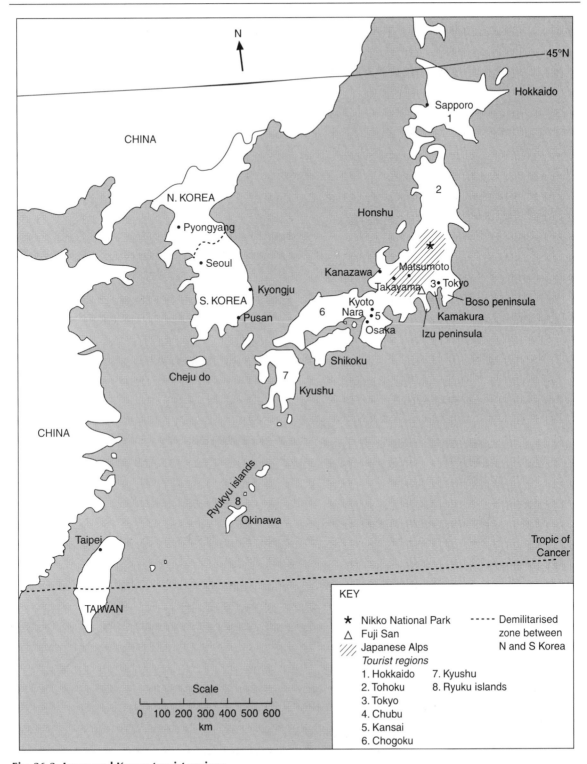

Fig. 36.3 Japan and Korea: tourist regions

ture of Japan was strengthened and maintained by Japan's resistance in the past to any foreign influences, particularly in the period 1600–1868.

The Resort Act of 1987 may increase the opportunities for sport, activity and resort tourism: the indented coastline provides many natural harbours and plenty of opportunity for marinas and boating activities. But the high cost of these pursuits may inhibit extensive inbound activity tourism: it is said that it is cheaper for the Japanese to travel to the Philippines to play golf than to participate in Japan. There are eight tourist regions in Japan, each with its own characteristic type of tourism:

1 Hokkaido. The cold, dry winter climate makes this a suitable region for winter sports and its landscapes (of volcanoes, lakes, hotsprings, wild flowers and forests) favour outdoor activities. The island has five important National Parks. The Winter Olympics were held at Sapporo in 1972 and the winter snow festival (held in February) is another major attraction. The island is popular with Taiwanese visitors.

2 Tohoku in the northern part of Honshu Island. This is also a scenic area. Some of Japan's best mountain scenery is said to be in the Bandari-Ashai National Park. The region attracts visitors for skiing, mountaineering, its hot springs, folk festivals and local crafts. Again, the region is becoming more popular among the Taiwanese.

3 Tokyo and its region.

(*a*) Tokyo

The city has a population of over 8 million and offers a wide range of urban attractions. It was the centre of the shogun government from 1603, although it was not the capital city. The main sights are the Imperial Palace, the Meiji shrine (one of the finest in Japan) and classical gardens (e.g. the Korakuen garden). The main entertainment and shopping district is the Ginza, with big department stores, speciality shops and boutiques, and a wide range of restaurants, theatres and nightlife. Tokyo Disneyland was opened in 1983, and attracted 10 million visitors a year in the 1980s, but caters mainly for the domestic market (only 6 per cent of its visitors were foreign tourists). Tokyo has a significant convention (business tourism) trade but its relative importance is declining. In 1991, it hosted only 14 per cent of Japan's conventions. The main international air-

port (at Narita City) is 66 km (41 miles) north east of Tokyo, and it is very congested.

(*b*) Fuji-Hakone-Izu area

Outside the city, the main landscape attractions lie to the south west, dominated by Mount Fuji (Fuji-San), Japan's highest mountain (3776 metres). Buses take the tourist two-thirds of the way up. Hakone is a mountain resort and spa town with hot springs. The Izu peninsula has beautiful coastal and island scenery. Nearer Tokyo, Kamakura is an old imperial city with temples and shrines, but is also a quiet seaside resort. There are also good beaches on the Boso peninsula.

4 Japanese Alps: Chubu region. These lie to the north and north west of Tokyo. There are seven national parks in this beautiful area of mountains, lakes, forests and waterfalls. The Nikko National Park (93 miles north of Tokyo) is one of the most popular; it is famous for the 330 foot Kegon waterfalls, Lake Chuzenji and the superb Toshogu shrine. The region contains many historic and picturesque towns and villages such as Matsumoto (famous for its medieval castle) and Takayama. Kanazawa, on Japan's east coast is another historic centre that is growing in popularity, with many ancient Samurai houses and beautiful gardens.

5 Kansai region. Kyoto, Osaka and Nara are the main cultural attractions of this region. Kyoto is one of the world's most attractive cities built in the classical Chinese style. It was the capital of Japan between 794 and 1868 and has many historic buildings (palaces, castles, temples and shrines) dating from 13th to 19th centuries. Nara, a town located 26 miles south of Kyoto, is even older (being the country's capital from 710 to 784 AD). It is particularly noted for its five-storey pagoda (Kofuku-ji) and the Great Buddha Hall, the largest wooden building in the world, housing the world's largest bronze statue of Buddha. Kansai is also a centre for business tourism. In 1991 it hosted 38 per cent of Japan's international conventions. Osaka's airport is very congested, but the region's accessibility and convenience as a conference location will be further improved when the Kansai International Airport (being built on a manmade island in Osaka Bay, 5 km off-shore) is completed: it is due to be opened in 1994.

6 Chogoku

7 Kyushu and

8 Okinawa and the Ryukyu Islands. These remaining three regions lie in the south of Japan (*see* Fig 36.3) and are in the subtropical climatic zone. Their attraction lies as much with their landscape and climate resources as with their historical and cultural features. Chogoku has beautiful beaches and the island-studded 'Inland Sea' National Park (between Honshu and Shikoku). The island of Kyushu is popular with both South Koreans and Taiwanese, while Okinawa has coral reefs.

In spite of the wealth of scenic and historic attractions throughout the whole of Japan, tourism is concentrated in the three regions in the centre of the country (Tokyo, the Japanese Alps and Kansai). The 'golden route' followed by most tourists includes Tokyo and Kamakura, the Japanese Alps, Fuju-Hakone-Izu, and finally Kyoto and Nara. The Japanese government wishes to spread tourism into the less heavily used regions through its 'New Sites of Discovery' promotional programme. It is thought that this may succeed with the Asian and repeat visitors, but long-haul travellers from Europe and the USA will probably stick to the 'Golden Route' due to time and money constraints. However, transport around the country is good: Japan has one of the best rail networks in the world and is famous for its 'Bullet' trains. Urban public transport is good but crowded.

On the other hand there is a severe shortage of both domestic and international airport capacity. The two main airports (Narita for Tokyo, and Osaka for Kansai) are limited by runway capacity and curfews on night flying. This is a major constraint on the continued rapid growth of both inbound and outbound tourism, as the vast majority (76.66 per cent) of tourists pass through these two gateways.

Inbound tourism

In the past, tourism into Japan was dominated by the US market. North America contributed 25–30 per cent of all Japan's tourists up to the late 1980s. Inbound tourism was inhibited by the strength of the yen (making it a relatively expensive destination) and a lack of local markets. Arrivals reached only 2 million in 1984 and the sharp appreciation of the yen in 1985/6 led to an 11 per cent drop in arrivals in 1986. However, the growing economic strength of the newly industrialised countries of South East and East Asia and the region's lack of major involvement in the Gulf War of 1991 meant that Japan's inbound tourism has continued to grow (albeit at a reduced rate) into the 1990s. The total reached 3.58 million in 1992. Asian visitors now make up two-thirds of Japan's tourists and the United States has been replaced by South Korea and Taiwan as Japan's main markets (*see* Fig 36.4). The relaxation of constraints on travel by South Koreans (*see* page 459) has created a new market for Japan.

Travel to Japan from most Asian countries, the US and Australia is mainly for holidays rather than for business purposes, while the long-haul European travel market is still dominated by business travel. There is a fairly even flow of

	Total (000s)	%	Pleasure/Tourist			Business		
				Total (000s)	%		Total (000s)	%
South Korea	864.1	24.1	Taiwan	622.7	29.6	South Korea	266.3	28.5
Taiwan	715.5	19.97	South Korea	502.9	23.9	USA	199.7	21.4
USA	560.9	15.66	USA	298.0	14.17	Taiwan	60.1	6.4
China	183.2	5.11	Hong Kong	136.0	6.46	UK	53.0	5.7
Hong Kong	177.7	4.96	Thailand	58.6	2.78	China	48.6	5.2
Philippines	105.2	2.94	Canada	43.7	2.07	Germany	29.4	3.14
UK	104.4	2.91	Brazil	36.3	1.73	Hong Kong	3.06	28.6
Thailand	97.2	2.71	UK	35.9	1.70	Thailand	2.47	23.1
Total	**3 581 540**			**2 103 046**			**934 508**	

Fig. 36.4 Japan inbound: visitor arrivals 1992
(*Source*: Japan National Tourist Organisation)

visitors through the year, but with a slight peak in October. This is partly due to the fact that Japan is a cultural (rather than climate and beach) destination and it also attracts a fairly high proportion of business tourists.

CHINA

China has a vastly larger population than Japan but its economic and political circumstances have inhibited the development of its tourist industry until very recently. In contrast to Japan, its major role has been as a tourist destination.

With 27.46 million tourist arrivals in 1990, China is the major destination in the Pacific in purely statistical terms. However, the vast majority of these (25.6m in 1990) were ethnic Chinese (categorised by China as 'compatriots') originating from Hong Kong, Macao and Taiwan. Only 1.7 million of the inbound tourists were 'foreigners', mainly visitors from Japan, USA, the Commonwealth of Independent States (CIS), UK etc. The explanation of these travel patterns lies in China's political history and its current relationships with Hong Kong, Macao and Taiwan. Although China has the oldest civilisation in the world (*see* Chapter 5), its 'modern' history dates from 1840 with the opium wars with Britain and other European powers. Hong Kong island was ceded to Britain in 1842 and developed as a trading base, while the Kowloon Peninsula was acquired by Britain in 1860. Additional land on China's mainland (the Hong Kong 'New Territories') was leased to Britain by China on a 99-year lease in 1898. Macau was established as a Portuguese colony in the same era. China's political development in the first half of the 20th century was characterised by political instability, culminating in civil war after the end of the Second World War. The communists won and become established (as the People's Republic of China) on the mainland from 1949, while the defeated Chinese Nationalists and their supporters fled to Taiwan and established their own government there (as the Republic of China): most international governments chose to recognise Taiwan's government as the legitimate Chinese government at the time. Thus, the mainland Chinese still perceive Hong Kong and Taiwan to be more a part of China than separate territories. However these events, plus increasingly strained relations between the Chinese and Russian Communists, led to the People's Republic of China being completely politically isolated from most of the world from the 1960s to the late 1970s. Travel into and out of China virtually ceased. The attitude of the Chinese government began to change in the 1970s, with the need for economic and political reform within the country.

In 1978, China, after years of isolation from the rest of the world, adopted an 'open door' policy. This encompassed both the modernisation of China's economy as well as its opening up to western travellers. One of the main incentives for China to promote tourism after 1978 appears to have been the country's need for foreign currency. In spite of teething troubles resulting from the lack of tourist infrastructure and experience, the number of non-Chinese visitors grew very rapidly in the 1980s to 1.8 million in 1988. These were essentially cultural and special interest tourists. The modernisation programme for the economy (with a move away from a centrally-planned economy towards a market economy) brought rapid growth in the GNP (up 11 per cent in the year 1987/8) but also 30 per cent inflation.

Along with economic development, the period 1978–88 brought significant political changes, both within China and between China and its neighbours. In 1984, Britain and China agreed that on 1st July 1997 (when the lease on the Hong Kong 'New Territories' runs out), not only the leased territory but also the whole colony will be handed back to China. Since then closer economic links have been developing between Hong Kong and adjacent regions of mainland China. As China began to be integrated into the world's political and economic system, international support for Taiwan waned, but relationships between China and Taiwan have gradually improved. Travel between them was still not possible up to 1987 but now Taiwan allows its people to visit friends and relatives in China although there is still no direct connection between them and Taiwanese travel to China via Hong Kong. Mainland Chinese are still not allowed to travel to Taiwan. However, the most profound effects of the 'open door' policy were felt inside China. The 'open door' policy and greater contacts with the west brought demands from China's students for greater democracy. In 1989 the regime reacted violently to quell these demands with protestors being killed in Tiananmen Square on 4 June 1989.

Western tourists (particularly Australasian and American) responded by staying away and tour operators withdrew. The Chinese are, however, keen to see tourists return and the UK and European market has begun to recover, although it inevitably takes time for confidence to return. Travel by the Japanese and other Asians to China was not so drastically affected. The way in which China approaches and solves its domestic economic and political problems will no doubt be reflected in the extent to which foreign tourism is encouraged or constrained. The internal economic and political reforms were also beginning to generate a domestic tourist market. By 1987 there were 290 million domestic tourists. The extent to which China becomes an international tourist generator and destination entirely depends on its political evolution. With such immensely varied resources and such a huge population it could radically alter the patterns of tourism in East Asia and, indeed, the Pacific region as a whole.

Current patterns of tourism into China

'Compatriot' travel

It has been noted that the vast majority of visitors to China are ethnic Chinese from Taiwan, Macao and Hong Kong (i.e. 'compatriots') (*see* Fig 36.5) and most of them travel into China via Hong Kong. Departures from Taiwan to Hong Kong jumped from 195 000 in 1987 to 1.245 million in 1990: it can be assumed that a high proportion of these travel on into China. China's National Travel Administration estimated 1 million Taiwanese entered the country in 1990. However, total crossings from Hong Kong to China in 1990 were around 20 million. Hong Kong had a population of only 5.8 million in 1990. Thus the majority of the travel into China by 'compatriots' must be frequent travel by Hong Kong residents across the border, to visit friends and relatives, for business purposes and even some daily commuting to work in China. This is, therefore, all but domestic travel.

'Foreign' tourism into China

The opening up of China in 1978 led to an immediate response from foreign tourists – inbound tourism grew to over half-a-million within two years. The mid-1980s saw a second spurt of rapid growth (after the recession of early 1980s) but the

Year	Foreigners	Percentage change	'Compatriots'	Percentage change
1978	0.229		1.561	
1979	0.362	57.8	3.820	144.7
1980	0.529	46.0	5.138	34.5
1981	0.675	27.6	7.053	37.2
1982	0.764	13.2	7.117	0.9
1983	0.872	14.1	8.564	20.3
1984	1.134	30.0	11.670	36.3
1985	1.370	20.8	16.377	40.3
1986	1.482	8.2	21.267	29.9
1987	1.767	16.6	25.087	18.0
1988	1.840	6.6	29.773	18.7
1989	1.460	−20.6	22.971	−22.8
1990	1.747	19.6	25.623	11.5
1991	2.710	55.1		
1992	4.006	47.8		

Fig. 36.5 Visitor arrivals in PR China (millions)
(*Source*: Yearbook of China Tourism Statistics/WTO)

	Ranking market (numbers of tourists in thousands)			
	1st	*2nd*	*3rd*	*4th*
1980	Japan (169.3)	USA (101.5)	UK (28.5)	Australia (28.5)
1985	Japan (470.4)	USA (239.5)	Australia (78.2)	UK (71.2)
1990	Japan (463.2)	USA (233.1)	USSR (109.8)	UK (78.9)

Fig. 36.6 China inbound: main markets
(*Source*: Yearbook of China Tourism Statistics)

rate of increase had appeared to slow down a little, even before the events of 1989, possibly due to overseas perception of poor management and congested transport infrastructure. The main market between 1979 and 1988 was Japan, followed by USA, with UK and Australia in 3rd or 4th place. In 1989 the USSR replaced Australia to become China's third most important foreign market (*see* Fig 36.6).

The expansion of the USSR market again has its origin in political change. China and Russia were political enemies since 1960, but the policy of *glasnost* and *perestroika* began in USSR in 1985 culminating with agreements between China and USSR to open borders for trade and commercial business. It is thought that the cross-border trading in the far north east of China accounts for most of this increase in travel between the Soviet Union and China. For the Japanese and western tourists China is predominantly a cultural tourism destination. The cities and historic sites are the main attractions, though China is promoting its festivals and landscapes. The number of areas open to foreigners has steadily increased from 122 cities in 1982 to 274 by 1986 and over 500 in 1990. Potential tourist resources are scattered far and wide throughout such a huge country (*see* Fig 36.1). The main historic attractions are located in the north east and central provinces (where the most ancient civilisations of China began, *see* Chapter 5). The southern and coastal provinces have many beautiful cities and landscape resources.

The main tourist destinations

Beijing and its region

Beijing is a city of over 6 million. At its centre lies the rectangular Imperial Palace Museum (the Forbidden City) which was built between 1406

and 1420 and was the residence of the Ming and Quing Emperors from 1644–1911. It covers 72 hectares, with about 800 buildings and over 9000 rooms. Tiananmen Square is just to the south of the Palace. This is the largest public square in the world. It contains monuments (e.g. the tomb of Mao) and is surrounded by museums, parks and the zoo (home of the famous giant pandas). Other historical attractions close by include the Temple of Heaven (in South Beijing) – China's largest temple and altar complex, and the Summer Palace complex of gardens, lakes, pagodas, courtyards and temples (10 km north-west of Beijing City).

Forty kilometres further out to the north west are the Ming Tombs (the burial place of 13 Ming Emperors) approached along a road lined with statues of men and animals. Several parts of the Great Wall of China are accessible from Beijing. The wall was begun in the period between 770–221 BC, and parts were repaired and rebuilt by succeeding generations. It stretches 6350 km east to west: the section at Badaling is 75 km north of Beijing, where it is very well preserved, with repair and rebuilding work dating from 1368–1644.

Beijing has bitterly cold but dry winters (with daily maximum temperatures only just above freezing between December and February), while summers are wetter and hot (maximum up to 30°C in June to August) with a peak of over 200 mm rainfall in July. Beijing is China's most important city for foreign tourists with 864 800 foreign visitor arrivals in 1989.

Central China

The historical city of Xi'an (the capital of 11 dynasties) is the main attraction of central China. The very well preserved city walls and moat date from the Ming dynasty and were built 1374–1378 AD. The city is the site of the tomb of Emperor Qin Shihuang (the first emperor to have united China). The terracotta army of 6000 life size warriors and horses, bronze chariots, soldiers and kneeling archers was buried with him and was only excavated in 1974. It now forms the centre piece of tourism in Xi'an, although there are many other historic buildings nearby, including the Big Wild Goose Pagoda, a seven-storey construction dating from 648 AD, the Famen Temple, and the Banpo Neolithic village museum. The Longmen caves at Luoyang (over 300 km to the east of Xi'an) contain inscriptions, pagodas and at least 100 000 Buddhas dating back to 494 AD. Xi'an has its own airport and 288 900 foreign visitors made the trip to Xi'an in 1988.

Southern half of China

This region is within the humid subtropical zone of China, with a warmer but wetter climate. Most tourism occurs on and near the coast, centred around Shanghai and Guangzhou, but there are many scenic attractions inland that the Chinese government is promoting.

1 Inland attractions. The Yangtze River flows west–east from its source near the Tibetan border, to Shanghai. It cuts through the Wushan mountains in a series of narrow deep gorges before it reaches the lowlands of south west China. The most dramatic scenery is along the Three Gorges (the Qutang, Wuxia and Xiling gorges) which run for 193 km between Fengjie and Yichang. River cruises take tourists along this stretch of the Yangtze. South of the Yangtze, there are several scenic mountain regions that the Chinese government is promoting including Wulingyuan, Huangshan, Wuyi and Guilin. Huangshan has been listed as a world heritage site, but Guilin has become most popular with foreign visitors (300 500 foreign visitor arrivals in 1988). It is a limestone region with a strange landscape of high hummocky topped mountains rising steeply out of flat rice fields among the rivers, with many caves.

2 The coast. The two main centres of tourism along the southern half of China's coast are Shanghai and Guangzhou (formerly Canton).

Shanghai is China's biggest city and is the centre of China's trade and industry but it also has many temples, pagodas and gardens and river trips can be taken on the Yangtze delta. It attracted 664 300 visitors in 1988. Nearby are the historic towns of Nanjing and Suzhou. Nanjing is a former capital of China and has many temples, tombs and museums. Suzhou is one of China's oldest cities and has many beautiful gardens, waterways and silk mills. Hangzhou is a centre for silk production but is also a famed beauty spot, particularly the Westlake region. Each of these three centres attracted over 120 000 foreign tourists in 1988. The climate here is humid, subtropical with cool winters and hot summers (maximum over 30°C in July and August) with rain all year round, though the summer months are wettest. Guangzhou is the other main centre of inbound tourism, with 479 400 foreign visitors, but it also receives millions of 'compatriot' Chinese visitors from nearby Hong Kong. The climate here is genuinely subtropical, with temperatures above 20°C from March to November and heavy rainfall (over 300 mm per month) from May to August. The typhoon season runs from July to September.

Developments in China's tourism

In the mid-1980s a shortage of hotel capacity appeared to be the factor limiting tourist growth in China. This was remedied by the rapid development of new 3- to 5-star hotels, many joint ventures (i.e. with some foreign involvement in their financing). With the decrease in foreign visitors coinciding with the opening of these new hotels (planned in the mid-to-late 1980s) there is now a major problem of hotel overcapacity, particularly in Beijing, Shanghai and Xi'an. Many hotels were in financial difficulty in the early 1990s: they are in the wrong locations and wrong price range to take advantage of the growing 'compatriot' tourist market that has sustained China's tourism since 1989.

A further difficulty concerns China's transport infrastructure – new airport developments lagged behind hotel construction. The rail system is very congested with domestic travel and the road system is poor and generally not used by foreign tour groups unless there is no other form of transport available. Between 1983 and 1989 tourism contributed between 4 and 5 per cent of China's foreign exchange earnings, and China's leaders still view tourism as an important element of its economic policy. It remains to be seen how long it takes for the western tourists' image of China both politically and as a tourist destination to change.

HONG KONG AND MACAO

Hong Kong is a tiny British colonial territory of only 1074 km^2 but with a population of 5.86 million (1991); it is densely populated and highly urbanised. It consists of Hong Kong island, plus 235 other islands and a portion of the Chinese mainland known as the Kowloon peninsula and the New Territories. Its history and future are very closely bound up with China's policies and politics (*see* page 452), as the whole colony is due to be handed back to become a part of China in 1997. Hong Kong has been developed during the last 100 years into a major world (and Pacific region) trading, commercial and business centre and port, as well as a major tourist destination. It functions as the major gateway for tourists into South China, as a destination in its own right and as a stopover destination for long-haul Europe–Australia routes and round-the-world trips. Tourism is Hong Kong's third largest earner of foreign exchange.

A political change as profound as that due in 1997 is bound to influence Hong Kong's economic and tourist functions, while the inevitable internal political instability and uncertainty within the colony in the years running up to 1997 may also have some effect on tourism. It is assumed that China, in its own economic self-interest, will wish to maintain Hong Kong's economic role and it has agreed to preserve Hong Kong's current economic system for at least 50 years, but there will inevitably be a difficult period of transition; continued economic growth depends on business confidence in the political system. A sign of the apprehension amongst the residents of the colony (brought on by the events in China in 1989) can be seen in the emigration statistics: since 1987, emigration has doubled from 30 000 per annum to over 50 000. Those who are leaving Hong Kong are more likely to be young (25–44-year-olds), have a University degree, and be professionals or executives. The implications of this 'brain drain'

for the colony's industries (including the tourist industry) are serious (*see* Hueng, 1993). The outbound tourist statistics for 1989–90 also indicate dramatic increases (of 87 to 136 per cent) in Hong Kong residents travelling to other countries such as Singapore, Canada and Australia. This increase is thought to be due to 'look–see' travel, i.e. visits by Hong Kong residents to assess migration possibilities and to make overseas investments in preparation for 1997.

Hong Kong is one of the more affluent parts of the Pacific, with a GDP per head of US $ 13 400 in 1991. Hong Kong's prosperity is currently based on manufacturing (textiles, electronics, toys), financial services, shipping and tourism. It has enjoyed the sustained growth typical of many of the 'newly industrialised countries' (or 'tiger economies') of the Pacific region, with growth rates well above world averages through the 1980s. Even in 1991 its GDP grew more than 3 per cent. It is well integrated into the Asian economic system, being a location for Japanese investment and as a source of investment in countries such as Indonesia, Taiwan, Philippines, and so on. But in the run up to 1997 its economic links with China are increasing. Hong Kong has made major investments in the adjacent Guangdong province of China, with trade, manufacturing and transport links being strengthened. In consequence travel between Hong Kong residents and Guangdong is very high. The pattern of Hong Kong's inbound tourism has changed as China's internal politics and its political relationships with neighbouring countries have altered. Hong Kong's touristic role has always been twofold: as a destination in its own right and as an entry point into China. Good road and rail links exist between Hong Kong and Guangzhou, and scheduled flights are available from Hong Kong to over 10 Chinese cities. Before the Tiananmen Square events, 28 per cent of all Hong Kong's arrivals went on into China. After 1989, only 13 per cent of Hong Kong's leisure visitors made the trip over the border. On the other hand, Taiwan's improving relations with China (*see* page 452) has led to a massive increase in Taiwanese visitors to Hong Kong (from 354 195 in 1987 to 1 344 641 in 1990) and two-thirds of all these visitors travel on into China. If diplomatic relations between Taiwan and China continue to improve, the Taiwanese may be allowed direct entry into China (rather than via a third country such as Hong Kong, as at present). Such changes might lead to just as rapid a decline of Taiwanese tourists into Hong Kong in future. Hong Kong's other major markets (which visit the colony as a destination in its own right) are dominated by Japan, followed by USA and Canada, Australia and New Zealand, UK, followed by a group of Asian countries (*see* Fig 36.7). Its climate is humid and tropical; it is on the border of monsoon Asia, so it has very hot, humid, wet summers (*see* climate of Guangzhou), and a typhoon season from July–September. Winter days are mild and drier but temperatures can drop to around 12°C at night. However, tourism is not particularly influenced by the weather and arrivals are spread fairly evenly through the year, with October being slightly more popular.

The scenery of the islands off Hong Kong is very attractive, but being such a small and intensively developed urban area, Hong Kong's main tourist appeal lies in its manmade facilities and living culture. Tours of the New Territories take only six hours. Because of the very intense development pressure, most of Hong Kong's traditional Chinese and colonial buildings have been demolished, although there are some splendid Chinese temples and monasteries left. Tourism is predominantly based on the shopping, nightlife, Chinese cultural events (theatre, opera etc.), sport (particularly horse racing), theme parks (such as the re-creation of the 1000-year-old Sung dynasty village, and the Ocean Park Oceanarium), and special events such as festivals (e.g. June's Dragon Boat Festival, the Chinese New Year and Spring Lantern Festival). Hong Kong is also actively promoting itself as an exhibition and conference

| | Visitor arrivals | |
	Numbers	%
Taiwan	1 625 231	23.3
Japan	1 311 884	18.8
USA and Canada	842 795	12.1
UK	348 739	5.0
Thailand	313 192	4.5
Australia and New Zealand	290 393	4.2
Singapore	253 110	3.6
Malaysia	244 263	3.5
Philippines	229 286	3.3
South Korea	201 386	2.9
Germany	174 950	2.5
TOTAL	6 986 163	

Fig. 36.7 Hong Kong inbound, 1992
(*Source*: Hong Kong Tourist Association)

centre: 18–29 per cent of western visitors were business or conference travellers in 1990 (*see* Fig 36.8). Hong Kong's size and range of attractions mean that visitors tend to stay only a few days, even the single destination pleasure travellers.

Hong Kong outbound

It has been noted that there is massive cross-border day-to-day travel between Hong Kong and China and Macao (20 million to China, 5 million to Macau in 1990). Hong Kong's role as a generator of tourism to other Asian countries has gradually grown from 1 million in 1981 to 2.04 million in 1990. Figure 36.9 shows the main destinations. Most travel is relatively short-haul to nearby countries – the pattern typical of a newly developing

| | Purpose of visit – % of visitors | | | | Average length of stay (days) |
	Vacation	VFR	Business	En route	
Taiwan	37	3	15	42	2.2
Japan	73	1	23	2	2.9
USA/Canada	51	3	29	14	3.9
W Europe	61	2	29	6	4.1
Australia/NZ	66	3	18	9	4.8
SE Asia	55	7	29	8	4.0

Fig. 36.8 Hong Kong inbound: purpose of visit and length of stay, 1990
(*Source*: Hong Kong Tourist Association)

outbound market. Thailand is a mainly holiday destination (with 90 per cent of Hong Kong travellers going for holiday purposes), while there are significant flows of business tourists from Hong Kong to the Philippines, Indonesia, Singapore and Japan (51, 26, 21 and 20 per cent of Hong Kong visitors respectively).

	Number (000s)
Thailand	316.6
Japan	291.7
Taiwan	270.9
Singapore	195.9
Philippines	166.4
USA	151.8
South Korea	124.7
UK	121.0
Other	N/A
TOTAL	2.232 million

Fig. 36.9 Hong Kong outbound, 1992
(*Source*: Hong Kong Tourist Association)

Macao is a tiny Portuguese colony (of 16.92 km^2) near Hong Kong, located at the mouth of the Pearl River. Most of its visitors arrive by jetfoil from Hong Kong, a journey of about 55 minutes. Nearly half visit on vacation, but 19.6 per cent of the visitors said they came for the gambling in the casinos. A total of 7.85 million visitors made the trip to Macao in 1992 (78.7 per cent of them came from Hong Kong).

TAIWAN (REPUBLIC OF CHINA)

This small island of 36 000 km^2 (halfway in size between Belgium and the Netherlands) has a population of 20.2 million (1990). Taiwan's role as a tourist destination and generator of outbound tourism has been controlled by its political history and current political status. The civil war on mainland China ended in 1949 with the retreat of the defeated Chiang-Kai-Shek to Taiwan with his supporters. The non-Communist government on Taiwan still claimed to be the legitimate government of the whole of China, Tibet and Mongolia, in spite of the establishment of the Communist

People's Republic of China on the mainland. The People's Republic of China also maintained territorial claims over Taiwan. Thus, the two rival governments remained hostile to each other for many years and travel between the two was prohibited by both governments. There is also no direct postal contact, no direct air services and no direct trade between them. Taiwan received the support of the USA until the 1970s when US relations with People's Republic of China began to improve and Communist China began to be accepted internationally. This left Taiwan diplomatically isolated, as other countries felt contacts with Taiwan would offend China. A new generation of younger Taiwan politicians in Taiwan have made moves to ease the tension between China and Taiwan by unilaterally abolishing the provisions calling for active resistance to the Communist regime in 1991. This has eased diplomatic relations between Taiwan and some of its other neighbours too. Alongside these developments, the Taiwan government has gradually lifted some of its controls on overseas travel by its own population. In 1987 Taiwanese were allowed to travel to PR China to visit friends and relatives (15 per cent of Taiwan's population originated from the mainland and moved to Taiwan in 1949), although 'leisure' travel to PR China is still not officially allowed and citizens of PR China are not allowed entry into Taiwan (except a very small number by special permit). The result of these changes has been a growth of direct international flights between Taiwan and some of its neighbours and a huge increase of outbound travel by Taiwanese to China via Hong Kong (as direct flights between Taiwan and PR China were still under negotiation in September 1992. There is a strong, pent-up demand for travel among the Taiwanese. The economy developed strongly, due to rapid industrialisation: its low overheads and low labour costs made it very competitive in world terms, and it now has one of the highest standards of living in East Asia with GDP per head of US $ 7896 in 1990. Economic growth slowed down in the early 1990s, but outbound tourism continues to grow. Taiwan's tourist role is thus as an increasingly significant generator of outbound travel (growing from 2.107 million in 1989 to a total of 4.21 million in 1992, an annual growth rate of 25 per cent) and as a destination for

Number of departures (000s)		
	1990	*1992*
Hong Kong	1245.8	1747.4
Japan	591.5	748.1
Thailand	356.0	359.8
USA	239.3	286.9
S Korea	221.5	302.1
Singapore	96.6	220.3
Malaysia		136.2
Others	–	–
TOTAL	2942.2	4214.7

Fig. 36.10 Taiwan outbound tourists 1990–92, main destinations
(*Source*: Taiwan Tourist Bureau)

Number of arrivals (foreign visitors and overseas Chinese) (000s)		
	1990	*1992*
Japan	917.2	799.8
USA	224.9	259.1
Hong Kong	193.5	193.5
S Korea	150.5	157.6
Singapore	59.4	56.5
Malaysia	49.4	51.7
Others	N/A	N/A
TOTAL		1873.327

Fig. 36.11 Taiwan inbound tourism, 1990–92
(*Source*: Taiwan Tourist Bureau)

the East Asian and Pacific region's tourists, for pleasure purposes and increasingly for business tourism – *see* Figs 36.10 and 36.11. Very few western tourists visit Taiwan.

Taiwan's tourist attractions

The island's historic resources are no match to those of mainland China for the western tourist. The island's appeal for Pacific region visitors is mainly its landscape, coast and manmade attractions (e.g. Taipei Zoo, Taiwan film studios and amusement parks). The main landscape resources (e.g. Sun Moon Lake and Taroko Gorge) are located in the mountains of central Taiwan, while good beaches and fine coastal scenery are found

on the north of the island. The climate is subtropical with hot wet summers. There are no significant high or low seasons, although the winters are cooler and less sunny, tourism is spread evenly through the year.

SOUTH KOREA

South Korea (along with Hong Kong, Taiwan and Singapore) is one of the thriving capitalist economies of the Pacific region which have grown in economic strength throughout the 1970s and 1980s. Its economic development has been based on heavy industry (steel and shipbuilding and overseas construction), as well as electronics. But tourism (both inbound and outbound) is a relatively recent development, with major growth dating from 1988 and 1989. Once again, changing economic and political policies paved the way and led to the increase in tourism activity in the late 1980s, even though the overall level of tourism is still quite small in world terms with just two million departures and 3.2 million arrivals in 1992.

Political history

Korea was divided into the Communist Democratic People's Republic of North Korea and the Republic of Korea (i.e. South Korea) in 1948 after the Second World War. Travel between the two is still not possible and relations between them remain strained. South Korea was governed by a series of repressive dictatorships, and martial law existed until 1981. This, combined with tough economic policies, severely limited travel into and out of the country although inbound tourism had been promoted as part of the country's economic development plan since 1962. Political reform slowly developed until multiple party elections were held in 1988. The coincidence of this political change with the holding of the Olympic Games in Seoul led to a 25 per cent increase in tourist arrivals that year. Meanwhile the economy had improved enough and the political environment had changed sufficiently for the restrictions on South Korean outbound travel to be gradually reduced. The removal of most restrictions led to a dramatic 67 per cent increase in overseas travel by South Koreans in 1989. While both numbers of outbound tourists and expenditure per head continue to grow, inbound tourism appears to have slowed its rate of growth while expenditure per head has declined. This had led to an increasing tourism deficit (*see* Fig 36.12) which prompted the government to try to reduce expenditure on outbound tourism with a 'frugality' campaign (although only 35 per cent of outbound travel was classified as pleasure travel).

Year	Tourist arrivals (000s)	Tourist departures (000s)	Tourism balance in US $ millions
1985	1426	484	178
1986	1660	455	937
1987	1874	510	1595
1988	2340	725	1911
1989	2781	1213	955
1990	2958	1560	393
1991	3196	1856	–357
1992	3231	2043	–522

Fig. 36.12 South Korean tourism
(*Source*: Korean National Tourist Corporation)

Patterns of travel into and out of South Korea

The biggest tourist flows in both directions are between South Korea and Japan. In 1992, 43 per cent of South Korea's arrivals were from Japan, while 44 per cent of the outbound travellers were destined for Japan. The Japanese tourists came mainly for holiday trips, while Korean travel to Japan was more or less evenly divided between pleasure, business and visiting friends and relatives (VFR) travel. The USA is the second most important market (again for both inbound and outbound travel) but much of this travel is for business or VFR purposes rather than holiday making (*see* Fig 36.13).

South Korea's main attractions to inbound tourists include the two main cities (Seoul and Pusan). Its main historic attraction is Kyongju, the capital of the Shilla Dynasty from 57 BC to 935 AD. Unesco designated the site as one of the ten most important historic cities of the world. The unspoilt Cheju Island is a semi-tropical resort island with dramatic mountain scenery and good beaches. It is a major Japanese honeymoon destination (with direct flights and ferry connections to Japan).

CONCLUSIONS

Tourism in the region is primarily dependent on the health of the Japanese economy. However, political change is continuing in the region and this too will no doubt cause further changes in the geographical pattern of travel flows within the region.

	Visitor arrivals in South Korea from each country (%)	Visitor departures from South Korea to each country (%)
Japan	43.4	44.1
USA	10.3	17.1
Taiwan	9.2	6.2
Philippines	3.6	–
Hong Kong	2.9	6.8
Thailand	1.8	5.8
Singapore	1.0	2.8
Others	N/A	N/A
	100 %	100 %
	Total number of arrivals = 3.231 million	Total number of departures = 2.043 million

Fig. 36.13 In- and outbound tourism: South Korea, 1992
(*Source*: Korean National Tourist Corporation)

REFERENCES AND FURTHER READING

Those texts marked with an asterisk are particularly recommended for further reading.

Japan

Bywater, M (1990) 'Japanese investment in South Pacific
tourism', *Travel and Tourism Analyst*, No. 3, EIU, pp.
51–64.

Dutton, I M (1991) 'Leisure in Japan', *Australian Journal of
Leisure and Recreation*, Vol. 1, No. 3, pp. 23–32.

*Mackie, V (1992) 'Japan and South-East Asia: the inter-
national division of labour and leisure', in Harrison,
D (Ed) *Tourism and the Less Developed Countries*,
Belhaven.

*Morris, S (1988) 'Japanese leisure patterns', *Travel and
Tourism Analyst*, No. 5, pp. 32–53.

*Morris, S (1992) 'Japan', *EIU International Tourism
Reports*, No. 4, pp. 5–35.

*Morris, S (1994) 'Japan outbound', *Travel and Tourism
Analyst*, No. 1, pp. 40–63.

China

*Economist Intelligence Unit (1990) 'China', *EIU
International Tourism Reports*, No. 3, pp. 22–48.

*Tisdell, C and Wen, J (1991) 'Foreign tourism as an ele-
ment in PR China's economic development', *Tourism
Management*, Vol. 12, March, pp. 55–67.

Yu, L (1992) 'Emerging markets for China's tourism
industry', *Journal of Travel Research*, Vol. 31, No. 1
(Summer), pp. 10–13.

Hong Kong and Taiwan

*Bailey, M (1992) 'Hong Kong and Taiwan outbound',
Travel and Tourism Analyst, No. 1, pp. 55–75.

*Bailey, M (1991) 'Taiwan', *International Tourism Reports*,
No. 4, pp. 73–93.

*Guangrui, Z (1993) 'Tourism crosses the Taiwan Straits',
Tourism Management, Vol. 14, No. 3, pp. 228–31.

Heung, V (1993) 'Hong Kong', in Baum T (Ed) *Human
Resource Issues in International Tourism*, Butterworth-
Heinemann, pp. 161–75.

*Hunt, J (1992) 'Hong Kong', *International Tourism
Reports*, No. 1, pp. 5–31.

South Korea

*McGahey, S (1990) 'South Korea', *International Tourism
Reports*, No. 2.

*McGahey, S (1991) 'South Korea outbound', *Travel and
Tourism Analyst*, No. 6, pp. 45–62.

QUESTIONS AND DISCUSSION POINTS

1 Explain the tourist role of Hong Kong.

2 How has the changing political relationship
between China and Taiwan affected the pattern
of tourism in East Asia?

3 To what extent does tourism in East Asia depend
on the health of the Japanese economy?

ASSIGNMENT

You are an employee in a tourism consultancy. The
firm has been commissioned to advise a company on
the long-term viability of developing European
tourism in China and Hong Kong. As part of this con-
tract you have been asked to prepare a brief report
outlining the background to the political situation
including the relations between China and Hong
Kong: if possible include an update on current developments, with reference to reports in the quality
press and magazines such as the *Economist*. Outline
at least two scenarios of how the political situation
might develop in the future and how this could affect
the prospects for tourism in the two countries.

CHAPTER 37

South East Asia

LEARNING OBJECTIVES

After reading this chapter you should be able to

- assess the tourist potential of the climatic, landscape and wildlife, historic and cultural resources of the region
- distinguish between the regional distribution of these resources and their development and use for tourism
- demonstrate a knowledge of the main tourist resorts and tourist centres
- be aware of the political constraints on the development of tourism in the region
- assess the role and impact of special interest tourism (particularly ethnic tourism) in the region.

INTRODUCTION

South East Asia forms a quadrant of the 'Pacific Rim'. In common with the rest of the Pacific region, tourism is growing rapidly from 8.3 million arrivals in 1980, to nearly 20 million by 1991. However, the eight countries of the region (*see* Fig 37.1) show distinctly different patterns of tourism, due partly to their differing physical character and partly to their political history. Malaysia, Singapore and Indonesia lie on, or within, 8° north or south of the Equator and have very hot and humid equatorial climates (*see* Chapter 2) which are generally not conducive to energetic outdoor activity.

Indonesia is the largest country of the region and it is a mainly Muslim country but has 366 different ethnic groups and has chosen to promote some of these unusual cultures and tribes specifically for ethnic and cultural tourism (e.g. Bali, Tana Toraja). The tiny island of Singapore, on the other hand, is an ultra-modern, western-style business and communication centre and its tourism is mainly short stay business and stopover holiday tourism. Indonesia and Singapore are thus important world destinations, with over 50 per cent of their visitors originating from outside Asia.

Malaysia, on the other hand, receives most of its visitors from Asia (predominantly from Singapore, Thailand and Japan). There is a particularly strong two-way flow of tourists between Singapore and Malaysia across the relatively unrestricted border.

The remaining countries of the region, the Philippines and the 'mainland' countries of Laos, Vietnam, Cambodia and Thailand, are located between 8° north and the Tropic of Cancer. They have tropical monsoon climates which, although hot all year round, have a slightly cooler and distinct dry winter season from November to March, with lower humidities. They have a wealth of landscape, cultural and coastal resources, but their differing political histories give them very different patterns of tourism. The Philippines were an American colony between 1898 and 1946 and were occupied by the Japanese during World War Two; in the past the country has depended heavily on the USA (and now the Japanese) markets as a source of inbound tourists for beach, sport and sex tourism, but internal political instability is just one factor that has inhibited the expansion of tourism to the Philippines in the last decade. Laos, Vietnam and Cambodia are also

Fig. 37.1 South East Asia

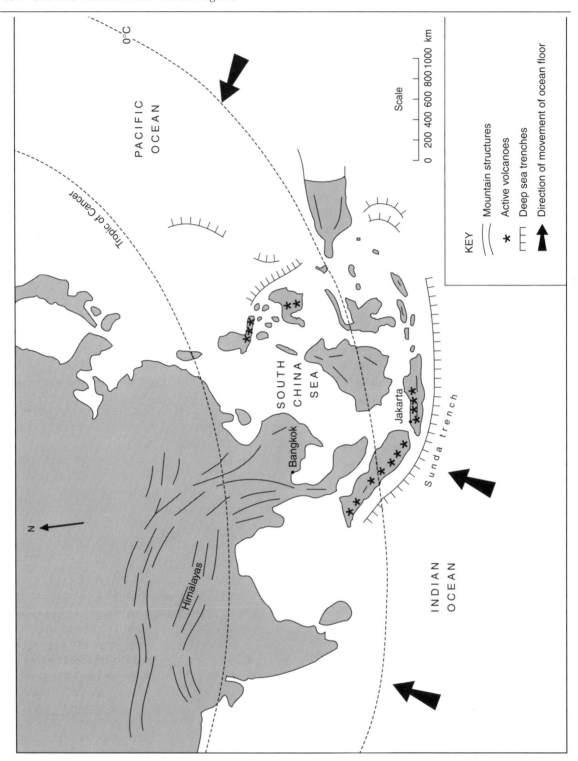

Fig. 37.2 Structure of South East Asia

countries emerging from political upheavals. Tourism is still in its infancy here as these countries try to create a new image after the end of the long, drawn-out Vietnam war. In contrast, Thailand has been independent and relatively stable politically for a long period and it has built up a varied portfolio of tourist attractions, including beach, sex, historic, cultural and ethnic tourism. As a result it draws very substantial proportions of its tourists from outside the immediate South East Asian region.

THE PHYSICAL CHARACTER OF THE REGION

The backbone of the countries of SE Asia is made up of a series of mountain ridges that run north west to south east through mainland SE Asia. They run from the Thailand highlands and then split into two: the Thai–Myanmar border follows the western branch and the Laos–Vietnam border runs along the crest of the eastern branch. The ridges then swing around to run roughly west–east to form the islands of Indonesia (*see* Fig 37.2). These mountain ridges are the eastern-most end of the series of ranges that run west–east through southern Europe and Asia (e.g. the Alps, the Himalayas), which were formed when the northward drifting continents of Africa, India and Australia were pushing up against the mainland mass of Asia. The floor of the Indian Ocean is being pushed under the continental land mass, creating the deep sea trench (the Sunda trench) off the southern coasts of the main Indonesian islands. These slow but inexorable earth movements cause some instability in the earth's crust: most of the region is subject to earthquakes and there is a string of 300 volcanoes in Indonesia, along the line of the Sunda trench (*see* Fig 37.2). One hundred and twenty eight of these are still active. To the north east of the region the Pacific Ocean floor is also creeping towards mainland Asia and is similarly being forced under the continental landmass. Here, too, there is a line of deep sea trenches, running north–south along the eastern edge of the Philippines (and extending north along the Mariana Islands, Japan and the Kuril Islands) and a line of active volcanoes. Mount Pinatubo in the Philippines has produced the most dramatic eruptions in the early 1990s.

It has been noted that the region falls into two climatic zones: the equatorial and the tropical monsoon zones.

1 The equatorial zone: most of Indonesia lies just south of the Equator and while the country has heavy rainfall, high temperatures and high humidity all year round, the heaviest rainfall occurs between November and April (coinciding with the wet season in Northern Australia). The south-facing shores of Sumatra and Java receive particularly high rainfall totals. North of the Equator, the wettest season is the opposite half of the year (May to October).

2 In the tropical monsoon zone (Thailand, Cambodia, Laos, Vietnam and the Philippines) there are three distinct seasons. The 'cool' season runs from November to February with temperatures ranging between an average minimum of 20°C and an average maximum around 30°C. There is little rainfall and humidities drop to 70–75 per cent. This, climatically, is the best season for tourism. The second season, running from February to May, is also dry but very hot: temperatures peak in the mid 30s°C. The 'monsoon' breaks in May/June with heavy rain until October, although the most torrential rain and the highest humidities occur in August–October.

SINGAPORE

Introduction

Singapore consists of one main island and over 50 small islets, totalling 625 km². With a population of 2.69 million (1990) the island is very intensively developed. Its economy is growing very rapidly (at 8–10 per cent 1988–1992) and is based on its role as a port, world trading, business and communication centre. It was a British colony from 1867 to 1963, when it was granted independence as a part of the Federation of Malaysia, though it broke away from the Federation in 1965 to become a separate republic. It is a clean, modern, international city and most of the older, traditional buildings have been demolished to make way for new high rise development, though some of the remaining parts of Chinatown (*see* Fig 37.3) are now being conserved and renovated, although in the process they are losing much of their original

Fig. 37.3 Chinatown, Singapore

character. With an uncomfortable equatorial climate (*see* Chapter 2) it would not seem an ideal tourist destination, but with nearly six million visitors in 1992 it is one of the leading South East Asian destinations. Its population is affluent enough to generate significant outbound tourism into the region, although the majority of trips are short distance and short duration trips to almost 'local' destinations across the border into Malaysia or Indonesia. This high level of outbound 'local' tourism is a function of the small size of Singapore's territory, its large population and its lack of space and natural leisure resources.

Singapore's tourist resources

With few natural resources and an uncomfortable climate, it is not surprising that Singapore's inbound tourism is based on its manmade attractions.

1 Shopping: Singapore is the major shopping centre for South East Asia, with a wide range of competitively-priced goods from the region e.g. antiques from China, Malaya, Bali, the Philippines, Chinese and Indian carpets, crocodile and snake-skin leatherware and, of course, electronic goods – cameras, videos, etc. However, the strength of the Singapore dollar may make such goods relatively more expensive for the mass market and the restoration of Chinatown and the relocation of its many small shops in modern multi-storey complexes may eventually reduce Singapore's attraction as a shopping destination. Orchard Road is the main shopping street.

2 Special events and festivals: The multi-racial nature of Singapore's society is reflected in the range of Chinese, Hindu, Islamic and Christian festivals that are regularly celebrated (e.g. Chinese New Year, and the Festival of the Hungry Ghosts, the Hindu Thaipusam, Diwali, and Christmas) and cultural events such as the Singapore Festival of the Arts, Singapore's National Day and Dragon Boat Festival.

3 Sports: The island has 17 golf courses as well as fishing and other watersports, horseracing, polo, badminton and cricket, though the climate is a major restraint on energetic outdoor activity.

4 Attractions: Sentosa Island, linked to the main island by ferry and cable car, is a complete pleasure resort with beaches and lagoons for swimming and boating, parks and gardens, nature areas and an underwater world, museums with waxworks of Singapore's significant pioneers and historic events; there are activities such as roller skating, plus a bazaar and night entertainment. Elsewhere on Singapore island, the zoo, Jurong Park Aviary, the Botanic gardens (with its huge display of orchids), the Tiger Balm gardens, the colonial era Raffles Hotel, many museums and nightlife, etc. add to the range of manmade attractions. Sightseeing river and harbour cruises are also new attractions.

5 Convention facilities: The island has good facilities for conventions and exhibitions and is the main Asian convention centre and is among the world's top conference venues. Many hotels have conference rooms but the main venue is the Raffles City Convention Centre, though additional facilities (e.g. a 12 000-seater indoor stadium and the Suntec City complex) are being developed.

6 Cruising: Singapore's port facilities are being used to develop Singapore into a major centre for cruises round the South China Sea.

Singapore's tourism

Inbound tourism

Tourism to Singapore grew steadily between 1965 and 1982 to a total of nearly 3 million. The number of arrivals levelled off in the early 1980s, but the late 1980s (1986–1990) saw the period of most rapid growth (at 14 to 15 per cent pa). In common with many Asian countries, the rate of growth slowed down sharply in 1991 (to 1.7 per cent) but had recovered by 1992 (to 10.6 per cent) when the total number of arrivals reached 5.989 million, (this figure excludes Malaysian inbound trips by road, *see* Fig 37.4).

Singapore's strong world role as a business and stopover destination has meant that the regional pattern of arrivals has changed relatively little over the years, with 60–65 per cent of visitors coming from Asia, 15–19 per cent from Europe, around 12 per cent from Australia and New Zealand and around 6 per cent from the Americas. (Singapore is Europe's second favourite Asian des-

tination after Thailand.) Figure 37.4 shows Singapore's leading markets in 1992. Some of the fastest growing markets in 1991, 1992 and the early months of 1993 continue to be Taiwan, Korea and Hong Kong (for the political reasons discussed in Chapter 36). There has also been a very rapid increase of visitors from China in 1992 and early 1993 (though the total number of Chinese travelling abroad is still very small). The success of Singapore's policy of promoting itself as a holiday destination can be judged from the fact that around 66 per cent of all its visitors come on holiday; business tourism accounts for 13 per cent and transit tourists make up less than 15 per cent of its visitor population. However different nationalities come for different purposes (*see* Fig 37.4). The Japanese and Taiwanese are most likely to come on holiday, while a higher than average proportion of American, Hong Kong and French people come on business trips, and more Australians, New Zealand, British, French and Dutch travellers are likely to be stopover visitors.

	1992		1989 (%)		
	Visitor arrivals (by country of residence)		Holiday	Business	Transit
ASEAN*	1 810 920 **				
Japan	1 000 775		81.0	11.7	2.8
Taiwan	386 061		70.1	13.0	5.1
Australia	385 079		65.4	10.7	14.6
UK	303 310		66.8	14.2	10.2
USA	287 576		51.3	20.5	13.1
Hong Kong	232 591		48.2	32.3	5.4
India	195 469		49.8	14.9	9.7
Germany	160 376		69.1	15.2	7.9
S Korea	156 399		49.3	16.3	7.8
Others	N/A		N/A	N/A	N/A
Total	5 989 940	Average 1989	66.5	12.8	15.5
		Av no. days stay	3.5	3.5	2.3

* ASEAN = Association of South East Asian Nations, which include Indonesia, Malaysia, Philippines, Thailand and Brunei. (NB Singapore is also a member of ASEAN.)

** The figures exclude Malaysian citizens arriving by 'land' across the causeway road link between Singapore and mainland Malaysia. These arrivals are estimated at 9.5 million trips in 1991.

Fig. 37.4 Singapore inbound tourism
(*Source*: WTO/Singapore Tourist Promotion Board)

Outbound tourism

With a GNP per head of US$ 7420 in 1988, Singapore is the wealthiest of the ASEAN nations and in 1991 its population generated 1.6 million trips (excluding trips to Malaysia). A high proportion of these were likely to be short breaks to Batam Island in Indonesia – only a 20 km ferry ride away. However, the mountain scenery of Lake Toba in Sumatra and the city of Jakarta are also popular Indonesian destinations for Singaporeans. Thailand and Hong Kong are the next most popular destinations.

Malaysia also provides many of the leisure resources that Singapore lacks, for example, the cooler climates of the Genting Highlands near Kuala Lumpur. Estimates of the number of cross-border trips from Singapore to Malaysia vary. Opperman reports 11.7m trips across the causeway in 1990, with 820 000 trips to Malaysia by air; it is estimated that 25–36 per cent of these may be tourist trips. The Economist Intelligence Unit, on the other hand, suggests a total of 3.2 million trips to Malaysia in 1991.

INDONESIA

Introduction

Indonesia is a large country: with an area of 1.919 million km² it is more than three times the size of France. It has a population of 180 million (in 1991); in terms of its total population it ranks as the fifth largest country in the world and it is the world's largest Muslim country. Its territory is split into 13 677 islands, strung out over 3000 miles of ocean (*see* Fig 37.5). The capital Jakarta is on the island of Java, which is not the biggest in the archipelago but with a population of 90 million, is the most densely populated. The Indonesian government faces a difficult task to forge a politically unified country from such a fragmented and scattered territory and such an ethnically diverse population and there are political tensions not far below the surface. There is conflict on the island of Timor, which is 'out of bounds' to tourists and at times the central government has taken a repressive attitude to some of its ethnic minorities.

Tourist resources

Indonesia has a wealth of historic buildings, e.g. Hindu and Buddhist temples date from 500 to 1500 AD, while Sultans' palaces (Kratons) were built during the early period of Islamic rule from 1520 to Dutch colonial times. Its landscapes range from lush, green, irrigated rice terraces to volcanic peaks, while wildlife is abundant in some areas of remaining rainforest. There are good beaches, although being an Islamic country, women are expected to dress modestly and restrict scanty swimwear to the tourist beaches. Eight new beach resort complexes have been completed in the early 1990s (*see* Fig 37.5) and beach tourism is the mainstay of Indonesian mass tourism. However, it is perhaps as well known for its cultural and ethnic tourist resources. Its performing arts (e.g. wooden and shadow puppets, traditional dances and gamelan orchestras of gongs) attract many tourists, while batik cloth is one of its most famous arts and crafts. The government has also promoted tourism in the Hindu island of Bali and in the Tana Toraja region of Sulawesi for ethnic tourism, as part of its policy of dispersing tourism more widely through Indonesia and particularly to some of the more remote islands of the archipelago. However, at present, tourism is concentrated on four islands: Java, Sumatra, Bali and Sulawesi.

Java

The capital Jakarta has interesting Dutch colonial architecture and museums with exhibits from Indonesia's different ethnic groups and cultural periods and a fine ceramics collection. The modern Istiqlal mosque is the biggest in Asia. On the eastern side of the city there is an outdoor cultural park with full-scale replicas of the traditional houses from Indonesia's twenty-seven provinces. Good snorkelling, diving and beach activities are available at nearby Pulau Senbu (Thousand Islands). Yogyakarta is the other major tourist centre on the island. Two important temples are close by: the 10th century Hindu temple at Prambana and the huge Buddhist sanctuary at Borobudur.

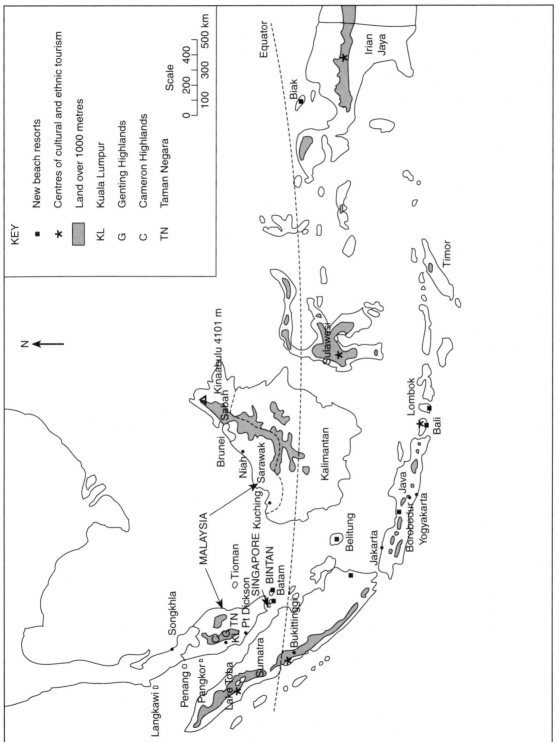

KEY

■	New beach resorts
✳	Centres of cultural and ethnic tourism
▨	Land over 1000 metres
KL	Kuala Lumpur
G	Genting Highlands
C	Cameron Highlands
TN	Taman Negara

Scale

0 100 200 300 400 500 km

Fig. 37.5 Indonesia and Malaysia tourist resources

Sumatra

This is Indonesia's second largest island (after Borneo) but has a much smaller population than Java (only 28 million). It has varied cultural, landscape and wildlife resources, e.g. the Batak people who live in the Lake Toba region and whose houses are built on stilts with high, saddle-shaped roofs and abundant carvings. The landscape of West Sumatra is perhaps the most spectacular with volcanic mountains, jungle-covered slopes and deep canyons (e.g. Sianok near Bukitinggi). The matrilinear MinangKabau people inhabit this region. Their houses are large, rectangular buildings with pointed horn-like ends to the roofs.

Bali

This small island lies just east of Java. It is perhaps the best known tourist destination in Indonesia. It combines beach tourism with landscape and cultural tourism. The Hindu religion is the focus of village life and ceremony. There are said to be at least 20 000 temples on the island and temple festivals with processions, music, dancing and rituals are held every year. On any given day there is likely to be a festival at one of the island's main temples. However, dances accompanied by gamelans, such as the Barong, Fire and Monkey dances, are performed regularly for the tourists at different locations (Ubud, Bona, Batubulan, Denpasar and Kuta) in the south of the islands.

Cultural tourism in Bali has gone through three phases of development over the last 60 years. A recurrent feature has been the promotion of the island's culture by non-Balinese and the Balinese response of using their cultural arts as a means of defining their own cultural identity and cultural tourism as a means of exerting political influence on their non-Balinese governments. The first phase of tourist development dates from the 1920s to 1942, a period when the island was under Dutch colonial rule. Picard (1993) suggests that the Dutch policy of conserving Bali as a 'living museum' of the original Hindu Javanese culture and its promotion as a tourist destination had as much to do with the Dutch need to improve their image as colonial rulers as it did with an understanding of Balinese culture. Whatever the motivation of the Dutch, by the 1930s tourism had grown to several

thousand a year, including visits from some well-known artists and anthropologists. This first phase ended with the invasion by the Japanese in 1942. A period of political turmoil followed until the creation of the new independent Indonesia in 1945.

The new President Sukarno's government, faced with a spatially fragmented and ethnically diverse country, became increasingly repressive and corrupt. Tourism was at a low ebb but Bali was adapted as the President's 'showplace' for state guests, so communications to the island were improved (with the building of the airport) and several luxury hotels were put up. The 1965 *coup d'état* closed Indonesia to foreigners and brought this second phase of tourist development to a close. In 1966 tourism to Bali consisted of only 2000 visitors. By 1967 Suharto was established as president and once again the Java-based government chose to promote Bali as a showcase of Indonesian tourism, and Balinese culture as an example of Indonesian regional culture.

This heralded the third phase of tourism development. By this time the Bali Beach Hotel had been built at Sanur and there was one hotel in Kuta. The Indonesian government commissioned a firm of French consultants (SCETO) to produce a tourism plan for the island, but the Balinese themselves were neither consulted nor involved in the plan. The master plan was produced in 1971: it was based on the assumption that exposure to tourism would spoil traditional Balinese culture, so tourism development was confined to an enclave on the south tip of the island at Nusa Dua. The accent was on beach tourism but a limited number of tour routes into the island were allowed – the restrictions were imposed in order to shield the Balinese villages from the impact of western tourism. At the time this was thought to be a form of sustainable tourist development. The plan was approved, and most of the luxury beach resort development at Nusa Dua and Sanur was financed by large (non-Balinese) corporate bodies of Indonesian or foreign origin. Thus the hotels were not owned or operated by the Balinese, so there was a high leakage of profits out of the island and the plan did not allow the Balinese regional government to pursue its own tourism policy. Picard (1993) suggests that the Balinese authorities would have preferred a greater emphasis on cultural (other than beach) tourism and a wider spread of tourism through the island with more involvement of the Balinese in tourism operations in order to spread the economic benefits. The expansion of tourism was slow to start with (*see* Fig 37.6).

Year	Number of hotel rooms	Number of tourists.
1966		2 150
1968		5 000
1969		10 000
1970		23 000
1975	3 072	
1978		133 000
1981		158 000
1988	11 000	
1989		700 000
1991	25 000	
1992		est. 1 million
1993	est. 34 000	

Fig. 37.6   The development of tourism in Bali

During the 1970s the Balinese regional government equated the promotion of culture with the promotion of tourism and there was a revival of interests in their cultural arts which led to the setting up of the Bali Arts festival in 1979. At the same time a Balinese (rather than a Javan) governor general was appointed. It was not until 1986, when Bali airport was opened to non-Indonesian airlines that tourism really began to grow rapidly (*see* Fig 37.7). This growth has brought increasing congestion and physical problems (e.g. with water supplies) in the south of the island, particularly around Nusa Dua. This has led to a virtual reversal of the 1971 tourism policies with a temporary ban on new hotel development in Nusa Dua and a policy to disperse tourism into 15 newly designated tourism areas throughout the island. Tourism development on Bali may be about to enter a new phase, with the setting up of yet another 'outside' tourism policy initiative – the Bali Sustainable Development Project, a joint study by several Canadian and Indonesian Universities started in 1991 (Wall, 1993). The project seeks to put together a sustainable development strategy

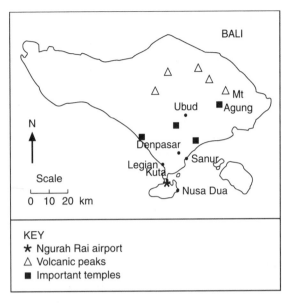

Fig. 37.7   Bali tourist resources

for the island, covering all its resources and not just tourism. First indications suggest the strategy might encourage more local Balinese participation in tourism businesses and a greater geographical spread of tourists through the island.

Cultural change in Bali

Chapter 12 discusses the ways in which tourism can affect cultures but it notes that tourism is only one of many agents of change. In Bali, it is clear that the development of cultural tourism has been caught up in the political relationships between the Balinese and their different political 'masters'. Some would argue that some aspects of Balinese culture have been strengthened in the process: Picard (1993) suggests that the religious foundation of Balinese society and its artistic expression are, indeed, thriving. However, the aspect of Balinese culture that may be most changed by tourism is the traditional social organisation of the villages (e.g. there are groups within each village that coordinate irrigation work and temple activities). The village 'bandjar', the council of heads of households which organises and controls ritual duties, is one of the most significant as it has the power to fine and discipline villagers who do not participate in religious and life cycle ceremonies. Wall reports that these duties may be time-consuming with up to a quarter of Balinese persons' working hours being devoted to such obligations. In the seasonal rhythms of agricultural work these duties are more easy to fulfil, but it has been noted (Snow and Wall, 1993, Guerrier, 1993) that some tensions are created for workers who leave their village to work in a tourism job (with regular hours). Attending to their village duties and holding a regular job (with defined holidays) may not be compatible.

Sulawesi

This mountainous island has dramatic scenery, with volcanic peaks, geysers, hotsprings, splendid beaches and waterfalls. However, ethnic tourism is the island's main attraction. The Tana Toraja (the 'Land of the Heavenly Kings') lies in the centre of the island. The Torajans' traditional religion includes very elaborate and spectacular rituals – particularly funerals. Up to 1971 the island was very isolated and the traditional people were viewed as backward by educated Indonesians. Christian and Islamic missionaries had worked on the island to educate and convert the traditional people. But in 1971, with the growth in interest in cultural tourism in Bali, it was realised that Tana Toraja could also be developed for tourism (*see* Fig 37.8) and this led the modernised Torajans to reorientate their attitudes to their traditional culture and traditional ritual practices are now encouraged by the modernised elite and are tolerated by the churches (*see* Crystal, 1989). So here again, the introduction of tourism has in some ways reinforced and helped maintain a traditional culture. The funeral rituals that attract the tourists are very elaborate and drawn out (up to seven days) and involve dancing, song, procession, animal sacrifice and feasting. The lavishness of the ritual is a way for families and

Year	Number of tourists
1971	58
1974	1 908
1975	6 008
1983	30 000
1985	40 000

Fig. 37.8 Development of tourism in Sulawesi

individuals to gain social status. The dead bodies are buried in caves carved in vertical cliffsides and almost life-sized effigies of the dead (tau-tau) are placed in galleries near the burial site. The tau-tau are the places of residence of the spirit of the dead person. The funeral rituals are held months or years after the death and are generally in the least busy months in the agricultural cycle (usually between May and September), thus avoiding the busy rice cultivation season. This also makes it possible to arrange for tourists to visit at the time of a funeral celebration. Although tourism may have helped preserve the culture from modernising forces and helped raise the prestige of the Torajans amongst non-Torajan Indonesians, tourism has inevitably had some impact on the Torajans and their home area (*see* Crystal, 1989). Perhaps the most serious is the growing theft of the tau-tau for the international art market.

Other tourist destinations in Indonesia

The Indonesian government is encouraging tourism to other islands, and new beach resort complexes have been developed on the Riau archipelago (e.g. Batam Island to meet the needs of the Singapore market), Lombok, Biak, etc (*see* Fig 37.5). Small, special interest tours also visit some of the remoter regions (e.g. wildlife tours to Komodo to see the big lizards known as Komodo 'dragons', *see* Hitchcock, 1993) and to Irian Jaya for ethnic tourism to the mountain tribes.

Inbound tourism and tourism policy

Looking at Indonesia tourism from a central government perspective, the motivations for promoting tourism have been twofold:

1 To create employment (the country has a large and rapidly expanding population).
2 To earn foreign exchange, much needed by the country since the fall in oil prices in the 1980s. Tourism has been promoted energetically particularly since 1987 and tourism is now the fifth largest foreign exchange earner for the country (after oil, gas, timber and textiles).

Up to 1987 tourism grew quite steadily (*see* Fig 37.9) and was dependent on long-stay, high-spending western tourists for 55 per cent of its

	Visitor arrivals (000's)
1983	685.9
1984	700.9
1985	749.3
1986	825.0
1987	1 060.3
1988	1 301.0
1989	1 625.9
1990	2 177.5
1991	2 569.8
1992	3 064.1

Fig. 37.9 The growth of Indonesia's inbound tourism

Country of residence	Number of visitors
Singapore	809 144
Japan	394 693
Malaysia	338 049
Australia	234 723
Taiwan	220 326
USA	125 337
Germany	118 244
UK	117 826
Netherlands	86 034
Republic of Korea	82 526
Others	
Total	**3 064 161**

Fig. 37.10 Visitors to Indonesia by country of residence, 1992
(*Source*: Indonesia Tourist Promotion Office)

visitors. Tourism has grown much more dramatically (at 20–34 per cent per annum) between 1987 and 1990 and has expanded at around 20 per cent per annum in the early 1990s. This growth has coincided with the expansion of outbound travel from East and South East Asian countries. By 1990, western countries contributed only 34.6 per cent of Indonesian visitors, while the ASEAN countries plus Japan make up 47 per cent of the total (*see* Fig 37.10). Between 1990 and 1992, American and European tourist numbers dropped slightly (as a result of the 1991 Gulf War) but this was more than counterbalanced by the rapidly increasing numbers of Asian tourists (particularly from Korea and Taiwan). Singapore has been Indonesia's main market for a long time but many are short stay

repeat visitors. By 1992 the total visitor arrivals from all countries topped 3 million and 82 per cent of these were holiday tourists.

Outbound tourism

EIU (1991) estimates that 400 000–450 000 Indonesians travel abroad: this is a minute proportion of the total population. Those who do travel are reputed to be high spenders. These are the characteristics of the tourism of countries at the earliest stages of the development of domestic and outbound tourism (*see* Chapter 15).

MALAYSIA

Introduction

Malaysia is a country of 329 758 km^2 and has a population of 17.5 million. It is divided into Peninsular Malaysia and Sabah and Sarawak on Borneo Island. It has a hot (daily maximum 30–33°C), wet, equatorial climate: the rainiest months on the west coast of Peninsular Malaysia are April, May and October, while November to February are the wettest on the east coast and Borneo. Being one of the more affluent countries of South East Asia, it has a good transport and tourist infrastructure and a well developed domestic tourist market (8.1 million domestic guest nights in 1989). Inbound tourism (including Singaporeans) grew steadily from 2.2 million to 3.6 million between 1980 and 1988. Peak numbers of over 7 million were achieved in 1990 ('Visit Malaysia Year') with huge increases of visitors particularly from other Asian countries, but in 1991 numbers fell back to 5.5 million. The main tourist destinations are concentrated on the more populated west coast of Peninsular Malaysia, in spite of the better beaches being located on the east coast.

Tourist regions

Kuala Lumpur

The capital city is the major gateway into Malaysia for air arrivals and departures. It is a modern city but has a blend of Malaysian cultures (Chinese, Malay and Indian). 'KL', as it is known, has its own Chinatown, national museums and urban attractions. Nearby are the Batu caves (limestone caverns housing a Hindu shrine), the Mimaland theme park (Malaysia in miniature) and the jungle sanctuary of Templers Park. The city is the leading destination for both domestic and international tourists and is the hub of Malaysian tourism network.

Genting Highlands

The hill resorts are very significant destinations. The most visited are the Genting Highlands: at an altitude of 1711 metres, the weather is about 10°C cooler than the lowlands. Genting is a modern hill resort with multi-storey hotels, golf, swimming and sports facilities and the only casino in South East Asia. It is only an hour's drive from KL and is a popular destination for domestic tourists and Singaporeans.

Penang

The island of Penang is the third major tourist destination, again popular with both domestic and mainly non-ASEAN international tourists. It is the northern gateway to Malaysia for air travellers. It has excellent beaches, good watersports and snorkelling, and mosques, Buddhist temples, a Batik factory, the Snake Temple, Botanical Gardens and Butterfly Farm provide a variety of other attractions.

Other destinations

In terms of tourist numbers, the west coast towns of Malacca (Meleka) and Selangor and Johor are the other most popular destinations. Malacca is a historic trading town with architecture from the Chinese, Dutch, Portuguese, British and Sultanate periods of Malaysia's history.

New beach resort areas are being developed and promoted on the west coast islands of Langkawi, Pangkor and Port Dickson and on Tioman Island off the east coast.

Special interest tourism

Malaysia's highland landscapes, jungle and wildlife have great potential for more active tourists. The Cameron Highlands region is an area of jungle and tea plantations with abundant wild flowers and pleasant landscapes. The Taman Negara is a forested, mountainous National Park (of 4343 km²) with many jungle walks, fishing areas and hides where wildlife may be observed. The jungle vegetation makes wildlife difficult to see and the hides are located at salt licks which attract animals such as tapir, wild boar, deer, monkeys and occasionally civet cats, tigers and elephants, and, of course, many species of birds may also be seen.

Sabah and Sarawak also have potential for ethnic, wildlife and wilderness tourism. There are 30 different races in Sabah and the Bidayuk and Melaney are the indigenous peoples of Sarawak. The Kinabalu National Park in Sabah is famous for the relatively easy climb to the top of Mount Kinabalu, the highest mountain in South East Asia (at 4101 metres). The limestone caves are the main attractions of the Niah and Gunung Mulu National Parks in Sarawak.

Inbound and outbound tourism

The close relationship between Singapore and Malaysia has been outlined earlier (*see* page 465). Peninsular Malaysia is very dependent on the Singapore market: in 1991 58.3 per cent of its inbound tourists came from Singapore. Thailand and Japan were the most significant markets (contributing 9.3 per cent and 7.1 per cent of Malaysia's tourists respectively). European visitors made up another 7 per cent. In the early months of 1993 the most rapidly growing markets were once again China, Taiwan and Hong Kong.

Malaysia's buoyant economy has generated significant outbound tourism. In 1991, over 9.5 million trips were made to Singapore (for shopping and entertainment). The other main holiday destinations are Thailand and Indonesia.

THAILAND

Thailand's pattern of tourist development has been significantly different from that of the other South East Asian countries. It is much more of a world holiday destination. Around 90 per cent of its visitors come for holidays and it draws a much higher proportion of its visitors from outside Asia: about 23 per cent come from Europe and 7 per cent from North America. Tourism grew rapidly (at an average of 10 per cent per annum) throughout the whole decade of 1980–1990 (from 1.85 million in 1980 to 5.2 million in 1990), but for various political, economic and environmental reasons, the total has stuck at around 5 million in the first few years of the 1990s. During this period the number of tourists from Europe began to recover but the number of visitors from the rest of Asia declined.

Tourist resources

Thailand has varied tourist resources (*see* Figure 37.11); beach resorts include Pattaya, Ko Samui and Phuket, while Bangkok offers a wealth of urban and cultural attractions. There are historic ruins of the old capital of Siam while ethnic tourism (hill tribe treks – *see* Chapter 12) are popular in the northern highlands. Although prostitution is officially illegal, Thailand has the reputation of being the sex capital of Asia; sex tourism was at its peak during the 1970s and early 1980s but has declined since the threat of AIDS began to change visitors' attitudes.

Thailand is made up of three physical regions, which roughly coincide with the location of these three main types of tourism:

1 The coast and peninsular Thailand, where beach, urban and sex tourism is concentrated.
2 The central lowlands where general sightseeing, historic and cultural tourism is dominant.
3 The northern hills where ethnic and adventure tourism occur.

Coastal Thailand

Thailand's territory extends south down the neck of the Malay peninsula: most of Thailand's coast faces the Gulf of Siam but a shorter stretch of coastline faces the Indian Ocean to the west. The climate of the southernmost parts (near the Malaysia border) are more equatorial (with all year round rainfall) but this becomes more seasonal as the climate makes the transition from equatorial to monsoonal as you go north; so at the island resort of Phuket there is some rain all year round, but further north at Hua Hin and Cha'Am it is concentrated between June and September.

Pattaya is currently the most developed beach resort (with nearly 20 000 hotel rooms in 1989) and it is the second most visited destination in Thailand after Bangkok (the capital). The resort started as an unspoilt weekend retreat for Thais from Bangkok in the 1960s but became known to westerners when it was visited by US military personnel from the US bases and soldiers on leave from the Vietnam war during the late 1960s and early 1970s. After the decline of visits by the military, the resort was marketed in Europe and Australia; it rapidly expanded and became an urbanised resort within 20 years (*see* Smith, 1992). But the resort has suffered from the lack of effective planning resulting in illegal and unapproved building, beach pollution and congestion and water shortages. Smith (1992) traces the growth of Pattaya in some detail and notes that the resort is now in its mature phase of development (*see* Chapter 8). There are few pressures for new development and Boyd (1992) reports some hotels with occupancy rates as low as 20 per cent. In spite of its environmental problems, the resort still has a reputation for 'vibrant' nightlife.

New resorts are being developed further south on peninsular Thailand, first on the island of Phuket, and then at Ko Samui where tourism has increased from a 'trickle' of backpackers (staying in bamboo huts) in 1976, to between 250 000–480 000 tourists by 1987/8 (*see* Parnwell, 1993), with an airstrip and 220 hotels. Phuket is also

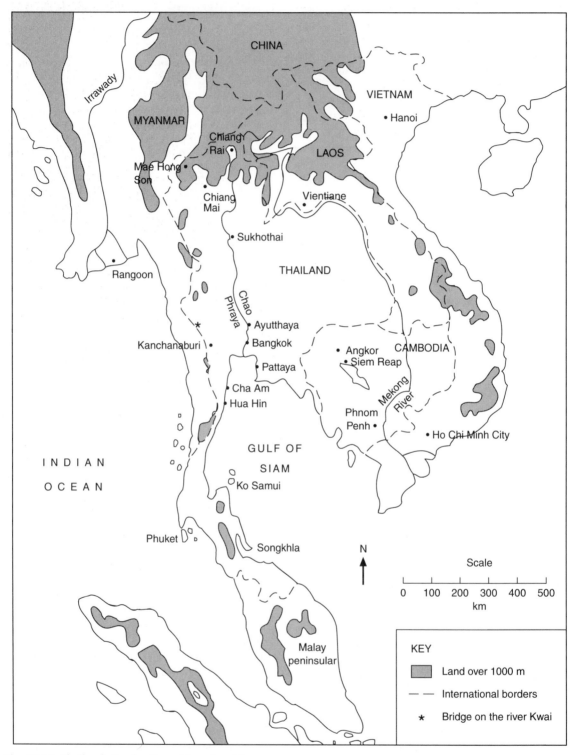

Fig. 37.11 Thailand, Cambodia and Laos tourist resources

reputed to be suffering the environmental consequences of very rapid unplanned resort expansion.
The greatest concentration of hotel rooms in
Thailand is now in this southern region (*see* Fig
37.12), and between 1991–1993 it is where the
greatest pressure for new hotel construction
existed. Songkhla is a popular resort for Malaysian
visitors. The rapidity of the growth of tourism in
the southern region is reflected in the fact that
hotel rooms have increased from 23 311 in 1986 to
48 276 in 1991.

Region	Hotel rooms 1991
South	48 276
Bangkok	45 548
East	37 880
North	28 140
Northeast	15 407
West	10 638
Central (excluding Bangkok)	4 564
Total	190 453

Fig. 37.12 Distribution of hotel rooms in Thailand's regions
(*Source*: Kitthaweerat, 1992)

Central lowlands

This region is the basin of the Chao Phraya river,
which flows southwards to the Gulf of Siam. It is
surrounded by the mountain ridge dividing
Thailand from Myanmar to the west, the highlands of Thailand to the north and a lower dry
plateau area to the east, which divides the Chao
Phraya basin from the basin of the River Mekong
on Thailand's eastern border. The capital, Bangkok
is located on the lower reaches of the river; the
canals and waterways (though quite badly polluted) are used as alternative thoroughfares to the
congested Bangkok roads and there are 'floating
markets' where, for example, fruit and vegetables
are sold from the small boats. In the city centre the
buildings are mainly of modern style. The
Buddhist temples (which are an integral part of
Thai life) and the Royal Palace are examples of
ornate traditional Thai architecture. The temples of
the Emerald, Gold and Reclining Buddhas are

Fig. 37.13 Thai temple, Bangkok

major attractions, as is the Temple of Dawn (*see* Fig
37.13). Bangkok is the main centre for Thailand's
tourism, with 62 per cent of tourist nights in 1991.
Shopping (e.g. for Thai silk), performances of Thai
dancing, the nightlife and massage parlours are
other urban attractions.

Ayutthaya, the old capital of Siam from 1350 to
1767, is 70 km upstream of Bangkok. The ruins of
palaces, temples and city walls cover a large area.
Even further north up the Chao Phraya is
Sukhothai, the site of the first independent Thai
Kingdom: these ruins, towers, moats and walls
date from 1238 AD. A tourist feature from modern
history lies to the west of the region, towards the
Myanmar border near Kanchanaburi: the 'Death
Railway', built by European prisoners of war
during World War Two, the war cemetery, and the
'Bridge Over the River Kwai' are visited by many
British and Dutch tourists.

The North

Chiang Mai is the centre for tourism in the mountainous, northern region of Thailand. There are

several beautiful temples, the summer palace of King Bhumibol and a cultural centre where traditional songs and dances are performed. Chiang Rai is the jumping off point for hill tribe treks (*see* Chapter 12) in the 'Golden Triangle' (where opium was and still is grown). Mae Hong Son is another growing tourist centre, and is not far from the villages of Padaung tribes (*see* Fig 6.2).

Inbound tourism

Thailand has a common land border with Malaysia and Malaysia is Thailand's leading market source (*see* Fig 37.14); however, many of the trips are short trips across the border to Songkhla (average stay 4.4 days in 1990) and Malaysians are among Thailand's lowest spending visitors. Japanese and Taiwanese are Thailand's next most important markets: these visitors stay longer and are Thailand's highest spending visitors. All Thailand's Asian markets have declined since 1990, along with Australia. On the other hand, after a dip in 1991, the European market continued to grow: the UK is now Thailand's fifth most important source of tourists. Europeans tend to stay longer (9 to 14 days) but are lower spenders (in terms of expenditure per day), though their longer stays make them important contributors to Thailand's tourism revenue. Tourism is now Thailand's top

	Million
1986	2.818
1987	3.482
1988	4.230
1989	4.809
1990	5.298
1991	5.086
1992	5.136

Fig. 37.15 Thailand: growth of tourism

foreign exchange earner (*see* Fig 37.15).

Thailand's tourism has faced some difficulties in recent years (in addition to the general effects of the 1991 Gulf War). Its reputation as a politically safe and stable country was dented by a military coup in February 1991, followed by political unrest in May 1992. This, along with the publicity given to its environmental problems and other tourist management difficulties, has led to several vigorous marketing campaigns (e.g. promoting the country as a golfing destination, encouraging more women to visit, etc.). Environmental legislation is being strengthened but it remains to be seen whether or not it will be effectively enforced. In spite of all these problems, Thailand is still Europe's most popular Asian destination and its combination of outstanding beaches, its cultural, entertainment and adventure tourism make it an attractive and exotic destination.

Originating country	Number
Malaysia	728 459
Japan	568 049
Taiwan	395 146
Hong Kong	316 683
UK	281 100
USA	278 580
Germany	276 336
Singapore	274 875
France	198 639
Australia	195 917
Scandinavia	142 265
S Korea	118 968
Italy	117 794
Others	N/A
Total	**5 136 443**

Fig. 37.14 Thailand: tourist arrivals, 1992
(*Source*: WTO)

LAOS, VIETNAM AND CAMBODIA

Introduction: political background

These three countries are just emerging from a long period of political instability and have only been considered as possible tourist destinations from 1989. All were involved in the Vietnam war, when the USA resisted the Communist North Vietnamese takeover of South Vietnam. The war ended in 1975 with the withdrawal of USA support for the South Vietnamese government and the subsequent fall of Saigon (now Ho Chi Minh City) to North Vietnam. Laos and Vietnam are now relatively stable, Communist countries. They were formerly supported by the Soviet Union, but political changes there have led to a reduction of Soviet financial support and this has led to a process of economic reform within Laos and Vietnam. Tourism and foreign investment in tourist infrastructure have both been welcomed.

Vietnam's tourism began in 1986 when foreign visitors were allowed into the country; Laos followed suit in 1989. The political situation in Cambodia is a little different: after a period of rule by the Maoist Khmer Rouge and civil war, the United Nations is supervising a period of transition to democratic government but the political outcome is (at the time of writing) still uncertain. The little tourism that does occur in Cambodia is mainly short, cross-border trips originating from and organised in Thailand.

Tourist resources

Cambodia has great potential for tourism: its resources are mainly cultural and historic features. Angkor is designated as a World Heritage Site and is located north west of Siem Reap. It is not accessible by road, but visitors can reach it via an airstrip at Siem Reap. Angkor was the capital of the Khmer empire which ruled over territory in Cambodia and adjacent parts of modern day Thailand, between 800 AD and 1370 AD. The ruins of the city cover a huge area of 25 by 10 km. The Angkor complex includes the ruins of many Hindu and Buddhist temples: Angkor Wat is just one of these, and was built on a 2.5 km^2 site between 1113 and 1150. In the seven years from 1986 to 1993, Angkor Wat has been cleared of jungle vegetation, cleaned and restored by an Indian team; the site has suffered some damage and loss of sculptures during the war years but much of the fighting bypassed the site. It is estimated that about 6000 foreigners visited the site in 1991.

Cambodia also has many other cultural and architectural resources, e.g. the Palace, pagodas and museum at Phnom Penh. Vietnam's resources, on the other hand, are mainly for coastal, scenic, ethnic and adventure tourism. The country has 3250 km of coastline with many untouched beaches and a hot climate fairly similar to that of Thailand's beach resorts. Inland, the territory is mountainous – the lower slopes clothed in tropical rainforest, where many hill tribes live. The country is also being promoted for activity holidays (e.g.

motorcycle and bicycle tours, parachuting and hiking). Hotel developments are expanding, with the help of foreign capital investment (e.g. from Hong Kong, Taiwan and France) in joint ventures with the Vietnamese Government, but there are still infrastructure problems and in 1993 there were only 4000 hotel rooms of international standard and there are still restrictions on foreigners' travel within the country.

International tourism to Vietnam grew from 4500 in 1986 to nearly 41 000 in 1989 and 300 000 in 1992 and has continued to grow. It is thought that these tourists come mainly from Taiwan, Japan, France, South Korea and Singapore. In 1989 there were an additional 115 000 visitors of Vietnamese origin, who are likely to be members of the 2 million Vietnamese expatriate population who now live scattered in some 80 different countries across the world. Most of Vietnam's tourist activity is located in the south, centred on Ho Chi Minh City.

The landlocked, mountainous country of Laos has more limited tourist resources and tourism in Laos is at an even earlier stage of development. The capital Vientiane (a small settlement of only around 175 000 people) is the only official point of entry for overseas tourists by air. The only overland crossing into Laos across the Mekong is via nearby Nong Kai. Most tourists arrive by air via Bangkok. There are two 'first class' hotels in Laos. Like Cambodia, most international tourists make a short package trip into the country as part of a main holiday visit to Thailand. There are, as yet, no reliable statistics on tourism to Laos.

THE PHILIPPINES

The Philippines is a group of over 7100 islands: the largest are Luzon in the north and Mindanao in the south. It has a longer coastline than the USA, although its total area is only 300 000 km^2 (roughly the same size as Italy). Its tropical monsoon climate results in a dry period extending from about November to May. This would seem an ideal recipe for tourism development, but although tourism has been established on the islands since the 1970s, its growth and development have been inhibited by political upheavals in the 1980s, with the assassination of the opposition leader Aquino in 1983, the subsequent overthrow of the Marcos regime and the installation of Aquino's widow as president by popular acclaim. In the early 1990s the political situation has been much more stable although there have been several coup attempts against Corazen Aquino.

During the 1970s tourism had grown strongly to just top the 1 million mark in 1980. But numbers dropped back during the turbulent 1980s and have only recovered to 1 million in 1992.

The Philippines' main markets are the USA and Japan (*see* Fig 37.16). The islands are well known to the American market as they were governed by America for a short period before the Second World War; they have housed American Military bases for many years and have been considerably influenced (culturally, politically and economically) by the Americans. The Japanese have been attracted to the islands for sex tourism and golfing holidays (there were over 40 courses on the islands in the early 1990s). In the 1980s 78 per cent of all Japanese tourists to the islands were male and in 1992 men still made up 66 per cent of all the Philippines' tourists. Sex tourism has been legitimised and regulated, and takes place on a big scale. In 1985 it was estimated that there were up to 300 000 'hospitality girls' in the country (Hall, 1992).

Nevertheless, the islands possess a wealth of natural tourist resources. Jenner and Smith (1992) (*see* Chapter 10) summarise the country as 'a potential paradise for ecotourism', but weak planning control over tourism development, other forms of economic exploitation and the pressures of rural poverty may severely limit this potential. Many coral reefs are under threat and coral is even mined for the building industry. The islands also have dramatic landscape resources with volcanic peaks (including Pinatubo which erupted in 1991), mountain sides terraced for rice cultivation (at Banaue), waterfalls and strange limestone hill landscapes.

The island's Spanish colonial past provides opportunities for heritage tourism but the many beach resorts, the nightlife, the golf and watersports provide the focus for tourism to the Philippines at present.

Originating country	Number	%
USA	221 630	19.22
Japan	221 578	19.22
Taiwan	122 177	10.60
Hong Kong	66 238	5.75
Korea	54 115	4.69
Australia	50 911	4.42
UK	38 916	3.38
Germany	36 031	3.13
Canada	26 794	2.50
(Overseas Filipinos)	109 764	9.52
Others	N/A	N/A
Total	**1 152 952**	

Fig. 37.16 Philippines visitor arrivals, 1992
(*Source*: Philippines Department of Tourism)

REFERENCES AND FURTHER READING

Those titles marked with an asterisk are particularly recommended for further reading.

Bali

Cukier-Snow, J and Wall, G (1993) 'Tourism employment - perspectives from Bali', *Tourism Management*, Vol. 14, No. 3, pp. 195–201.

Guerrier, Y (1993) 'Bali' in Baum, T (Ed) *Human resource issues in International Tourism*, Butterworth-Heinemann, pp. 108–15.

*Hussey, A (1989) 'Tourism in a Balinese village', *Geographical Review*, Vol. 79, pp. 311–25.

Picard, M (1993) 'Cultural tourism in Bali: national integration and regional differentiation' in Hitchcock, M, King, V T and Parnwell, M J G (Eds) *Tourism in South-East Asia*, Routledge, pp. 71–98.

*Wall, G and Dibnah, S (1992) 'The changing status of tourism in Bali Indonesia' in Cooper, C P and Lockwood, A (Eds) *Progress in Tourism, Recreation and Hospitality Management*, Vol. 4, Belhaven, pp. 120–30.

Wall, G (1993) 'International Collaboration in the search for sustainable tourism in Bali, Indonesia', *Journal of Sustainable Tourism*, Vol. 1, No. 1, pp. 38–47.

Tana Toraja

*Adams, K M (1984) 'Come to Tana Toraja Land of the Heavenly Kings' – travel agents as brokers in ethnicity', *Annals of Tourism Research*, Vol. 11, No. 3, pp. 469–85.

Crystal, E (1989) 'Tourism in Toraja (Sulawesi, Indonesia)' in Smith, V L (Ed) *Hosts and Guests*, Second Edition, University of Pennsylvania Press, pp. 139–68.

Indochina and Philippines
*Choy, D J L (1991) 'National tourism planning in the Philippines', *Tourism Management*, Vol. 12, No. 3, pp. 245–52.
* King, B and Fahey, S (1993) 'Indochina - Vietnam, Cambodia and Laos', *International Tourism Reports*, No. 2, pp. 59–81.
Hall, C M (1992) 'Sex tourism in South East Asia' in Harison, D (Ed) *Tourism and the Less Developed Countries*, Belhaven, pp. 64–74.
Jenner, P and Smith, C (1992) *The Tourism Industry and the Environment*, EIU Special Report no. 2453.

Indonesia
*EIU (1991) 'Indonesia', *International Tourism Reports*, No. 3, pp. 23–40.
Hitchcock, M (1993) 'Dragon tourism in Komodo, Eastern Indonesia' in Hitchchock, M, King, V T, Parnwell, M J G (Eds) *Tourism in South East Asia*, Routledge, pp. 306–16.

Malaysia
*Cochrane, J (1993) 'Tourism and conservation in Indonesia and Malaysia' in Hitchcock, M, King, V T and Parnwell, M J G (Eds) *Tourism in South East Asia*, Routledge, pp. 317–26.
*Cockerell, N (1994) 'Malaysia', *International Tourism Reports*, No. 2, pp. 41–61.
King, V T (1993) 'Tourism and culture in Malaysia' in Hitchcock, M, King, V T and Parnwell, M J G (Eds) *Tourism in South East Asia*, Routledge, pp. 99–116.
*Opperman, M (1992) 'International tourist flows in Malaysia', *Annals of Tourism Research*, Vol. 19, pp. 482–500.
Ping, O L and McVey, M (1992) 'Malaysia and Singapore outbound', *Travel and Tourism Analyst*, No. 4, pp. 27–47.

Thailand
Boyd, A (1992) 'Thailand', *International Tourism Reports*, No. 1, pp. 68–81.
Kitthaweerat, B (1992) 'Thai tourism', *Bangkok Monthly Review*, Vol. 33, November, pp. 23–9.
Parnwell, M J G (1993) 'Environmental issues and tourism in Thailand' in Hitchcock, M, King, V T and Parnwell, M J G (Eds) *Tourism in South East Asia*, Routledge, pp. 286–302.

Smith, R A (1992) 'Beach resort evolution – implications for planning', *Annals of Tourism Research*, Vol. 19, pp. 304–22.
(For hilltribe trekking, see references for Chapter 12.)

QUESTIONS AND DISCUSSION POINTS

1 What are the arguments for and against the development of sex tourism in South East Asia?

2 Given that Singapore has few natural tourist resources and an uncomfortable climate, why has it been such a successful tourist destination?

3 Does Malaysia have the potential to become a world (rather than a regional) tourist destination?

ASSIGNMENTS

1 You work in a travel agency. A well-educated, middle-aged couple wish to visit South East Asia and they have a particular interest in ethnic and cultural tourism. However, they are 'good' tourists who are concerned about the cultural and environmental impact of tourism, so they wish to minimise their impact on the cultures they visit. They seek your advice on where they should go and whether they should travel independently or join a special interest tour group.

Write out some notes for your next appointment with the couple, outlining the advice you would give them; also explain why you would give them this advice. Add some notes as to how they can minimise their impact on the people and places they visit when they get there.

2 You have been asked to write a short article for a tourist trade journal on 'New opportunities for tourism in South East Asia'. Your brief is to indicate the locations where there is the potential for investors to develop new destinations, or where tour operators might start new (or different special interest) tours. Explain why you suggest these new opportunities and outline any risks or problems that developers or operators might have to face. Write the first draft of your article.

CHAPTER 38

South Asia: The Indian Subcontinent

LEARNING OBJECTIVES

After reading this chapter you should be able to
- assess the tourist potential of the climatic, landscape and wildlife, historic and cultural resources of the region
- distinguish between the regional distribution of these resources and their development and use for tourism
- demonstrate a knowledge of the main tourist resorts and tourist centres
- be aware of the political constraints on the development of tourism in the region.

INTRODUCTION

This region, although structurally part of Asia and adjacent to the focus of tourism in the Pacific region (see Fig 17.6), is functionally quite separate from the Pacific region. It shows all the economic, political and tourist characteristics of the economic periphery (see Figs 15.2 and 17.4).

Like subsaharan Africa, all the countries of the region are very poor: in 1988 the GNP per head ranged from US $ 150 in Bangladesh to US $ 380 in Pakistan, although India and Pakistan have a growing middle-class and a growing domestic tourist market.

Again, in common with Africa, and indeed Latin America, it is the local political circumstances that determine the extent to which international tourism is developed. Myanmar (formerly Burma) has been ruled by a military regime which has kept this Buddhist country effectively closed to tourists. The regime was defeated in democratic elections, but in 1993 had still refused to give up power.

Sri Lanka had a growing beach tourist industry until intercommunal strife broke out and the north of the island was effectively closed for tourism in the 1980s. Pakistan, too, has had a turbulent political history, encompassing both military dictatorships and democratically elected governments, while India has been the most stable democracy of the region, although it has its own local internal ethnic and intercommunal problems. The main region of long-term political instability has been the Pakistan/Indian border region of Kashmir and the Punjab, where international border disputes and the Sikh separatist movement have caused intermittent problems. However, the intercommunal friction that led to the partition of India and Pakistan is never far below the surface. These problems have constrained the growth of tourism to a very low level indeed, in spite of the region having a wealth of scenic and cultural resources.

Tourism in the region has grown slowly since 1988 (from 2.88 million visitors to 3.24 million in 1991) but this still represents only 0.71 per cent of total world tourist arrivals. The tourists come from two main sources: either from within the region (between 1987 and 1991 South Asian tourists made up 30–34 per cent of the total) or from Europe, which continues to be the region's main market (contributing 36–41 per cent of the tourists). Of the remainder, 11 to 12 per cent come from East Asia and the Pacific, while the contribution from the Americas has steadily dropped from 10.35 per cent in 1987 to 7.9 per cent in 1991.

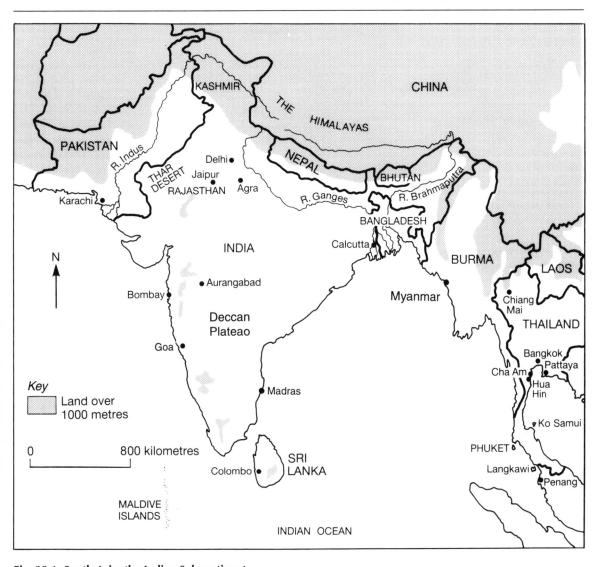

Fig. 38.1 South Asia: the Indian Subcontinent

TOURIST RESOURCES

The region consists of four physical subdivisions, each of which has a distinctly different type of landscape, and different tourist resources and tourist potential.

1 The Himalayas, which form an arc of mountainous territory extending from Afghanistan and Pakistan in the west, through North India, Tibet and the mountain kingdoms of Nepal, Sikkim and Bhutan, to the ridges which curve south through Myanmar. The mountains are geologically young and produce the same dramatic scenery of parallel ridges, jagged, eroded peaks, with deeply cut, steep-sided river valleys. The terrain makes the land remote and inaccessible. The Himalayan chain is the highest and most extensive mountain range of the world.

2 The Valleys of the Indus and Ganges. These two rivers and their tributaries drain from the Himalayas and they flow across immense, flat and fertile plains stretching in a virtually unbroken arc from Karachi to Calcutta. Their lower reaches are subject to flooding and Bangladesh (whose territory is mainly the delta and lower flood plains of the Ganges and Brahmaputra) is subject to repeated flooding from both the sea and river.

3 The Deccan plateau of South India. The much dissected plateau is highest along India's west coast and slopes gently downwards towards the north and east.

4 The islands. The biggest island, Sri Lanka, lies off the east coast of India, and the Maldives are a group of much smaller islands which offer sun, sea and sand tourism, with coral reefs for diving and snorkelling in a tropical climate.

East of the Thar Desert, the region has a 'three season' climate. The winter (November to February) is the coolest season and is most suited to tourism. Temperatures begin to rise through March to peak in May, when the average daily maximum is 40°C in Delhi and Jaipur, and 41°C in Agra. In South India it is even hotter. Although this hot season is dry, it is too hot for most sightseeing activity in the plains and in peninsular India, though it is cooler in the mountains. The monsoon breaks in June and lasts until October. This rainfall is variable in its amount but torrential in nature. The high land on the west coast of peninsular India is in the path of the rainbearing winds and receives particularly heavy rain (Goa has 752 mm in the month of June alone). Similarly the west-facing coast of the Bay of Bengal (Assam and Myanmar) has exceedingly heavy rain at this time of year. Rainfall decreases inland but June still marks the abrupt change from hot and dry to hot and wet conditions. Delhi and Agra have their rainfall peaks in July with a monthly total of 177 mm and 228 mm respectively. Most cultural tours of India operate from October to March, while the mountain regions are best in April and September/October. The cultural resources of the region are rich and varied, ranging from ancient archaeological sites in Pakistan, to magnificent Hindu and Mughal buildings in India; the modern Muslim, Hindu and Buddhist cultures and ways of life also provide a great variety of experiences for the tourist. Although the countries are very densely populated and there is great pressure on the land, there are pockets of wildlife interest where national parks and reserves provide opportunities for wildlife tourism.

INDIA

India is the seventh largest country in the world in area, but with over 840 million people it has the second largest population. Although it is a secular state, the majority of the population is Hindu, but there are also substantial Islamic and Buddhist minorities. In such a large country which ranges physically from desert to jungle and from open flat plains to the heights of the Himalayas, it is not surprising that there is considerable regional cultural variation. The country possesses a wealth of landscape, wildlife, beach and adventure tourism resources, but it is perhaps best known for its cultural, historic and architectural heritage.

Cultural attitudes to tourism in India

Popular interest in Indian culture became trendy and widespread among young people in the west in the 1960s and early 1970s when many hippies and other young people made the overland journey from Europe to India. Some aspects of contemporary Indian culture (e.g. Indian food) are now familiar to westerners but the contrasts of India, the relative poverty and the more simple way of life still came as a shock to some western travellers. There were many opportunities for western tourists to misunderstand the complexities of Indian society (e.g. the caste system and the role of the cow in religious life, the economy and the environment) and for western habits to offend Indian social and religious customs. These frictions were familiar to older generations of Indians as a result of their experience of being a British colony up to 1946 and to younger Indians as a result of their experiences of the hippies.

Perhaps for these reasons or perhaps because India was preoccupied with other political and economic development issues, India remained relatively indifferent to tourism up to 1990. It is only during the 1990s that tourism has been more positively promoted, but among the government's key objectives for tourism was to encourage tourism that preserves, retains and strengthens Indian social and cultural values and allows India to present itself on its own terms. The fact that most Hindus are vegetarian, many do not drink alcohol, some do not smoke, that women are expected to dress with sobriety and that some castes would be unable to take service type jobs in the tourist industry mean that the trappings of modern western style tourism fit uneasily into contemporary Indian culture. Western style 'nightlife' hardly exists in India. Facilities for the rapidly developing domestic tourist industry are not adaptable for western use. However, inbound tourism is now the country's major generator of foreign exchange and tourism promotion is now a key economic policy. This, most of all, is beginning to overcome the country's ambivalent attitude towards tourism development.

Cultural and historic resources

Indian civilisation is very ancient, tracing back to at least 2500 BC. Excavations in Delhi have shown the site to have been occupied as far back as 1000 BC and Hinduism and Buddhism were established in these epochs. Hindu and Buddhist empires extended over most parts of India up to about the 4th century AD (*see* Chapter 5). Islamic dynasties took over as rulers of North India from 10–12th centuries AD and continued up the 18th century, but were soon replaced by the British as the colonial power over the whole of India. Tensions between Islamic and Hindu cultures are deep seated, culminating in the partition of the subcontinent into the predominantly Islamic Pakistan and a majority Hindu India and its associated bitter conflicts and massive population movements. India has a wealth of historic buildings representing these various cultural periods. In northern India there are many cities, palaces and tombs of the Islamic dynasties dating from 12th to 15th centuries, mixed with Hindu temples and Hindu religious sites. In South India, the architecture and buildings are mainly Buddhist and Hindu, as Islamic influence did not spread throughout the whole of Peninsular India.

Wildlife and landscape resources

India consists of three physical and landscape units: the Deccan plateau of Peninsular India, the flat plains of the Ganges, and the Himalayas. Apart from the Thar desert the natural vegetation is monsoon forest, dry woodland and thorn scrub (i.e. 'jungle') with temperate forest and scrub on the slopes of the Himalayas. The population pressure is such that most natural vegetation has been replaced by agricultural land, or is harvested for forest products (e.g. fuel for local villages and grazing for domestic animals). There are relatively few pockets of unmodified natural habitat left. Many of India's most spectacular wildlife (e.g. tiger, leopard, Indian elephant, Indian rhinoceros) have dwindled in numbers due as much to the continuing habitat loss and competition with agriculture as to profligate shooting for sport in the past. The wildlife is often difficult to see because of the undergrowth and tall grasses that grow in the wet season, but wildlife viewing from elephants (available in several wildlife sanctuaries and National Parks) makes it possible to get quite close to some species. The growth in the ecotourism market (*see* Chapter 10) may make this more popular.

Adventure and activity tourism

The cooler conditions of India's hill and mountain areas make trekking a popular activity. The higher parts of the Himalayas (e.g. in Nepal) are perhaps more renowned for trekking but the Indian sections have spectacular landscapes where there are ex-colonial hill stations that provide bases for trekking expeditions. Jammu, Kashmir and Ladakh were the most popular areas with the highest peaks, but Kashmir has not been accessible to tourists for some while, firstly because of friction between India and Pakistan along their mutual border and more recently due to internal political disturbances. Fishing, skiing, river running and rock climbing are all being promoted in the mountain and hill regions, while camel safaris take place in the Thar desert and water sports and scuba diving are available at the coastal resorts.

Beach tourism

India possesses some very beautiful and unspoilt beaches. Some resorts have been developed (both for the international and domestic markets), for example, around Bombay, Goa, Madras and on the Malabar and Coromandel coasts south of Goa and Madras.

INDIA'S TOURIST REGIONS

North India

Delhi and the 'Golden Triangle' (made up of Delhi, Agra and Jaipur) is the focus of most of India's cultural tourism. Delhi is strewn with historic buildings, tombs, mosques and monuments, dating from successive dynasties of Islamic Sultans (1206–1526) and the later Mughal (1526–1707) rulers. Many of the ancient Hindu temples that predated these dynasties were destroyed, though some of the materials from these were incorporated in the early Islamic constructions. The first four cities of Delhi lie to the south of the modern city centre. Lal Kot (dating from 1193) is the first and is the site of the Qutb-Minar (*see* Fig 38.3), a 72.5 m-high stone tower and the beautifully carved colonnades and walls of the ruined Quwwatu'l-Islam Mosque. The seventh city (begun in 1638 by the Mughul ruler Shahjahan) is at the centre of Old Delhi. The Red Fort (a massive citadel and palace made of red sandstone walls and marble palaces) overlooks the River Jumana and was part of Shahjahan's city. New Delhi was built during British rule and its wide straight roads and colonial British Victorian architecture are in great contrast to the rest of Delhi. Agra is a 40-minute flight or a 3.25 hours'

rail journey from Delhi. It was the seat of government of Akbar (a Mughal king from 1556–1605) who built his city of Fatehpur Sikri here instead of at Delhi. The now empty buildings of Fatehpur Sikri are very well preserved, seemingly untouched from the date they were abandoned when the Mughal court returned to Delhi. Agra is more famous as the location of the Taj Mahal, the mausoleum built by Shahjahan for his wife. The white marble of the graceful building is delicately inlaid with other semi-precious stones but it is the way in which the marble absorbs and reflects the changing quality of the light throughout the day and the reflections of the building mirrored in the pools in front of it that add to the impact of the architecture. Trips are arranged to view the building by moonlight. Its reputation as one of the most beautiful buildings in the world is not overstated. Much Mughal architecture was enhanced by water (pools, fountains and waterfalls and lights), but apart from the Taj, these are rarely restored. Jaipur is the third city of the 'Golden Triangle' and appears on most tours of India. It is known as the 'Pink City' due to the colour of many of the buildings. This 18th century city has broad avenues and many palaces (e.g. Hawa Mahal – the Palace of the Winds). Elephants carry tourists up to the now deserted hilltop city of Amber, just outside Jaipur. Another attraction of Jaipur is the Jantar Mantar (or observatory of masonry-built astronomical instruments) built by Maharaj Jai Singh II (between 1699 and 1743). The observatory is one of six built in North India during this period (one is also located in Delhi). These three cities are the most visited in India, but the northern part of the country has a variety of other attractions. The sacred river Ganges is a focus for Hindu pilgrims who perform various religious rituals at Varanasi (and at Hardwar where the river emerges from the Himalayas). The ruins of Gwalior fort and the temples at Khaturaho (a complex of 10–11th century temples with many erotic carvings) are not far from the Ganges. One of the best tiger reserves in India is at Ranthambhor (between Jaipur and Agra). The desert state of Rajasthan lies south west of Delhi. Its landscape is a great contrast to the intensively cultivated and fertile plains; there are opportunities for adventure camel treks and the cotton fabrics and handicrafts of the region are very colourful. The foothills of the Himalayas are

Fig. 38.2 Jantar Mantar Observatory, Delhi

Fig. 38.3 Qutb Minar, Delhi

not far (about 200 miles) north of Delhi: hill stations such as Dharamsala, Simla, Mussoorie, Rishikesh and Nainital are all bases for treks into the more dramatic mountain regions.

Peninsular India

Bombay is a modern city that is another focus for tourism. The Ajanta and Ellora caves dating from 5th to 7th century AD are accessible from Bombay via Aurangabad. The Ajanta caves consist of Buddhist temples cut into the rock face of a deep gorge. The caves contain extensive and well-preserved paintings. The Ellora cave temples are Hindu. The former Portuguese colony of Goa is a centre for beach tourism, while Kovalem further south also has unspoilt beaches with modern facilities. Madras and the southern tip of the Peninsula is the part of India least affected by the invasions from the north and the heritage of ancient India has been protected from the influence of other cultures. There are many temples in the classic Hindu style, for example, at Kanchipuram (with 150 temples dating from the 7th–13th centuries), Madurai, Thanjavor and Mahabalipuram that has temples carved out of rock on the seashore. The western Ghats and the Nilgiri Hills provide less dramatic landscapes than the Himalayas but the hill stations provide attractive settings for trekking and climatic relief from the heat of southern India.

The East of India

The busy city of Calcutta is the biggest settlement in eastern India. North of Calcutta is the hillstation of Darjeeling, set among tea plantations. It is the base for trekking trips north into the Himalayas in Sikkim. The railway to Darjeeling and settlements further east is very spectacular. Assam is famous for its tea plantations and wildlife reserves.

Inbound tourism

Tourism has grown steadily up to the mid-1980s when political problems and the assassination of Prime Minister Indira Ghandi checked the growth rate. But the numbers of international tourists (the figures exclude visitors from Bangladesh and Pakistan) recovered in the late 1980s when Asian tourism was expanding rapidly. In 1986 arrivals reached the 1 million mark, but growth has slackened since 1990 as a result of the Gulf War and further internal political instability, associated with Sikh separatism in north-west India and Hindu fundamentalists who have again raised the ever-present Muslim–Hindu tensions. However, a large proportion of India's tourists are Indians resident in other countries who are returning for holidays and to visit friends and relatives. The statistics make it difficult to separate this element of inbound tourism from non-Indian visitors. India's main markets are the UK, USA, France, Germany, Sri Lanka and Japan (*see* Fig 38.4). A

Originating country	Number	%
Bangladesh	251 260	14.97
UK	212 052	12.64
Pakistan	190 128	11.33
USA	117 322	6.99
Germany	71 964	4.28
Sri Lanka	70 088	4.17
France	69 346	4.13
Japan	46 655	2.78
Italy	41 129	2.45
Canada	36 142	2.15
Others	N/A	N/A
Total	**1 677 508**	

Fig. 38.4 India's main markets, 1991
(*Source*: WTO)

relatively high proportion of the total comes from western Europe (33.5 per cent in 1991), while the rest of South Asia accounts for another 35.24 per cent of India's visitors, 9.85 per cent are visitors originating in the Americas, while 7.08 per cent come from the Middle East (though these are thought mainly to be migrant Indian workers returning on leave). East and South East Asia contribute relatively few visitors.

India is functionally separate from the east and south east Asian economic and tourist systems. The Gulf War and further political disruption hit India's tourism in 1991. Nevertheless, India's potential for special interest and cultural tourism is huge; the need for foreign exchange has switched the government's attention from the needs of the domestic market to catering more for the international visitor. Improvements to the tourist infrastructure (in terms of its quality and capacity) will ease the growth of tourism. The frustratingly slow bureaucratic procedures and the internal transport network need particular improvement to allow tourists quick and easy access around the highlights of such a big country. Although long-term tensions exist within Indian politics, the current unrest is localised in a few regions: much of the country is unaffected, and tourism is being expanded in the south.

NEPAL AND BHUTAN

These two kingdoms are sandwiched between India and Tibet. Their territory covers half of the southern flanks of the Himalayas and rises from the plains of the Ganges and Brahmaputra to the highest peaks of the Himalayan chain: Mount Everest (8848 m). Annapurna (8091 m) and Kanchenjunga (8598 m) are both inside Nepal's boundaries. The climate ranges from tropical in the foothills and lower valleys, to temperate at mid-altitude, to alpine at high altitude where the temperatures drop below freezing and there is permanent snowcover. Mountain sickness (*see* Chapter 2) is a danger for tourists visiting the higher mountain areas. The monsoon season (with high rainfall) lasts from June to October. The best seasons for tourism are spring and autumn; March, October and November are the

peak months for arrivals in Nepal. The main tourist activities are adventure tourism, mountain trekking and cultural tourism.

Nepal

Kathmandu, the capital of Nepal, is sited in a wide valley at 1337 m above sea level. Kathmandu is the gateway to Nepal. Most (88 per cent) visitors arrive here by air: road and rail access is difficult. The city is rich in Buddhist and Hindu temples and life centres round Durbar Square (*see* Fig 38.5). The city was the goal of the overland hippie trail in the 1970s but now has some international class hotels (though not luxury accommodation), as well as lodges and hostels in the old town round Durbar square. In 1988, three-quarters of the country's hotel capacity was concentrated in the capital, with a total capacity of 47 000 beds. The second main settlement is Pokhara, set on a lake with spectacular views of the Himalayas. This, too, is the starting point for many treks.

Fig. 38.5 Traditional architecture Kathmandu, Nepal

Mountain trekking

Trekking permits are required for treks beyond Kathmandu and Pokhara. The number of permits issued has increased from 27 000 in 1980 to over 60 000 by 1988. The treks vary from easy to moderate (with 5 to 6 hours' walking, up to 2800 m) to strenuous and serious mountain walking (e.g. up to 7 hours' walking, reaching 6000 m on the Annapurna circuit starting from Pokhara). The trekkers stay in lodges or camp out, but Sherpas act as porters and pack animals are used to carry the equipment. The Annapurna route is the most popular (with over 30 000 trekkers in 1990), followed by the trek to Everest base camp, then the Langtang valley (north of Kathmandu). The more serious mountaineers climb some of the peaks, but again permits are required. Much of the country is in fact not accessible to tourists. The concentration of these numbers of campers along restricted and well-used routes has led to some serious environmental problems. The campers need fuel wood for cooking, heating and light during the trek, as do local people living in the mountain regions. The trees and scrub on the higher slopes have been used up at unsustainable rates and the thin soils on the bare mountainsides are consequently exposed to accelerated soil erosion. A second problem concerns the disposal of litter and sewage. The thin soils and the rock terrain make it difficult to bury the waste material and burning is culturally unacceptable to local people. A conservation project set up in the Annapurna region seeks to resolve some of these problems by planting tree nurseries producing seedlings to restore the tree cover, providing toilets at the main nodes on the route, and alternative fuel supplies (e.g. bottled gas) have been considered. Jenner and Smith (1992) maintain that better management of both tourists and environment by the Nepalese could reduce many of the impacts of trekking in the mountains. Trekking is not the only adventure activity available: white water rafting is expanding and canoeing, mountain biking, and jungle safaris are also promoted. Wildlife tours (including wildlife viewing from elephants) are offered in some of the National Parks. Perhaps the best known is the 1431 km² Royal Chitwan National Park which is easily accessible from both Kathmandu and Pokhara. It has lodges, camps and resorts inside its boundaries and is noted for its tigers and rhinos. Given the character of Nepalese tourism, it is not surprising that

two-thirds of the tourists are male and half are between 16 and 35 years old, although only 13–15 per cent of arrivals come specifically for trekking or mountaineering. Tourist arrivals plateaud at 150–175 000 between 1978 and 1986, when there was a sharp increase of arrivals to over 250 000. India was Nepal's biggest market but otherwise the destination is very much a western taste (*see* Fig 38.6). The main markets (after India) were USA, UK, Germany, France, Japan, Italy, Australia and the Netherlands. Although the government is not heavily involved in developing or promoting tourism, it is an important sector of the economy, contributing 20 per cent to the country's foreign exchange earnings.

Originating country	Number	%
India	92 506	31.57
UK	24 968	8.52
Germany	19 897	6.79
USA	19 128	6.52
France	18 106	6.17
Japan	17 874	6.10
Italy	11 728	4.00
Australia	8 289	2.82
Netherlands	6 491	2.21
Spain	6 347	2.16
Others	N/A	N/A
Total	**292 995**	

Fig. 38.6   Nepal tourist arrivals, 1991
(*Source*: WTO)

Bhutan

Bhutan is physically similar to Nepal but its approach to tourism development is very different. It has remained isolated from the outside world for hundreds of years; its kingdom has never been invaded or conquered by foreigners. It eventually became a member of the UN in 1971 and tourists were first allowed to enter the country in 1974. It has very strictly controlled the number of inbound tourists, what they can do and where they can go, and thus sought to minimise tourism's environmental impact while maximising earnings (through the limited number of high-priced, all-inclusive packages available). The main attractions are the dramatically located Buddhist monasteries, the traditional festivals, the mountain landscape and the trekking. Access to the monasteries was limited in 1988–1990, while trekking is limited to six set routes. In 1988, 73 per cent of the visitors came on cultural tourism, while 26 per cent went trekking and mountaineering. Tourism has been limited to 2000 a year but plans exist to increase this to 4000 a year by 1996. In 1991, the main markets were USA (24.1 per cent), Germany (12.77 per cent), Japan (29.6 per cent), UK (7.4 per cent), Italy and France. Access is only via India.

SRI LANKA

The mainly Buddhist island of Sri Lanka (formerly known as Ceylon) has an area of 65 610 km^2 (a little smaller than Ireland) with a 1585 km coastline. It has many sandy beaches and a hot wet climate (maxima around 30°C all year and minima never falling below 20°C) but two wetter monsoon periods (which peak May–July and October–November). Its main tourist attractions are beach and cultural tourism. Tourism grew steadily to just over 400 000 in 1982, when political problems curtailed its expansion. The Hindu

Originating country	Number of tourist arrivals (excluding India*)
Germany	85 443
France	40 227
UK	34 605
Japan	28 797
Italy	25 575
Netherlands	17 541
Switzerland	11 487
Australia	10 995
Belgium	10 128
USA	8 511
Scandinavia	8 256
Others	N/A
Total	**393 669**

* Sri Lanka received 20 352 Indian visitors in 1991.

Fig. 38.7 Sri Lanka's main markets, 1992

Tamil population of the north of the island (which comprises 18 per cent of the island's population) wanted their own separate state (along with Tamils on the Indian mainland). Terrorist activity and the involvement of the Indian army in the north of the island were all part of the turbulence of the 1980s which has died down since 1990. Tourist arrivals dropped to 182 000 during the conflict but has recovered remarkably quickly since 1990 to 393 669 in 1992. Before the political problems, Sri Lanka marketed itself as mainly a winter season beach destination for the European market and the government intended to restrict tourism to coastal resort enclaves. However, the rapid expansion of tourism thwarted this policy and in the 1990s there has been a marked swing towards cultural tours or combined beach and cultural holidays. Cultural tours are particularly favoured by French and Japanese visitors, while the British and Dutch mix the two. However, the Scandinavians are still primarily interested in winter sun beach holidays (80 per cent of them going on beach-only holidays in 1992). A high proportion (60 per cent) of Sri Lanka's tourists come from western Europe (see Fig 38.7); it is mainly a winter destination and the peak months for arrivals are December to March.

Tourist resources

The beaches

The main tourist resorts are on the south-west coast between Negombo and Galle. Most of these beaches are sheltered from surf waves and have safe bathing. There are many coral reefs and most resorts offer a range of watersports. The east coast has good beaches particularly between Trincomalee and Pottuvil but this side of the island has been more affected by the political disturbances.

Cultural attractions

Colombo is the island's capital and has the main airport. It has a mixture of Buddhist and Hindu temples along with buildings from its British, Dutch and Portuguese colonial past. The island has several world heritage sites (e.g. the ancient city of Anuradhapura, and Polonnaruwa built in 1100 AD in the interior).

Anuradhapura was established in the 3rd or 4th century BC and has bell-shaped white temples dating from the 2nd and 3rd centuries BC (although some have been restored in recent years) and kings' and priests' palaces, ritual baths and irrigation reservoirs. Another dramatic historic site is the Sigiriya, a citadel perched on the summit of a granite mountain, containing beautiful frescos dating from 600 AD. Polonnaruwa was the capital from the 11th century. The ruins have not been restored and include palaces, temples and statues of the Buddha. Dambulla is another heritage site: it is a series of caves containing shrines and frescos. The hill town of Kandy is another centre of cultural tourism, with palaces of the kings who resisted colonial rulers in the 16th century, and many temples and museums. Daily ceremonies are held at the Temple of the Tooth (containing the Buddha's tooth). The dancers and drummers are an integral element of these religious festivals. The island has many festivals, some of which also involve processions and dancing. Masked dancing also occurs in folk dramas, in the festival processions and in some rituals of exorcism and healing (performed by a specific caste located in the south of the island). These rituals and the demon masks used in the dancing have been commoditised (see Chapter 12) for the tourist and they are performed as the 'devil dance'. The masks are produced for sale to the tourists.

THE MALDIVE ISLANDS

This group of islands is located 450 miles south west of Sri Lanka. The archipelago consists of 1500 islands strung out over 500 miles of ocean. About 200 islands are inhabited and 50 are set aside for tourism. The islands are so small that the different functions are spread out. For example, the capital Male is on one island, but the airport is

on the adjacent Hulule island. Motor launches meet the planes to take the tourists to their island. The islands were converted to Islam in 1153 but this does not inhibit beach tourism, which began in 1972. There is little sightseeing: activity is concentrated on the beach and sea – some of the best diving in the world (snorkelling and deepsea diving) is found here. Tourism has grown from 131 399 visitors in 1987 to 196 112 in 1991; 23 per cent came from Germany, 19.6 per cent from Italy, and between 6 and 8 per cent each from Japan, UK and France.

BANGLADESH, PAKISTAN AND MYANMAR

These remaining countries of South Asia have relatively little international tourism due to their political or physical characteristics – see Fig 38.8.

Pakistan has had an eventful political history since its creation in 1947, with periods of military rule and a fairly turbulent period of democratic rule. It is an Islamic state. Its territory is predominantly made up of the flat Indus valley where the climate is hot and dry but it has dramatic rugged mountainous territory in the north. But it borders three countries where political problems exist: Iran to the west, Afghanistan to the north west, and the disputed Kashmir region on the Pakistan–Indian border. It has the potential for adventure and trekking tourism in its Himalayan north and cultural tourism in the historic city of Lahore (where there are tombs and mosques built by the Mughals and the Shalimar gardens built in 1637) and at Mohenjo Daro, the huge ancient city site that dates back 5000 years. But tourism is still small scale and visitors are mainly from India, or are overseas Pakistanis returning to visit family and friends.

	Number of tourists	Percentage from South Asia	Europe	Main markets
Bangladesh	113 242	58.33	14.91	India, Nepal
Pakistan	438 088	N/A	29.2	
Myanmar	21 000	N/A	N/A	

Fig. 38.8 Tourist to the rest of South Asia, 1991
(*Source*: WTO)

Bangladesh is one of the world's poorest countries. It consists mainly of the flat plains and deltas of the Ganges and Brahmaputra rivers. It has a hot tropical climate, with a heavy monsoon between May and September. Although it has historic and cultural resources, its infrastructure is poorly developed and it has relatively few visitors – most come from India or other Asian countries. Those from Europe may include immigrants returning to visit family and friends.

In contrast **Myanmar** (formerly known as Burma) has a wealth of tourist resources, particularly its ancient culture and many Buddhist temples, shrines, pagodas and palaces and the ancient ruined city of Pagan (dating from 1044–1287). The country has been virtually closed to the outside world since 1960 and in the late 1980s and early 1990s there were major internal political difficulties, with the violent suppression of popular dissent and political deadlock whereby the regime in power refused to allow the new democratically elected government to take over. Some special interest tourists do go into Myanmar but until its internal political tensions are resolved and it changes its policy of political isolationism, it is unlikely to develop any significant tourist industry.

REFERENCES AND FURTHER READING

Those titles marked with an asterisk are particularly recommended for futher reading.

India

*Andrews, S (1993) 'India' in Baum, T (Ed) *Human Resource Issues in International Tourism*, Butterworth-Heinemann, pp.177–91.

*Cockerell, N (1991) 'India', *EIU International Tourism Reports*, No. 2, pp. 5–25.

*Goonasekera, A (1993) 'India outbound', *Travel and Tourism Analyst*, No. 6, pp. 19–29.

Nepal

*EIU (1991) 'Nepal and Bhutan', *International Tourism Reports*, No. 1, pp. 32-51.

Jenner, P and Smith, C (1992) 'The tourism industry and the environment', *EIU Special Report*, No. 2453.

*Stevens, S (1993) 'Tourism, change and continuity in the Mount Everest region, Nepal', *Geographical Review*, Vol. 83, No. 4, pp. 410–27.

Sri Lanka

*Cleverdon, R (1993) 'Sri Lanka', *EIU International Tourist Reports*, No. 1, pp. 43-67.

*O'Hare, G and Barrett, H (1993) 'The fall and rise of the Sri Lankan tourist industry', *Geography*, Vol. 78, pp. 438–42.

QUESTIONS AND DISCUSSION POINTS

1 Compare and contrast the patterns of tourism in the Alps and the Himalayas. How can you explain the differences?

2 Pakistan has a population of over 112 million, and India of 843 million, yet according to the statistics less than 200 000 tourists cross the border in each direction. What explanations can be put forward for this?

3 India, Nepal and Bhutan are relatively popular destinations for the North American market but very few Americans visit Sri Lanka or the Maldives. Why do you think this is?

ASSIGNMENTS

1 You work for a tour company that specialises in tours to India and Nepal. Tours to the 'Golden Triangle' (Delhi, Agra and Jaipur) are successful but customers are expressing an increasing interest in visiting other parts of India and seeing other aspects of the region's culture and environment.

   Can you meet this need by providing short optional additions to the 'Golden Triangle' tours and, if so, for how long, and to which destinations? Or are there other parts of India that could be developed for separate tours (if so, where, and to what attractions)? Write a report to your Chief Executive identifying the opportunities for expanding and diversifying your tours to the Indian Subcontinent.

2 The company also wishes to be updated on the political situation in India and Nepal (as it may affect the development of the new tours you have identified). The company is also keen to expand into other parts of South Asia as and when political conditions allow. Review the current press (e.g. quality papers and journals such as the *Economist*) and write a brief report updating the company on the political situation in South Asia, highlighting the regions it would be prudent to avoid.

PART 4

Conclusions

CHAPTER 39

The dynamics of change

INTRODUCTION

Three of the regions described in this book – Europe, North America and the Pacific – account for most of the tourist activity of the world. They show well-established patterns of tourist development, trends that evolve slowly following a fairly predictable course during each successive decade. Their relative political and economic stability has enabled this to occur.

There are many other countries of the economic periphery that have the climatic and natural resources to make them highly attractive tourist destinations; few have yet reached the stage of economic development to make them potential international tourist generators. Although there may be economic incentives for encouraging inbound tourism from affluent countries (i.e. the need for foreign currency), there is much debate about the undesirable impact (social and environmental) that such tourist developments may have in very poor countries. Furthermore, many of these countries are not politically stable, and few tourists will risk travelling to a country of uncertain political stability or where the enforcement of law and order is doubtful. There are a few islands of political stability where tourist industries of some size have been established, but patterns of tourism here are perhaps more prone to sudden changes. Events such as natural disasters, political unrest or changes in transport services may stop tourism virtually overnight. Thus tourism is an activity open to sudden decreases in volume, particularly in politically unstable areas.

Tourism tends to increase in response to political change or new opportunities rather more slowly, over a period of several years as markets readjust to new circumstances.

The five-year period between 1989 and 1993 has seen great changes in world politics, firstly the revolutions in the countries of the Communist bloc, secondly in the Islamic world of the Middle East, and thirdly in parts of Africa.

The dominant effect of these changes has been to increase tourism, though the short term impact of the Gulf War in 1991 was to constrain the growth of world tourism a little for that one year. The post-1989 'new world order' appears to have enabled international tensions to have been lessened, but the political vacuum left in some of the ex-Communist countries has allowed long suppressed nationalism and inter-ethnic disputes to reappear. This has been the case in former Yugoslavia and the conflict has caused a well established, large scale tourist industry to melt away.

Tourism is one of the world's economic activities that is particularly sensitive to political and economic events and the patterns of tourism described in this book could change fairly suddenly in the short term.

However, it is long term economic change that fuels the growth of world tourism and the focus of the world's economic development appears to be shifting towards the Pacific region. The health of the world economy will continue to dictate the speed at which world tourism grows and if the trends of the 1990s continue, the Pacific region will become an increasingly important tourist generating and tourist destination region.

However, the world's natural cultural, historic and climatic resources for tourism remain essentially unchanged by these events. The challenge to politicians and the tourist industry itself will be to manage the inevitable increase in tourism so that the world's limited supply of tourist resources can meet future demands. The general concepts of sustainable development and sustainable tourism are attractive to politicians, tour operators and tourists alike, but require difficult and sometimes unpopular decisions to be made to implement them effectively in practice. Past experience suggests that short term economic interests generally prevail.

The early chapters of this book have suggested ways in which travel patterns evolve, and highlighted the factors and processes that appear to influence tourist flows and later chapters have illustrated patterns of tourism in various regions of the world. These factors will continue to exert an influence and will play a part in both modifying existing flows and moulding new patterns of tourism in changing political contexts in the world in future.

It is hoped, therefore, that this book has not simply described world tourism as it was up to the early 1990s, but enhanced the readers' ability to interpret and understand these new patterns of tourism as they evolve.

ASSIGNMENTS

1 You are a tourism consultant with special expertise on world cruising. Your client, a Greek shipping magnate, has spare capacity in his shipyards and is considering building a new seagoing cruise ship. He wishes to be briefed on the main cruise destinations in the world, and the main world cruise markets before he decides whether to build the ship.

Your brief is to:

(a) Provide a brief comparative assessment of the major world cruise destinations, their size, location, geographical character and attractions.

(b) Provide a brief comparative assessment of the main world markets for cruising, their character, size and geographical location.

(c) Provide an outline of the existing level of competition and the potential for new cruise developments.

(d) Make a reasoned recommendation of which cruise market and destination the new cruise ship should be designed for.

(e) Provide a detailed account of the chosen market and particularly the travel links between market and cruise destination.

(f) Provide a full account of the geographical attractions of the cruise destination area, and the choice of ports of call.

(g) Make a reasoned recommendation of which location in the destination region should be chosen as the port of embarkation. Suggest at least two different itineraries, starting from this embarkation point. The length of the itinerary and the nature of the cruise should be appropriate for the chosen market.

You should present your work in report format.

2 A young couple living in the UK have been left some money by an eccentric aunt who has directed that it should be spent on a year's round-the-world trip. They wish to visit:

(a) the historic sites of Greece, Egypt, China, and India and the Andes mountains:

(b) the wildlife of East Africa, the Amazon rainforest and the Great Barrier Reef;

(c) the landscapes of the Himalayas, the Rockies and Alaska;

(d) the attractions of Disneyland and New York; and

(e) two different tropical islands.

They would like to stay at least one month in each of India, China and Australia and two in the United States. Are there any locations on their list that you (as a travel agent) would advise them to avoid due to political problems?

Arrange an itinerary for them: the itinerary should minimise time spent travelling between destinations; it should indicate the starting date and time of year that they will arrive in each destination. Is it possible to arrange an itinerary that allows them to enjoy ideal climatic conditions in each and every destination? Are there any destinations that they might have to leave out on climatic grounds?

3 You are the editor of a journal for the UK travel trade. Write a brief editorial article reviewing the current political and economic circumstances of the world, and assessing the general prospects for world tourism in the coming year.

INDEX

Note: Most subject entries only refer to the general information on the subject in question. Information on climate, physical geography, and cultural and other resources is not separately indexed for most places but will be found in the general references for the place concerned. Information on main tourist movements is summarised under countries. References to maps (which are in **bold** and follow other page references) are given selectively based on the assumption that (as suggested in the Preface) this book will be used in conjunction with an up-to-date atlas.